William Conyngham Plunket

Speeches at the bar and in the senate

Edited with a Memoir and historical notices

William Conyngham Plunket

Speeches at the bar and in the senate
Edited with a Memoir and historical notices

ISBN/EAN: 9783337150655

Printed in Europe, USA, Canada, Australia, Japan

Cover: Foto ©ninafisch / pixelio.de

More available books at **www.hansebooks.com**

SPEECHES

AT

THE BAR AND IN THE SENATE,

BY THE RIGHT HONOURABLE

WM. CONYNGHAM, LORD PLUNKET,

LORD HIGH CHANCELLOR OF IRELAND.

EDITED,

WITH A MEMOIR AND HISTORICAL NOTICES,

BY JOHN CASHEL HOEY.

DUBLIN:
JAMES DUFFY, WELLINGTON QUAY,
AND
22, PATERNOSTER ROW, LONDON.
1867.

I DEDICATE THIS BOOK,

TO MY FRIEND,

CHARLES GAVAN DUFFY,

MEMBER OF PARLIAMENT FOR THE BOROUGH OF NEW ROSS,

THE BEST MAN AND THE BEST IRISHMAN

I HAVE EVER KNOWN,

IN FAREWELL MEMORIAL

OF HAPPY DAYS THAT ARE NO MORE,

AND OF ALL THAT I OWE TO HIS COUNSEL, EXAMPLE,

AND AFFECTION.

November, 1855.

CONTENTS.

	PAGE
Memoir	3
The Press, March 3, 1798	25
The State of the Nation, March 5, 1798	30
The Sheares' Case, July 4, 1798	35
The Union, December 9, 1798	39
The Union, January 22, 1799	40
The Union, January 28, 1799	52
The Place Bill, May 16, 1799	53
The Union, May 18, 1799	56
The Union, January 15, 1800	58
The Union, May 26, 1800	75
Robert Emmet, September 19, 1803	82
The Threshers, December 5, 1806	96
Catholic Relief, April 9, 1807	106
The Catholic Claims, February 25, 1813	111
The Speaker's Address to the Regent, April 22, 1814	135
The War of 1815, May 25, 1815	143
The Navy Estimates, March 27, 1816	147
The State of Ireland, April 26, 1816	150
The Window Tax, April 21, 1818	157
The Peterloo Massacre, November 23, 1819	161
The Seditious Meetings' Bill, December 13, 1819	174
Reply to Brougham, December 22, 1819	180
Dublin City Election, June 24, 1820	183
Catholic Relief, February 28, 1821	187
Doctor Milner, March 16, 1821	221
The Catholic Bills, March 16, 1821	223
The State of Ireland, April 22, 1822	238

MEMOIR.

The heralds and annalists tell us that among the Danes of Dublin who mingled with our Norman conquerors and helped them to carry their castles and their marchmen to the very edge of Ulster, within a few years after Strongbow's landing, was an Ostman chief, named Plunkett of Bewley. The name meets us often in the early chronicles of the Pale—now in border battles with the Clan Colla, or the Irians of Dalaradia, now in high administrative and judicial office at the Castle. Three peerages, the baronies of Killeen (merged in the earldom of Fingall), of Dunsany, and of Louth, had ennobled the old Norse blood with honours as ample as their estates, which dotted the whole country from the fair margin of Lough Crew, to the low park lands of the City—when in the reign of King Henry the Eighth, Sir Patrick Plunkett, a knight of the house of Louth, married the grand-daughter of the Lord High Chancellor, Sir William Welles.* From one scion of their family the martyr primate, Oliver Plunkett of Armagh, derived the innocent blood shed on Tyburn Hill. From a younger son of the same Sir Patrick, the Reverend Patrick Plunket of Glennan, in the county of Monaghan, more than a century ago, claimed descent. The particulars of the pedigree baffle Ulster King-at-Arms, but it rests, to the family satisfaction, at either end on the Chancery woolsack.

A son was born to the Rev. Patrick Plunket in 1725, and entered upon the Presbyterian ministry by license of the presbytery of Monaghan in the year 1747. The following year the young Levite was unanimously called to the congregation of Enniskillen. He was early distinguished among his brethren for the keen, wiry wit, the subtle, hard-headed logic, and the free-thinking turn which are characteristic of the Ulster Presbyterians, and for twenty years he preached the gospel, with occasional Socinian strictures, in the chief kirk of Fermanagh. There he married "Mary, sister of Redmond Conyngham, Esq.," and there, in the year 1750, was born his son Patrick, afterwards as eminent in physic as William was in politics and law. In July, 1764, while the minister and his wife were on one of those long excursions which the duties of a yet neglected ministry sometimes entailed, late at night, Mrs. Plunket was taken ill in a country part of Fermanagh, fortunately within reach of the manse of a brother minister, and there delivered safely of the son, who was afterwards named William Conyngham Plunket.

Next door, under the same roof with the minister's house in Enniskillen, was the house of a Protestant burgess named Magee, to whose wife was born a son at the same time. The two children were often nursed at the same breast, shot

* Burke's "Peerage."

marbles, pegged tops, learned the rudiments and the humanities, entered college, and proceeded *pari passu*, faithful friends and steadfast allies through life together, to the highest dignities of the Anglo-Irish constitution in Church and State. This young William Magee, with the hot no-Popery blood of the Inniskilling Dragoons in his veins, was afterwards Archbishop of Dublin, and author of the famous Protestant tractate on the Atonement.

In the year 1768, the Rev. Thomas Plunket obeyed a call from Strand-street congregation, the oldest of the Irish Socinian chapels, and shifted his pulpit to Dublin. The memoirs mention his intimacy with the eccentric, benevolent parson, *Premium* Madden, and with that gentle genius, his curate, Philip Skelton ; and that he was particularly appreciated and courted by all the wits and politicians of the time of Charles Lucas and Anthony Malone. He died poor in 1778, and his congregation undertook the charge of his family. From the subscription raised, all the minister's little debts were paid off and the cost of his funeral defrayed ; and with the balance of the fund his widow and daughters established a quiet tea warehouse, patronised by pious elders and the Strand-street matrons, on the profits of which the family was decently maintained and the sons liberally educated. After they had become wealthy and famous, their sisters still, with true northern independence, kept the little shop, and sold the best Bohea in Dublin.

In 1779, William Magee and William Plunket stood for sizarship together in Trinity College, and were rejected, but entered as non-decremented pensioners, and chummed during their college course. In the same examination Mr. Sealy Townsend, afterwards Master in Chancery, and Dr. Miller, the gifted author of " History Philosophically considered," were candidates.* Townsend took the first place, Plunket the third or fourth, Miller the fifth—neither was so distinguished during the under-graduate course as Townsend, until the second examination of the fourth year when Plunket stopped his certificate on equal answering. He is said to have been dull in the college course ; but it was not in the lecture-hall or the tutor's room that the students of Trinity then received the most valuable elements of that education, which for half a century afterwards supplied Ireland with so distinguished a list of lawyers, politicians, and preachers. It was in the gallery of the House of Commons where Grattan's glorious eloquence was preaching the new born nationality. It was in the Historical Society, where the rights of man and the principles of history were debated with a force and a fire which their practical application to a revolutionary period inspired and made real among a generation of young men, perhaps the most splendid in abilities and acquirements who have ever studied together in Ireland.

A grand group might be selected from any *seance* of the Historical Society in these days of the triumphant Volunteers. A versatile, impetuous revolutionist, intensely insubordinate, always meditating love or murder, with a reputation for military, political, literary, any and every kind of talent, when he pleases to apply it, which is by no means perpetually—him they call Theobald Wolfe Tone. A gentle youth, fresh from the country, with softly winning manners, and a tongue from which language flows with a peculiar happy murmur, is named Charles Kendal Bushe. A calm, self-possessed, young citizen, with a Spartan purity of character, and a serene loftiness of intellect, which exercises a strange sway over all his comrades —this is Addis Emmet, younger brother of the great dead lion of the Historical Society, Temple Emmet. Philosophic Miller, ready of speech, racy of hard study, but never dull with it, for his brain was an alembic able to fuse any sub-

---

* Memoir of Dr. Miller in the *Dublin University Magazine*.

ject. Honest Peter Burrowes, who, when his generous human heart was stirred to its tranquil depths (seldom, indeed, it must be allowed) could utter beyond any other man among them what would make you burn or shudder with genuine passion. Whitley Stokes, of a most amiable nature, and a beautifully classic and cultivated mind. Magee, who rushed into a controversy at a charge, trusting to the sheer force of his intellect and character to carry him through. Wild Tom Goold, acting the admirable Crichton, flirting for half a day in Sackville-street with all his heart, and then giving half an hour and half his head to astrology, Roman law, or some equally useless abstruse and absurd study. Saurin, somewhat senior to the rest, with his dry and unrelenting logic, which you saw cut in every line of that hard Huguenot head.* The heads were all heads of mark indeed, and there were more of as good quality, some of which were lifted dripping on the gibbet twenty years afterwards, some of which wore judges' wigs or bishops' mitres, and one or two in Spanish breaches, waved cocked hats with the tricolour and eagle of Napoleon's Irish Legion on them. But all these young men admitted one master mind in the grand game of debate. None of his cotemporaries has challenged the supremacy of Plunket in the talent of oratory. As it is said now that his reported speeches are nothing to what they were when delivered, so it was long before his youthful comrades could be induced to admit that his finest efforts at the Bar or even in Parliament could be compared to the impromptu sallies of that earlier and more familiar forum. Even then they spoke, not so much of the figurative brilliancy and poetic harmony of his language, which young men most admire in eloquence, and which, in Grattan's dithyrambic days were all the fashion, as of an irresistible roll of argument which swelled like wave after wave, clear, rapid, and overwhelming. It was vain to play rhetorical fireworks against such an element. Then you aroused the keen excoriating irony which flowed like bile off his vigorous intellect.

Plunket entered Lincoln's Inn in 1784, and was called to the Bar in 1787. Old attorneys say, that his circuit practice at first was of a humble class, and of a popular character; and that he began by moving Civil Bills at Trim, where the northern circuit then commenced for half-guinea fees—according to the custom of the junior bar before assistant barristers were known. He was so poor that he had to sell his gold medal, and rode his first circuit on a horse lent for the service by Peter Burrowes. In these early difficult days, he lodged with a young Catholic merchant from Monaghan, in Eccles-street, and in the faithful intimacy which he always maintained with his old friends, in after days of pride and place, often said, half in jest and half in earnest, that the Catholics of Ireland owed much of the service he gave to their cause, to his ancient regard for honest Michael Hughes. The following anecdote tells the accident which is said to have first revealed his particular power as a pleader:—

"While yet unknown, he happened to be acquainted with a gentleman who conducted the business of an eminent solicitor. The proprietor gave his man of business instructions for a bill in a very heavy suit, who, trusting to the abilities of his young friend, gave him the instruction and the fee. The bill, a voluminous one, was quickly despatched; the name of the pleader was inquired and introduced; he became the confidential adviser and constant guest of the solicitor, and a connexion of a closer nature soon followed."†

Hereby we learn how Plunket came to marry into the house of John M'Caus-

---

* Journals of the Historical Society.

† A valuable Memoir in the *Metropolitan Magazine*, by John O'Donoghue, Esq., of the Irish Bar.

land, the great northern solicitor, and to devote himself at so early a period to the practice of the Equity Courts.

Magee and Bushe, Tone and Burrowes, all rising young men, were of his more particular friendship in these days; and although he did not join the little Political Club in which Tone brought together the rest of his college mates, with his adjutant Tom Russell, and his reformed aristocrat Sir Lawrence Parsons, and the rising national writers, Drennan and Pollock, yet there seems to have been between the two young men a racy, hearty appreciation and genuine regard for each other. One day in November Term, 1792, Tone, who has been working the Catholic cause with an ardour, activity, and courage, quite new in the councils of the committee, walks down from their office to the hall of the Four Courts to take note of the vane of opinion there. "Wonderful," he writes in that wonderful journal of his, "wonderful to see the rapid change in the minds of the bar on the Catholic question; almost every body favourable. Some for an immediate abolition of all Penal laws; certainly the most magnanimous mode, and the wisest. All sorts of men, and especially lawyer Plunket, take a pleasure in girding at Mr. Hutton (himself), who takes at once all their seven points on his buckler, thus!" Exceeding good laughing. Mr. Hutton called Marat. Sundry barristers apply to him for protection in the approaching rebellion. Lawyer Plunket applies for Carton, which Mr. Hutton refuses, inasmuch as the Duke of Leinster is his friend, but offers him Curraghmore, the seat of the Marquis of Waterford. This Mr. Hutton does to have a rise out of Marcus Beresford, who is at his elbow listening. Great laughter thereat." A few years afterwards, it was one of the same Beresfords whose black and brutal heart suggested to the Castle the too atrocious idea, that Tone should be dragged out while life was yet oozing through the unhappy death wound he had inflicted, and hanged in his very agony according to the letter of the law.

Even so soon a vast difference of opinion was beginning to exhibit itself among the generation of young men who had worshipped Grattan and Liberty at college, and who had been proud to couple the names of George Washington and Edmund Burke together. The French Revolution had been for several years in action, and was fast erupting into anarchy and general dissolution of law, order, and religion; spreading, by a kind of volcanic sympathy, into all surrounding nations. Edmund Burke had taken his memorable stand against democracy, far in advance of the general opinions of his party, but was gratified to find that his doctrines had found several zealous disciples among the rising young men of his native country. Bushe, who had lived a little in France, wrote a pamphlet to sustain his side of the controversy; so did Goold. Tone at once took the opposite side, and vowed that Paine was the prophet. Plunket was early in his life and to its last day in all his politics a disciple of Burke, tempered by Blackstone, He hated despotism much, but he hated anarchy more. He had a great and equal antipathy to the constructiveness and to the destructiveness of democracy—the antipathy to ancient establishments, and the rage for system-building which it engendered. He saw in the English constitution reformed and unclogged as it had been by the early American republicans, the ideal of a great system of political dynamics, in whose careful balance of powers, a civilized and Christian community might hope to enjoy all the happiness and liberty which government can confer. He added to these principles the intelligence and the reverence of a constitutional lawyer for a state system, to which so much had been contributed by the sagest authorities of his own profession. And he believed that if the parliamentary patriots of Ireland, undazzled by reent democratic conquests in America and France, and undismayed by the terrorism and corruption which rendered the king's government scandalous, should take their stand upon the concessions compelled by Grattan, they might in time succeed in widening the basis of the constitution of '82, so as to admit all its subjects to equal rights and franchises, and to perfectly conserve the estates of the realm in just and co-ordinate relations, by gradual internal reform. All his interests and ambition went the same way. His daily business was with rights and properties, which had grown with or under the existing system. His ambition was the same which had raised Pery and Burgh, Wolfe and Yelverton, to fame, office, and fortune. Tone on the other hand was a thorough revolutionist by nature, station, and ambition. From his boyhood, revolt had been the very breath of his being—now and then against his father whom withal he so tenderly loved, but who *would* insist upon the boy's wearing a wig or a fellow's gown instead of a shako; against the Provost and Fellows, against the Benchers and Bar; but above all, against the atrocious injustice which was then, denominated Government in Ireland. He detested his profession. The existing system afforded him no other fixed arena for his eminent and various abilities—abilities equal to any of the positions which daily fell to men of his *genre* in the democratic countries; compared to which any position he could hope to attain in Ireland was a mere vegetation. But ardent as his ambition was, it is only just to him to say that he never allowed it to have more than a secondary influence in his plans for the subversion of the English government. With all his heart and soul, he abominated the loathsome corruption and the unmerciful tyranny of that system. At the time it presented to the view a suspicious and ferocious executive; a parliament, powerless unless for shame or evil, and as much a byeword for corruption as any bagnio in the city; the ascendancy political and religious, therefore social also, and in all the three aspects intolerant and intolerable, of a small privileged sect over two vast segments of the population, the Catholics and the Dissenters, who had no communion in the constitution, and hardly the least influence with the administration. Grattan's constitutional revolution had utterly failed to remedy this system. The government of Ireland had relapsed into a worse state than the state before '82. If it could by possibility be destroyed by an unconstitutional revolution, any result whatever could hardly have failed to be more gratifying to God and man. The people failing, the English minister did, in fact, effect a result as extreme by an unconstitutional counter-revolution, the Union. Such results as America, Holland, and even France, before the bloody era of Robespierre, had attained, by armed revolutions, it was Tone's ambition and mission to produce in Ireland—Republican Institutions based upon a Declaration of the Rights of Man, guided by the patriotic elements youth and genius, and fortified by a vigorous military spirit.

It is right to remember, in judging Plunket's subsequent conduct, especially at the time of Robert Emmet's trial, that at so early a period and with a man whom he regarded so highly as he did Tone, right or wrong, he had taken decided issue against the Irish republicans.

Long before Tone was obliged to leave Ireland, the political opposition had even bred a personal estrangement between the two friends. One day after a long successful interview with "my friend, citizen Carnot, the organiser of victory," Tone writes in his journal, "Well, my friend, Plunket, (but I sincerely forgive him) and my friend Magee, whom I have not yet forgiven, would not speak to me in Ireland because I was a Republican. Sink or swim, I stand to-day on as high ground as either of them." Indeed Tone always speaks of Plunket with such a fondness as shows that he believed in the perfect sincerity of his convictions; and on the very eve of Tone's exile, Plunket writes to him thus:—

DEAR TONE:—I embrace with great pleasure the idea and opportunity of renewing our old habits of intimacy and friendship. Long as they have been interrupted, I can assure you that no hostile sentiment towards you ever found admittance into my mind. Regret, allow me the expression, on your account, apprehension for the public, and great pain at being deprived of the social, happy, and unrestrained intercourse which had for so many years subsisted between us, were the sum of my feelings. Some of them, perhaps, were mistaken, but there can be no use now in any retrospect of that kind. It is not without a degree of melancholy I reflect that your present destination makes it probable that we may never meet again, and talk and laugh together, as we used to do, though it is difficult to determine whether these jumbling times might not again bring us together. In all events, I shall be most happy to hear from you, and write to you, often and fully, and to hear of your well-being, wherever you may be. If I had known your departure was to have been so very immediate, I would not have suffered you to slip away without a personal meeting. I shall hope to hear from you as soon as you get to America. I formerly had friends there. The unfortunate death of my brother you have probably heard of; perhaps however, I may still have some there who might be useful to you. Let me know where, and in what line you think of settling, and, if any of my connections can be of use, I will write to them warmly.—I beg you will give my best regards to Mrs. Tone, and believe me, dear Tone, with great truth, your friend,

W. PLUNKET.

May 29th, 1795.

Tone sailed for America, thence to France, and within the next three years, had engaged the French and Dutch governments to direct three expeditions to the shores of Ireland; had served with the French army as adjutant-general; was acting in confidential council with Hoche, Bonaparte, Carnot, and as well known and accredited in the *bureaux* of the Directory and at the Hague, as the official of any regular legation. Three years of miraculous work! While Bushe lamented in the House of Commons that he should be " wasting on the desert air of an American plantation, the brightest talents that I ever knew a man to be gifted with"—doubting withal, perhaps, if in such quick and teeming times, the elements of a revolutionary statesman and soldier, were indeed or would long remain mouldering among Yankee maize and tobacco. Plunket lived in Dominick-street; sat under Chancellor Clare as regularly as his register; got his silk gown, and among the innumerable titles, mortgages, jointures, attainders, remainders, and reversions, with which five or six generations of good old Irish gentlemen, rake-helly, and rapacious, had incumbered their rights of property, made much money and a great name in equity. When the Rebellion of '98 broke out, he subscribed to the Patriotic Fund; and on that famous night, when the rebels were to have taken Dublin, and General Craig packed all the lawyers and attorneys in Smithfield to meet the first rush of the Kildare pikes, Plunket was out in battle array, like the rest of Captain Saurin's Lawyers' corps. Once he emerged from his pleadings, while that other battle, fiercer than any that General Craig commanded was going on between the lawyers and the rebels—venue changed from Smithfield to Kilmainham. He was counsel with Curran for Henry Sheares, and did his duty well; but when Curran, that same sad winter, made such a gallant effort to save Tone from the hangman, it is gratefully told by the patriot's son, "that Peter Burrowes* ably exerted himself"—and there is no mention made of Plunket.

He had entered parliament in the spring of that awful year for the borough of Charlemont. At the time there was no more honoured constituency in all Ireland, than the tidy village which rests under Mountjoy's old fort, beside the Northern Blackwater. The good old lord, who took his title thence, throughout his life had exercised his *conge d'elire* as a trust for the people, and was always proud to award its honours where he saw, or fancied he saw, genius, patriotism, and youth struggling into public life, under the discouraging auspices of a system in which counties were family appanages, and boroughs cost £4000 a seat. Grattan had entered Parliament as member for Charlemont, and represented it when he carried the revolution of '82. Among the names which we find on its list of burgesses, is that of Sheridan, a cousin of Richard Brinsley, to whom the earl, struck on a short acquaintance, by the brilliant wit and high ideality which belong to that old Celtic blood, forthwith offered a seat in Parliament. He died young; and then Lawyer Jephson, full of parliamentary promise, is spoken of with a proper *pater patriæ* pride; but ungrateful Lawyer Jephson took a judgeship at Gibraltar. Lord Caulfield and he had occupied the two seats from the general election of 1797, until parliament met in the following February. Then the viscount, elected to sit for the county of Armagh, by which he had also been returned; Jephson took office; the Speaker's writ was moved, and the answer that came to it was—that Francis Dobbs, Esquire, Barrister-at-Law, and William Conyngham Plunket, Esquire, one of his Majesty's counsel, had been duly elected by the Portreeve and burgesses of the Borough of Charlemont to serve in the Commons house of Parliament.†

When Plunket entered parliament, the patriot party had dwindled to a miserable minority of seven or eight steady votes, and about twice as many fluctuating tallies. The great assembly, which as Grattan told the English Commons, had "in fourteen years acquired for Ireland what you did not acquire for England in a century—freedom of trade, independency of the judges, restoration of the final judicature, repeal of a perpetual mutiny bill, *habeas corpus* act, *nullum tempus* act," had, since the secession of the opposition, sunk into a mere divan of the minister. With whatever ambitious anxiety the honourable member for Charlemont may have looked forward to his entrance upon that high arena, he must have felt the position a forlorn hope as he looked round the splendid chamber, from whose gallery he had often longingly gazed upon the assembled magnates of Ireland. The seats of the opposition were almost vacant. Grattan, under his beloved oaks of Tinnehinch, chafed like some war-worn soldier, bound by parole, while the trumpet of his cause called all good men and true to the rescue. Curran stood day after day in the bloody assize of the rebellion, pleading in such tones of courage, pity, and wrath, as never were addressed to any tribunal on the earth before for mercy to the young, the gifted, and the true—as well ask mercy from the famished tiger. The familiar faces that used to cluster round Grattan were gone—some dead and gone, and their ancient places knew them no more. Tone's old friend, Sir Laurence Parsons, still kept his seat, and

---

* Burrowes prepared Tone's defence before the court-martial. I owe this interesting fact, never before published, to my friend, Waldron Burrowes.

† Hardy's "Charlemont." Journals of the House of Commons.

occasionally harrassed Mr. Pelham. George Ponsonby frequently attended, and his upright character, high connexion, and trained capacity were always an honour to his party. Bushe had been for some months in the House, and was creating a sensation by his elegant and spirited eloquence. Tighe of Wicklow, Stewart of Killymoon, O'Donnell of Donegal, and a few more of the country gentry remained faithful. But parliament was hardly attended during the session of '98, by the squires. They were busy in their counties; some were dragooning the rebels, others had grown indifferent to the character of parliament since Grattan's retirement. A herd of colonels, commissaries, revenue commissioners, members of ballast boards, and barrack boards, castle clerks, and black leg barristers, composed the ministerial majority—suppressed the constitution whenever they were bid, and boasted they had been sent into parliament to put an end to it. The task of the little opposition during this dreary period consisted in an ineffectual effort to thwart and mitigate Pitt's *Thorough*—the policy bayonet in one hand and bribe in the other, by which he was preparing for the Union. After a few months more the Union itself roused all Ireland like the sound of the last trumpet.

On the 16th of November, 1798, Mr. Pitt writes to Lord Cornwallis enclosing a rough draft of the articles of Union, and appointing Viscount Castlereagh Chief Secretary for Ireland.* On the same day, the late Lord Lieutenant, Earl Camden, congratulates the young minister, his nephew; and begs he will write letters frequently, as Mr. Pitt has confidentially complained that the Lord Lieutenant is rather remiss in correspondence—write long letters often, and make his excellency sign them. Neither Mr. Pitt nor Earl Camden seems to have perfectly discerned the amazing elements of power which lay latent in this extraordinary young man. Who indeed could have believed that under that bland adolescent air, that lithe and dazzling front, and, stranger still, that tongue so awkward and maladroit, were hidden a heart as subtle, a will as truculent, a courage as cold, and a conscience as unscrupulous as Cæsar Borgia's. For a model of Castlereagh's character, we naturally refer not to the generous ambitions, and the gallant rivalries of the British parliament; but to the crafty, impassable, and implacable ideal of Machiavelli's Prince, or the inexorable volition, passionless wisdom, and atrocious cold blood of the Third Napoleon. He was then not quite thirty years of age, and wore them with such a blooming, patrician beauty, that it was the custom of the opposition to speak of the secretary as a smooth-faced minion of Mr. Pitt. He had that order of mind, difficult and ungraceful of display in the liberal air of public assemblies which " men of intellect," *par excellence*, are always so vain to contemn. To the last days of his life, Castlereagh's mixed metaphors and rigmarole reasoning were the sport of the wits of opposition. But sneer, stricture, and invective, alike glanced aside from his imperturbable, polite placidity, and his callous pluck. Few men have ever possessed such extraordinary executive faculties, such reticence, tact, and duplicity, such skill in deceiving, and such address in managing men, and so intense and even an energy in the conduct of great affairs.

In a few months he earned a name the most hateful in Ireland since Cromwell's. During the last months of the rebellion, acting as secretary, *ad interim*, he had served a rapid noviciate in the corrupt system of the castle at one of its worst periods. Bloody Carhampton, domineering Clare, and Toler, a ferocious vampire, composed the real executive of the country at the time. At such

* The Castlereagh Correspondence.

a council board he learned to "dabble his sleek young hands in Erin's gore"—and learned the lesson with all the rancorous zeal of a renegade; for a very few years before his lordship had been a very ultra-democratic Northern Whig. Already an audacious and unscrupulous ambition possessed him. It was said that he even ventured to emulate the fame, and imitate the methods of Mr. Pitt. But perhaps the brilliant success, which another young Irish noble, Lord Mornington, had rapidly won in the wider field of imperial politics, obtained a more natural incentive for him. Fifteen years afterwards, he and the two brothers Wellesley concluded that awful contest, in which Pitt himself had succumbed. Its secret history is that of an alliance between these three Irish adventurers. It was Castlereagh who appointed and maintained the Duke of Wellington as British generalissimo—Wellesley who suggested and Castlereagh who conducted the diplomatic arrangements which banded all Europe against Napoleon at the congress of Vienna.

Yet had the young Secretary been of a less aspiring and active temper, there sat in his office an old familiar of the Castle, whose mind took a perfectly Satanic pleasure in the arts of intrigue and the darker passions of power, and whose influence he could hardly have escaped. It is likely that Edward Cooke had quite as much to do with the formation of Lord Castlereagh's character as either nature or accident. In the correspondence of that strange being, we observe an intellect of keen, cold, wily energy; a heart without passion, prejudice, or scruple; a temperament of preternatural activity, but which loved to sit still in the shade and move men about like puppets. To prompt an informer; to instruct a spy; to know the precise price of every member in the House; how to manage the "Popish titulars;" how to infuriate the Orange Lodges; how to master the weak points by which the Lord Lieutenant and the Lord Chancellor, and the Lord Chief Justice, and the Attorney-General and the Secretary could all be moved, so as to be of one purpose (*his*, Edward Cooke's purpose)—such were the arts which he loved and in which he was versed beyond any man who has filled his office before or since. Into Castlereagh he infused, with the zeal of a master who has at last found a fit pupil in the rare art he loves, all the tortuous schemes and all the dark experience of his life.

A rival is almost as essential to the passion of ambition, as a mistress is to that of love. Almost from the very hour he entered the house, Plunket pitted himself against the secretary. There was no extremity of insult to which he did not proceed, in speeches, to which every man who listened must have felt that they were destined to live as long as Irish history and the English language. Their honest passion and fertile eloquence, hardly redeem passages of that surpassing invective from the character of unjustifiable vituperation. But the Secretary sat silent—perhaps stunned before it all. There is no doubt whatever that Castlereagh was a man of courage.—

> "Fearless, because no feeling dwells in ice,
> His very courage stagnates to a vice."

But he neither ventured to reply to those savage onslaughts, nor to seek the coarser and in those days common satisfaction of the duel. It is perhaps the most extraordinary proof we possess of the Secretary's elaborately stern and thick-skinned nature that then or afterwards he never resented all this deadly animosity. When Plunket entered the English House of Commons, Castlereagh was one of the first to hail his success in terms of unstinted admiration. On the questions of the war and the Peterloo Massacre, he led the Irish lawyer, yet independent of government, and an important parliamentary personage away from his party. And afterwards when Plunket took office, he speaks of Castlereagh's influence upon him in such terms as these :—" His friendship and confidence were the prime causes which induced his majesty's government to desire my services ; and I can truly add that my unreserved reliance on the cordiality of his feelings towards me, joined to my perfect knowledge of the wisdom and liberality of all his public objects and opinions, were the principal causes which induced me to accept the honour which was proposed to me. Nothing can ever occur to me in political life so calamitous as the event, which, in common with all his country and Europe, I so deeply deplore." This was written to the Marquis of Londonderry a few days after the minister's suicide.

Plunket appears to have entered upon the contest of the Union at first with despondency. Cooke writes of the Bar Meeting, that " Plunket was cunning, and changed his ground from the violence he had used in a former debate to a tone of moderation, and by that device had good effect." A very good effect in Mr. Cooke's mind—for he frankly declared his decided belief that the Union would be carried! " Fear, animosity, a want of time to consider coolly the consequences, and 40,000 British bayonets will carry it." He might have added the chronic apathy which had affected the national parliamentarists ever since Grattan had withdrawn from public life; he might have added, but his audience would have laughed the assertion to scorn that grand cause, which Grattan afterwards admitted in the most memorable words he ever spoke to the British Parliament—" When the Irish Parliament rejected the Catholic Petition, on that day she voted the Union; many good and pious reasons she gave, and she lies there with her many good and her pious reasons." As the session of 1799 advanced, the lobbies and galleries of the houses and the closets of the castle became as busy as the Stock Exchange, with peerages and boroughs to be bought and sold, applications for the escheatorships, tenders for the manufacture of situations and sinecures, and applications now seldom neglected for places of every species by persons of all possible denominations. When Mr. Cooke has a little leisure, we find him writing to Doctor Troy to ascertain if any more of his brother Titulars have given in their adhesion; and by return the *comharba* of Saint Laurence writes back to the castle, to say that all is right in Armagh, that he is almost sure of Tuam, and that his own priests have got the hint. At last the old fire began to kindle into a flame. When the measure of the Union was really revealed, first consternation, then wrath spread from man to man, and shore to shore. Two classes were foremost to combine and resist—the independent country gentlemen ; old volunteer colonels, toparchs of their counties, and owners of boroughs, who anticipated not merely the national dishonour, but the injury of their influence and property. It afterwards cost at least two millions of money, not to speak of titles and places, to buy their acquiescence. The second class was the Bar, then the most powerful, influential, and intellectual order in Irish society, and having even stronger obvious motives of interest, honour, and ambition, than the gentry in the maintenance of a national legislature. The most considerable men of the first class in parliament were the Speaker Foster, Sir Laurence Parsons, Sir Henry Parnell, Sir Edward O'Brien, Tighe of Wicklow, and Stewart of Killymoon. To the second class, the Prime Sergeant Fitzgerald, George Ponsonby, Saurin, Bushe, Goold, Barrington, and Plunket belonged.

But in that brief parliament no man, squire, lawyer, or minister made such a figure as Plunket. The debates were generally led by Parsons or Ponsonby ; he was always content to follow, but he invariably spoke the speech of the night, and Grattan significantly recognized the place he had attained, by taking his seat next to him when he re-entered parliament. His later efforts never excelled these grand orations. The *sæva indignatio*—the pestering sarcasm that stung like a swarm of hornets, the clear, icy irony that flayed its adversary like a razor, and the fiery factfull invective that riddled a reputation like grapeshot—the classic structure, the stately, luminous, and ample language of these magnificent speeches are unsurpassed in oratory—but these were only the ornaments or variations of argument that has all the accuracy of mathematical proof; in which every word is a link of one perfect chain; in which all the ingenuity of logic cannot suggest one superfluous sentence. And there is great moral grandeur in the attitude which he sustains throughout—that of a jurist pleading before the High Court of Parliament, for the constitution of which it is the depository, and which it is bound to guard against the lawless violence of the minister as well as of the mob. Even in the utmost length to which he carried the doctrine of the incompetency of Parliament to enact the articles of Union, we observe that there is not a syllable of sympathy with the attempts lately made by the people against the constitution. He treats the rebel in the same category with the minister, and when he justifies a resort to the *ultima ratio*, as he very plainly does, it is on the same constitutional principle as applied to an abuse of parliamentary authority, that justified the English Revolution of 1688, in consequence of a *malfeasance* of the sovereign power. How far he urged this doctrine, the following passage, taken from one of the speeches of which only a fragmentary report is extant, will tell:—

"I boldly assert, staking whatever professional character I may possess as a constitutional lawyer, that if the parliament of Ireland pass this measure against the consent of the people of Ireland, their act will want all the attributes of a law. This is a plain, simple proposition, which I am ready to maintain, and I call on any learned or honourable gentleman in this house to contradict it. It is said by gentlemen on the other side, that Parliament is omnipotent. Sir, the omnipotence of parliament, if literally understood, is impious blasphemy, and if it be understood with limitations, it proves nothing for the gentlemen of the other side, for it implies a limit to its omnipotence. Sir, there are acts which but to name, proves that no parliament can be authorised to perform them—acts, to which no authority can give the force of laws, and which all mankind are justified in resisting. It is true indeed, that under and within the constitution, there can be no power to control the legislature, because the legislature is the highest power known to the constitution; but who is the driveller will say, that therefore any act of that legislature, however contrary to national justice, or inconsistent with the constitution itself, is rightful, and that they have a legal competency to perform them. If then there are acts which no power in the state is competent to, it remains only to ask is this not one of them—I contend that it is, because it is an act which goes to alter the constitution."

At the close of the same speech, he says in a spirit only too prophetic:—

"Who will say, that when the imperial parliament shall have got an uncontrolled power over Ireland, that they will not make local laws for the government of this country? Who will answer that when the *Habeas Corpus* shall be suspended in Ireland, it shall also be suspended in Great Britain? Who will say, that the miserable inhabitants of this remote and barbarous province shall not be smarting under the fetter and the whip, while the British Parliament, in its imperial dignity, shall sit unconcerned at our sufferings and out of the reach of our cries?"

B

He lived to see the full extent of all he had foreseen. The last words, spoken against the Union in the Irish Commons, say the reports, were spoken by Plunket and Goold—words of what anguish and indignation we can faintly conceive. With the fall of Ireland's independence, the grand ambition of his life, and of all the great Irishmen of that day, seemed to succumb. To Plunket especially, the shock must have been terrible. Had the minister been defeated, such a career lay before him, as no Irishman had yet attempted. He had acquired in a few months, a rank in parliament equally splendid and solid. It is hardly an exaggeration to say, that he stood in a position to fulfil Grattan's labours, and to anticipate O'Connell's. To resume the old policy of the opposition, to reform the House of Commons, to emancipate the Catholics and the Dissenters, to erect a popular ministry in the Castle, and in the fulness of time, make himself its Chancellor—such might have seemed a not unreasonable ambition, for the man who had so easily attained such an ascendancy in his native legislature. Instead of a destiny so brilliant, only the dull and daily-degenerating routine of an Irish practising barrister's life awaited him. One of the first curses of the Union, was that it subverted the natural order of legal promotion, and for twenty years afterwards filled the Benches of the Four Courts with judges, who had no claim to the ermine, but that of having corruptly opposed the leaders of their profession on the question of national independence. To an Irish barrister without office or private fortune, a seat in the British Commons was the road to ruin, in times when all the expenses and troubles of a parliamentary life may be epitomised in the fact, that the mail took four days to go from London to Dublin. Even in the present age of cheap and easy communication, it is in some cases a rather risky speculation for honourable and learned members who have got a country to sell—the competition is so undue, and the first self-denying pangs of a lessening fee book so sharp. In despair, it is said, Plunket meditated for a time emigration to England or the United States. Finally, he settled down to make the leading and most lucrative practice at the Irish Bar—to make money—to watch opportunities of making power. Already it was said that he was far fonder of money and of power than of mere fame.

The next time he appeared in public life, it was to cloud in an unaccountable hour his character as an Irish patriot and as an advocate, with that merciless speech for the Crown, in the case of Robert Emmet. No palliation can mitigate the simple censure, that his speech to evidence upon that occasion was a cruel and uncalled for assault upon a young heroic martyr, who had already surrendered himself frankly to his doom. But the publicists of the day, who sympathised with Emmet, or who, like Cobbett, hated Plunket's party or person, did not rest there. They declared that Emmet had attacked Plunket from the dock—which was a lie; that Plunket had been under the deepest obligations to Emmet's father and brother—which was also a lie; and that Emmet declared he had imbibed the opinions upon which he had acted from Plunket's teaching—opinions, now abandoned by Plunket for corrupt motives. This also is an assertion equally without foundation; but which has never yet been properly met by the apologists of Plunket's conduct. There is to it one simple and sufficient answer. Ten years before, towards Tone, Plunket had evinced precisely the same sentiments. Violent and unfeeling as he was in their utterance, it is impossible to deny that they were in perfect consistency with the settled opinions which he had for many years held and expressed. In every one of his Union speeches, he speaks of the attempt of the United Irishmen and the attempt of the minister with equal abhorrence. There can hardly be a doubt that he regarded Emmet's

experiment, as one more dangerous in every sense than even that of '98—more
likely, but for the merest chance, to have succeeded, and certain to have led to
an atrocious anarchy, or a French deputy-despotism, if it had. It was now not
merely horror of democracy—horror of Bonaparte too had seized upon men's minds.
And those who doubt the extent to which both feelings may have fairly influenced Plunket in warning the country against such designs, will find that Curran, speaking not for the Crown, but for the defence of one of Emmet's partizans,
Owen Kirwan, a few months afterwards, used language of the same spirit, and if
possible, more vehement. Perhaps, too, the very sense that the rebellion had
considerably contributed to aid the minister in carrying the Union,* added its
rankling bitterness to the animosity which he exhibited against all who had
hand, act, or part in this last attempt of the United Irishmen.

It is certain, however, that Plunket's speech against Emmet had the effect of
establishing good relations between him and the government, and led directly to
his acceptance of office under Mr. Addington's ministry. He became Solicitor-
General in October, 1803, on the promotion of Standish O'Grady to the Court
of Exchequer; Attorney-General under Mr. Pitt, in 1805; and retained office
with Bushe as his colleague under the Cabinet of "all the talents," worthily sustaining their intellectual reputation in Ireland. They gave him an English sea ,
and tempted him, not reluctant, to a British ambition. His brief career in Parliament at this time, bred in him an extraordinary attachment to that high and
select party, of which Earl Grenville was the head. He followed the Stowe sect
ever afterwards. Nor is it difficult to conceive, what an effect the influence of
that family of statesmen, by birth and profession, aristocrats in the noblest sense
of the word, and engaged to the public service with a zealous, unselfish, and industrious devotion—must have had upon a man, fresh from the Union's experience of borough-mongering rottenness in the lower House, and miserable self-
emasculation in the upper. In their resolute sincerity for the Catholics, and
against the French, he founded the basis of his future political career. He left
office honestly with them, in 1807, gave up his seat, and came home to make a
fortune sufficient to enable him to live independently in Parliament; showing,
as Grattan said, "a contempt for salary equal to his regard for law." There is
no doubt that at the time he could have continued to hold his office, as Bushe
did, and secured to himself the fifteen years of absolute power and unlimited
lucre upon which his rival, Saurin, then entered.

This is a view of him, at the height of his fame as a lawyer, in the period
which followed, from the vivid pen of William Henry Curran :—

"Of all the eminent lawyers I have heard, he seemed to me to be the most admi-
rably qualified for the department of his profession in which he shines. His mind
is at once subtle and comprehensive; his language clear, copious, and condensed;
his powers of reasoning are altogether wonderful. Give him the most complicated and doubtful case to support—with an array of apparently hostile decisions
to oppose him at every step—the previous discussion of the question has probably
satisfied you, that the arguments of his antagonists are neither to be answered or
evaded—they have fenced round the rights of their clients with all the great
names in equity—Hardwicke, Camden, Thurlow, Eldon :—Mr. Plunket rises:

* "If Mr. Pitt is firm, he will meet with no difficulty; the misfortunes of the present
time are much in favour towards carrying the present point on the same grounds that
the rebellion assisted in carrying the Union. Timid men will not venture on any change
of system however wise and just, unless their fears are alarmed by pressing dangers."
—*Lord Cornwallis to Lord Castlereagh*—CASTLEREAGH CORRESPONDENCE, vol. iv., p. 30.

which a perpetual pallor overspread the whole visage. While he pleaded before the Bench, there was a natural authority about him, that embarrassed the Chancellor on his wool-sack. He lorded it over Mr. Speaker, too, and chained the Commons when he rose. His manner had the same austere energy and studious simplicity as his language. It was perfectly natural and unaffected; the only peculiarity of his delivery on record is, that as he reached each climax of his statement, point after point, he would raise his two hands gradually above his head, and then suddenly swing them down, as though he would drive the argument home with a sledge-hammer. It was a singular gesture, and almost seemed to say *quod erat demonstrandum*.

Plunket's course in British politics illustrated the principles of Burke, and was identified with the party of Earl Grenville. He was an Anti-Jacobin Whig. In 1813, we find him in savage attack upon the Liverpool Cabinet for compromising the Catholic Question; but in 1815, he sustains the same cabinet against Earl Grey and the Gallican Whigs, upon the question of renewing the war. The following year, we find him again in violent opposition to the financial measures of the ministry. But when the discontents which ensued upon those very measures assumed a revolutionary character, he gave to Lord Castlereagh all the immense aid of his ability, his independent position, and his forensic fame. His speech upon the Peterloo massacre had the same result, in opening direct relations between him and the government, that had followed his speech in Emmet's case. " 'He saved the cabinet by that one speech,' said one of the ablest and most critical of the Whigs."* The Cabinet were more than willing to acknowledge the obligation—but Plunket was slow to admit an interested adhesion. He would not even accommodate them with a full report of his Peterloo speech. Nevertheless, he was heartily abused as a corrupt deserter by Earl Grey in the House of Lords, and by the advanced Reformers in and out of Parliament. There was now, indeed, an open breach in the ranks of the opposition. The structure of the Cabinet had also considerably changed. It contained at once the most unrelenting enemies and the most eminent advocates of Emancipation in the house. Indeed there never was a cabinet in England, not even Chatham's, which so completely deserved the epithet of a Patch-work Cabinet as that which is called Lord Liverpool's, from the year 1812 to the year 1827, but which in reality consisted of the same integral elements, for five years before, and for three years after that statesman's premiership. It had originally been formed on a pledge to the king, never to propose any redress to the Catholic Claims—and consisted on the one hand of ministers like Perceval and Eldon, who were his majesty's particular advisers in this question, and on the other hand, of Pitt's peculiar disciples, the young Tory tribunes, Canning and Castlereagh, who accepted his design of emancipating the Irish Catholics as a doctrine of imperial policy. One could not by possibility traverse a wider difference of view upon this subject, than existed between the minister who kept the king's conscience, and the minister who stood next to the people, between the liberal zeal of Plunket, and the incurable bigotry of Eldon. By its later Irish appointments, this government had adopted a system, which amounted to a precursorship of emancipation. But whenever the question came into the House of Commons, the opposition could afford to look on, and halloo one set of his majesty's ministers against the other. Imagine such a debate as this! The Irish Attorney-General rises to present the petition of the Catholic Association, and to de-

* Mr. Owen-Madyn's " Ireland and its Rulers."

clare that the laws affecting Catholics are an unconstitutional, impolitic, and useless injustice. The Secretary for the Home Department denounces the Catholic Association as the greatest peril of the public peace, and the Catholic Claims as incompatible with the system and institutions of the empire. The Secretary for Foreign Affairs has come down to the house on crutches, to declare his solemn belief, that England will forfeit her position in Europe, if she persists in refusing to do justice to her Irish subjects. The Irish Chief Secretary assures honourable gentlemen, that the Irish people are a rabid and rebellious horde, who will only swamp the State if admitted. Finally, the minister who carried the Union, and who has the most profound experience of the policy of the Castle, takes a last opportunity of assuring the house, before his elevation to the peerage, that this measure must sooner or later be passed, and the sooner the better. What is his Majesty's opposition to do while his Majesty's ministers are at such cross-purposes? The House of Lords with calm contempt listens to this exterior uproar; but Eldon, on his woolsack, that had almost become a second throne, now and then shudders with a foreboding terror; hearing afar off " the tramp of seven millions of men."

There is no more signal retribution in all history, than that which has followed the cruel and impious injustice of the Irish Penal Laws. Despised and persecuted, the miserable Celtic Papist pursued the British minister like the monster of Frankenstein, breathing perpetual vengeance, and harassing his policy at every point. A tithe of the armies that met his generals in Flanders or Spain was recruited at the mass houses of Connaught and Munster. It was the arm of the Irish Catholic in the enemy's uniform, which covered the retreat of Ramillies and decided the victory of Fontenoy. The most dangerous antagonist of the English conquest in India was one of the expatriated, Lally Tollendal. It was a Munster Papist who led the Russian arms to the spot where Sebastopol lately stood. In all the armies and courts of Europe, this outlawed and excommunicated Pariah disgraced the policy of England, by his heroic valour, his loyalty in service, and his capacity in command. At home, meantime, he kept the Ascendancy which had been established over him, in constant terror of a war at once servile, civil, religious, of property, and of the succession. He was by turns a Jacobite and a Jacobin. When the Ascendancy took up arms against England, their citizen array rested on the unarmed masses, who hated their Irish masters much, but their English enemy far more. When the Ascendancy refused the Catholic petition, they revenged the wrong by that passive attitude which allowed the Union to be carried. Then they shared the prostration which befel their country; but although apparently insignificant in the policy of the empire, the dead weight of their pressure mysteriously destroyed its equilibrium. In 1801, in 1807, long before O'Connell had elevated them into a political power, Pitt and Grenville, the two ablest ministers of the two greatest parties in England, had to abdicate office, because the conscience of a British statesman could no longer tolerate the indefensible injustice of their position. They cowed Wellington— they checkmated Peel. The Irish Catholics have wrecked more ministries since the Union than all other political questions and parties put together. The old king, George the Third, had, with a dogged and malignant bigotry devoted all his authority to maintain his hostility to their claims; but in the end the task broke his brain. The Duke of York publicly declared that the Catholic Question had driven his father mad. The crown at last had to give way before that monstrous moral force, filled with such spirit and *solidarite*. George the Fourth, with tears, told the Irish Protestant Bishops that "they had done their duty" in assuring him he was about to break his coronation oath, "but what could he do? He could not command a ministry capable of conducting affairs in the position to which they had come." To this conclusion it had come at last; and largely owing to Plunket's endeavours.

"Lord Plunket was, in my opinion, the most powerful and able advocate the Catholics ever had. I will say, that he, more than any other man, contributed to the success of the Roman Catholic Question." Such is the striking testimony of Sir Robert Peel, expressed when an interval of nearly twenty years had cast the sober hue of history between him and that momentous political crisis. Such too was the emphatic and authoritative testimony of Canning. And it is true testimony. We, Irish Catholics, are wont to regard our extraordinary agitation with its plenary arrogation of the functions of government, its weekly parliament in the Corn Exchange, its exchequer of Catholic rent, its arbitration courts of justice, its omnipotent tribune, and his brilliant staff of orators—his skilful application of the administrative mechanism of the church—his masses of passive-obedient or stormy-passionate peasantry—all culminating to the grand *coup* which completely clogged the Protestant Constitution at Clare; we are too much accustomed to treat these things as the whole of the history of Catholic liberty. But it had a splendid parliamentary history besides—and to parliament Plunket impersonated the cause as completely as O'Connell did to the people. He did more to reconcile the mind of the House to the policy and justice of the Catholic Claims than any other, than all the other advocates of them. His clear, calm, lofty argument reads strangely beside the passionate appeals, the clamorous complaints, the taunts and threats of the Catholic Association. The grand grounds of that argument were: I. That the Catholics were not slaves at all; that they were already practically admitted to the substantial privileges of the Constitution, and only denied its honours in such a way as to offend their loyalty without lessening their power. II. That the machinery of exclusion by oath under the Test and Corporation Acts was immoral, imperfect, and inconsistent in itself, and with all the internal and external polity of England. III. That the true safety of the Church Establishment consisted in a generous policy, whereas its identification with the existing system of civil disabilities exposed it to the perilous enmity of a whole people. IV. That a system of religious disabilities was alien to the spirit of the British Constitution, and had only been provisionally attached to the legislation of the empire, under circumstances which had gradually expired—sustaining this branch of his argument by a masterly historical study of the progress of penal religious legislation from the Reformation to the Revolution, and the re-actionary tendency towards a total repeal of the peculiarly Protestant laws afterwards. V. That the safety of Church and State against Popery might in the present age be amply provided for by accompanying the grant of civil privileges to the laity with a system of administrative relations with the clergy; a concordat—the Veto, the Pension, what the Catholics called the Wings.

The House had been in the habit of considering Catholic Relief merely as a measure of expediency, and even of an immoral and unconstitutional expediency. Arguments so different from those which it was in the habit of hearing—arguments which rested the case of the Catholics upon an indisputably constitutional basis, created, we may well believe, a profound and original sensation. Plunket has obtained the whole glory of this unrivalled political pleading. But Plunket perhaps unconsciously had drawn its leading principles and method from that grand depository of political wisdom, the writings of Edmund Burke. The

Tracts and Letters of that master of statesmen on the Catholic Disabilities—although loosely and hastily written, and, like his other Irish political studies, almost forgotten in the fame of his labours for the people of India and America, and against the principles of the French Revolution—had long before exhausted the subject, and left only corollaries and deducibles for those who followed in his rear. He "who saw everything and foresaw everything," had from the first moment that his splendid mind surveyed the condition of "that municipal country in which he was proud to have been born," urged that the civil emancipation of the Catholics and the freedom of their Church from the influence of the state, were essential principles of imperial policy and Irish government.

On the latter point, the question of the independence of the Catholic Church, Burke stands honourably alone among British statesmen. Upon this point the parliamentary question and the popular agitation moved always aloof, and yet always approaching to each other. British statesmen and the British Parliament would gladly have conceded civil privileges to the laity at any time, provided they obtained an influence over the Church. Pitt's plan contemplated the reduction of the Irish bishops and clergy to a state of dependence upon the crown as complete as that of the Established Church; and Pitt's was the project of law which his successors always contemplated. Even the liberal Protestant body, even Plunket and Grattan, were anxious, while they conceded full political rights to the laity to encourage them to what they conceived an independent use of them by weakening the influence of the clergy. It would seem to have been by a special Providence that legislation upon the question was so long delayed; for had it taken place at any earlier date or under any other ministry, the old national Church of Ireland should inevitably have been the subject of a department in the Castle. Pitt had perfected all his arrangements with the principal bishops and the leading aristocrats of the Catholic body. A strong body of the laity, a strong body of the bishops for many years afterwards eagerly supported the Veto. Immortal honour to Daniel O'Connell and to the faithful Catholic instinct of the people, who sustained him in repudiating any concession that would have brought the taint of a state connection upon the free Church of St. Patrick and St. Laurence! For years of patient hope deferred, of glorious indefatigable effort, they laboured not in vain; they had at last so widened the breach and weakened the enemy, that the final effort carried the question by storm, and ministers had to surrender Wings and all. The history of these persistent parliamentary approaches is the history of Plunket's career in the British House of Commons. He moved with the progress and grew with the growth of the Catholic question. It made his fame as the first parliamentary orator of his period. He went into office, with it and Lord Wellesley. He went on the English Bench as Sir William Plunket, Master of the Rolls, when Canning's premiership denoted another advance in the ministerial dispositions to concession. Finally, he went to the House of Lords with the certainty that it was safe in the Commons, and sat by the Duke of Wellington's side, watching every turn of the debate, and not less impressive in that cold and stately atmosphere, than he had been among the knights and burgesses of the three kingdoms.

And with the enactment of Catholic Emancipation, Plunket's political career may be said to terminate. His arguments in the Upper House are as powerful, as profound, as well adapted to his audience, as those which for years he had addressed to the Commons. But after he came home with that great measure of peace and good-will, he seldom reappeared in the political arena

He did, indeed, once or twice put forth the old lustre and vigour of his mind in that matchless debate in which, with him, the great law lords, Lyndhurst, and Eldon, and Brougham, closed in the lists of Reform. But his speaking, which was frequent for several years after 1829, was generally upon Irish business, and was only a superior order of common-place.

His career in office was distinguished by a high-minded fearlessness and impartiality. He gave the example of a crown prosecutor, who, in the most violent times, was never known to pack a jury. If he strained the authority of his office in the Bottle Riot prosecution, we are bound to remember the position in which the first officer of the law was then placed in Ireland. He stood between two factions, which equally domineered over the law in their respective spheres; and he had determined to try issue with both. He had to deal with Orange judges, sheriffs, juries, and officials upon the one hand—he had to assail a cause indentified with his own personal predilections and antecedents upon the other. He failed in both. What could he hope to do against the Orange Ascendancy, pleading in a hostile court, before a packed jury, with Mr. Solicitor-General, a well-known partizan of the prisoners at the Bar—and scandalously deserted by ministers when the case afterwards came before the Commons! If ever a man was justified in pushing authority to the extreme, it was in such a position. We may be sure that he secretly rejoiced when the counter-prosecutions which he undertook against Sheil and O'Connell also failed; and may well fancy his feelings realised in Sheil's passionate appeal;—

"When Mr. Plunket read the words attributed to Mr. O'Connell, did he ask himself—What is the provocation given to this man? Who is he, and what am I? Who is His Majesty's Attorney-General, the Right Honourable William Conyngham Plunket? I know not whether he administered that personal interrogatory to himself; but if he did, this should have been the answer. 'I raised myself from a comparatively humble station by the force of my own talents to the first eminence in the state. In my profession I am without an equal. In parliament I had once no superior. When out of office, I kindled the popular passion.—I was fierce, violent, vituperative; at last I have won the object of my life; I am Attorney-General for Ireland; I possess great wealth, great power, great dignity, and great patronage. If I had been a Roman Catholic instead of an enfranchised Presbyterian, what should I have been?' I can tell him. He would have 'carried up and down a discontented and repining spirit;' he would have felt like a man with large limbs who could not stand erect; his vast faculties would have been cribbed and cabined in; and how would he have borne his political humiliation? Would he have been tame and abject, servile and sycophantic? Look at him, and say, how would that lofty forehead have borne the brand of 'popery?' How would that high demeanour have worn the stoop of the slave? No, he would have been the chief demagogue, the most angry, tumultuous, and virulent tribune of the people—he would have superadded the honest gall of his own nature to the bitterness of political resentment—he would have given utterance to ardent feelings in burning words; and in all the force of passion, he would have gnawed the chain from which he could not break. And is this the man who prosecutes for words? If the tables were turned; if Mr. O'Connell were Attorney-General, and Mr. Plunket were the great leader of the people; if Antony were Brutus, and Brutus Antony, how would the public mind have been inflamed; what exciting matter would have been flung amongst the people? What lava would have been poured forth? 'The very stones would rise in mutiny.' Would to Heaven, that not only Mr.

Plunket, but every other Protestant that deplores our imprudence in the spirit of a fastidious patronage, would adopt the simple test of nature, and make our case his own, and he would confess that, if similarly situated, he would give vent to his emotions in phrases as exasperated, and participate in the feelings which agitate the disfranchised community to which it would be his misfortune to belong."*

He was not a great judge in the opinion of the Four Courts—rather, be it said, he was not so great a judge as his former fame had led men to expect he would prove. But after a position at the Bar, in which his character had towered by its moral and intellectual elevation, over a bench filled by much inferior men, and after the illustrious and powerful station which he had so long occupied in the senate, it is easy enough to understand that neither the Common Pleas nor the Court of Chancery was likely to excite his faculties, or administer a fresh impulse to his ambition. As he grew old, it began to be observed that he was of an intensely indolent disposition. The three score years and ten allotted to man's life had almost elapsed ere he reached the woolsack—and, spent in such arduous and unremitting exertion, might well have wearied and worn away even that massive intellect and those athletic energies. In his most vigorous days, indeed, it is said that his best work was the fruit of rapid, ready, and intense effort rather than the result of patient and plodding industry. Old attorneys say that he was seldom known to note a brief, and that he digested his business as he drove into town from the beloved shades of Old Connaught. Of the method of his public speaking he told Sheil, who told George Henry Moore (so that the tradition reaches us through a line of orators accomplished in the art) that he always carefully prepared to the very syllable the best passages and the best only of his great speeches, and used these as a kind of rhetorical stepping stones, trusting to his native fluency and force for sustaining the style. Sheil said, what all who ever heard and all who read Plunket will confirm, that so consummate was the art with which this was done, one could never discern where the prepared was welded into the extemporaneous. But certain it is believed to be, that many of his great sentences—that for instance in which he did *not* say that History was no better than an old Almanack—had been carefully constructed and finished *ad unguem* long before the occasions came upon which they were applied. It is easier to believe this of a style with the corruscating brilliancy of Grattan's than of one with such a stately and sustained rhythm, and out of whose own innate and vivid vitality, the grand, simple figures seem to flash. Of his wit,† Parliament seldom saw a specimen; but some of the best anecdotes of the Four Courts are those which record its virile ease and attic finish.

His later life preached two striking political morals. One was reflected from the passionate nationality of his early life. He had submitted to the Union; he had devoted his mighty talents to the service of the empire; he had become a West Briton to all intents and purposes. But the curse of Swift was on him withal Being an Irishman, he was used while he was useful, and afterwards flung aside with indignity. When he was appointed Master of the Rolls in England by Canning—the first attempt that had been made to place an Irish Barrister on the English Bench—the Bar of England rose in rebellion at the outrage to their nationality, and the minister was obliged to cancel the appointment. So

---

* Speech in Catholic Association, 6th January, 1825.
† I may be excused for mentioning here, the last witticism of Plunket's of which there is record. "What is the tone of the *Nation* to day, my lord?" asked some one in '43. "Oh, Wolfe Tone, of course," was his answer.

much for the reality of the Union! But when in his old age, the Whigs wanted to get the Irish woolsack for Sir John (afterwards Lord) Campbell, Lord Plunket was disgracefully hustled into a reluctant resignation. He had thus lived to approve in his own person the prophetic spirit of his earlier days. There was another moral too in this later life of his—his price. When he did sell himself, it was on the grand scale of his character. After making, as it was believed, £120,000 at the Bar, he took, one after another, the most honourable and productive offices of his profession, and the British Peerage. He made one son a Bishop, another a Chairman of a County, a third Commissioner of Bankrupts, a fourth Vicar of Bray—and scattered the *spolia opima* of Church and State among a clan of kinsmen to the third and the fourth degree.

In private life, among the few to whom he opened his heart, he was greatly beloved always. The affection which Peter Burrowes had for him was womanly in its fondness, and childish in its simplicity. Between him and Bushe, and Magee, and Millar, and the surviving few of his early circle of college friends, to the last a loyal and generous friendship subsisted. Of them all, he remained alone and the last, and his heart seemed to grow stern and gloomy, and the bright light of his intellect to fade, as one by one they fell around him, and he remained weathering year after year like an old oak, the last of a forest—and going, as the stern cynic, to whom he was much alike in many of his moods, said of himself, going atop.

Decay first crept into his frame through the subtle valves of the intellect. For years before his decease, he had sat in the valley of the shadow of death. Mournfully the once giant intellect dwindled away, and his last days were like those of Swift, Moore, and O'Connell. In one of the wayward moods of these later days, he is said to have destroyed all his political papers. He often drove from Old Connaught, along the margin of the bay, towards the city that had once been the arena of his ambition, and that had proudly hailed every phase of his fortunes—and a last trait told of him by one bright-eyed girl, who loved the white-haired "old man eloquent," is, that he was very gentle with children, and stopped to speak with them always—a child himself again of the second childhood; he whose manhood had been of so stately and masculine a mould. At last, on the 5th of January, 1854, came the merciful release of death, startling rather than saddening all who heard the news; for the name of Plunket had long been irrevocably blended with the past. He sleeps in the Cemetery of Mount Jerome, under a massive altar-base of granite, beside a walk that leads from the old lawn of John Keogh, and that was familiar many and many a long year ago to the footsteps of Tone in the gay and brilliant days, when Lawyer Plunket and he began the warfare of the world.

THE SELECT SPEECHES

OF

WILLIAM CONYNGHAM PLUNKET.

THE PRESS.

March 3, 1798.

THE last of the Irish parliaments assembled on the 9th of January, 1798 Plunket took the oaths and his seat on the 6th of February. It is mentioned in the *Journals*, that having been named on an election committee within the following week, he claimed, and obtained exemption in consequence of his recent return. His name appears in the *Debates* for the first time on the 3rd of March, in committee on "a bill for amending the act of the 23d and 24th of George III., for securing the liberty of the press by preventing the abuses arising from the publication of traitorous, seditious, false, and scandalous libels by persons unknown."

The express design of this bill was to suppress the *Press* newspaper, the organ of the United Irishmen. The *Press* had been started in the autumn of 1797, with funds supplied by Arthur O'Connor, and with the aid and inspiration of Addis Emmett, MacNevin, Lord Edward Fitzgerald, and, in fact, the whole Dublin directory of the United Irishmen. It was written from the first number to the last with a daring and eloquence unknown in Irish journalism since the days of the Drapier. It probably furnished a model for Mr. Mitchel's *United Irishman*. The leader was ordinarily a philippic at the Lord Lieutenant. The moderates, Grattan and his party, were stigmatised or ridiculed. Every article was "in red ink." The *Press* would not condescend to report the debates in parliament—even the debates in which its own existence was decided—and totally ignored that institution, until one morning Major Sirr and his myrmidons marched into the office, carried off their type cases, and smashed their presses. The principal writers were Sampson, formerly of the *Northern Star*, O'Connor, Emmett, Deane Swift, and, it was suspected, Dr. Drennan.

In the course of February, Mr. O'Donnell, of Donegal, moved for a committee to examine into the character of certain articles recently published and attacked the government for not prosecuting. The articles which he quoted were rather strong. One of them dared Major Sirr to say in their office at Abbey-street what he was reported to have said elsewhere of the writers of the *Press*, and promised him a horsewhipping if he should. Another begged to inform a noble peer that if he should desire to apply more particularly the general censure he had lately passed upon the society of United Irishmen, there were gentlemen, nay men of his own rank, to be heard of in Abbey-street, who would be pleased to treat such reflections as personal. The attorney-general (Toler), in reply, stated that there was no lack of inclination to prosecute; but the state of the law precluded his proceeding. The statute gave no remedy, unless against the registered publisher, and that individual had left the country.

Arthur O'Connor was at this date the registered publisher. Peter Finnerty who first filled that dangerous post, had been set in the pillory—on which occasion Lord Edward Fitzgerald and Arthur O'Connor took their places at his side—and sent to gaol the previous Christmas. Samuel Neilson, who succeeded him, was also instantly arrested and prosecuted Then O'Connor avowed himself proprietor and editor; but went to England a few days afterwards, and on his way to France was arrested on the charge of high treason, upon which he was afterwards tried at Maidstone. Meantime there was no way of instituting a prosecution in Ireland. The registered proprietor was the person properly indictable, and he was out of the realm.

Mr. O'Donnell's committee recommended an abominable bill. Besides imposing the obligation of large securities upon newspaper proprietors, it enabled grand juries to present newspapers containing seditious or libellous matter as nuisances; and empowered magistrates, upon such presentation, to seize and destroy the printing materials and suppress the publication of such newspapers. The opposition to it was quite insignificant, however. Mr. Tighe, of Wicklow, Plunket, and his colleague, Francis Dobbs, were the only members who took part in it. They succeeded in diminishing the stringency of particular provisions, but not in spoiling the main force of the measure.

On the 3rd of March, the house resolved into committee on the third reading. The attorney-general moved a clause making it necessary for the publisher of a newspaper to give securities, to be approved by the authorities, himself in £1000 and two or three others in the like sum. Mr. Tighe spoke against this clause with great spirit, on the ground that it would give the minister almost an arbitrary power of fixing who should or who should not publish a newspaper. "At present," he continued, " the jealousy of government with respect to libels and slanderous publications seemed to be entirely at one side; for though publications of that kind appeared perhaps in all the public prints, yet none but those whose politics were of a certain cast were ever noticed by them: he instanced the *Dublin Journal*, in which there frequently appeared the most gross and scandalous libels on the best and brightest characters of both countries—libels in which the first and most respectable men in the community were falsely, basely, foolishly, and meanly aspersed, for no other reason but because they did not pour fulsome adulation and undeserved praise upon the ministers. This paper was in the pay of administration, and for aught he knew administration, if they were capable of writing their thoughts, conveyed them through this foul channel to the public."

Toler replied, declaring that all the government wanted was securities. Let the journalist print treason, sedition, or scandal if he pleased, but let him be properly responsible, amenable, and liable for it. " What, he would ask, was the satisfaction to that society which might be injured by the promulgation of seditions, or to the individuals whose good fame should be blasted by the publication of the most foul and unfounded calumnies, if the printers and publishers of such mischievous publications were either men destitute of property or fugacious in their persons?" He would be no party to reducing the amount of security.

Plunket followed him:—

Finding from the tendency of every clause in the bill, that it went, not to restrain the licentiousness of the press, but to restrict its liberty, he gave his opposition to the whole of it. The bill, he understood, had originally been called for by a case which had occurred where the printer of a paper was not responsible. So far as any measure went to provide for that case, and make the printers of newspapers responsible for what they published, he would support it. But this bill went not merely to that point—its great object seemed to be to lay such previous restraints on the liberty of publishing as would, in his mind, utterly abolish that liberty.

So far as he had been able to learn in what the liberty of the press consisted, he had always believed that it consisted in this—that every man should have full liberty to communicate his sentiments to the public, without any restriction whatever but that if he published anything inconsistent with the peace, good order, or morals of society, or anything tending to injure others in their property, persons, or character, he should be liable to such punishment as the law should inflict for such misconduct. Nor was this merely his private sense on the subject; it was corroborated by one of the highest authorities who had ever written on the laws and constitutions of these countries. Speaking of the liberty of the press, that great man said: "The liberty of the press is indeed essential to the nature of a free state; but this liberty consists in laying no previous restraints upon publications." "Every freeman has an undoubted right to lay what sentiments he pleases before the public, and to forbid this is to destroy the freedom of the press." "And to this we may add, that the only plausible argument heretofore used for restraining the just freedom of the press, ' that it was necessary to prevent its daily abuse,' will entirely lose its force when it is shown by a seasonable exertion of the laws that the press cannot be abused to any bad purpose, without incurring a suitable punishment." Such was the opinion of Justice Blackstone.

Did the present bill, then, lay any previous restraint on publication? Certainly it did. What else can it be considered to prevent a man from publishing until he gets security to the amount of £2000. Justice Blackstone says, every freeman has a right to lay his sentiments before the public. This bill says no man shall lay any sentiment before the public unless he be worth £2000. Was not this curtailing the liberty of the press?

But who were the men that were called on to find security for so large a sum? Not certainly a very wealthy class of men, who could be supposed to be able to find it without inconvenience. They were printers; a business not in the very highest degree of repute, probably not so high as it ought. They were men who entered into the business of news printing to make a livelihood, and who generally began with little or no property, and made a living of it principally by their manual labour. If such men were called on to give security to the amount of £2000 they would be compelled to resign the business. Even of men worth that sum, the minister might refuse the securities at his discretion, while the favourite print might be suffered to publish without any security at all. Thus the liberty of the press in Ireland would receive a vital wound. Every channel of communication with the great bulk of the people would be shut up, except those which government might think proper to keep open to blazon their own praise and their own virtues. There would reign throughout the country a deadly silence, except where the venal voice of some hireling print might break in upon it by mutilated and false statements of facts, by misrepresentation of principles, or by base and servile adulation of its masters!

What was the occasion of introducing a bill thus aiming at the vital essence of the liberty of the press? It was that some publications had appeared aspersing the government, and tending to excite disaffection and sedition. Why had not the law officers of the crown noticed them then, and applied to the law of the land for punishment?

[Here it was said by some gentlemen on the other side of the house that they had done so.]

I believe gentlemen will find themselves mistaken on this subject. The prosecution which has been instituted against Mr. O'Connor is for an offence committed long prior to his becoming the proprietor of *The Press;* and though so many complaints have been made of the publications in that paper, within the last five or six weeks, I have the best reason to believe that no steps whatsoever have been taken to prosecute him or them. It will be said he is not in the kingdom—true; but he has already given security for his appearance to the full amount exacted by this bill, so, that if any argument can be drawn from the situation of Mr. O'Connor, that argument must bear against the bill, as it appears the government have already the same hold of him which this bill would give them. And yet they complain that he evades justice.

The licentiousness of the press has been complained of: I will tell government a better remedy against it than this bill affords them. Let them act in such a manner as to be above its obloquy. Let them restore the constitution. Let them reform the abuses which pollute every department. Let them reform the parliament. Let them mitigate their system of coercion. Let them conciliate the people. Then may they laugh at the slanders of a licentious press. They will have a better defence against its malice than this unconstitutional measure can afford them. If they want proof of the efficacy of this remedy, I refer them to what has occurred on the case of that unfortunate man, William Orr, of which so much has been said. The falsest calumnies have been thrown on the judges who presided at that trial. Do the public believe those calumnies? Are the names of Yelverton or Chamberlaine less loved and revered because they have been thus calumniated? No! The shafts of malice have been blunted by the virtue, the integrity, the humanity of those learned and upright men; so will they ever fall innoxious from the seven-fold shield of public and private virtue! Sir, the constitution of these countries rests on two great pillars—the liberty of the press and the trial by jury. The imperious necessity of the times (a necessity of which the existence cannot be denied, but into the causes of which it is not now time to inquire) has made it necessary to suspend for a time the trial by jury. If the liberty of the press is also to be given up, in what situation will this country be? What security any longer remains to the people to guard them against the encroachments of power? what vestige of constitution or liberty? On broad principles I oppose this bill altogether—I decline to go into objections to particular clauses.

---

[1] This speech appears to have startled ministers. The chief secretary himself, Mr. Pelham, replied. He shirked the "broad principles," canvassed any details to which Plunket had alluded, and ended by advising his right honourable friend, Mr. Attorney-General, to concede the principal point, the amount of security. The security was accordingly reduced to £500.

A swarm of speakers followed, defending the principle of the bill, wholly on account of the intolerable audacity of the *Press*, which treated College-green quite as ill as Cork-hill, and either side of the house as if it were no better than the other. There was no further resistance, and the bill passed.

Afterwards, the *Press* was forcibly stopped. A curious fact may be mentioned here—that one of the printers in the *Press* office on that occasion, Mr. T. O'Flanagan, was also in the *Nation* office fifty years afterwards, when the authorities effected a similar exploit.

THE STATE OF THE NATION.
March 5, 1798.

The ambition of Pitt's Irish policy was the Union. In more peaceful times he might, perhaps, have attempted it by raising the Catholic element against the parliament, as he afterwards half reconciled the leading Catholics to the sacrifice of national independence by promising emancipation. But when he found the French Republic really determined upon dismembering the British empire by revolutionising Ireland, it became necessary to precipitate his designs. On the one hand, therefore, he utterly destroyed the character and acquired the control of the parliament by the most open and infamous corruption. On the other, he tried a policy as wicked as Alva's, to drive the people into a premature rebellion. Thus the state at which Ireland had arrived, in 1797, was the most execrable that could be conceived. The patriot opposition, headed by Grattan, had formally seceded from parliament in disgust with its corruption and slavishness. Martial law was proclaimed throughout the country, and this martial law was administered by an army which, in the words of its own general, Sir Ralph Abercrombie, was " in such a state of licentiousness, as to render it formidable to every one but the enemy."

A convulsion was evidently imminent. The Irish Whigs made a last effort after the meeting of the new parliament to avert it, in which they were aided by Fox and his friends, in the English Commons, and Lord Moira came over expressly to move conciliation in the Irish House of Lords.

He lost no time, but early in the session attacked the government for the policy they had during the previous year pursued towards the people. He recapitulated the abominable acts of cruelty and torture, flogging, picketing, and half-hanging, by which the confession of crimes had, in innumerable instances, been extorted from persons against whom no legal evidence could be adduced, and no reasonable cause even of suspicion—persons who, unless under the momentary pressure of excruciating agony, still persisted in the avowal of their innocence. He declared his intention, if his statement of facts was denied, to move for the examination of witnesses at the bar of the house. He admitted the probable existence of conspiracy in the kingdom: but asked were they " on a loose charge of partial transgression, to inflict punishment on a whole community. The state of society was dreadful, indeed, when the safety of every man was at the mercy of a secret informer; when the cupidity, the malevolence, or the erroneous suspicions of an individual were sufficient to destroy his neighbour. His lordship's humane and able speech was concluded by moving an address to the Lord Lieutenant, praying for conciliatory measures; but after a long debate the motion was, of course, rejected by a large majority.

On the 5th of March Sir Lawrence Parsons introduced a similar motion in the House of Commons. Parsons was one of the more liberal of the Irish aristocrats, who had been bitten in their youth with the political doctrines of the French revolution. He was a friend of Tone, and in parliament had always been an advocate of the most sweeping reform. In the absence of Grattan and the old parliamentary opposition, he found himself, for a short time, in the lead of that side of the house, and spoke upon this occasion, as upon several others, where pluck and power were called for, with an energetic and vehement eloquence. The substance of his speech is given in the following passage:—

"The distractions of the country were too obvious and too lamentable for him to dwell on its circumstances: but he called upon the house, by the motion which he was about to make, to inquire into the causes of that distraction, to examine into the demands of the people; it was their duty, as representatives of that people, to conciliate that people, by conceding those demands, if they were just, or convincing them by argument, if they were inadmissible. This would be adopting a conduct worthy of the representatives of the people: this would be better than continuing a system of coercion which had failed, or branding a whole people as factiously and irreconcileably turbulent."

His motion, seconded by Lord Caulfield (son of the Earl of Charlemont) was—
"That this house do forthwith resolve itself into a committee of the whole house, to consider whence the present discontents in this country arise, and what are the most effectual means of allaying the same."

Lord Castlereagh flatly opposed the motion, declaring that the United Irishmen were not men to be contented or conciliated by any measures of concession short of a separation from Ireland, and fraternity with the French Republic; that they were in open rebellion, and therefore only to be met by force; that the coercive measures of the government had been the consequences, not the causes of the discontents; and that the excesses charged on the soldiery were naturally to be expected from this state of things.

No fewer than twenty-nine speakers followed on the government side. The opposition could only command nineteen votes. Dr. Browne, member for the college, Tighe, of Wicklow, Newenham, author of the *View of Ireland*, Hans Hamilton, of Dublin county, and a few more, briefly gave their reasons for supporting the motion, which was attacked by several of the government members, as an exhibition of disaffection. Plunket also spoke as follows:—

It is contrary to my original intention, that I rise to say a few words on this question; nor should I have risen at all, but because it is made incumbent on every man who intends to vote for the motion to state his reasons for doing so. Such has been the obloquy that has been thrown on those who support it.

Sir, I feel as strongly as any man can the awful situation of this country; and I feel as much detestation for the wicked combination which has brought it into that situation as any gentleman who has spoken this night. If I could more emphatically express that detestation than they have done, I would do it. That situation, however, it is which imposes on the house a peculiar and imperious necessity of adopting every fair and honourable measure which may probably lead to lessen or avert the difficulties which press upon the state; and could I believe that by any sentiment which I shall utter this night those difficulties or the discontent of the country would be in any degree aggravated, my lips should be closed. No wish can be farther from my heart than to say anything which by possibility may have such a consequence.

It has been said by an honourable gentleman in the course of this debate [Mr. Daly], that there exist in Ireland only two parties—those who distrust and those who support the laws. The state of Ireland is not such as this division insinuates ; for if it means anything, it must mean that there are only two parties in the country, one who support and the other who oppose the government. I say there are in this country hundreds of thousands who, though they are neither in favour with the administration nor friends to their measures, but, on the contrary, dislike their principles and their system, yet are not with the United Irishmen, but entertain a more strong disapprobation of them and their plots. In the north of Ireland there are numbers of men who understand the constitution as well as any of the respectable assembly whom I address—men who not only know the constitution, but the best interests of this country better than any man who hears me, because their understandings are unsophisticated by that prejudice which I suppose it will not be denied is the natural result of peculiar situations and peculiar interests. These men are not combined with the traitors of the society of United Irishmen, and yet these men, however well inclined they may be to the British constitution, may entertain a very strong dislike to government and to their measures. If they see seats in this house bought and sold—if they not only see them bought, but made a retailable commodity in which government traffics—

[Mr. Plunket was called to order by Mr. Bagwell, who said such language was unparliamentary, and ought not to be tolerated.]

Sir, the honourable member quite mistakes my meaning. I am as confident as the right hon. gentleman I address that no seat in this house was ever bought or sold. No member in the house knows that this is impossible better than I do. But, sir, suppose those ignorant and foolish people of the north, of whom I have been speaking, were told, among many other equally false and slanderous tales that are every day circulated against our innocent government, and against this most honourable and immaculate assembly—suppose they were told that seats were really bought and sold, and suppose they should be foolish enough to believe the story, what conclusion must they not draw from these premises? The learned members of this house who know what is meant by "knowledge of the world" and "the usage of parliament," probably would call this practice by a soft name, but those unpolished people would certainly call such a traffic base. They would, no doubt, say it was a violation of the constitutional rights of the subject, a shameful debauchery of the morality of the nation, a scandalous departure from morals, the commencement of a crime among the higher ranks, which must soon descend with accelerated velocity to the lower orders, where it will vitiate whatever is sound in their principles, and make loyalty itself venal. If such errors can possibly have crept among any class of the king's subjects, would it not be wise to conciliate such men, and make so many honest, intelligent men fast friends to the constitution and the government, instead of leaving them to vibrate between loyalty and disaffection—a prize to reward the industry of sedition? Will you freeze that blood which, if you act as you ought, is ready to flow for your state?

Let me not be told that to agree to a motion of this kind is to conciliate traitors. Give me leave to tell you, sir, that the United Irishmen dread nothing so much as your granting such a measure—they tremble lest you should, because if you do you tear off the mask with which they have hitherto covered themselves, and strip them of those pretexts by which they have crowded their ranks. It is by this mode you must put them down. The rebellion of the mind, by which you are assaulted, is dreadful, and not to be combated by force. You have tried that remedy for three years, and the experiment has failed. You have stopped the mouth of the public by a convention bill —have committed the property and liberty of the people to the magistrate by the insurrection act—you have suspended the Habeas Corpus act—you have had, and you have used a strong military force—as great a force as you could call for; and there has been nothing that could tend to strengthen your hands or enable you to beat down this formidable conspiracy that you have not been invested with. What effect has your system produced? Discontent and sedition have grown threefold under your management. What objection, then, can you urge against trying another mode? If on trial it shall not be found to do good, you are only where you were. If it succeed, you have secured an inestimable benefit. Do not let me be understood as if I meant to withdraw from the hand of government any of the strength which they possess at this moment. No, if more were wanted I would give it, if the traitors could be put down by it; but while you go with the sword in one hand, I would have you carry the olive in the other.

Gentlemen have talked of French principles. These principles have grown indeed, but it is because they were not resisted by proper means. I wonder not that when assailed by these principles, the rotten fabric of the French monarchy tumbled into atoms; nor do I wonder that they carried terror and destruction through the despotisms of Europe. But I did hope that when the hollow spectre of French democracy approached the mild and chaste dignity of the British constitution, it would have fled before it. It would have done so had you not destroyed the British constitution before it reached us. You opposed it then with force, and its progress grew upon you. Restore the constitution, and it will defend you from this monster. Reform your parliament. Cease to bestow upon the worthless the wealth you extract from the bowels of your people. Let the principles of that revolution, which you profess to admire, regulate your conduct, and the horrid shade will melt into air before you.

You complain that French principles have taken hold of Ulster. The connexion then must have been forced, for they are not congenial. The people of the North are an industrious, plain, and sensible people. They have acquired property, and they know the worth of it. They have got a religious education, and they know the value of it. What have the atheism and frippery of France to do with such a people? What voluntary connection would the religious people of the North have with the mad wickedness of those who have pulled down God from Heaven to establish anarchy upon earth? I warn the minister not to treat this as a mere colonial question; it is one in which the interests of the empire are deeply concerned. He has already passed a bill of indemnity for crimes committed against the people. It is now time he should pass one for the nation. I call on him to recollect how severely he will be liable to account to his country and to his own conscience, if he suffers this question to be made an instrument to separate the two countries.

Isaac Corry, afterwards Castlereagh's Chancellor of the Exchequer, replied, with a malicious, but clumsy inuendo. To whatever barristers and Presbyterian ministers it applied, it certainly touched neither Plunket nor his father.

"The hon. gentleman who spoke last (he said) had stated that there were hundreds and thousands among the industrious and sensible people of the North, who were intent only on reform, and were not involved in the conspiracy. He wondered where the learned gentleman found those men; he knew some of a learned profession there who were among the first that engaged in that conspiracy—he knew others in a sacred profession, who had gone so far as to abuse their pulpits for the purpose of treason."

The motion was negatived by 156 to 19.

THE SHEARES CASE.

July 4, 1798.

THE only case in which Plunket appeared during the rebellion was that of the brothers Sheares, in which he was second to Curran. I refer the reader to Davis's edition of Curran for a graphic sketch of the trial. Plunket opened for Henry Sheares. Half of his speech is an argument on points of law, which I omit, and as Curran was to follow, he allowed himself little latitude to expatiate on the general merits of the case; but the following passage on Armstrong's evidence is in his most trenchant style. The evidence against Henry Sheares was very slight. The only evidence, in fact, was that of Captain Armstrong; and at the interview which took place with that miserable informer, John Sheares, the ablest and boldest of the brothers, was always spokesman. Henry only listened and assented.

A VERY few observations remain in point of fact. What I have hitherto said applies to both the prisoners, so far as respects the law of the case. But with regard to the facts, I must trouble you, upon the case of Mr. Henry Sheares, much less indeed than I would otherwise do, if I was not to be followed by a very able advocate, who will speak to the evidence.

With regard to Mr. Henry Sheares, the evidence against him rests upon the testimony of Captain Armstrong alone. As to the law stated by Mr. Ponsonby, of two witnesses being necessary, I will not give any positive opinion upon it. I do not pretend to say whether the statute in England enacted a new law, or only declared the old. There are great authorities, who say it is only a declaratory statute—among others, Lord Coke says, two witnesses were necessary by the common law. If he be right, we are entitled to the benefit of the common law, and will claim it. But I throw that out of the case—not concluded indeed; but supposing that, in point of law, the testimony of one witness is sufficient to convict, I beg leave to observe upon the nature of that testimony. What the kind of story it is which fell from the lips of the witness—how far it is natural or probable, or entitled to credit, merits your consideration, when compared with your observance upon life and manners. That so rash and indiscreet a confidence should be reposed in this stripling, without any previous acquaintance of himself, his life, or manners—without any pledge of secrecy—but rashly and suddenly, as if he had fallen in love with him upon first interview—is matter for your conjecture. How far it was an honourable ministry, is for your judgment.

In the case of a common informer, his evidence is weighed with caution. Every circumstance throwing a doubt upon it is to be attended to. If the testimony exceeds the common rules of life and course of experience, the jury are cautious in admitting it. But this is not the case of a common informer. It is not the case of an accomplice, who repents of his crime. That might be the fate of an honourable mind. A man may be involved in the guilt of conspiring or treason, and retrieve himself nobly by making an atonement to his country and his God, by a fair and full confession of the crime. But that is not the case here. This is the case of a man going for the purpose of creating and producing guilt, that he might make discovery of it. Does it not appear that the conception of the guilt was entertained in the mind, if not fomented by the witness. You are to consider the different motives and movements of the human heart, and how wavering dispositions may be taken advantage of, and urged on by dexterous persuasion to a conduct which the seduced may abhor. You are not now trying whether the prisoner be a man of strong frame—of firm nerves and mind, capable of resisting allurements of guilt and temptation to vice. But you are to try whether the evidence has satisfied you that he has been guilty of treason.

Suppose now the evidence to be true: would it not shake the mind of an ordinary man, not of the most strong and firm disposition, if he saw an officer of the camp making declarations hostile to government—making a sacrifice of his situation, saying, " I will betray the camp which I am appointed to guard" —if he goes and persecutes another with his volunteering treason, fastens upon him in the streets, follows him abroad, and haunts him at his house ; I say, are you surprised at seeing the other listen for a moment to the temptation, when he perceives that the man whose more immediate duty it is to resist the treason, has adopted it ? I say this, supposing for a moment that the evidence is true: I will show you presently it is not.

Was it the part of an honest man to seek repeated interviews —to follow the other to his house and into the bosom of his family, until at last he lodged him in a gaol? Did he know the prisoners before?—was he acquainted with their lives and characters? No; but, seized with a sudden zeal of turning informer against them, he insinuates himself into their acquaintance. I can conceive the zeal of an honest mind in the moment of mistaken enthusiasm to be led into an act of vice to save his country. I can conceive an exertion of Roman virtue flinging morals into the gulf as a sacrifice to patriotism. But what a life must there have been to claim praise for that act of enthusiastic ardour? There must have been a life of religious feelings, of continued virtue, and disinterested, honourable views. In such a case you can, by exerting your imagination, account for an act of perfidy to save the country. But does this witness stand in that point of view? No, gentlemen, by his own confession he is convicted, and we shall show by a crowd of witnesses, whose characters are above imputation, that he does not believe in the existence of a God, or a future state of rewards and punishments—that he is a notorious republican, and devoid of the principles of loyalty. Hear his own account. Was he a man of decided loyalty—attached to his king and country? No; he confessed he had been in the habit of reading Paine's pamphlets —his *Rights of Man* and his *Age of Reason*—his creed was founded upon these, and he drinks republicanism as a toast—and this man, the companion of Byrne, and who had been foolishly democratic, engages in conference with Mr. Sheares, and enters upon the new office of informer for the good of his country! It is surprising that between the violence of republicanism and the zeal of an informer for the crown, the mean proportion of virtuous patriotism could not be found! The friend of Mr. Patrick Byrne—the drinker of republican toasts, suddenly becomes a spy for the good of his country! You see, gentlemen, the evidence which has been laid before you. Is there any one fact brought forward, except the naked testimony of this informer, to fasten guilt upon Mr. Henry Sheares? He has chosen his time of interview with great discretion; no person has been present at the conversations, but the prisoners, who cannot give evidence for each other. Has the person who introduced them been brought forward, or the serjeant of the militia? They are in the power of the crown; or did the counsel for the prosecution conceive this witness to be so immaculate, that he could not be impeached, and not necessary to be supported? Why not produce Connors? He is in the barrack. Why not produce Byrne? He is in prison. Why not produce Fannan? Why not produce any one to give steadiness to the tottering evidence of this man?

Gentlemen, as to the proclamation which has been commented upon, it is not in the handwriting of the prisoner, Mr. Henry Sheares. It was not in his possession; he knew nothing of it; he had an opportunity of destroying it, if he chose, or knew of it. Whatever the effect of it may be, as applying to the other prisoner, I meddle not with it. But I do not think it affects the other, and most certainly, gentlemen, the court will tell you, that this evidence is not to weigh a feather upon your minds in determining the case of one man, to whom it does not apply, although it may be thought to have some relation to another. It is an unpublished, blotted, and unfinished paper. The mere circumstance of that blotted paper being found in the house of Mr. Henry Sheares, where Mr. John Sheares resorted—not received by Mr. Henry Sheares, not acknowledged by him; on the contrary, from the evidence you must infer he knew nothing about it—cannot weigh with you, nor affect his life. Is it proved that Mr. Henry Sheares did any act—corrupted any man or frequented any society, or took any political step, beyond the mere colouring which Captain Armstrong gives to the conversation between them? And how is that, with regard to Mr. Henry Sheares? Did he appear eager to gain proselytes? At the first interview, Mr. Henry Sheares declined to say anything; he departed, and did not return that day. Did that show an eagerness to gain a proselyte? He deserted Captain Armstrong, is hunted and persecuted by him; he infests the society of his wife and children—still no act is done; it rests in conversation; not a single act done; no men corrupted; no societies frequented, arms taken up, or furnished to others; no act countenancing rebellion, or hostility to the crown.

Gentlemen, we will prove by a crowd of witnesses that this gentleman, Mr. Henry Sheares, has been unconnected with and unconcerned in politics, devoted to pursuits of a different nature, to literature, to science, an attention to private affairs; enjoying the society of an amiable wife and children, beyond whose company he sought no pleasure. You certainly are not to be influenced by humanity. But your verdict must be founded in justice and in truth. You cannot suppose that a man in possession of every comfort and enjoyment, with a wife and six children, would voluntarily engage in treason; would rashly confide his life, his fortune, and his family to this stripling of an informer, whom he never before beheld.

Gentlemen, I have troubled you too long. I now conclude, and with a firm hope, I trust my client to your hands.

On the following morning, the brothers walked hand in hand to the gibbet.

THE UNION.
December 9, 1798.

The rebellion had been completely crushed. Its leaders had been exiled or executed. The last French expedition had failed. The insurgents had all surrendered, save a few outlying rapparees in the Wicklow mountains. The country lay palpitating under a reign of terror as suspicious and remorseless as Robespierre's. So the time had come to moot the Union. So strong, however, was the feeling against annexation to England, that the first rumour which appeared upon the subject in the newspaper press (*Evening Post*, Oct. 13, 1798) was couched in the following daring terms:—" The public ear has been filled for three days past with the report of a meditated Union; but, although we cannot wholly pass unnoticed a subject so much engaging the public attention, yet we do not deem ourselves authorised to treat it as an admitted fact; or by a base and coward compliance to the times, or an honest and dangerous expression of resentment, seem for a moment to accredit what, according to the established laws and constitution of this kingdom, must be high treason in the person who should propose it."

The rumour grew, however. Soon appeared the Castle pamphlet, " Arguments for and against an Union," written by the Under-Secretary Cooke. Bushe replied in the witty brochure, "Cease your funning." Thenceforth the press teemed with pamphlets. Above a hundred remain on library shelves, the relics of that momentous controversy.

The first meeting of any national importance was that of the Irish bar, called by requisition which fourteen of the king's counsel signed. Saurin opened an animated debate by moving, " That the measure of a legislative Union of this kingdom and Great Britain is an innovation, which it would be highly dangerous and improper to propose at the present juncture in this country." Mr. St. George Daly moved an adjournment. In the course of the debate,

Mr. Plunket urged the extreme danger and impropriety of agitating the question of Union at such a time as the present. Should the administration however propose a Union now, he had no doubt but it would be carried. Fear, animosity, a want of time to consider coolly its consequences, and forty thousand British troops in Ireland, would carry the measure. But, in a little time the people would awaken as from a dream, and what consequences would then follow, he trembled to think. For himself, he declared that he opposed an union, principally because he was convinced it would accelerate a total separation of the two countries. He dissuaded the meeting from adopting the motion of adjournment, because it would give a handle for further misrepresentation to those libellers who had already dared to misrepresent the motives and conduct of the bar. It would give them an opportunity to say that the adjournment of the question argued the sense of the bar to be for a Union. Those audacious libellers had already ventured to misrepresent, in a public print, the meeting of the bar as a military body on Friday last. He could not believe the insolent libeller was one of the body. But some person, within or without, had taken occasion in ten minutes after that meeting was held to carry to the Castle the falsehood, that the meeting broke up because the good sense of the bar thought it not right in them to agitate in any manner the question of an Union.

The original resolution was carried by 166 votes to 32. Of these 82, every man was afterwards promoted at the expense of his seniors and superiors in the profession. St. George Daly, of whom it was said that his first brief was the Union, was immediately appointed to the prime sergeantcy (then the highest law office in Ireland), from which Mr. Fitzgerald was dismissed for his hostility to the measure. He and seven of his supporters were subsequently made judges—fifteen assistant-barristers, and the other ten appointed to valuable commissionerships or legal offices.

THE UNION.

January 22, 1799.

THE first of the Union debates occurred upon the occasion of the Viceroy's speech in opening the session of 1799. During the previous six weeks, the country had been full of agitation and anxiety, the Castle busy with intrigue and corruption. After the bar meeting, the City of Dublin, the University, the freeholders of Galway, Westmeath, Louth, and Dublin counties declared against the Union. The opposition began to concert their tactique, the government to purchase every vote they could, and to intimidate where they could not hope to buy. The prime sergeant, Mr. Fitzgerald, and the chancellor of the exchequer, Sir John Parnell, the most respectable members of the Irish administration, were dismissed on avowing themselves anti-Unionists, and threats of discharge were held over all office-holders who should dare to oppose the government.

In the following passage of his speech, Lord Cornwallis raised the question before parliament :—

"The more I have reflected on the situation and circumstances of this kingdom, considering on the one hand the strength and stability of Great Britain, and on the other, these divisions which have shaken Ireland to its foundation, the more anxious I am for some permanent adjustment which may extend the advantages enjoyed by our sister kingdom to every part of the island. The unremitting industry with which our enemies persevere in their avowed object of endeavouring to effect a separation of this kingdom from Great Britain must have engaged your particular attention, and his majesty commands me to express his anxious hope that this consideration, joined to the sentiment of mutual affection and common interest, may dispose the parliaments in both kingdoms to provide the most effectual means of maintaining and improving a connexion essential to their common security and of consolidating, as far as possible, into one firm and lasting fabric, the strength, the powers, and the resources of the British empire."

A most animated and protracted debate followed, continuing for twenty-two hours, from 1 o'clock on the 22nd to 11 o'clock on the 23rd.

Sir John Parnell opened the opposition in a vigorous and statesmanlike argument. He was followed by Mr. Tighe, who, on objecting to concur in the address as a Unionist document, was assured by Lord Castlereagh that an acquiescence in the address did not at all involve an approbation of legislative Union. It only premised that the house would deliberate on the best means of improving the connexion. George Ponsonby spoke next, the leading speech of the anti-unionists, and ended a trenchant attack upon the measure and the ministry by moving as an amendment, that the house would maintain the constitution of 1782. Sir Lawrence Parsons, Mr. F. Falkiner, Lord Clements, Mr. Fitzgerald (late prime sergeant), Colonel Vereker, Mr. O'Hara, Mr. Lee, Mr. Crookshank, Colonel Maxwell, and Colonel Archdall followed in support of the amendment, in speeches that, as the debate tolled deep into the night, seemed to rise with every speaker and every sentence into bolder and loftier peals of eloquence. In a speech of a few sentences, Colonel Archdall declared that nothing could induce him, or, as he believed, any man in the north-west of Ireland, to vote for so infamous a measure. Mr. Jonah Barrington followed. The only speakers upon the government side to this stage of the debate had been St. George Daly, Sir Boyle Roche, and the Knight of Kerry; and none of them had dared to treat the opposition offensively or to openly avow the design of government. Castlereagh, who had occupied himself during the debate with completing the purchase of some of his doubtful votes, appears at this stage to have perceived that it was necessary to stop the victorious career of the opposition, and accordingly, when Barrington stated that corrupt and unconstitutional means had been used by the government to carry the measure, he at once changed his course, assumed the insolent and defiant tone which he preserved through the subsequent debates called Barrington to order, and threatened to have his words taken down. On the instant Plunket addressed the Speaker, reiterated Barrington's words as expressing his opinions also, and said that if the noble lord was in a humour of taking down words he would give him an opportunity, as it was his intention before the debate closed to use the same language and stronger. On this, Castlereagh did not press the question, and Barrington continued his speech in the same tone. He was followed by Francis Dobbs, George Knox, Sir J. Freke, and Hans Hamilton against, and by Sir J. Blaquiere for the Union.

At last Castlereagh rose, and said that he "trusted no man would decide on a measure of such importance as that in part before the house, on private or personal motives; for if a decision were thus to be influenced, it would be the most unfortunate that could ever affect the country. What was the object of this measure but such as every loyal man, who really loved his country, must feel the strongest attachment to. By an incorporation of our legislature with that of Great Britain, it would not only consolidate the strength and glory of the empire, but it would change our internal and local government to a system of strength and calm security, instead of being a garrison in the island. Here was but a part of many and numerous advantages, which the stage of the business did not then render necessary to be entered into, and which would come more suitably at a future period. As to the argument of the parliament's incompetence to entertain the question, he did not expect to hear such an argument from constitutional lawyers, or to hear advanced the position, that a legislature was not at all times competent to do that for which it could only have been instituted —the adoption of the best means to promote the general happiness and prosperity. After the melancholy state to which this country had been reduced, his majesty's ministers would feel that they abdicated their duty to the empire, if they did not seriously consider that state, and adopt the best remedy for the evils which it comprised. It was the misfortune of this country to have in it no fixed principles on which the human mind could rest—no one standard to which the different prejudices of the country could be accommodated. What was the price of connection at present with Great Britain? A military establishment far beyond our natural means to support, and for which we are indebted to Great Britain, who is also obliged to guarantee our public loans. It is not by flattery that the country could be saved—truths, however disagreeable, must be told— and if Ireland did not boldly look her situation in the face and accept that Union which would strengthen and secure her, she would perhaps have no alternative but to sink into the embrace of French fraternity. You talk, said his lordship, of national pride and independence, but where is the solidity of this boast? You have not the British constitution—nor can you have it consistently with your present species of connection with Great Britain: that constitution does not recognise two separate and independent legislatures under one crown—the greater country must lead—the lesser naturally follow, and must be practically subordinate in imperial concerns; but this necessary and beneficial operation of the general will must be preceded by establishing one common interest.

"As the pride of this country advances with her wealth, it may happen that you will not join Great Britain in her wars—it is only a common polity that will make that certain. Incorporate with Great Britain, and you have a common interest and common means. If Great Britain calls for your subjection, resist it; but if she wishes to unite with you on terms of equality, 'tis madness not to accept the offer."

Plunket, who had apparently been waiting for an opportunity of reply to the Secretary, followed in a speech of which Sir Jonah Barrington speaks in terms that are hardly an exaggeration:—

"At length Mr. Plunket arose, and in the ablest speech ever heard by any member in that parliament, went at once to the grand and decisive point, the incompetence of parliament: he could go no further on principle than Mr. Ponsonby, but his language was irresistible, and he left nothing to be urged. It was perfect in eloquence, and unanswerable in reasoning. Its effect was indescribable; and Lord Castlereagh, whom he personally assailed, seemed to shrink from the encounter. That speech was of great weight, and it proved the eloquence, the sincerity, and the fortitude of the speaker."

Judging from the length of the preceding debate, this speech must have been spoken after daybreak on the morning of the 23rd.

Sir, I shall make no apology for troubling you at this late hour, exhausted though I am, in mind and body, and suffering, though you must be, under a similar pressure. This is a subject which must arouse the slumbering, and might almost reanimate the dead. It is a question whether Ireland shall cease to be free. It is a question involving our dearest interests and for ever.

Sir, I congratulate the house on the manly temper with which this measure has been discussed: I congratulate them on the victory, which I already see they have obtained; a victory which I anticipate from the bold and generous sentiments which have been expressed on this side of the house, and which I see confirmed in the doleful and discomfited visages of the miserable group whom I see before me. Sir, I congratulate you on the candid avowal of the noble lord who has just sat down. He has exposed this project in its naked hideousness and deformity. He has told us that the necessity of sacrificing our independence flows from the nature of our connexion. It is now avowed that this measure does not flow from any temporary cause; that it is not produced in consequence of any late rebellion, or accidental disturbance in the country; that its necessity does not arise from the danger of modern political innovations, or from recent attempts of wicked men to separate this country from Great Britain. No; we are now informed by the noble lord, that the condition of our slavery is engrafted on the principle of our connexion, and that by the decrees of fate, Ireland has been doomed a dependant colony from her cradle.

I trust that after this barefaced avowal there can be little difference of opinion. I trust that every honest man who regards the freedom of Ireland, or who regards the connexion with England, will, by his vote on this night, refute this unfounded and seditious doctrine. Good God, sir, have I borne arms to crush the wretches who propagated the false and wicked creed, "that British connexion was hostile to Irish freedom," and am I now bound to combat it, coming from the lips of the noble lord who is at the head of our administration.

But, sir, in answer to the assertion of the noble lord, I will quote the authority of the Duke of Portland, in his speech from the throne, at the end of the session, 1782, " that the two kingdoms are now one, indissoluble, connected by unity of constitution and unity of interest, that the danger and security, the prosperity and calamity of the one must mutually affect the other; that they stand and fall together." I will quote the authority of the king, lords, and commons of Ireland, who asserted and established the constitution of our independent parliament founded on that connexion; and the authority of the king, lords, and commons of Great Britain, who adopted and confirmed it. With as little prospect of persuasion has the noble lord cited to us the example of Scotland; and as little am I tempted to purchase, at the expense of two bloody rebellions, a state of poverty and vassalage, at which Ireland, at her worst state, before she attained a free trade or a free constitution, would have spurned.

But, sir, the noble lord does not seem to repose very implicit confidence in his own arguments, and he amuses you by saying, that in adopting this address you do not pledge yourselves to a support of the measure in any future stage. Beware of this delusion. If you adopt this address, you sacrifice your constitution. You concede the principle, and any future inquiries can only be as to the terms. For them you need entertain no solicitude, on the terms you can never disagree. Give up your independence, and Great Britain will grant you whatever terms you desire. Give her the key, and she will confide everything to its protection. There are no advantages you can ask which she will not grant, exactly for the same reason that the unprincipled spendthrift will subscribe, without reading it, the bond which he has no intention of ever discharging. I say, therefore, that if you ever mean to make a stand for the liberties of Ireland, now, and now only, is the moment for doing it.

But, sir, the freedom of discussion which has taken place on this side of the house has, it seems, given great offence to gentlemen on the treasury bench. They are men of nice and punctilious honour, and they will not endure that anything should be said which implies a reflection on their untainted and virgin integrity. They threatened to take down the words of an honourable gentleman who spoke before me, because they conveyed an insinuation; and I promised them on that occasion, that if the fancy for taking down words continued, I would indulge them in it to the top of their bent. Sir, I am determined to keep my word with them, and I now will not insinuate, but I will directly assert, that base and wicked as is the object proposed, the means used to effect it have been more flagitious and abominable. Do you choose to take down my words? Do you dare me to the proof?

Sir, I had been induced to think that we had at the head of the executive government of this country a plain, honest soldier, unaccustomed to, and disdaining the intrigues of politics, and who, as an additional evidence of the directness and purity of his views, had chosen for his secretary a simple and modest youth, *puer ingenui vultus ingenuique pudoris,* whose inexperience was the voucher of his innocence; and yet I will be bold to say, that during the viceroyalty of this unspotted veteran, and during the administration of this unassuming stripling—within these last six weeks, a system of black corruption has been carried on within the walls of the castle which would disgrace the annals of the worst period of the history of either country.

Do you choose to take down my words?

I need call no witness to your bar to prove them. I see two right honourable gentlemen sitting within your walls, who had long and faithfully served the crown, and who have been dismissed, because they dared to express a sentiment in favour of the freedom of their country. I see another honourable gentleman, who has been forced to resign his place as commissioner of the revenue because he refused to co-operate in this dirty job of a dirty administration.

Do you dare to deny this?

I say that at this moment the threat of dismissal from office is suspended over the heads of the members who now sit around me, in order to influence their votes on the question of this night, involving everything that can be sacred or dear to man.

Do you desire to take down my words? Utter the desire, and I will prove the truth of them at your bar.

Sir, I would warn you against the consequences of carrying this measure by such means as this, but that I see the necessary defeat of it in the honest and universal indignation which the adoption of such means excites. I see the protection against the wickedness of the plan in the imbecility of its execution; and I congratulate my country, that when a design was formed against her liberties, the prosecution of it was intrusted to such hands as it is now placed in.

The example of the prime minister of England, imitable in its vices, may deceive the noble lord. The minister of England has his faults. He abandoned in his latter years the principle of reform, by professing which he had attained the early confidence of the people of England, and in the whole of his political conduct he has shown himself haughty and intractable; but it must be admitted that he is endowed by nature with a towering and transcendent intellect, and that the vastness of his resources keeps pace with the magnificence and unboundedness of his projects. I thank God, that it is much more easy for him to transfer his apostacy and his insolence than his comprehension and his sagacity; and I feel the safety of my country in the wretched feebleness of her enemy. I cannot fear that the constitution which has been founded by the wisdom of sages, and cemented by the blood of patriots and of heroes, is to be smitten to its centre by such a green and sapless twig as this.

Sir, the noble lord has shown much surprise that he should hear a doubt expressed concerning the competence of parliament to do this act. I am sorry that I also must contribute to increase the surprise of the noble lord. If I mistake not, his surprise will be much augmented before this question shall be disposed of; he shall see and hear what he has never before seen or heard, and be made acquainted with sentiments to which, probably, his heart has been a stranger.

Sir, I, in the most express terms, deny the competency of parliament to do this act. I warn you, do not dare to lay your hands on the constitution. I tell you, that if, circumstanced as you are, you pass this act, it will be a nullity, and that no man in Ireland will be bound to obey it. I make the assertion deliberately—I repeat it, and I call on any man who hears me to take down my words. You have not been elected for this purpose. You are appointed to make laws, and not legislatures. You are appointed to act under the constitution, not to alter it. You are appointed to exercise the functions of legislators, and not to transfer them. And if you do so your act is a dissolution of the government. You resolve society into its original elements, and no man in the land is bound to obey you.

Sir, I state doctrines which are not merely founded in the immutable laws of justice and of truth. I state not merely the opinions of the ablest men who have written on the science of government, but I state the practice of our constitution as settled at the era of the revolution, and I state the doctrine under which the house of Hanover derives its title to the throne. Has the king a right to transfer his crown? Is he competent to annex it to the crown of Spain or any other country? No—but he may abdicate it and every man who knows the constitution knows the consequence, the right reverts to the next in succession—if they all abdicate, it reverts to the people. The man who questions this doctrine, in the same breath must arraign the sovereign on the throne as an usurper. Are you competent to transfer your legislative rights to the French council of five hundred? Are you competent to transfer them to the British parliament? I answer, no. When you transfer you abdicate, and the great original trust reverts to the people from whom it issued. Yourselves you may extinguish, but parliament you cannot extinguish It is enthroned in the hearts of the people. It is enshrined in the sanctuary of the constitution. It is immortal as the island which it protects. As well might the frantic suicide hope that the act which destroys his miserable body should extinguish his eternal soul. Again,

I therefore warn you, do not dare to lay your hands on tne constitution; it is above your power.

Sir, I do not say that the parliament and the people, by mutual consent and co-operation, may not change the form of the constitution. Whenever such a case arises it must be decided on its own merits—but that is not this case. If government considers this a season peculiarly fitted for experiments on the constitution, they may call on the people. I ask you are you ready to do so? Are you ready to abide the event of such an appeal? What is it you must, in that event, submit to the people? Not this particular project; for if you dissolve the present form of government, they become free to choose any other—you fling them to the fury of the tempest—you must call on them to unhouse themselves of the established constitution, and to fashion to themselves another. I ask again, is this the time for an experiment of that nature? Thank God, the people have manifested no such wish—so far as they have spoken, their voice is decidedly against this daring innovation. You know that no voice has been uttered in its favour, and you cannot be infatuated enough to take confidence from the silence which prevails in some parts of the kingdom : if you know how to appreciate that silence, it is more formidable than the most clamorous opposition—you may be rived and shivered by the lightning before you hear the peal of the thunder!

But, sir, we are told that we should discuss this question with calmness and composure. I am called on to surrender my birth-right and my honour, and I am told I should be calm and should be composed. National pride! Independence of our country! These, we are told by the minister, are only vulgar topics fitted for the meridian of the mob, but unworthy to be mentioned to such an enlightened assembly as this; they are trinkets and gewgaws fit to catch the fancy of childish and unthinking people like you, sir, or like your predecessor in that chair, but utterly unworthy the consideration of this house, or of the matured understanding of the noble lord who condescends to instruct it! Gracious God! We see a Pery re-ascending from the tomb, and raising his awful voice to warn us against the surrender of our freedom, and we see that the proud and virtuous feelings which warmed the breast of that aged and venerable man are only calculated to excite the contempt of this young philosopher, who has been transplanted from the nursery to the cabinet to outrage the feelings and understanding of the country.

But, sir, I will be schooled, and I will endeavour to argue this question as calmly and frigidly as I am desired to do; and since we are told that this is a measure intended for our benefit, and that it is through mere kindness to us that all these extraordinary means have been resorted to, I will beg to ask, how are we to be benefited? Is it commercial benefit that we are to obtain? I will not detain the house with a minute detail on this part of the subject. It has been fully discussed by able men, and it is well known that we are already possessed of everything material which could be desired in that respect. But I shall submit some obvious considerations.

I waive the consideration, that under any union of legislatures the conditions as to trade between the two countries must be, either free ports, which would be ruinous to Ireland; or equal duties, which would be ruinous to Ireland; or the present duties made perpetual, which would be ruinous to Ireland; or that the duties must be left open to regulation from time to time by the united parliament, which would leave us at the mercy of Great Britain. I will waive the consideration, that the minister has not thought fit to tell us what we are to get, and, what is still stronger, that no man amongst us has any definite idea of what we are to ask; and I will content myself with asking this question—is your commerce in such a declining, desperate state, that you are obliged to resort to irrevocable measures in order to retract it? Or is it at the very moment when it is advancing with rapid prosperity, beyond all example and above all hope— is it, I say, at such a time that you think it wise to bring your constitution to market, and offer it to sale, in order to obtain advantages, the aid of which you do not require, and of the nature of which you have not any definite idea.

A word more, and I have done as to commerce. Supposing great advantages were to be obtained, and that they were specified and stipulated for; what is your security that the stipulation will be observed? Is it the faith of treaties? What treaty more solemn than the final constitutional treaty between the two kingdoms in 1782, which you are now called on to violate? Is it not a mockery to say that the parliament of Ireland is competent to annul itself, and to destroy the original compact with the people and the final compact of 1782, and that the parliament of the empire will not be competent to annul any commercial regulation of the articles of Union? And here, sir, I take leave of this part of the question; indeed, it is only justice to government to acknowledge that they do not much rely on the commercial benefits to be obtained by the Union—they have been rather held out in the way of innocent artifice, to delude the people for their own good; but the real objects are different, though still merely for the advantage of Ireland.

What are those other objects? To prevent the recurrence of rebellion, and to put an end to domestic dissensions? Give me leave to ask, sir, how was the rebellion excited? I will not inquire into its remote causes; I do not wish to revive unpleasant recollections, or to say anything which might be considered as invidious to the government of the country; but how was it immediately excited? By the agency of a party of levellers actuated by French principles, instigated by French intrigues, and supported by the promise of French co-operation. This party, I hesitate not to say, was in itself contemptible. How did it become formidable? By operating on the wealthy, well-informed, and moral inhabitants of the north, and persuading them that they had no constitution; and by instilling palatable poisons into the minds of the rabble of the south; which were prepared to receive them by being in a state of utter ignorance and wretchedness. How will an Union effect those pre-disponent causes? Will you conciliate the mind of the northern by caricaturing all the defects of the constitution, and then extinguishing it, by draining his wealth to supply the contributions levied by an imperial parliament, and by outraging all his religious and moral feelings by the means which you use to accomplish this abominable project; and will you not, by encouraging the drain of absentees, and taking away the influence and example of resident gentlemen, do everything in your power to aggravate the poverty, and to sublimate the ignorance and bigotry of the south?

Let me ask again, how was the rebellion put down? By the zeal and loyalty of the gentlemen of Ireland rallying round—what? a reed shaken by the winds; a wretched apology for a minister, who neither knew how to give nor where to seek protection? No! but round the laws and constitution and independence of the country. What were the affections and motives that called us into action? To protect our families, our properties, and our liberties. What were the antipathies by which we were excited? Our abhorrence of French principles and French ambition. What was it to us that France was a republic? I rather rejoiced when I saw the ancient despotism of France put down. What was it to us that she dethroned her monarch? I admired the virtues and wept for the sufferings of the man; but as a nation it affected us not. The reason I took up arms, and am ready still to bear them against France, is because she intruded herself upon our domestic concerns—because with the rights of man and the love of freedom on her tongue, I see that she has the lust of dominion in her heart—because wherever she has placed her foot, she has erected her throne; and to be her friend or her ally is to be her tributary or her slave.

Let me ask, is the present conduct of the British minister calculated to augment or to transfer that antipathy? No, sir, I will be bold to say, that licentious and impious France, in all the unrestrained excesses which anarchy and atheism have given birth to, has not committed a more insidious act against her enemy than is now attempted by the professed champion of civilized Europe against a friend and an ally in the hour of her calamity and distress—at a moment when our country is filled with British troops—when the loyal men of Ireland are fatigued with their exertions to put down rebellion; efforts in which they had succeeded before these troops arrived—whilst our Habeas Corpus Act is suspended—whilst trials by court martial are carrying on in many parts of the kingdom—whilst the people are taught to think that they have no right to meet or to deliberate, and whilst the great body of them are so palsied by their fears, and worn down by their exertions, that even this vital question is scarcely able to rouse them from their lethargy—at the moment when we are distracted by domestic dissensions—dissensions artfully kept alive as the pretext for our present subjugation and the instrument of our future thraldom!

Yet, sir, I thank administration for this measure. They are, without intending it, putting an end to our dissensions—through this black cloud which they have collected over us, I see the light breaking in upon this unfortunate country. They have composed our dissensions—not by fomenting the embers of a lingering and subdued rebellion—not by hallooing the Protestant against the Catholic and the Catholic against the Protestant—not by committing the north against the south—not by inconsistent appeals to local or to party prejudices; no—but by the avowal of this atrocious conspiracy against the liberties of Ireland, they have subdued every petty and subordinate distinction. They have united every rank and description of men by the pressure of this grand and momentous subject; and I tell them that they will see every honest and independent man in Ireland rally round her constitution, and merge every other consideration in his opposition to this ungenerous and odious measure. For my own part, I will resist it to the last gasp of my existence and with the last drop of my blood, and when I feel the hour of my dissolution approaching, I will, like the father of Hannibal, take my children to the altar and swear them to eternal hostility against the invaders of their country's freedom.

Sir, I shall not detain you by pursuing this question through the topics which it so abundantly offers. I shall be proud to think my name may be handed down to posterity in the same roll with these disinterested patriots who have successfully resisted the enemies of their country. Successfully I trust it will be. In all events, I have my exceeding great reward; I shall bear in my heart the consciousness of having done my duty, and in the hour of death I shall not be haunted by the reflection of having basely sold or meanly abandoned the liberties of my native land. Can every man who gives his vote on the other side this night lay his hand upon his heart and make the same declaration? I hope so. It will be well for his own peace. The indignation and abhorrence of his countrymen will not accompany him through life, and the curses of his children will not follow him to his grave.

Mr. Ball and Mr. Arthur Moore, two of the most eminent of the Irish bar, Dr. Browne, and the Hon. Mr. Knox, members for Trinity College, Lord Corry, Colonel O'Donnell, Sir Edward O'Brien, Colonel Bagwell, Mr. Stewart of Killymoon, Mr. Richard Dawson, and several of the highest of the country gentry, followed against the Union. The Attorney-General, Sergeant Stanley, the Chancellor of the Exchequer, and Mr. William Smith, were the chief speakers upon the side of government. In all, upwards of sixty members had spoken, when, at eleven o'clock a.m. the house divided, and Mr. Ponsonby's amendment was defeated by a majority of one—which majority was obtained by the purchase, a few hours before, in the very house, of two members. One of them, Mr. Trench, of Woodlawn, afterwards Lord Ashtown, had actually spoken against the Union early in the debate; the other was Mr. Luke Fox, afterwards judge, who, having by mistake gone into the opposition lobby, would, had he been counted, have made the numbers equal for and against the government, in which case the Speaker's casting vote would have dismissed the question. Driven to his wits' end, Fox declared, upon his honour, that he had accepted the Escheatorship of Munster (the Irish Chiltern Hundreds), and accordingly had no right to vote. The statement was false, as subsequent reference to the record proved, but it sufficed for the night to give ministers the majority.

The debate was renewed on the report of the address two days afterwards, and after again lasting until near noon of the following day, ministers were defeated on Sir Laurence Parsons' amendment to expunge the paragraph of the address relating to the Union, by a majority of five. Through these wintry nights College-green, and all the avenues of the house, were crowded with people, and the moment the ministers' defeat was announced from the chair, the cheers of the opposition were re-echoed at every corner of the city. "A due sense of decorum," it is said, "restrained the galleries within proper bounds;" but Sergeant-at-arms tried in vain to still the triumphant treble of the ladies. Sir Jonah Barrington's narrative of those memorable nights is very graphic, but not literally accurate in the order which he gives of the debates. For instance, he states that Plunket's speech of the 22nd was spoken on the 24th, in reply to Castlereagh's second speech, in which, abandoning all restraint, the secretary denounced the opposition as "a desperate faction," led by "levellers and pettifoggers," and trading on the prejudices of a "barbarous and ignorant people;" and he proceeds to account for the unusual vehemence and asperity of Castlereagh's tone by the severe attack which Ponsonby had made upon him. Now the fact is, according to all the regular reports of the debates, that Castlereagh spoke second and Ponsonby third in the debate of the 24th, and that Ponsonby's attack upon the ministers did not provoke, but was in answe. to Castlereagh's insolent strictures upon the opposition. The speech which Castlereagh really tried to answer was evidently Plunket's terrible philippic, under which he quailed at the time, and which, two days afterwards, he hesitates directly to refer to, though every sentence of his speech is evidently aimed at it.

One withering allusion, which was said to have stung the Secretary to the quick, is interpreted in a memoir of Lord Plunket which appeared in the *University Magazine*. The passage referred to is that in which he calls Castlereagh " a green and sapless twig":—" This last stroke was felt at the time to have more in it than met the eye. Lady Castlereagh, who was remarkable for her beauty, was sitting in the gallery, and although married for some years, it was Lord Castlereagh's misfortune to be childless. Plunket's tomahawk sarcasm was felt to bear not merely upon his imputed political, but upon his suspected personal imbecility." In the revised report the phrase is " green and limber twig," but I believe the traditional version is correct.

THE UNION.

January 28, 1799.

MEANTIME the Union had been discussed in the British Houses of Parliament Sheridan heading the opposition in a speech full of Irish feeling, and of his characteristic loftiness, vigour, and brilliancy. " My country," he nobly exclaimed, " has claims upon me which I am not more proud to acknowledge than ready to liquidate to the full measure of my ability." He was replied to with almost equal power by George Canning; and the debate on Irish independence was, in fact, a duel between the two great Irish orators, until Pitt rose and developed his plan of consolidating the empire, in a long and magnificent speech, ending by a declaration of his intention to carry the Union at all hazards.

Meanwhile, however, contrary to his expectation, the Irish cabinet had been beaten upon the address. On the 28th, Lord Castlereagh moved an adjournment of the house until the 7th of February, in order to obtain advices from England. In the course of debate,

MR. PLUNKET condemned the declaration of the British minister, which was made under the influence of ignorance and delusion, as to what were the real sentiments of the parliament and people of Ireland on the subject of Union. He must suppose that the British minister had been taught to reckon upon the certain and infallible success of his project for influencing the Irish parliament, and he could not have discovered his error in the decision of that parliament, when he had the temerity to utter the speech alluded to, and of the authenticity of which there was pretty good evidence in a confidential paper of the minister (the *Sun*). The public mind (as the honourable member had observed) stood in need of repose after so much agitation as it had recently sustained upon this topic, and therefore he should not oppose the motion for adjournment; but if it should appear on the next meeting of the house, that the British minister still persisted in his rash design, he would call upon every gentleman on this side of the house who had already voted against the measure, and upon any gentleman on the other side, who, through false delicacy, had not resisted the proposal for entertaining it, to come forward in vindication of the honour, the dignity, and the independence of the Irish parliament and the Irish nation, and by some strong and decided declaration put an extinguisher upon this odious and abominable measure. The noble lord had intimated that the time might come when the parliament and the country would be glad to solicit the measure, as the only means of effectually securing tranquillity. He hoped the noble lord did not mean to insinuate that measures would be adopted to produce such a situation in the country as would create the necessity of such a solution, in order that " what was spoken by the prophets might be fulfilled." He was not over fond to see a minister ruling the country, who seemed to have a taste for verifying his own predictions as to the necessity he foretold; and he wished to see that minister and his British colleague removed from office, a circumstance which could not much affect them, as they seemed too cool to feel for any event.

THE PLACE BILL.
May 16, 1799.

THE proceedings during the rest of the session were unimportant. In a discussion having reference to the number of seats vacated under the place bill, by which means ministers were gradually making a Unionist majority, Plunket said:—

SIR, I think that the question put to the noble lord by my honourable friend (Mr. Dawson), was put with such candour and moderation, that it merited a respectful answer, instead of being treated, as it has been, with contemptuous silence. But as I find that the noble lord has yielded to the all-powerful and eloquent injunction of his learned friend the prime-serjeant (Mr. St. George Daly), I am justified in supposing that no answer could have been given, but such as would confirm the house in an opinion of the justness of the observations made by my honourable friend.

But what stuff, sir, does the noble lord think this house and the country made of, that they should bear with such contemptuous silence—with a treatment so insulting? It has been said that the question of Union ought not to have been introduced into the discussion; but I must say, that the question before the house is intimately connected with that of a legislative Union, because the noble lord is making use of the prerogative of the crown as a means and instrument of filling the benches of this house with the supporters of his favourite measure.

Baffled in this house at the time that the question of Union was openly brought forward, administration have now recourse to other modes; and every little means, artifice, and agency, is made use of indirectly to attain those ends which the minister wants only the mockery of an artificial majority in parliament to sanction in order then to enforce.

Sir, how has the measure of a Union been introduced into this house? Have the inducements of office been held out to any member on this side of it? Have the old and faithful servants of the crown been dismissed and their places pointed to in order to tempt the integrity of political virtue? Have bribery and corruption been resorted to for the purpose of making that majority which the unbiassed play of honest principle would never make? Sir, let the minister answer, for he is one of those who can best tell; but thus much, sir, I will say, that nor place, nor power, nor bribery, nor corruption influenced any man who voted against the minister's measure, but in the strength of honest principle was it rejected.

The true sense of parliament has been declared; it is manifested to the world. The unbought sense of parliament has been declared; and that virtue which protected the independence of this house and of this kingdom, will again save it, should any ministry foolishly and wickedly persist in hostility against them. I would then warn the noble lord how he again attempts the liberties of his country. I would warn the noble lord to profit of the experience which he has already had, and not court another defeat and another shame. I would warn that minister who exhibits a political phenomenon in this house, who, contrary to every precedent after having failed in measures odious to his country, odious to parliament, and injurious to his sovereign, yet retains his place and has not sought refuge from public notice in private situation. I would warn him not to persist in his destructive course, or continue to urge a measure which the people of Ireland never will accept; and which, if forced on them, will, to use the noble lord's own words, be the most rash, fatal, and unfortunate conduct, that ever has been adopted by any minister?

Sir, it is meanly and insidiously attempted to impute motives of personal interest to gentlemen at this side of the house, for the part they have taken on the question of the legislative Union. The odium of corrupt motives is attempted to be divided; but I will ask is there one instance—one solitary instance that can be pointed out?

"Yes," said Mr. Martin, from the other side of the house.

Let me hear that name then.

Here Mr. Martin cried out that he was ready. But he was stopped by a general exclamation of "Shame, shame!" and a cry of "proceed" addressed to Mr. Plunket.

I waited, Mr. Speaker, to hear the solitary name of him who on this side of the house in opposing the Union had acted on any motive of interest, but that which he felt in common with his country. I have heard of 116 placemen and pensioners; I will not say whether any of these voted for it, but I am sure if any independent gentleman has given his support to the measure, he has been betrayed into that support by circumstances, acting not on his conviction, but on those temporary feelings which they have excited; and, sir, I hail, as most propitious to the freedom of this country, the successes of his Majesty's allies on the Continent; because, I hope, they will lead to a speedy peace. When fears of invasion and rebellion are removed, I am sure there will not be found a single independent gentleman in this country to support the minister in this abominable measure.

Sir, I have heard the opposers of Union, branded also with the name of faction. But who are they who form this faction? It is they who have put down rebellion. It is these men who, even in the young memory of a young minister, have saved this country, and to whom it is owing, that the connexion between it and Great Britain subsists at this moment.

Sir, it is a fact, and I speak it under correction of the noble lord if I am wrong, that he has said that none shall vacate their seats in this house, whose successors will not support the measure of a Union. And it is another fact, sir, which the minister may contradict if he can, that in almost every instance since the commencement of the present session, the escheatorship of Munster has been given to members whose only qualification for the office has been, that their successors were conditioned to vote for an Union. This condition the honourable colonel, whose case has given rise to the present discussion, would not, could not make for his successor. On the contrary, it was known that his intended successor was one who, like himself, loved the free constitution of Ireland, and therefore it was that the colonel was refused, and the escheatorship of Munster for the first time converted into an instrument of prerogative, injurious to parliament and to the people. The noble lord has professed—every man in this house has heard him profess—that he will carry the measure of Union only by the free consent of parliament and of the country; has this refusal of the escheatorship of Munster been a consequence of tha', profession? Have the instructions given to sheriffs not to call meetings of their counties been in conformity with that profession? Is it to carry the Union by the free consent and unbiassed judgment of the people that all the public prints have been bought up, and either bribed to silence on the subject of Union, or filled with publications in support of it? Sir, it is very easy for a minister to clasp his hands and to implore the house to refrain from pledging itself on the measure of a legislative Union until the sense of the country shall be known. It is very easy thus to implore parliament, and set this entreaty to notes of most pathetical cadence, but acts are the strongest testimonies of intention—the strongest witnesses of motives, and the actions of the noble lord, loudly speaking against his professions, cannot be misunderstood by any man who is not senseless and heartless to the interests of his country, against which the noble lord has arrayed himself in sincere, but I trust futile hostility.

THE UNION
May 18, 1799.

Towards the close of the session, one day St. George Daly summoned up courage, made a furious attack upon the opposition in general, and the opposition barristers in particular; had ventured a savage onslaught upon Bushe, and was proceeding to assail Plunket, when the latter, who happened to sit near him, caught his eye, and, as it were, shot him through with one keen glance of merciless scorn. Daly faltered, stammered, and after a few awkward struggles to regain the flow of his speech, sat down. Plunket followed him, and these are his last words to the government in the session of 1799:—

You, Mr. Speaker, have already, on a former occasion, proved a Union to be inconsistent with the interests of the people of Ireland, and the honourable gentleman who spoke last but two has proved it to be inconsistent with the interests of any member of this house, and of every Irish gentleman of £3000 a-year; and after this I trust there can be but one sentiment in execration of this abominable measure. Another learned gentleman has expressed much indignation at the language used at this side of the house; and when he arose, I was afraid that his indignation would have hurried him beyond the bounds of prudence; but very seasonably he happened to be "so angry that he could not speak," and thus he found a tolerably good chance of not being able to offend. I wish, however, that he had bestowed some of his indignation on the conduct which gave rise to the present debate; and if a conduct the most base and flagrant could inspire terms of disapprobation, the honourable and learned member must certainly have recovered the use of his tongue. He would then have to reprobate the most shameful hypocrisy— the most scandalous effrontery; and the warmth of his eloquence and the freedom of his manner would be well employed in reprehending the conduct of a minister who had not only thrown away the substance, but the semblance of virtue.

The honourable and learned member has asked why the house does not now act with that cordiality in support of government which it did last session, and most pathetically he asks if the spirit of loyalty has fled from this house. I will tell the honourable gentleman why government does not find that warm support in this house which it was wont to do. It is because the conduct of the administration has been such as to freeze the warm blood of loyalty—and if it should again dilute at the approach of public danger, it will not be owing to that administration, which did all it could to put down the loyalty of the country. Sir, the conduct of the noble lord this night, and of his friends, has proved that although the administration may wish to do mischief, it has not talents sufficient to effect it, and I warn the noble lord how he proceeds in such a line of conduct. I warn him how he shows to the people of Ireland that the question of Union is to be carried by force or fraud, and as far as my humble voice can go, I take this last opportunity of cautioning the people and ministry of England how they suffer themselves to be deceived by the false representations of the noble lord. After the boasts with which he ushered in the question at the commencement of the session, it was rejected with ignominy and disgrace: the same cant is used now. The people are said to be changing their minds. The members of this house are said to be changing their minds; but I challenge the treasury bench to name the man who has changed his mind. Again and again I do remind the noble lord of the weight of responsibility which rests on him, if by misrepresentation he commits the two countries on this subject. On his head will be the consequences—and poor indeed will that compensation be which such a head can make for the public evils which its errors may create.

THE UNION.
January 15, 1800.

The government were busily occupied during the parliamentary recess. Lord Cornwallis made a tour of the country, carefully selecting places where he could elicit a semblance of public opinion in favour of the Union. His progress was like the canvass of a potwalloping borough. Country gentlemen were promised titles, public functionaries promotion, the Catholics emancipation, the Protestants ascendancy; the *shebeen*-keeper was licensed, and the prisoner pardoned if he would only agree to support the Union. The Lord Lieutenant was all things to all men.

The Secretary and Under-Secretary were equally active in operating upon the parliament. Peerages and pensions were scattered like largesse. Honourable members who would not sell their votes could sell their seats. Thus between actual purchases and changes in the representation, Castlereagh carried off forty-three votes from the opposition in the course of 1799.

Parliament met on the 15th of January, 1800; and to the great surprise of the opposition, the Viceroy's speech had no allusion direct or indirect to the Union. The address was moved by Viscount Loftus and seconded by Colonel Crosbie—yet no reference whatever by either speaker to the ministerial policy. Sir Laurence Parsons then rose; called upon the clerk to read the Lord Lieutenant's speech at the close of last session, in which the king's recommendation of an incorporating Union was embodied; lamented that the sudden prorogation had then unfairly prevented the house from giving a suitable answer to his majesty; and said the same object was now aimed at by a studious omission of the subject from the opening speech. His speech ended by an amendment to the address, declaratory of the house's adherence to the constitution of '82. In the course of his reply, which was a malignant attack upon opposition, Castlereagh stated that it was his intention to have moved a call of the house for that day fortnight, in order to consider the formal proposition of an Union. After this declaration the debate proceeded in regular order—the Right Hon. David Latouche, the Right Hon. Denis Browne, the Attorney-General, Sir John Blaquiere, and a few minor stars of the treasury bench on the side of government. The speaking of the opposition was all powerful and impassioned; and Bushe's, Ponsonby's, and O'Donnell's speeches were of a high order of eloquence. Plunket spoke late in the night. Doctor Browne, an American by birth, and member for Trinity College, whom Castlereagh had converted during the recess from a violent anti-Unionist into a proselyte of the Castle, preceded him, and thus met the rough edge of his wrath:—

Sir, I have no right to sit in judgment on the motives of the hon. member who has just sat down. The secrets of his heart and the springs of his conduct must be left to the great Searcher of hearts; but by his public actions his public character is to be judged, and on those I will beg leave freely to comment. He has stated his reason for refusing to concur in the amendment of the hon. baronet to be, that it would pledge him irretrievably against the measure of a Legislative Union: how would that concurrence pledge him more solemnly than the amendment of the last session, proposed by my hon. friend (Mr. G. Ponsonby), in which he then concurred? That was a resolution, that we would support our free constitution as finally established in 1782. This is a resolution declaring that we are in possession of that constitution, and that it is the wish and interest of his Majesty's Irish subjects to remain in possession of that constitution, and in the state of union and amity with Great Britain which we now enjoy. What has happened to change the sentiments of the hon. gentleman? I have heard that when he was elected to the dignified situation which he now fills, representative of the university of Dublin, he declared to his constituents that only one possible event could make him harbour the idea of an Union, and that was, to save this country from a separation.

Cries of "hear, hear," from the treasury benches.

I am glad the new friends of the hon. gentleman have found an excuse for him which he did not suggest for himself; if they do not furnish him with an argument, they must relieve him from an anxiety —he was much alarmed, because he knew his opinions would be unpalatable to both sides of the house: but whatever sentiments they may have excited amongst us, they certainly have been received with acclamation by the minister. The hon. gentleman departs from the pledge which he entered into to his constituents, not because he apprehends any separation between the countries, but because so much corruption has taken place in parliament, in the course of the last session, and so many bad laws have been passed, that he really feels the constitution not worth preserving. Will the hon. gentleman recollect, that in the last session he not only declared against the measure, but argued with much ability that parliament was incompetent to adopt it. What has done away their incompetence? Their corruption! He then believed them incapable of sanctioning this measure, and he now rises to pronounce a libel on the parliament; and on the strength of their iniquities, for which he arraigns them, he declares them armed with authority to dispose of the liberties of Ireland. Not of his country—I rejoice that he has no claim to the name of Irishman. He has been raised into station by the bounty of the country, and he shows his gratitude by conspiring for the destruction of her liberties. So much for the hon. gentleman— to the comfort of his own reflections, and to the gratitude of his constituents I consign him. But whilst I express an honest indignation against those who have left our cause, and whilst I turn back to shed a tear of regret over the tomb of an honourable and honest man who is now no more (I mean Colonel O'Donnell, the late member for Donegal), I must congratulate the relations of that gallant man that a phœnix has risen from his ashes—I must congratulate the country on that splendid blaze of eloquence with which his successor has this night delighted and illuminated the house.

Sir, I feel no ordinary sensation on this question being again introduced to the consideration of parliament. It was ushered into the last parliament with the same boyish boasting which now accompanies it, and rejected with the same contumely which ultimately awaits it. Without any change in the circumstances of the country, without the production of any new argument, the same men who fled like detected thieves at the close of the last session, and who in the precipitance of their flight stumbled over and overturned all public decency and parliamentary decorum, now exhibit themselves to challenge the national observation, and to brand with the name of faction every man who has honesty and courage to spurn their degrading purposes. What change has taken place? Has the measure changed its nature, or the minister his objects, or the countries their relations? No, you shall know the changes which have taken place—I will unmask the men who have dared to come into the midst of parliament and people to pamper their liberties by sordid bribery and to subdue their spirits by lawless force, and if I cannot excite the feelings of honour or virtue in their hearts I will call the blooming blush of shame into their cheeks.

You are told with puny sophistry that you ought at least to discuss the question. What is meant by this? That you should discuss the principle? You have already done so; no principle ever underwent a more ample discussion in parliament, and after examining it for two entire days in all its relations, and after supposing all the details the most favourable which possibly could be offered to Ireland, the principle was rejected by a majority not only free from any influence, but resisting every influence. If by discussion is meant that we should discuss the detail without examining the principle, I utterly refuse it. We now stand on the high ground of national independence, secured by solemn compact; and we are called on to declare our readiness to surrender that independence and relinquish that compact, for the purpose of treating about we know not what possible advantages, and this is called discussion. In answer to this demand, I say, first, you have not stated any one definite advantage which Ireland can gain, or evil which she can avoid, to induce her to relinquish guaranteed independence. The measure has now been agitated above a year, and we have not to this hour heard stated in definite terms, such as a plain understanding can comprehend, any one specific advantage which we are to gain, or any one evil which we are to escape, by its adoption. We have heard a deal of lofty language—increased resources and consolidated strength—wealth and morals of England imported—present benefits from England secured—possible evils deprecated—corruption of our own parliament destroyed—to be made partakers with the most dignified assembly in the world—danger of separation to be avoided—and political and religious differences closed for ever. This all sounds magnificently; but analyse it, and where a definite meaning can be extracted, no man pretends to say how an Union can forward the thing meant.

Again, I will not admit the principle, because it is a barter of liberty for money, even supposing your advantages as real as they are visionary. The nation which enters into such a traffic is besotted. Freedom is the parent of wealth, and it is an act of parricide to sacrifice the constitution which generates and nourishes your commerce for the supposed improvement of that commerce. This is, indeed, under all its circumstances, the most extravagant demand ever made by one nation from another. Ireland, a happy little island, with a population of between four and five millions of people —hardy, gallant, and enthusiastic—possessed of all the means of civilization—agriculture and commerce well pursued and understood —laws well arranged and administered—a constitution fully recognised and established—her revenues, her trade, her manufactures thriving beyond the hope or example of any other country of her extent, within these few years advancing with a rapidity astonishing even to herself; not complaining of her deficiency in any of these respects, but enjoying and acknowledging her prosperity—is called on to surrender them all, to the control of whom? To a great and powerful continent, to which nature intended her as an appendage? To a mighty people, totally exceeding her in all calculation of territory and population? No, but to another happy little island placed beside her in the bosom of the Atlantic, of little more than double her territory and population, and possessing resources not nearly so superior to her wants; and this, too, an island which has grown great, and prosperous, and happy by the very same advantages which Ireland enjoys—a free and independent constitution, and the protection of a domestic, superintendent parliament. The wealth, and power, and dignity of Great Britain (of which no man rejoices more sincerely than I do) are the most irresistible arguments against an Union.

A little clod of earth, by the enjoyment of freedom, has generated strength, and wealth, and majesty. She has reared her head above the waters, and has dictated to the unwieldy, lethargic despotisms, and to the unripened, fertile dependencies of Europe. And does she therefore call upon Ireland to cast from her her constitution, and to resign the same never-failing means to the same ends? No. I must take leave to consider the example of Britain more persuasive and more disinterested than her advice. Further, we are called on by this sister island not to connect ourselves in alliance with her; we have already done so in the most indissoluble way; the crown of Ireland necessarily annexed to the crown of England, and the responsibility of the British minister as a pledge for their continuance; not like Scotland, where the crowns were accidentally united in the person of the reigning monarch, and where the parliament had proceeded to sever that solitary bond of connexion; not like Scotland, where a Jacobite parliament had proposed to appoint a king not only different from the king of England, but actually claiming title to the English throne against the lawful monarch; not like Scotland, thus put into a state of war with England, with her shores blockaded, and her trade interdicted; but with full and perfect alliance, founded on unity of executive, unity of interest, and similarity of constitution; and all of them not only uninvaded by, but uniformly strengthened and secured by, the parliament of Ireland.

Again, sir, I will not admit the principle of Union, because we are not only called on to abandon our tried prosperity and the free constitution which gave birth to it, and without any necessity for so doing, or any specific advantage to be derived; but we are called on to do so on the faith of compact, and by the very persons who, in making the demand, violate the most solemn of all possible compacts, I mean that of 1782. The minister acts consistently in arraigning that settlement. It is at variance with all his plans, and in contradiction to all his sentiments. That settlement acknowledged the independence of the Irish parliament on this sound principle, "That the two countries were united by sameness of interest and similarity of constitution; that the strength and security of the one mutually affected the other; that they stand and fall together." You now avow to us that we have no sameness of interest; that we never had and never can have the British constitution; that there are no principles of union in our connexion, that the elements of hostility are essentially intermixed with it; that our weakness is your strength; that our subjugation is your safety; and that you cannot stand unless we fall, and are trampled on. Consistently, therefore, do you arraign that settlement, and candidly do you tell us that it was no compact, but a delusion; that on our part it was an arrogant claim, taking advantage of the weakness and distress of Great Britain, and that on your part it was a political finesse, humouring ou. childish insolence, yielding to our accidental strength, and that you will resume in the hour of force what you granted in the hour of feebleness.

Act your part in its full extent—resume it; but do not resort to the mockery of calling on us to relinquish what you tell us we have no right to retain. Do not insult us by offering compacts, when you avow that no compact can bind. Do not hold out to us the taunting pledge of faith and sincerity, when you boast of your total want of faith and sincerity in the compact of 1782. It is not merely by your licensed scribblers that the fraud of 1782 has been flated. Posterity will scarcely believe the page of history, when they see it recorded by the British minister. In 1782 you pledged the royal word, you pledged the solemn honour of the parliaments of both countries. You called on Almighty God to witness the truth and sincerity of that final adjustment; and you now call on us, by the pledge of the same royal faith, by the authority of the same parliament, and under the same religious sanction, to enter into a new treaty whose basis must be the violation of the former one.

Who is to guarantee it? If by your own authority you claim a right to violate a compact made amongst equals, and you call on us not to contract with, but to surrender to the same persons who have overturned it; if that treaty is not binding on you whilst we are both alive and strong and able to support our mutual pretensions, will this treaty of 1800 be binding when we are extinct by the terms of it, and you survive alone to expound and to enforce it—call down whatever sanction of king or parliament or God on your new contract, and how will it be treated twenty years hence, in an imperial parliament? If they wish to extinguish your 100 representatives and make you a province in form as well as substance, may they not then with some colour say, "we told you in 1800 that you had no constitution: your pretended compact you then gave up, we admitted you to our parliament by courtesy and for a time, and we now at our pleasure dismiss you from it." Would that act of 1820 be so shameless a violation of the articles of 1800 as these articles of 1800 would be of the compact of 1782.

I say, therefore, I will not quit the vantage ground of freedom and compact to admit the principle of an Union.

But it is said we press the discussion—that no mention of Union has been made in the speech, and that it is unbecoming in us to urge the rejection of a measure which has not been announced. Sir, this is very idle talk. If gentlemen do not feel a due respect for themselves, they should at least have some for the representative of majesty. Is it not more than ludicrous that the lord lieutenant should at the close of the last session propose the measure of Union, when parliament could not answer him, and that he should be utterly silent on it at the commencement of this session, when parliament is ready to answer him? You well know the reason of this inconsistency. You wait to have your troops recruited. You do something more than conjecture how those members mean to vote whose seats have been vacated since the last session of parliament. This trick is of a piece with the rest, and the conduct of the measure from first to last is the true expositor of its merits. May I be indulged in taking a very short review of it?

It is admitted by the minister that the alleged necessity of Union flows merely from the constitution of 1782. From Henry the Second until that time Great Britain never suggested the idea. It then was suggested not as a measure to be granted on the constitution of 1782, but as a substitute for it. It was found that no man could be hardy enough to utter the sentiment in this country, and it was abandoned. You thereupon acknowledged our independent constitution, and said that all grounds of constitutional disagreement between the two countries were thereby for ever precluded; and yet you now tell us that thereby, and thereby only, they were created. In 1785 commercial differences arose; there were long negociations between the two countries, yet the name of Union never hinted at. They broke off; still Union never hinted at. At a later period they are renewed and settled, and still Union never hinted at; in 1789 the question of regency arose, and Union never hinted at. And it is worthy of remark, that at those latter periods both countries were in profound peace, foreign and domestic, and nothing existed to prevent the fair sense of every man in this kingdom, in or out of parliament, being had upon the subject. At last, in 1795, we see the measure peeping out of the British cabinet, and the propriety of its adoption mentioned as the reason for dashing the hope which had been held out to the Catholic. The admission of the Catholic, says Lord Carlisle, would deprive the empire of advantages greater than any which she has derived since the revolution, at least since the Union! And it is to be observed, that the Catholic claim is rejected in order to enable the minister to effect Union, and not Union adopted for the purpose of rejecting the claim. Still, however, the scheme is not avowed to parliament or people, we only discover it by the accidental disclosure of a ministerial correspondence.

During the administration of Lord Camden, of whom I wish to speak with every degree of personal respect, a system was adopted certainly not calculated to soften religious animosities, or to endear the parliament to the Irish people. I do not mean to comment on the propriety of those measures, but when I reflect that the British minister had hatched the plan of Union before they were adopted, and when I see the supposed alienation of people from parliament in consequence of those measures, and the religious and political animosities excited by them used as the instruments for effecting that plan, I cannot divest my mind of the suspicion that the plan was adopted to effect the purpose. During the administration of that nobleman the most extensive, deep, well-planned, and wicked conspiracy that ever nation escaped from was hatched, matured, and prepared to burst upon the country. It was detected in all its parts, and published in all its details, and the energies of the nation called out to resist it, by the vigilance, information, and resources of a resident, superintending Irish parliament. If this wicked plot of Union had then been effected, and our parliament at Westminster, every vestige of British connexion would have been swept off the face of the land. Well, sir, this rebellion burst on the public with hideous and unexampled atrocity, and it was substantially put down by the resident, loyal men of Ireland; by native valour and native honour, before any reinforcement had arrived from Great Britain; and it is because the connexion has been preserved by the wisdom of the resident parliament, and by the valour and loyalty of the resident gentlemen of Ireland, that you now propose to banish both. In the summer of 1798 Lord Cornwallis arrived in this country, a man of high character and great military fame, not for the purpose of repelling invasion, not for the purpose of subduing rebellion, but to apply all his character and all his powers to the achievement of a political purpose. I will not dwell on the glories of his military campaign; I mean him no personal disrespect; but this I must observe, that whilst the military lord lieutenant was in the field, with an army of 60,000 men to support him, history will have it to record that we are indebted to a gallant Irishman (Mr. Vereker), at the head of about 800 native troops, for having withstood the enemy, and prevented the capital of Ireland from being entered in triumph by a body of not one thousand Frenchmen.

I do not wish to inquire too minutely why the embers of an extinguished rebellion have been so long suffered to exist; I do not wish to derogate from the praise to which the noble lord may be entitled for his clemency. Its very excesses, if they do claim praise, are at least entitled to indulgence; but when I see that all the rays of mercy and forbearance are reserved to gild the brow of the viceroy, and that all the odium of harshness and severity is flung upon the parliament; when I see the clemency of the chief governor throwing its mantle over the midnight murderer; when I see it holding parley with the armed rebel in the field; and when I see the task of making war against the victim in his grave and the infant in the cradle thrown by the same government upon the parliament, I cannot avoid suspecting that there is something more than the mere milk of human kindness in the forbearance on the one part, and something more than mere political caution in the severities of the other. But, sir, this rebellion was subdued by the parliament and people of Ireland; and before the country had a breathing time, before the loyalist had time to rest from his labours; before the traitor had received his punishment or his pardon; whilst we were all stunned by the stupendous events which had scarcely passed; whilst something little short of horror for all political projects had seized the mind of every man; whilst the ground was yet smoking with the blood of an O'Neill and of a Mountjoy, the wicked conspiracy was announced which was to rob their country of its liberties and their minor children of their birthright. With a suspended Habeas Corpus Act, with military tribunals in every county, the overwhelming and irretrievable measure of Union was announced for the free, enlightened, and calm discussion of an Irish parliament, and with all these engines of terror still suspended over their heads it is again submitted to them.

How was it brought forward? A hireling of the Castle employed to traduce parliament and insult the country; hopes held out to the Catholic that he should be established if he adopted; threats to the Protestant that he should be annihilated if he rejected; the constitution of 1782 openly treated as a system of force on our part and of compulsion on the part of England, and the right to resume it openly asserted. Whilst this impolitic insult was circulated through the country by the authority of government, the lord lieutenant sent to some of the principal gentlemen, merely to request their attention to the subject, but at the same time to assure them that he did not wish it to be carried unless by the uninfluenced opinion of the wealth and sense and loyalty of the country. What was the first parliamentary step? The chancellor of the exchequer and prime sergeant turned out of office because they ventured to declare an opinion against it. The measure was brought forward without hinting at the opinion of the people, but, on the contrary, asserting the full competence of parliament to decide without them. An insidious speech prepared by the minister and delivered from the throne, affecting to advise merely general strengthening of the empire, but which the secretary was compelled to avow meant Union, and Union only. What followed? The measure was justified by the noble secretary on account of the poverty and wretchedness of Ireland, and the necessity of separation flowing from the constitution of 1782. The principle of influence which had been exerted was justified, and the intention fairly avowed of following it up to the full extent of prerogative. The question was discussed for two days in all its relations, the principle examined and the details supposed the most favourable which possibly could be granted to Ireland, and after that full discussion, in despite of the calamities and terrors of the times, in despite of the surprise with which it was brought on, in despite of the influence exercised and avowed, the preliminary principle was rejected by a majority not only not acting under any corrupt influence, but against all corrupt influence.

I need not remind you of the transport with which that determination was received in every corner of the kingdom. Whatever might have been the former errors of parliament, they were lost in the virtue and splendor of that event. What, sir, was the consequence? In opposition to the declared sense of parliament and known wishes of the people, you were told, by one whom I may, without offence, call, if not a boy, at least a very young man, "that you were all in error; that you should hereafter implore as a blessing what you now deprecated as a curse; and that he would never lose sight of the measure, but would govern you for the purpose." I ask, was such language or conduct ever ventured on by a defeated minister; or would this insolence have been dared, if you had been considered as a free parliament or a free people. What was the conduct of Great Britain? Exactly corresponding in contemptuousness with that of their minister here. On the very day of the defeat in the Irish parliament, the minister of England, confiding in the dark promises of his partizans here, and taking our acquiescence to the surrender of our constitution as a thing of course, announces the measure to the British parliament, and gains their ready assent—no reluctance on their part, as when the free trade was obtained—no reluctance as on the repeal of 6th of George, or on the renunciation, or on the Commercial Propositions, which we thought so bad that we rejected them, although they acceded to them with regret, as much too good for us. No, sir, knowing that Union would make them masters, their ready acquiescence is procured. Well! by the temerity and boasting of a very young man, the parliament of one country is committed against the other. What is done by the minister when the disappointment is announced? Is he overwhelmed with shame? Anxious to extricate himself? No; he proceeds with as much composure as if he had our complete assent; he treats us like silly, passionate children, and goes on to adjust the terms. He makes a lofty, turgid speech, talks in high-sounding general terms of increased resources and consolidated strength; a couple of powdered lacquies of epithets waiting upon every substantive. Whatever we may think of the wisdom or justness of the oration, we cannot but admire its fashion and its pomp; and after all this absurd jargon, which has been so often exposed, he proceeds to inform the British house, that he is satisfied an enlightened majority must proceed to adopt the measure; and after the great leviathan has concluded his tumblings, a young whale puts up his nostrils, and spurts his blubber on this country, and tells a British senate, that when he came over to Ireland to put down the rebellion he discovered the true character of the country, and that it is best summed up by Swift's verses on the town of Carlow, " High church and low steeple, poor town and proud people ;" and all this to the great admiration of the wisest and most liberal assembly in the world. Give me leave, sir, here to advert to the declaration made in the House of Lords on the same subject by my Lord Auckland, who had been an Irish secretary in the administration of Lord Carlisle, and he declares, " that he knows enough of the theatre of action, and of the principal actors on that theatre, to do them the justice to believe, that their resistance will give way to the commanding voice of reason and of truth." Whoever remembers the administration of that noble lord in this country, when he was Mr. Eden, would be able to comprehend the full force and delicacy of the strain of irony in which he proves the candour and docility of the Irish parliament.

On such grounds as these, in defiance of our proceedings, the crown is addressed, and the father of his people is made to say, that he will take the first opportunity of laying before his Irish parliament the same principle in the detail which they had already rejected in the general.

(Here it was said from the treasury bench, that his Majesty's expression was not " the first," but a proper opportunity.)

I thank the noble lord for the correction; we shall see presently in what the propriety of the opportunity consisted. Has the royal word been kept in that respect by the minister? The resolution passed early in the session. The Irish parliament was adjourned at the request of the noble lord, for the express purpose of our being apprized of the result of the English deliberations. And yet, during the whole course of the session not a word is said upon the subject. The proper opportunity had not arrived; but the noble lord was certainly not remiss in his efforts to create that opportunity; he proceeded to accomplish the predictions of the British minister and of himself; to endeavour to corrupt and pack the parliament, so that an enlightened majority should pass the measure, and so to govern the country, that they should implore Union, or anything rather than remain as they were; how effectual the latter part of his plan has been you perceive, from the declaration of the hon. member (Doctor Browne), who declares that he is made a proselyte to the measure by the abominable proceedings of the minister and the parliament. The minister in the meantime proceeded to execute his threats of dismission from office. Every man, whether in a confidential situation or not, who had dared to express his free opinion was dismissed. When men would not be base enough openly to apostatize—their resignation was purchased—the place bill, which had been enacted to preserve the liberties of the subject, converted into an instrument to oppress them; and no man suffered to vacate his seat, unless he would stipulate an Unionist for his successor. The same lord lieutenant who first had declared his intention to submit the question to the uninfluenced sense of the country, frankly avowed his determination to abuse the prerogative for this scandalous purpose; and the noble lord who had declared, in full parliament, that he never would press the measure, even with a majority, against the free sense of parliament, heard himself publicly branded with his shameful departure from that promise, in the case of Colonel Cole, without having the hardihood to deny it! The British minister thought this last act too indecent even for the meridian of Ireland, and the parliament was the next day prorogued.

The public will not easily forget that memorable day, when the usher of the black rod was stationed within the doors of the commons, to watch the instant at which the house assembled. The public will not easily forget the indecent precipitation with which the message from the throne was delivered, without allowing time even for the ordinary vote of thanks to you, sir, for your conduct in that chair. They will not easily forget, not the absence, but the disgraceful flight of the minister of the country, to avoid the exposure and the punishment of guilt. When the functions of this house were thus superseded, his excellency, for the first time, thought proper to inform them of the resolutions of the British parliament; and he was further pleased to insinuate, that it would be a great satisfaction to him in his old age, if we would be so good as to adopt this measure of an Incorporating Union.

I must, for one, beg to be excused from making quite so great a sacrifice, from mere personal civility, to any lord lieutenant, however respectable he may be. The independence of a nation, I must own, does not appear to me to be exactly that kind of bagatelle which is to be offered by way of compliment, either to the youth of the noble lord who honours us by his presence in this house; or to the old age of the noble marquis, who occasionally sheds his setting lustre over the other. To the first, I am disposed to say, in the words of Waller—

> "I pray thee, gentle boy,
> "Press me no more for that slight toy;"

and to the latter I might apply the language of Lady Constance—

> "That's a good child—go to its grandam—give grandam kingdom—and its grandam will give it a plumb, a cherry, and a fig—there's a good grandam."

I hope, therefore, sir, I shall not be thought impolite if I decline the offer of the constitution of Ireland, either as a garland to adorn the youthful brow of the secretary, or to be suspended over the pillow of the viceroy.

Thus ended that never-to-be-forgotten session. What has since been done? During the whole interval between the sessions the same barefaced system of parliamentary corruption has been pursued. Dismissals, promotions, threats, promises. In despite of all this, the minister feared he could not succeed in parliament; and he affected to appeal to what he had before despised—the sentiment of the people. When he was confident of a majority, the people were to be heard only through the constitutional medium of their representatives. When he was driven out of parliament, the sense of the people became everything. Bribes were promised to the Catholic clergy—bribes were promised to the Presbyterian clergy—I trust they have been generally spurned with the contempt they merited. The noble lord understands but badly the genius of the religion in which he was educated. You held out hopes to the Catholic body, which were never intended to be gratified; regardless of the disappointment, and indignation, and eventual rebellion, which you might kindle—regardless of everything, provided the present paltry little object were obtained. In the same breath you held out professions to the Protestant, equally delusive: and having thus prepared the way, the representative of majesty sets out on his mission, to court his sovereign, the majesty of the people.

It is painful to dwell on that disgraceful expedition—no place too obscure to be visited—no rank too low to be courted—no threat too vile to be employed—the counties not sought to be legally convened by their sheriffs—no attempt to collect the unbiassed suffrage of the intelligent and independent part of the community—public addresses sought for from petty villages—and private signatures smuggled from public counties. And how procured? By the influence of absentee landlords; not over the affections, but over the terrors, of their tenantry. By griping agents and revenue officers. And after all this mummery had been exhausted; after the lustre of royalty had been tarnished by this vulgar intercourse with the lowest of the rabble; after every spot had been selected where a paltry address could be procured, and every place avoided where a manly sentiment could be encountered; after abusing the names of the dead, and forging the signatures of the living; after polling the inhabitants of the goal, and calling out against the parliament the suffrages of those who dare not come in to sign them till they had got their protection in their pocket; after employing the revenue officer to threaten the publican, that he should be marked as a victim, and the agent to terrify the shivering tenant with the prospect of his turf-bog being withheld, if he did not sign your addresses; after employing your military commanders, the uncontrolled arbiters of life and death, to hunt the rabble against the constituted authorities; after squeezing the lowest dregs of a population of near five millions—you obtained about five thousand signatures, three-fourths of whom affixed their names in surprise, terror, or total ignorance of the subject: and after all this canvass of the people, and after all this corruption wasted on the parliament, and after all your boasting that you must carry the measure by a triumphant majority, you do not dare to announce the subject in the speech from the throne.

You talk of respect for our gracious sovereign. I ask, what can be a more gross disrespect than this tampering with the royal name —pledged to the English parliament to bring the measure before us at a proper opportunity—holding it out to us at the close of the last session, and not daring to hint it at the beginning of this. Is it not notorious why you do not bring forward the measure now? Because the fruits of your corruption have not yet blossomed; because you did not dare to hazard a debate last session, in order to fill up the vacancies which the places bestowed by you, avowedly for this question, had occasioned ; and because you have employed the interval in the same sordid traffic ; and because you have a band of disinterested patriots waiting to come in and complete the enlightened majority who are to vote away the liberties of Ireland.

Will you dare to act on a majority so obtained? Fatal will be your councils, and disastrous your fate, if you resolve to do so. You have adopted the extremes of the despot and the revolutionist; you have invoked the loyal people and parliament of Ireland, who were not calling on you; you have essayed every means to corrupt that parliament, if you could, to sell their country; you have exhausted the whole patronage of the crown in execution of that system ; and to crown all, you openly avow, and it is notoriously a part of your plan, that the constitution of Ireland is to be purchased for a stipulated sum. I state a fact, for which, if untrue, I deserve serious reprehension; I state it as a fact, that you cannot dare to deny, that £15,000 a piece is to be given to certain individuals, as the price for their surrendering—what? Their property? No; but the rights of representation of the people of Ireland; and you will then proceed in this, or in any imperial parliament, to lay taxes on the wretched natives of this land to pay the purchase of their own slavery. It was in the last stage of vice and decrepitude that the Roman purple was set up for sale, and the sceptre of the world transferred for a stipulated price; but even then the horde of slaves who were to be ruled would not have endured that their country itself should have been enslaved to another nation.

Do not persuade yourselves that a young, gallant, hardy, enthusiastic people like the Irish are to be enslaved by means so vile, or will submit to injuries so palpable and galling. From those acts of despotism you plunge into the phrenzy of revolution, at a time when political madness has desolated the face of the world; when all establishment is staggering under the drunkenness of theory ; when in this country, which it is said has been peculiarly visited by the pestilence, even the projects, which the noble lord may recollect to have been entertained by the Northern Whig Club, have been necessarily suspended, if not abandoned ; when you have found it necessary to enact temporary laws, taking away almost every one of the ordinary privileges of the subject of a free constitution ; with the trial by jury superseded, and the whole country subject to martial law—a law, by which the liberty and life of every man rest merely on the security of military discretion ; a law which you have not yet ventured to repeal, and the necessity of whose continuance is strangely hinted in the speech from the throne; with a bloody rebellion only extinguished, and a formidable invasion only escaped; you call on this distracted country to unroof itself of its constitution, and having been refuted by the wisdom and virtue of parliament, you desire the rabble of every description to array themselves against the constituted authorities, and to put down the parliament, because parliament would not put down the constitution.

Are the people of Ireland cured of their frenzy? Take off their fetters—restore the Habeas Corpus—give back the trial by jury—repeal the martial law bill—let the ordinary laws resume their course. Are they maniacs, and are they manacled?—do not erect them into law-givers and judges. Do not insult them by a mock appeal—do not at the same time trample on them as slaves and worship them as masters. These, sir, are not the times for theory—let us cling to experience; it tells us we can exist with a common king and separate parliaments, because we have done so for ages; and therefore, when I see a modern Solon taking to pieces the different parts of our constitution, like those of a watch, and asking, "If you have a common king, would it not be better, *a priori*, to have a common parliament," I laugh at his visions. Will he answer to me, that if the people are called on to pull down the parliamentary part of their constitution, they will stop precisely there?

I ask him further, what is there in his theory of equal value to the proof from experience, that a common king and separate parliaments produce a good practical system of liberty and connexion. The two parliaments may clash! So in Great Britain may king and parliament; but we see they never do so injuriously. There are principles of repulsion! Yes; but there are principles of attraction, and from these the enlightened statesman extracts the principle by which the countries are to be harmoniously governed. As soon would I listen to the shallow observer of nature, who should say there is a centrifugal force impressed on our globe, and, therefore, lest we should be hurried into the void of space, we ought to rush into the centre to be consumed there. No; I say to this rash arraigner of the dispensations of the Almighty, there are impulses from whose wholesome opposition eternal wisdom has declared the law by which we revolve in our proper sphere, and at our proper distance. So I say to the political visionary, from the opposite forces which you object to, I see the wholesome law of imperial connexion derived—I see the two countries preserving their due distance from each other, generating and imparting heat, and light, and life, and health, and vigour, and I will abide by the wisdom and experience of the ages which are past, in preference to the speculations of any modern philosopher.

Sir, I warn the ministers of this country against persevering in their present system. Let them not proceed to offer violence to the settled principles or to shake the settled loyalty of the country. Let them not persist in the wicked and desperate doctrine which places British connexion in contradiction to Irish freedom. I revere them both—it has been the habit of my life to do so. For the present constitution I am ready to make any sacrifice. I have proved it. For British connexion I am ready to lay down my life. My actions have proved it. Why have I done so? Because I consider that connexion essential to the freedom of Ireland. Do not, therefore, tear asunder to oppose to each other these principles which are identified in the minds of loyal Irishmen. For me, I do not hesitate to declare, that if the madness of the revolutionist should tell me you must sacrifice British connexion, I would adhere to that connexion in preference to the independence of my country. But I have as little hesitation in saying, that if the wanton ambition of a minister should assault the freedom of Ireland and compel me to the alternative, I would fling the connexion to the winds, and I would clasp the independence of my country to my heart. I trust the virtue and wisdom of the Irish parliament and people will prevent that dreadful alternative from arising. If it should come, be the guilt of it on the heads of those who make it necessary.

On the 16th of May, 1799, Plunket had commented upon the case of Colonel Cole, to which he again adverts in this speech. A word may be useful to explain both allusions. Castlereagh had already secured a number of votes in the course of 1799 by inducing members, who were not shameless enough themselves to support the Union, to vacate their seats and allow Castle candidates to be returned. The regular compensation in a case of this kind was £15,000. But in the course of the year he discovered another way of weakening the opposition, which, however, could only be practised upon a small scale. It was to refuse the escheatorship to any of the opposition who might desire to retire, or be compelled for private reasons to resign their seats, unless on the condition of allowing an Unionist to be returned in their stead. Colonel Cole, going on foreign service, wanted to withdraw from the representation of Enniskillen. A member of opposition was certain to be elected in his place. But the escheatorship was refused, and thereby the seat kept in suspension until the following year.

In the passage alluding to the Lord Lieutenant's campaign against Humbert, Plunket refers to Colonel Vereker, a member of the opposition, and admitted by the French general to be the only British officer he had found who was fit to command fifty men. With two hundred of the Limerick militia, half a troop of dragoons, and two curricle guns, he had given the advance guard of the French such a check at Collooney as entirely diverted Humbert's line of advance,

In the reference to the English debates, beside Pitt's speech, those of Mr. Pelham, chief secretary under Lord Camden, and of Mr. Eden, chief secretary under Lord Carlisle, are alluded to. I suppose the reference to Castlereagh's early Presbyterian breeding, his sympathies with the extreme reform doctrines of the Northern Whig Club (and even, it was said, of the first United Irish societies—for he began political life as a violent reformer), need no particular explanation.

St. George Daly followed Plunket in a virulent harangue, which surprised the house by its audacity and volubility. Bushe replied tartly to a reference which it contained to him. Barrington and Sir John Macartney spoke in succession against ministers, and (Bully) Egan was rising, when along College-green and through the courts and corridors of the house such another thunder of popular enthusiasm was heard as had announced, a year before, the triumph of the opposition to the city. At last the doors opened, and, leaning upon Arthur Moore and George Ponsonby, the opposition and the galleries recognised, with tears and cheers, the thin gray hairs, the stooped and shattered body, the prophet eyes and Titan brows of Henry Grattan, advancing like an Avatar to the rescue of Ireland. Even Castlereagh was so moved by that venerable and commanding figure, in which life seemed to be only sustained by the intense will within, that he rose at the head of the whole treasury bench, bowed, and remained standing as the grand old tribune moved feebly to his place, in which, after taking the oaths, he spoke, sitting, for hours a speech full, fertile, brilliant, and convincing beyond any speech spoken on the subject, and beyond almost any of his own previous efforts. When he sat down, Isaac Corry was put up by Castlereagh to make a formal closing of the debate, and when the house divided, government had a majority of 42.

THE UNION.

May 26, 1800.

The resolutions of the English parliament suggesting articles of Union, were laid before the Irish Commons on the 5th of February. They were debated during the ensuing month. Grattan led the opposition with all the ancient lustre and electric vigour of his eloquence. By him, and by Saurin, Burrowes, and Goold, who had all been returned within the session, the brunt of these debates was borne. Plunket spoke but seldom. When George Ponsonby, on the 10th of March, raised the question of bribing members under the pretence of compensating for the loss of parliamentary influence, Plunket challenged Castlereagh to declare whether he really meant to raise £1,500,000 for such a purpose.

"Because, if the noble lord had decency enough to abandon so infamous, so base a part of his plan, as that of employing the money of the people to buy up their representatives, he deserved credit for it; and he called upon him now to stand up in his place and avow his abandonment, if he really had given up the measure, that the public mind might be calmed upon a subject of such abomination, so irritating to their feelings, so insulting to the honour of their country; and that no base miscreant, however honourable or noble his rank, however powerful his influence, who had the meanness and criminality to listen to the corrupt and degrading proposal of purchasing from him the representative rights of his country, for fifteen, twenty or forty thousand pounds, to be wrung from the bowels of his miserable country, and afterwards have the baseness to boast of his venality, should continue to exult in his infamous and corrupt triumph over every principle of national honour and justice."

Castlereagh coolly answered, that he had no notion whatever of abandoning any part of his plan, and he was only waiting until the articles of Union were adopted by both houses, to propose "the exact quantum and mode of ompensation." Plunket could only make this caustic retort:—

"Gentlemen on one side, it appears, are to have compensation for past services, and gentlemen borough proprietors on the other side are promised compensation in hope of future services. But neither are to have compensation unless the Union is carried.

"Here then is a poor country that has travelled, according to the noble lord's account, so rapidly in the career of bankruptcy, that her finances are unequal to her war establishment, or her civil establishment. a nation almost engulfed in the jaws of beggary and ruin—yet this poor country is now told by the minister, he must find a million and a half of money, to be raffled for by the members of this house—but that every man who takes the dice-box in his hand, to throw for his share of the plunder, must first pledge himself to vote for the Union.

"What will the people of Ireland say to so base and flagitious a piece of plunder, as this juggling from them, by taxes on their wants and miseries, the enormous sum of a million and a half, to reward the betrayers of their rights and liberties?"

He did not speak again until the 26th of May, when the bill for settling the commercial relations of the two countries under the Union, was in the stage of second reading. Grattan opened the debate in a masterly statistical statement, followed by passages of glowing appeal and exquisite imagery. Castlereagh answered with his natural cold-blooded insolence:—

"He called in question the patriotism of those who took every opportunity of inflaming the public mind against a settlement, which was on the very eve of conclusion; whatever might be their views, however strong their allusions to rebellion, government was energetic and able enough to defend the constitution against all future attacks, as it had against the past."

Mr. May more moderately supported the Secretary. In his mind it was an excellent argument for Union, that the Irish house might by admixture reform the English house. One of the articles of Union, however, provided that not more than twenty Irish members holding office should be eligible to sit in the united parliament; so that Mr. May and his friends were, as it were, innocently supporting a self-denying ordinance.

MR. SPEAKER, I rise to reiterate my opposition to this measure—an opposition which I will never cease to make until the constitution is finally extinguished. I cannot subscribe to the new doctrine of the noble lord, that this bill must now be considered as passed, and that whoever ventures to oppose it in its second reading is guilty of insolent disrespect to the law of the land. I congratulate the noble lord on his recent discovery, that it is insolence in any man to set up his private opinion against the declared sense of parliament. If, when an unbought majority of parliament had reprobated a certain measure as a violation of the liberties and constitution of the land, a young man, with intemperate and ill-advised obstinacy, should declare himself determined to persevere in pressing that very measure, and that he would never lose sight of it—if such a man, slighting the sense of the legislature, abusing the power he possesses, and practising against the virtue and independence of parliament, should come back here in less than twelve months, and, with a miserable venal and packed majority at his back, propose and carry that very measure against the former unbought and avowed opinion of the parliament and the people, such a man must indeed be insolent and audacious. So far is it from being treason to expose and resist the attempt of such a man in every stage of it, it is loyalty and virtue to do so—it is of use to the country—it tends to preserve its peace—to show the people of Ireland that they are not destitute of friends, and to hold out a hope, which I have no doubt will be realised, that the constitution shall again be restored, and that better days are yet to come. It may prove, too, that, notwithstanding the treachery and the insolence with which our constitution and our liberties are now attacked, the people of Ireland are not yet abandoned, and that they have friends who will stand by them to the last. This bill I oppose, not as a bill of union, but of separation—as a bill calculated to dismember the empire—a bill to put down the loyalty of the country—a bill of robbery, not of legislation. (He then adverted to the doctrine of Lord Clare respecting the competency of parliament, and to the idea of Mr. May that this change would be a reform of the British parliament). This argument, so ingenious, I will not attempt to refute; nor do I wish to deprive a British parliament of any advantage they may derive from the infusion of such virtue and independence as that of the honourable gentleman; but I cannot help calling the attention of the house and of the country to the opinion expressed by the British minister himself of that class of men who are now to decide on the fate of Ireland. Into a British parliament twenty men only will be admitted of that description which now constitutes the minister's majority. Let no more than twenty placemen vote on the present question, and I would freely and cheerfully submit the fate of the country to their decision. Let the minister even retain all his placemen, and let him put the question on the constitution of Ireland to a ballot, and I will abide the issue. Let the gentlemen who hold places vote uninfluenced by the fear of losing their situations, and even they will act like Irishmen. Who, then, are this body of men to whose opinion we are asked to look up with so much reverence? They are men whom a British minister had declared too foul to pollute the walls of a British senate. Those men who are too base to enter the door of one parliament are to vote the extinction of another, and decide for ever upon the liberties of this country! I again repeat it emphatically, you are incompetent to pass this measure against the sense of the nation. Such an act in such circumstances must want the binding obligation of a law. If any petulant and ignorant should accuse me of treason for this sentiment, I answer him but by scorn. My habits, my known principles, and the whole tenor of my life give the lie to the imputation.

The noble lord has talked in high-sounding terms of the ease with which he would put down another rebellion, should this measure produce one but if a future rebellion should not rouse the noble lord to more valorous exertion than he made during the last, the country cannot safely depend much upon the prowess of the noble lord. Sir, who put down that rebellion? I look around me, and I see the men to whose exertions we owe our deliverance These are the men whose courage and loyalty restored peace to the country while the noble lord was lounging about the Castle—if not more wickedly employed in plotting the destruction of the constitution of his country. As to the part which I have taken in opposing this measure, I look upon it as the proudest honour of my life. By it I wish to be remembered by posterity—it is an inheritance I am glad to transmit to my children. The recollection of the part I hav taken in common with the one hundred and twenty honest men who with incorruptible steadiness have defended the liberty of their country against the machinations of the noble lord and those under whom he acts, will soothe me at my last hour, and soften the blow of death: nay, when I am called before the Almighty Power, in whom I believe and trust, I am willing to take in my hand the record of my opposition to this measure, in humble confidence that it may afford some atonement for the errors of which I have been guilty.

Of course, ministers had a majority of 37. The votes which they had secured during the previous year sustained them at every division, and during the debates of 1800 they could always calculate upon whipping a majority averaging 40 votes.

THE UNION.

June 7, 1800.

The last of the Union debates were those of the 5th and 7th of June, in committee. The resistance of the opposition was still gallantly, though hopelessly protracted. On the 5th, Mr. O'Donnell proposed an amendment, of which the reporters profess not to have learned the exact import, but say it excited a great flame in the house. It appears to have been a declaration that the people ought to resist the Union by force. After a scene, with closed doors and galleries cleared, the amendment was withdrawn.

On the 7th, O'Donnell moved a postponement of the third reading, and in supporting him, Francis Dobbs, Plunket's colleague, delivered an extraordinary harangue. A learned lawyer and an accomplished gentleman, Dobbs was mad on one subject—the millenium, and firmly believed that Ireland was decreed by Providence to remain for ever an independent state, to be the birth-place of Antichrist, and the temporal kingdom of the Messiah. The last remarkable speech made against the Union was couched in this extraordinary style. Pointing to the divided and convulsed state of Europe as the realization of one of Daniel's prophecies, and as a sure sign that the millenium was at hand, he declared he was not alarmed at the progress of a measure which he detested, as he was convinced it could never be operative. The house listened with mingled ridicule and horror. And O'Donnell's motion was defeated, of course.

The house having resolved itself into committee, the Hon. Mr. Annesley in the chair, the detailed parts were read, and some amendments proposed by Lord Castlereagh adopted.

On the clause regulating the representation in the first session of the united parliament being read,

MR. PLUNKET, after observing that any observations which he should offer on any part of this bill were not offered by him with a view of suggesting amendments that could or ought to make it less an object of abhorrence to the country than it was at present, but bad and destructive as the bill was and must be in every possible shape, he wished its enactments might be certain and explicit, so that the country should know what they had to look to. For this reason, therefore, he observed that by this article, as it now stood, there was one very material case left totally unprovided for, and that was the case of his majesty's dissolving the British parliament and calling a new one before the first of January next. The article stated that if his majesty should think proper so to declare under the great seal, that they, the present representatives of Great Britain, and the delegated members for this country should constitute the first united parliament; but the article did not provide for the case which possibly might occur—that he should dissolve the British parliament before the 1st of June, 1800, and therefore he would be glad to know whether, in that case, the delegates to be sent from the present Irish parliament were to be continued as representatives in the united parliament until the term of the British representatives should elapse, which would be seven years from the first of January next. Should the king think proper to dissolve the present British parliament and call a new one before the Union should take place—or was it intended that when the united parliament should have sat three years, at which time the term of the Irish representatives would have expired, the counties and towns of Ireland were to be sent to new elections, while the British representatives only continued to legislate for the two countries; Ireland during the interval of the election having no representation whatsoever in the united parliament. One or other of these two things which he had now stated he conceived must inevitably happen, if this article stood as it was at present, and the crown should think proper before the next year to call a new British parliament: the first case he had supposed would be one of flagrant injustice to this country, by continuing the representatives in that office four years beyond the time for which they were elected, and the other would be not only unjust, but an absurdity on the face of it.

After a good deal of time taken to consider, the Attorney-General replied by observing that the case supposed by Mr. Plunket, and on which the difficulty rested—namely, that the king should dissolve his British parliament before next year, rested merely on a violent presumption, and was not reasonably to be looked for. The King could never be supposed to do that which would tend to defeat the measure of Union which he himself had recommended to his parliament.

The Attorney-General's argument was followed by that of William Johnson, who contended that if the King should dissolve both his parliaments, he might call two distinct new parliaments, which, under the provisions of this act, would sit in January next as the united parliament.

The Speaker supported the objection of Mr. Plunket, and insisted that the article as it now stood, though drawn up by the officers of the crown, went to abridge in a very material instance the prerogative of the crown by preventing it from dissolving the British parliament before January next, unless it incurred one or other of the absurdities which Mr. Plunket had stated.

Lord Castlereagh and the Chancellor of the Exchequer spoke in support of the article as it stood; but confined themselves to stating more at large the arguments of Mr. Johnson, namely, that the crown might dissolve both parliaments before January next, and call new ones for each country distinctly, which under this law would, in January, 1801, constitute the united parliament, thus leaving Plunket's objection unanswered.

This and several other clauses having been agreed to, when the chairman came to the part regulating the proportion of contribution between the two countries,

MR. PLUNKET objected to the data on which the proportion was founded. He insisted that there were no regular parliamentary documents to go by; that the House and the country had no other guide than the noble lord's assertion, which, however it might in other cases be entitled to confidence and respect, was not to be deemed sufficient in a case of such great and vital importance as that before the committee. The British minister, when he was laying on a tax only for a year, entered into calculations of the cultivated acres in the country—of the profit resulting from them—of the home trade of the country—of the profit made on the capital of the country—and laid authentic documents before the house on every one of these points. The noble lord, on the other hand, though deciding for ever upon the capacity of the country to bear taxation, had taken no account of the quantity of cultivated land in Ireland—none of the home trade of either country, though by that criterion England would be found more able to bear taxation than Ireland as thirty to one ; he had taken no account of the profit made upon Irish capital; he had reckoned only the capital itself—and even for these calculations he had furnished the house with no authentic documents on which they could rely.

He then proceeded to prove by a variety of calculations, founded on irrefragable facts, that the proportion which Ireland ought to pay compared with that of England should be, instead of one to seven and a half, the proportion established by the bill, not more than one to twelve. He urged this point with great force, and pointed out the ruin and misery which must result to both countries from imposing upon us a proportion of taxation so inequitable in itself, and so much beyond our possible means of paying.

Three days afterwards occurred the closing scene of the Irish parliament. The last words of resistance to the Union were spoken by Plunket. In the parliamentary report of the 10th of June, we find it stated, that on the motion for a third reading of the Articles of Union Bill—

" Mr. Plunket rose and began to arraign the means by which the Union had been carried, and having charged the minister with having employed bribery,

" The Hon. Mr. Butler called him to order. He said that he represented one of the most respectable counties in the kingdom, and no man could or should dare to say that the influence of bribery could reach him."

The Hon. Mr. Butler probably felt that the imputation was particularly pointed at him. He had been a staunch anti-Unionist until the month before, when he joined the government on Lord Corry's motion, and, like the rest of Castlereagh's later converts, it was supposed for a consideration of hard cash.

The report proceeds :—

" Mr. Plunket again rose, and a cry of 'order!' 'chair!' resounded from both sides of the house, until at length the gallery was cleared, and strangers were not admitted until the house adjourned. While the house was in discussion, a great many of the anti-Union members seceded, and the Union bill passed, and was ordered to the Lords for their concurrence."

ROBERT EMMET.
September 19, 1803.

THE life of Robert Emmet is one of the most affecting episodes in Irish history Of all the United Irishmen, there is not one who has left memory invested with so much sympathy at home and abroad. His last speech has been ever since his death a gospel of rebellion against England. Even in the American schools it is as popular a recitative as Patrick Henry's defiances; and Robert Emmet trampling on the British crown figured as often on a western signboard, thirty years ago, as General Jackson. There was such purity, chivalry, and devotion in his nature—his life, his love, his death, are full of a romance so true and so touching—that in thinking of him, men unconsciously elevate his character above the poor failure—an hour's scuffle with the police and the picquet, stained by an atrocious murder—which history asserts his insurrection to have been. They wonder how that wild attempt can have won for its leader a character like Bayard's; but so it is.

Moore and Washington Irving have wafted the legend of his love for Sarah Curran and for Ireland wherever the English language is spoken; and to Irish readers, the pious care of Doctor Madden has made every step in his attempt, from the hour he left his brother Addis at Amsterdam to that of his execution, familiar. The noble integrity and courage of his character are above vindication. Even the British Lord Lieutenant, in a dispatch to his government, could not forbear to express his sense of "that sentiment of magnanimity with which, whatever his crimes may have been, he certainly conducted himself." Even Curran, who beheld in him the cause of a sore family sorrow, declared that he would rather trust the word of Robert Emmet than the oath of any other man in the world. Even the hardened gaoler, who turned the key of the condemned cell, fell senseless as the young rebel passed forth, with a face bright and serene as an angel's, to the scaffold.

For all the sacred obligation of his dying words, his name will not "sleep in the shade," but be the theme of song and story for many a day in Ireland. I would rather see his memory acquitted, if it may be, of that imputation of reckless rashness which rests upon it, and which is the point of Plunket's speech. It is difficult. He alone held and guided all the threads of the conspiracy. When the first blow was struck and had failed, his lips were sealed, and his confederates, with the exception of those who were actually engaged in the attempt to surprise the Castle, were saved. But I think there remains evidence enough to show that his designs were not the mere Quixotic enterprise they are represented, and that an hour's success might have brought not merely "the bricklayer, the baker, the old clothesman, the hodman, and the ostler" to his side, but peers and merchants, the disgusted anti-Unionist and the disappointed Catholic agitator, the bankrupt city, and the peasantry of the south.

The revolutions of '48 have taught the world that one well-directed blow in a capital city, against a government to which the people are disaffected, is like a spark of fire touching choke-damp. Emmet evidently acted upon some such idea. He did not attempt to revive the old ramified organization of the United Irishmen, of which government had got all the clues. He used its remaining links only so far as to prepare the peasantry for a general rising, whenever they heard that the green flag had been set up on the Castle. The question is, had he a reasonable hope of carrying the English executive in Ireland by a *coup de main*, and was he certain of sufficient support at home and abroad if he had succeeded?

I doubt if any man can examine his masterly plan of attack, check, and defence in Dublin, the calculations upon which it rested, and the accidents by which it was baffled, without feeling that the government had almost a miraculous escape. The rebel depot had been for months in the immediate neighbourhood of the Castle, yet until a few hours before the actual explosion of the insurrection the Lord Lieutenant had no information, and was quite unprepared when it burst upon him. The only force that could be got together to guard the Castle was a police patrol and a lieutenant's guard of fencibles. It was even without military stores at the time. Emmet, on the other hand, had certainly provided more than sufficient force in men and armament. His supplies of arms and ammunition were immense. At the depot in Thomas-street alone, Lord de Blaquiere found nearly 12,000 pikes, and abundance of powder, rockets, and grenades. Within the last few hours, however, beginning with the explosion of one of his magazines, everything fell asunder through a series of accidents and mistakes, which no human sagacity could have foreseen or ingenuity repaired. Napoleon Bonaparte might have failed in the same circumstances.

Had Emmet reason to suppose that if he could seize on the capital he would be supported by the country? I think he had. The disaffection in Ireland at this date was more intense and pervading than it ever had been in Tone's time. The Union was ruining Dublin. The national gentry remained disgusted with the government. The Catholics perceived that they had been deceived. The whole country was again ripe and alert for revolt. "If Ireland be not attended to, it will be lost;" wrote Lord Charles Bentinck to his brother in India; "these rascals are as ready as ever for rebellion." "I hope to see you next year," wrote Lord Grenville, by the same mail, to the Marquis of Wellesley, "supposing at that period you have still a country to revisit." Shortly after Emmet's arrival in Ireland he dined with John Keogh, at Mount Jerome. Keogh was a cautious, but resolute and forecasting man. He agreed that if Emmet could rely upon even two counties rising, the experiment might succeed. Emmet counted upon nineteen, and he certainly had the zealous co-operation of five or six. General Tarleton's evidence is that "the conspiracy extended to the south beyond Cork, where the rebels learned by means of telegraphic fires the ill success of the insurrection in Dublin, before the king's officers knew it in Cork. It was by this information only that the insurrection was prevented from being general over the country."

Again, Emmet did not rely merely upon the masses. In his speech from the dock he declared that in this design he was only the subaltern of men before whose virtues and genius he bowed with respectful deference. He referred, I dare say, chiefly to the United Irish leaders then in France. But, perhaps, he also included men like Keogh, Lord Wycombe (afterwards Lansdowne), Colonel Plunket, Colonel Lumm, and Mr. Fitzgerald, of Glyn, who were, if not compromised, at least in direct communication with him. I need only add on the subject of foreign assistance, of which Emmet, however, had always a strong suspicion, that in 1803 Bonaparte had really taken up the cause of Ireland—was organizing an Irish legion—had agreed to the future relations between the two republics—gave Emmet a long interview before he left for Ireland, and was also cognizant of several conferences between him and Tallyrand.

I do not state these facts merely to acquit Emmet's character of the absurd and injurious imputation that he was a rash and visionary enthusiast, but to show the grounds upon which Plunket afterwards rested his defence of the speech which follows, and upon which I observe elsewhere.

The trial occurred before the special commission presided over by Lord Norbury, on the 19th of September. Standish O'Grady, attorney-general, Mac Lelland, solicitor-general, and Plunket, were leading counsel for the crown; Peter Burrowes and Leonard Mac Nally, for the prisoner.

Evidence was duly given of Emmet's residence at Butterfield-lane, of his preparations at Thomas-street, of his appearing in green uniform with his lieutenant, the brave veteran Michael Quigley, Dowdall, and Stafford, of the brief career of the insurrection in arms, his subsequent flight to the mountains, and arrest. The proclamations and other documentary evidence were then given in, and the case closed on the part of the crown. I quote the scene which follows from the report:—

Mr. Mac Nally.—My lord, Mr. Emmet says, he does not intend to call any witness, or to take up the time of the court by his counsel stating any case, or making observations upon the evidence; and therefore I presume the trial is now closed on both sides.

Mr. Plunket.—It is with extreme reluctance that under such circumstances, and in a case like this, I do not feel myself at liberty to follow the example which has been set me by the counsel for the prisoner.

Mr. Mac Nally.—I beg pardon; I am, then, to call on the court to decide a matter of practice, No doubt, the crown is entitled to the last word—that is a reply; but if I understand anything of the arrangement of criminal trials, it is this: the counsel for the prosecution states the case; after the evidence given in support of it, the prisoner is called upon to state his case; and if he does, the counsel for the prosecution has a right to reply; but I conceive that the word REPLY, according to its true meaning, is this:—observing upon that which has been urged in answer to the charge; but if there has been no answer, there can be no reply. I believe the case is new; at least since the proceedings in treason were regulated by statute, there is no instance where there had not been a defence made by the prisoner's counsel, and an answer given to the evidence against him; therefore, I say, it is a new case. However, we do not intend to press the objection further, unless my learned friend, with whom I have the honour to act, should think proper to add anything in support of it.

Lord Norbury.—Were it a matter of any doubt, it would be our duty to have it spoken to; but as there can be no doubt that the counsel for the crown have a right to speak to a great body of evidence, and that the counsel for the prisoner cannot by their silence preclude the crown from that right—we cannot prevent the reply; if we did we should introduce a novel practice, which never prevailed in any of the state trials; into many of which for some time past I have looked.

Mr. Attorney-General.—My lord, we feel that stating a case and observing upon evidence are different duties. I have had the burden upon me of stating the case for the crown. The prisoner declining to go into any case, wears the impression, that the case on the part of the crown does not require any answer, that is the most charitable way of considering his conduct, and therefore it is at my particular desire that Mr. Plunket rises to address the court and the jury upon this occasion.

My lords and gentlemen of the jury, you need not entertain any apprehension that at this hour of the day I am disposed to take up a great deal of your time, by observing upon the evidence which has been given. In truth, if this were an ordinary case, and if the object of this prosecution did not include some more momentous interests than the mere question of the guilt or innocence of the unfortunate gentleman who stands a prisoner at the bar, I should have followed the example of his counsel, and should have declined making any observation upon the evidence. But, gentlemen, I do feel this to be a case of infinite importance, indeed. It is a case important, like all others of this kind, by involving the life of a fellow subject; but it is doubly—and tenfold important, because from the evidence which has been given in the progress of it, the system of this conspiracy against the laws and constitution of the country has been developed in all its branches; and in observing upon the conduct of the prisoner at the bar, and in bringing home the evidence of his guilt, I am bringing home guilt to a person who, I say, is the centre, the lifeblood and soul of this atrocious conspiracy.

Gentlemen, with respect to the evidence which has been offered upon the part of the crown to substantiate the guilt of the prisoner, I shall be very short indeed in recapitulating and observing upon it —I shall have very little more to do than to follow the statement which was made by my learned and eloquent friend who stated the case upon the part of the crown; because it appears to me that the outline which was given by him has been with an exactness and precision seldom to be met with, followed up by the proof. Gentlemen, what is the sum and substance of that evidence? I shall not detain you by detailing the particulars of it? You see the prisoner at the bar returning from foreign countries some time before hostilities were on the point of breaking out between these countries and France. At first avowing himself—not disguising or concealing himself—he was then under no necessity of doing so; but when hostilities commenced, and when it was not improbable that foreign invasion might co-operate with domestic treason, you see him throwing off the name by which he was previously known, and disguising himself under new appellations and characters. You see him in the month of March or April going to an obscure lodging at Harold's-cross, assuming the name of Hewitt, and concealing himself there.

For what purpose? Has he called upon any witness to explain it to you? If he were upon any private enterprise—if for fair and honourable views—or any other purpose than that which is imputed to him by the indictment—has he called a single witness to explain it? No; but after remaining six weeks or two months in this concealment, when matters began to ripen a little more, when the house was hired in Thomas-street, which became the depôt and magazine of military preparation, he then thinks it necessary to assume another character and another place of abode, accommodated to a more enlarged sphere of action—he abandons his lodging—he pays a fine of sixty-one guineas for a house in Butterfield-lane, again disguised by another assumed name, that of Ellis. Has he called any person to account for this; or to excuse by argument, or even by assertion, this conduct? Why for any honest purpose should he take this place for his habitation, under a feigned name?

But you find his plans of treason becoming more mature. He is there associated with two persons. One of the name of Dowdall; we have not explained in evidence what his situation is, or what he had been; the other is Quigley; he has been ascertained by the evidence to have been a person originally following the occupation of a bricklayer; but he thought proper to desert the humble walk in which he was originally placed, and to become a framer of constitutions and subverter of empires.

With these associates he remains at Butterfield-lane, occasionally leaving it and returning again; whether he was superintending the works which were going forward, or whatever other employment engaged him, you will determine. Be it what it may; if it were not for the purpose of treason and rebellion, he has not thought proper by evidence to explain it. So matters continued until some short time before the fatal night of the 23rd of July. They became somewhat hastened by an event which took place about a week before the breaking out of the insurrection. A house in Patrick-street, in which a quantity of powder had been collected for the purpose of the rebellion, exploded. An alarm was spread by this accident; the conspirators found that if they delayed their schemes and waited for foreign co-operation, they would be detected and defeated; and therefore it became necessary to hasten to immediate action. What is the consequence? From that time the prisoner is not seen in his old habitation. He moves into town, and becomes an inmate and constant inhabitant of this depôt. These facts, which I am stating are not collected by inference from his disguise, his concealment, or the assumption of a feigned name, or the other concomitant circumstances; but are proved by the positive testimony of three witnesses; all of whom positively swear to the identity of his person: Fleming, Coghlan, and Farrell, every one of whom swears he saw the prisoner, tallying exactly with each other, as to his person, the dress he wore, the functions he exercised; and every one of whom had a full opportunity of knowing him. You saw him at Butterfield-lane, under the assumed name of Ellis—you see him carrying the same name into the depôt, not wishing to avow his own, until the achievement of the enterprise would crown it with some additional eclat.

The first witness, Fleming, appears in the character of a person who was privy to the conspiracy—he was acquainted with the depôt from the moment it was first taken—he had access to it and co-operated in the design—he was taken upon suspicion, and under these circumstances, he makes the disclosure. If the case of the prosecution rested upon the evidence of this man alone, though an accomplice in the crime, it would be sufficient evidence to go to you for your consideration, upon which you would either acquit the prisoner or find him guilty. In general, from the nature of the crime of treason—from the secrecy with which it is hatched and conducted, it frequently happens that no other evidence can be resorted to than that of accomplices; and therefore, notwithstanding the crimes of such witnesses, their evidence is admissible to a jury. But doubtless every honest and considerate jury, whether in a case of life or not, will scrupulously weigh such evidence. If it be consistent with itself, disclosing a fair and candid account, and is not impeached by contradictory testimony, it is sufficient to sustain a verdict of guilty.

But, gentlemen, I take up your time unnecessarily, in dwelling upon this topic, which I introduced rather in justification of the principles which regulate such evidence, than as attaching any particular weight to it in the present instance. Because, if you blot it altogether from your minds, you have then the testimony of two other persons not tainted with the conspiracy; one of them brought in while in a state of intoxication, and the other taken by surprise when he was watching at the door, in every respect corroborating the testimony of Fleming, and substantiating the guilt of the prisoner. You heard the kind of implements which were prepared, their account of the command assumed by the prisoner—living an entire week in the depôt, animating his workmen, and hastening them to the conclusion of their business. When the hour of action arrived, you see him dressed in military array, putting himself at the head of the troops who had been shut up with him in this asylum, and advancing with his party, armed for the capture of the Castle, and the destruction of his fellow-citizens.

Gentlemen, what was the part which the prisoner took in that night of horror I will not attempt to insinuate to you. I hope and trust in God, for the sake of himself, his fame, his eternal welfare, that he was incapable of being a party to the barbarities which were committed —I do not mean to insinuate that he was—but that he headed this troop, and was present while some shots were fired, has been proved by uncontroverted testimony. At what time he quitted them—whether from prudence, despair, or disgust, he retired from their bands, is not proved by evidence upon the table; but from the moment of the discomfiture of his project, we find him again concealed. We trace him with the badges of rebellion glittering upon his person, attended by the two other cousuls, Quigley, the bricklayer, and Dowdall, the clerk—whether for concealment or to stimulate the wretched peasantry to other acts of insurrection, you will determine; we first trace him to Doyle's and then to Bagnall's: one identifies him, the other, from her fears, is incapable of doing so. But the same party, in the same uniforms, go to her house, until the apprehension of detection drove them from her. When he could no longer find shelter in the mountains, nor stir up the inhabitants of them, he again retires to his former obscure lodging, the name of Ellis is abandoned, the regimental coat is abandoned, and again he assumes the name of Hewitt. What is his conduct in this concealment? He betrays his apprehensions of being taken up by government. For what? Has any explanation been given to show what it could be, unless for rebellious practices? There he plans a mode of escape, refusing to put his name upon the door. You find him taken a reluctant prisoner, twice attempting to escape, and only brought within the reach of the law by force and violence. What do you find then? Has he been effecting to disguise his object, or that his plan was less dignified than his motive—that of treason? No such thing. He tells young Palmer that he was in Thomas-street that night—he confesses the treason—he boasts of his uniform, part of which was upon his person when he was taken. He acknowledges all this to the young man in the house—a witness, permit me to remark, not carried away by any excess of over-zeal to say anything to the injury of the prisoner, and therefore to his testimony, so far as it affects the prisoner, you may, with a safe conscience, afford a reasonable degree of credit.

Under what circumstances is he taken? In the room in which he was—upon a chair near the door is found an address to the government of the country; and in the very first paragraph of that address, the composer of it acknowledges himself to be at the head of a conspiracy for the overthrow of the government, which he addresses, telling them, in diplomatic language, what conduct the undersigned will be compelled to adopt, if they shall presume to execute the law. He is the leader, whose nod is a fiat, and he warns them of the consequences!

Gentlemen of the jury, you will decide whether the prisoner at the bar or Mrs. Palmer was the person who denounced those terms, and this vengeance against the government. What is found upon him? A letter written by a brother conspirator consulting him upon the present posture of the rebellion, their future prospects, and the probability of French assistance, and also the probable effects of that assistance, if it should arrive. What farther is found at the depôt?— and everything found there, whether coming out of the desk which he appears to have used and resorted to, or in any other part of the place which he commanded, is evidence against him. You find a treatise upon the art of war, framed for the purpose of drilling the party who were employed to effect this rebellion; but of war they have proved that they are incapable of knowing anything but its ferocities and its crimes; you find two proclamations, detailing systematically and precisely the views and objects of this conspiracy; and you find a manuscript copy of one of them, with interlineations, and other marks of its being an original draft. It will be for you to consider who was the framer of it—the man who presided in the depôt, and regulated all the proceedings there; or whether it was framed by Dowdall, the clerk, by Quigley, the bricklayer, or by Stafford, the baker, or any of the illiterate victims of the ambition of this young man who have been convicted in this court, or whether it did not flow from his pen, and was dictated by his heart.

Gentlemen, with regard to this mass of accumulated evidence, forming irrefragable proof of the guilt of the prisoner, I conceive no man capable of putting together two ideas can have a doubt. Why then do I address you, or why should I trespass any longer upon your time and your attention? Because, as I have already mentioned, I feel this to be a case of great public expectation—of the very last national importance; and because, when I am prosecuting a man, in whose veins the very life-blood of this conspiracy flowed, I expose to the public eye the utter meanness and insufficiency of its resources. What does it avow itself to be? A plan, not to correct the excesses or reform the abuses of the government of the country; not to remove any specks of imperfection which might have grown upon the surface of the constitution, or to restrain the overgrown power of the crown; or to restore any privilege of parliament; or to throw any new security around the liberty of the subject. No; but it plainly and boldly avows itself to be a plan to separate Great Britain from Ireland, uproot the monarchy, and establish "a free and independent republic in Ireland," in its place! To sever the connexion between Great Britain and Ireland! Gentlemen, I should feel it a waste of words and of public time, were I addressing you or any person within the limits of my voice, to talk of the frantic desperation of the plan of any man who speculates upon the dissolution of that empire, whose glory and whose happiness depend upon its indissoluble connexion. But were it practicable to sever that connexion, to untie the links which bind us to the British constitution, and to turn us adrift upon the turbulent ocean of revolution, who could answer for the existence of this country, as an independent power, for a year? God and nature have made the two countries essential to each other—let them cling to each other to the end of time, and their united affection and loyalty will be proof against the machinations of the world.

But how was this to be done? By establishing "a free and independent republic!" High sounding name! I would ask, whether the man who used it understood what he meant? I will not ask what may be its benefits, for I know its evils. There is no magic in the name. We have heard of "free and independent republics," and have since seen the most abject slavery that ever groaned under iron despotism growing out of them.

Formerly, gentlemen of the jury, we have seen revolutions effected by some great call of the people, ripe for change and unfitted by their habits for ancient forms; but here from the obscurity of concealment and by the voice of that pigmy authority, self-created and fearing to show itself, but in arms under cover of the night, we are called upon to surrender a constitution which has lasted for a period of one thousand years. Had any body of the people come forward, stating any grievance or announcing their demand for a change? No; but while the country is peaceful, enjoying the blessings of the constitution, growing rich and happy under it, a few desperate, obscure, contemptible adventurers in the trade of revolution form a scheme against the constituted authorities of the land, and by force and violence to overthrow an ancient and venerable constitution, and to plunge a whole people into the horrors of civil war!

If the wisest head that ever lived had framed the wisest system of laws which human ingenuity could devise—if he were satisfied that the system were exactly fitted to the disposition of the people for whom he intended it, and that a great proportion of that people were anxious for its adoption—yet give me leave to say, that under all these circumstances of fitness and disposition, a well-judging mind and a humane heart would pause awhile and stop upon the brink of his purpose, before he would hazard the peace of the country, by resorting to force for the establishment of his system; but here, in the frenzy of a distempered ambition, the author of this proclamation conceives the project of "a free and independent republic;" he at once flings it down, and he tells every man in the community, rich or poor, loyal or disloyal, he must adopt it at the peril of being considered an enemy to the country, and of suffering the pains and penalties attendant thereupon.

And how was this revolution to be effected? The proclamation conveys an insinuation that it was to be effected by their own force, entirely independent of foreign assistance. Why? Because it was well known that there remained in this country few so depraved, so lost to the welfare of their native land, who would not shudder at forming an alliance with France; and therefore the people of Ireland are told, "the effort is to be entirely your own, independent of foreign aid." But how does this tally with the time when the scheme was first hatched—the very period of the commencement of the war with France? How does this tally with the fact of consulting in the depôt, about co-operating with the French, which has been proved in evidence? But, gentlemen, out of the proclamation I convict him of duplicity. He tells the government of the country not to resist their mandate, or think that they can effectually suppress rebellion, by putting down the present attempt, but that "they will have to crush a greater exertion, rendered still greater by foreign assistance;" so that upon the face of the proclamation they avowed, in its naked deformity, the abominable plan of an alliance with the usurper of the French throne, to overturn the ancient constitution of the land, and to substitute a new republic in its place.

Gentlemen, so far I have taken up your time with observing upon the nature and extent of the conspiracy; its objects and the means by which they proposed to effectuate them. Let me now call your attention to the pretexts by which they seek to support them. They have not stated what particular grievance or oppression is complained of, but they have travelled back into the history of six centuries—they have raked up the ashes of former cruelties and rebellions, and upon the memory of them, they call upon the good people of this country to embark into similar troubles; but they forget to tell the people, that until the infection of new-fangled French principles was introduced, this country was for an hundred years free from the slightest symptom of rebellion, advancing in improvement of every kind beyond any example, while the former animosities of the country were melting down into a general system of philanthropy and cordial attachment to each other. They forget to tell the people whom they address that they have been enjoying the benefit of equal laws, by which the property, the person, and constitutional rights and privileges of every man are abundantly protected. They have not pointed out a single instance of oppression. Give me leave to ask any man who may have suffered himself to be deluded by those enemies of the law, what is there to prevent the exercise of honest industry and enjoying the produce of it? Does any man presume to invade him in the enjoyment of his property? If he does, is not the punishment of the law brought down upon him? What does he want? What is it that any rational friend to freedom could expect, that the people of this country are not fully and amply in the possession of? And therefore when those idle stories are told of six hundred years oppression and of rebellions prevailing when this country was in a state of ignorance and barbarism, and which have long since passed away, they are utterly destitute of a fact to rest upon; they are a fraud upon feeling, and are the pretext of the factious and ambitious, working upon credulity and ignorance.

Let me allude to another topic: they call for revenge on account of the removal of the parliament. Those men who, in 1798, endeavoured to destroy the parliament, now call upon the loyal men, who opposed its transfer, to join them in rebellion; an appeal vain and fruitless. Look around and see with what zeal and loyalty they rallied round the throne and constitution of the country. Whatever might have been the difference of opinion heretofore among Irishmen upon some points, when armed rebels appeared against the laws and public peace, every minor difference was annihilated in the paramount claim of duty to our king and country.

So much, gentlemen, for the nature of this conspiracy and the pretexts upon which it rests. Suffer me, for a moment, to call your attention to one or two of the edicts published by the conspirators. They have denounced, that if a single Irish soldier, or in more faithful description, Irish rebel, shall lose his life after the battle is over, quarter is neither to be given nor taken. Observe the equality of the reasoning of these promulgers of liberty and equality. The distinction is this: English troops are permitted to arm in defence of the government and the constitution of the country, and to maintain their allegiance; but if an Irish soldier, yeoman, or other loyal person, who shall not within the space of fourteen days from the date and issuing forth of their sovereign proclamation, appear in arms with them; if he presumes to obey the dictates of his conscience, his duty, and his interest—if he has the hardihood to be loyal to his sovereign and his country, he is proclaimed a traitor, his life is forfeited, and his property is confiscated. A sacred palladium is thrown over the rebel cause, while, in the same breath, undistinguishing vengeance is denounced against those who stand up in defence of the existing and ancient laws of the country. For God's sake, to whom are we called upon to deliver up, with only fourteen days to consider of it, all the advantages we enjoy? Who are they who claim the obedience? The prisoner is the principal: I do not wish to say anything harsh of him; a young man of considerable talents, if used with precaution, and of respectable rank in society, if content to conform himself to its laws. But when he assumes the manner and the tone of a legislator, and calls upon all ranks of people, the instant the provisional government proclaim in the abstract a new government, without specifying what the new laws are to be, or how the people are to be conducted and managed—but that the moment it is announced, the whole constituted authority is to yield to him; it becomes an extravagance bordering upon frenzy: this is going beyond the example of all former times. If a rightful sovereign were restored, he would forbear to inflict punishment upon those who submitted to the king *de facto*, but here there is no such forbearance. We who have lived under a king, not only *de facto* but *de jure* in possession of the throne, are called upon to submit ourselves to the prisoner—to Dowdall, the vagrant politician—to the bricklayer, to the baker, the old-clothes-man, the hodman, and the ostler. These are the persons to whom this proclamation, in its majesty and dignity, calls upon a great people to yield obedience, and a powerful government to give " a prompt, manly, and sagacious acquiescence to their just and unalterable determination!" "We call upon the British government not to be so mad as to oppose us." Why, gentlemen, this goes beyond all serious discussion; and I mention it merely to show the contemptible nature of this conspiracy, which hoped to have set the entire country in a flame. When it was joined by nineteen counties from north to south, catching the electrical spark of revolution, they engaged in the conspiracy—the general, with his lieutenant-general, putting himself at the head of the forces, collected not merely from the city, but from the neighbouring counties; and when all their strength is collected, voluntary and forced, they are stopped in their progress, in the first glow of their valour, by the honest voice of a single peace officer, at which the provincial forces were disconcerted and alarmed, but ran like hares, when one hundred soldiers appeared against them.

Gentlemen, why do I state these facts? Is it to show that the government need not be vigilant, or that our gallant countrymen should relax in their exertions? By no means; but to induce the miserable victims who have been misled by those phantoms of revolutionary delusion, to show them, that they ought to lose no time in abandoning a cause which cannot protect itself, and exposes them to destruction, and to adhere to the peaceful and secure habits of honest industry. If they knew it, they have no reason to repine at their lot. Providence is not so unkind to them in casting them in that humble walk in which they are placed. Let them obey the law and cultivate religion, and worship their God in their own way. They may prosecute their labour in peace and tranquillity; they need not envy the higher ranks of life, but may look with pity upon that vicious despot who watches with the sleepless eye of disquieting ambition, and sits a wretched usurper trembling upon the throne of the Bourbons. But I do not wish to awaken any remorse, except such as may be salutary to himself and the country, in the mind of the prisoner. But when he reflects, that he has stooped from the honourable situation in which his birth, talents, and his education placed him, to debauch the minds of the lower orders of ignorant men with the phantoms of liberty and equality, he must feel that it was an unworthy use of his talents; he should feel remorse for the consequences which ensued, grievous to humanity and virtue, and should endeavour to make all the atonement he can, by employing the little time which remains for him in endeavouring to undeceive them.

Liberty and equality are dangerous names to make use of; if properly understood, they mean enjoyment of personal freedom under the equal protection of the laws; and a genuine love of liberty inculcates a friendship for our friends, our king, and country—a reverence for their lives, an anxiety for their safety; a feeling which advances from private to public life, until it expands and swells into the more dignified name of philanthropy and philosophy. But in the cant of modern philosophy, these affections which form the ennobling distinctions of man's nature are all thrown aside; all the vices of his character are made the instrument of moral good—an abstract quantity of vice may produce a certain quantity of moral good. To a man whose principles are thus poisoned and his judgment perverted the most flagitious crimes lose their names; robbery and murder become moral good. He is taught not to startle at putting to death a fellow creature, if it be represented as a mode of contributing to the good of all. In pursuit of those phantoms and chimeras of the brain, they abolish feelings and instincts, which God and nature have planted in our hearts for the good of human kind. Thus by the printed plan for the establishment of liberty and a free republic, murder is prohibited and proscribed; and yet you heard how this caution against excesses was followed up by the recital of every grievance that ever existed, and which could excite every bad feeling of the heart, the most vengeful cruelty and insatiate thirst of blood.

Gentlemen, I am anxious to suppose that the mind of the prisoner recoiled at the scenes of murder which he witnessed, and I mention one circumstance with satisfaction: it appears he saved the life of Farrell; and may the recollection of that one good action cheer him in his last moments! But though he may not have planned individual murders, that is no excuse to justify his embarking in treason, which must be followed by every species of crimes. It is supported by the rabble of the country, while the rank, the wealth, and the power of the country are opposed it. Let loose the rabble of the country from the salutary restraints of the law, and who can take upon him to limit their barbarities? Who can say, he will disturb the peace of the world and rule it when wildest? Let loose the winds of heaven, and what power less than omnipotent can control them? So it is with the rabble; let them loose, and who can restrain them? What claim, then, can the prisoner have upon the compassion of a jury, because in the general destruction which his schemes necessarily produce he did not meditate individual murder? In the short space of a quarter of an hour, what a scene of blood and horror was exhibited! I trust that the blood which has been shed in the streets of Dublin upon that night, and since upon the scaffold, and which may hereafter be shed, will not be visited upon the head of the prisoner. It is not for me to say what are the limits of the mercy of God, or what a sincere repentance of those crimes may effect; but I do say, that if this unfortunate young gentleman retains any of the seeds of humanity in his heart, or possesses any of those qualities which a virtuous education in a liberal seminary must have planted in his bosom, he will make an atonement to his God and his country, by employing whatever time remains to him in warning his deluded countrymen from persevering in their schemes. Much blood has been shed, and he perhaps would have been immolated by his followers if he had succeeded. They are a bloodthirsty crew, incapable of listening to the voice of reason, and equally incapable of obtaining rational freedom, if it were wanting in this country, as they are of enjoying it.

They imbrue their hands in the most sacred blood of the country, and yet they call upon God to prosper their cause, as it is just!— But as it is atrocious, wicked, and abominable, I most devoutly invoke that God to confound and overwhelm it.

Norbury's ferocious charge, the verdict, Emmet's glorious speech, the last sentence of the law quickly followed, and next day dogs were lapping the young rebel's blood under the scaffold in Thomas-street.

THE THRESHERS.
December 5, 1806.

IN the year 1806, agrarian disturbances had risen to an extraordinary pitch in north Connaught and in parts of Ulster—throughout that district, famous for bogs, rack-rents, poteen, and Whiteboys, stretching from Cavan across the country to Sligo—a district which, in disturbed times, has always exhibited a certain uniform character and correspondence of action, like the subterranean sympathies of a volcanic district. The five counties of Cavan, Leitrim, Longford, Sligo, and Mayo were included in a special commission, issued in the winter to Chief Justice Downes and Baron George, upon which they at once proceeded to strike terror into the Threshers. The Threshers formed one of the most formidable, well-organized, and levelling secret societies that ever existed in Ireland, and bore the peculiar character that its principal object of attack was neither rent, cess, nor excise—but the priest's dues and the minister's tithes. In some places they undertook to regulate wages, and in all, were armed, badged, and drilled.

The special commission first sat at Sligo—Plunket and Bushe appearing for the crown, as attorney and solicitor-general—and the first indictment tried was that "John M'Donough and William Kearney, with many others, on the 2nd of September last, after sun-set and before sun-rise, did maliciously and feloniously break and enter the dwelling-house of Peter O'Neill, at Cartron Watts, in the county of Sligo, that they maliciously assaulted and injured the habitation of O'Neill, and forcibly took away his money; and that prisoners provided an instrument, to wit, weaver's cards, for inflicting bodily pain and punishment upon O'Neill, in order to compel him to enter into an unlawful confederacy, called Threshers; that they inflicted punishment with that intent, and by menaces and intimidation exacted money and goods from him." Plunket stated the case :—

My Lords and Gentlemen of the Jury, in this case, as counsel for the crown, it is my duty to lay before you the grounds of the present prosecution. The indictments upon which the prisoners are arraigned have been read, and you are thereby apprised of the nature of the charges preferred against them. The charges go to a variety of acts, all, by the law of the land, capital, and if the prisoners are guilty of all or any of them, the consequence is death : the charges in their nature are such as draw down the highest punishment of the law. The prisoners are charged with breaking and entering the dwelling-house of a fellow-subject in the night time; with robbing that fellow-subject of his money, and with inflicting torture upon his person, for the purpose of compelling him to become a member of their own lawless and dangerous associations. These are crimes, gentlemen, which no civilized society can tolerate. They bid defiance to all law, and assert a claim of unconditional submission to those who avow themselves the bearers of that defiance. These are conditions under which no government can exist. But if the crimes with which the unfortunate men are charged, however atrocious, did not involve consequences of a peculiar nature, they would have been left to the ordinary visitation of the law, and would be tried at the regular assizes of the county. It is because they form part of a class of atrocities which disturb the tranquillity, and in their progress endanger the safety of the country, that you have been assembled at this season of the year for the immediate and solemn dispensation of justice. Gentlemen, it is with great satisfaction I see, upon a subject of this emergency, so full and respectable an attendance, calculated to impress every mind with a sense of obedience to the law. Every gentleman of character—of rank—of consideration and of property, appears at his post on this important occasion, to give his personal sanction to the law. Judges of the land are sent, armed with his majesty's commission, and armed with a character resulting from their learning and virtues, which reflect lustre and dignity on that commission. Gentlemen, everything has been done on the part of the government to let the wretched people of this country see that there are laws for the punishment of guilt, and that no nerve will be left unstrained to give effect and vigour to them. I therefore rejoice to see such an array of rank and property upon the grand jury which has found the bills, and such a respectable description of gentlemen composing the petty jury which I now address because it must remove from the minds of the wretched people, engaged in these outrages, the delusions which have been industriously spread to excite the hope of impunity. In aid of the magistracy, from whom information has been procured, they see the whole body of the county—every man who has talent, character, and property, rallying round the constitution. It is not, therefore, merely for the purpose of inquiring into the guilt of the persons now on trial, but to bring home punishment to the great body of the guilty —protection to the great body of the innocent—to undeceive the abused, and give confidence to the disheartened, and to restore peace and tranquillity to the country, that this special commission has been issued; and you, gentlemen, to perform your sacred part, have been sworn upon the jury.

Gentlemen, it is far from my purpose or my wish, that by having your minds strongly moved with a sense of the mischiefs prevailing in the country, any of the prisoners should be visited with peculiar hardships. On the contrary, upon an occasion of this kind, it is my duty to caution you against the suggestions of rumour or prejudice: it is our duty to vindicate, not to strain, the law. If the prisoners are guilty, the guilt should be brought home by clear legal evidence. God forbid, gentlemen, that your abhorrence of the crime should work injustice to the criminal or the accused. But, gentlemen, you will feel that it is not irrelevant to the subject to call your attention to what is, and what has been, the state of the country; because it grows out of the association imputed to the prisoners, and it is therefore that the consequence of guilt and punishment attaches upon them. And therefore, gentlemen, in calling your attention to the state of the country, and the nature of the outrages, I feel that I do not transgress my duty in the case now before you.

Gentlemen, it is unfortunately too notorious to need any minute statement, that for some time past the peace of this county has been infested by a set of persons assuming the name of *Threshers*. Their outrageous associations have been in direct defiance of the law. The business has originated with men possessing no situation—whom nobody knows—a set of men who dare not avow themselves—a description of persons not possessed of any rank—of any property —of any talent—of any education—men who are not placed in any situation, either by the conventions of society or their own fitness, entitling them to dictate to their fellow-subjects, or to take upon themselves the task of reformation and of legislation. These persons have discovered that the existing laws are not to their mind— they have found out that there are errors in the state and in the church, and they have conceived that they are the proper persons to undertake the task of reforming them. But not satisfied with infringing the law in their own persons individually, they become associated for the purpose of saying, that no other person in the community shall dare to obey the law. So that the first act of those who profess to interfere upon principles of liberty is to exercise compulsion over the consciences of others, and to say, that no man shall presume to form an opinion for himself, nor act upon it, unless it meet the approbation of those self-created reformers. The pretext upon which these illegal confederacies is formed is, a repugnance to the payments in support of the legal establishment of the church of the country, and also of the fees which have been usually paid, without any law to enforce them, to the clergymen of the Catholic persuasion. The mode taken to accomplish this object has been by assembling themselves at night in disguise, sometimes with arms, going to the houses of such persons as refuse to associate themselves in their body, and if necessary for their purpose, breaking open the houses of those persons, and robbing them of their property, inflicting torture upon those who become objects of their enmity, and if necessary for the final completion of their designs, if any person be honest or bold enough to give information against them, the business, which began in lawless combination, is consummated by murder.

Gentlemen of the jury, this is the natural progress of associations of this kind. When men enrol themselves for the purpose of resisting the law, whatever the pretext may be upon which they originally associate, the foulest crimes are generated in its progress; that which begins in anarchy ends in murder; and even murder itself, in the progress of outrage, may be only a preparation for the blacker horrors which are to ensue.

Gentlemen, there remains one circumstance of peculiar atrocity, with which this matter is connected. In the various forms and associations under which their designs have been conducted, it has been the policy of those people to administer oaths to the persons called upon by them, binding them to association and to secrecy. This offence is by law punished with death. The person who commits it must pay the forfeit of his life. The person taking such an oath is banished for ever from his country: the mere circumstance of going to a magistrate and telling him of the oath being taken, will not absolve the party; the oath must be taken against his will; for if it be taken voluntarily, he is, notwithstanding such information, liable to be transported for life. Gentlemen, this is no new-devised punishment, it is the established law of the land; it has been so for many years; it has been provided, and wisely, by the legislature to meet the outrages which from time to time have infested this country: there is no disproportion between this punishment and the crime; it strikes at the roots of morality and religion, and tends directly to destroy those principles, which are essential to civilized society. Gentlemen, an oath is the sanction, by which under the law of the country we call upon the Creator to attest the truth and purity of our words; and this solemn sanction which our civil institution has borrowed from our religious code, is prostituted to bind together an association of traitors, robbers, and murderers. The name of the living God is appealed to for the purpose of witnessing and ratifying the infernal compact, by which these wretches league themselves against law and religion. Gentlemen, it produces a revulsion of every moral feeling to hear of such conduct; not that it is a violation of the laws and usages of society, but, because it is an outrageous blasphemy against our Creator to call upon him to attest and sanctify the crimes of his creatures.

Gentlemen, it is not necessary now to dwell upon the illegality of those associations, but while they profess to attack the property of the church, I cannot pass them by without a few observations. The tithes of the clergy of this country are their property; they are secured to them by the same laws which secure to every man amongst you his estate or his property, whatever the description of it may be; the same laws and the same right by which any gentleman who hears me holds his estate, transmitted to him from his ancestors; the laws which secure the fruits of each man's individual industry are the title by which the property of the clergy is secured to them; and I do trust, gentlemen, that there is no man so selfish as to look to any system by which the property of one part of the community shall be protected, and that of another spoliated. If there be any man so selfish as to wish it, let no man think it can be done. Let a multitude be assembled under the empire of *Threshers* and *Shakers*, armed and arrayed in order to make head against the rank and property of the country, and what shall stop their career? I wish my voice to extend to every man within these walls—to every man of sense and reflection. I would tell him, that there is no protection for rank, for property, for the state, but by resisting those disturbers, and making them feel the irresistible weight of the law. They say, they rise to redress grievances! But, gentlemen, there is a mode known to the constitution of redressing grievances; there is no law to prevent men from stating them; and there is a legal mode of claiming relief. This, I will say, that the constitution of the church is intimately connected with the constitution of the state; it is a part of the same fabric, which has been handed down to us from our ancestors, and if there be anything imperfect in it, no reflecting man will approach it, for the purpose of alteration, without extreme caution; he will be careful in the attempt to remedy its imperfections not to affect the substance, or even the proportion, or beauty of the ornaments. But this task of reformation is undertaken. By whom? By the dregs of the community—anonymous ruffians, who fear the face of day, whose title is founded in anarchy, and whose pretensions are enforced by robbery and murder!

I cannot pass by another part of these associations; I mean their attack upon the priests. I meddle not with religious rites; but I mean the attack which is made upon the support derived from the voluntary bounty, which the members of the Roman Catholic persuasion have been in the habit of giving to the ministers of their religion, for celebrating the rites of that religion. It is not, that they say, we will not pay, for there is no law to compel them to pay. But they proclaim this, that no man, who chooses to do so, shall dare to pay his priests their fees! For what purpose are these fees given? They are given to obtain the rites of their religion: they flow from a sense of religion; they flow from voluntary bounty; they are enforced by no compulsion, the unfortunate men who receive them are armed with no law for their support; and yet these associations are formed—To do what? To rob the priest of his benedictions and his prayers! Do these men, besmeared with blood and covered with crimes, imagine that the ceremonies of religion which are plundered from their clergy can give them a passport to a better world? I cannot help feeling and deploring that this view of the subject suggests an apprehension, that the devisers of this plan could have had nothing less in their contemplation, than eradicating from the minds of those upon whom they could operate all sense of religion. Nothing but their hellish machinations could have devised such a scheme. If they expect that the people will be ripe to perpetrate crimes worse than these; if they wish them to be the ready instruments of every design which is diabolical, there is no plan so effectual, as the extinction of every sentiment of religion in the minds of the common people. What may be the form of the religion of the several classes of the people, I care not to inquire. If the principles of Christianity prevail; if the sense of obedience to a supreme ruler of the world; if the conviction of the existence of a future state, in which rewards and punishments are distributed, be kept alive in the minds of the people, they will never become the instruments for the commission of abominable crimes. But if these sentiments be extinguished; if they shall be taught to cast off all regard for a future world, the ties which bind them to earth as well as to heaven are rent asunder.

Gentlemen, we have had a miserable example in our own time. You may recollect, that not many years back, in a neighbouring country, the most dreadful atrocities were committed; you recollect the overthrow of an ancient monarchy. That overthrow, deplorable as it was, was not the most dismal scene of the tragedy. The horrors of that unfortunate revolution, in which the hands of the father were imbrued in the blood of the son, in which all moral and social relations were raised in mutual warfare, could not be perpetrated until the sentiments of religion were previously extinguished in the minds of the people. Human nature was not outraged by gross and unexampled crimes until a solemn decree was framed, declaring that there was no God in heaven! What the consequences were, every man knows. But this I state, that as soon as a settled form of government was established, it was found that atheism and infidelity, which were the ready instruments to throw down an ancient throne, were an insecure foundation for a new one; and one of the first acts of the founder of the new dynasty was to restore the consolations of religion to his thirsty and supplicating subjects.

Gentlemen, it is no wonder, that those who searched after democratic equality should be the foes of religion. Religion is the genuine equality of mankind. It is the poor man's friend. During the troubles of this life it renders him content with the lot of inferiority, which is the condition of his nature, and in the last awful hour of existence it puts him upon a level with the highest and most exalted.

Gentlemen, it is a melancholy and disheartening thing, that our wretched peasantry can be deluded by such arts, and that they should be thus imposed upon after such miserable examples. For half a century attempts have been made upon the infatuated people of this country. What has been the consequence? Disgrace to the perpetrators; failure of their plans; ruin and death to themselves. Yet what is the condition of the poor unhappy people of this country? As soon as any disaffected mountebank appears, proclaiming his laws, and imaginary benefits, they become the willing instruments of his schemes, and their own destruction. Is it possible they can for a moment imagine that a great empire like this, armed with the law, protected by an army, with a regular administration of justice—are they so infatuated as to imagine, all these will yield to a few miscreants like those under whom they have enlisted themselves? It is therefore principally to undeceive these miserable wretches; to rescue them from the grasp of fiends, who are working their destruction, that the law is sent down here, at this unusual season, to speak its emphatic language. What the law is, I will tell you. What the consequence of infringing it is, you, gentlemen, will tell; and I cannot help feeling, that in the consequence of this commission, we may look to an end of the confusion and anarchy which has prevailed, and that the vicious may again be brought within the ordinary channels of subordination.

Gentlemen, in speaking as I do, with indignation for those crimes, I feel compassion from the very bottom of my heart for the victims of them. Seeing the mischiefs which have been spreading in the country by the artifices of miscreants, it does not surprise me at all, that many persons should be of opinion, that measures more summary should have been adopted, for the purpose of at once extinguishing these mischiefs. I am satisfied that the opinion of such men is dictated by a feeling of the truest regard for the interests of their country; of genuine compassion and mercy towards the unfortunate delinquents themselves. But yet, my lords and gentlemen of the jury, I trust that the government of the country will ultimately acquire credit from those who entertained the opinion I have mentioned, for the course which has been adopted in the present instance. The feeling of the government has been, that the insult which has been given to the laws of the country is best vindicated by those laws themselves. The persons whom we are now called upon to cope with, do not compose multitudes too strong for the arm of the law. It is not an assembly daring to stand before exertions of the magistracy, but it is a lawless association of men, who find their safety in their obscurity. And I cannot help feeling a confidence, that when the victims of delusion shall have been undeceived; when they find that the law is adequate to their punishment; that the laity make a common cause with the clergy; when they see atonement made to the laws by the speedy and energetic administration of justice, now in progress amongst you—I say, I feel a confidence, that after they have seen the array of this country drawn up for the investigation of their crimes; after they have seen the assemblage, this day, of every man of rank, character, and property, feeling their interests united with those, who have been the subject of lawless attack; that the most salutary consequences will be experienced, and that these people will at length be convinced, that when they dare to raise their hands against the laws of their country, those laws will be found to have weight enough to fall down upon and crush them. What, gentlemen, would it not be a miserable state of our country, to suppose that, armed as we are by the law—supported as we are by the aid of every gentleman in the country, and with an armed force, if such be necessary; that associations of men, whose names are not known—of no rank, property, or station—could not be put down, without doing away, for a time at least, the ordinary constitution of the land? If the time should unfortunately come, when, what is now a tumultuous rising, should assume an aspect of a different nature; if ever, which God forbid! those scenes shall be renewed, which we formerly witnessed; if treason shall rear its head in the country, and supersede the law, these wretches will have to sink under the tide of ruin, which will be let in upon them. But

I trust that no visitation of that kind will occur; but that, with the ready assistance of the government, and the aid of every loyal man, we shall be able to bring punishment upon the guilty, and that the law will be strong enough to wrestle with and put down these disturbers of the public peace.

Gentlemen, I shall say only a few words more. The laws in being, of which I shall make a short statement, will appear to every one, particularly calculated to meet the outrages which at present exist. They are laws which have not been recently introduced. For half a century, the country has been visited with partial insurrections: during a portion of the reign of the late king, and during the entire of the present, laws have been enacted calculated to meet these crimes. These laws are still in full force and operation. If the insurgents assemble with arms; if they assume any particular denomination, or wear any badge, to the terror of his majesty's subjects, by that mere act of assembling, though no further act be done, they are punishable by law. The magistrates are authorised to disperse and apprehend them. If they resist, and any be killed, the magistrate is indemnified; and if he has just cause to suspect that any person can give information respecting such outrages, he may summon the person, examine him, bind him in a recognizance to appear, and commit him, in case he refuses. I wish this was generally known, that if any man meet such an assembly, he is called upon to disperse it, and to apprehend the persons assembled; and if death unfortunately ensue, the magistrate is indemnified.

The magistrate is also armed with extraordinary powers to preserve the public peace. He is entitled to call for the assistance of every man in the county. The power which the law has, in ordinary cases, intrusted to the sheriff, that of raising the posse comitatus, is, in this instance, given to every magistrate; and if any man refuses to give this assistance, he is guilty of a misdemeanor. Persons not entitled by law to carry arms, are liable to have their houses searched, and the law protects the person making the search. If any persons, tumultuously assembled, shall assault, or injure the habitation or property of another, they are punishable with death; every person who administers an oath, whatever the nature or purport of it may be, binding the person taking it, to be of a particular party or association, is punishable with death; any person who voluntarily takes such oath, is liable to be banished for ever; and he is not to suppose that after voluntarily taking such an oath, the mere circumstance of going to a magistrate and telling him, will protect him; two circumstances must concur to save him from punishment: first, that he was compelled to take the oath; and secondly, that he gave immediate information of his being so compelled; so that here are abundant provisions for the punishment of these offences. But, gentlemen, it has been industriously circulated that these laws are expired: I tell you, and those who hear me, what was stated yesterday from the high authority of the bench, that these laws are in full force and existence; and every man joining in unlawful confederacies is liable to pay the penalty inflicted by those laws.

Gentlemen, I have also to inform you, that under the statute of the 15th and 16th of his present majesty's reign, commonly called "The Whiteboy Act," any person who harbours, conceals, or gives assistance to any person concerned in such outrages, is as much guilty as the person so concealed; and any person who supplies horses, arms, or ammunition, for the purpose of these confederacies, is liable to forfeit his life. Gentlemen, armed with these laws, which have been found competent to put down insurrections, as alarming as the present, with the honourable zeal and activity of the magistrates, which you may confidently look to, and with the sincere desire of government to protect the loyal, and reclaim the guilty, are we to despair of the laws being able to cope with the mischiefs, and not to look for the restoration of tranquillity and peace? I cannot so persuade myself, and I am not uneasy as to the result. Gentlemen, with regard to the particular case now before you, it will appear that the prisoners, on the night of the 2nd of September last, with many others, attacked the house of Peter O'Neill, at Cartron Watts in this county. He had been audacious enough to say, he would pay the dues which he had been accustomed to pay; he was not prepared at the instance of these legislators to renounce his obedience to the laws; he said he would pay as he had formerly done; this was high treason by their law: they repaired to his house; they broke it open; they dragged him naked from his bed; they asked him for money; that is part of their system for redress of grievances; he had only one tenpenny piece; he had no more; but he was desired to send more to the house of a person whom they named, but who is not now upon trial; they took him away naked, and one of the party had an instrument for carding wool, with which they inflicted punishment upon him, by severely excoriating his back; the prisoners will be identified by O'Neill, his wife, and son, who plainly saw them; so that there are three witnesses to the transaction. If these facts shall be proved, there can be no doubt of the melancholy necessity which will be imposed upon you. O'Neill gave information to Mr. Soden, the magistrate, and exhibited his back, which was excoriated with the torture which had been inflicted upon him; so that with regard to this being a case within the statute no question can arise; but if the evidence be not clear and satisfactory, no sense of danger or alarm should induce you to find a verdict against the prisoners. It will, in that case, be your duty to acquit them; but if you have no doubt of their guilt, I will not humble you or myself by supposing, that any of you would shrink from a firm and manly discharge of his duty.

The prisoners were acquitted. Several of the other leading prosecutions of the commission failed; but in Mayo, where that renowned toparch, the Right Hon. Denis Browne, had pioneered the operations of the commission, there were about a dozen of the Threshers hanged.

CATHOLIC RELIEF.
April 9, 1807.

PLUNKET, who had accepted office from Pitt, remained attorney-general to the ministry of "all the talents," and was returned to parliament by their influence for Midhurst, a little borough in Sussex, for which Fox and Sheil have also sat.

The Catholic question had lain dormant since the Union. The King had become frantically hostile to their claims. Pitt, on retiring from office in 1801, sent word to the Irish Catholics, through Dr. Troy, the archbishop of Dublin, that "the leading part of his majesty's ministers, finding insurmountable obstacles to the bringing forward measures of concession to the Catholic body, had felt it impossible to continue in office under the inability to propose it with the circumstances necessary to carrying the measure with all its advantages;" and he held out hopes that he would never return to office unless on the condition of being allowed to redress their claims. Nothing was attempted in the ministry of Addington, and Pitt returned to office in 1804, and died at the height of his contest with Napoleon, without a thought of Ireland, which had been half deluded and half crushed into a state of torpor. At last, when Lord Grenville formed an administration containing so many statesmen pledged to support their claims, the Catholic committee began to agitate. Yet their auspices were gloomy enough. Pitt was dead, and Pitt might well be believed in these days to be the only British minister strong enough to bend the bigotry of King and parliament. The councils of the Catholics were rather distracted. Many of the bishops and most of the gentry were for patience, and prudence, and all possible trust in the King's kindness and the ministry's charity. John Keogh had grown suddenly old and wayward; now violent out of time, now over cautious. A new era was dawning, of which the brave old tribune could not read the signs. Catholic emancipation was destined never to come until the people of Ireland had proved themselves stronger than King and Lords and Commons. Twenty years of dreary agitation lay before the persecuted race; and from this time forth a young Kerry barrister, named Daniel O'Connell, became the Moses, the man of men among them.

Lord Grenville was quite sincere in his friendliness to the Catholic claims, but neither he nor one of his party dare attempt what Pitt would have done, had he done anything—that is, at once admit the Catholics to political power, and endow their clergy, on the basis of a concordat admitting to the crown a right of veto in the election of bishops. A Whig ministry, however well disposed, could only attempt the same work by insignificant and dilatory instalments. Even Sheridan, with his hot Celtic heart—and in opposition too—declared, at the close of the session of 1807, that his notion of Catholic emancipation was to conciliate the peasantry, by relieving them of tithes: to admit the Catholic gentry to be judges and generals and members of parliament, was like "decorating the topmasts of a ship when there were ten feet of water in the hold, or putting a laced hat on a man who had not a shoe to his foot." Lord Grenville attempted very little, but his fate was a warning to the Whigs and a terror to the Catholics for many a long year. He lost office for merely attempting to assimilate the state of the law in England to the Irish Relief Act of 1793.

In Ireland the law allowed Catholics to hold all military commissions under the rank of colonel, but the law enabled the king to grant such commissions only in Ireland. The Whigs attempted to extend this provision to the entire empire, and to all ranks in the army. To this effect, Lord Howick, afterwards the great Earl Grey, prepared a bill. At first the king made no opposition to its introduction. At a second audience, he expressed, to Lord Howick, a general dislike and disapprobation of the measure; but as he did not continue the subject with Lord Grenville, who entered the closet immediately after Lord Howick, they presumed they might proceed with the second reading of the bill. A few days afterwards, however, he became so furiously obstinate, that the ministry were obliged first to postpone, and finally to withdraw it altogether. Even this however was not enough for the wrong-headed old bigot—his majesty's servants in the cabinet must pledge themselves never under any circumstances to recommend a redress of the Catholic claims. This was too much. "All the talents" retired. The Duke of Portland came in with a thundering no-Popery cry, and the Catholics learned a little more of Castlereagh's sincerity by seeing him in office. Parliament was dissolved in the mid-summer. "The Church in danger" sounded at every British hustings, and one of the most bigoted Protestant parliaments that had sat in England since the Revolution was returned.

Before the dissolution, long explanations were given in both houses on the causes of the change of administration; and on the adjourned debate, Plunket spoke the only speech he delivered in parliament during the short period for which he represented Midhurst.

Mr. PLUNKET declared that he was not one of these men, whom an hon. baronet (Sir T. Turton) had supposed were anxious to load the persons of his majesty's new ministers with obloquy and reproach. He was sure that his majesty was the kind father of his people, and had acted only on the representations of others that the church was in danger. Those, however, who had been the foremost to set up this cry, and to sound this alarm, had thrown upon him a great weight of responsibility. It was incumbent upon them to prove the existence of that danger. He had yet to learn, and the house had yet to learn, how and from what quarter danger was to be apprehended to the Established Church. No man felt more strongly than he did, the advantages to both countries from the connexion with Ireland; no man wished more, that that connexion should be finally cemented, and no man was more attached to the Protestant establishment of Ireland, which he conceived to be no less important than the connexion itself. If, then, he could see any ground for supposing the Protestant establishment was in danger, he would be as ready as any man to raise his voice in its support, and to ring the alarm to the country. He was at a loss, however, now to discover from what quarter this danger was threatened; and it did appear to him, that men who, upon such slight grounds, or rather upon no grounds at all could come forward and wantonly disturb the peace of that country, did not show themselves to be men possessed of such discretion as should be expected from those to whom the administration of the affairs of the empire were to be committed at a crisis like the present. After the measure had been abandoned, still the cry was artfully kept up that the church was in danger. He should therefore beg leave to call the attention of the house to the act of 1793, and he would first observe that that Irish act did not apply merely to Irish Catholics, but to all Catholics serving in the army of Ireland. Since the Union, however, there no longer existed any separate army of Ireland, nor any separate establishments. But before the Union, English Catholics, if serving in the army of Ireland, were entitled to the benefit of the act of 1793. At present, by the law of the land, the king is empowered to grant commissions in Ireland to Catholics, and it would be certainly a strange thing to tell those Catholics, that although they were very fit to be trusted in Ireland, yet they were not fit to be trusted in any other part of the world. If the artful endeavours to keep up the cry of the church being in danger had been confined to placards stuck up against the walls, or to Protestant songs and religious choruses, perhaps those endeavours would not merit any severe reprehension; but he had been informed of other attempts, which he thought were deserving of more serious attention. The peace of the University of Dublin had lately been disturbed with attempts from a very high quarter to procure an address to his majesty, stating that the church and the Protestant religion was in danger. Two letters had been written to the university by its chancellor (the Duke of Cumberland) to procure such an address. The first produced but very little effect; but in the second, the royal duke to whom he alluded stated (as he was informed) that such a step would be the only means of recommending that university to the favour of his majesty. He considered that nothing could be more unconstitutional than this mode of using his majesty's name o procure an address or petitions parliament. He thought, however, that it would be necessary to consider the time at which such exertions were made to get a petition from the University of Dublin. It was either after the bill had been abandoned that it was endeavoured to raise the ferment and outcry, or it was in contemplation of its serving the new ministers. If the attempt was made before his majesty had exhibited the slightest disapprobation, it was evident how far the machinations of secret advisers operated; if it was after the bill was abandoned, it was equally evident that it was then the purpose of effecting a change of administration, which was stated to have been produced by other causes. He could not state at present the date of this last letter; but he must say generally, that whether it was before the bill was abandoned or immediately after, it equally showed what sort of engines had been set to work to spread the alarm that the church and the Protestant religion were in danger. When he heard the name of religion mentioned, he felt that everything that was most dear to his heart was touched; but when the name of religion was so dear to him, it was from its intrinsic value, from its dictating and concentrating all the amiable charities of life, from its breathing the spirit of toleration and mutual affection, and not as being the rallying word of a persecuting party. He knew there were many in that house to whom true religion was dear, and he therefore called upon those who possessed it in their hearts, and who did not use it as a watch-word for persecution, to show it in their votes in favour of a system of toleration and benevolence to all classes of his majesty's loyal subjects. He should, then, call the attention of the house to the pledge which was required from the late ministers. This pledge he considered in the highest degree dangerous and unconstitutional, and tending directly to substitute secret whispers in the place of the responsible ministers and advisers to the crown. He conceived it of the most dangerous consequences to have it supposed that the ministers of this country could have one duty to their master and sovereign, which was directly opposite to their duty to their country. He conceived that this particular pledge would compromise the safety of Ireland. The state of the Catholics of Ireland was this : during the course of his majesty's reign, many concessions had been made to them, and many of the advantages to which they had been entitled had been granted them. In consequence of this, many of them had arrived to wealth, and honour, and distinction. It would be asked by many—Ought not this content them? and ought they press for anything more? It was not, however, in human nature to be so contented. He should appeal to the individual feelings of the members of that house, who all of them enjoyed wealth, honour, and distinctions in society—if they were to be told, you ought to be well satisfied with those advantages, and should be content not to be admitted to the full participation of the constitution, would they be so contented? They would not: it was not in human nature that they should.

The Catholic gentry of Ireland were now in that situation of exclusion, and anxiously wished to be received into the bosom of the constitution. The Catholic priesthood were at present unpaid and degraded, and they wished also to be put into a more respectable situation. The Catholic population of Ireland, which was by far the greatest part of its inhabitants, also felt themselves degraded by the humiliation of their nobility, their gentry, and their priesthood. It was impossible that they should not feel in that manner; and it was impolitic to disappoint their natural and just feelings and expectations. Such was the actual situation of Ireland: he would not pretend to point out the specific remedy; but this he would say, that it was impossible for Ireland to continue much longer in the state in which it was at present; it might be thrown into a worse state, but every one that was acquainted with its actual situation, and he would appeal to the right honourable gentleman who was lately secretary for that country (Mr. Elliot), must know and agree that it was impossible that it should remain long as it is at present. We might as well shut our eyes, and then say there was no danger, as remain longer in indifference and apathy respecting the situation of Ireland. The pledges that were demanded from the late ministers would have a most important effect upon the situation of that country. The ministers were to be absolutely prevented from even proposing anything in favour of its population. Every paltry corporation, the lowest individual in the empire, had by the constitution a right to present his petition to the king or to the legislature; but now, for the first time, it is stated that four millions of the people of Ireland shall be debarred of the right of petitioning, or, what is equivalent, they are told that no petitions they may present will be paid any attention to. This was not only a novelty, but a prodigy, an alarming appearance in the constitution, and which seemed to portend the greatest danger. This general interdiction appeared more like some divine chastisement to a people, than like any measure which human policy could have adopted. What must have been the effect of those transactions which have recently taken place? The Catholics of Ireland would be given to understand that the royal ears were hermetically sealed against them; that the ministers of the crown were bound by some pledge, expressed or implied, never to propose any redress for them, but always to resist their claims. This consideration filled him with the most serious apprehensions; and when he said so, he must take notice of an expression that had fallen from an honourable baronet (Sir T. Turton), that those who prophesied those dangers intended to act in such a manner as to bring their prophecies to their accomplishment. Nothing could be more unparliamentary or indecent than this observation. He should not, however, be prevented by it from expressing fully those apprehensions which he felt. He had in Ireland so many dear pledges, that no man could suspect him of lightly wishing to offer any observations which could tend to disturb its tranquillity or endanger its security; he knew, however, that there were many fiends and demons waiting to seize on every opportunity to effect a separation of the two countries, and he conceived that they would take every advantage of the discontent which the Catholics might feel. He felt that we were walking *per ignes suppositos cinere doloso:* he did not mean to say that the danger was immediate; it might be smoothed over for a year or two, but it would continue to keep Ireland the most vulnerable part of the empire. If a measure of such unnecessary outrage as this was persevered in, he thought it might shake to the centre the connexion between the two countries, and the prosperity, if not the existence of the empire.

THE CATHOLIC CLAIMS.

February 25, 1813.

PLUNKET was again returned to parliament by Trinity College, in 1812, after an interval of five years.

The parliamentary progress of the Catholic question meantime may be told in a few words. In 1808, Grattan proposed the petition of the Irish Catholics, and moved that it be referred to a committee of the whole house; he was defeated by a majority of 153. Again, in 1810, he was beaten on the same motion by a majority of 104; and in 1812 by a majority of 85. In the House of Lords, Lord Donoughmore, who had charge of the petition there, was beaten at the same dates by majorities averaging 80 votes. The question made progress, nevertheless. The most eminent English statesmen then living, or lately dead, Pitt, Fox, Burke, Tierney, Windham, Sheridan, Canning, Castlereagh, were positively pledged to sustain it. So the prince regent was also supposed to be. The king's insanity had settled one great obstacle. The pamphlets and debates —and particularly Sir John Cox Hippisley's documentary collections and parliamentary papers upon Catholic doctrine and practice touching the civil authority and sects without the pale of the church—had disabused the English public mind of much prejudice. But the most powerful argument of all was the fact that the Irish Catholics had become a formidable political power, and every day grew more determined in their tone, more coherent and organised in action. Napoleon Bonaparte and then Daniel O'Connell were the two weightiest troubles of the imperial minister.

At last the scale turned a little. On the 22nd of June, 1812, Mr. Canning moved that the house would, early in the next session, take into its consideration the state of the laws affecting his majesty's Roman Catholic subjects, with a view to a final and conciliatory adjustment compatible with the Protestant constitution in church and state. A brilliant debate ensued, and the motion was carried by a majority of 235 to 106 votes.

Accordingly, in the following February, Grattan proposed a committee of the whole house in the terms of Canning's motion. Before he rose, Mr. Yorke called on the clerk to read from the Bill of Rights the passages guaranteeing a Protestant constitution in church and state. Grattan began by declaring his opinion that these very passages might and ought to be contained in the preamble of any bill for the relief of the Catholics. His speech throughout was a singularly clear, simple, and earnest argument. Exception was taken to the fact that he seemed to speak of Ireland as a distinct and independent country— a lapse that might well happen to the man who had once made Ireland a nation. Plunket spoke early in the debate—after Mr. Bankes, who had taken Grattan to task for the use of such terms in an imperial parliament, and had referred to the recent controversy between the Pope and Napoleon, as a proof that the Papacy was still inspired by a spirit of utter intolerance.

A generation of Irish Catholics has grown to manhood since emancipation, and lost the memory of the old bondage; so, many readers may find it difficult to understand the exact bearings of the masterly argument in which Plunket pleaded the rights of our fathers. I may therefore state in a few sentences the condition of the then existing penal laws. In many particulars, the laws against Catholics differed in the three kingdoms; in Scotland they were most severe, even touching freedom of worship. In Ireland they had been relaxed so as to recognise full freedom of worship, the right to practise professions, to act under the royal commission in peace and war, to serve on juries, and to exercise the parliamentary franchise. But the acts of real grievance affecting the general body of the Catholics throughout the three kingdoms, and especially in England, were: 1. The 13th Charles II., commonly called the Corporation Act, by which they were excluded from offices in cities and corporations. 2. The 25th Charles II., commonly called the Test Act, by which they were excluded from all civil and military offices—unless in the cases in which the test was abolished by the Irish act of 1793. 3. The 30th Charles II., by which Catholics were interdicted from sitting in either house of parliament. An act of William and Mary, operative in England, prevented the use of the parliamentary franchise. The mutiny and admiralty laws enabled officers to compel Catholic soldiers and sailors to attend Protestant worship. There were many other statutes, especially in England and Scotland, unrepealed, but practically inoperative. The machinery of exclusion was either the oath of supremacy, declaring the king's civil and ecclesiastical pre-eminence within the realm, or the sacramental test of taking the Protestant communion before the acceptance of office, or a declaration denying transubstantiation, and denouncing the invocation of saints and the sacrifice of the mass as idolatrous. In parliament, the oath and declaration were both taken. Whenever Catholics were admitted to office, they disclaimed upon oath the temporal authority of the Pope outside his own states, and the doctrine that the infallibility of his holiness was an article of faith.

Mr. Speaker, I am induced to rise, at so early a period of the debate, for the purpose of obviating the mis-statement (certainly unintentional) of the expressions and sentiments of my right honourable friend Mr. Grattan, which has been made by the honourable gentleman who has last spoken. My right honourable friend did not call Great Britain a foreign country; and even if such an expression had accidentally been used by him, the uniform tenor of his opinions and of his language in this house might have suggested to the honourable member the propriety of abstaining from a verbal criticism upon it. My right honourable friend unites to the enthusiasm of an Irish patriot the comprehensive views of a statesman and a legislator; and his affection for his native country, to which his life has been devoted, has expanded into love of the general weal, and zeal for the glory of the empire. In every sentiment which he has uttered I most cordially concur. My right honourable friend has not been so absurd as to propose to re-enact the bill of rights and the act of settlement; but absurd and extravagant calumnies having, with no laudable industry, been propagated, as if the present motion were intended to invade the church and to overturn the state, my right honourable friend has placed in the front of his resolution a denial of the calumny.

The honourable gentleman has said there is nothing specific or intelligible in the motion or in the statement. The motion appears to me to be perfectly distinct, and perfectly intelligible. It proposes to remove all the civil disabilities which affect a great portion of our fellow subjects, on account of their religion; offering, at the same time, to accompany the measure with every security which may be required for the protection of the Protestant interest. This seems not very difficult to comprehend; but I own I do not find it equally easy to ascertain the meaning of the honourable gentleman himself. In some part of his argument he relies on objections, which, if they have any weight against the measure now, must always operate; in other parts, he insinuates as an opinion that the objections are only accidental or temporary. Why the honourable member voted for the measure in the last parliament, and intends to oppose it in this, seems to require some further explanation than he has thought proper to afford. The intolerant declarations of the Pope, which he has referred to, were surely as strong an argument at that time as they are now. The honourable gentleman seems to have spoken with an anxiety to anticipate what is to be said by a right honourable friend of his who is hereafter to express his opinions; and he has alluded to the proposal of some plan which, he fears, will not be acceptable to the petitioners, and which he himself does not approve of; or, if he does, why he cannot agree to the going into a committee for the purpose of considering it, the house are left to conjecture.

Much has been said of the question of right. It appears to me to be a very unnecessary metaphysical discussion, and one which cannot have any practical application in the present instance. In the same sense in which religious toleration is a right, a due share of political power is a right. Both must yield to the paramount interests of society, if such interests require it. Neither can be justifiably withheld, unless their inconsistency with the public interest is clearly established. But in the present case the question does not, in any respect, arise; for we have already admitted the Roman Catholics to substantial power, and what we seek to exclude them from is honour. The privileges which are withheld are impotent as protections to the state, but most galling and provoking to the party who is excluded. No candid mind can hesitate to admit that these exclusions must be severely felt as subjects of grievance, and grievances of the most insulting kind. That the man of the first eminence at the bar should be prevented from acting as one of his majesty's counsel, or from sitting on the bench of justice; that the gallant officer who has distinguished himself in the battles of his country, when his heart is beating high with the love of honourable fame, should be stopped in his career, and see his companions in arms raised above him, to lead his countrymen to victory and glory, must be felt as wounding and humiliating. In this house, does it require argument to show that exclusion from parliament must be considered as a privation and indignity? What assembles us here? The honest ambition of serving our country—the pride of abiding by honourable engagements—or motives perhaps of a less elevated description. Whatever they may be, honourable and dignified, or otherwise, they subsist in their minds as much as in ours; and though the elective franchise, which has been granted to the Irish Catholic, gives him a substantial representation, yet the exclusion is calculated to operate as a severe and humiliating disability; and the more humiliating, because it is a mark of inferiority branded on the Catholic, merely for the purpose of marking inferiority!

The topic that toleration admits of one consideration and political power of another has little application to this case, even if it were true; for here it must be contended that rank, and station, and honour are not the proper appendages of wealth, and knowledge, and education, and of everything which constitutes political and moral strength. In every system of human policy the few must govern the many, but, putting military force out of the case, their legitimate government must arise from their superiority in wealth and knowledge ; if, therefore, you exclude the wealthy and the educated from the government of the state, you throw into the scale of the many the only weight which could have preserved the balance of the state itself. This is universally true ; but when you reject the opulent and the educated, on account of a condition which they have in common with the many, you add the attraction of politics and party to the operation of general and moral causes ; and, if the principle of exclusion be a religious one, you organize not merely the principles of revolution, but of revolution furious and interminable. Put the policy of the separation of political rank from property and education, in the extreme case of their total division, or in any intermediate degree, the conclusion is equally true, that the attempt so to separate, establishes a principle, not of government, but of the dissolution of all government! So sensible of this truth were our ancestors, that when they saw, or thought they saw, a necessity for dishonouring the Roman Catholic, they adopted, as a necessary consequence, the policy of impoverishing and barbarizing him. When they degraded him, they felt that their only safety was to steep him in poverty and ignorance. Their policy, good or bad, was consistent— the means had a diabolical fitness for their end. Is it not a perfect corollary to this proposition, is it not the legitimate converse of this truth, that, if you re-admit them to wealth and to knowledge, you must restore them to ambition and to honour ? What have we done? We have trod back their steps ; we have rescued the Catholics from the code, which formed at once their servitude and our safety. And we fancy we can continue the exclusion, from civil station, which superinduced that code. Theirs was a necessity, real or fancied, but a consistent system ; we pretend no necessity; we have voluntarily abdicated the means of safety, and we wilfully and uselessly continue the causes of danger. The time to have paused, was before we heaved from those sons of earth, the mountains which the wisdom or the terrors of our ancestors had heaped upon them ; but we have raised them up and placed them erect—are we prepared to hurl them down and bury them again ?

Where is the madman to propose it ? Where is the idiot who imagines that they can remain as they are ? The state of the Catholics of Ireland is, in this respect, unparalleled by anything in ancient or modern history. They are not slaves, as some of their absurd advocates call them, but freemen, possessing substantially the same political rights with their Protestant brethren, and with all the other subjects of the empire: that is, possessed of all the advantages which can be derived from the best laws, administered in the best manner, of the most free and most highly civilized country in the world. Do you believe that such a body, possessed of such a station, can submit to contumely and exclusion? That they will stand behind your chair and wait upon you at the public banquet? The less valuable, in sordid computation, the privilege, the more marked the insult in refusing it, and the more honourable the anxiety for possessing it! Miserable and unworthy wretches would they be if they ceased to aspire to it; base and dangerous hypocrites if they dissembled their wishes; formidable instruments of domestic or foreign tyranny if they did not entertain them! The liberties of England would not, for half a century, remain proof against the contact and contagion of four millions of opulent and powerful subjects, who disregarded the honours of the state, and felt utterly uninterested in the constitution.

In coming forward, therefore, with this claim of honourable ambition, they at once afford you the best pledge of their sincerity, and the most satisfactory evidence of their title. They claim the benefit of the ancient vital principle of the constitution, that the honours of the state should be open to the talents and to the virtues of all its members. The adversaries of the measure invert the order of all civilized society. They have made the Catholics an aristocracy, and they would treat them as a mob; they give to the lowest of the rabble, if he is a Protestant, what they refuse to the head of the peerage, if he is a Catholic. They shut out my Lord Fingal from the state, and they make his footman a member of it; and this strange confusion of all social order, they dignify with the name of the British constitution; and the proposal to consider the best and most conciliatory mode of correcting it, they cry down as a dangerous and presumptuous innovation.

Sir, the Catholics propose no innovation. They ask for an equal share, as fellow-subjects, in the constitution, as they find it; in that constitution, in whose original stamina they had an undisputed right, before there was a reformation and before there was a revolution, and before the existence of the abuses which induced the necessity of either. They desire to bear its burdens, to share its dangers, to participate its glory, and to abide its fate. They bring, as an offering, their hearts and hands, their lives and fortunes, but they desire also the privilege of bringing with them their consciences, their religion, and their honour, without which they would be worthless and dangerous associates.

The position, therefore, to be maintained, by those who say that the first principles of the constitution are in opposition to their claim, is rather a critical one. They must show why it is that a Roman Catholic may vote for a member to sit in parliament, and yet may not himself be a member of it; why he may be the most powerful and wealthy subject in the realm, and the greatest landed proprietor, and yet may not fill the lowest office, in the meanest town upon his estates; why he may be the first advocate at the bar, and be incapable of acting as one of the counsel of his sovereign; why he may be elector, military officer, grand juror, corporator, magistrate, in Ireland, where the danger, if any, is immense, and why none of them in England, where the causes of apprehension are comparatively trifling and insignificant. Besides all this, arguing as they do, that the Roman Catholic religion necessarily includes hostility to the state, on the very points which, by the oaths which the Roman Catholics have taken, are solemnly disavowed, they must show the safety of harbouring, in the bosom of the state, and admitting to its essential and substantial benefits, a body of men whose only title to admission has been perjury; a body of men who, in addition to religious opinions, inconsistent with our particular constitution, have violated the solemn obligations which bind man to man, and therefore are unworthy of being admitted into any society. in which the sacred principles of social intercourse are respected.

Sir, if these things are so, the petitions of the public should be, not to be protected against the dangers which are to come, but to be rescued from those which have already been incurred. Nay, more, if oaths are no longer to be regarded, we should not rely on the vain securities which our ancestors have resorted to, and which consist of oaths, and only of oaths; but we should devise some new means of proving their religion by the testimony of others, and of chaining them down to it, without the possibility of disowning or escaping from it.

But, let us examine, somewhat more accurately, these supposed principles of public policy which oppose an insuperable bar to the admission of the Roman Catholic. They join issue with you on this point. So far as concession is inconsistent with the true principles of the constitution, the safety of the Established Church, and of the Protestant throne, they admit that they are entitled to nothing; so far as it is not inconsistent, they claim to be entitled to every thing. Let it be shown that these great foundations of our liberties and of our civil and ecclesiastical polity are their enemies, and they must yield in silence. They must receive it as the doom of fate; it must be submitted to, as part of the mysterious system of Providence, which, whilst it has embarked us in an awful struggle for the preservation of its choicest blessings, has ordained that, in this struggle, we may not unite the hearts and affections of our people. We must cherish the hope that the same incomprehensible wisdom, which at once impels us to this mighty contest and forbids us to use the means of success, may work out our safety by methods of its own. If it can be made to appear that the imperious interests of our country pronounce, from necessity, this heavy and immitigable sentence upon millions of its subjects, I trust that they will learn submission, and not embitter their hopeless exclusion by the miseries of discontent and of disorder; but, before they bow down to this eternal interdict, before they retire from the threshold of the constitution to the gloom of hopeless and never ending exclusion, I appeal to every candid mind, are they not entitled to have it proved by arguments, clear as the light of heaven,.that this necessity exists? I now challenge the investigation of those supposed maxims, step by step, and inch by inch. Let it be stated in some clear and intelligible form, what is this fundamental prop of the constitution; what is this overwhelming ruin, which is to tumble upon us by its removal. Let us meet and close with this argument. But beware, I warn you, of attempting to outlaw the Irish people, by an artificial and interested clamour! Let not those who have encouraged the Irish people to expect redress, now affect to be bound by this spell of their own raising! This would be to palter with their own consciences and the public safety, and can entail no consequences, other than calamity and disgrace.

The only obstacles, which appear to stand in the way of the Roman Catholics, are the oath of supremacy and the declaration against transubstantiation. The former of these, in its original enactment and application, had a very limited political relation. I speak not of the capricious fury of Henry VIII., which made it treason to refuse the oath. He considered himself, under God, the supreme head of the Church, in all things spiritual and temporal; and bound the subject to submit to all his ordinances made, and to be made, under the penalty of death. But the application of the oath, as it was modified by Elizabeth, had chiefly (and with the exception of offices immediately derived from the crown, or concerning the administration of justice) a religious, and not a political, application. Subject to these exceptions, it professed not to control the private opinion, nor to make it a ground of exclusion. But it subjected the public profession, or non-conformity, to penalty. And, accordingly, Roman Catholics were admissable to parliament and to corporate offices for more than one hundred years after the introduction of the oath of supremacy. Then came the laws of Charles II., which, for the first time, superinduced general exclusion from office, as a political consequence of the religious opinion.

Here, then, were before us, two principles, the first, that of the Reformation, which proscribed the religion; the second, that of Charles II., which presumed that certain unconstitutional tenets must be held by those who professed that religion, and therefore made civil incapacity the consequence of the religious belief. Here were two principles perfectly distinct, but perfectly consistent. Now what have we done? We have, in fact, abrogated the principles of the Reformation, for we have repealed the laws against recusancy, and legalized the religion. Having done this, it was a necessary consequence to say that we could not infer, from a religious tenet which we legalized, a political opinion inconsistent with the safety of the state; otherwise we should have been unjustifiable in legalizing it. We therefore substituted instead of the renunciation of the religious doctrine, from which the political opinion had been formerly inferred, a direct denial, upon oath, of the political opinion itself. If then the Roman Catholic may lawfully exercise the religion, and if he will take the political oath, how can we consistently make objection, either in a religious or political point of view, to his being admitted to the remaining privileges of citizenship? If there is anything inconsistent with the true principles of our religion, in permitting the Catholic to enjoy civil offices, the authors of the Reformation were deeply criminal in permitting him to enjoy them, while they denounced his religion; and we have been doubly traitors, to our religion and to our constitution, in sanctioning by law the free exercise of that religion; throwing away the religious test and substituting a political one in the place of it. If the political oath, either from its supposed insincerity, or from any other cause, is an insufficient substitute for the religious abjuration, how can we be justifiable in allowing it to give the Catholic admission to the high constitutional privileges which he now enjoys? If it is a sufficient substitute, we prevaricate with our own consciences, in refusing him admission, on the strength of it, to the remaining privileges which he requires. In direct violation of the policy which substituted the political oath for the religious declaration, we now say that we require this declaration that he does not hold the religious doctrine which implies the political. But he is ready to swear that he does hold the political doctrine, and still you prefer his declaration that he does not hold the opinion, which furnishes the presumption, to his oath that he does not hold the opinion, which is the thing presumed. Is not this a perfect proof that the political apprehension is a pretext, and that it is bigotry, or something worse, which is the motive? Is not this also a full attestation of your perfect reliance on the honour and sincerity of the Catholic, as well as of your own intolerance? You will accept his word as a proof that he has abjured his religious tenets, but you will not receive his oath as long as he abides by them. Is it that he is insincere in his oath? Then why trust his declaration? Has the oath a negative power? It is not merely that his oath is not binding, but, that which shall be full evidence, if he merely asserts it by implication, shall become utterly incredible if he swears to it directly. Why, this is worse than transubstantiation; it is as gross a rebellion against the evidence of demonstration as the other is against the testimony of sense. Again, the oath of supremacy extends to a renunciation, as well of the spiritual as of the temporal authority of the Pope; and its object appears to have been two-fold: first, to exclude the interference of the Pope in the temporal concerns of the realm; and secondly, to secure the Protestant hierarchy against the claims of the sect which had been evicted. As to the first, the Roman Catholic tenders an oath, utterly denying the Pope's right to exercise any kind of temporal jurisdiction in these kingdoms; as to the second, he tenders an oath, abjuring all interference with the Protestant establishment and hierarchy. What then remains in difference? The right of the Pope with respect to their clergy. Now, to this the oath of supremacy never had any reference, nor could have had: their clergy were not recognised as having any legal existence when the oath of supremacy was enacted, nor as the subject of any other regulation than that of heavy punishment if they were discovered. This part of the oath merely looks to the preservation of the Protestant hierarchy, and all this is effectually provided for by the oath which is proffered. If the Catholic swears that he will not disturb or question the establishment, it would seem to concern us very little whether he admires or approves it, or what may be his abstract opinion of its fitness. We have already the effect of the oath of supremacy, so far as it concerns practical and conscientious submission, now, and at all times, and it is perfectly childish to say that we will not accept their present acquiescence, and their oath that they will continue to acquiesce, unless they also swear that they ought, as matter of abstract right, to do so. That is, they must not only submit to our title, but swear to our argument. I do not mean to say that the mode of appointing their clergy and the Pope's interference with respect to it is not a very important topic, and one which we are well warranted in looking to and regulating; but what I rely on is, that it is a new subject, resting on its own merits, and calling for and requiring r conciliatory adjustment, but in no respect involving anything which affects the oath of supremacy or the principles of the reformation.

As to the Corporation Act, every person acquainted with its history knows that it was introduced, not with an aspect to the Roman Catholics, but to sectaries of a very different description, who had got into the corporations during the government of Cromwell, and were supposed to be disaffected to the politics of the court. Part of the oath, as it was originally framed, was, that it was unlawful, under any pretence, to take up arms against the king, or those commissioned by him; and the amendment, which sought to qualify it by adding the word "lawfully," before commissioned, was thrown out. One of the first acts of William and Mary was to repeal this scandalous and slavish enactment, which was at direct variance with the first principles of the revolution; and yet we are told, in patriotic petitions, from loyal Protestant bodies, that this Corporation Act was one of the great bulwarks of the revolution. This mutilated fragment, one half of which was lopped off by the revolution, is one of its pillars, and the Test Act is the other. Its history is known to everybody. It was the child of my Lord Shaftesbury, who, on the score of religion, possessed a most philosophical composure, but had a very pious horror of the court, and levelled this act personally against the Duke of York[*]; and, as the Corporation Act was the first offering of overflowing servility, brought in on the full tide of the Restoration, so was the Test Act the result of deep and bitter repentance, subsiding at its ebb; and yet these conflicting, partial, and temporary regulations are dwelt on, as if they formed part of that great event which we all consider as the foundation of our liberties. But I beg to ask has the charter of our liberties become obsolete? If not, why are those mighty instruments hung up like rusty armour? Does not every man know that they are endured only because they are not exercised, and that they are never men-

---

[*] The act passed the House of Commons without much opposition; "but in the upper house," says Hume, "the Duke of York moved that an exception might be admitted in his favour. With great earnestness, and even with tears in his eyes, he told them that he was now to cast himself on their kindness in the greatest concern which he could have in the world; and he protested that whatever his religion might be it should only be between God and his own soul. Notwithstanding this strong effort in so important a point, he prevailed only by two voices."

tioned, by any constitutional writer, without pleading their inactivity as the only apology for their existence? The taste and sense of the public is, in this respect, a reproach to the tardy liberality of the legislature.

Sir, a right honourable gentleman (Mr. Yorke), to whom I wish to allude with every possible degree of public and private respect, has desired that the Bill of Rights should be referred to; give me leave to ask, do you find in the Bill of Rights the principle of exclusion of Roman Catholics from the legislature or from the state? It is required, no doubt, by the Bill of Rights, that the new oath of supremacy, thereby substituted for the former one, should be taken by all who were bound to take the former one, but this is not introduced as one of the grievances redressed or rights declared, but it merely incidentally mentioned, in consequence of the substitution of the one oath for the other; and the declaration against Popery is in no respect adverted to; but one fact, most decisive and important on this point, is this, that when this act was passed the Roman Catholics of Ireland were not, by any law or usage, excluded from parliament or from civil or military offices. The articles of Limerick (3rd Oct., 1691) stipulated for all such privileges in the exercise of religion as were enjoyed in the reign of Charles II., and as were consistent with the laws of Ireland. They required the oath o allegiance, as created in the first year of William and Mary; and the oath to be administered to the Roman Catholics, submitting to his majesty's government, was to be that oath and no other; and it was further stipulated that, so soon as their affairs would permit them to summon a parliament, their majesties would endeavour to procure them such further securities as might preserve them from any disturbance on account of their religion. At this time Roman Catholics were not excluded from parliament in Ireland, nor were there any test or corporation laws in force against them. On the faith of these articles, all of which were punctually performed on their part, they surrendered the town, and left King William at liberty to apply his arms to the great cause in which he was sustaining the liberties of Europe. The stipulation, on the part of government, was to protect them against any additional oaths, and to endeavour to procure for them additional securities. What was done? The act of the 3rd of William and Mary was passed, giving them no additional securities, but excluding them, for the first time, from parliament and from offices civil and military, and from the bar, unless they subscribed the declaration against Popery, and swore the oath of supremacy. The stipulation in the articles had been, not for those in garrison, but that the Roman Catholics of Ireland should enjoy their privileges: for the garrison, they had stipulated for liberty to serve abroad, and to be conveyed accordingly. These victims of mistaken loyalty, when they were about to leave their native land, and, with the characteristic generosity and improvidence of their country, to commit themselves with the fortunes of a banished monarch, stipulated, not for themselves, but for the country they were about to leave for ever; and the parliament, by a cruel mockery, enacted, not for the country, but for them, that they should not lose the privileges of—what? Of being barristers-at-law, clerks in chancery, attorneys, practitioners of law and physics, but that they might freely use the same!

Why, sir, do I mention these historical facts? Not for the purpose of raking up the embers of ancient animosities, but for the purpose of showing that, in restoring the privileges of the Catholics, we are performing an act of justice, and vindicating the Revolution from the stain of this act of perfidy. Men who have forgotten every circumstance of that great event, which connects it with the cause of civil and religious freedom, affect to call this breach of faith and honour one of the sacred principles of our constitution. It is a miserable perversion of understanding which can forget everything sacred and animating in that glorious struggle, which can fling away as dross the precious attestation which it bears to the just rights of the people, which would bury in eternal oblivion the awful lesson which it has taught to their rulers; but consecrates and embalms this single act of injustice, which disgraces it.

Sir, I am satisfied that the illustrious persons who perfected the Revolution were not aware of the injustice done to Ireland. In the crowded events of that day the stipulations might not have been fully known, and there have been at all times a set of slaves ready, in this country, to defame and to defraud their native land, to traffic on the calamities of their countrymen. I will go further, and suppose that the severe necessity of the times may have made it impossible to avoid an act of injustice; but I will not therefore confound the deviation with the rule; I cannot trample on the principle and worship the exception. It might as well be said that to restore the Danish fleet would be a violation of the laws of nature and of nations, because a deplorable necessity had compelled us to violate these laws by seizing it. I have, perhaps, dwelt too long on this part of the subject, but I felt anxious to meet the cry of this great charter of our freedom being at variance with the rights of the people. The great men of that day had deeply studied the laws and constitution of their country; with ardent feelings and sublime conceptions they made no unnecessary breach on any ancient usage; no wanton encroachment of any rights of people or of king; not like our modern improvers, who hold for nothing the wisdom which has gone before them, and set up their own crude conceptions, with an utter contempt for all the sacred lore of their ancestors. They committed no rude outrage on those who had gone before them; they entailed no odious bondage on those who were to succeed them: with the modesty and simplicity which characterize great minds, they declared the essential rights of the constitution. They saw that the system of the reformation would be incomplete, unless the king, who was the temporal head of the church, should be in communion with that church; they therefore enacted that he should hold his crown only while he adhered to his religion. They declared the throne unalterably Protestant—they declared the religion of the state unalterably Protestant; and, having thus laid the firm foundation of civil and religious freedom, they left all other considerations open to the progress of time and to the wisdom of posterity.

That time has come and that posterity is now called upon to decide. We are fighting the same battle, in which the illustrious deliverer of these countries was engaged—we are defending the liberties of Europe and of the world, against the same unchangeable and insatiable ambition which then assailed them—we are engaged with an enemy far more formidable than Louis XIV., whether we consider the vastness of his plans, the consummateness of his skill, his exhaustless resources, or his remorseless application of them. But if our dangers are aggravated, our means of safety are increased. William III. was obliged to watch, with a jealous eye, the movements of one half of his subjects, whilst he employed the energies of the other. We have it in our power to unite them all, by one great act of national justice. If we do not wantonly and obstinately fling away the means which God's providence has placed within our grasp, we may bring the energies of all our people, with one hand and heart, to strike against the common enemy.

Sir, there is a kind of circular reasoning which seems, at some public meetings, to pass for full proof. They say that this measure invades the constitution, because it endangers the church; and they say it endangers the church, because it invades the constitution. Sir, it is not sought to affect the church establishment—to take away its possessions, to degrade its rank, or to touch its emoluments. Its doctrines and its discipline are not interfered with. This is no attempt to include the Catholic within the pale of the Protestant church, nor to give him any share in its establishment. What is meant by the cry of danger to the church? Is it that the measure will be immediately injurious to the church, or that it will endanger the church, by enabling the Catholics hereafter to overturn it? In the first point of view, the only immediate effect it has is to open the honours of the state to all other descriptions of subjects, as well as to those who profess the established religion. Is it meant to be argued that the Protestant religion will be deserted, unless a temporal bonus is held out to those who adhere to it? Do they mean to recruit for the establishment by a bounty from the state? The supposition is too abhorrent from the spirit of Christianity, and too degrading to the dignity of the church. Then as to danger—the overthrow of the Protestant establishment—how is this to be effected? In parliament or out of parliament? By force or by legislation? If by force, how does the removal of civil disabilities enable them? Does it not make it much more unlikely that they should make the attempt? And if they should make it, will not the removal of the real grievance deprive them of the co-operation of the moderate and the honest? If the latter, is it really apprehended that the number of members let in would be strong enough to overrule the Protestants, and force a law to pull down the establishment? Would you have the returns much more favourable to the Catholics than they are at present? If the entire one hundred members were to be Catholics, could such a measure, in the range of human possibility, be successful, or could it seriously enter into the contemplation of any man in his senses? The apprehension, when it undergoes the test of close examination, is perfectly chimerical. These are not the fruits of the wholesome caution of statesmen, but the reveries of disordered brains. But if you reject this measure now, and postpone it to times of difficulty and danger, will the interests of the Protestant church be better guarded? Grant it now and you grant it as a matter of grace, to which you may annex every fair and reasonable condition; but if you find it necessary to resort to it in some hour of dismay and adversity, when the storm is blowing and the public institutions are rocking and toppling, will the establishment be perfectly secure? Again, if you grant it now, you give it to a class as much inferior in property as they are superior in numbers. Now, it is a truth, as certain as any in political economy, that at no very distant period the wealth of the country must become diffused pretty nearly in proportion to its relative population. Will the Protestants of Ireland thank you for deferring the adjustment of this question until it shall be demanded by people having as great an ascendancy in wealth as in population? Sir, these are serious practical considerations, and the clergy of this country would do well to weigh them and to reflect upon them. These are questions much more of policy than of religion, and it is not without deep regret that I see any portion of that respectable body interpose themselves between the wisdom of the legislature and the temporal interests of the subject, with such a tone and such a manner as some of them have assumed on this occasion. If the interests of religion or the rights of their order are at stake, they are entitled to come forward as a body—even if the matter is merely political, they are entitled to come forward as individuals; but that any of them should adopt the present tone of unqualified remonstrance, because the Commons of England propose to consider the political claims of their fellow Christians and fellow subjects, with a view to a final and amicable adjustment, does not seem calculated to advance the real interests of religion.

Sir, religion is degraded when it is brandished as a political weapon—and there is no medium in the use of it; either it is justified by holy zeal and fervent piety, or the appeal to it becomes liable to the most suspicious imputation. Sir, I consider the safety of the state as essentially interwoven with the integrity of the establishment. The established religion is the child of freedom. The reformation grew out of the free spirit of bold investigation: in its turn it repaid the obligation, with more than filial gratitude, and contributed, with all its force, to raise the fabric of our liberties. Our civil and religious liberties would each of them lose much of their security if they were not so deeply indented each with the other. The church need not be apprehensive. It is a plant of the growth of three hundred years; it has struck its roots into the centre of the state, and nothing short of a political earthquake can overturn it: while the state is safe it must be so; but let it not be forgotten that, if the state is endangered it cannot be secure. The church is protected by the purity of its doctrines and its discipline; the learning and the piety of its ministers; their exemplary discharge of every moral and Christian duty; the dignity of its hierarchy, the extent and lustre of its possessions, and the reverence of the public for its ancient and unquestioned rights: to these the Catholic adds the mite of his oath, that he does not harbour the chimerical hope, or the unconstitutional wish to shake or to disturb it; and, therefore, all that is requisite for the security of the church is that it should remain in repose, on its own deep and immoveable foundations; and this is the policy which the great body of the church of Ireland, and I believe I may add, of the church of England, have adopted. If anything could endanger its safety, it would be the conduct of intemperate and officious men, who would erect the church into a political arbiter, to prescribe rules of imperial policy to the throne and to the legislature.

Sir, a reason assigned by the honourable member who last spoke for his change of opinion is, that the sense of the people of England is against the measure. Supposing, for a moment, that the fact were so, to a much greater extent than it really is, would it afford a fair argument for precluding an inquiry and adjustment? I consider it, under any circumstances, an invidious and dangerous topic, to cite the opinion of the people of one part of the empire against the claims of the people of another part of it; but to cite it as an argument against the full discussion of their claims seems utterly unwarrantable. But, when it is recollected that the Union was urged upon the Catholics of Ireland, under the strong expectation that facilities would be consequently afforded to the accomplishment of their wishes, is it not something very like dishonesty to press into the service, against their claims, the opinion of the people of England, and its authority with an English parliament? If this question were now under discussion in an Irish parliament, granted to be in itself just and expedient, called for by all the Catholics and by a great majority of the Protestants of Ireland, would it be endured as an argument that the cry of the people of England was against it? You have taken away that parliament, under the assurance that, in a British parliament that might be safely done, which, in an Irish parliament might be difficult or dangerous, and now you say, " true, the measure is right, but the difficulty grows from its being discussed in an English parliament, because such a parliament must defer to the prejudices of the English, at the expence of the rights of the Irish people." It may be said that the people of England are no parties to such a compact; but I would appeal to the noble lord,* who, if he did not guarantee it as a compact, was at least a very principal mover in holding it out as an inducement, whether he can countenance such a topic; or can he link himself with those who have, by every indirect method, endeavoured to excite the people of England, in order to fabricate the argument?

Sir, the opinion of the people is undoubtedly entitled to a respect-

* Castlereagh. One of Pitt's principal arguments for the Union was, that in a British parliament, where the weight of the assembly and the constituencies represented would be Protestant, there would be less difficulty in reconciling the claims of the Catholics with the principles of the British constitutional system than in Ireland, where the nation was Catholic, and only the governing class Protestant.

ful attention; it is to be listened to—to be canvassed, and, if sound and reasonable, to be deferred to; but the clamour of the people of either country is not to silence the deliberations of parliament; still less the opinion of a partial and very limited portion of that people; still less an opinion founded on imperfect views; still less an opinion founded upon gross prejudices, excited and kindled by artful and interested misrepresentation, and for the very purpose of preventing fair discussion. The opinion of the people of both countries is to be looked to, and the reasonable foundations of the opinions of both; and in so doing, it is always to be recollected that the sentiments of the Catholics are not to be the less regarded on account of their being principally condemned in one part of the united kingdom; but if, either from prudence or affection, they would be respected if interspersed through the counties of Great Britain, they are not the less entitled to attention because they constitute four-fifths of the most vulnerable, and not least productive portion of the empire. The question, it is true, is an imperial one: why? Because Ireland is identified with your interest and happiness and glory; her interests are yours, and therefore Irish policy is imperial policy; but it seems rather inconsistent to take cognizance of the question, on the supposition that the interests of the two countries are absolutely the same; and to decide it upon the principle that the rights of the one are essentially and unalterably opposed to the wishes and the safety of the other. But, sir, I utterly deny the fact, that such is the sentiment of the people of England. A pretty bold experiment has been made, and it has failed. The intelligent class of the English public, those who, from property and from education, and from place in society, are entitled to sway the opinion of the legislature on this, or on any political subject, are, I firmly believe, friendly to a full discussion of the Catholic claims, and with a strong leaning in favour of liberality and concession, if they can be made to appear consistent with public safety. This is a tribunal to which an appeal may be fairly made, and to which adequate and ample satisfaction should be given; and there is no concession or sacrifice, not inconsistent with the essential principles of their religion, which the Catholics are not bound to make for the purpose. But, sir, beyond this public, and to the very dregs of the community I fear there are some desperate enough to look. I have heard something like a muttered threat of such an appeal; but I do not believe, though there is much valour at present on this subject, that we need fear a repetition of the outrages of St. George's Fields; I do not fear that our ears will be again assailed by the hell shout of "No Popery." I have heard something more than an insinuation, within these walls, that this is a question in which the lower classes of the people are very deeply interested, and that their voice is, on this occasion, to be particularly attended to.

Sir, the doctrine is rather novel in the quarter from which it proceeds, nor am I disposed to give it an unqualified denial. I should be sorry to contend, that the voice of any portion of our fellow-subjects, however humble, should be disregarded. If they complain of grievances by which they are oppressed, of justice withheld, or of anything trenching upon their freedom or their comforts, they are to be heard with patient and with deep attention; and the more humble the situation of the complainants, the more bounden the duty of the representative to listen to them. But, on a subject like the present, where the legislature is called on to withhold the privileges of the constitution from a great proportion of the people, upon supposed principles of state government; when claims of common right are withheld, in deference to sacred and mysterious maxims of imperial policy: on such a subject, I say, it is something more than absurdity to affect a deference for the shouts of the lower orders of the people. Sir, the apprehension of such an appeal being resorted to need not affect our deliberations; those who intimate such an intention know full well that, though the threat may be endured, the times would not bear the execution of it; they know full well that, if parliament determines to pursue its steady course of calm investigation and liberal adjustment, there is no faction in the state which can effectually interpose between the sovereign authority of the legislature and the just demands of the people.

The conduct of the Roman Catholics of Ireland has been resorted to as an argument for abandoning the pledge of the last session. Sir, I am not the advocate of their intemperance; I am free to say that there have been some proceedings, on the part of the public bodies, who affect to act for them, altogether unjustifiable. Their attempts to dictate to the entire body how they are to act on each particular political occurrence, their presuming to hold an inquisition on the conduct of individuals in the exercise of the elective franchise, and putting them under the ban of their displeasure, because they vote for their private friends and abide by their plighted engagements; all this is a degree of inquisitorial authority unexampled and insufferable; and this, by persons professing themselves the advocates of unbounded freedom and unlimited toleration, at the moment when they are extending their unsparing tyranny into the domestic arrangements of every Catholic family in the country. Sir, I am equally disgusted with the tone of unqualified demand and haughty rejection of all condition or accommodation, so confidently announced by them; nor can I palliate the intemperance of many of their public speeches, nor the exaggeration and violence of some of their printed publications. To this tone I never wish to see the legislature yield; but, as this indecent clamour is not to compel them to yield what is unreasonable, I trust it will not influence them to withhold what is just.

Sir, it appears to me most unfair to visit on the Roman Catholic the opinions and the conduct of such public assemblies as profess to act for them; if they labour under a real and a continuing grievance, and one which justifies, on their part, a continued claim, they must act through the medium of popular assemblies, and must, of course, be exposed to all the inconveniences which attend discussion in assemblies. In all such places, we know that unbounded applause attends the man who occupies the extreme positions of opinion, and that the extravagance of his expression of such opinion will not be calculated to diminish it. That there may be many individuals anxious to promote their own consequence at the expense of the party whose interest they profess to advocate, is an evil inseparable from such a state of things; and, amongst those who sincerely wish to promote the interests of the cause, much may fairly be attributed to the heat naturally generated by long continued opposition; much to the effects of disappointed hope; much to the resentment excited and justified by insolent and virulent opposition. But, sir, I should unworthily shrink from my duty, if I were not to avow my opinion, that the unfortunate state of the public mind in Ireland is, above all things, imputable to the conduct of the government. Without recurring unnecessarily to subjects which have been already discussed in this house, I may be allowed to say that the rash interference with the right of petitioning has given deep and just offence to the entire Catholic body. They have been compelled to rally round their constitutional privileges, and make common cause. Those excesses, which two years since would have been eagerly repressed by the Catholics themselves, might now, I fear, be regarded with some degree of favourable allowance on their part.

I must say that the country has not been fairly dealt with on this subject. It is the bounden duty of the government to make up their mind, and to act a consistent part. If this measure is utterly inadmissible, expectation should be put down by the certainty of rejection; resentment should be allayed by the clear exposition of the necessity which bars; the fever of the public mind should be subdued, and all the means of conciliation consistent with such a system should be resorted to. If, on the other hand, this claim may and ought to be acted on, it should be frankly received and honestly forwarded; every facility for its accomplishment should be afforded, by tempering and directing the proceedings of those who seek it; by suggesting the conditions and terms on which it should be granted; and by arranging the details, as well as planning the outlines, of such a system. But how can any honest mind be reconciled to the ambiguity in which the cabinet has concealed itself from public view on this great national question, or with what justice can they complain of the madness which grows out of this fever of their own creating.

This is not one of those questions which may be left to time and chance. The exclusion of these millions from the rights of citizenship is either a flagrant injustice or its necessity springs out of the sacred fountains of the constitution. This is no subject of compromise. Either the claim is forbidden by some imperious principle too sacred to be tampered with, or it is enjoined by a law of reason and justice, which it is oppression to resist. In ordinary cases it sounds well to say that a question is left to the unbiassed sense of parliament and people; but that a measure of vital importance, and which has been again and again discussed by all his majesty's ministers, should be left to work its own course, and suffered to drift along the tide of parliamentary or popular opinion, seems difficult to understand. That government should be mere spectators of such a process is novel. But, when it is known that they have all considered it deeply, and formed their opinions decidedly in direct opposition to each other, that, after this, they should consult in the same cabinet, and sit on the same bench, professing a decided opinion in point of theory and a strict neutrality in point of practice; that, on this most angry of all questions they should suffer the population of the country to be committed in mutual hostility, and convulsed with mutual rancour, aggravated by the uncertainty of the event; producing, on the one hand, all the fury of disappointed hope, on the other side, malignity and hatred, from the apprehension that the measure may be carried, and insolence from every circumstance, public or private, which tends to disappoint or to postpone it; one half the king's ministers encouraging them to seek, without enabling them to obtain—the other half subdivided; some holding out an ambiguous hope, others announcing a never-ending despair. I ask, is this a state in which the government of the country has a right to leave it? Some master-piece of imperial policy must be unfolded, some deep and sacred principle of empire, something far removed from the suspicion of unworthy compromise of principle for power, to reconcile the feelings of the intelligent public, or to uphold a rational confidence in the honesty or seriousness of the government. The consequences of such conduct are disastrous, not merely in the tumult and discord which, in this particular instance, they are calculated to excite, but in their effect upon the character of the government and the times.

Sir, I repeat it, the Irish Catholics have not been fairly dealt with ; the government has not, in any instance, come into amicable contact with them ; it has not consulted, nor soothed, nor directed them ; it has addressed them only in the stern voice of the law, in state prosecution, and it is most unjust to charge against them the anger which has been kindled by such treatment. But, sir, I ask what have the Catholics done ? Look to their actions for the last century, and do not judge them by a few intemperate expressions or absurd publications—these are not the views of statesmen—you are considering the policy of centuries and the fate of a people, and will you condescend to argue, on such a subject, the merits of a pamphlet, or to scan the indiscretions of an angry speaker at a public meeting ? Of this I am sure, that if the violence with which the demand has been urged by some of its advocates is to create a prejudice against it, the virulence with which it has been rejected by some of its opponents ought to be allowed to have some operation in its favour ; perhaps under these opposite impulses of passion a chance may be afforded of reason having fair play, and a hearing may be procured for the merits of the case. This, too, should not be lost sight of: that the Catholics are seeking their rights ; that they are opposed by an adverse government, many of whom declare that no concession on their part could be effectual, but that their 'doom is interminable exclusion. May I ask, whether it is fair to require, or reasonable to expect, that the Catholics should, under such circumstances, exercise a fastidious delicacy in the selection of their friends ; and say to those who profess themselves their advocates, " We refuse your aid, your language is not sufficiently measured ; you urge our demands in too warm and too unqualified a tone, and we prefer the chances which may arise from throwing ourselves on the mercy of our enemies."

Sir, I will not affect to disguise the fact, that there are persons in Ireland who look to revolution and separation. I certainly do not mean to say, nor do I believe, that those whose warmth of expression has been so much and so justly complained of are, in the most remote degree, liable to the suspicion of being joined with such a party. The separatists are, in my judgment, neither numerous nor in themselves, formidable ; and of this I am sure, that they tremble at the prospect of the adjustment of the Catholic claims, as a measure deadly to their views. Is it a wise policy, is it a course which any government can justify to the country, to recruit for these public enemies, by endeavouring to embody the legitimate claims of the Catholics with their wild and pernicious projects ? Is it not madness to oppose the same blind and indiscriminate resistance to the honest objects of the great untainted landed and commercial interests of the Catholic people, and to affect to confound them in a common cause with those miserable enemies of public freedom and safety?

Sir, if I am asked what course, in my opinion, should be pursued in this momentous business, I cannot answer without doubt and distrust in my own judgment, where I may differ from many whose opinion I highly respect ; but it is fair to say that the opinion which I have always entertained and always expressed, publicly and privately, on this subject, is, that this measure cannot be finally and satisfactorily adjusted, unless some arrangement shall be made with respect to the Roman Catholic clergy, and some security afforded to the state against foreign interference. On the best consideration I have been able to give the subject, and on the fullest communication I have been able to obtain on it, I am satisfied that such security may be afforded without interfering in any degree with the essentials of their religion ; and if so, the mere circumstance of its being required is a sufficient reason for conceding it. This is not a struggle for the triumph of one party of the state over another ; it is a great national sacrifice of mutual prejudices for the common good ; and any opportunity of gratifying the Protestant mind should be eagerly seized by the Catholic, even if the condition required were uncalled for by any real or well-founded apprehension. But I must go a step further, and avow that the state has, in my opinion, a right to require some fair security against foreign influence in its domestic concerns. What this security may be, provided it shall be effectual, ought, as I conceive, to be left to the option of the Catholic body. I am little solicitous about the form, so that the substance is attained. As a veto has been objected to, let it not be required ; but let the security be afforded, either by domestic nomination of the clergy or in any shape or form which shall exclude the practical effect of foreign interference. Let them be liberally provided for by the state, let them be natives of the country and educated in the country, and let the full and plenary exercise of spiritual authority by the Pope, which forms an essential part of their religious discipline, remain in all its force ; leave to their choice the mode of reconciling these principles, and stand not upon the manner, if the thing be done.

An honourable gentleman asks, will this satisfy the Catholics? I will not be so indiscreet as to answer for what will satisfy them—I believe it will. But it is enough for me to know that this ought to satisfy them; and of this we may be convinced, that we do not enable them to obtain what they ought not, by granting them what they ought, to have. But what is the use, it is asked, of a measure proposed as an instrument of peace, if it is likely, on the contrary, to produce nothing but dissatisfaction? I answer, first, I believe it will produce full satisfaction, if frankly proposed and honestly acted on. But if you doubt of this, do not make your proceeding an absolute and a final one; reserve the operation of the act which grants relief (if you think it necessary), until the accompanying measure of security shall be ripened, so as to ensure satisfaction in their enactment; declare your principles of security, and your conditions, and let the operation of your law, or the effect of your resolution, await the desire of the Catholic body, signified or fairly understood, with respect to them. Pursue this course, put this measure into the hands of those in whom the Catholics can place confidence, or give them such a parliamentary pledge, that they may see that the accomplishment of their wishes is dependant on their own good sense and moderation; and, I have no doubt, they will not be wanting to contribute their part to this great national work of strength and union. In all events you will have discharged your duty. You will have given satisfaction to the honest and to the reasonable. You will have separated the sound from the unsound, and you will leave the bigot or the incendiary, stripped of all his terrors, by depriving him of all his grievances. Sir, I have done. I may be in error; but I have not sacrificed to interest or to prejudice, and I have spoken my sentiments in the sincerity of my heart.

Plunket sat down amid cheers from all sides of the house. This grand effort was regarded as his maiden speech in the British Commons, and had a success beyond parallel. Almost every speaker who followed him upon either side of the question referred to it in terms of unmeasured admiration. "A speech," said Peel, "which has called forth many compliments; but none which the eloquence and abilities which he has displayed do not fully justify." "A speech," said Whitbread, "the excellence of which with painful regret recals to my recollection the golden days when this house contained a Pitt, a Fox, a Sheridan, and a Windham." "A speech," said Sir William Scott, "not more to be admired as an exhibition of talents than for the honourable and manly candour by which it was still further dignified and adorned." "A speech," said Canning, "to whose merits it is superfluous to add my feeble testimony: a speech displaying not only the talents of an accomplished orator, but the large views and comprehensive mind of a statesman; but still more commendable for a still greater excellence—that of manfully disclaiming all meretricious popularity, and courageously rebuking the excesses of those whose cause he came forward to plead." But the most remarkable tribute of all was that of Castlereagh, when we remember the ferocious collisions between him and Plunket in the Irish house. In answering Plunket's attack upon the government, he said he hoped whatever he said would be "imputed to the sincere respect which he thought due to everything which fell from so distinguished a character as the right honourable and learned gentleman, whose talents excited the highest admiration, and whose convincing speech could never be forgotten."

The house went into committee on the 9th of March, and produced, after various sittings, extending to the 20th of May, a Roman Catholic Relief Bill, which afterwards formed the basis of the Emancipation Act—hampered, however, with securities on the subject of episcopal nomination, which were exceedingly obnoxious to the Catholics of Ireland. Plunket did not speak in committee, and was obliged to return to Ireland before the final debate. This was on the 24th of May, when, on considering the bill in detail, the Speaker moved, in a speech of virulent bigotry, an amendment to the effect of excluding Catholics from parliament. After a long debate, in which Canning spoke with signal earnestness and eloquence, the committee divided, and the amendment was carried by a majority of four. Instantly on the division being declared, Mr. Ponsonby rose and said that as the bill, without this clause, was worthless to the Catholics, it would now be abandoned.

THE SPEAKER'S ADDRESS TO THE REGENT.
22nd April, 1814.

AT the close of the session of 1813, the Speaker, addressing the Prince Regent at the bar of the House of Lords, alluded to the defeat which he had been the instrument of administering to the Catholic cause in the following terms:—

"Other momentous changes have been submitted to our consideration. Adhering, however, to those laws by which the throne, the parliament, and the government of this country are made fundamentally Protestant, we have not consented to allow that those who acknowledge a foreign jurisdiction should be authorised to administer the powers and jurisdictions of this realm—willing as we are, nevertheless, and willing as I trust we shall ever be, to allow the largest scope for toleration."

This language, based upon a majority of merely four votes, naturally excited great indignation, and early in the session Lord Morpeth moved that the language of the Speaker, commenting in such a way upon a question under the consideration of parliament, should not be drawn into a precedent, and that a minute to that effect should be entered upon the journals of the house. This being virtually a vote of censure upon the Speaker, a warm debate ensued, early in which Plunket spoke:—

SIR, after the long and able arguments which we have heard on this subject, and more particularly after the ample justice which has been done to it in the eloquent and admirable speech of the honourable gentleman below me (Mr. Grant), it may appear unnecessary or presumptuous further to occupy the attention of the house. Feeling, however, as I do on this important occasion, I own I cannot reconcile myself to remaining wholly silent on it. I completely concur with you, sir, that the present question is one wholly unconnected with the question of Catholic emancipation. We are not now to consider what it may or may not be right to do with respect to this latter. We are not to ascertain the present opinion of the house upon it. The question is, whether, the house having come to a resolution with respect to the Catholics, you, sir, were authorized to convey to the throne an intimation of that proceeding, accompanied by a censure on those who had endeavoured to follow it up by a legislative measure.

Sir, I declare most solemnly, that if the sentiments which you expressed to the throne had been as friendly to the Catholic cause as they were certainly hostile to it, I should equally have concurred in the present motion. It is true, as it has been justly said, this is not a party or a personal question. Nothing, sir, but the most imperious sense of duty could justify the censure of your conduct. But if any man feels that a vital and important part of the constitution has been assailed, and that you have done that which, if it were established as a precedent, would overturn and destroy the constitution itself; and if that man should refuse to accede to the motion of the noble lord, either out of deference to you, sir, or from any unworthy exultation at the attack made by you on so large a portion of the community, no words are sufficiently strong to describe the meanness of such a dereliction of duty on the one hand, or of such an unworthy betraying of the trusts reposed in a representative of the people on the other.

Sir, I am free to say, that the speech made by you to the throne, at the close of the last session, was one of the most formidable attacks on the constitution of parliament that has occurred since the revolution. It was an attack materially aggravated by its having proceeded from a person the natural guardian of that constitution. And, sir, it is peculiarly unfortunate, that we cannot assert our own rights without impairing your dignity; however anxious we may be to abstain from everything like asperity, and to treat you, sir, with all that respect to which you are so amply entitled. Subject to this last consideration, I shall make my observations upon the question with as much freedom and latitude, and discharge my duty as unrestrainedly, as you, sir, have done, in what I have no doubt you conscientiously conceived to have been yours.

Sir, there is no subject upon which this house has always evinced so much anxious jealousy as that its proceedings should be exempt from all control and interference on the part of the crown. Some communication between the throne and parliament must undoubtedly exist; but the mode of this communication is perfectly defined and ascertained. If the throne wishes to communicate with parliament, that communication is made either by a formal speech from the throne or by a message. But the object of such communication always is to invite parliament to deliberate on some proposed measure, and never to control or interfere with any deliberations already entered into. So on the other hand, if either house wish to communicate with the throne, that communication is made either by address or by resolution; and the object of such communication is, not to ask the advice of the throne on any subject upon which parliament may be deliberating, but to give to the throne any advice that parliament may think it expedient to offer; for this plain reason, that we are the constitutional advisers of the throne, but that the throne is not the constitutional adviser of parliament. Advice from the throne would have too much the air of command, to be consistent with the freedom of discussion in this house. Beyond the limits which I have mentioned, there is no constitutional channel of communication between the throne and parliament, save when we present our bills for the royal assent or dissent. This is so clear, that it is generally acknowledged that if, sir, you had no bill to present, you would have no right to address the throne at all. Accordingly when you uttered the address which is the subject of our present deliberation, you held in your hand the vote of credit bill, and you concluded that address with praying the royal assent to the bill. Had you not held such a bill, your speech would have been an absolute intrusion, wholly unwarranted by parliamentary usage, or by the constitution.

I do not mean to say, sir, that you were under the necessity of strictly confining yourself in your address to the subject of the bill which you presented. It was perfectly allowable, that your speech should be graced and ornamented by allusions to other matters. If, sir, you had described generally the measures adopted by parliament, or had descanted on topics of general policy, however we might have considered your opinion as a mistaken one, the promulgation of it could never have been deemed a violation of our privileges. Unless you had alluded to matters pending in parliament, the observations which you had thought proper to make might have been thought light or unnecessary, but could not have been characterised as unconstitutional. This remark applies to what has been said of my right honourable friend, the late Speaker of the parliament in Ireland

(Mr. Foster). My right honourable friend did certainly make the question of Catholic emancipation and Protestant ascendancy the subject of a speech to the throne: and in doing so he had no reason to congratulate himself on his prudence; for in the very next session, his principles and his predictions were overturned all together. But this was imprudence only, and not a violation of parliamentary privilege. It has not been so considered. A solitary petition was presented to the house on the subject; but no member of the Irish parliament had made it a question of parliamentary discussion.

It is on these grounds, sir, that I perfectly concur in the propriety of the general observations contained in your speech at the close of the last session. In that style of dignified congratulation which so well becomes you, you spoke of the success of our brave fleets and armies, and conferred the just meed of your eloquent praise on their gallant leaders. I am sure, sir, that every one of us must be proud and gratified when he hears you deliver yourself on such subjects with so much elevation and propriety of manner. But when, because you are the organ of communication between this house and the throne, you proceed to notice subjects controverted in this house, you will find it difficult to discover precedents in justification of your conduct; and still further, when you mention propositions made here, and not acceded to, but rejected, you place yourself in a situation still less capable of defence. On this part of the subject, the remarks made by the honourable gentleman below me (Mr. Grant) are unanswerable. As that honourable gentleman justly observed, if a measure passes in parliament no single person is responsible for that which is an act of the whole house. But it is impossible for you, sir, to state that a proposed measure has been rejected without implying a censure on the individual or individuals by whom that proposition was made. Accordingly, our rule of proceeding with respect to bills is founded on this consideration. When a bill is sent to the other house, or is presented to the throne for the royal assent or dissent, it does not bear on the face of it whether or not it passed unanimously, or what was the amount of the majority by which it was carried. And why? Because this house will never suffer the state of its divisions and parties to be subject to the direction or to be under the influence or control of any other tribunal.

The authority of Mr. Hatsell has been dwelt upon with much emphasis. As members of the legislature, I deny that, in our decision on great constitutional questions we are to take Mr. Hatsell's publication as a text-book. We are not to be told that we must learn the principles of the British constitution from Mr. Hatsell's work,

But, after all, what is there in that work which bears on the present question? Mr. Hatsell states, and states truly, that when the Speaker presents a money bill at the foot of the throne, he may advert, not to the subject of that bill alone, but to other business which parliament may have transacted. But does he say that the Speaker may advert to pending or rejected measures? Nay, up to this very moment, after all the inquiries made by yourself, sir, so capable of deep research, and after all the inquiries made by all your numerous friends, has a single precedent been found of a Speaker's having referred in his speech to the throne to any measure which had been rejected by the house?

And let it be recollected, that the measure to which you thought proper to refer was still pending. For, what was the state of the proceedings on the Catholic question? A resolution had been agreed to, to take into consideration, in a committee of the whole house, the laws affecting the Roman Catholics, with a view to their amicable adjustment. The committee met, and resolutions were passed, declaring it expedient to admit the Catholics to seats in parliament, and to other powers and jurisdictions, under certain provisions for the security of the Protestant establishment. A bill was introduced to that effect, and the second reading agreed to by a considerable majority of the house. Everything, therefore, sir, of which you could properly take cognizance was favourable to the Catholic cause. But in the speech which you made to the throne you passed over what alone you had a right to know, and what, if communicated, would have made an impression favourable to the cause of the Catholics, and you resorted to that which you had no right to know, and by an unjustifiable perversion sought to make an impression inimical to that cause. For, sir, you were no more competent to report to the throne the proceedings of the committee of this house than any other member of the committee. It was not even necessary that you should be present in that committee. Mr. Hatsell so says. It happened, however, that you were there, and that you gave your opinion on the bill in progress. Was it as Speaker that you gave that opinion? Certainly not. You gave it as member for the University of Oxford.

But it may be said that this is a question of mere form. Sir, the forms of parliament are essential to the preservation of the privileges of parliament. But, sir, in taking the liberty to report the opinions of that committee, did you truly report them? On the contrary, you totally, though I am sure not wilfully, misrepresented them. The opposition to the proposition rejected in the committee was grounded on a variety of considerations. Some opposed it in consequence of the intemperate conduct of certain public bodies in Ireland; others because of the writings which had been diffused in that country; some wished the change to be deferred until a time of peace; others were desirous that the see of Rome should first be consulted.

With all this variety of sentiment, how, sir, were you competent to say what were the opinions by which the majority of this house on that occasion were swayed? I will venture to assert, that not ten of that majority were perfectly agreed on that subject; and yet you took upon yourself, in the name of that majority, to declare your own opinion as theirs. Nay, even in that respect you were incorrect. The member for the University of Oxford has a right to complain that the Speaker misrepresented him. That right honourable member declared, that in his opinion, many powers and jurisdictions might be safely conferred on the Catholics. He declared that they might be eligible to the magistracy—there was jurisdiction; he declared that they might be raised to any rank in the army, except that of commander-in-chief—there was power; a jurisdiction and a power by no means harmless, if improperly used. Again, a great number of those who composed the majority, voted on the ground that the question was a religious one. Have those individuals no right to complain of the Speaker, for declaring that the house considered the question not as a religious, but as a political one; and that if the see of Rome were released from foreign influence, the danger of allowing Catholics to sit in parliament would cease? Will the member for Armagh, and those who think with him, consent thus to have their opposition disrobed of all those important considerations, which arise out of religious views of the subject? Will they allow the Catholics, if they disavow the supremacy of the Pope, to come here and legislate for Protestant England? In my judgment, therefore, sir, you misrepresented the opinion of the majority of this house, as well as your own.

One striking fact you wholly abstained from mentioning. You never told the throne that, notwithstanding all the means used on the occasion, notwithstanding the temporary difficulties arising out of various causes, notwithstanding the powerful influence exercised in various quarters, there were still two hundred and forty-seven members of this house who declared their readiness to admit the Catholics into parliament on the principles of the bill which was then under discussion. Will any man lay his hand on his breast, and declare upon his honour, that he thinks you were authorized, on a decision by a majority of four, to represent to the crown, that the question was put finally at rest? Was it not evident that the subject must return to be considered by parliament? And if so brought back, with what impartiality could parliament proceed with respect to it, if, by any indirect means, the artillery of royal influence was brought to bear on their march?

Suppose, sir, that in reply to you his royal highness the Prince Regent had been pleased to say to you, " I feel great surprise and indignation that two hundred and forty-seven members of the House of Commons are so lost to a sense of their duty, as to wish to change those laws by which the throne, the parliament, and the government of the country are made fundamentally Protestant;" would any member of that minority have endured such an expression? On the other hand, suppose his royal highness had said, " I lament that the laborious exertions of so large a number of members of the House of Commons as two hundred and forty-seven have been disappointed; and I trust when temporary obstacles are removed, and when the suggestions of reason and wisdom become prevalent, their efforts will prove successful;" would such a declaration have been endured by any member of the majority? Would it not have been asked, what right the throne possessed to interfere with the proceedings of parliament, to school their past conduct, and to lecture their future?

And here, sir, I must observe, that an honourable gentleman on the floor (Mr. Bankes) has contended that there is no difficulty in this question, because your speech was not made until the end of the session. It is then of no importance if we subject ourselves to be schooled and lectured by the throne; it is of no importance that we should be liable to this annual audit and account, provided it take place at the close of our sittings! Such an occurrence would have no affect on the deliberations of the next session! And, besides, if this annual audit were once established, the honourable member for Corfe-Castle is too fond of accuracy not to think it necessary, sir, to add to your report a specification of the numbers of those who might vote on any particular measure, the names of the voters, and so on, until the whole of our mystery is exposed to the eye of royalty!

With respect to your speech, sir, I have another observation to make; it regards its ambiguity. The words of it are capable of two opposite constructions—of a construction unwarrantable, intolerant towards the Catholics, and of a construction as tolerant as their warmest friends could desire. You say, sir, that we have determined to exclude them from the privileges which they require " as long as they shall obey a foreign jurisdiction." Now, what does this expression mean? If by "foreign jurisdiction" is meant the spiritual jurisdiction of the Pope, then the Catholics will be excluded as long as they remain Catholics. But if it merely means temporal, or indeed ecclesiastical jurisdiction within the realm, then no friend of the Catholic cause in this house would, I am sure, wish it to prosper on any other terms. Again, sir, you say in your speech that parliament have not consented to do so and so. I am persuaded that no special pleading will be resorted to in defence of this passage, and I appeal to the common sense of all who hear me, whether the statement that "momentous changes had been proposed for our consideration, but that adhering to those laws by which the throne, the parliament, and the government of this country are made fundamentally Protestant, we would not consent to those changes." Is it not a distinct implication of an intention in some persons, by proposing such changes, to destroy "the laws by which the throne, the parliament, and the government of this country are made fundamentally Protestant?" Sir, recollecting that one of the essential features of the resolutions on which the Catholic bill was founded was, the distinct declaration that the Protestant establishment should be effectually secured, I ask you, how you can reconcile to any feelings of justice the implied statement that two hundred and forty-seven members of this house were anxious to introduce changes subversive of that establishment? For one, I loudly disclaim my share of such an imputation. If there be here one man of that number who deserves it, let him take the only opportunity of proving his demerit, by voting for your exculpation. Sir, it is a proposition which every honourable gentleman present would not merely not consent to, but which he would reject with scorn and indignation.

One word more. This speech, which in my opinion was a violation of the privileges of parliament, and which misrepresented the conduct and sentiments of all parties, appears to me to have been wholly uncalled for. There was nothing, sir, in the bill which you held in your hand at the time you uttered it, or in any other bill which passed during the last session, that required such an exposition. When you adverted to the splendid victories of our illustrious commander who has gained such transcendant fame—when you spoke of the passage of the Douro, of the battles of Roleia, of Vimiera, of Talavera, of Salamanca, of Vittoria, the feelings of all who heard you vibrated in unison with your own. Every heart exulted; and every Irish heart peculiarly exulted that Ireland had given birth to such a hero. Was that a well-chosen moment, sir, to pronounce the irrevocable doom of those who, under their immortal commander, had opened the sluices of their heart's blood in the service of the empire? It was the custom in Rome to introduce a slave into their triumphal processions, not for the purpose of insulting the captive, but to remind the conqueror of the instability of human glory. But you, sir, while you were binding the wreath round the brow of the conqueror, assured him that his victorious followers must never expect to participate in the fruits of his valour, but that they who had shed their blood in achieving conquests were to be the only persons who were not to share by the profits of success in the rights of citizens.

THE WAR OF 1815.
May 25, 1815.

IMMEDIATELY after Napoleon's escape from Elba, the Prince Regent communicated to parliament by a message that he had resumed action with the allies, to redress the violation of the treaty of Paris. A large section of the Whigs, affected by the universal enthusiasm with which Napoleon had been received in France, were averse to a war that had merely for its purpose the proscription of one man, and he the favourite ruler of a powerful and warlike people. Accordingly, an amendment was moved to the address, expressly condemning the principle and policy of a war undertaken for the purpose " of personally proscribing the present ruler of France." Grattan led the debate, and his voice was still for war, in a speech the most celebrated of all his efforts in the British house, and which stirred England and Europe with the tones of a tocsin. It is curious to observe in this debate, decisive of the destinies of the world as it was, that the great voices are all Irish—Grattan, Plunket, Ponsonby, and Castlereagh. Plunket's speech is spoken of in contemporary accounts as an amazing effort; but it appears to be clumsily condensed in the reports, with the exception of the concluding passages, which I print in the first person:—

MR. PLUNKET thought that the house was now, for the first time, called upon to give an opinion of the policy of peace or war, under the present circumstances of the country and of Europe. This was a question of the utmost importance, at all times, and under all circumstances. It was important as it involved the fate of many human beings, who must be sacrificed in war: it was still more important, as it involved the fate of this country, and the other nations of Europe. He was ready to admit that, to which ever side we turned, we were encountered by dangers; and that we were so surrounded with evils, that nothing was left us but a choice of evils. He should consider that man as precipitate in his judgment, and a very rash counsellor, who would pretend, at present, to foretell either the duration or the issue of this war. He would have as little confidence in the judgment of any person who would say, that he considered that a peace negociated with Bonaparte would afford sufficient security to the country.

He should have been well contented to have given a silent vote on the present occasion, if he had not found himself under the necessity of differing from those friends whom he so highly respected, with whom he had so long acted, and with whom he hoped long to act. Differing, however, so materially from them upon this question, he felt it necessary for his own justification, to explain to the house the grounds of his difference. In rising to answer the arguments of his right honourable friend who spoke last, he felt some consolation in being protected by the paramount ability of another right honourable friend who sat near him (Mr. Grattan). It appeared to him that his right honourable friend who spoke last was completely mistaken, when he conceived that the house was now called upon to give its sanction to all the stipulations of the treaty negotiated at the congress of Vienna. The house was not called upon for any such opinion. He could see no absurdity or impropriety in calling upon the house to sanction one part of a treaty, without calling for their opinion on all the points of it. Even if he were to admit the force of all the objections which had been made to other parts of the arrangements made at the congress of Vienna, he should still be most decidedly of opinion on the question now before the house, that we ought, in conjunction with our allies, to prosecute the war against Bonaparte. He really wished to hear the sincere opinion of the right honourable gentleman and his friend, as to what conduct the country ought to pursue under the present circumstances. Would any man say that we ought to make peace with Bonaparte, and war with our allies? or would they say, that we should altogether desert our allies? It had been said, that we ought to negotiate with Bonaparte in concert with our allies. If it were then admitted, that we ought to negotiate in concert with our allies, it must also be allowed, that if those negotiations were not successful, we must go to war with France in concert with those allies. How, then, was it possible to separate the cause of this country from that of the allies, even upon the supposition of trying negotiation instead of war?

He did not believe that any of those who recommended negotiations with Bonaparte would deny that those negotiations might be unsuccessful; and if they were carried on in concert with our allies, we could no more desert them in war than in the negotiation. He was really at a loss to perceive how the argument on the present occasion could be at all helped, by finding faults in the conduct of the allies upon former occasions. The faithlessness of those powers (if they had been faithless) did not apply to the present question. If it was Austria and Prussia that were preparing an attack upon this country, then we might talk about their faithlessness on former occasions. It was, however, from France and the faithlessness of her government that danger to this country was apprehended. What answer was it to this apprehension, to say that other powers had been faithless too? Such an answer had evidently nothing to do with the question now before the house. As long as France chose to submit to the government of Bonaparte, he could see that neither honour, nor peace, nor anything that was desirable for this country could be expected by entering into a negotiation with him.

Sir, as to the right of interfering with the internal affairs of another country, I must admit, that so long as those internal arrangements do not menace the peace and security of other countries, there can be no right to interfere; but when the internal arrangements of one country do plainly threaten the peace and security of others, it appears to me as clear as the light, that interference is justifiable. If it be asked, whether anything in the personal character of a ruler can justify other nations in not treating with him, I will answer by stating a supposed case. Suppose, then, that any nation should, in time of peace, put itself into an extraordinary state of preparation for war—if that nation should organize itself in such a manner as to be perpetually prepared for commencing offensive war—if that nation should embody itself under the command of a military chief of great talent and experience in the art of war—if, for 15 years, Europe had experienced that the efforts of that nation were uniformly directed to aggression, conquest, and spoliation—if Europe had been obliged in self-defence to carry its arms into the heart of that country—if the capital of that country were taken—if the conquerors in their magnanimity and moderation offered a peace which was accepted with gratitude—if that treaty was accepted with gratitude by the individual who abdicated the throne—and yet if, after ten months, that guilty individual should be recalled by a licentious soldiery, for the purpose of fresh aggression—am I then to be told in this house, that neither we nor the other nations of Europe have any right of interference with the internal arrangements of such a nation? How does it happen that the just and legitimate sovereign of France has been driven from his throne? It is because his unambitious virtue made him appear to the soldiery, not to be a proper instrument to wield the unsocial and unnatural energies of the French empire. If it be said that personal character has nothing to do with the question, then I ask, why was the treaty of Paris ever entered into? That treaty turned entirely on personal character, and stipulations were considered satisfactory when made with the lawful sovereign of France, that would never have been entered into with Bonaparte. If we are to take the common feeling of mankind upon this subject, we must recollect how universally the abdication of Bonaparte was hailed in this country, as an event more important than the most brilliant victories. But the question now is not merely with Bonaparte, it is with France. She has purchased the benefits of the treaty of Paris, by giving up Bonaparte, and taking her lawful sovereign, in whom Europe has confidence. If we are now to declare that we are ready to treat with Bonaparte, it will at once put an end to the coalition. If we are to tell the French people that we are ready to negotiate with Bonaparte as their ruler, it will at once destroy all the hopes that might now fairly be entertained of the co-operation of a considerable portion of that nation. When, however, we see the situation in which Bonaparte now stands; when we see him reduced to make professions contrary to his very nature; when we see the vessel in which his fortunes are embarked labouring with the storm, and its mast bowed down to the water's edge, it would be the height of impolicy and absurdity to hesitate on the course that we ought to pursue. We have now a most powerful combination of allies, not fomented by us, but acting from the moral feeling which pervades all Europe. If we are foolish enough to throw away those means, we can never hope to recall them. Such of my friends as have talked the most about husbanding the resources of the country, have confessed that when an occasion should arrive, when some important blow might be struck against the enemy, that system should no longer be persevered in. The important crisis has now arrived. It is vain to expect that a more favourable opportunity will ever arise. All the great powers of Europe are now with us, and a considerable portion of the population of France.

It has been said, that invading France would be the way to unite the population of that country. The fact, however, is directly the reverse. The not invading France would be the sure means of reducing the whole population under the power of the present ruler. I consider that we have, in fact, no option between peace and war. As for peace, we can have no more than a feverish, unrefreshing dream of peace, still haunted by the spectre of war. 'In point of finances, we would find a peace with a war establishment, an evil much greater than war itself. If we do not now go to war in conjunction with all the great powers of Europe, we shall soon be reduced to a war single-handed against France. If we do not now invade France, and carry on the war upon her territories, the time may arrive when our country will become the seat of war, and we shall fall unpitied and despised. If we now turn our back upon the great powers that are our allies, we shall deserve that all nations should turn their backs upon us, when we begin to feel the consequences of our impolicy.

THE NAVY ESTIMATES.
March 27, 1816.

INSTANTLY upon the declaration of peace, economy and retrenchment became the cry of all the country—a cry which Castlereagh, who professed a profound contempt for "the ignorant impatience of taxation" which prevailed, was not disposed to gratify too abruptly. Such retrenchments as he did allow were, as the opposition complained, in many cases made rather with a reference to personal than to public interests. About forty millions of taxes were abated. In almost all the departments salaries and allowances were reduced by regular rule from a war to a peace standard.; but in the admiralty, where Castlereagh's *protegè* and Plunket's opponent, Croker, was secretary, a special order decreed that the war salaries should be continued. This order produced several angry debates, in which the inconsistency of Castlereagh's economy was exposed by Brougham, Tierney, Methuen, Ponsonby, Cavendish, and defended with a continual shifting of his ground by Castlereagh himself and by Croker. Plunket's speech reminds us of his old harangues against Castlereagh in the Irish house :

Mr. PLUNKET, in rising to address the committee, was too well aware of the lateness of the hour, to encroach at any length on their time. At the same time he felt it would be doing injustice to his own feelings, to the interests of his constituents, and the sacred rights of British subjects, not to express the sentiments he entertained on the line of conduct adopted by administration. Before proceeding further, he would beg leave to ask, whether the salaries of the secretaries of the admiralty were to be regulated by the difference between a state of peace and war? or, in other words, whether the salary of Mr. Croker was to be reduced to £3000 in peace?

[This question being answered in the affirmative, the honourable and learned member proceeded.]

He was gratified to learn that this distinction had at last been reluctantly acceded to by his majesty's ministers. The line of conduct adopted by the noble lord, was one of the most extraordinary that the House of Commons or the British nation had ever witnessed in any minister of the crown. On a former occasion when that distinction had been pressed in a forcible manner on the attention of the house by an honourable member (Mr. Methuen), the noble lord had decidedly given his negative to it: and yet now, with an inconsistency which must strike even the most careless observer, he gave it his support.

I call on the noble lord, I call on his honourable colleagues in office, I call on the gentlemen who usually support his measures, to say, if in that line of conduct there has been the least justice or fairness. I call on country gentlemen on the opposite side of the house to lay their hands on their hearts, dispassionately to weigh every circumstance which has characterized the proceedings of the noble lord, and to ask themselves how they can, consistently with a regard to conscience, face their constituents and say they have honestly done their duty? I do not impute to the noble lord any unworthy motives. I cannot for one moment suppose that he is actuated by any desire of degrading this house in the eyes of the world. I trust in God there will never be a public functionary in Britain capable of such conduct. But when I consider the procedure of the noble lord—when I contemplate the inconsistency which has characterised him throughout, I must appeal to the feelings of every honest man in this house, whether there is not an evident design to oppose whatever is proposed on this side of the house, without the smallest regard to whether the measure proposed by us be right or wrong? The honourable member for Wiltshire one day proposes a measure which the noble lord reprobates as improper, and yet next day he comes down to the house and adopts the very measure he had reprobated. Sir, it is high time for gentlemen accustomed to follow in the noble lord's train to think whether, in consistency with their own credit as British senators, with their fidelity to their constituents, and, I will add, with their dignity as men, they can any longer be so blinded by prejudice as to become the tools of the noble lord. For, I will ask, how does the noble lord use them? He gives them the odium of supporting measures which he afterwards takes to himself the grace of retracting. Sir, I regret to be under the necessity of saying so much, but I feel it to be my duty, and should certainly consider myself guilty of an omission of duty had I not so spoken. I do not believe, indeed it is impossible for me to believe, that gentlemen wish to degrade the House of Commons, but how can they vote in consistency with their own character, if they for one moment consider the tactics of the noble lord. The resolution for economy is now agreed to. This is so far very well; but why was it not agreed to before? The answer is obvious. It was for the best of all possible reasons—because the noble lord and his colleagues would not suffer so dangerous a term as the word economy to be registered on the journals of this house.

In a very fine pompous manner the committee are told of the difference between the last year of war and the first year of peace. No doubt, sir, the expenses of the first year of peace must be admitted to equal those of the last year of war. But there are elements for retrenchment which a minister alive to the interests of his country might lay hold of. These have in a satisfactory manner been pointed out by my right honourable friend (Mr. Tierney), who, in a manner that must flash conviction on every mind, has, item by item, showed that instead of being lessened they have been increased. No symptoms whatever of a voluntary nature have been shown by government for any retrenchment. Government now stand in the situation of men on their trial. Clamour, an ignorant impatience for relaxation from taxation, and a thousand similar motives has been applied to the people for expressing their detestation of the policy of ministers. But I call on gentlemen in this house, whose minds are unfettered by prejudice, I call on them in conscience to say whether they can believe ministers had ever one serious thought of retrenchment, had it not been for this clamour, this "ignorant impatience." I tell the noble lord that that clamour has compelled him to do his duty so far, and may perhaps, if he does not take care, clamour him out of office.

A very nice distinction has been made between clamour out of doors and clamour within doors. Sir, what does this mean? Why, it means simply this. Had the members who presented petitions—or rather the remonstrances of "ignorant impatience"—to the house, ushered them quietly, with all that suavity and smoothness so happily practised on the opposite side, there would have been no clamour. But because they did, in a manly constitutional manner, scorn to abandon their duty—because they introduced the clamours of the people, excited by the dereliction of the ministers from their fidelity—because they have made these walls to re-echo with their determined opposition to the attempts made to press down a people already worn out, they are charged by the noble lord with making a clamour. The people have, however, assembled and asserted their rights; they have expressed their abhorrence of a most detestable, unjust, and inquisitorial tax; they have declared their indignation at the attempt of the government to cover the soil of the country with armies; in a word, they have called loudly and unanimously for retrenchment and economy; and the members of this house will grossly abandon their duty, if they do not attend to the voices of their constituents. This may be clamour in the opinion of the noble lord, but let the country gentlemen remember, that it is in consequence of these sentiments re-echoed through the country, that anything has been obtained. The people have put their representatives on their trial, and the house has been electrified. The noble lord and his colleagues are doubtless alarmed at these proceedings; but there is a general cry for retrenchment and economy which cannot be put down. The noble lord may attempt it, but the result of his experiment will be, that the voice of the people will only be raised more loudly, and they may very soon put down him and his colleagues.

THE STATE OF IRELAND.
April 26, 1816.

SIR JOHN NEWPORT, in one of the ablest speeches ever delivered upon Ireland in the House of Commons, called upon the government to change their coercive policy. 25,000 men were quartered upon the country, and six counties proclaimed under an insurrection act of atrocious rigour. Peel was then chief secretary, and believed in no remedy for Irish ills but the bayonet and gibbet. He replied to Newport, and was followed by Plunket:—

MR. PLUNKET began by expressing his warmest gratitude to his right honourable friend, for calling the attention of the house to this most important subject, and for the peculiarly able manner in which he had sustained the motion. The state of Ireland was indeed a question in which Great Britain must feel a direct and immediate interest, and therefore it claimed, as no doubt it would receive, the fullest consideration in that house. To illustrate that interest, and enforce that claim, he could not think it necessary to add much to the impressive speech of his right honourable friend. For that speech presented the most valuable variety of local, political, and constitutional knowledge. It was indeed so distinguished for accuracy of information, that he should have to occupy the attention of the house but for a short time. He particularly applauded his right honourable friend's speech in consequence of its complete freedom from any alloy of party spirit. The question was indeed too important to b   into any mixture with party or faction. Last year the insurrection act was passed, and though he was not present, he had no hesitation in saying, that if he had been so, he would have supported the measure, although it did go the length of suspending the enjoyment of the constitution during the period in which it remained in force. In the year 1796, and on other occasions, similar acts had been passed, but they were seldom enforced. It was now two months, however, since the right honourable gentleman who was the author of this measure last session, had mentioned to the house the necessity of carrying it into execution. The county of Tipperary, and that of Westmeath, were disturbed, and the country was in such a state as to render a military force of 25,000 men necessary for suppressing the spirit of revolt and tumult. Soon afterwards two other counties were added to this mass of confusion and disorder, and now there were no fewer than six declared in a state of disturbance. The military force was increased, but the evils were not diminished; tumult and disorder were rather augmented than suppressed; and he would tell the right honourable gentleman, that if matters did not soon change, 40,000 men would be found insufficient to perform the duty for which 25,000 were now deemed adequate. This was such an alarming state of things, that it could receive no aggravation from fancy—could admit of no additional colouring from fear or apprehension. It pressed upon the house with a weight of interest which no consideration could increase. The natives of Ireland were celebrated for their gratitude for benefits conferred—their fine and ardent feelings were almost proverbial—nor could slight injuries rouse them to revenge. The present deplorable state of that country showed, therefore indisputably, that some intrinsic vice was in the government, which must be removed before tranquillity was restored.

He did not find that the right honourable gentleman professed to apply any remedies to those evils which he admitted to exist; and, in truth, if certain doctrines which he had advanced were to be considered as the sort of remedy which the right honourable gentleman might feel disposed to apply, he most cordially and most sincerely thanked him that he had abstained from the application. The two remedies of the right honourable gentleman, if he might venture to call them such, were referable, first to absentees, and secondly to forty shilling freeholders. With respect to the absentees, he wished with all his heart they were fewer; he wished for the sake of Ireland, that she possessed a more numerous resident gentry. But how was that to be accomplished? The right honourable gentleman had suggested no means, but seemed to trust merely to the powers of persuasion. He did not wish to underrate the right honourable gentleman's eloquence, though he was certainly afraid it would not be found an instrument sufficiently powerful to induce the gentry of Ireland to reside on their estates. If the right honourable gentleman meant to go further than persuasion—if he contemplated the idea of legislative interference—then he would say to him, repeal the Union, send back again to Ireland her parliament, restore that portion of rank and property and influence which she possessed before, and which had been drawn from her by the inevitable operation of that measure. If the right honourable gentleman was prepared to go so far, then, indeed, he would admit that his observations were a proper forerunner of his intentions; but, otherwise, situated as Ireland now was, the question of absentees was one which no wise statesman would venture to touch. As to any connexion that might be supposed to subsist between the present disturbances in Ireland, and the effects produced by absentee gentry, he would venture to say that in those districts where outrage was most prevalent the grievance of the absentees was least felt.

The next topic to which he wished to refer, was that of the forty shilling franchises. He was not quite sure whether he accurately comprehended what fell from the right honourable gentleman, and he was most anxious to avoid anything which might be construed into misrepresentation. The right honourable gentleman would set him right if he erred; but he understood him to speak of the act of 1793, as that act by which the elective franchise was originally granted.

Mr. Peel rose to explain. He said he mentioned the act of 1793, not as having originally granted the elective franchise, but as having extended its privileges to the Catholics.

Mr. Plunket continued. The act of 1793, then, was alluded to by the right honourable gentleman, merely as having extended those privileges which had previously been enjoyed by the Protestants of Ireland, to the Catholics of Ireland. Taking the argument upon that ground, he was prepared to contend, that if that act were repealed, it would be disfranchising the Catholics. He would say further, that if the right honourable gentleman had studiously contrived a firebrand calculated to precipitate into immediate explosion the combustibles now scattered all over Ireland—if he had laboured night and day to discover what means were most likely to consummate the mischief—he could not have hit upon a more certain one than to propose to disfranchise the Irish Catholics.

Mr. Peel rose to explain. He said he was sorry to interrupt the right honourable and learned gentleman again, but he was tempted to avail himself of his candid offer, and that desire which he had manifested not to misinterpret him. In speaking of the act of 1793, he expressly said that he did not complain of it because it extended the elective franchise to the Catholics. What he complained of was, the great abuses to which that act had been perverted. The way in which the Catholic freeholders acquired their right presented opportunities for the grossest perjury. It had never entered into his contemplation to withdraw those franchises, but he lamented the way in which those fictitious franchises were created.

Mr. PLUNKET said, he was most happy at being set right, though he believed he had erred in common with a great number of persons as to what had fallen from the right honourable gentleman. He should now proceed to the consideration of the question generally, and he must say, it struck him as somewhat extraordinary, that the government did not seem prepared to propose any specific remedies for the many evils, the existence of which no one denied. He would except, indeed, what had fallen from the right honourable gentleman upon the nomination of the sheriffs. For that he was entitled to much approbation, for he was sure it would be productive of infinite good to Ireland; but if he imagined it was calculated, alone, to allay the ferments that now existed, he had much mistaken the real influence and operation of that system. The only thing upon which the right honourable gentleman seemed to rely as an effectual method of remedying the grievances felt in Ireland, was the diffusion of education; and he hoped he should not be considered as undervaluing the importance of education in what he was about to say. The most beneficial effect of education, in his opinion, was, that it brought the lower and the higher classes into connexion by acts of beneficence and kindness. But if, by education, the right honourable gentleman meant merely that the Irish should be instructed in reading, writing, and accounts, he really believed it would be found that the people of Ireland were no more deficient in those things than the people of this country. Nay, if a distinction were taken between the two countries, he believed it would be in favour of Ireland. In those public bodies of men, where the inhabitants of the two countries were brought together, as the army, for instance, he would venture to say that the number of Irishmen who could read and write, was greater in proportion than the number of Englishmen. But really, to talk of carrying on the education of a people, by teaching them to read and write merely, was a gross and childish misapplication of the word. The education of a people must grow out of the government of the country. It must spring from that paternal care, and from that equal protection of the laws which insensibly formed the habits of the citizen to a peaceable and correct demeanor. What was it that made every man in England interested in the preservation of public order, tranquillity, and obedience to the laws? Because every man in England knew that the law was his friend and his protector: he cherished it as his birthright, and he regarded those who administered it, as labouring with himself for the general good of the commonwealth. Give that education to Ireland, and Ireland would receive it as a boon. Teach the people how to respect the laws, and they would be taught how to be happy But where was the utility of teaching them reading and figures? To count property which they did not possess, and to read about that liberty which they did not enjoy?

With respect to the motion of his right honourable friend, he protested he could not comprehend why it should be frittered down in the way which was proposed by the amendment. What reasons had been urged to show the probability that less than 25,000 men would be wanted for Ireland next year? And if 25,000 men were then wanted, why not forty, nay, a hundred thousand, hereafter? The evils which afflicted Ireland, whatever they were, would not remain stationary. They must be put down, or they would progressively increase. If, then, it was intended to maintain a force of 25,000 men permanently in Ireland; and if the insurrection act was to be continued; if the people of that country were to be subjected to domiciliary visits in the night, to be liable to be imprisoned, and even transported, not by the verdict of a jury, but by summary commitment: if all these terrible miseries were to be inflicted by the aid of the bayonet, he would say that that house would neglect—would grossly abandon—its duty, if they refused to inquire why such things were necessary, and how they might be avoided. Where was the use of knowing the extent of the mischief, if they were to be precluded from examining into the causes? The reason why it was wished to have information upon the one was, that they might afterwards inquire into the other. He would willingly admit that he must be a bold man who would pretend to affirm that he knew what remedies would effectually remove the evils now existing; but he would be a much bolder man who should presume to leave the country under the hopeless curse of those measures which had so long afflicted and degraded it. Exile and death were not the instruments of government; but the miserable expedients which showed the absence of all government. The sources of public authority were dried up; and that house ought to rescue the people of Ireland from such a desperate state of outlawry and degradation.

The state of Ireland was a sort of gordon knot which they could not untie, and refused the aid of parliament, whose duty it was to interpose in behalf of a suffering people. His right honourable friend had prudently abstained from discussing the question of Catholic emancipation, and he would follow his example; but at the same time, when they were called upon to decide so important a subject as the present, he would not be deterred by the fear of having one vote less, or the hope of one vote more, from expressing his opinion. He would not say that Catholic emancipation was a charm which would allay every discontent and remove every grievance; but he would say that it was a *sine quâ non*, and that without it no other system of measures could be entirely prosperous.

He would now take the liberty of pointing out a few of those causes which, he conceived, had contributed to place Ireland in her present unfortunate condition. He declared that he felt no personal animosities towards any member of the Irish government; on the contrary, for the lord lieutenant, and for his noble friend at the head of the law department, he entertained the highest respect. In the first place, it was but too well known that there were a number of discontented agitators in that country, who sought every means of disturbing its tranquillity. But it was equally true that there was a great proportion of the Catholic population as different in their principles and conduct from those unprincipled agitators as if they were not of the same class. Those persons cherished legitimate and honourable objects of ambition, and earnestly desired to be admitted within the pale of the constitution; but he would put it to the candour and sincerity of the right honourable gentleman, whether the government of Ireland had ever attempted to separate the sound from the unsound portion of the Catholic body? He could not say that such an attempt had ever been made; and that, he firmly believed, was one cause of the present infuriated and inflamed state of the country.

The state of the press in Ireland had been referred to, and no man could deny that it was most licentious, having been made the instrument of wild demagogues to advance their own projects of ambition. But was this all? Had it not been also most unjustifiably employed on the other side? Had not those papers which were paid highly for the insertion of government proclamations, been made the vehicles of the most scandalous, malignant, and indiscriminate libels upon the whole Catholic body? Was this dealing fairly by the people of Ireland, distracted by political and religious differences? He did not accuse the government of encouraging these disgraceful practices, but he complained that it had not interfered to control them. The Orange societies were another source of the present evils, and in speaking of them the right honourable gentleman, without his usual candour, had perverted, in his absence, the argument of his right honourable friend. The objection to them was, not that they celebrated anniversaries, or that they played particular tunes, but that they were societies exclusively Protestant, bound by an illegal oath to continue their allegiance only so long as the king supported what they termed a Protestant constitution. What steps would not the right honourable gentleman have thought it right to take, had Catholics been so illegally united for the purpose of supporting only a Catholic sovereign? It was no answer to state that the Orange societies would be punished when their acts were illegal, for their very constitution was a breach of the law, for which they were amenable. It might be true that the evil was less among the higher classes; but among the lower these associations of Protestants degenerated into the most brutal and offensive assertion of superiority over the whole Catholic body. Another point likewise deserved notice. It would not be denied, that of all people the Irish were most subject to the influence of their priesthood, and the first act of a prudent government would have been to establish with that priesthood an amicable connexion; yet no attempt of the kind had been made; on the contrary, in the only instance that had occurred, they had given, as it were, designed offence to that very respectable body. A priest of the county of Limerick had been instrumental in quelling a disturbance, for which a letter of thanks from the right honourable gentleman was sent to him; but, before it could reach his hands, it was published in the newspapers, and this reverend gentleman was thus held up to the suspicion of all his fraternity and his flock as a person aiding the tyrannical purposes of government. There were many important differences between the present and former disturbances. From the highest authority it had been stated, that within the last fifty years the commerce of Ireland had doubled, her agricultural produce had increased fourfold, and her population had trebled. Thus it appeared that she was capable of becoming the dangerous rival, or the powerful friend, of England; a gigantic form was rising at the side of Great Britain, and the question now was, whether it should be converted into a friend or an enemy. Sixteen years had elapsed since the union had professed to give to Ireland the benefits of the British constitution; yet now that constitution was to be suspended, and the natives of that country were to be deprived of its benefits. What would be thought of a proposition of the like kind with respect to any portion of Great Britain, however small? And yet upon the whole of Ireland this calamity was to be inflicted almost without repugnance. Such a state of things —such gross injustice and inequality—could not be endured with patience; and the longer the system was pursued, the greater would be the evil to be remedied. It was erroneous, too, in point of expenditure. The whole military force must be paid by this country, for Ireland could not produce any revenue, in consequence of the miscalculation at the time of the union as to the contribution she was to provide. Her debt, since the year 1800, had increased fourfold, no part of which was expended in the country, as was the case in England. On the whole view of the case, the only advice he would take upon himself to give ministers was, that they should retrace as exactly as possible the steps they had pursued in the government of Ireland; instead of establishing themselves on the narrow, odious principle of Protestant exclusion, which kept alive the spirit of dissension, he earnestly recommended them to adopt measures calculated to secure the union and happiness of all classes.

THE WINDOW TAX.

April 21, 1818.

MR. SHAW (afterwards Sir Robert) was an uncompromising anti-Unionist, and, continuing to represent Dublin in the British parliament, acted with the small party—Grattan, Plunket, Ponsonby, Newport, and their friends, who worked together in an Irish spirit on Irish questions. Sir Robert had neither the statesmanlike conceptions nor the natural eloquence of his friends; but his clear common sense, his skill in business, and the independent probity of his character did them service and honour. The great event of his parliamentary career was the abatement of that uncomfortable and oppressive impost, the window tax. It had been imposed upon Ireland in the last days of the Irish parliament professedly as a war tax, and with a pledge of its removal whenever peace came to pass. Peace came; but although at one stroke fourteen millions of property tax were taken off the people of England, the Chancellor of the Exchequer manifested very little disposition to decrease the burdens of Ireland. The case for reference to a committee, with a view to the repeal of the tax, was stated with care, moderation, and point by Mr. Shaw, and Plunket rose to support him, after the Chancellor had replied on the part of the government:—

MR. PLUNKET regretted that the motion of his honourable friend, introduced as it was with so much candour, moderation, and propriety, had not been acceded to by the right honourable gentleman. In the course of his speech, the right honourable gentleman had expressed the utmost desire to grant every relief in his power to the people of Ireland; but the line of conduct he had pursued was by no means an exemplification of such a disposition. To prove that this was not a war tax, the right honourable gentleman had referred to observations made by the Irish chancellor of the exchequer. He begged leave, in addition to this, to refer the right honourable gentleman to the language of the acts of parliament themselves. The right honourable gentleman would there see clear, direct, and specific evidence, that the tax was only intended as a war tax. It was first introduced in 1799, and the house would find, by the 40th of the King, cap. 4, that the tax was granted for the purpose of keeping up an effective force of 49,973 men—that was for the express purpose of maintaining a war establishment. It was recited, in the body of the act, that the tax was laid on for this purpose, and for no other. If it were not then a war tax—completely incapable of being explained away —he was utterly at a loss to know what a war tax was. In the same session the act of the 40th of the king, c. 52, was passed. By this act, certain regulations were introduced, "for the better collecting rates and taxes on dwelling-houses inhabited, in respect of windows and lights therein, and to prevent frauds—be it enacted, that those houses built before the 1st of January, 1799, shall be rated, according to the windows they then had, for three years from and after the passing of the said act, provided the present war shall so long continue." Now it did surprise him, how the right honourable gentleman, whose acute mind could not have suffered this act of parliament to have passed unnoticed, could, after a reference to it, have had any doubt on the subject of the nature of the tax. But, if he still retained a doubt, he hoped it would not extend beyond the precincts of his own mind, and that the house would agree in opinion, that the tax was clearly a war tax. If, then, it was a war tax, he would proceed to examine the ground on which the right honourable gentleman refused to put an end to it, when an end had been put to the war. He stated, that at the peace of Amiens, the chancellor of the exchequer, Mr. Corry, who had proposed the tax, did not think it right to move for a repeal of it. Now, it did not appear to him to be a fair inference, because a chancellor of the exchequer was not in the greatest hurry—did not seize the earliest opportunity—to remove the burdens of the people, that therefore no pledge for their removal had been given. In the short period during which peace then prevailed, it was not surprising, perhaps, that the tax was not taken off. But the people having suffered injustice for a certain period of time, did not furnish a good argument for refusing to do them justice, when their eyes were opened and they applied for redress. The right honourable gentleman said, it would be a breach of faith with the public creditor, if it were repealed, when it was pledged as a security for a part of the charge on the consolidated fund. The right honourable gentleman had, he conceived, supplied him with an answer to this argument. He was himself ready to give up 25 per cent. of this tax. He was willing to break one-fourth of his good faith with the public creditor. In point of principle, he here gave up his whole argument : he left it without support.

He (Mr. P.) would wish to keep faith inviolate with the public creditors. Some other tax must be found to pay them ; but it was for the right honourable gentleman to devise a tax for that purpose, and not for his honourable friend, who made the present motion, to supply him with ways and means. He protested, the more he considered the admissions contained in the right honourable gentleman's statement, the more he was surprised at his opposing the proposition for a committee, since a committee was the proper place to consider what modifications ought to be made in the tax. He should now shortly advert to the produce of the tax. In 1810, it produced £173,509. An additional duty of 50 per cent. was then laid on ; which, supposing the same number of windows continued to be used, ought to have produced £347,018. An additional duty of 25 per cent. was afterwards imposed, which, on the last-mentioned sum, should have given £86,750. The whole amount of the tax, then, according to his calculation, supposing the entire number of windows to have been used, which were taxed in 1810, would be £427,277. Now what was the fact ? In the last year, it amounted to £302,014, which left a deficit nearer to one-third than one quarter of the estimated produce of the tax. If this were the fact, it was not difficult to discover the quantity of windows stopped up, and the measure of light and air of which the people of Ireland had been deprived. The right honourable gentleman said that Ireland had not paid her fair contribution to the exigencies of the empire. This was a position to which he could not accede. Ireland certainly had not paid the 2-17ths stipulated for at the time of the Union ; and for the plainest of all possible reasons, because she could not—because a burden utterly disproportioned to her strength had been imposed on her. What had been her exertions ? The sum now paid into the treasury was three times the amount of her nett income at the time of the Union, and, notwithstanding this, the debt of Ireland had increased nearly fivefold since that event. Was not this a proof that, at the time of the Union, a mistaken estimate had been made of her powers? The statement sounded very well at the time. It was gratifying to the people of this country to be told—"You are very much in debt, it is true—but Ireland is to pay a considerable portion of it." They were now, however, dealing with sober realities. Ireland would not, for she could not pay it. On this country it must fall. Ireland could not exert herself beyond her strength—she could not pay beyond her means. Every part of the empire ought to support the state, and contribute to its exigencies, according to the extent of its ability. He hoped he should not be looked on as an individual, who, in his place in that house, would advise any portion of the people to shrink from bearing their fair share of the public burdens; but resources could not be wrung from an exhausted population. This tax was utterly odious and hateful in Ireland. It was, therefore, the duty of the right honourable gentleman to find some means of filling up any deficiency which its repeal might create, and to bow to the generally-expressed sense of the country. Those who called for the repeal, stood on the ground of the faith of parliament, and on the principle that a war tax should not be continued in time of peace. War taxes to the amount of £17,000,000 were remitted to the people of this country, while a trifling relief of £200,000 or £300,000 was alone granted to Ireland.

The right honourable gentleman had stated, in his place, that it was most important to continue the income tax; he had declared that the business of the country could not be carried on without it. But the house thought it was just and proper that it should be removed. And, after parliament had declared its sentiments on the subject, what was the conduct of the right honourable gentleman? He felt that it was necessary to pay due deference to their opinion—he came down to the house, and, voluntarily, gave up the war malt tax. He begged leave to ask, how the right honourable gentleman, acting in his financial capacity for the whole empire, having listened to the voice of the English people, conveyed through their representatives—having obeyed their call, and given up the income tax—could now refuse to bow to the sentiments of the people of Ireland, expressed in the most unequivocal and most constitutional manner? He spoke warmly—nor was it wonderful that he should, seeing what he had seen in that country with which he was immediately connected—but he meant nothing offensive to the right honourable gentleman, whose wishes for the welfare of Ireland, were, he believed, sincere. The right honourable gentleman had observed, that some relief, granted at the present time, would have a much better effect than any that could be produced by waiting for the result of the deliberations of a committee. He, however, could see nothing to prevent the right honourable gentleman from granting that relief, and acceding also to the proposition for a committee. The committee, he might rest assured, would throw no impediment in the way of any relief he might be inclined to grant. Indeed, having received the boon of which the right honourable gentleman had spoken, the committee could go to work with more spirit. Were the right honourable gentleman to go back to Dublin—were he to notice the unhappy beings whom he would meet in every direction —were he to mark their meagre and famished countenances, and to witness the despair which characterised their looks—were he to know the disappointment which had settled in the minds of the better order of people, deprived as they were of their ordinary comforts —he could not avoid feeling a great anxiety, if it could be reconciled with the public interest, to remove those burdens which pressed most heavily on the people of Ireland.

The motion was defeated by a majority of 16; but the Chancellor consented to an abatement of 25 per cent. of the tax. Sir Robert Shaw obtained and deserved the credit of abolishing it.

THE PETERLOO MASSACRE.
November 23, 1819.

The extraordinary English prosperity of the year 1818 was by a single act of parliament, passed without a dissentient voice, turned in the course of a few months into violent and universal distress, which lasted for three years. This was the new Bank of England Act. It contracted the currency of the country by no less a sum than eight millions. The paper in discount fell from twenty millions to four—exports from forty-five millions to thirty-five—imports from thirty-six millions to twenty-nine—and the profits of every trade and the wages of every labour. There was almost universal distress, dismay, and bankruptcy.

Cobbett, when he heard the news in America, prepared to return to England, feeling certain, he said, that the cause of reform in parliament could now no longer be averted; and all the English reformers, who know as well as the Irish that the British governing classes listen respectfully to the claims of justice only when danger makes the opportunity, commenced a violent agitation for the reform afterwards partly carried by the Whigs and Manchester party, and embodied in their entirety by the Chartist points. Meetings of immense masses of men, marching in disciplined order, were convoked during the summer of 1819 throughout the manufacturing districts, and as the year advanced became more and more formidable in their aspect and violent in their tone.

At last a bloody collision occurred between the people and the authorities. A great meeting was summoned at Peterloo, near Manchester, on the 9th of August, to elect "a representative and legislatorial attorney for the city of Manchester." The local magistrates declared that such an object was illegal, and the meeting was adjourned to the 16th, and convened again "to petition for a reform of parliament." Henry Hunt was announced as tribune of the day, and 60,000 of the artisan class gathered to hear him.

The magistrates still conceived the meeting to be illegal, and resolved to arrest Hunt in the midst of it. Accordingly, after the business had begun, the chief constable got orders to execute the warrant at once. He attempted to make his way to the hustings, but the crowd was so dense as to render passage impossible. Then the Manchester yeomanry were ordered up to clear the way. Advancing two by two amid the dense and excited crowd, they were hooted, separated, surrounded, and in some instances unhorsed. But no blood was shed, until the chief magistrate turned to the regular cavalry and gave them orders to rescue the yeomen. In a minute they were forward at the charge, and dashed into the meeting with drawn swords. Four or five persons were killed, about twenty wounded; several hundreds crushed and otherwise injured. Hunt and two of his friends were arrested for high treason—and another collision with the military took place on his way to gaol. A sense of indignation and horror spread among the people, and the outrage was resented by popular opinion throughout the empire. On the other hand, the home secretary, Lord Sidmouth, at once conveyed the "approbation and high commendation" of the Prince Regent and the ministry to the magistrates of Manchester for their conduct.

Three months elapsed before the meeting of parliament. England resounded with execrations of the government and the magistrates. The common council of London framed a petition condemning their conduct. Meetings were held in Liverpool, York, Westminster, and in almost all the great manufacturing towns, to stigmatise the proceedings of the executive. At some of the meetings violent riots broke out; others were forcibly dissolved. At the York meeting, Lord Fitzwilliam attended, and was instantly dismissed from the lieutenancy of his riding. The people organized, agitated, threatened. The government embodied the disbanded soldiers of the war, and drafted the famous six coercion acts.

In the Prince Regent's speech opening the session, he called the earnest, speedy, and careful attention of parliament to the state of the country. "A spirit is now fully manifested," he said, "utterly hostile to the constitution of the kingdom, and aiming not only at the change of those political institutions which have hitherto constituted the pride and security of this country, but at the subversion of the rights of property and of all order in society." On the address in reply violent debates arose.

In the House of Lords, Earl Grey, Lord Erskine, and the Marquis of Lansdowne in strong language proposed an amendment condemnatory of the conduct of the magistrates; and the Dukes of Kent and Sussex voted in the minority with them. In the House of Commons, Tierney led the opposition in a long passionate speech denouncing ministers and magistrates, and calling for inquiry and vengeance. Castlereagh replied, admitting the "awful responsibility of ministers to God and their country," but vindicating their conduct on the grounds that the meeting was one held to intimidate the executive and the legislature, and that the magistrates had used all reasonable means to disperse it peaceably before resorting to force. On the case of Lord Fitzwilliam he asserted that "it was essential to the due administration of public affairs, and to the dignity of the crown, that none of its servants should hold opinions of it derogatory to its honour and character. Lord Fitzwilliam when he went to the meeting at York, virtually tendered the resignation of his office. * * * Never thanks to the meeting for being allowed to address them with the radicals * * * He had lived long enough in Ireland during a disastrous period of its history to know how far delusions might be carried on by popular agitators; and he had seen those who had been so deluded afterwards become faithful subjects and zealous supporters of the laws." Several minor speakers followed, and then Sir James Mackintosh rose, denounced the dismissal of Lord Fitzwilliam as "an outrage the most gross on honour and virtue, on rank and fortune, that had ever degraded any administration in modern times"—and urged the house to adopt the amendment; to inquire, "if the inquiry should be gone into, it would rub out as foul a blot and black a stain as ever disgraced the history of the country."

Plunket's speech is next in the debate, and from his antecedents and connexion astounded the house. Their surprise was possibly increased by Castlereagh's apposite reference to his experience in Ireland of "agitators," who, however, afterwards became "zealous supporters of the laws"—meaning, of course, the anti-Union tribunes. But Plunket never heeded, and spoke like an attorney-general with an unflawed indictment and a packed jury. The speech, although reported in the third person, is printed from the authorised edition.

Mr. Plunket commenced by observing that the question before the house had not been very fairly treated. Much had been introduced which did not necessarily connect itself with the subject, and which had a tendency to divert the attention of the house from the deeply important matters which pressed for their consideration. There had been some address in making the case of Lord Fitzwilliam so principal a topic. As a ground of argument applicable to the present question, it could not be justly resorted to by any person who did not go the length of asserting that the dismissal of that nobleman would warrant parliament in the refusal to consider, or to make provision against, the dangers with which the country was threatened, and which were announced in the speech from the throne. No person, on any side of the house, had laid down so extreme a position; on the contrary, the amendment of his right honourable friend admitted the danger and the necessity of meeting it by suitable provisions. He would, therefore, in his view of the subject, relieve himself from a discussion which he could not approach without feelings of great embarrassment. His habitual reverence for that distinguished nobleman was such that he could scarcely hope to bring his mind, fairly and impartially, to any investigation which affected him. He considered his character as uniting everything noble and generous in freedom, with everything that could exalt or dignify the aristocracy of the country; and he therefore took leave to dismiss this subject as one not connected with the debate, and in doing so, he felt much satisfaction in the statement of the noble lord (Castlereagh), that the dismissal of Earl Fitzwilliam was founded, not on any personal imputations, but on a difference of opinion with his majesty's government on points involving the exercise of his duties as lord lieutenant of the West Riding.

Again, he thought the subject had, in another respect, not been very fairly treated by his right honourable friend who immediately preceded him. It was stated in the speech from the throne that a revolutionary spirit was at work in the country, which threatened its safety and its existence; and the truth of this statement was not denied, but indeed admitted, by the amendment. Was it then perfectly fair to call the attention of the house from the consideration of the public danger and its remedies—from the machinations and arts of those who were preparing measures for the subversion of the state and the overthrow of every constituted authority—to the plans and objects of that portion of the peaceful and loyal subjects of this country who respected the law and constitution, and were desirous of improving them. This latter description of persons were entitled to the most attentive and respectful consideration. However he might differ from them on the subject of parliamentary reform, he considered their objects as honest, and their means of effecting them as constitutional. Whenever, at any proper time, and in any proper form, their claims should be brought before parliament, they should be listened to with attention and with respect. Their proposals, if reasonable, should be yielded to; if not so, they should be met with fair argument and calm discussion; and the result, in either event, would be satisfactory and conciliating. The people of England were a reasoning and reasonable people; but was it fair, either to them or to the country, to confound their cause and their objects with the persons whom we now were called upon to deal with, whose undisguised aim was to pull down the entire fabric of our constitution and to effect a revolution by force? Against this immediate and overwhelming danger it was the first duty of parliament to provide. And to turn aside from this urgent and paramount duty to the discussion of subjects of inferior importance and of distinct consideration, would be an abandonment of the interests of the country. When he saw a revolutionary project ripe for execution—when he saw that sedition and blasphemy were the instruments by which it worked, and that open force was to be employed for its accomplishment, he felt it to be trifling with the duties of the house, and with the safety of the country, to turn their minds to any other object until the terrors that hung over our existing establishments were first dispelled.

No person, he was happy to see, denied the existence of these dangers; but he thought there was some tendency to underrate their extent, and to undervalue their consequence. It was said that the public mind in general was sound : he trusted and firmly believed it was so. He was convinced that the strength and spirit of the loyal subjects were sufficient to put down the enemies of law and of order; he, therefore, was apprehensive, not of revolution, but of the attempt at revolution, which he believed in his conscience would be made, if not prevented by the vigilancy and energy of parliament; and what he contemplated with the deepest alarm was the miseries which such an attempt, in its progress to certain and necessary failure, must produce. If this mischief should once burst forth, he anticipated a series of horrors which must shake the safety and happiness of the country to its foundations. The very circumstances which must ensure the ultimate failure of the enterprise aggravated its dangers. Revolution, always calamitous, yet, when pursued for some definite purpose, conducted by abilities, tempered by the admixture of rank and of property, may be effected, as it had been before in this country, without any incurable shock being given to the safety of persons of property. But here was a revolution to be achieved by letting loose the physical force of the community against its constituted authorities—a revolution for the sake of revolution, to take away the property of the rich, and to distribute it among the rabble, a rabble previously debauched by the unremitting dissemination of blasphemous libels, and freed from the restraints of moral or religious feeling. On this subject he felt sufficient confidence to express his opinion, without waiting for any of those documents which the noble lord proposed to lay before the house.

These were facts of public notoriety, known and seen by every man who did not choose to shut his eyes. Had not meetings been proposed for the purpose of assuming the functions which belonged only to the sovereign power of the state—meetings which, if they actually had been held, would have been acts of high treason. When it was found that matters were not sufficiently ripe for this undisguised act of public rebellion, had not the same masses of the populace been again convened, under the directions of the same leaders, under the pretext of seeking universal suffrage and annual parliaments—their very pretexts such as the constitution could not survive, if they were effectuated; but their real object being to overawe the constituted authorities by the display of their numerical strength, and to prepare for direct, immediate, forcible revolution. Had we not seen the same itinerant mountebank,* who set their powers in motion publicly assisting at the orgies of the blasphemous wretch† lately cou-

---

* Hunt.   † Carlile the publisher.

victed; and could we doubt that treason was the object, and that blasphemy and sedition were the means? When he saw these fiends in human shape endeavouring to rob their unhappy victims of all their consolations here, and of all their hopes hereafter; when he saw them with their levers placed under the great pillars of social order, and heaving the constitution from its foundation, he was rejoiced to see parliament assembled. Their first duty was to convince these enemies of God and man, that within the walls of parliament they could find no countenance; and through the organ of parliament to let them know, that nothing awaited them but indignant resistance from the great body of the people.

They were bound to assure the throne of their loyal and cheerful co-operation for these purposes; and on this ground alone the amendment was objectionable, even if the measure suggested by it were in itself desirable, inasmuch as by tacking it to the address, and not proposing it as a separate resolution, it declared the measure of inquiry so essential as to preclude all exertions for the safety of the state until that inquiry should be disposed of. But, waiving this objection, he should proceed to consider it on its own merits. It was said then that the dispersion of the meeting at Manchester on the 16th of August called for parliamentary inquiry; and here he begged leave to remind the house that parliamentary inquiry, though certainly a proceeding recognised by our constitution, was still not the ordinary mode for investigating either the conduct of magistrates in the execution of the laws, or the conduct of those who were the objects of the execution of those laws. A case, therefore, for inquiry was to be made out by those who called for it. What, then, was the inquiry proposed? Was it into the conduct of government for thanking the magistrates? Such a proceeding, he owned, appeared to him most premature and uncalled for. If the magistrates had issued orders for dispersing the king's subjects peaceably and legally assembled—if, in consequence of such orders, the blood of innocent and unoffending persons had been shed, the conduct of ministers in advising his royal highness the Prince Regent to thank them for such acts would call for inquiry and for censure. If, on the contrary, bodies to the amount of twenty thousand or seventy thousand, he cared not which—but to an amount beyond the means of the civil power to deal with—had marched in regular columns and in military array, with seditious banners, into the heart of one of the most populous and most inflammable towns in the empire; if these men had been previously drilled to military exercises; if they had been shortly before convened for a treasonable purpose; if they resisted the authority of the peace officers executing the warrant of the magistrates; if, in short, the case stated by the noble lord and by the honourable member for Dover were correct, then, he had no hesitation in saying that his majesty's ministers were not only justified in returning thanks to the magistrates, but that it was their bounden duty to do so; and that those gentlemen, acting in the discharge of a most important duty, in a crisis of public peril, and undertaking an awful responsibility for the public service, were entitled to have the sense of the executive government on their conduct. When it was said that this was prejudging the question, it seemed to be taken as granted that the executive power of the country is not in any degree lodged in the government. Would it not have been their duty to have given previous advice and instruction to the magistrates on such a subject and with a view to such an emergency? When they direct the public prosecutor to proceed against any individual, can that be considered as a prejudging of the question? To this extent it is the exercise of their proper functions, which they cannot neglect without an abandonment of duty; and if they felt, under all circumstances, that the conduct of those most meritorious public servants deserved their praise, it would have been unjust and mean to have withheld their expressions of it. How, then, could the propriety of the letter of thanks be judged until the facts were ascertained? True, it was said; and therefore inquire. Certainly; but how? Clearly by the regular course of law, and by the regular tribunals of the country, unless some case were previously established, showing that these tribunals were inadequate or unsuited for the purpose. Bills were found against several of the persons alleged to be actors in this seditious meeting: on these trials the legality of the meeting would be necessarily the subject of investigation. And why was it that these trials had not taken place, and the public mind, through the regular constitutional channel of a trial by jury, been informed of the real nature of these transactions? Why; because the persons so accused had availed themselves of the delay which the law unfortunately allows, and had postponed their trials until the spring assizes.

But, it is said that although the legality of the meeting might be decided on in those cases, still the conduct of the magistrates in dispersing it might be illegal; and this would not necessarily, in them, come under discussion. Why, then, were not proceedings taken on the part of the persons alleged to be aggrieved or injured by the acts of the magistrates? The honourable and learned member made the absence of such proceedings a ground for parliamentary inquiry; but was not the fair inference from the absence of such proceedings this, that no reasonable foundation for them existed? But the grand jury had thrown out the bills preferred on behalf of these persons. Was this a ground for parliamentary inquiry? Was it to be presumed that the grand jury of the county of Lancaster had violated their oaths? An artifice had been resorted to, for the purpose of rendering the administration of justice suspected in the public mind, by publishing the informations which had been sent up to the grand jury; but every gentleman must be aware of the difference between an information in which the party states the facts according to his own views, and a *vivâ voce* examination before the grand jury, in which the entire truth is extracted from the witness. But, supposing the grand jury had erred in ignoring the bills, fresh indictments might be sent up to any succeeding grand jury. Was the entire county of Lancashire to be pronounced incapable or unwilling to exercise such functions? But magistrates refused to receive informations. Was not their conduct examinable in the Court of King's Bench; and might not all the facts connected with such a transaction be fully examined on affidavits? And if any doubt existed for a jury, on an information under the sanction of the court, was the Court of King's Bench also to be included within the ban of this proscription of all the constituted authorities? But the honourable and learned member said that the Court of King's Bench would not interfere unless the magistrate acted wilfully, and that he might commit an error which would not subject him to punishment. Was this, then, a ground for parliamentary interference, to stop the course of law, and subject the public functionary to an extraordinary visitation of public vengeance? Were the different points of the argument of the honourable and learned member altogether reconcileable? When his object was to make out a case so important as to call for parliamentary inquiry, he stated the conduct of the magistrates as a daring violation of the subjects' privileges, a triumph of authority over law, a foul stain upon our laws, forming a black era in the annals of our country; but when it became an object to show that there might be a case in which the courts of law would be incompetent to investigate the truth, then this foul deed, this portentous violation of the laws and of the constitution dwindled into an error in judgment too slight and too pardonable to warrant the interference of the Court of King's Bench.

Was such an error, if it did exist, he would ask, a case for parliamentary inquiry? Was this the way in which the conduct of magistrates was to be examined by parliament? He owned he was not one of those who were disposed to examine too critically the conduct of magistrates acting in perilous times, under heavy responsibility; and sure he was, that if the benignant principle of the law shielded their errors, it was not the province of parliament to deprive them of that protection. Further, he would ask, if any individual was aggrieved, where was the bar to his remedy by civil action, in which the whole merits of the case would be discussed in a court of law, and decided on by a jury of his country? What pretence was there for saying that justice had been denied, or even delayed? Unless the house was prepared to bring to its bar the grand jury of Lancashire; unless they were prepared to say that the whole body of public functionaries, petty juries, grand juries, magistrates, and judges, were linked in one common conspiracy against the peaceable petitioners who assembled at Manchester on the 16th of August, they had not ground or principle on which they could order this inquiry. He deprecated such a proceeding as calculated to give efficacy to the plans of the revolutionary party for the degradation of the public functionaries, and to stamp with the authoritative seal of parliament what hitherto had rested on vulgar calumny and on popular clamour. He believed that such an inquiry, instead of being calculated, as was alleged, to allay dissatisfaction, and to conciliate the public mind, could have no other effect than to raise the hopes and spirits of revolutionists, and to strike damp and panic into the heart of every loyal subject. Besides this, the course was wild and impracticable. How was this inquiry to be conducted? At the bar of the house or in a committee? Was this inquiry to supersede the proceedings already instituted in the king's courts? Or were the two classes of proceedings to be carried on simultaneously? If the former was to be the course, the laws were to be robbed of their authority, and the subject of his redress, by a proceeding utterly unsuited to the purposes either of punishment or of compensation. If the latter, we were to have the anomalous and unprecedented spectacle of persons being tried on charges affecting their persons and properties, perhaps their lives, in proceedings before juries, and with witnesses on oath, in the regular courts of law; while the very same facts were undergoing a discussion without oath, before the extraordinary tribunal of parliament. Was it possible that either public or individual justice could be obtained by such a course, or that any result could be derived from it calculated to maintain the authority of the laws or the dignity of parliament? Such a proceeding, he must say, appeared to him wild, unprecedented, and impracticable.

His honourable and learned friend had adverted to three cases as precedents to warrant such a course as that now recommended: the first was a case in the year 1714, in which the House of Lords, for the purpose of procuring the removal of magistrates who were supposed to entertain Jacobitical principles, had addressed the throne for a list of the magistrates, and entered into a strict inquiry; in consequence of which, several of those magistrates were dismissed. Was there any trial then pending in the court of law? Was there any specific fact that could be inquired into in a court of law? Or was it anything more than a proceeding to enable parliament to advise the crown with respect to the wholesome exercise of its prerogative? The second was the case of the murder of Porteous by the mob of Edinburgh (which had derived much celebrity from a late popular work). Was that a proceeding affecting any trial depending, or with a view to any individual punishment? It was, as fairly stated by the honourable and learned member, an inquiry in order to ground a bill of pains and penalties against the town of Edinburgh, and which was accordingly passed. The third instance alluded to was, the inquiry instituted before the secret committee in 1794: that was an inquiry for the purpose of grounding measures for the public safety; and was, with reference to the general state of the country, not in the conduct of local magistrates, and on a particular occasion. Again, the danger of its incidentally affecting the rights of individuals, who were liable to be tried in the courts of law, was so strongly felt, that the inquiry was a secret one. When published, the names of individuals were suppressed; and even under all these circumstances, the possibility of an impression unfavourable to these individuals having been made by the report was so strongly felt, that Mr. Erskine relied on it, and successfully, and in some instances, as he (Mr. P.) believed, acquittals were obtained on that ground. When his honourable and learned friend, with his extensive knowledge and research, could produce no other instances than these, he felt himself justified in repeating the assertion, that the measure was unprecedented. But there was a case not alluded to by his honourable and learned friend, as he recollected, about the year 1715, in which a parliamentary inquiry having been directed into the nature of a certain meeting at Oxford, which was alleged to be riotous, a number of affidavits were produced on one side, and after an unavailing demand of examination on the other, the inquiry was found so impracticable that it was dropped, and no further proceeding founded on it.*

* The reference appears to have been made from memory, and though substantially true, was certainly inaccurate in expression. The facts were these: A tumult having arisen at Oxford on the prince's birth-day, and the loyalty of the mayor and of the heads of the university being called in question, the lords of the council examined into the case on affidavits, not with reference to the

The case for inquiry, he therefore contended, was unsupported by precedent, and was not bottomed on any ascertained fact, or even on any statement made by any member in his place of any case which, if true, would warrant its adoption; indeed, he had not heard any member assert the legality of the Manchester meeting. He was confident that no man acquainted with the laws and constitution of the country would venture to do so.

The house, he trusted, would excuse him, if he trespassed a little further on their patience, by stating his opinion as to those public meetings. The right of the people of this country to meet for the purpose of expressing their opinions on any subject connected with their own individual interests, or with the public welfare, was beyond all question; it was a sacred privilege belonging to the most humble as fully as to the highest subject in the community : they had a right to the full expression and to the free communication of such sentiments; to interchange them with their fellow-subjects, to ani-

---

riot, but with respect to their conduct as to rejoicing on the prince's birth-day—a matter which could not be the subject of any legal inquiry. The council came to the following resolution :—Resolved, that the heads of the university and mayor of the city neglected to make any public rejoicing on the prince's birth-day; but some of the collegiates, with the officers, being met to celebrate the day, the house where they were was assaulted, and the windows were broken by the rabble, which was the beginning and occasion of the riots that ensued as well from the soldiers as the scholars and the townsmen, and the conduct of the mayor seems well justified by the affidavits on his part.

On the 25th of March, 1717, the Lords addressed the crown, that the proper officer should lay before the house the complaints and depositions relative to the riots and disorders complained of at the city of Oxford, and the proceedings which had been had thereon. In consequence of this address, the documents, consisting among others of fifty-six affidavits by the officers and soldiers, and fifty-five affidavits on the part of the mayor and city, were laid before the House of Lords, and referred to a committee of the whole house. On the 3rd April, 1717, the committee repealed two resolutions, viz., an approbation of the resolutions of the lords of the council already stated; and secondly, that the publication of depositions, while the matter was depending in council, was disrespectful to the prince and tending to sedition. A petition against this resolution was offered on behalf of the vice-chancellor, the mayor, and magistrates, who desired to be heard in reply. Their application was refused, and the resolutions already stated were adopted by the house, and no further proceedings were taken; and even from this mere adoption of the resolution in council twenty-eight peers dissented, assigning this among other reasons—namely, that the matters of fact were not sufficiently inquired into, from want of opportunity of replying to the affidavits; and because of such proceedings the magistrates may be discouraged from doing their duty on such occasions. These facts appear on the journals of the Lords, and it is conceived they substantially warrant the statement of this case as one tending to show the futility of such inquiries, although they do not confirm the exact words of the statement.

mate and catch fire each from the other. He trusted that to such rights he should never be found an enemy; but he must say that these rights, like all others, to be exercised in civil society must be subject to such modification and restriction as to render them compatible with other rights equally acknowledged and equally sacred. Every subject of this realm had an undoubted right to the protection of the laws—to the security of his person and his property—and still more, to the full assurance of such safety. And he had no hesitation in asserting that any assembly of the people, held under such circumstances as to excite in the minds of the king's peaceable and loyal subjects reasonable grounds of alarm, in this respect were illegal assemblies, and liable to be dispersed as such. ' He thought it important that it should be understood that these rights were restricted not merely to this extent—namely, that they must not assemble for an illegal purpose; that they must not assemble with force and arms; and they must not use seditious language; that they must not revile the laws or public functionaries; but beyond all this, that they must not assemble under such circumstances, whether of numbers or otherwise, as to excite well-grounded terror in the minds of their fellow-subjects, or to disturb their tranquil and assured enjoyment of the protection of the laws, free from all reasonable apprehension of force or violence. A vulgar notion may have prevailed, that if the avowed and immediate purpose of such meetings were not illegal, or if they had not arms in their hands, or if no force was actually used or immediately threatened, the assembly was legal: no opinion could be more unfounded, and he did not fear contradiction from any constitutional lawyer when he asserted that any assembly of the people, whether armed or unarmed; whether using or threatening to use force, or not doing so; and whether the avowed object was illegal or legal: if held in such numbers, or with such language, or emblems, or deportment as to create well-grounded terror in the king's liege subjects for their lives, their persons, or their property, was an illegal assembly, and might be dispersed as such.

Such had been the law as laid down by the ablest of our lawyers and of our judges from the earliest period of our jurisprudence, and in the best times of our history and constitution, before the revolution and since the revolution, independent of the Riot Act or of any statuteable enactment, by the principles of our common law, which was always founded on the principles of common sense. The application of this principle to each particular case must always be a matter of discretion, but in cases like the present it could not admit of doubt or difficulty. When meetings became too strong for the civil power to deal with them, the laws must prohibit them; if not recourse must be had to military force. When the citizen becomes too strong for the law, the magistrate of necessity becomes a soldier; and those who justified these unrestricted meetings were the worst enemies to the liberties of their country, and laid the foundation of military despotism. If bodies of the people, not convened by any public functionary, but called together by mountebanks whose only title was their impudence and folly, were entitled to assemble, not in thousands but in tens of thousands; to march with banners displayed in military array, into the hearts of populous cities; and if the laws were not competent to assure the people of this country against the panic and dismay excited by such proceedings, there was an en ! to the constitution. He implored the house to protect the country from the effect of these desolating plans which were now in operation. Even though they should not break out in actual rebellion, their mischiefs were beyond calculation. The principles of respect for the laws and orders of the state, the reverence that was due to the sacred obligations of religion, these were not the results of momentary feelings which might be thrown aside and resumed at pleasure; they were habits which if once removed could not easily be restored. If those sacred sources from which were the issues of public happiness and virtue, were once tainted, how was their purity to be restored? He had reason to believe that the blasphemies which had excited the horror of all good men, had been fashioned by these miscreants into primers for the education of children, that these helpless beings in receiving the first elements of knowledge might be inoculated with this pestilence. He again implored the house to act with decision and energy while yet it was in their power. If the great foundations of public safety were once shaken, the united exertion of all the honest men of every party might come too late. On these grounds he deprecated the amendment, as calculated to give encouragement to the worst enemies of the state; and cordially concurred in the original address.

The debate was adjourned, and on the second day strong references were made by Hume, Burdett, and several others of the opposition speakers, to the course taken by Plunket, who, on the other hand, was warmly complimented by Canning—"The right honourable and learned gentleman, himself a host, had pledged his authority and reputation as a lawyer (pledges of which the house and the United Kingdom know, and posterity will acknowledge, the value) that the meeting was an illegal meeting," &c. Brougham was of quite another opinion. The government, however, carried their address by a large majority.

THE SEDITIOUS MEETINGS BILL.

December 13, 1819.

INSTANTLY after ministers had felt their way with the house by the address, they introduced the six acts—the training, seizure of arms, misdemeanour, seditious meetings, blasphemous libels, and newspaper stamp acts—a series of measures devised to environ the Radicals with a complete *cordon* of legislation. The Seditious Meetings Prevention Act was a peculiarly severe measure. It made the least resistance to any magistrate who called upon any meeting to disperse, a felony, and indemnified justices for killing and maiming in dispersing any meeting that so refused.

Mr. Hutchinson, "a blood relation of my Lord Donoughmore," delivered a rattling Irish speech on the third reading, attacking the government for wantonly and unnecessarily including Ireland in the bill. Turning to the Irishmen who supported it, "Perhaps," said he, "the most novel and singular circumstance attending these debates was the conspicuous lead the Irish gentlemen had taken on the occasion. The member for the university of Dublin (Mr. Plunket), one of the first legal characters in that country, had come over to declare the law, to strengthen and to shield the minister. The president of the Board of Control (Mr. Canning), also an Irishman, had exhausted all the powers of his extraordinary eloquence, in a three hours' speech, in order to guide or rather beguile the house into an adoption of these measures. The noble lord (Castlereagh), the author of this notable system, himself an Irishman, seventy other Irish members, crowding the ranks of ministers, and making their victory decisive—a noble duke, the first, the great captain of the age, one of Erin's most favoured sons, covered with honours and with glory, forming one of the cabinet where these measures were devised, and prepared, no doubt, to lead the armies of the empire, if necessary, even against the people of Great Britain, should they in their despair and madness unhappily be goaded on to violence and to mischief. One felt disposed to ask whether this be revenge?—revenge for the injuries inflicted by Great Britain on that country for so many centuries?—whether it was the hand of Providence interferfering to punish, through Irish agency, the sufferings of millions, though thus tardily? He asked whether those gentlemen he had mentioned now wished to give chains to Great Britain, in return for the misery and desolation inflicted on their own country by the barbarous policy of Briti h cabinets." Another passage in his speech was an urgent personal appeal to Plunket against extending the bills to Ireland.

MR. PLUNKET trusted the house would indulge him for a short time, while he expressed his sentiments on the measure then before them. He did not intend to have occupied their attention at this stage of the debate, nor should he have offered himself, but for the very pointed manner in which he had been alluded to by his honourable and learned friend who had spoken last but one. He held it to be rather unusual to call particularly upon any member for his opinion upon what was passing before the house, and perhaps he might, with a full sense of duty, decline to comply with the demand;

but he confessed he had so much of the Irishman in him as not to refuse the challenge. He thanked his honourable and learned friend for the compliments which he had paid him in the course of his speech; but he conceived the allusion made to his character, as affected by the vote which he had given or might give on this subject, was wholly uncalled for. He must say that he did not think his character was likely to sustain any injury or diminution from the course of conduct which he had felt it his duty in that house to follow. He thought that his character could never be implicated by the conscientious expression of a conscientious opinion. His honourable and learned friend, in what he had expressed, was not inconsistent with his politics; and he (Mr. Plunket) maintained that he, in what he had said, was not inconsistent with those politics which he had always supported. In the course of his parliamentary experience, he had frequently been compelled to differ from his honourable and learned friend, and he had never seen occasion since to regret that difference. He had heard a great deal of the claim set up to exclusive loyalty by the gentlemen on the other side; but he considered the claim to exclusive patriotism, which was set up by some gentlemen, equally as arrogant and unfounded. His honourable and learned friend had talked a great deal of liberty, and of the inroads which had been made upon it. He should be glad to learn from him what that liberty was, and what were those attacks which were so much to be feared. That liberty would not, he was certain, be defined to mean the unlimited power of each individual to do whatever he pleased. He should rather define it to be "*Potestas faciendi quicquid per leges licet.*" It was not the unbridled license of disturbing the community at the caprice of all who sought only for confusion. The outcry of the present day was not in support of any enjoyment—it was not to uphold a legal and recognised right, but the uproar was shouted to secure the power of disturbance, to perpetuate an abuse with whose existence constitutional freedom was incompatible. Could such a misapplication of right be called liberty? Was that liberty which was preached up as such in so many parts of the country? No, it was a screaming harpy, an obscene bird of prey, that polluted every social and every natural enjoyment, and sought only to poison all those who allowed themselves to be brought within its influence. He had heard many assertions on the subject on that side of the house, and though he was certain that anything which fell from his honourable and learned friend was not said with any evil intention, yet it should be recollected that in the present state of the country the slightest assertion might be sufficient to unsheath the sword of civil discord, which unhappily was already half drawn from its scabbard. Many gentlemen talked of the introduction of military power and the substitution of a government of force for a government of law. He could not participate in such apprehensions—he read the answer to such fears in the application to parliament for the wholesome laws in the passing of which the house was then engaged.

He had made those few observations from having been so pointedly called upon by his honourable and learned friend, but he trusted the house would excuse him if he went a little farther into the subject than he originally intended; for he was anxious to state what his reasons were for giving his support to the present measures. That support was not founded on any suggestions of temporary policy—nor on the information which was disclosed in the papers before the house, but with the conviction that the proposed measures did not infringe on the constitution; while they were essential to its conservation. The state of society in this country, every man who reflected on the subject must admit, had within the last twenty or thirty years undergone a greater change than from the period of the conquest until the time of which he spoke. Within that interval the public attention had been called to the consideration of every measure connected with the administration of the government, in a degree hitherto unprecedented. There had been an intensity of light shed upon all subjects, civil, political, and religious; so that measures were now scanned with minuteness, which were scarcely looked into, or at most, but generally known before. Did he complain of that change, or of the means by which it had been produced? No; he rejoiced at it. The freedom of the public press, directing its efforts under the institutions of the constitution, was the most effectual security of public freedom. He was persuaded that where every action of every man connected with public affairs was laid before the public in the fullest manner, and most strictly canvassed and examined; where the press exercised this kind of guardianship we had the best guarantee of all our rights. Then why did he allude to the public press? Because there was under the same title another description, a blasphemous, seditious, mischievous press, of which the members of that house knew but little, but which had been unremittingly at work in destroying every honest and good feeling in the heart of man, and in loosening all those moral and social ties, without which civilization could not exist. It was not against the respectable press but against this under-current, which, setting with great force, was drifting the great mass of the humbler classes of the community into sedition, atheism, and revolution, that the house sought to guard. It was for the consummation of such atrocious objects that this battery was brought to play upon their passions and their ignorance. Did he mean to say that the lower class of the people had no right to be informed on public transactions? Did he mean to say that the lower orders of the people had not a right to inquire into and discuss subjects of a political nature? No such thing. Did he mean to say that they ought not to have the power of expressing their sense of any grievance under which they might think themselves to suffer? Far from it; but when he was willing to allow to them the enjoyment of every constitutional privilege, which they were entitled to possess, he never could consider that nice discussions on the very frame of the constitution —on the most essential changes in the institutions and fundamental laws of the country, were calculated for minds of such intelligence and cultivation. They ought rather to be protected from the mischiefs which such a misapplication of their minds must entail. Every capacity was capable of understanding the nature and the extent of the restrictions which government, from the purport of its institution, necessarily imposed on the natural freedom of man; but to the task of contemplating the more than usurious repayment which in long and various succession was received for that surrender, the generality of persons were not quite so adequate. The penalties of government stood at the threshold, but its benefits were to be traced through a long interval of ages—in the distribution of equal laws—in the control of public wisdom, producing, even through apparent contradiction, the grand harmony of the social system— these he conceived were subjects which could not be well discussed by men whose time was chiefly devoted to daily labour. It had been wisely said that "a little learning was a dangerous thing." It was true in literature, in religion, in politics. In literature, superficial reading too frequently formed the babbling critic. In religion the poor man, who, unsettled as to his faith, became curious upon his evidences, and who, if he possessed the capacity and had time and means to extend his inquiries, would in the end reach the moral demonstration which religion unfolded—shaken, but not instructed, became a shallow infidel. It was equally so in politics; men who indulged in the perusal of every species of invective against the institutions of their country, who read on their shopboard of all the evils, and did not comprehend the blessings of the system of government under which they lived, these men the nature of whose employment and whose education disallowed them to be statesmen, might however learn enough to become turbulent and discontented subjects. Was not this the case in France, where persons were called from their daily labour to give opinions upon the most difficult points of legislation?

But he heard from his honourable and learned friend, and from other honourable members, a great deal about overturning the constitution of the country, and the wish that the practices of the good old times should be restored. He should be glad if the persons who made these observations would prove their present applicability. If it were said that the measures now introduced were against the practice of the good old times, he should only state, that before he could agree to the proposition he must unlearn all that he had known of those good old times, and all that he had read in history respecting them. He should be glad to know when had such meetings as it was now attempted to control been considered as the ordinary exercise of the constitution? Why, until the present reign had far advanced there were no such meetings known, and the reason why such laws as the present were not before thought of was, that no grounds ever before existed for their necessity. Where a spirit of disaffection existed, some restrictive measure should be passed to check its operation. The house were called upon to provide against an evil not of ancient, but of recent origin, and, in the wise spirit of the constitution, it proceeded to apply new remedies to a new mischief. Let any man who read the bill contradict him. Did it in its enactments interfere with any right of the subject according to the spirit of the constitution? It was, and he said it with sincerity, a remedial measure. He appealed to the common sense of every man who heard him, whether the expression of the public voice was possible to be obtained at these screaming, howling, hallooing meetings which the measure went to suppress? Could any discussion, any deliberation, any fair, impartial decision result from such assemblages? Let him ask whether, if ever there came a question of deep importance, on which it was of the greatest moment to procure the authoritative expression of the public opinion, that opinion would not be better ascertained, and its influence more powerfully felt at a hundred meetings, held in apartments, where every man would be allowed to deliver his sentiments and to hear distinctly those of others, than at a meeting of 10,000 persons assembled together in the open streets, and where what was said by one could not be heard by hundreds? Why, the spirit of the constitution was more likely to be preserved in those meetings than in the large and tumultuous ones. He would admit that it was of importance that the public voice should be frequently expressed; but then he would not sanction meetings where, under the mask of expressing that opinion, the use of physical force was recommended in bringing about alterations not only of the law, but the constitution. He would agree with what had fallen from an honourable baronet, that perhaps the opinions of lawyers might not be the best on these subjects; but he would ask whether the first step from barbarism was not this—to prevent the elements of society from being let loose against those laws which were enacted for the benefit of all; and thus throwing mankind back into a state of nature, in which the institutions of government possessed neither respect nor power. The first principle of society was, that care should be taken to prevent the exercise of physical force from bearing down those bounds which that society had placed to human action in particular cases. He would admit that there were states of society where those bounds were broken, but then they were states of revolution, and never existed without the destruction, for the time, of all order and harmony in the country where they rose. In conclusion, he begged to state his opinion that the same reason which existed for the extension of the bill to all parts of England, also existed for its extension to Ireland. His honourable and learned friend had, on this occasion, mixed up the question of the Roman Catholic claims with this bill. In his opinion, there was no connexion between them. No doubt his honourable and learned friend was a warm and sincere advocate for the question in which the Roman Catholics were concerned; but he (Mr. Plunket) should say, that any man who could mix up their question with such measures as the present, was not, in effect, acting the part of a friend to them. His honourable and learned friend must admit that most, if not all the meetings which were held on the subject of the Roman Catholic question were held within doors, and therefore the present bill could not affect their assembling to petition; and he knew his Catholic countrymen so well as to feel that even if, under the present circumstances, they were to suffer some privations, they would freely acquiesce in them, in the hope that the time was not far distant when they might be enabled to participate in the benefits of that constitution which they were ever ready to support and defend.

REPLY TO BROUGHAM.
December 22, 1819.

In debate on the third reading of the Newspaper Stamp Duties Bill, Brougham took the opportunity of attacking Plunket merely for the two preceding speeches.

MR. PLUNKET said, that every person who had heard the honourable and learned gentleman who had just sat down, must be sensible that he owed it to himself and to the house, not to suffer the allusion which had been made to what had fallen from him on a former occasion to go unanswered. It was now nearly a month since he had taken the liberty of offering his humble sentiments on the situation of the country. At that distance of time he had made use of expressions, which, he ventured to say, had been that night most completely, although he was sure not intentionally, misquoted. He would take the liberty of stating what he believed he had said, and thus the mistake which had arisen would be set right. He was first charged with having said, "that the conduct of magistrates ought not to be too critically inquired into." Now he begged permission to state, that at the time he made use of this expression, there was no appearance of an indemnity being asked for on the part of the magistrates, nor, as he was apprised, of any intention existing of screening them from the operation of the law as it affected their conduct. He conceived that their conduct was open to inquiry in the Court of King's Bench, and he did say that it was inconsistent with the dignity of the house to stop short in the task which their public duty imposed upon them, for the purpose of critically inquiring into their conduct, and for parliament to exercise a degree of criticism which could not have been exercised in a court of justice. This was what he meant to say, and what, he believed, he had said. The next charge brought against him was, that he had looked for a definition of liberty among the records of the Roman empire, and in the Justinian code. He had defined personal liberty to be *potestas faciendi quicquid leges licet;* but he had at the same time said that there was as well as a personal a political liberty. It would have been candid in the honourable and learned gentleman to have stated that he made that distinction. His honourable and learned friend had brought another charge against him, which was that he had asserted, that the "intensity of light" which was thrown on the people unfitted them for the enjoyment of liberty.

Mr. Brougham.—I did not say that you directly said so, but such an inference was deducible from your expressions.

Mr. Plunket resumed. He would now state what he did say on that occasion. He had said that an intensity of light (which he did not regret but rejoiced at) was thrown upon every subject for the last few years, that public curiosity, with respect to the affairs of government, was excited to such a pitch that the faculties of the great portion of the people were not sufficiently exercised to consider well and thoroughly—that therefore it was likely to lead them into error, and that it was the duty of parliament to see that good and wholesome food was administered to the minds of the people. His honourable and learned friend had said that he had charged some of the schools in England with teaching blasphemy and sedition. He admitted that he had said he believed blasphemous libels, which had been made the subject of public prosecution, had been formed into primers for the purpose of inculcating into the minds of children that description of pestilence. His honourable and learned friend had stated that it was a mistake to say that anything like blasphemous or seditious doctrines were taught in certain schools. But admitting the statement of his honourable and learned friend to be quite correct, would that serve to prove the fallacy of the information which he (Mr. P.) communicated to the house upon a former evening? That information he still believed to be correct; and surely his honourable and learned friend was not prepared logically to maintain, that because he was acquainted with certain schools where no such mischievous system of education was admitted, that therefore this system was not pursued in any other schools. His honourable and learned friend's contradiction could not, indeed, be effective, unless it applied to the precise schools in which he (Mr. P.) had the best authority for stating that instruction in blasphemy and sedition actually prevailed. But he had this evening had a letter put into his hands by a member of that house not then in his place, from which letter it appeared that the blasphemous doctrines which had of late been so widely circulated, and so justly censured, were inserted in primers, for the purpose of inoculating children in a particular school, the name of which he felt it would be indelicate to mention. The letter he should be happy to communicate to his honourable and learned friend, but he did not feel that he should be justified in pointing out the particular school, as the individual concerned would have no opportunity of defending himself. And now, having said so much as to his personal vindication, he begged leave to say a word or two with respect to the merits of the bill under consideration, which, in concurrence with the language of his right honourable friend on the other side of the house, he could not conceive in any degree an infraction of the liberty of the press. In the first place, this measure did not in any degree interfere with the great standard and truly useful works which were published by the respectable booksellers: and then as to those ephemeral publications which were called newspapers, which were highly respectable, and in which facts were fully stated—in which productions were generally tolerated, as they ought to be, far beyond the line of argumentative disquisition, this measure only proposed to put other periodical publications on the same footing as those newspapers. What, then, could be fairly urged against the adoption of such a measure? It was said that there was a class of publications containing ribaldry and trash which no respectable newspaper would admit, because any newspaper inserting such offal would not be read long or continue respectable; and that such publications should be tolerated for the indulgence of a certain part of the people. All that was intended was, to impose the same duty on those publications which were now sold for twopence as upon newspapers; and this he would say, that if any portion of the people required such a supply of filthy luxury —if they would have such a separate table, they must pay for the gratification of their depraved appetites. His honourable and learned friend, whose eloquence he heard with the admiration which the whole house must have felt, had deplored the fate of young literary aspirants, who, he said, would suffer by the operation of this measure. But how suffering was to be apprehended he could not at all imagine, and he could not help expressing his astonishment that this distinguished individual, who was so worthy to be the great historian of his country, could condescend to fall in with the clamour that was raised upon this occasion, and to contend that the restriction of the filth and ordure was calculated to restrain the liberty of the press, and to injure that freedom of discussion which was the pride and glory of the constitution of England. The aspirants alluded to by his honourable and learned friend would have ample opportunity, notwithstanding this measure, to send forth their productions to the country, and therefore there could on that score be no reason to oppose the enactment of such a law. The bill was only calculated to suppress those publications which were likely to abuse rather than to maintain the liberty of the press. In the whole course of his political life he had never done anything more satisfactory to his own mind, or which appeared to him more deserving the approbation of his country, than the part which he had taken on this and the other measures which, with a view to the public safety, the house had lately felt it necessary to adopt.

DUBLIN CITY ELECTION.

June 24, 1820.

On the death of Henry Grattan, his son offered himself to represent Dublin in his place. He was opposed and defeated, after an exciting contest, by Master Ellis, of the Court of Chancery. Plunket appeared at the hustings to nominate him, and I quote the following imperfect, but interesting, report from the election pamphlet:—

Mr. Sheriff, I shall endeavour, as well as I can, to perform the mournful duty which has fallen to my lot.

[Here the right honourable gentleman's utterance became quite choked, and after a struggle for a few moments against his feelings, he was overcome by their violence, and he burst into tears. As soon as he recovered some composure, he proceeded.]

My friend the lord mayor has pronounced a deserved panegyric upon my learned friend, Mr. Ellis. He has told you that he is a man of honour, of integrity, of independence, and to the justice of the panegyric, I most cordially subscribe. But when I heard my worthy friend, Mr. M'Quay, say he was a fit person to succeed Henry Grattan, I felt the situation to which that gentleman was reduced: I felt the humiliation he was undergoing, when announcing Master Ellis a fit person to represent Henry Grattan! If I were to stop here, and only pronounce that name, without further comment, I know ten thousand responsive feelings would burn in the breast of every man who regards the independence and honour of his country. But, sir, I must discharge my painful duty to my young friend—I cannot—I am unable —every affection of my nature is drawn back to the tomb of him who honoured me with his friendship.

[Here his powerful emotion again overcame him, and again the whole auditory sympathised in his sorrow. As for Mr. Grattan, he wept bitterly during all the time the right honourable gentleman was speaking.]

I would deem it sacrilege and impiety, if I were to suffer any feeling of faction or party to interfere with this solemn duty. When I see Protestants and Catholics intermingled in this assembly, I feel I am surrounded by friends, and cursed be the wretch who, by any art or expression, would endeavour to kindle the flames of contention amongst them. I will not here attempt the vain task of recapitulating the services and the virtues of the friend we have lost. They are far above the reach of my humble powers to do them justice. But great as his patriotism was, no feeling was ever more grateful to his heart, than the support of the Protestant constitution. It was the rare felicity of that immortal man, to have been at once the advocate of every class of his majesty's subjects, and to have given equal satisfaction to all; and in the highest soarings of his enthusiasm, and in the warmest zeal of his exertions, the pole star that guided both, was his wish to strengthen the connexion. I do not now talk of Protestant or Catholic. It would be profanation to the dead to make any distinction. I came here to talk of Ireland! And never could I perform a duty more serviceable to my countrymen, than to implore them not to degrade themselves by trampling on the ashes of their father, and their benefactor. And I tell my learned friend, that I could never offer him a sincerer mark of friendship, than by advising him to retire from a contest, in which he could not triumph, without sharing in the degradation of those who have thrust him forward. How I should compassionate his feelings, when paraded through those streets, his memory would return to the days when that great man, now no more, passed those same streets, between the files of his countrymen, resting on their arms, as it was well said, in admiration of his virtues.

> Even when proud Cæsar 'midst triumphant cars,
> The spoils of nations, and the pomp of wars,
> Ignobly vain and impotently great,
> Show'd Rome her Cato's figure drawn in state,
> As her dead father's reverend image past
> The pomp was darkened and the day o'ercast.
> The triumph ceased—tears gushed from every eye,
> The world's great master passed unheeded by;
> Her last good man dejected Rome adored,
> And honoured Cæsar's less than Cato's sword.

When I look at my young friend who sits beside me, my mind is led back to the times when I saw his great father scaring and blasting with his lightnings the ranks of venality and corruption. It is led back to those hours, when, disarmed of his lightnings, I beheld him in the bosom of his family, surrounded by innocence, and domestic tenderness. My young friend beside me inherits those virtues —his father's image walks before him, and when a mean idea could enter his breast, he must be possessed of a boldness in infamy beyond the share of moderate degeneracy. If, then, it be asked what security exists for his parliamentary conduct, I will answer—" HIS NAME."

The son of the man, unequalled in the annals of history—the man who raised his country from the degradation of a province, to the rank of a nation—the man who has been honoured by the great, the good, the illustrious—he who sleeps amidst kings and patriots, and the most distinguished statesmen—for the empire claims the honour of entombing him, and his very ashes confer a glory upon Britain.

I am now led to consider the claims of my learned friend, who I admit to be a man of honour, of integrity, and of talents. I will not ask what are the acts he has done, the proofs he has given, the trials he has undergone; but I will say in direct terms, if he possessed every qualification—if he possessed a genius as transcendent as the immortal man he claims to succeed—if he manifested as ardent a patriotism—if he had procured a free trade for his country—I say that still, Master Ellis ought to be rejected by the citizens of Dublin. Are you aware, that he is at this moment under a responsibility as awful as the trust you are called upon to repose in him? Are you aware of the duties he is bound to discharge by his office, which he has said (inadvertently, no doubt) he holds independently, but in which he has deceived you, for he only holds it during pleasure. He is bound by his oath, to sit in his office from eleven to three o'clock during term, and out of term from twelve to three. He is obliged, as he himself has sworn, to attend ten months of the year in his office, and to spend his evenings in preparing his decisions for the next day. Let me now ask, how he can realize the promise of Mr. M'Quay, that he will assiduously attend to his duties in Westminster! Will he keep that promise? He gives you bad security for it, when he abandons the old trust confided to him, and for which he is well paid. Who is capable of doing all that? Is Master Ellis capable of discharging his duties in Dublin, and in Westminster together?

[Mr. Plunket then read an account, from Mr. Ellis's own examination in the commissioners of inquiry's report, of the different important and difficult duties he had to perform in all matters of account, taxing of costs, &c., in the Court of Chancery.]

These are not like the duties of a judge, with the intervention of a jury; they are not like the decisions of a judge pronounced in open court, with the wholesome check of the public eye upon him. He has a difficult and complicated duty to discharge, in which he must exercise the soundness of his own discretion. I do not mean to say, that Master Ellis would suffer any improper feeling to sway his mind in the administration of justice; but when a disappointed suitor leaves his office, who has been opposed to another suitor who has a vote, and he himself has none; will he, however justly he be condemned, utter no murmur when retiring? Justice must be not only pure, but unsuspected. Will that man be unsuspected, who is deciding the cause of a person in the evening, to whom he has doffed his hat in the morning, supplicating him for his vote? I do not say this lightly; I am not now upon a topic calculated to catch popular applause, or tickle the ears of some individuals, but I pledge myself this circumstance shall not pass, without being made a subject of legislative investigation. I am aware that there are instances of English masters in chancery having been in parliament. My answer to that is twofold. It is physically possible for a master in London to discharge the duties of both offices. But how is a man, who is obliged to remain in his office in Dublin for ten months in the year, able to attend to his parliamentary duties in London? He can only be absent from his office for two months in the year, as he himself has sworn, and that in the middle of the long vacation, when the parliament is not sitting; therefore, if he is so anxious to assist the legislature, he can only do it with his advice, and he can do that as he is. If he is so eager to enlighten them by his advice, in God's name let him give it to them now. But I assert, there never was such a thing heard of as a master in chancery, even in England, canvassing for a contested election. If such a flagrant outrage of the first principles of justice were attempted in the sister country, the delicacy of English notions of right would shrink with alarm from it. And let me ask my honest friends, are they acting a worthy part, when they propose, to a man, to do an act which would be considered an outrage to justice in London? They think they are now serving themselves—that they are promoting their interests, and forwarding certain schemes—but I predict, that before many months will have elapsed, every man who has taken a part in this degrading transaction, will wish he was not born on the day he first interfered in it.

Mr. Plunket then adverted to the Catholic cause and the late Mr. Grattan's advocacy of it, whose object, he said, he knew was to give strength to the Protestant connexion, and security to the empire.

It is the basis of liberty, and I shall therefore be their advocate. They are not storming the constitution, by wild theories and dangerous innovations, but are calmly, temperately, and constitutionally seeking for their rights; and if they desisted, they would be degraded—if they were contented to be the creeping slaves they are, and abandoned their lofty aspirings after liberty, I would warn every Protestant in the land against the contagion of their society.

The right honourable gentleman concluded by saying—

I am probably shortly to lay their claims before the legislature, but I shall feel disabled and paralyzed if I do not see my young friend beside me, sheathed in the armour of his immortal father.

He then proposed Henry Grattan, Esq., as a fit and proper person to represent the city of Dublin in parliament.

CATHOLIC RELIEF.
February 28, 1821.

For eight years the claims of the Catholics were utterly disregarded in parliament. After the defeat of Grattan's bill in 1813, the House of Commons relapsed into its old temper of indifference, and peace brought back such a sense of security in England that no British minister would peril his place by devoting himself to a measure merely Irish, and so hateful to the House of Lords. In 1814 the petitions were simply presented. In 1815 Sir Henry Parnell attempted to get a committee on the Irish petition, but was defeated by a majority of 81. In 1816 Grattan brought forward the question, and was beaten by a majority of 31. In 1817 Lord Donoughmore in the House of Lords, Grattan in the House of Commons, again moved. Although the majorities grew every year less and less, still the annual motion had become a mere parliamentary sham-battle. In May, 1818, General Thornton elicited what was considered a favourable debate, by moving directly the repeal of the test acts; but neither the Catholics nor the government had given him any sanction, and on Castlereagh's motion the house passed unanimously to the previous question. Next year, however, the majority against Grattan was only two; and the tone of the debates, the growth of public opinion outside, and the abilities, union, and courage which had begun to be displayed in the Irish Catholic agitation, indicated that some decisive attempt at a settlement should soon be made.

Grattan died in 1820, and Plunket succeeded to his parliamentary position towards the Catholic cause. In that session nothing was attempted, owing to the queen's trial. But in the first session of the new parliament, a combined attempt of the English and Irish Catholics was made, and Plunket appeared in formal charge of their case. On the 28th of February, the debate preceding the second great effort to remove the Catholic disabilities occupied the house.

Lord Nugent opened the business by presenting the petition of the English Catholics, signed by 8000 persons. The Duke of Norfolk, earl marshal of England, headed that long roll of aliens for conscience sake. Seven peers and fourteen baronets of the oldest and purest blood in England followed his name. Seven of the churchmen, who then discharged the duties of the dormant Catholic hierarchy of England, signed among the aristocratic laity of their caste— but the name of the vehement polemic Doctor Milner was missed from the list. Then followed the scanty thousands of the Saxon people, scattered all over the length and breadth of Britain, who through bloody persecutions and the systematic contumely of the law for continued centuries, had clung faithful to the faith of Bede and of Becket, of Alfred and of More.

Since the debate of 1813, the question had undergone anxious discussion in the House of Lords, and the bench of bishops had with natural eagerness entered upon the controversy. In the Bishop of Norwich the Catholics found an able and zealous advocate. Plunket, in the course of his speech, argues in reply to one of the most conspicuous prelates upon the other side. Dr. Marsh, who had been advanced to the bishopric of Llandaff, and thence translated to that of Peterborough, opposed Lord Donoughmore's motion in an ingenious speech, the object of which was to show that the Catholics were not excluded from the blessings of the constitution for their belief respecting transubstantiation, the invocation of the saints, or their other speculative religious opinions, but because they divided their allegiance, giving part of it to their own sovereign, and part to a foreigner—were therefore deficient in civil worth, and ought not to be placed in the same rank with those who gave all their allegiance to their native king. This was new ground, and elicited from Plunket one of the most masterly displays of sheer logic ever heard in the English House of Commons.

Another branch of his argument is in reply to Peel, and on the mere political grounds—that the Catholics were too strong a body to be entrusted with full civic faculties, bound as they were by all their instincts and passions to use whatever powers the constitution should endow them with to plot and perpetrate the subversion of the Protestant church establishment—therefore, that emancipation really meant the separation of Ireland and ruin of church and state. The rest of this long and powerful speech is an exact analysis of the historical and legal relations of the Catholics to the constitution, and a demonstration that in consistency the house was bound to continue the reactionary course of legislation which for the last half century had been in their favour, and that their complete emancipation was a measure *dignum, justum, et salutare*, fraught with security to existing establishments, and for the general good of the commonwealth.

The first of the Irish petitions was that of the Catholic committee.

SIR, I hold in my hand a petition, signed by a very considerable number of his majesty's Roman Catholic subjects of Ireland. From the names attached to it, which amount to many thousands, distinguished for rank, fortune, talents and everything which can confer weight and influence,—from the means which these persons possess of collecting the opinions of the people in that part of the United Kingdom—the petition may be fairly considered as speaking the sentiments of the great body of the Roman Catholics of Ireland.

A similar petition was presented, from the same body, the year before last. It is unnecessary for me to remind the house that, on that occasion, it was presented by the late Mr. Grattan. It was sanctioned by the authority of his name, and enforced by all the resistless powers which waited on the majesty of his genius. I have no design to give vent to the feelings with which my heart is filled, or to mingle with the public mourning the mere peculiar and selfish regrets, which have followed to the grave the friend by whose confidence I was honoured, by whose wisdom I was instructed, by whose example I was guided. His eulogium has been heard from the lips of kindred eloquence and genius. The last duties have been rendered to his tomb by the gratitude and justice of the British people. In his death, as in his life, he has been a bond of connexion between the countries.

I will not weaken the force of that eulogium, or disturb the solemnity of those obsequies, by my feeble praise, or unavailing sorrow; but with respect to the sentiments of that great and good man on this particular question, I wish to say a word. Sir, he had meditated upon it deeply and earnestly—it had taken early and entire possession of his mind, and held it to the last. He would willingly have closed his career of glory in the act of asserting within these walls the liberties of his countrymen; but still, regarding them as connected with the strength, the concord, and the security of the empire. Sir, he was alive to fame—to the fame that follows virtue. The love of it clung to him to the last moments of his life; but though he felt that "last infirmity of noble minds," never did there breathe a human being who had a more lofty disdain for the shallow and treacherous popularity which is to be courted by subserviency, and purchased at the expense of principle and duty. He felt that this question was not to be carried as the triumph of a party or of a sect, but to be pursued as a great measure of public good, in which all were bound to forego their prejudices, and to humble their passions for the attainment of justice and of peace.

In the humble walk, and at the immeasurable distance at which it is my lot to follow the footsteps of my illustrious friend, I pledge myself to be governed by the same spirit. I have a firm and entire persuasion, that justice and policy require that the prayer of this petition should be complied with; but I am equally convinced, that if this question is pressed, or carried on any other terms but such as will give full satisfaction to the Protestant mind, it cannot be productive of good. All these objects appear to me to be attainable; with this view, and in this temper only will I prosecute them.

Mr. Plunket then moved, that the petition should be brought up.

Mr. Denis Browne seconded the motion. The petition was brought up, read, and ordered to be printed.

Petitions to the same effect, from the Roman Catholic inhabitants of the parishes of St. Anne's, St. Andrew's, St. Mark's, and St. Peter's, in the city of Dublin, and from the Roman Catholic inhabitants of the county and city of Waterford, were brought up by Mr. Plunket, read, and ordered to be printed; after which Mr. Plunket, having resumed his place, spoke in substance as follows:—

Sir, having presented the petitions confided to me by so respectable portions of the Roman Catholics of the empire, it now remains for me to discharge my duty as a member of this house, by bringing forward a motion founded on their prayer, and calculated for their relief. I desire to be considered as applying, not on the part of the Roman

Catholics, praying to be relieved from the pressure of a grievance; but, as a member of the legislature, on behalf of Protestants and Roman Catholics both. I require of this house to take into their consideration, earnestly and immediately, the relative situation of both; a situation which, on the one side, involves the charge of harshness and injustice; which excites on the other a sense of injury and oppression, and which, in its consequences, must be degrading and dangerous, as well to the party which inflicts as to the party which suffers. My primary object, therefore, is to arrive at public good by doing an act of public justice. I am sure that if it is an act of justice, it will be the foundation of ultimate concord. I believe besides, that it will be productive of a high degree of immediate satisfaction, and will be followed by a warm feeling of gratitude.

But these are advantages secondary and inferior, although certainly desirable, and not to be left out of the account. To suppose that the allaying of present discontent is the principal object of the measure which I have the honour to bring forward, is utterly to undervalue its importance, and to misconceive its bearing. Sir, the Roman Catholics of both countries have nobly disentitled themselves to such a topic. On their part, I am bold to say, that determined as they are never to abandon their claims on the justice and on the wisdom of parliament, their resolution is equally fixed to await, with patience and confidence, the result of that wisdom and justice in which they know they cannot be finally disappointed. That there does exist an anxious and eager desire in that body to share in the rights of Englishmen, I should be ashamed, for them, to deny. That there may grow a sickness of hope deferred, which ought to be administered to them, I will not attempt to conceal. Neither am I so sanguine as to think, or so silly as to assert, that the adoption of any measure which can be proposed to parliament, will have the effect of allaying at once every unpleasant feeling which a long course of unwise policy may have produced. I do not entertain the childish expectation that concession will operate as a charm, and that at the very moment in which the storm has ceased to blow, the waves will subside and the murmurs will be hushed; but I feel convinced that agitation cannot be formidable or lasting, and that in rendering justice we must obtain security.

And, sir, these are not the questions of statesmen. Our duty is to inquire whether injustice is offered to our fellow-subjects, and if so, to atone for it; whether grievances press on them at which they have reason to be dissatisfied, and if so, to remove them; whether injurious distinctions exist, and if so, to obliterate them. If these things excite discontent, the more our shame to suffer injustice, and grievances, and injurious distinctions to remain, and the more imperious the call on every honourable mind to do them away.

I desire, therefore, in the outset, to have it distinctly understood, that my object is not to apply a palliative to temporary or accidental humours. I call on the deliberate wisdom of this house to look at things, and into their causes. If they find any institution pressing heavily and unnecessarily on the rights and feelings of any portion of the subjects, they know that it must ultimately generate discontent; that the longer it is continued, the deeper that discontent must sink into the hearts of the aggrieved parties. And if, sir, these grievances bear not on individuals, or on small classes, but on the great mass of the people, in one of the most important portions of the empire, the house must feel that not a moment should be lost in averting the evils, which must grow from a state of society so alarming and unnatural. Admitting, then, that this great measure is exposed to the lot of all human measures for the happiness of human beings; that the unreasonable will not be convinced; that those who wish for war, will not rejoice in peace; that the bigots in politics and in religion will remain true to their bigotry and blind to their interests; still, I say, you do your duty as legislators, and doubt not that they will do their duty as subjects. The lasting fruit of honest government is lawful obedience, as certainly as insubordination and resistance grow from insolence and injustice.

Before I enter on the considerations which appear properly and necessarily to belong to the subject, I beg leave, sir, to deprecate a mode of dealing with it which has been uniformly, and, I fear, not unsuccessfully resorted to,; I mean the argument that our plan is not perfect: that there are incongruities in the detail; that some of the offices, which we propose to open, are as dangerous as some of those which we propose to keep closed; that some of the oaths which we propose to retain, are unwise and affrontful as those which we desire to abrogate; that we are not all agreed as to the conditions which we would impose, or as to the necessity of at all imposing them.

Sir, this appears to me to be neither a fair nor a manly mode of meeting the question.

If the measure, in any shape or form, is altogether inadmissible, be it so: show this, and there is an end of it.

But, be it good, or be it bad, no man can doubt that it is a question of deep and vital importance. Does justice require it? Does the constitution admit of it? Does policy allow it? All these are fair and open questions, and must be met. But if, without impeaching it on these solid and substantial grounds, you content yourselves with saying, that the particular measure is not well matured, or that there are inconsistencies in the detail, or that the proposed arrangements are not clear or accurate; these, I say, are considerations to excite every man, who feels an interest in the public good, to come at once to the discussion, to join his labours in reconciling the difficulties, and in rounding the arrangements. But it is neither a manly, a patriotic, nor, give me leave to say, an honest part, to condemn the principle because the plan is weak. To him who says that the principle of concession is, in itself, radically vicious, I have no other answer than to join issue on its soundness. But to him who admits that the matter is of deep and earnest interest, but who, without saying whether it ought or ought not to be effected, demurs to its consideration, because he sees imperfections in the means proposed, I have a right to answer, where is your privilege for neutrality or indifference in that which concerns you as much as me, because it involves the best interests of your country? If your objection grows solely from the difficulty, assist me in getting rid of the difficulty; help me to clear up what is obscure, to reconcile what appears inconsistent, to facilitate what appears difficult to reduce to practice; join with me in removing the obstacles to that which, if it is not public evil, is public good.

Sir, this is not a question on which any party has a right to lurch, and practise stratagems, and take advantage. If it be not utterly inadmissible, the state has a claim on every man who feels that he has that within him which is capable of rendering public service, to join in the consideration of this question as its friend and auxiliary. These claims are not to be encountered as an invading enemy, or avoided by device and stratagem. We come forward with no innovation on ancient practice, with no attack on constituted authority, no quarrel with existing establishments, no storming of the strongholds of the constitution, no theoretical experiment for new rights, no resting on unvouched professions; but an unanimous body, consisting of millions of the king's liege subjects, come before parliament, humbly and peaceably, men whose undeviating loyalty stands recorded on your journals and your statute books; they come forward petitioning to be admitted to the privileges enjoyed by their ancestors, in order that they and their posterity may enjoy and exercise them, in cordial support of all the establishments, of all the lawful authorities of the state, according to the well-known principles, and the sound, tried, practical doctrines of the constitution.

Sir, such claims are entitled to an honourable meeting. Let them be put down by reason and by truth; but, if that cannot be done, every able and honest man is bound to assist me in the details which are necessary (and most difficult I admit them to be) for carrying them into effect.

I really do not apprehend that I have to encounter any feeling of hostility in this house. I am sure no man wishes that the plan of conciliation should be impossible. That there cannot be discovered such a plan, I believe no man has sufficient grounds for asserting, I have some confidence in expressing the hope and opinion that there may, because I know that, within the last few years, nearly a majority of this house was of opinion in favour of a specific plan, of which admission to parliament formed a part; and had it not been for the indiscretion of some of those who fancied they were friends to the Roman Catholics, that measure would then have probably been carried.

Sir, at that time the empire was reeling to its centre under the heaviest tempest that ever was weathered by a great nation. I will not believe that any person who, in that hour of danger and dismay, yielded his assent to the desires of the Roman Catholics, will now be disposed to retract it. It will not easily be forgotten that, proud and noble as the exertions of the whole British people have been in bringing that contest to a triumphant issue, no portion of them have been more distinguished than the Roman Catholics. They have shed their blood in defence of our laws and liberties, with a prodigality of self-devotion which proves them worthy to share in them. This house and this country, I trust, have not hot and cold fits; and I know that the question will now receive an attention as anxious and favourable as if the enemy were pressing to land upon our shore, and our hopes of immediate safety rested on the cordial union of every portion of our people.

Whatever difference of opinion exists on this subject, there is little of hostility, nothing of rancour. Prejudices, I must say, I believe there are; but when I call them so, I acknowledge them to be derived from an origin so noble, and to be associated with feelings so connected with the times when our civil and religious liberties were established, that they are entitled to a better name; and I am confident that they are accessible to reason and open to conviction, if met by the fair force of argument without rudeness and violence. Sir, it is impossible to mistake the feeling of the house and of the enlightened part of the country on this subject, or to doubt that it is a growing one.

The liberal and gentleman-like temper in which the question has been discussed, is in itself of the highest value; not merely from the hope it holds out that the cause, if just, must ultimately prevail, but from the soothing influence with which it gains on the minds of our fellow-subjects. With respect to the Roman Catholics of Ireland, I am satisfied that the tone in which the rejection of their claims has of late years been uttered, has considerably softened their disappointment at that rejection; and I do not think I injure the interests of my countrymen, when I say that the character of fair and liberal discussion with which the question has been met in the united parliament, the absence of invidious party feeling, the freedom from bigotry, the forbearance and moderation which has generally marked the opinions and governed the language of the opponents of the measure, has done more to conciliate their minds than many of the concessions which had formerly been made; yielded, as they too generally were, with grudge and reluctance, and accompanied by reproachful charges and degrading insinuations.

And now, sir, I shall proceed, without further preface, to the main argument. The question presents itself in three distinct points of view; as a question of religion, as a question of constitutional principle, and as a question of policy and expediency, in reference to the stability of our existing establishments.

On the first topic it is not necessary that I should say much. I am led to advert to it, not so much from the bearing that the application of the religious principle to civil rights has upon the argument as it regards the Roman Catholic, as from a feeling of the serious injury which it is calculated to work to the cause of Christianity. As an argument affecting the Roman Catholics, merely as such, it has of late been altogether abandoned. So far the cause of religion and of truth is much indebted to a right reverend prelate* of the Established Church, to whom I shall presently have occasion more particularly to allude. He has fairly acknowledged, (and no one of the right reverend bench, in whose presence he made the acknowledgment, disavowed his sentiments), that the profession of the Roman Catholic religion, merely as a religious opinion, or otherwise than as affording an inference of a want of civil worth, was not properly the subject of any political disability. Perhaps therefore, so far as the present measure is concerned, I might safely dismiss the further consideration of this topic; but on my own behalf, and on behalf of all the members of this house, who are obliged to make the declaration now required by law, I hope I shall be excused if I make a few observations.

In the first place, it appears obvious that the requiring a religious

* The Right Rev. Herbert Marsh, Bishop of Peterborough.

pledge to the state, as a qualification for civil rights, makes religion an affair of state; because you cannot lay it down as a rule to be applied only in a case of true religion; for every religion is the true one in the opinion of its own professors; and therefore, if the position is true in our instance, it must be equally true that, in every state, Protestant or Catholic, Christian or Pagan, the interests of true religion require a pledge to the state that the person admitted to its privileges is of the religion of that state. All this leads to the unavoidable inference that, in the opinion of those who so argue, there is no truth in any religion, and no criterion other than its adoption by the state. I do not say that such a principle may not be taken on trust by an honest man, and hotly insisted on by him, if he happens to be a zealous man, but I say it cannot be deliberately and rationally maintained by any person who believes that there is any absolute truth in any religion.

Again, if religion is to be an affair of state, why not require some positive profession of faith, as a qualification? Such as that he is a Christian, or that he believes in God, or in a future state, or that he has an immortal soul? Why does the declaration sound only in horror, and antipathy, and denunciation of another religion? If the law is to be put into a state of electricity by the church, why not of positive electricity?

Again; if we are to denounce, why denounce only one particular sect of Christians? Why not Socinians? Why not those who deny the divine nature of our Lord? Why select those who believe all that we do, merely because they believe something more? Why not Jews, Mahometans, Pagans? Any one of these may safely make the declaration, provided he is willing to commit the breach of good manners which it requires. He may not only deny our God and our Redeemer, but he may worship Jupiter or Osiris, an ape or a crocodile, the host of heaven or the creeping things of the earth; let him only have a statutable horror of the religion of others, and agree to brand with the name of idolatry the religion of the greater part of the Christian world. But further, if the Roman Catholic religion is to be singled out as that, by the common bond of hatred to which we are all to be united in the ties of brotherly love and Christian charity, why select only one particular article of their faith, and say that the sacrifice of the Mass is impious and idolatrous? Why leave them their seven sacraments, their auricular confession, their purgatory, all equally badges of superstition, evidences of contumacy and causes of schism? Why make war exclusively upon this one article? We all declare solemnly that we consider the sacrifice of the Mass as superstitious and idolatrous. Now I entreat each member of this house to suppose that I am asking him individually, and as a private gentleman, does he know what is said, or meant, or done in the sacrifice of the Mass; or how it differs from our own mode of celebrating the communion, so as to render it superstitious and idolatrous? If I could count upon the vote of every member, who must answer me that upon his honour he does not know, I should be sure of carrying, by an overwhelming majority, this or any other question I might think it proper to propose. Were I now to enter on a discussion of the nature of these doctrines, every member would complain that I was occupying the time of statesmen with subjects utterly unconnected with the business of the house or the policy of the country. Can there be a more decisive proof of its unsuitableness as a test?

Still, even at the hazard of being censured for my irrelevancy, I must venture one or two observations on the point denounced. It is important that I should do so, because the truth is that at the reformation the difference between the two churches on this point was considered so slight and so capable of adjustment, that it was purposely left open. Our communion service was so framed as to admit the Roman Catholics, and they, accordingly, for the first twelve years of Elizabeth's reign, partook of our communion, and there is nothing to prevent a conscientious Roman Catholic doing so at this day. The sacrament of our Lord's Supper is, by all Christians, held to be a solemn rite of the Church, ordained by its divine founder as a commemoration of his sacrifice, and most efficacious to those who worthily receive it with proper sentiments of gratitude and contrition; so far, all Christians agree, and we are on the grounds of Scripture and of common sense; but beyond this the Roman Catholic is said to assert that the body of our Lord is actually present in the sacrifice. Now this, in the only sense in which I can affix a meaning to it, I must disbelieve. It is contrary to the evidence of my senses and to the first principles of my reason. But the Roman Catholic states that he does not believe the body of our Lord to be present in the Eucharist, in the same sense in which it is said to be in heaven; for he admits that the same body cannot be in two places at the same time, but it is present in a sense; the council of Lateran says sacramentally present. Now what this sense is I own baffles my faculties. The proposition which states it I can neither affirm nor deny, because I cannot understand it any more than if it was laid down as a dogma, that it was of a blue colour, or six feet high. I feel satisfied, as a sincere Christian, resting on Scripture and reason, that it is not necessary for me to involve myself in these mysteries; and of this I am sure that I should act a very unchristian as well as a very ungentleman-like part, if I were to join in giving foul names to the professors of this, to me, incomprehensible dogma.

Whether it be a fit subject for polemical controversy I will not pretend to say. Queen Elizabeth certainly thought it was not, and forbade her divines to preach concerning it; and they thought her judgment too good on such points not to render an implicit obedience to her commands. I will beg leave, sir, to read a short extract from Burnet's History of the Reformation, bearing on this point:—" The chief design of the queen's council was to unite the nation in one faith, and the greatest part of the nation continued to believe such a presence (the Real Presence), therefore it was recommended to the divines to see that there should be no express definition made against it; that so it might be as a speculative opinion, not determined, in which every man was left to the freedom of his own mind." Such were the opinions of Queen Elizabeth, the founder of the Reformation. Perhaps no monarch ever swayed the British sceptre who had so profound an acquaintance with the royal art of governing. To the Protestant religion, certainly, no monarch ever was more sincerely and enthusiastically attached. On the truth of these opinions she hazarded her throne and life. But she respected the opinions and the sincerity of others, and refused to make windows to look into the hearts of her subjects. She, Queen Elizabeth, the founder of the Reformation, altered the liturgy, as it had been framed in the reign of Edward the Sixth, striking out all the passages which denied the doctrine of the Real Presence; and this for the avowed purpose of enabling the Roman Catholics to join in communion with the Church of England; and am I to be told that this was done in order to let in idolaters to partake of, and to pollute our sacrament? But it seems some of the divines of our day are better Protestants than Queen Elizabeth. If she were alive again I should be curious to see them tell her so. Indeed, sir, these things are calculated to injure the cause of true religion. The Christian is a meek and well-mannered religion, not a religion of scolding and contentious reviling; it is an outrage on that religion and a dangerous attack upon its evidences, to say that the mission of its divine Founder has hitherto served only to establish superstition and idolatry among mankind; and that, except for a favoured few, his blood has been shed in vain. In whatever point of view we turn this question, the absurdities increase upon us. We have legalized their religion and the sacrifice of the Mass; and if that is idolatrous, the king, lords, and commons are promoters of idolatry. By the 31st of the late King we require the party claiming certain privileges to swear that he is an idolater. By the same act we excuse him from coming to our church only on condition of his going to mass; that is, we inflict on him penalties which are to be remitted on the express terms of his committing an act of idolatry. By the same act we inflict penalties on any person who disturbs him in the exercise of his idolatry. In Ireland, we admit him to the magistracy, and to administer the laws of a Christian country, requiring from him, as a preliminary condition, his oath that he is an idolater. When we reflect on all this, and remember that we have established their religion in Canada, and that we are in close alliance, for the purpose of protecting religion and morals, with great nations professing the Roman Catholic religion, is it not obvious that the perseverance in such a declaration is calculated to bring our religion and our character into contempt, and to make thinking men doubt the sincerity of our professions? Whatever may be the fate of the other part of this question I cannot bring myself to believe that this outrage upon the religious decencies of the country will be suffered to remain on our statute book.

Sir, I shall now proceed to the consideration of the question, so far as it involves the objection derived from the supposed existence of certain principles of the constitution, inconsistent with the claims of the Roman Catholics. I shall endeavour to show that the exclusion of the Roman Catholics from franchise and from office, is repugnant to the ascertained principles of our free monarchy; that these principles existed before the reformation, and were coeval with the first foundation of our constitution; that they were not touched at the reformation, or at the revolution, or at either of the unions; that the restriction or suspension of them grew out of temporary causes; that they were so declared and acknowledged at the time; that, when well considered, they afford a confirmation of the principle; that these causes have long since ceased to operate; that we have acknowledged it; that we have acted on this acknowledgment in concerns of the deepest moment; that we have framed a course which, if the acknowledgment be true, is imperfect justice; if false is absolute folly and rashness; and that, if we stop where we are, we are precisely in the situation of exciting every discontent, and organizing every mischief which can be generated by a sense of injury, and arming the party aggrieved with all the strength, and all the means of wreaking that resentment, which belong to solid and essential power; a situation from which we cannot be relieved by shifts or devices; a situation, whose difficulties must every day augment, and, if only put aside, must recur with aggravated pressure; that there is only one mode of dealing with the difficulty; that the part of justice and of safety is the same; that we are called on to try the principle on which we have acted during the entire of the late reigns, and if we find it a sound one, to carry it to its full extent.

By the constitution of England, every liege subject is entitled, not merely to the protection of the laws, but is admissible to all the franchises and all the privileges of the state. For the argument I have now to deal with is this: " that by some principle of the constitution, independent of the positive law, the Roman Catholic is necessarily excluded." What then is this principle of exclusion? Merely this, " that the Roman Catholics acknowledge the spiritual supremacy of the Pope." Why then if, independently of the positive law, this acknowledgment deprives them of the privileges which belong to the liege subjects of the realm, the exclusive principle must have been in force before the law. If so, there did not exist in England a liege man entitled to the privileges of the constitution before the time of Henry the Eighth; for till then all acknowledged the spiritual supremacy of the Pope. Magna Charta was established by outlaws from the state. Those gallant barons, whose descendants have been so feelingly alluded to by my noble friend,* though they were indeed permitted to achieve, yet were not entitled to share the liberties of their country. They might not dare to open the great charter which had been won by their hardihood and patriotism. Nay, more, if this principle be true, there is not, at this moment, a liege subject in any Catholic country in Europe. Sir, such trash as this shocks our common sense, and sets all argument at defiance.

What is this spiritual supremacy of the Pope, and how does it affect the civil allegiance of the subject? The Roman Catholic submits to the authority of the common and the statute law; he acknowledges the force and bindingness of all constituted authorities and jurisdictions, civil and ecclesiastical; he claims no coactive or contentious jurisdiction, or other than a merely conscientious one; and the fullest illustration of this may be found in the fact—that although spiritual censure might, in this conscientious forum, attach to a marriage which our law allows, yet still the Roman Catholic fully admits the legality of the marriage for all civil purposes, and would visit with spiritual censures any member of his church who transgressed against the civil rights which belong to the wife or to the issue.

* Lord Nugent.

This I believe they are ready to testify, in any form of words you may think it right to introduce, or to take the oath of supremacy, if altered or explained in that sense; and for the purpose of trying the practicability of some such measure, I propose going into committee. Sir, if it is said that the spiritual power may be abused for temporal purposes, and that the appointment of their bishops may be an instrument for such purposes, I admit both; I shall allude to them more particularly before I conclude, and I, for one, shall most cheerfully concur in the appropriate remedies; but to say that, therefore, the allegiance of the Roman Catholic is imperfect, is an abuse of terms. After the repeated declarations of the legislature of both countries on this subject, it would seem not unreasonable to require from those who take upon themselves to graduate the scale of allegiance, for the purpose of exclusion from common right, to show where, in the principles of our law and constitution, or where, in the regions of common sense, they find the canon on which this exclusion is founded. Sir, it has been with no ordinary degree of regret that I have heard the opinion of the distinguished and learned prelate,* to whom I have before alluded, on this subject. With a candour which does him honour as a minister of religion, he fairly avows that the religious consideration is entirely to be thrown out of the case, save so far as it bears on the civil worth of the party. But he says, that "inasmuch as the Roman Catholic yields that spiritual homage to the Pope which (as he thinks) the Protestant of the Established Church of England yields to the King, and which the Protestant of the Established Church of Scotland yields to no man, he conceives himself warranted to infer that he possesses less of what he calls civil worth; and not only this, but that this difference is so important as to become a specific difference, and therefore to warrant the separation of the Roman Catholics into a distinct species, necessarily excluded from offices and franchises, while the two others continue entitled to the enjoyment of both." Sir, this is the kind of reasoning which Mr. Locke describes as "seeing a little, presuming a great deal, and so jumping to a conclusion." It might have occurred to the mind of the learned prelate, accustomed to the precision of mathematical proof as he is, that if the Roman Catholic, for the reason assigned, really had less civil worth than the Protestant, it would not therefore follow that he should be excluded, unless the Protestant's quantity of civil worth were first proved to be the minimum which would warrant admission. But what may be the nature of this quality which he is pleased to designate under the new appellation of "civil

* Dr. Marsh.

worth," he has not thought proper exactly to state. It leaves out, I presume, all consideration of birth or fortune, or such like; also the accidental circumstances of education and learning and talents; also the unessential attributes of truth and honour and probity, these all are circumstances too mean to form any part of his abstractions. I must presume so; for the person who possesses them all in the highest degree, if he happens to acknowledge the spiritual supremacy of the Pope, is actually excluded, is below zero in his scale of " civil worth;" and the person who is utterly destitute of all of them is admitted, provided he is not so punctilious as to refuse to deny that supremacy.

To the English dissenter, and to the orthodox Scotchman, he manifests a degree of indulgence which does more credit to his liberality than to his logic. They, it seems, are deficient in this " civil worth;" but still he admits them rather, I suppose, to a kind of limbo, between the enjoyments which belong to perfect allegiance and the curse of utter exclusion. But he has, by some process, ascertained that the Roman Catholic has reached the exact degree of deficiency which necessarily draws down the sentence of condemnation.

Sir, it would have become the gravity and station of the person who made this assertion to refer to some authority or analogy of our constitution to warrant it, and not arbitrarily to draw a line of such fatal denunciation, merely because he has discovered a circumstance which distinguishes from each other two classes of his fellow-subjects and fellow-Christians. Mr. Burke truly says, that " there is no description of men more absurd than the metaphysician, who, dealing in essences and universals, rejects the consideration of more and less;" and never was the justice of this truly philosophical remark more strongly exemplified than in this argument, which excludes from the pale of the state, and from the hope of the royal favour, the Howards and the Arundels, and the long line of illustrious persons who have shone with the brightest lustre on the noblest periods of our history, who have gained the charter of our liberties, and fought the battles of law and freedom; and all for this want of " civil worth;" while it lets in the lowest and the vilest, no matter of what description, slaves or traitors, outcasts from everything connected with truth or virtue, merely because their " civil worth" is authenticated by denying the spiritual authority of the Roman Pontiff.

Sir, neither in this nor in anything is our constitution metaphysical or pedantic. Political constitutions are not like natural ones·

they grow out of the action of man on man; there must be choice, approbation, distinction founded on moral differences. The wisdom, and justice, and discretion, by which the moral order is administered, are all unlike the laws of matter and of motion, which govern the physical world; and, therefore, when we hear of a machinery so constituted as to be capable of letting into trust everything that is unworthy, and of shutting out everything that is exalted, we may be assured that we have to do with idle dreams, and that they do not proceed from any waking, sober, practical views of British law and constitution. If it is said that this touchstone does not let in the rabble I have described, but merely makes them eligible, then we come back to the true principles of our policy; the power of the crown to reject the base, and to select the worthy; the power of the people to exclude from the franchises which depend on their favour the candidates who are not deserving; and above all, the controlling good sense and vigilance of the public mind to see that these privileges are not abused.

These, sir, are the sound, and rational, and practical principles on which our constitution has been formed; by these it must be preserved, and not by the affectation of what Mr. Pitt, with peculiar felicity, calls " a harsh uniformity;" not by inert abstractions, which are fit only for the school and the cloister, but become ridiculous when applied to the concerns of states and to the business of life.

I speak in the presence of enlightened constitutional lawyers and statesmen, and I do not fear a contradiction when I assert, that the doctrine of exclusion is not to be found in the principles, or in the analogies of our constitution, or in the history of our country, or in the opinion of any statesman whose name or memory has reached us. It is, at once, inconsistent with the subject's rights and with the king's prerogatives. Ours is a free monarchy, and it is of the essence of such a government that the king should be entitled to call for the services of all his liege subjects, otherwise it is not a monarchy; and that no class of his subjects should be excluded from franchise, otherwise it is not a free monarchy. I use the word franchise, not in the lawyers' technical sense of it, as a right supposed to be derived by prescription or grant from the crown, but in the sense of Mr. Burke, when he applied it to the right of voting for members to sit, and to the right of sitting in parliament. Sir, these are privileges not derived from the grace of the crown or the permission of the legislature, or from the positive declaration of any written law, but drawn from the great original sources from which crown and law and legislature have been derived; from the sacred fountains of British constitution and freedom; the denial of which, as justified by any supposed principles of our constitution, I take on me to denounce as founded on a radical ignorance of the essence and stamina of our civil polity.

Such was not the opinion of Lord Bacon. With the permission of the house I will read the words of that illustrious statesman and philosopher. In his bird's eye view of our constitution, after enumerating the classes of alien enemies, alien friends, and denizens, he goes on thus: "The fourth and last degree is a natural born subject, and he is complete and entire; for, in the law of England, there is *nil ultra;* there is no more subdivision, no more subtle distinction beyond these; and hence it seems to me that the wisdom of our law is to be admired, both ways, both because it distinguisheth so far, and because it doth not distinguish farther; for I know that other laws do admit more curious distinctions of this privilege; for the Roman law, besides "*jus civitatis*," which amounts to naturalization, has "*jus suffragii;*" for though a man were naturalized to take lands of inheritance, yet he was not entitled to have a vote at the passing of laws, or at election of officers, and yet further they have "*jus petitionis,*" or "*jus honorum;*" for although a man had a voice, yet he was not capable of honour or office; but these are the devices commonly of popular or free estates, which are jealous whom they take into their number, but are unfit for monarchies, but by the law of England, the subject that is natural born hath a competency or ability to all benefits whatever."

This principle of exclusion, therefore, is equally at war with the prerogative of the crown, and the title of the subject. It wrests the sceptre from the king that it may strike at the liberties of the people, and obtrudes an unconstitutional monopoly on the just rights of both. It is an insolent republican principle, which has more than once been publicly and universally reprobated in this house; the principle of lawless association, for the purpose of lawless exclusion, and which promises a conditional allegiance to the monarch, so long only as he shall uphold the arrogant and exclusive claims of one class of his subjects against the inherent rights and privileges of the other.

I shall now proceed to show that this principle of common right was not touched, or meant to be touched, at the Reformation. The house will be so good as to excuse my dwelling somewhat on this part of the question, as no portion of our history is less understood than that of the Reformation, in as far as it affects the civil rights of the Roman Catholics. Sir, the act of supremacy was intended, not as a test of religion, but of loyalty; not to distinguish the

Roman Catholic from the Protestant, but the well-affected Roman Catholic, who acknowledged the queen's title and authority, from the disaffected, who denied both. The title of the act is, "An act for restoring to the crown the ancient jurisdiction over the state, ecclesiastical and spiritual." The queen's injunction and admonition were issued to explain the oath for the express purpose of enabling the Roman Catholics, as well as other classes of dissenters, to take it. After ordering all offensive words, such as Papist, heretic, schismatic, to be forborne, under severe pains, she declares "that she does not pretend to any authority, save that which had at all times belonged to the imperial crown of this realm, namely, that she had the sovereign rule over all persons under God, so that no foreign prince had rule over them; and if those who formerly appeared to have scruples about the oath were willing to take it in that sense, she was well pleased to accept of it, and did acquit them of all penalties in the act." This explanation so given by the authority of the queen is adopted by the legislature and incorporated into the act of the 5th of Elizabeth, which is the first that requires the oath of supremacy from the members of the House of Commons. The 17th section of this act is particularly entitled to attention; it recites in these words, "whereas the queen is otherwise sufficiently assured of the loyalty of the temporal lords of her high court of parliament; therefore the act shall not extend to them." Here, sir, is a legislative proof that the act of supremacy was a test, not of religion, but of loyalty, not of exclusion but of selection; and accordingly it enumerated a class of acknowledged Roman Catholics, of whose faith and loyalty she was assured, and as such admitted them to the high court of parliament, and to all offices whatsoever. I have already adverted to the alteration of the litany and communion service for the express purpose of admitting the Roman Catholics; and any person who will take the trouble of looking into the history of the times, will see that for the first twelve years of her reign the Roman Catholics attended the service of the Church of England; so it is stated by Lord Coke in Cawdry's case, and so by Rapin, Burnet, and Hume. Nor was it until the twentieth year of her reign, when the Spanish schemes against her crown and life were aided by the machinations of the foreign priests imported into England, that the punishment and exclusion of the Roman Catholics commenced. Sir, all this is well explained in Walsingham's letter to Monsieur Critoy, which is to be found in Burnet. The queen there recognises two principles, "first, that consciences were not to be forced, but to be won and reduced by force of truth, with the aid of time and all good means of instruction and persuasion; the other, that causes of conscience, when they exceed their bounds and grow to be matters of faction, lose their natures; and that sovereign princes ought distinctly to punish their contempt and practices, though coloured with the pretence of conscience and religion; not to make windows into men's hearts, but to punish their overt acts;" and he defends her majesty from the charge of being a temporizer in religion. "It is not (he says) the success of things abroad, or the change of servants here at home can alter her; only as the things themselves altered, she applied her religious wisdom to methods correspondent with them, only attending to the two distinctions above-mentioned, first, in dealing tenderly with conscience; and secondly, distinguishing faction from conscience and softness from singularity." These, sir, I repeat it, are the dictates of royal wisdom, and thus, I humbly trust, our gracious sovereign will apply his royal and religious wisdom, that as the things themselves have altered, he may adopt methods correspondent with them. During the entire reign of Elizabeth, some of the highest and most confidential offices in the state were filled by Roman Catholics; and Mr. Hume states, as a thing notorious, that James the First gave preferment indifferently to his Roman Catholic and Protestant subjects.

That Roman Catholics sat and were considered as entitled to sit in the House of Commons as well as in the House of Lords, until excluded by the act of the 30th of Charles the Second, is evident from Sir Solomon Swaile's case; in the year 1677, (the year before the 30th Charles the Second,) he was expelled, not for being a Papist, which was admitted and notorious, but for being a recusant. Sir Robert Sawyer's argument is this, " a Popish recusant cannot come near the king's person, and *à fortiori* he cannot be of the great council of the realm; whoever disables himself from his attendance in parliament you ought to discharge;" and the resolution of the house is, " that Sir Solomon Swaile is convicted of Popish recusancy, and therefore discharged." So that for one hundred and twenty years after the reformation had been completed by Elizabeth, the notion that any merely religious tenet should disqualify for civil rights was never acted on or announced; the very title of the act of the 30th Charles the Second is decisive, it being " for the more effectually preserving the king's government by disabling Papists to sit in either house of parliament." Sir, the reason is obvious why the measure was then resorted to; the religion of Charles was more than suspected, and the presumptive heir was known to be a Roman Catholic; and had he been at liberty to fill the offices of the state with Papists (in the most offensive sense of the word), and to pack a Popish parliament, there would have been no safety for the Protestant establishment, or for the civil liberties of the country. This case properly formed an exception to the universality of Lord Bacon's rule; for the king's power of selection ceased to afford any security. The functions of royalty were so far paralyzed, or worse, and the exception proves the justness of the rule. But were the exceptions then introduced made fundamental articles of our constitution? Were they incorporated with the great principles declared at the Revolution? No; but the particular mischief is for ever guarded against, by making it a fundamental law of the land, that the king shall be of the Protestant religion as by law established; thus applying a remedy precisely commensurate with the evil, not declaring that the valves of the constitution should be for ever closed against any portion of the people, but putting them under the control and guardianship of the king, declaring that he should execute that sacred trust no longer than while he continued a member of the Established Protestant Church. Sir, if I am asked, why then, when the Protestantism of the throne was thus secured, did the provisions of the 30th of Charles the Second continue? I answer, because the danger was not in fact done away, or at least the apprehension of it; because the return of the exiled family still impended over the country; that we have narrowly, by God's providence, escaped that calamity; and that it was not until nearly the period of his late majesty's accession that all apprehensions on that score were effectually removed. But any person acquainted with the history of that period knows that the 30th of Charles the Second was merely a substitute for a bill of exclusion; and that if the latter could have been obtained the former never would have been resorted to; and Bishop Burnet tells us that King William mainly rested the policy of that law on the Popery of the throne, stating that, while the king was not a Protestant, that law was the only security of the establishment.

Sir, I think I have now shown that these notions of exclusion are at war with the original spirit of our constitution, and that they form no part of the system either of the reformation or of the revolution. I will now proceed to demonstrate, from the records of parliament and the authentic history of the times, that this act of Charles the Second, which had been adopted as a necessary restriction for the time, was always refused as a permanent law, and carefully kept out of the wholesome circulation of the constitution; and that the period was always looked to, and the means anxiously preserved, of recurring to its true principles when the accidental obstruction should be removed. Sir, by the act of the 4th and 5th of Queen Anne, cap. 8, the lords justices were empowered to act in the event of the queen's death, until the arrival of her successor; the 16th section of the act disables them from giving the royal assent to any bill for repealing the act of uniformity. And why? Because it was held to be a perpetual and fundamental law. But it was proposed in the House of Lords to introduce a clause disabling the commissioners from assenting to the repeal of the 25th of Charles the Second (the test act), or the 30th of Charles the Second, (the act requiring the declaration), and the proposition was rejected; here then is a direct and positive proof that the statesmen and legislature of that day did not contemplate the perpetual continuance of that law, and that they considered it as of a different class and order from that which secured the Protestant established church fundamentally and unalterably; yet now it seems it has become a sacred element of the constitution, which it would be sacrilege to touch. When, on the following year, the Scottish Union was brought forward, they did not venture even to propose the 30th of Charles the Second, as a provision to be incorporated as fundamental, but the zeal of bigotry did propose the test and corporation acts. The proposition was made in the House of Lords, on the 1st of February, 1706, for the insertion of the test act as a fundamental law, and, in the House of Commons, for a similar insertion of the test and corporation acts, and on full debate, the propositions were, in both houses, rejected. What the parliament intended as fundamental, it expressly declares, namely, the Scotch act for the security of the church of Scotland, and the English act for the security of the church of England; and they declare, that the said acts shall, for ever, be held and adjudged to be observed as fundamental and essential conditions of the said union, and shall, at all times coming, be taken to be, and are thereby declared to be, essential and fundamental parts of the said articles and union; but when they come to state the oaths to be taken on admission to parliament, the words are these, that every one of the lords of parliament of Great Britain, and every member of the House of Commons, until the parliament of Great Britain shall otherwise direct, shall take the oath of allegiance and supremacy, and shall subscribe the declaration contained in the act of the 30th of Charles the Second.

What are the terms of the act of union with Ireland? "That every one of the lords of parliament, and every member of the House of Commons of the United Kingdom, shall, until the parliament of the United Kingdom shall otherwise provide, take the oaths and subscribe the declaration now by law required to be taken, made, and subscribed by the lords and commons of the parliament of Great Britain." Sir, here is the clear and express recognition by the legislature of both countries of the temporary nature of these oaths. In the words and in the spirit of both the unions, I call upon you now "otherwise to determine." Backed then by the known principles of the constitution, growing out of the nature and essence of our free monarchy; backed by the history and well authenticated objects of the Reformation, by the public declaration of Queen Elizabeth, and of her ablest ministers; supported by the declarations of the 5th of Elizabeth, expressly stating that the oaths required were tests of loyalty and not of religion, and admitting the Roman Catholic peers on the ground of their known loyalty, independent of the oath; supported by the admitted practice of one hundred and twenty years from the 1st of Elizabeth to the 30th of Charles the Second; having the clear evidence of history to show that the innovation then made grew out of circumstances accidental and temporary; supported by the Bill of Rights and Act of Settlement, which provide the proper remedy for the temporary evil, by a perpetual and fundamental law, securing the Protestantism of the throne; supported by the positive refusal of the House of Lords, in the 4th and 5th of Queen Anne, to treat it as a fundamental law; by the facts of its not being ventured to be proposed as a final regulation at the Scottish Union, though the test and corporation acts were so proposed, and unsuccessfully; with the provision in the articles of that Union, which, while it defines the articles that were to be held fundamental, declares that the oath and declaration shall continue to be taken only until the British parliament should otherwise provide; and with the express provisions of the legislatures of Great Britain and Ireland, at the Irish Union, to the same effect; supported as I am by the records of parliament, and the undeniable facts of history, by the acts of the last fifty years, which, if this principle were a sound one, would have been a continued outrage on the constitution; with the authority of the illustrious men who were cotemporary with that system of conciliation; Dunning, Pitt, Fox, Burke, Sheridan, Wyndham, enlightened statesmen, who saw their way, and engaged in this order of restoration on no light or superficial views, but on careful results, as wise and deliberate as they were liberal and noble, and who were well aware that if this course were to end in anything short of the full renovation of civil rights, it would have been, not a plan of policy, but a paroxysm of frenzy; supported by these great names, and not encountered by one which has had sufficient buoyancy to float along the stream of time; with these authorities, I ask, have I not redeemed (I had almost said triumphantly) the pledge which I threw down, when I arraigned the principle of exclusion as founded on a radical ignorance of the essence and stamina of our constitution. Triumph, sir, I cannot feel when I miss the ornaments of this house, when there is painfully obtruded on my mind the recollection of the losses which this cause and this country has more recently sustained; of Mr. Whitbread, the watchful and incorruptible sentinel of the constitution; the more than dawning talents and virtues of Mr. Horner; the matured excellencies of Sir Samuel Romilly, a light extinguished, which threw a steady lustre, not merely on his profession and his country, but over all the interests of mankind; Mr. Ponsonby, the constitutional statesman, who led the ranks of opposition with disinterested honour, equally revering the constituted authorities and the people's rights; my ever-lamented friend Mr. Eliot, noble in his nature as he was liberal in his sentiments, a model of what aristocracy ought to be, a bond between the people and the throne; Sir Arthur Pigott, the genuine representative of the sound, honest, constitutional English lawyer; above all, when I revert to this last and heaviest disaster, this dark and overwhelming calamity on which I dare not trust myself to speak—I feel anything but triumph; I feel that in passing before the images of these illustrious men, there is a funeral gloom thrown over this great procession, in which we are moving to offer up our bad passions and angry prejudices upon the altar of freedom and of concord. But, sir, though I feel no triumph, I boldly appeal to the sense and candour of the house, whether what I have endeavoured to demonstrate does not require some better answer than vague and general assertions, that the principles of the constitution, and of the reformation, and of the revolution, are hostile to the claim of civil rights, and whether the Roman Catholic can consider himself as fairly dealt with while his exclusion is rested on such gratuitous and arbitrary dogmas.

I am conscious that I press on the indulgence of the house, but there remains one topic to which it is absolutely necessary that I should closely and earnestly address myself, because I know that there are many persons, most worthy, respectable, and liberal, who on the score of religion, and of constitutional principle, are quite alive and friendly to the claims of the Roman Catholics, but who, at the same time, have serious apprehensions that the removal of their disabilities might endanger our establishments in church and state. Could I believe that the measure of redress involved consequences of injury or of danger to these establishments, dear to my heart as I hold the interests of my Roman Catholic countrymen, I should abandon their long-asserted claims, and range myself with their opponents; but having the most entire conviction of the groundlessness of the apprehension, and entertaining a sanguine hope that such alarms may be removed from the minds of those who are sincere in their profession of them, I particularly entreat the attention of the house. To the right honourable member for the university of Oxford,* I beg leave especially to address myself, and I assure him I do so with all the respect due to his talents, his acquirements, and his integrity; to his high principles as a statesman and as a gentleman; I am well aware that there is no member of this house whose opinions are so likely to have influence on this subject, or whose being confirmed in his prejudices (if they are prejudices) is so likely to produce serious injury to the country.

Is it true then, that the church is not exposed to any danger? I certainly will not take it on myself to make the assertion; but I say that this danger, whatever it may be, exists at this moment, and that the proposed measure, therefore, cannot produce it; I say, that it is not calculated to increase it; I go further, and I assert that it is, in the highest degree, calculated to diminish it.

Sir, the question is unfairly dealt with when it is asked what security have we for the Protestant church, if we adopt this measure? I answer, every security which you have if you do not adopt it, and a great many more. The fallacy consists in supposing that we propose to pass from a state of security and ease, to an untried scene of difficulty and danger; whereas the danger at this moment exists— the disproportion between the Roman Catholic population, and that of the establishment (I speak of Ireland) is not produced by this measure; the insecurity is in the narrowness of the basis, which neither this nor any other measure can either cause or remove, though it may in some degree remedy it; and it is beyond the reach of human art to provide an adequate remedy in any other way than by making it the interest and duty of this population to abide by and to support the establishment. Let those who propose not to meddle with this question, but to leave it to tide and time, consider the nature of the dangers as stated on a former occasion by the right honourable member for Oxford, or suggested by him, and every one of which exists at this moment in all its dimensions, without any reference to this measure. I shall endeavour to enumerate them subtantially as put forward by him, or as necessarily resulting from the statements made by him.

First, the exceeding disproportion of the Roman Catholic to the

* Mr. Peel (afterwards Sir Robert).

Protestant population in Ireland. The right honourable member did not, I believe, profess to state it exactly ; I myself believe that it is much greater than is generally supposed,—certainly more than four to one—but for the purpose of this argument it matters not.

Next, this great majority principally contribute to the support of the establishment to which they do not belong. Besides this, they exclusively support their own clergy.

By the principles of their religion they are in direct communication with a foreign potentate, through the medium of their clergy. This communication is uninterrupted and uncontrolled by the state.

Though the Roman Catholic clergy possesses a most extensive influence over the passions, opinions, private and political principles and actions of the laity, yet the state neither exercises nor possesses any control over their appointment.

The established religion is not merely that of the small minority, but one which has dispossessed the great majority. This has been effected, not as in England, by a reformation of public opinion, but by an act of state, leaving the necessary consequences, irritation and hostility.

This great majority is in the unprecedented situation of being excluded from a great proportion of the franchises, offices, and honours of the state, not on account of any moral or political delinquency, but merely on account of its religion. They are at the same time admitted to the full enjoyment of substantial power, including the command of our fleets and armies.

This ejected majority, if they are actuated by the motives by which man is ordinarily actuated, and by the feelings which nature inspires, must have views hostile to the religious establishments of the state.

Though they disavow such principles on their oaths, still they must entertain them, and therefore they have been admitted to their present privileges on the faith of oaths which, if they are sincere in their religious opinions, cannot bind them.

They are, therefore, required by the legislature, and have accordingly stooped to stain themselves with the odious crimes of hypocrisy and perjury; the liberal feelings of the right honourable gentleman will, no doubt, induce him to say that he does not impute to them the wilfulness of perjury, but that they deceive themselves; be it so; as to the extent of the danger it matters not; they are swearing against nature, and their oath affords no security; our danger is as great as if they were admitted without the oath, with this difference, that it is admitted that the oath which they are ready to take, cannot, on such a subject, bind them.

Being thus incapable of being bound by oaths, they are, at this moment, shut out from what is sought by oaths only.

The country in which all these dangers and anomalies exist is separated by nature from that to which it is united by law. It once had an independent existence; within twenty years had an independent legislature, and still has its separate courts of justice and distinct departments of executive government.

Now, sir, mark, if these are at all to be considered as causes of danger. Such is our existing state. An ejected majority of four to one; irritated and hostile; subject to the unbounded influence of a clergy appointed by a foreign potentate, unregulated by the state; placed in a portion of the empire separated by nature, recently and imperfectly united by law; and observe, this hostile majority, not an uneducated rabble, but the leaders now, and all of them, in the natural course of things, growing to be a wealthy, powerful, thriving, prosperous body; actually admitted to every thing which constitutes real power in the state; and this on the strength of oaths which cannot bind them, without overturning the laws of nature; and at the same time, the remaining barriers and bulwarks of the state, resting on oaths and on oaths alone!

Sir, I ask any man really anxious for the safety of the Established Church of Ireland, is this the state in which it ought to be left? Is this the bed of roses on which the right honourable gentleman is disposed to rest himself? These, if he is right, are the existing dangers, which at this moment threaten the safety of the establishment; and amidst this rocking of the battlements we are told that the true and statesman-like conduct is to share in the repose of the right honourable gentleman.

Sir, no man sensible of the dangers which really exist, and duly impressed with the vitality of the connexion between church and state, can suffer this momentous question to depart from his mind; it is a problem of difficulty the most extreme, but until it is solved, there is no safety for the country.

The way in which the right honourable gentleman has argued the question is, to my mind, most alarming. The Roman Catholics, he says, if they have organs, senses, affections, passions, like ourselves, nay, if they are sincere and zealous professors of that faith to which they belong, will aspire to the re-establishment of their church, in all its ancient splendour. Why, sir, according to this view they ought to aspire to it! They ought to be sincere and zealous in their faith, and if so they will aspire to it. Why then, this subversion of the establishment, which we are bound to the last extremity to resist, they are bound by an equally imperious duty to aim at! And then the right honourable gentleman tells them they have before their eyes the example of Scotland, which, with her Presbyterian Church, has been united to England with her Episcopal Church, all jealousies buried in oblivion and the political union completed.

Why then, having left the country committed in this manner; the establishment of the Protestant minority in Ireland opposed, not only to the schemes, but to what he considers as the rightful, natural, and necessary views of the Roman Catholic majority, who, if they are sincere in their religion, must desire to restore the ancient splendour of their church, backed as they are by a sound constitutional precedent in the establishment of Presbytery in Scotland; we being determined, nevertheless, as I trust we all are, to hold our establishment; bound to do so as we value our laws, our liberties, and the connexion between the two countries; and they being equally bound to subvert it—urged by the irresistible impulses of nature, by their organs, senses, affections, and passions, and sanctioned by the awful calls of religion in doing so—Sir, this is to leave the Protestant establishments, and the Roman Catholic people of Ireland, committed in necessary and interminable hostility, the one side insisting on subversion, and the other struggling for existence; and the right honourable gentleman says, it is a shame to come forward with indigested schemes, and to disturb this happy and halcyon state of security and comfort.

Sir, if I could view the question in the same light with the right honourable gentleman, I should indeed not propose to legislate; I should, like him, abandon it; but not like him with satisfaction; not under the impression that, in doing so, we were to continue in possession of the freedom and the glory derived from the constitution of our ancestors; but under the deep and afflicting conviction that our glories and our freedom were doomed to perish. I should, like him, remain inactive, but not at rest; I should turn from the question, not to a state of tranquillity, but of torpor; the prelude, not to repose, but to dissolution.

Sir, I am sure the right honourable gentleman is not aware of the consequences to which his position would lead. It goes to establish this monstrous doctrine, that the Roman Catholic who is sincere in his belief is bound to aim at the subversion of the establishment, and so divides society into two classes, those whose duty it is to support the establishment, and those who are bound to overthrow it. It leaves no alternative. Every honest man in the country must be ranked on the one side or on the other. The bigotry which he imputes to the Roman Catholic imposes the duty of intolerance on ourselves. If it is of necessity a principle of their religion to overturn our establishment, it becomes our duty to put down their religion. If this serpent is fostered under their altars, we must put down their altars. This alarming doctrine makes the distinction between tolerating their religion, and giving power to those who profess it, mere rant and folly. If that religion contains the spark which is to consume our establishments, we must extinguish that religion. Toleration would be a crime. This imputed duty frightfully recoils upon ourselves, and the doctrine resolves itself into the most sublimated spirit of bigotry.

It is, therefore, most consolatory to me, that, in resisting the argument of the right honourable gentleman, I at the same time vindicate the Roman Catholics from the unmerited charge of hostility which is imputed, and relieve the Protestant from the hateful duty of intolerance which results from the imputation.

Sir, on behalf of the Roman Catholics, I am bold to say that, though they prefer their own religion to ours, yet that they find the Protestant religion established by law, by the same law by which their own lives, liberties, and properties, along with those of all the other subjects of this realm, are secured; that, if the right honourable gentleman were to state, to any well-informed Roman Catholic, the precedent of Scotland, he would laugh at his precedent; because he knows that the Presbyterian religion was the reformed religion of Scotland, that it was so established at the reformation, that it was so confirmed at the revolution, and so ordered and perpetuated by solemn compact between the two countries at the Union; that on the contrary, the Protestant established religion of England was, in Ireland, established at the reformation, confirmed at the revolution, and perpetually incorporated at the Union; that it forms a part of the fundamental unalterable law of the empire; that he therefore prefers a Protestant establishment and an unimpaired state to a Roman Catholic establishment and a subverted one; that he considers the possessions of the Protestant clergy as their absolute property, secured to them as sacredly as the private possessions of any individual are secured to him; that he abides by the oath which he has taken, to maintain that establishment, and that, so far from considering himself under any obligation to subvert it, he holds himself obliged, by the most solemn ties which can bind him to society, as a man, a citizen, and a Christian, to resist all attempts at its overthrow, from whatever quarter they may proceed. Most iniquitous and absurd would it have been in the legislature to require that such an oath should be taken by the Roman Catholics, if, as such, they were under a religious and moral obligation to violate it; the supposition would be equally degrading to the legislature which imposed, and to the Roman Catholic who submitted to it.

On what authority does the right honourable gentleman, in opposition to their oaths, burn and brand on the Roman Catholics this odious stigma? What have they done? What have they said? What have they sworn? He will not try them by their declarations, their oaths, or their actions; but, on views of what he calls human nature, he not only proscribes the great mass of the Irish people from the honours of the state, but on principles which, if justly imputed, ought to shut them out from the pale of human society.

Sir, the sources from which the right honourable gentleman derives his view of human nature are not those to which I have had access. I cannot find in them that a Roman Catholic gentleman, enjoying every privilege of the British constitution, and with every avenue to wealth, and power, and place, and honour opened to him, should wish for the subversion of the state, in order that his priest may have a mitre. The alliance between church and state is not founded on any such supposed propensity in the nature of man, but on a principle of policy, for the security of the state, and of all religion within it, and by which all sects are benefited by having the principles of religion incorporated with the state; and therefore to suppose that a man, sincere in his religion, must wish it to be the established one, argues an equal want of acquaintance with the nature of man and the institutions of society. There is a profound political wisdom in this alliance, and every man who regards the welfare of the state, be his religion what it may, is bound to uphold it; and he would be an absurd sectarian, as well as a wild politician, who, on such motives as are imputed, would engage in the experiment of heaving the establishment from its centre, and overturning along with it the constitution of Great Britain.

But, sir, this I *can* read in the book of human nature, that if men are harshly excluded from the privileges of citizens; if the door of the state is closed against them; if they are stopped short in the career of honourable ambition; if they are made an invidious exception to the principle which allows the talents and virtues of every man to rise to the level, that it may flow in the bed of the constitution; if they are told that they and their children, to the end of time, *nati natorum, et qui nascentur ab illis*, are to be stigmatized as a caste, and to be for ever excluded from honour, and station, and confidence; I *do* read in the book of human nature, that such persons have ground for discontent. And I cannot but admire the persevering cordiality with which men so circumstanced have fought the battles, and shared the dangers, and borne the burdens of their country. But I would disdain to make their patience an argument for their exclusion, nor can I shut my eyes to the danger which may result from its continuance.

What then is my remedy for the dangers which really exist? And what is the difference in this respect between the views of the right honourable gentleman and mine?

First, I propose to regulate and legalize, within its proper limits, the intercourse with the see of Rome, so as to satisfy the state that the communication for spiritual purposes shall not be perverted to become an instrument of political intrigue. What is the remedy of the right honourable gentleman? To leave the intercourse as it is, secret and uncontrolled.

Next, I propose to regulate the appointment of the Roman Catholic bishops, so as to assure the government of the country, that they, and through them all the Roman Catholic clergy, shall be well affected to the state. What is the remedy of the right honourable gentleman? To leave the appointment as it is, unregulated and subject to the unmixed influence of a foreign power, which may be friendly, which may be neutral, or which may be hostile. The right honourable gentleman really seems so much in love with the perfection of his danger, that he is afraid of having it spoiled by any alteration.

But, sir, my third proposition, and that to which all others must be secondary and subordinate, is to incorporate the Roman Catholics with the state. So to bind them to the present order of things, that their interest shall be our security. To give to the well-affected the reward of his loyalty, to take away from the revolutionist the pretext and the instrument of his treason. To rivet the honest Roman Catholic to the state by every good affection of his nature, by every motive that can affect his heart, by every argument that can convince his reason, by every obligation that can bind his conscience; not by adding the weight of a feather to his power, but by relieving his feeling from everything that is contumelious, insolent, and personal, by abolishing every odious distinction, every affrontful suspicion, every degrading exclusion. What is the remedy of the right honourable gentleman? To leave them as they are. Gracious heaven! To leave the great body of the Irish people bound by the law of their nature to plot the subversion of the state! I say of the state, because I trust that every man who hears me will say, that to subvert the Protestant establishment is to subvert the state.

I propose, not to take the shackles from his limbs. He is u--

shackled, free, and strong as we are. But to take the brand from his forehead, and the bitterness from his heart, and the sense of debasement from his mind.

The plan of the right honourable gentleman is, to leave him for ever a marked man and a plotting sectary. Mine is to raise him from exclusion and disability to the consciousness of having the full possession of the highest situation that can be occupied in civilized society; I mean the full participation of the rights, the privileges, and the honours of a free-born British subject. Do not, I conjure you, turn your backs on this proposal of grace, of justice, and of security. Do not drive your Roman Catholic brother from your bar, as a sulky and discontented outcast. You have admitted him into the bosom of the state, civil and military; do not in the same breath insult him by saying that he is, and that he ought to be, its enemy.

Sir, in considering the argument of the right honourable gentleman, I have not stopped to meet the supposition that the power of the Roman Catholic body to effect any hostile purposes can be augmented by, or grow out of this measure. He has, I think, truly said, that "in the natural, and therefore certain order of things, the Roman Catholic must constitute by far the most powerful body in Ireland." The right honourable gentleman has notions far too just and statesman-like to suppose that their power can, in any material degree, be effected by their obtaining seats in parliament or admission to the excepted offices. No; their number, their wealth, their exercise of all professions, their possession of land, of commerce and manufactures, their constituting and commanding our fleets and our armies; these the right honourable gentleman well knows are the imperishable materials of political power, and that wherever the wealth, and knowledge, and arms of a state reside, there is its real power. Since the first foundations of the civilized world, steel and gold have been the hinges on which its gates have hung, and knowledge has been the guardian of their keys; any attempt on the part of man to overturn this eternal scheme of nature, this fixed law of Providence, is shallow and presumptuous. The power, therefore, to subvert cannot be created by this act of justice: will the desire be kindled by it? Will the Roman Catholic feel a respect for the establishment only on the condition of its being the cause of his exclusion from the state? gratified by the injury, indignant at the redress? These are puerilities to which the right honourable gentleman will not condescend. I agree with him in his manly view of the subject; if this measure is carried, we are to expect and wish that in progress of time (probably a very gradual one) the admission of the Roman Catholics may have a fair proportion to their qualifications; but I trust he will agree with me, that the power of making an impression on the government, or on the people of this country, will depend, not on the circumstance of their claims being personally asserted within these walls, but on the justice and exigency of the claims themselves. The voice of the humblest subject of the realm, claiming the privileges of a citizen, will find its way to the honest members of this house, and to the honest people of this country, from the remotest corner of the empire; it will find an echo in every independent mind and in every generous breast.

In all continued struggles between a lawful government and a free people there can be but one issue. That party must prevail which has truth and justice on its side, otherwise there is an end of freedom or of government, it must end in despotism or anarchy. While you resist the claim of civil right, the Roman Catholic is armed with truth and justice. Grant him what he ought to have, and if he refuses the reasonable conditions or aspires to more, you transfer to yourselves these invincible standards, and you may look with confidence to the result.

If it is said that the objection is not so much to any particular measure as to the principle of concession, and to the difficulty of ascertaining its limit; I do not find it easy to ascertain the exact meaning of the argument. Is it meant that no concession should ever have been made? That Ireland should have been left in the situation to which the penal laws had reduced her; a jungle fit for the habitation of wild beasts—a moral waste, in which every principle of social order, and of political regulation, and of honourable feeling was defied? No; the right honourable gentleman says he rejoices that the system was departed from; he says so consistently; he must say so; he justly admits that restriction is in itself an evil, and if so, the removal of it must in itself be good.

It must mean then that there is a point at which concession ought to stop. I admit it. Have we passed that point? Where ought we to have stopped? And are we to retrace our steps? No; the right honourable gentleman says, we have not gone beyond it, but we arrived at it precisely in the year 1793, and by the arrangement then made he abides.

He will not, I know, condescend to the disingenuity of saying that our measure is bad because it involves a principle of concession, and that the principle of concession is dangerous because our measure is a bad one.

Well then, the concessions of 1793 were wise and salutary, but anything more would be dangerous and unconstitutional.

The Irish parliament, it seems, was so fortunate as to hit the exact point to which concession ought to go, and beyond which it ought not to be carried ; why then, may I ask, is it not to be carried to the same extent in Great Britain ? Why should not this just and critical measure, which has admitted the Irish Roman Catholic to the grand inquest, to the magistracy, to the constituency, and to various high offices in the state, be extended to the English Roman Catholic, who is shut out from all of them, though with every claim, from rank and dignity, from patience and long suffering, and who is unaffected, besides, by those circumstances of danger which have excited so much alarm as to Ireland ? Surely, were it for this purpose alone, the house ought to go into a committee. But, sir, I think there would be some difficulty, if we examine the details of the Irish act of 1793, in demonstrating their perfect wisdom and consistency. The Roman Catholic there may be chief commissioner of the revenue, and yet may not hold the lowest office in the most petty corporation. He may be owner in fee of the estate to which the whole corporation right is annexed, he may transfer it, he may entail it, he may name every corporator and every officer, and yet he has not " civil worth" to entitle him to the meanest of these offices. He may be proprietor of a borough, so as substantially to nominate the member to serve in parliament, and yet the state would be shaken if he were himself that member.

Sir, to enumerate all the inconsistencies of this supposed measure of final adjustment would be endless; but there is one so glaring that I must beg leave particularly to allude to it. You admit the Roman Catholic, both here and in Ireland, to the bar, you invite him to study the laws of his country, to display his knowledge on a public theatre, where his talents and his acquirements are tried and known; you engage him in a career of honourable competition ; you see him distinguished by the approbation of his countrymen ; you see every relative connected with him gladdened and gratified by his successful progress; and when his heart is beating high with the consciousness of desert, and the hope of fame and honour, you stop him in his course, you dash his hopes, you extinguish his ambition, you leave him disgraced and mortified, sitting on the outer benches of your courts of justice, and imparting the gloom of his own hopeless exclusion to every one connected with him by consanguinity, friendship, or religion. Sir, in the name of the Protestant bar of both countries, I call on parliament to rescue us from this disgrace, to relieve us from the odium and shame of this degrading monopoly, and to restore us to the privilege of equal and generous and honourable emulation.

One word more and I have done. It has been asked, where is concession to stop? I say, precisely where necessity, arising from public good, requires the continuance of the restriction. Exclusion is like war, *justum quibus necessarium*. Beyond this it would be folly to proceed. Short of this it is folly and injustice to stop. By this test let the claim be tried. If there is any office the possession of which by a Roman Catholic would be dangerous or injurious to our establishments, let him be excluded from it. If there is any franchise, whose exercise can be attended with real danger, let it be withheld. Such exclusion, or withholding, is not an anomaly, or inconsistency, in our system of conciliation, because, when the exclusion is not arbitrary and gratuitous, there is no insult. Such an exclusion forms no link of the chain, and the Roman Catholic will submit to it cheerfully; just as it would be the duty of the Protestant if, for similar reasons, a similar sacrifice were required from him. Let him know, in intelligible terms, the reason and the necessity, and he is satisfied. But do not, in so momentous a concern, give him words, and think to reconcile him. Talk to him of the Protestant establishment, and he understands you; he bows to it; he sees it engraved in capitals on the front of the political fabric. But if you tell him of Protestant ascendancy, or Protestant exclusion, he asks in vain where its title is to be found; he looks in vain for it in the elements of our law or its traditions, in the commentaries of its sage expositors, in the reformation, the revolution, or the Union—he sees in it nothing but insult and contumacy; and he demands, in the name of the laws, and in the spirit of the constitution, that he may be no longer its victim.

Sir, I move, "That this house do resolve itself into a committee of the whole house, to consider the state of the laws by which oaths or declarations are required to be taken or made, as qualifications for the enjoyment of offices, or for the exercise of civil functions, so far as the same affect his majesty's Roman Catholic subjects; and whether it would be expedient, in any what manner, to alter or modify the same, and subject to what provisions or regulations."

The reports state that "the right honourable and learned member was heard throughout with the most profound attention, interrupted only by the loudest expressions of admiration and respect."

Peel replied, avowing, as he commenced, the charge of presumption to which any man would be liable who attempted to answer such a speech. "He knew well that under any circumstances his adversary would be an overpowering antagonist; but under the present, when he replied to a speech which he (Mr.

Peel) had made five years ago, and which he, having the power of tearing to pieces then by that extraordinary faculty of reasoning which he possessed, chose to leave unanswered until that night, when, besides his great talents, he had every other advantage, the difficulty was beyond calculation increased." Alluding then to the virtues and genius of Grattan, he hailed his successor "in the person of the right honourable gentleman, one than whom no man was more worthy to wield the arms of Achilles." After a long and vehement speech against the motion, he concluded by declaring that "no result of the debate could give him unqualified satisfaction. He was, of course, bound to wish that the opinions which he honestly felt might prevail; but their prevalence would still be mingled with regret at the disappointment their success must entail upon others." Sir James Mackintosh, who spoke next in support of the motion, began with rapturous applause of Plunket's speech—"That great display of the prodigious talents of his right honourable friend, who had often been admired for his commanding powers, never so greatly exercised as upon that night, when he had shown himself to be the greatest master of eloquence and reasoning now existing in public life." Dawson of Derry, Charles Grant, and Castlereagh spoke the only other remarkable speeches of the debate. It was the last time Castlereagh addressed the house on the subject, and "differing from those friends with whom he usually agreed on other political and national questions," he emphatically repeated his opinion that the Catholics ought to be emancipated, and that as an insurance of the Protestant church establishment, the Catholic clergy ought to be pensioned. The house then divided, and the motion was carried by a majority of 6, in a house of 448.

DR. MILNER.
March 16, 1821.

On the 2nd of March, Plunket stated to the house the course which he proposed to pursue. He would, in the first instance, submit resolutions to the committee on which a bill was proposed to be founded—the first reading of which would be taken on the next Tuesday, and the second on the Monday following. The house then went into committee, the resolutions were agreed to, a bill or bills ordered to be brought in thereupon, and the house ordered to be called over on the 16th.

On the 16th, Mr. Wilberforce presented a petition from "certain Roman Catholics of Staffordshire and Warwickshire against the bills now in progress for the relief of the Catholics," declaring, at the same time, that he did not concur in their prayer. Among the petitioners was Dr. Milner, who alone of the English vicars apostolic, had refused to sign the petition presented by Lord Nugent, and whose acts and writings on the question had led to angry and varied controversy among the Irish and English Catholics. At one time violently and almost disrespectfully assailed by O'Connell as a vetoist, at another expelled from the English Catholic Board for a too temerarious zeal, and detested by all the Protestant partizans of the cause as an unmanageable bigot, it is difficult to understand the prelate's position. In noticing the petition, Sir T. Lethbridge triumphantly pointed to his signature as a proof that no measure could or would satisfy the Catholics. Upon this Plunket rose and said—

THE honourable baronet has thought proper, in some degree, to anticipate the discussion of the subject, to which the attention of the house will shortly be directed, and I feel it necessary, therefore, to make one or two observations in reply to what has fallen from him. With respect to the signature of Dr. Milner, from which the honourable baronet appears to derive so much satisfaction, I cannot help saying that in that individual it is only an act of undeviating, consistent bigotry. If I have felt some exultation in my mind that a measure of the highest possible public good should now be apparently on the point of attainment, it is with the deepest regret that I witness an attempt to darken the prospect of happiness and security. The same evil spirit which in 1813 came forward to blast the hopes of the Catholics, is once more at work. The name of Dr. Milner is not at the head of this petition, but I am persuaded that he is the prime instigator of it—I am satisfied that he is at the bottom of a measure, the object of which is, to destroy once more the hopes of his Catholic fellow-subjects. Sir, I have a right to say, that the sentiments of the Roman Catholics of this country cannot fairly be collected from this petition. The petition of the Roman Catholics of England, which was laid before the house a few nights ago, was signed by seven apostolic vicars. Now, there are eight apostolic vicars in this country, and the eighth apostolic vicar, whose name was not annexed to that petition, who has disavowed that spirit of conciliation which animates his brethren, is the same upon whose intervention the honourable baronet has this night thought proper to congratulate the house. That gentleman is the same person, who, in 1813, came forward on the eve of the adoption of a measure for the relief of the Catholics, and by whose interference that measure was abandoned. He has been censured and disowned by the Catholic board; and the house will judge of the bigoted spirit of a man, who could publicly declare, that the day on which Catholic emancipation was granted, would be a day of downfall of the Catholic religion in this country. What is the object of this man? What, but to prevent the possibility of Roman Catholic emancipation —to destroy all hopes of conciliation—to keep alive religious dissension—and render discord and dissatisfaction interminable, by perpetuating the distinction between Protestants and Catholics.

Certainly, sir, I never expected a general concurrence; for it is visionary to expect the concurrence of bigotry. Bigotry is unchangeable. I care not whether it be Roman Catholic bigotry or Protestant bigotry—its character is the same—its pursuits are the same. True to its aim, though besotted in its expectations —steady to its purpose, though blind to its interests, for bigotry time flows in vain. It is abandoned by the tides of knowledge—it is left stranded by the waters of reason, and vainly worships the figures imprinted on the sand, soon to be washed away. It is inaccessible to reason—it is irreclaimable by experience.

THE CATHOLIC BILLS.
March 16, 1821.

THE debate on the second reading was then gone into, and Plunket rose to explain the bills:—

He said it was not then his intention to trespass at any great length on the time of the house; indeed, after the indulgence which he had so largely experienced on a former night, it would furnish but a bad specimen of taste to go a second time into a general consideration of the question. When he took the liberty of opening his views on the question, he had described the measure as having for its primary object a great end of public justice. He had expressed a hope that it would be favourably regarded by all those whose interests it was designed to promote; and he had received great pleasure in finding, from all that had passed in the country with which he was most nearly connected, that his hopes had been more than realized; for he must take leave to say, that he never entertained the chimerical notion of being able to conciliate the approbation of all persons on such a subject. There were persons by whom that general satisfaction would be felt as a grievous calamity, who prized the religious hostility which they bore to other Christian sects and denominations as a valuable inheritance descended to them from their ancestors, and which it was incumbent on them to leave as a legacy to their children. With such persons he would not argue; they lived in a territory of their own, wholly inaccessible to any reasoning which he could employ. It was however some consolation to know that the measure, if carried, could not interrupt their happiness, but that they would rise the next morning in possession of as much comfort and security as they had ever before enjoyed, and as he hoped, —for they were very worthy and respectable persons—they would long continue to enjoy. He must take that opportunity also of remarking, that he had never applied the term "bigotry" to the great body of Protestants with whom he had the misfortune to differ on this subject. Nothing could be more foreign from his disposition; and in truth, he felt the utmost degree of deference for sentiments, which, although they appeared to him to originate in prejudice and error, might be so regarded by him through his own prejudices and errors. Those errors, if they were such, he was ready to yield to the force of argument, and to a proof of actual danger arising to the establishments so justly dear to us, from admitting the Roman Catholics to share in the full advantages of the constitution.

It had been his endeavour, and that of the distinguished individuals who were associated with him in the preparation of this bill, to proceed with the greatest caution, and to evince a deference for the opinions of those classes to whom he was now alluding. Their object was not only to give security against danger, but to satisfy every reasonable apprehension. They had felt it to be their duty also to defer to the apprehensions and jealousies of the Roman Catholics. It was their wish to reconcile both Protestants and Catholics, by not yielding on the one hand what was necessary to the security of the establishment, nor demanding on the other what must violate the religious scruples of the Roman Catholics. The present state of public affairs, and the state also of the public mind, seemed to him peculiarly favourable to the success of this important measure. He considered that the indifference and apathy spoken of by an honourable member, as characteristic of the public mind, proved only that the people willingly left the decision of this question to the wisdom of their representatives. They were satisfied that nothing would be done by parliament to endanger the constitution, and they suppressed their own feelings from their confidence in the legislature. The time, therefore, was most favourable to a full consideration of those claims which had been so often and hitherto so unsuccessfully urged on behalf of the Roman Catholics. Without further preamble, he should proceed to state the substance of the bill, endeavouring only to set himself right with the house, as to what had fallen from him in the former discussion. He had then asserted, that admission to the franchises and offices of the state was the right of every Roman Catholic liege subject, and that exclusion from eligibility was inconsistent with the first principles of the constitution. In the sense in which he had stated, and in which alone he could be supposed to have stated it, he now re-asserted that proposition. The right of the Roman Catholic was precisely the same as that of the Protestant; but he never was so absurd as to maintain that that right could not be controlled by the exigencies or necessities of the state. If ever a clear case were made out to him of expediency arising from danger serious enough to countervail a general principle, he would say at once that the Roman Catholic must yield to the imperious rule which that expediency would dictate. But whence did the Protestant derive his claim to vote at elections, or to hold himself eligible to sit in parliament? Not from any written law or charter that he had ever met with; but from the first elements, from the essence and the stamina of the constitution. The Roman Catholic complained that since the reign of Charles the Second he had been subjected to certain disabilities. He did not deny the right of parliament to impose them, but stated that they were originally designed to be temporary, and were enacted in consequence of a suspicion that the reigning monarch was not a Protestant. The Roman Catholic added, that those circumstances had gone by; that there no longer existed any danger of a Popish king, or of a Popish successor. Therefore, he submitted, as the danger had ceased, so ought the restrictions which that danger alone had justified. If the Protestant could show no overruling necessity for the exclusion of the Catholic, could he show any principle by which it was made an essential or fundamental part of the constitution? The Catholic denied it: he challenged discussion; he contended that such a proposition was at war with the first principles on which that constitution was founded.

He was the more anxious to set himself right upon this point, because he had been supposed to argue the case of the Protestant dissenter, as well as of the Roman Catholic. But the truth was, that each question stood on its own special grounds; that of the Protestant dissenter was altogether distinct. As regarded the Roman Catholic, it was a question of danger between letting him in and shutting him out; but the situation of the dissenter was extremely different. Perhaps the house would allow him to explain the actual state of the Protestant dissenter in Ireland, as he believed the public was in general ignorant of it. The Protestant dissenter was not then subject to any test in Ireland, nor had he been for the last forty years. An act passed in the year 1780 exempted him from the operation of the Test Act; the exclusion of the Roman Catholic did not, therefore, involve the Protestant dissenter. As he was now on this subject, he could wish to put the house in possession of a curious fact. The act of 1780 relieved the Protestants from the sacramental test; the words were distinct and positive, that from and after the passing of the act the Protestants should not be bound by the sacramental test. In 1793, an act passed to relieve the Roman Catholics: and it went on to state, that the Roman Catholics should be subject to no other disqualification or disability in this respect than those to which the Protestants were liable. Some persons, however, thought that the Protestants of the Established Church were not included, and that the act exempting from the sacramental test did not apply to them; and as some doubts and difficulties arose in consequence with regard to the Catholics, a statute passed the Irish House of Commons to explain the act of 1780, and to exempt the Protestants of the Established Church. It was sent up to the House of Lords, and there, on consulting the journals, it appeared that it had been read with unexampled celerity three times in one day; that an amendment by the insertion of the simple word *not* was introduced, in fact negativing the whole object of the measure; and that being returned to the Commons, it passed in that shape unanimously. Under the operation of the law thus explained, the Roman Catholic in Ireland was therefore still liable to the sacramental test. He had thought it right to put the house in possession of this fact, to show how what had been meant here as a piece of justice, grace, and favour to the Catholics was marred in Ireland, by trick, artifice, and management.

He would now proceed to state particularly the nature of the bill, as framed by the committee on the resolutions of the house. The bill for removing disqualifications comprised two distinct objects. First, the disqualification by reason of the oath of supremacy; and secondly, the disqualification by reason of the declaration of transubstantiation. As to the last, he need not long occupy the time of the house; for he had never heard any man, whether clerical or lay, contend for the propriety of that declaration; it was justly considered injurious to the best interests of Christianity, and incapable of affording any real benefit or security. Though it contained several points besides transubstantiation, such as the invocation of saints and the sacrifice of the mass, yet it formed but a small portion of the faith of the Roman Catholics; and if in the progress of investigation, or in the course of time, those points were to be changed, there would still remain the doctrines of purgatory, the sacraments, and auricular confession. It was also imperfect in this respect; for if the object were to exclude the Roman Catholics, it did not effect that object. A man might subscribe this declaration for his convenience, and yet continue a Papist; and therefore it was not the sort of security the house ought to have. A Roman Catholic might say, "I choose to sacrifice to my interest the strictness of my religion, and become a member of parliament. If this were discovered, it would be the duty of the house to expel such an individual. And why? Because he had sacrificed his religion, because he had complied with the strictness of the penal laws of the Protestants, which tempted men to set the desire of the honours of the state above the clear dictates of conscience. On this account he stated, that the law carried on the face of it the marks of haste and imperfection.

He would now pass without further remark to that part of the bill that related to the oath of supremacy. It had struck him to-night with some degree of surprise to find that the right rev. gentleman who presided over the Catholics in the midland district of this country had taken upon himself to say that the explanation or modification of the oath of supremacy in the intended bill was inconsistent with the doctrines of the Roman Catholics; because, if any point could be established by undeniable documents anterior to the Reformation itself, it was, that the condition of the complete and absolute dominion of the king of these realms, as to all civil and religious rights, was perfectly reconcileable with the doctrines of Catholicism. He would state one or two facts upon this subject. Before the Reformation, the great body of the acts was passed by a Roman Catholic parliament, and the exclusion of the see of Rome from interfering with the political concerns of the kingdom was perfect before one of the doctrines was changed in it. In the time of Henry VIII., any one who would have been hanged as a traitor for decrying the authority of the king would have been burned as a heretic for impugning the doctrine of transubstantiation. When the statute of Philip and Mary, which restored all the Roman Catholic doctrines, passed, it contained in itself an express saving of all the acts prior to the 28th Henry VIII. He next came to the proceedings of Queen Elizabeth; and he had already noticed her admonition published at the beginning of her reign, and the accompanying admonition and injunction afterwards incorporated in the act passed in her fifth year. He begged to recal the attention of the house to the precise words of the queen's admonition: they were these:—
" For certainly her majesty neither doth nor ever will challenge any authority other than that was challenged and lately used by the said noble kings of famous memory, King Henry VIII. and King Edward VI., which is and was of ancient time due to the imperial crown of this realm; that is, under God, to have the sovereignty and rule over all manner of persons born within these her realms, dominions, and countries, of what estate, either ecclesiastical or civil, soever they be; so as no other foreign power shall or ought to have any superiority over them. And if any person that hath conceived any other sense of the said oath shall accept the same oath with this interpretation, sense, and meaning, her majesty is well pleased to accept every such in that behalf as her good and obedient subjects, and shall acquit them of all manner of penalties contained in the said

act against such as shall peremptorily and obstinately refuse to take the same oath." Thus, what the vicar of the midland district denied was expressly stated. The honourable gentleman, in further confirmation, read the opinion and explanation given by Bishop Burnet upon the subject, which showed the policy of the queen, and the obstacles that stood in the way of what she desired to accomplish. The only other point on which he would trouble the house was that of supremacy, which was fully explained in the 37th article of our church:—" The king's majesty hath the chief power in this realm of England and other his dominions; unto whom the chief government of all estates of this realm, whether they be ecclesiastical or civil, in all causes doth appertain; and is not, nor ought to be, subject to any foreign jurisdiction." There was not a word in the whole of it which the Catholics were not ready to adopt. It proceeded: " Where we attribute to the king's majesty the chief government, by which titles we understand the minds of some slanderous folks to be offended, we give not to our princes the ministering either of God's word or of the sacraments; the which things the injunctions also lately set forth by Elizabeth our queen do most plainly testify; but that only prerogative which we see to have been given always to all godly princes in Holy Scriptures by God himself—that is, that they should rule all states and degrees committed to their charge by God, whether they be ecclesiastical or temporal, and restrain with the civil sword the stubborn and evil doers." Such were the terms of the articles—such the terms of the admonition—and such the terms of the act of parliament in which it was incorporated; and after all this, it was really too much to say, that in putting this interpretation on the word, the framers of the bill were at war with the principles of the Reformation.

He now begged permission to read the terms in which the explanation of this oath had been framed in the bill upon the table. They were the following:—

" And whereas by certain acts passed in the parliaments of Great Britain and Ireland, the oaths of abjuration, allegiance, and supremacy, therein provided, are required to be taken for certain purposes therein mentioned; and the said oath of supremacy is expressed in the following terms:—' I, A.B., do swear, that I do from my heart detest and abjure, as impious and heretical, that damnable doctrine and position, that princes excommunicated or deprived by the Pope, or any authority of the see of Rome, may be deposed or murdered by their subjects or any other whatsoever; and I do declare that no foreign prince, prelate, state, or potentate hath, or ought to have, any jurisdiction, power, superiority, pre-eminence, or authority ecclesiastical or spiritual within this realm. So help me God.'

" And whereas his majesty's Roman Catholic subjects in Great Britain and Ireland have been at all times ready and desirous to take the said oath of allegiance in common with his majesty's other subjects, but entertain scruples with respect to taking the oath of supremacy, so far as the same might be construed to import a disclaimer of the spiritual authority of the Pope or Church of Rome in matters of religious belief.

" And whereas it appears from the admonition annexed to the injunctions of her majesty Queen Elizabeth, published in the first year of her majesty's reign, and sanctioned by the act passed in the fifth year of her reign, entitled, ' An act for the assurance of the queen's regal powers over all estates and subjects within her dominions,' that such disclaimer was originally meant only to extend to any such acknowledgment of foreign jurisdiction, power, superiority, pre-eminence, or authority as is or could be incompatible with the civil duty and allegiance which is due to his majesty and successors from all his subjects."

Here he proposed to introduce an amendment by the insertion of the following words:—" or with the civil duty and obedience which are due to his courts, civil and ecclesiastical, in all matters affecting the legal rights of his majesty's subjects." He had added these words to meet the doubts and accommodate the fears of all parties. Neither he nor the honourable friends whose assistance he had had in framing the bill, were tenacious of words. All he entreated was this—that no gentleman would look at this bill with the eye of a metaphysician, a casuist, or a critic; but with the plain good sense that the subject demanded, in order to see whether the distinction was not plainly marked between what was merely conscientious and what was an interference with the rights and powers of the king. Coming to the clause relating to the declaration against transubstantion, he proposed to strike out the words " and may therefore properly and safely be abrogated," and insert the following—" as a qualification to enable his majesty's subjects to take, hold, or enjoy any civil right, office, or franchise." The house was aware that by the disabling code, the Catholics were shut out from the inheritance of landed property, but certain relaxing statutes removed the disability on the taking of the prescribed oaths of abjuration, allegiance, and supremacy. If the words as they now stood were adopted, they could succeed without any such oaths; and if he were to act according to his own views, he should abolish all distinctions between the

Catholics and Protestants, but still he thought that so important a change of the law ought not to be effected indirectly. He did not know that all the Roman Catholics would adopt the construction put in the bill upon the oath of supremacy; the greater number were unquestionably ready to do so, but he could not answer for the scrupulousness of some nice consciences. A few might complain that they had received an injury from this bill—that at present they could succeed to landed property on taking certain oaths, with a certain interpretation which they could allow; but that their conscience would not permit them to take the oaths with the interpretation now annexed. To avoid this objection, he had framed a separate clause which gave the Roman Catholic the opportunity, at the time the oaths were administered, of stating the interpretation he gave to the oath of supremacy. It appeared to him most desirable that there should be no division or separation of oaths; nothing to make the Catholic separate or distinct from the Protestant, but that as much uniformity as possible should be introduced. It might be desirable not to part with oaths, to the continuance of which the great body of the Catholics had no objection. With reference to this part of the subject, he must say that he thought the oath a question of theoretical discussion. It could be considered and discussed in the committee, and it would be very easy, if then there should appear an imperative necessity for continuing this oath, to engraft it upon the bill.

Having stated what was the general scope of his bill, he now came to the exceptions which it contained. It provided, in the way of exception, as follows:—" That nothing herein contained shall extend, or be construed to extend, to enable any person, being a Roman Catholic, to hold and enjoy the office of lord high chancellor, lord keeper, or lord commissioner of the great seal of Great Britain, or of lord lieutenant or lord deputy, or other the chief governor or governors of Ireland." The exceptions in the bill went no farther than these offices. It would be open for any honourable member to propose other exceptions if he thought proper; but the reason he felt these enough was, because he was quite satisfied with the propriety of admitting the Catholics to possess eligibility to all other offices. These offices were essentially vested in the choice of the crown, and he saw little necessity for apprehending that the Catholics would ever look up to them. He was aware that a right honourable gentleman opposite (Sir W. Scott), and others who thought with him, were decidedly hostile to admitting Catholics to an eligibility to seats upon the bench. He felt peculiar respect for those who conscientiously differed from him, but he really thought the right honourable gentleman's argument in support of his objection quite insufficient. The right honourable gentleman candidly admitted that, if Catholics were elevated to the bench, he did not mean to insinuate that, in their general administration of justice, they would act unbecomingly; but his apprehension was, that if a question arose upon any subject connected with religious feeling between a Protestant and a Catholic, the Catholic judge must necessarily lean to the interest of his own religious persuasion, and against that of the Protestant. He begged the right honourable gentleman to consider the consequences of his argument, and to what a dangerous extent it might be carried. If the Protestant were justified in raising this inference on account of the naturally religious partiality of the judge, what must be the feeling of the Catholic when his rights are at stake, from the Protestant judge sitting alone, without the assistance of a judge of another religious community? But this inference could never be maintained; the apprehension was perfectly groundless. Away with such unworthy distrust! It went at once to dash the cup of conciliation from the lips of the Catholic, and to bereave him of his just hopes. He was satisfied no Catholic had the least idea that he did not receive the fullest justice from the judges on the bench. The Catholics had the most perfect confidence in them; and he entreated that Protestants would view with the same just and liberal feeling the acts of their Catholic fellow-subjects in whatever situation they might happen to be placed. With respect to the two universities of Oxford and Cambridge, the bill provided that all their existing institutions should remain in exactly the same situation in which they stood at present. The test laws were left as they stood, and liable only to the operation of the annual indemnity bill.

He would now come to the second bill, the title of which was, "To regulate the intercourse between persons in holy orders, professing the Roman Catholic religion, with the see of Rome." It set out with stating, that it is fit to regulate the intercourse and correspondence between the subjects of this realm and the see of Rome. It states that, " whereas it is expedient that such precautions should be taken in respect to persons in holy orders professing the Roman Catholic religion, who may at any time hereafter be elected, nominated, or appointed to the exercise or discharge of episcopal duties, or functions of a dean, in the said church, within any part of the United Kingdom, as that no such person shall at any time hereafter assume the exercise or discharge of any such duties or functions within the United Kingdom, or any part thereof, whose loyalty and peaceable conduct shall not have been previously ascertained to the satisfaction of his majesty, his heirs, or successors." On the subject of the intercourse between the Catholic clergy and the see of Rome, he was entitled to assert that it had long been carried on merely for spiritual purposes, and that in no single instance was it found to have been carried on for any factious or party purposes. With respect to the appointment of the Roman Catholic bishops by the Pope, the nomination was formally made in that manner, but to all intents and purposes not practically. In no instance did the Pope, in point of fact, practically exercise this right: so that in making any provision respecting the appointment of the Catholic bishops by the Pope, he was providing a theoretical remedy against a theoretical danger. Although there was no practical evil to be guarded against, there was yet that sort of apprehension upon which the Protestant mind had a right to be satisfied. As to the actual nomination of the Catholic bishops in Ireland, there had been a series of disputes and a variety of claims. It was first among the Catholics contended, that the bishops of the province should elect one to fill the vacant see; then, that the dean and chapter should; and, lastly, the parish priests put in a claim to the right of election. But, in all these instances, the nomination by the Pope was practically excluded. The Pope had, therefore, practically as little to do with originating the nomination of the Catholic bishops in Ireland as he had with the nomination of the Protestant bishops in England. But to give satisfaction to particular scruples, he had introduced this proviso into his bill, however practically unnecessary; and it stipulated that an oath in the following terms should be taken by every Roman Catholic individual who was initiated as a clergyman into holy orders, for the purpose of satisfying the state that their intercourse with the see of Rome should be confined exclusively to ecclesiastical matters. The proposed oath was as follows:

" I, A. B., do swear that I will never concur in or consent to the appointment or consecration of any Roman Catholic bishop, or dean, or vicar apostolic, in the Roman Catholic church in the United Kingdom, but such as I shall conscientiously deem to be of unimpeachable loyalty and peaceable conduct; and I do swear that I have not and will not have any correspondence or communication with the Pope or see of Rome, or with any court or tribunal established or to be established by the Pope or see of Rome, or, by the authority of the same, or with any person or persons authorized or pretending to be authorized by the Pope or see of Rome, tending directly or indirectly to overthrow or disturb the Protestant government, or the Protestant

Church of Great Britain and Ireland, or the Protestant church of Scotland, as by law established; and that I will not correspond or communicate with the Pope or see of Rome, or with any tribunal established or to be established by the Pope or see of Rome, or by the authority of the same, or with any person or persons authorized or pretending to be authorized by the Pope or see of Rome, or with any other foreign ecclesiastical authority, on any matter or thing which may interfere with or affect the civil duty and allegiance which is due to his majesty, his heirs, and successors, from all his subjects."

He would not say that this bill was likely to receive the unqualified assent of the Roman Catholics at large: that it would be at once received as a popular or favourable measure; but he did think and expect that it would be gratefully received by the great majority of the Catholic clergy and laity. He begged to assure the right honourable gentleman (Mr. Peel) that if he referred to the resolutions of the Catholic clergy in 1813, as indicative of their permanent opinion or wishes upon the subject of a legislative measure for their relief, he greatly deceived himself. Their declaration in 1813 was not that the bishops would not give the crown a voice in the nomination of their body, but that they could not then grant it without incurring schism, until they received the consent of the Pope. So far only went the resolutions of the Catholic prelates in 1813. The case was altered since; for the Catholic clergy of Ireland had had an opportunity of communicating upon the subject with the Pope, who had given his consent to the arrangement, and had declared that he saw nothing in it inconsistent with the principles of his church. The Catholic prelates had received this opinion of the Pope: they had pronounced no expression of disapprobation thereon. The right honourable gentleman did not put the point fairly, when he declared that he wanted the bishops' approval of the bill of 1813. To expect this public expression of approbation was neither just to the Catholic clergy nor respectful to the legislature. Was it right that the legislature, before it enacted a measure which it conceived founded in justice and necessity, should canvass about for the opinions of particular individuals upon the specific measure? If any measure were in its accomplishment calculated to sow discord among a large portion of the people, it would be wrong to press it. But, was it right to call upon the bishops, in the first instance, for a public avowal of their sentiments, where no reason existed for supposing that they entertained a contrary opinion? It had been said that although the Pope was desirous for the veto, the great majority of Catholics were against it. This certainly showed how groundless were the fears of those who apprehended so much mischief from the direct influence of the Pope upon the Catholics; for they, it seemed, were generally determined to have an opinion of their own, notwithstanding the power of the Pope. For his own part he believed the measure would be very palatable, and that the people would gladly receive what parliament was, he trusted, disposed liberally to grant. When the measure was before parliament, he had expressed his opinion in favour of domestic nomination. But in framing the bill he knew not how to arrange it for domestic nomination; for he could not find that the Catholics had any definitively fixed system of domestic nomination among themselves. It was therefore impossible to fix one upon them without unjustifiably obtruding upon them laws for the internal regulation of their own ecclesiastical regulations.

He owed it also to the house to state the reason why he did not, as in the bill of 1813, consolidate the ecclesiastical and civil arrangements of the question, and why he preferred that they should be kept distinct, and made the subject of two specific bills. The one bill did not necessarily arise out of the other, as cause and effect; for the Catholic layman was entitled to his civil rights, without any connexion with the ecclesiastical rules of his communion. When he drew this distinction he admitted the propriety of their legislating upon both points at the same time. They were now, he hoped, going to put his majesty's Roman Catholics upon the same footing as the rest of the people, and to put an end for ever to these impolitic and jealous distinctions. When performing this great work he thought it expedient to embrace the whole of the question in one comprehensive view, and to legislate for it at once. They were, in doing so, justified in guarding against the possible abuse of the control of a foreign potentate over a clergy in the dominions of another sovereign who had naturally considerable influence over the subjects of that prince. He still thought it right that the ecclesiastical parts of the measure should be separated from those which were purely belonging to the laity. He had also another reason. The clergy might feel disposed to assist in carrying the ecclesiastical arrangements into effect, and yet might not wish to do so at the actual time when the particular question of the laity was at issue:—that is, they might have some delicacy in seeing the two matters mixed up together, lest the one should appear like a compromise or a barter for the other. When he stated this necessity for keeping the bills separate, he claimed credit from the house when he said, that both he and the gentlemen who had assisted him in preparing the bill were perfectly ready to admit that, if the first bill were passed, the second must go on. Indeed, if the first bill went in its present shape through a committee, he was ready to say that there might arise no objection to the consolidation of the two bills in the committee. Of course he made this observation with reference to the event of the main principles of the first bill being adopted. The bill he proposed consisted of various parts; it might have been granted *in toto*, or in part. It might be either in a small or in a great part conceded. If only in a trifling part (which he could not possibly anticipate), the concession might not justify them in calling upon the Catholics for these ecclesiastical arrangements. A case might arise—he hoped it was very unlikely— that the first bill should pass in such a shape as to be stripped of those inducements upon which the concessions were grounded and justified. Suppose, for instance, the house should decide upon merely granting the English Catholics the same privileges which the Irish had long enjoyed, that concession to the English would be no boon to the Irish Catholic, and would not justify the legislature in exacting conditions from him, where it conferred no advantage. The Irish Catholic would gain nothing by the alteration, and ought certainly, in such an event, not to be called upon for any alteration of ecclesiastical arrangements. It was therefore desirable that the house should, in the first instance, proceed with two bills, and when in the committee it would be time enough to consider how far it would be proper to consolidate their principles.

An honourable gentleman (Mr. Croker) had suggested that it would be right to propose a provision for the Roman Catholic clergy. He could not concur with the honourable gentleman in the expediency of pressing his suggestion at the present moment. When the principles of the present bills were admitted and acted upon, then such a suggestion might be made with propriety, and, he doubted not, with success. The present time was, however, quite unsuitable for its introduction. The clergy would look at it as if it were a treaty into which they were called upon to enter as a condition for securing to the laity their civil rights. Indeed, he doubted the competency of any member to bring it forward without the concurrence of his majesty's advisers. The moment was favourable for enabling the crown to derive whatever popularity might attach from a boon to the clergy. When Queen Elizabeth manifested a desire to extend the liberality of her toleration, she was thwarted by the foreign measures in which she was compelled to embark. Such was the state of things up to the time of the revolution; and, unfortunately, after that event, the measures of the Pretender continued to assume such a character, as prevented liberal sovereigns from acting upon their own feelings towards the Catholics. Ireland during the same length of time was still more unfavourably circumstanced; for, before the English possessed Ireland, a pure religion, considering the state of the times, was professed in that country, and Popery was introduced there by the English, and made to supplant the form of religion which had preceded it. Ireland, he repeated, became essentially Popish by the act and effort of England. It was not till the revolution that the Catholics of Ireland were in a settled state in the country. In England there have been two rebellions and one insurrection since that period, and yet the Catholics of Ireland have been uniformly tranquil; and upon that proof of their allegiance they ground their claim for a removal of those disabilities which are now prolonged against them. It is the uniform tenor of this conduct which justifies the proviso of the bill.

Can the rebellion in 1798 justly be called a Catholic one? Did it not originate among Protestants? Were not the leaders in it Protestants? Was it not commenced amongst the Protestant population of the north of Ireland, while, at the same time, the Catholic population of the south of Ireland remained tranquil? Did it not appear, that when the French invasion took place in 1796, there was not a single rebellious organization of men in the whole southern population, from Dublin to Cork? Not a single Catholic in that extensive province? It was the uniform tenor of this conduct which justified the recital in the bill which he had brought into the house—" that after the due consideration of the situation, dispositions, and conduct of his majesty's Roman Catholic subjects, it appeared just and fitting to communicate to them the full enjoyment of the benefits and advantages of the constitution and government happily established in this United Kingdom;" thus putting an end to religious jealousies, consolidating the union between Great Britain and Ireland, and uniting and knitting together the hearts of all his majesty's subjects in one and the same interest, for the support of his majesty's person, family, crown, and government, and for the defence of their common rights and liberties.

I have now trespassed longer upon the time of the house than I had at first intended, in submitting to them the details of the two bills. I implore the house to adopt them; to conciliate that kind-hearted, enthusiastic, and loyal people; to enable the throne, at the moment when happily it might do so with safety and advantage to the state, to confer the high and generous privileges, which belonged to the free subjects of a free government, upon the Roman Catholics of this realm—to enable the monarch to enjoy the highest gratification of which his enlightened mind can be susceptible; namely—the gratification of seeing the hearts of his subjects throb with gratitude for his gracious acts, and approach his throne ready to shed the last drop of their blood, and to spend the last shilling of their treasure, in support of those laws and that constitution, in the whole benefits of which they were now allowed to participate.

He then moved the order of the day for the second reading of the Roman Catholic Disabilities Removal Bill, and the speaker put the question that, "the bill be now read a second time." After a short silence, Mr. Bankes opposed the motion by a long, a temperate, and an argumentative speech: his objections to it were, that it would not satisfy the Catholics, and would endanger the Protestant ascendancy. Mr. Wilberforce replied to him.

"Of those who advocated the bill in this stage of it," says Charles Butler, "the voice of none was more grateful to the Catholics, or heard by the house with greater attention and respect, than that of Mr. Wilberforce. The high opinion entertained universally of his ability, integrity, and beneficence, and the reputation which he has deservedly acquired by his successful exertions for the abolition of the slave trade—the greatest triumph obtained in our times in the cause of humanity—have endeared him to the public, and rendered his patronage of any cause of incalculable value. His mild and persuasive eloquence was exerted in this, as it is on every other occasion in behalf of the aggrieved. 'When I see,' said this excellent person, 'Roman Catholics possessed of intelligence, rank, and property, how can I but wish to see them furnished with the means of using that intelligence, holding that rank, and enjoying that property, in a manner which, while it best conduces to their own happiness, will most contribute to the welfare of their country. Their disabilities are the relics of a long course of oppression. They are not restrictions; they are a degradation: to continue them is making them wear a prison-suit, after they are left to go at large. Is it in the order of things, is it reasonably to be anticipated, that a great, a high-minded, a gallant people, when treated with kindness, should not feel, should not be sensible of that kindness?—should not be grateful for it?—should not serve with fidelity and zeal those from whom they had received it?' Mr. Wilberforce concluded by stating, that 'with whatever apprehension he approached the subject, a feeling with which, from his sense of its importance, he was deeply impressed, a feeling which, from his heart, he did certainly entertain;—(for there were many who knew with what tenderness and caution he had at length come to a conclusion, which was somewhat in contrariety to that which he had formerly entertained on the matter),— yet, after hearing much, and reflecting much, he then thought that the object of the motion before the house was calculated to ensure the ultimate security of the country.' This explicit declaration in favour of the bill, by a member so greatly loved and venerated, could not but recommend it to every part of the house."

Mr. Wilberforce was followed by Mr. Bragge Bathurst, who moved, as an amendment, that "the bill should be read a second time that day six months." This, Sir James Mackintosh opposed in a speech, not of much length, but of great power. Mr. Peel followed him. He admitted that excluding Catholics from high office and power was both an evil to them and an evil to the state;

but contended that doing away the exclusion would be a greater evil than continuing it. Mr. Canning replied to Mr. Peel, and the house finally divided—for the original question, 254; against it, 243: so that there was a majority of 11 for the second reading of the bill.

THE STATE OF IRELAND.

April 22, 1822.

THIS session again, Sir John Newport brought forward a motion to inquire into the state of Ireland, in a speech manly, vivid, and statesmanlike. The historian of this period will find no documents that throw such light upon the condition of the Irish people as the speeches of this model Irish member. The reader will remember that Plunket suported his former motion on the subject, and Sir John early expressed his regret that on this occasion the motion would no longer be benefitted by his right honourable and learned friend's assistance. Plunket spoke late in the debate, and shortly after a bigoted rigmarole from Master Ellis, of the Court of Chancery, the successful rival of young Henry Grattan for the representation of Dublin:—

MR. PLUNKET said, he would not at that late hour trespass long on the time of the house, and in a few remarks he had to make on the motion of his right honourable friend, he should confine himself strictly to the main question. The house might feel assured that it was far from his intention to follow the honourable and learned gentleman who spoke last, through the details of his disgusting attack upon the population of that country which had returned him to parliament. He owned, that when the honourable and learned member was first about to desert the duty which belonged to him in the Irish court of chancery, in order that he might devote his attention to parliamentary duties, he (Mr. P.) felt very great regret; but he now withdrew from the bottom of his heart, every regret on that account, and rejoiced that the honourable and learned gentleman had had an opportunity of displaying to the British parliament, and in the face of the whole country, the tone, and temper, and manner, which had long distinguished the treatment received by the great body of the people of Ireland from those who ought to be the advocates of their rights. It was often asked, in a tone of triumph, by the enemies of the Catholics, "Why are you not satisfied with the boon granted to you? Why are you not content with the concessions you have received?" The reason was, because concession had been followed in every stage, by the curse and malediction of those bigots, whose prejudices neither time nor circumstances could remove—who, like an unwholesome blight, like a destructive mildew, intercepted every ray of royal favour, or of legislative beneficence. He was free from alarm as to any argument which the honourable and learned gentleman might please to bring forward, but argument he adduced not. The honourable and learned gentleman relied upon what he denominated facts, and those facts would, in all probability, produce a very different effect from that which the honourable and learned gentleman had anticipated. The honourable and learned gentleman had spoken of transactions with respect to the disturbances that now prevailed in Ireland, and he (Mr. P.) must say, as he had been an eye-witness of those transactions, that if any part of the statements of the honourable and learned gentleman were literally true, in spirit and in application to the question they were totally and absolutely false. The truth was, that the insurrectionary movements in Ireland were confined entirely to certain districts of the south. Limerick, Cork, Kerry, and a part of Tipperary, were in a state of disturbance. The entire population, speaking of the lower classes of the people in those districts, were Roman Catholics. It was a well-known fact that the disturbances were confined to the lower orders, and did not extend beyond them; but, overlooking this fact, the honourable and learned gentleman had traced the disturbances to a religious feeling—those who were engaged in them being the dregs of the people, and all the lower classes professing the Catholic faith. The object of those insurrectionary movements was, in fact, to level the property of the country; and, in the pursuit of that object, the unfortunate persons who were engaged in this design directed their efforts against both Protestants and Roman Catholics. The respectable Catholics were, as much exposed as the Protestants to their depredations, and they exerted themselves with the same zeal and energy in repressing those disturbances, as the members of the Established Church did. When, as public prosecutor, the painful task of bringing some of those misguided men to punishment devolved on him, the direction he gave to the persons who were to empannel the juries was, that no distinction should be made, in admitting Protestants and Roman Catholics to serve on those juries. They were indiscriminately empannelled; and it could not be asserted—it could not be suspected—that the Roman Catholics did not perform their duty in every instance. These were facts which he positively knew. With respect to the Roman Catholic clergy, he would affirm, that from the highest dignitary of the Church to the lowest parish priest, they exerted themselves zealously and energetically, and honestly, to put down the spirit of insubordination. It was not merely a formal discharge of their duty—it was not merely making declarations from the altar, which as the honourable and learned gentleman had said, might be true or untrue—might be sincere or hypocritical—no, it was an active interference ; and he would assert, that if the lives, if the eternal happiness of the Catholic clergy depended on their exertions, they could not do more to put an end to those disturbances than they had done. If these men, instead of being zealous opponents of the discontented, had remained neutral, and still more, if, as had been insinuated, they had countenanced this—he would not call it contemptible conspiracy, because, if not put down in time, it might assume a form that would require the whole strength of the country to subdue it—if these men had proceeded in a different course from that which they had promptly adopted, would not the danger have been infinitely more terrific ? The honourable and learned gentleman told them that his great measure was to put down every symptom of insubordination by force, without inquiring into the cause in which it had originated. The honourable and learned gentleman would employ 50,000 or 100,000 men to effect this object. He (Mr. P.) would indeed have been surprised if such a doctrine had not been marked by the indignation of the house. For if such a principle were once adopted, the two countries would be opposed to each other in endless hostility.

He begged pardon for having been led away from the consideration of the immediate motion before the house, by the observations of the honourable and learned gentleman, which had already been sufficiently answered, by the effect they had produced in the mind of every person who had heard him on both sides of the house. There was one particular transaction, however, which had been mentioned by the honourable and learned gentleman, and in which he (Mr. P.) was personally concerned, to which he must shortly advert. The Roman Catholic priesthood had undoubtedly an opportunity of exerting a most powerful influence on the minds of their flocks; but their influence in restraining their flocks from the perpetration of crime must depend on their power of preserving the confidence of their flocks. It had been well observed by an eminent historian, Dr. Robertson, that the influence of the priesthood was most strong when united with the discontented portion of the population; but that when allied with the government, their influence over the minds of their flocks was proportionally diminished. Subject to this drawback, their influence was undoubtedly strong in restraining from the commission of crime ; but if, instead of exerting their influence as clergymen, they came forward as witnesses in cases of imputed crime, they would lose the confidence of their flocks, and the government would consequently lose all the advantages which it now derived from their influence and interference in the prevention of outrages. In the transaction to which the honourable and learned member had alluded, the priest had rescued the unfortunate man from the crowd by which he was surrounded, at the extreme hazard of his own person, and had succeeded in conveying him to a place of safety. After this the party returned, seized upon the priest, and threatened him with the loss of life if he did not immediately deliver the man into their hands, declaring at the same time that he should receive no injury. The unfortunate man was delivered up, and after an interval of half an hour he was put to death. The priest did not know the persons who actually perpetrated the murder: he did not even believe that those who were apprehended were the most guilty individuals. He knew, it was true, some of the faces of those who composed the numerous crowd; and, though he did not think that those whom he knew were the individuals who had actually imbrued their hands in blood, he was aware that, composing part of a multitude who had committed murder, they were considered as having joined in the deed, and were liable to be executed as murderers. The priest, therefore, refused to give evidence, or to disclose the names of those who were present. He (Mr. P.) was willing to admit that a Catholic clergyman could, no more than a Protestant, conceal a crime, and that this priest was therefore liable for the consequences of illegal conduct; but in this case he did not think it would have been advisable to inflict the punishment. By giving evidence against these persons, the priest not only exposed himself to personal danger, perhaps to assassination, but deprived himself of all capacity of being employed as an instrument to prevent future crimes. Having a choice, therefore, of compelling him to appear in the witness-box, and of punishing him if he refused to give evidence, or of employing the confidence which he enjoyed with those whose lives would be affected by his testimony to prevent future outrages, he (Mr. P.) notwithstanding that by so doing he exposed himself to the censures of the honourable and learned gentleman, had preferred the latter course, and he now appealed to the house from the decision of the honourable and learned gentleman, and asked if he was not entitled to their approbation and thanks for having so done?

He would now address himself to the motion of his right honourable friend. His right honourable friend, he was sure, could intend no unkindness towards him by the manner in which he had alluded to his conduct in 1816, and stating that he then joined with him in a motion similar to the present. Neither could his other honourable friend who had so ably supported his views, and who had quoted passages from his speech on that occasion. But as every man was anxious to maintain his character and to defend his consistency, he might be excused for offering some explanation by which his conduct in then supporting his right honourable friend's motion was reconcilable with his negative vote on the present occasion. The motions, then, he would say, were not exactly similar, nor brought forward under similar circumstances. On the former occasion, a vote had been proposed in the army estimates for 25,000 men, for preserving the peace of Ireland, and the motion of his right honourable friend was intended to obtain a previous inquiry into the state of the country, for the purpose of ascertaining whether such a force was necessary; in the present instance the house had voted the necessary force, and had, to arrest existing outrage, conferred additional powers on the Irish government. The latter fact was even embodied in the resolution now before the house. With respect to the latter part of the resolution, which pledged the house to assist his majesty in carrying into execution the most beneficial measure for the peace and prosperity of Ireland, and was intended to stimulate the government to more active exertions in the cause, he could not adopt it without declaring by his vote, that government required reproof for its indifference, and consequently did not enjoy its confidence. Now, that it enjoyed his confidence was proved by his sitting on that side of the house. To those who knew him best he would leave the decision, whether he had placed that confidence in the present administration because he had joined them, or had joined them because they had obtained his confidence. He believed in his conscience, that government was doing all in their power to find a cure for the evils with which Ireland was afflicted. His right honourable friend (Mr. C. Grant) who had that night spoken with such eloquence, and evinced so much statesmanlike talent and views, and who by his speech had acquired additional claims to the gratitude of his country, had enumerated the causes of the present state of Ireland. Many of these causes, it would be obvious, could not be immediately counteracted, and many of their effects could not be immediately remedied; but he was convinced that the government of that country was sincerely desirous of discovering a remedy, and would be zealous in applying it. Everything that could be done, he was convinced would be done. With respect to the great question of Catholic disabilities, he would at present say nothing, although he hoped that it would soon be satisfactorily settled. The house would recollect that the question last year obtained a new position; that a bill had been agreed to in that house, had passed through all its stages, and was only lost in another place. He confessed that he, therefore, looked forward with increased confidence to the final success of that great measure of security, of strength, and of justice; but it was too important a question to be mixed up with the discussion of that evening. A part of it would shortly come before the house on the intended motion of his right honourable friend (Mr. Canning) for the admission of Catholic peers into the other house of parliament; and at an early period of the next session, as he (Mr. Plunket) had formerly announced, he intended to submit the whole question to parliament; when he had no doubt it would receive that full, temperate, and satisfactory discussion which its momentous consequence deserved.

Among the circumstances which had had a beneficial tendency with regard to Ireland, and which, without reference to the success of the question to which he had alluded, increased his confidence in the future tranquillity of Ireland, was the late visit of his majesty to that part of his dominions. That gracious proceeding had been undervalued, and viewed with affected indifference, by the various descriptions of persons with various objects; but a wiser and more beneficial measure, he was convinced, could not have been taken. Its importance had been under-rated by those who were averse to see any lustre thrown around the throne, and by the petty factions of both sides who distracted that unhappy country; but the great body of the people had appreciated the visit as it deserved. His majesty had knocked at the hearts of his Irish subjects, and had been answered with inexpressible enthusiasm and gratitude. That visit had been followed by another measure of conciliation, on which they likewise set its proper value—he meant the appointment of the Marquis Wellesley to the government of Ireland. He would not then enter into any eulogium on that noble lord, who did not require any praises of his; but he should be wanting in that justice which he owed to him, if he did not state the wise and impartial views with which he entered upon his office—the zeal and vigour with which he applied himself to discover a remedy for the existing evils of Ireland, and the anxiety which he showed to administer the law, and to put down those who rose up against it, in whatever party, and under whatever banners, they appeared. He (Mr. Plunket) entertained from these and from other circumstances great hopes of approaching prosperity to Ireland; and he begged leave to say that some of his honourable friends had drawn too gloomy a picture of its past condition, when they spoke of an uninterrupted misgovernment of three centuries. Within the latter part of this period they might have found many subjects of consolation. The penal laws for religion had been within the last forty years entirely repealed; nothing now remained but one great measure of policy and justice that should remove all civil disabilities on account of religious faith. It should also be recollected that since the year 1782 that country had been restored to commerce and to all the commercial rights enjoyed in other parts of the empire. These advantages had been followed by an Union which placed Ireland on a footing with Great Britain, in all other privileges and rights. He had opposed that Union; he had done so openly and boldly, nor was he now ashamed of what he had done; but though in his resistance to it he had been prepared to go the length of any man, he was now equally prepared to do all in his power to render it close and indissoluble. One of the apprehensions on which his opposition was founded, he was happy to say, had been disappointed by the event. He had been afraid that the Irish interests, on the abolition of her separate legislature, would come to be discussed in a hostile parliament: but he could now state, and he wished when he spoke that he could be heard by the whole of Ireland, that during the time that he had sat in the united parliament, he had found every question that related to the interests or security of that country entertained with indulgence, and treated with the most deliberate regard. When he considered all these things—when he considered the privileges granted and the disabilities removed—and when he considered the effects that must result from the cordial efforts of a united legislature, he could not entertain gloomy ideas on the subject of the future prospects of Ireland. If an improved system of police were established in that country, and if the landed gentry discharged with zeal the duties of their character and station, we should soon see a manifest amelioration of the state of the sister island, and should find that, instead of being a source of weakness and distraction, it would become an arm of security and strength to the whole empire.

His right honourable friend (Mr. Grant) had adverted to the causes of the present state of society in Ireland, under the heads of the tithe system, the police, the magistracy, and education; and though he, when he rose did not intend to say one word upon them, he would now, as he was on his legs, address himself briefly to them. He confessed he approached the tithe system with great reserve and delicacy. The legislature had a right to meddle with that property, because there were no limits to its power; but, on the same principle that it could interfere with tithes, it might interfere with any other species of property. As to any forcible diminution of their amount, or compulsory commutation of them, he could never agree to any measure for that purpose, nor could parliament, on any just principle, entertain the question for a moment. In opposition to frequent complaints, he was of opinion that the clergy of Ireland were not adequately provided for. They did not receive what they were entitled to demand, and the clamour raised against their alleged exactions was most unfounded and most unjust. He wished to speak with respect of the great body of Irish landlords; but he was compelled to say, that, generally in the west and in the south of Ireland, they exacted so much rent themselves, that they left little for the tithe of the clergy, and joined in the cry of exaction when that little was attempted to be recovered. They sometimes let their land at from seven, eight, nine, or ten pounds per acre. Whatever the poor occupier could spare beyond mere subsistence, the proprietor claimed in the shape of rent, and thus left the clergyman, in the recovery of his tithe, to deal with an insolvent fund. If the latter surrendered his rights, he was left without an income, and praised for his generosity; if he exacted them, the cry of rapacity was raised against him. In the meantime, the poor occupier of the land gained no advantage by the clergyman's forbearance; as what was remitted in tithe was exacted in rent. The cry raised against the clergy for their enjoyment of that portion of the produce which the law awarded them from the land, always appeared to him illiberal and ill-founded. He knew of no class of country gentleman more useful than the clergy, even independent of their sacred duties, and none better entitled to the property which they enjoyed. They spent their income in the country, in the encouragement of industry, as usefully as laymen; they were better educated; they were more capable of directing their inferiors; and, independently of the religious instruction which they conveyed, they set a better example of morals and private conduct. But he agreed with those who thought that some change might be made with advantage, in the mode of collecting tithes, though he was opposed to any measure for compulsory commutation. The subject was certainly surrounded with difficulty, but he thought some means might be contrived, by which the clergy might be enabled to treat with the proprietors instead of the occupiers of land. In this manner an agreement, not amounting to a commutation of tithes, might be entered into, by which the clergyman might receive a certain sum for a certain number of years; and this arrangement might be farther perfected by making the tithe an actual charge upon the land into whatever hands it might fall. This would prevent that perpetual recurrence of vexatious pretensions which was now the source of so much dissension between the clergyman and the occupier of the land, and the effect would be extremely beneficial in another point of view. The occupier of land was generally a Roman Catholic, who was naturally disinclined to contribute to the support of a religion which he did not profess; but if the transfer which he had just alluded to were adopted, the Protestant clergyman would no longer have to deal with a Catholic occupier, but with the proprietor, who was generally a Protestant. He did not despair of some such measure being matured so as to be capable of being laid before parliament. This subject was now under the consideration of wiser heads than his; but he must deprecate the introduction of any measure, unless that measure had been precisely limited and ascertained; for he thought the Protestant clergy ought not to be exposed to the consequences of any indefinite arrangement, the exact limits and extent of which were not known previously to its being made the subject of deliberation. With regard to the system of police and the magistracy of Ireland, he could assure his right honourable friend, that those subjects were now occupying the serious attention of his majesty's government. The system of education had often received the attention of the house, and many measures had been passed with regard to it. Whether all the beneficial effects which had been expected had resulted from those measures, he would not pretend to say; but he was sure that the government would readily give its attention to any propositions which might be brought forward on the subject. He begged pardon for having trespassed so long upon the house. Indeed, it was not his intention to have occupied any portion of their attention, had he not felt himself called upon to make some counter statement to the evidence of the honourable and learned member for Dublin.

THE BOTTLE RIOT.

February 3, 1823.

ALL the facts concerning this celebrated prosecution are so clearly, fully, and consecutively narrated in the speech that it needs no introduction. I quote part of Sheil's description of the trial:—

"The grand jury, composed in a great degree of affiliated Orangemen, threw out the bills of indictment tendered by the crown against the perpetrators of the outrage at the theatre. Mr. Plunket announced his resolution to proceed by *ex officio* information; and a day was appointed for a trial at bar. The most anxious suspense awaited its arrival A deep pulsation throbbed through the city. The ordinary occupations of life appeared to be laid aside in the agitating expectation of the event which was to set a seal upon the future government of Ireland. It engrossed the thoughts and tongues of men, and exercised a painful monopoly of all their hopes and anticipations. At length the day of trial appeared amidst the heaviness of a gray and sombre morning. As soon as the doors were opened, one tremendous rush filled in an instant the galleries and every avenue of the court. There was not a murmur in the court; but the first glance at the auditory would have satisfied you that deep passions were working there, and could not long be hushed. The signs of this were most apparent in the galleries. You saw it in the scowling brows of the Orange partisans, and few else were there—in the compressed lip—in the roll of ferocious confidence with which their eyes went round the scene that reminded them of their strength—in the glare of factious recognition with which they greeted the accused, and assured them of a triumph. My eye next rested upon the crowded benches of the bar. They, too, betrayed a consciousness of being themselves upon their trial. Instead of the legal *nonchalance* with which they usually await the coming-on of the most important cause, they now presented a series of countenances quivering with political resentment. It was easy to trace their emotions in their looks—in the fixed and deadly sneer—in the flush of haughty indignation—in the impassioned gestures with which, in whispers among themselves, they arraigned the whole proceeding, and foretold the disasters it would bring upon the land. The business of the day opened with a joke. Mr. Plunket rose 'to call the attention of the court to a matter of some importance:' a dead silence prevailed. The attorney-general proceeded with much gravity to state, 'that he had been anxiously waiting the arrival of his colleagues, the solicitor-general and Mr. Serjeant Lefroy; and that, after a long search for them in all directions, it had been just discovered that they were both in one of the avenues of the court, firmly wedged in among the populace, with a prospect of immediate suffocation, unless their lordships should be pleased to interfere in their behalf.' The political tenets of the two learned sufferers were well known; and the most bigoted Orangeman in the galleries could not refrain from a loud giggle at the notion of two such personages writhing under the horrors of a popular embrace. Mr. Plunket's speech was on a level with his subject, but scarcely with himself. The solicitor-general's was tame and technical he felt too much sympathy with Orange principles, and he openly avowed them, to prove a formidable denouncer of Orange excesses."

My Lords and Gentlemen of the Jury,—It becomes now my duty to lay before you the case on behalf of the crown, and to put you in possession of the grounds on which the present prosecution has been instituted, and of the evidence by which it is intended to be supported. It has often been my lot, in the eventful history of this country, to appear in the character of a public prosecutor, and still more frequently to be a witness of the course and conduct of public prosecutions. But certainly never in my life have I approached a court of justice with sensations of more deep anxiety, or with a more intense feeling of the importance of the subject to be decided on, than I feel at the present moment. It is a case, my lords and gentlemen, not touching the life of the parties; the offence as laid amounting only to a misdemeanor. It is undoubtedly, however, to them a case of no small importance; involving them, if the facts charged be proved, in very heavy penal consequences. But with respect to the public at large, it is a case of as deep and vital importance, as for the last fifty years has been brought under the consideration of a court and of a jury. It is a great satisfaction to me, and a great part of my object has been achieved in knowing, that this case is now ready to be brought fully before an intelligent court and jury; and that whatever its merits may be, it is impossible they can be stifled or extinguished, but must be fairly brought under the consideration of the court, the jury, and the public. The charge is one of no light or ordinary character. You are already, my lords, probably apprised of it from public rumour; the nature of it has been more particularly stated by my learned friend who has opened the informations. It imports no less a crime, than having assaulted the person of the king's representative in this country; of having committed a riot in his presence for the purpose of insulting him; and of having done so in pursuance of a deliberate conspiracy previously entered into for the purpose.

This is a charge which ought not lightly to be made; and one, gentlemen, on which you ought not to act, unless fully and distinctly proved. But I should consider it as an insult to your character and understandings, to urge any argument to establish the enormity of the crime, if fully ascertained to have been committed. I should blush for our country, were it necessary to state in a court of justice, that a deliberate insult to the king's representative, in a public theatre, the result of a previous conspiracy, is no light or trivial or ordinary offence. In the mind of every man who has not banished the feelings of a gentleman, and who is not lost to every public and private consideration, there can be but one sentiment—a deep sense of indignity at the outrage, and an entire conviction of the necessity of vindicating the national character and the dignity of the laws, by affixing punishment, if deserved.

But, my lords, daring and unexampled as is the crime, I hesitate not to say, that the enormity of the act is lost in the boldness and description of the motives. I fairly tell you, that I come not here on the part of Lord Wellesley, to ask for personal redress, or even to call for public justice so far as he is personally concerned; not even on the part of the lord lieutenant of Ireland, to seek atonement for the outrage committed against the king's representative: but on behalf of the country and its laws; on behalf of its hopes of peace and safety; to claim your aid, backed by all the authority of opinion, in putting down a desperate and insolent attempt to overawe the king's government in Ireland; and to compel his representative, by the arm of personal violence, and by the demonstration of a force above the law, to change the measures of his government. I call on you to put down a base conspiracy of a contemptible gang, who have associated to put down the laws and to overbear the king's representative, because he has presumed to execute the king's commands. I think I know the feelings of the illustrious personage against whom this villany has been directed; with respect to his own personal safety, much as it has been endangered, the attack was fitted only to rouse his gallant mettle; indignant as he must have felt to be "hawked at by such mousing owls" as these; their base attempt excited no terror, it left no resentment. That there should have been in this land hearts capable of conceiving, and hands capable of executing, such an outrage against their countryman, must have excited sensations of regret and pain; but in this respect the national character has been redeemed, by the universal expression of indignation which has issued from the hearts of the Irish people. But beyond all this, much remains to be done; it is necessary to put down the daring pretensions of those who have associated themselves for the purpose of defying the king and the law, and setting up an authority superior to them both. They and all others who announce such projects, must be taught that their plans are vain and hopeless as they are insolent.

This I freely avow as my object. I trust that no unworthy prejudices, that no angry feeling, that no sentiment other than that which belongs to the conscientious discharge of public duty, has been suffered to mingle itself in the course of public justice. I shall go away from this court humiliated and under the heavy sentence of self-reproach if, after the evidence in this case shall have been disclosed, any honest or impartial man shall censure me for instituting this prosecution; or shall hesitate to think that it would have been a mean abandonment of duty to have shrunk from it.

You are apprised, by lords, that this is an *ex officio* information filed by his majesty's attorney-general upon his own authority; you are also probably aware that this *ex officio* information has been filed, after bills had been perferred against the same persons for the same offence, and had been ignored by a grand jury of the country. Before I proceed to trouble your lordships with any observation upon the exact nature and on the legality of this proceeding, I wish to disembarrass the case of a few topics which may attach to it. In the proceeding which I have thought it my duty to institute, though I have been governed by my strong impression that public justice had not been effected, I do not involve in this conclusion any imputation on the sheriff who returned the grand jury; still less on the grand jury themselves, who have acted on their oaths in throwing out those bills. For the purposes of the present trial, whatever opinions I may entertain on that subject, I have no right to advert to them. The sheriff who returned that grand jury is not on his trial, and it would be gross injustice to arraign his conduct when he cannot defend it. The grand jury are not on their trials, and it would be injustice equally gross to make a charge against them, where they can have no opportunity of vindicating themselves; a time may come, and an occasion may arise, in which these considerations may be proper and necessary; and most certainly I will not, in that event, be found wanting to the discharge of any duty, however painful, which may devolve on me. But in the meantime, and with reference to the present proceeding, I wish distinctly to be understood as disclaiming all imputations upon either; I am ready to suppose, for the purposes of this trial, that if the parties and the cause were the exact reverse of what they now are; that if it had been the pleasure of the government to direct that the statue of King William should be dressed on the 4th of November, and a body of Roman Catholics feeling themselves insulted, had risen against the law and the magistracy, and had flung a bottle or other missile at the lord lieutenant's head, and these facts had been before the grand jury, they would have ignored the bills; as, so help me God, I would, under the same circumstances, had I remained the king's attorney-general, have filed my information *ex officio*. I claim only for myself equal credit for the purity of my motives, and the fair discharge of my sworn duty.

I am told that it has been alleged that this proceeding on the part of the attorney-general, by an *ex officio* information, is illegal. I do not know whether what has been said in this respect has been rightly reported; or whether it is meant, that the proceeding is in point of law invalid, or that the resorting to it, though a legal right, is not a fair exercise of discretion. I am led naturally, without going out of the pleadings, to make a few observations upon this part of the subject; for although all the traversers have put in pleas amounting to not guilty, yet two of them have thought proper to put upon the record what cannot properly belong to that plea—a sort of preamble or inducement, in which they state that those informations have been filed against them after a grand jury had ignored bills for the same charge. My learned friends, who framed those defences, knew perfectly well that on that allegation no issue could be joined, either of law or of fact. It amounts, therefore, to nothing else than a plea of not guilty. But I presume they thought it might be made use of (though scarcely to your lordships or the jury whom I address) to swell the cry, which amongst the vulgar of the public has been raised against the legality of this proceeding.

I think that on that subject I need occupy but little time in addressing the court, before which I have now the honour to appear. What I am about to say is rather with a view to set right the public mind, and that it should be known that I have stated, in the presence of this enlightened court, what is the law upon this subject. I assert then, that the ignoring of a bill by a grand jury is, according to the known and established principles of our law, no bar to any subsequent legal proceeding against the same individual for the same offence. It is competent to the crown or the prosecutor to send up another bill to the same or any other grand jury; and the same power belongs to that public authority in which is vested the right of filing an information. A party who has been already tried, may protect himself against a subsequent prosecution for the same offence. He may do so by plea; it is a principle of our law that no man shall be twice tried for the same offence; if he has been already acquitted there is a known legal form of pleading as old as the law itself, by which he can defend himself. But it is settled by authorities coeval with the law itself, that the plea of *autrefois acquit* is not supported by evidence, that a bill of indictment for the same offence has been preferred to a grand jury and ignored. It must be an acquittal by a petit jury. Your lordships would consider it a waste of time to refer to authorities in support of such a position. It is laid down by Lord Hale, Lord Coke, and every writer on the subject of crown law. I shall not consume time by adverting to cases for recognition of known principles; the thing can only be doubted by those who are ignorant of our laws and constitution. That another indictment could be sent up is clear; and I think I go a good way to show its legality, by calling upon those who deny it, to show me any form of pleading by which it can be resisted. There is no legal right belonging to any subject of this realm, which the law has not afforded him a mode of setting forth; and therefore if there be no form of pleading, (and if there were such, my learned friends, in whose hands the interests of the traversers are so effectually secured, would have discovered it) by which the throwing out of a bill by a grand jury, may be set up as a bar to a subsequent information, that is in itself a full proof of the legality of such a proceeding. They have indeed distinctly admitted it, by putting in pleas not denying the competence of the attorney-general to file, or of the court to entertain, the present information. but asserting their innocence of the charge imputed to them. In an ordinary case, not affecting the rights of the crown, this court is in the habit of granting criminal informations; the right formerly exercised by the master in the crown office has been narrowed by statute, and is now subject to the discretion of the court. Has it ever been heard of, that the Court of King's Bench would refuse an information, because a grand jury had ignored the bill?

So much trash has been circulated, and the public mind so much abused upon this subject, that I hope your lordships will excuse my calling your attention to it. So far from its being considered an objection, that a grand jury has ignored the bill, it is often a reason why the Court of King's Bench grants an information. I have often applied for liberty to file an information, when I had the honour of practising in this court; and the court has asked me whether I had tried a grand jury; saying, that if they refused to find a bill, they would then entertain the application. The Court of King's Bench in England in the last term granted an information in a case where bills had been twice ignored by a grand jury, and because they had been ignored. So far therefore is that circumstance from being considered an objection to putting a party on his trial, that it is frequently insisted upon as a requisite condition. Thus it is where application is made to the Court of King's Bench. This is an information filed by the sworn officer of the crown, in whom the law has vested that privilege. Were I to come in as attorney-general, and apply for liberty to file an information against these parties, what would be your lordship's answer?—the same as was given by my Lord Mansfield to De Grey, and I think to Sir Fletcher Norton; namely, " We will not file an information at your suit; the law has made you the sole judge of its propriety; if you think it proper, you have a right to file it; if not, why should we do so?" I am not now applying myself to the soundness of this exercise of discretion, but to the new-fangled notion of the illegality of this information. It is the privilege of the lowest subject in the realm, if by the error or impropriety of a grand jury he do not obtain justice, to apply to the Court of King's Bench for a criminal information; but the king, it is said, is to be in a totally different situation; and though for an offence indictable the court would grant an information because a grand jury has ignored the bill, the sovereign himself shall not have that redress which is open to the meanest of his subjects. A proposition this too monstrous to bear debate. I am asked for an authority; permit me to say, this is not quite a fair requisition; where a circumstance is totally immaterial, it is not to be expected that it should be the subject of notice; and therefore we are not to be surprised, if in the greater number of reported cases of informations it should not appear whether a grand jury had previously thrown out bills or not; such a fact would be totally immaterial. It cannot be stated in a plea; it could not be proved in evidence, and therefore it would be too much to say that because it is not mentioned the case has not existed.

It has been my principle to hold in utter contempt the vile and scurrilous publications which have been circulated through the city, in order to prejudge the matters to be tried, and affect the characters of the persons employed as public functionaries. But I have, by the generosity of some of their authors, been furnished with a case directly in point, in which, by accident, the fact of bills having been ignored by the grand jury before the information filed does distinctly appear.

I shall detail the facts as they appear in the Commons' Journals. In the latter end of the reign of Queen Anne, in the year 1713, on King William's birthday, the play of Tamerlane was to be represented. King William, as your lordships are aware, was compared to Tamerlane, and very deservedly so, if the possession of every virtue that could ennoble a monarch entitled him to the distinction. The name of Tamerlane had been connected with his. A prologue to the play, written by Doctor Garth, was very generally repeated at the time. The doctor it seems was more happy as a poet than as a courtier, and his reverence for King William led him to compliment that monarch in terms not sufficiently guarded to avoid giving offence to Queen Anne. The government therefore thought it right that the prologue should not be repeated. When the play therefore came on for representation, the actor omitted to repeat it, and by so doing, gave great offence to the audience. They were full of respect for the memory of William, and did not wish that attention to Queen Anne should break in on the ancient practice. Mr. Dudley Moore, a zealous Protestant, who was in the house, leaped upon the stage, and repeated the prologue. This gave rise to something like a riot. The government indicted Mr. Moore for the riot. The bills were sent up to a grand jury, who returned a true bill, and were then dismissed. In about half an hour after, the foreman came into court, and made an affidavit that "*billa vera*" was a mistake, and that they meant to return "*ignoramus*." The court refused to receive his affidavit; but then came in the three and twenty, and swore positively to the same fact to which their foreman had deposed. The party was notwithstanding this, in my opinion very unwisely, put to plead to the indictment. But the attorney-general, thinking it would be hard to compel him to plead when the bill had been in fact ignored, moved to quash the indictment, which was done. Do I overstate the matter when I say, that things were then in the same situation as if the bill had been ignored by the grand jury? And yet under these circumstances, the attorney-general thought himself at liberty to file an *ex officio* information against the same person for the same offence. Sir Constantine Phipps, who was then lord chancellor, and one of the lords justices, was considered by many as a great Tory and Jacobite, and as an enemy to the Protestant interest. History has done more justice to him in that respect than in the heat of party he received from his contemporaries. He interfered with the prosecution; he sent for the lord mayor, and lectured him as to the mode in which he was to conduct himself. He was even supposed to have interfered with the return of the jury. The whole matter was brought before the House of Commons, who addressed the throne to remove Sir Constantine Phipps for intermeddling in the trial. No fault was found with the information though directly before them, but the trial was treated as legally depending, and a petition presented against the chancellor for interfering with that trial. Do I not here show a case in which an *ex officio* information had been filed after a bill had been thrown out, and where though the zeal of party generated an anxiety to lay hold of anything that could warrant an imputation on the proceeding, as the information filed was never questioned, but the chancellor and chief governor petitioned against for interfering with the proceeding.

I shall not trouble your lordships farther upon the legality of this proceeding. With respect to the soundness of the exercise of my discretion, under the circumstances, in resorting to the prerogative right, I shall reserve myself until I shall have laid before the court and the jury the facts which will be proved in the case. I have already said, that I will prove that an attempt has been made by a gang in this city for the purpose of controlling the law, and putting down the authority of the king's lieutenant. It is unfortunately necessary to show, that the individuals concerned in this outrage are persons belonging to a society known by the name of the Orange society. But it is particularly necessary, gentlemen of the jury, that you and the court and the public should understand what was formerly uttered by me, and what I now repeat. I am desirous of expressly stating, that with the general nature of the Orange societies, in relation to the laws, the interests, and happiness of the country, I have on this trial nothing to do. Upon this subject I have my opinions, which at a proper place and season I shall not shrink from avowing. But with the present investigation they have no concern. I do believe in my conscience, that the greater proportion of persons associated in that society feel as strong and lofty a contempt for those concerned in this disgraceful attack as I do, and are as incapable of participating, authorizing, vindicating, or palliating it. Every public man must expect to be the subject of no very candid criticism. I wish distinctly to have it understood, that this is no after-thought of mine, for the purpose of qualifying expressions either inadvertently or too strongly used. Had I applied these expressions indiscriminately to the Orangemen of Ireland, I should have violated my duty, and stepped beyond that line of conducting this prosecution, which was distinctly agreed upon between me and the eminent and respectable persons by whom I have been advised. I am glad to take this opportunity once for all, of returning my thanks to my learned colleague, by whose high talents, enlightened information, and extensive knowledge, I have been assisted in every stage of this proceeding, and to whose cordial zeal and co-operation no terms can be too strong to render justice and express my gratitude.

My lords, I am anxious to proceed to an immediate statement of the facts of this case, and to disperse that mass of scurrility and falsehood which for some weeks past has disgraced this city. I must however first trespass on your time with some preliminary observations.

It is impossible to lay this case truly before the public without briefly reverting to the political events in which the conspiracy originated.

The foundations of it were laid so long back as the period when his majesty was pleased to honour this country with his presence.

It is not, my lords, my intention to occupy your time by attempting a description of what took place on that occasion. From the minds of those who witnessed the transaction, the splendour and glory of that day never can be effaced. To those who have not, no powers of mine can give an adequate description. It falls to me to have the less pleasing task of remarking, that even then some indications were to be found, that his majesty's gracious dispositions were not likely to be met with that degree of gratitude and respect to which they were entitled, and that even before he left the Irish shore the elements of mischief were at work. It was understood that the king, before he honoured the Mansion House with his presence, had signified his desire that the glorious memory should not be given as a toast. I must entreat your excuse, my lords, (it connects itself intimately with the matter of this trial) if I advert more particularly to this topic, and endeavour to disabuse the public mind upon the subject.

Perhaps, my lords, there is not to be found in the annals of history a character more truly great than that of William the Third. Perhaps no person has ever appeared on the theatre of the world, who has conferred more essential or more lasting benefits on mankind; on these countries, certainly none. When I look at the abstract merits of his character, I contemplate him with admiration and reverence. Lord of a petty principality—destitute of all resources but those with which nature had endowed him—regarded with jealousy and envy by those whose battles he fought; thwarted in all his counsels; embarrassed in all his movements; deserted in his most critical enterprises—he continued to mould all those discordant materials, to govern all these warring interests, and merely by the force of his genius, the ascendancy of his integrity, and the immoveable firmness and constancy of his nature, to combine them into an indissoluble alliance against the schemes of despotism and universal domination of the most powerful monarch in Europe; seconded by the ablest generals, at the head of the bravest and best disciplined armies in the world, and wielding, without check or control, the unlimited resources of his empire. He was not a consummate general; military men will point out his errors; in that respect fortune did not favour him, save by throwing the lustre of adversity over all his virtues. He sustained defeat after defeat, but always rose *adversa rerum immersabilis unda.* Looking merely at his shining qualities and achievements, I admire him as I do a Scipio, a Regulus, a Fabius; a model of tranquil courage, undeviating probity, and armed with a resoluteness and constancy in the cause of truth and freedom, which rendered him superior to the accidents that control the fate of ordinary men.

But this is not all—I feel, that to him, under God, I am, at this moment, indebted for the enjoyment of the rights which I possess as a subject of these free countries; to him I owe the blessings of civil and religious liberty, and I venerate his memory with a fervour of devotion suited to his illustrious qualities and to his godlike acts.

Did our gracious sovereign come here to trample on the memory of the most illustrious of his predecessors? No, my lords; the high errand on which he landed on our shores was worthy of him, and bespoke a kindred mind to that of the immortal personage whose name and character he vindicated. He knew that the whole life of King William was a continued struggle against intolerance; that the policy of his reign was opposed, and his most favourite objects for the peace and happiness of his people were baffled, by the folly and bigotry of those who surrounded him; and that the career of his glorious life was obstructed, as the lustre of his glorious memory has been tarnished, by the absurd and intolerant dogmatism of those who were rescued by his exertions from that yoke which they sought, in opposition to his eager wishes, to impose on others. It was the unhappy but inevitable result of the circumstances in which the people of this unfortunate country were placed, that they had to meet that great man, not as subjects, but as enemies. The peculiar good fortune of the British people was, that every feeling of religion corresponded with their innate love of freedom to alienate them from the cause of the exiled monarch. His designs, his determinations against their civil and religious liberties, were notorious and unalterable. An inflexible bigot and despot, he was too intense in both characters to endure the appearance of a compromise with toleration or with freedom. Yet every man knows through what difficulties and dangers they had to struggle before the house of Brunswick was firmly seated on the throne. Even with the full tide of religion running in their favour, the principle of loyalty to an hereditary succession was so indigenous to the British character, that it was not until after the lapse of nearly a century that the principles of Jacobitism were finally subdued.

But in unhappy Ireland the exiled king was the professor and patron of the religion to which they were enthusiastically devoted. He must be a preposterous critic who will impute as a crime to that unhappy people, that they did not rebel against their lawful king, because he was of their own religion, even if they had been so fully admitted to the blessings of the British constitution as to render them equally alive to the value of freedom. They seem, therefore, by the nature of things, almost necessarily thrown into a state of resistance; nothing could have saved them from it but so strong a love of abstract freedom as might subdue the principles of loyalty and the feelings of religion. No candid man can lay so heavily on poor human nature; nor fairly say, that he thinks worse of the Roman Catholic, for having on that day abided by his lawful sovereign and his ancient faith. What was the result? They were conquered—conquered into freedom and happiness—a freedom and happiness to which the successful result of their ill-fated struggles would have been destructive. There is no rational Roman Catholic in Ireland who does not feel this to be the fact. Even the name of the exiled family is now unknown ; the throne rests on the firm basis of the unanimous recognition of the entire people. The memory of their unfortunate struggles is lost in the conviction of the reality of those blessings, which have been derived from their results equally to the conqueror and to the conquered. What wise or good man can feel a pleasure in recalling to the minds of a people so circumstanced the fact that they have been conquered ? What but the spirit of folly and of mischief can take a satisfaction in interrupting them in the enjoyment of the blessings of their defeat, by taunting them with the recollection that they were defeated? Why is conquest desirable to any one but the trooper ? Because it opens the way to peace and harmony; but to those I have now to deal with, the fruits of the conquest are valueless, without the perpetuation of the triumph.

He is a mischievous man who desires to remind the people of this country that they are a conquered people. He is a mischievous man who, for the gratification of his own whim, desires to celebrate, in the midst of that people, the anniversary of their conquest. Never was there a subject more loudly calling for and justifying the gracious and saving interposition of the royal wisdom.

In the history of royal lives there seldom has occurred an instance affording a more gratifying subject for the historian to dwell on, than the royal visit to Ireland. The statement of splendid victories, the development of profound schemes of policy, the application of able counsels, and of powerful resources, the defence of the liberties of the world; all these are the subjects of historic detail, and may be the fair subjects of political controversy. But here, by the mere impulse of his own feelings, the heartiness of his nature, a moment was created in which, without calling on any of the common places of royalty, without the aid of force, or fear, or flattery; without arms, or power, or patronage ; by the mere indulgence of his kind and generous nature, he gained to himself the most exalted privileges which a human being can exercise—that of bestowing happiness on, and sharing it with, millions of his fellow-creatures. The promptness with which this moment was seized—the gracious and condescending manner by which it was improved—the thousand and ten thousand blessings which are to be derived from it—all these may be subjects of just applause and of sober criticism. But here the true value of the act is its simplicity. To enter into the hearts and become master of the enthusiastic affections of an entire people, merely by showing himself the friend and father of them all, was a felicity to him and them unparalleled in the eventful history of this nation; it was worthy of a successor of the great monarch, whose talents and virtues he emulated, and whose memory he rescued from the disgraceful orgies by which it had been tarnished. Equal in the motive and the feeling—happier in this, that the hard fortune of William the Third compelled him to visit this country as a conqueror; but it was reserved for the peculiar felicity of George the Fourth, that he was the first British king who ever placed a friendly footstep upon the Irish soil.

I have already had occasion to remark, that the intimation of his majesty's pleasure on the subject of public concord was not perfectly agreeable to a certain portion of his subjects. Some little clouds were seen flitting along the horizon, which indicated the probability of a future storm. How far the government of the country were enabled to act on the personal recommendation and parting injunctions of the king—what were the difficulties the Irish government had to encounter —what were the means they used to surmount them, these are matters which do not belong to the present subject. I pass to the period of Lord Wellesley's arrival in this country. He found a great portion of the south of Ireland in a state of licentiousness, surpassing the worst excesses of former unhappy times. He had to deal with dangerous and secret conspiracies in other parts of the country. In what manner the lord lieutenant applied the powerful energies of his great mind to meet these complicated difficulties does not fall within the compass or limit of this trial. It would ill suit with my notions of what is due to the Marquis Wellesley, and of his temper and character, to offer up the suspicious praises which an Irish attorney-general is supposed bound to tender to the lord lieutenant. I am too sensible of the well-formed taste of this illustrious person, not to be convinced that he would reject with disdain the vulgar incense of official adulation, if I could stoop to offer it. No, my lords, it would be an unsuited return for the kindness, the confidence, I will presume to say, the friendship, with which he has honoured me; I know too well his lofty feelings and noble nature, "*cui male si palpere, recalcitrat undique tutus;*"—but I will not be deterred by the apprehension of a suspicion which I disdain, and to which I trust the character of my life renders me superior, from expressing my sentiments of that exalted personage, when he has become the object of vulgar scurrility, and when an open and desperate attack is made upon his person and his government. I will not be deterred from saying, that had our gracious sovereign surveyed the extent of his dominions in search of one fitted to execute the magnificent purposes of benevolence to his people, with which his royal breast was filled, he could not have found a person whom the gifts of nature, improved by every noble art, and mellowed by a long and arduous experience in the most difficult exigencies of this great empire, so eminently qualified for the task : or one whose heart so entirely and cordially vibrated in unison with the gracious and paternal interest which was felt for the welfare of his native land. That noble peer entered on the government of this country under this royal instruction ; he had to explore a very difficult and dangerous and untried path, but he had the parting admonition and the renewed injunctions of his sovereign for his pole star. He entered on that government, carefully distinguishing his opinions and duties as a politician and a legislator, from those which necessarily involved the system of government of the country committed to him. Never abandoning, but carefully distinguishing, his individual opinion from his official duties, he applied himself strictly and exclusively to effectuate the orders of the king, by the equal administration of the existing laws, and by the promotion of peace, happiness, and concord among all the various classes of his subjects. I defy the malignity of criticism to point out a false move in the government of that noble person; one instance in which he departed from the spirit of that mission of conciliation which was confided to him ; an act or an expression calculated to excite offence or disapprobation in the mind of any honest man or lover of his country, be his sect or his party what it may. Pursuing his clear and undeviating course ; raised above all party, the laws for his guide, and the public happiness for his object, his fame is independent of the praise of his friends, and above the malice of his enemies. It is our business, my lords, to guard his person and his government against their secret machinations and their open violence.

The discontinuance of the public insults to which I have already alluded, and which has been so highly disapproved of by the king, necessarily had a place in the system of the lord lieutenant. The offensive toast which had been renewed in the presence of the late lord lieutenant was withheld in the presence of Lord Wellesley. I grieve to say that a spirit of mutiny and dissatisfaction on this subject was giddily and rashly encouraged by many who knew and ought to have reverenced the king's commands. The lord lieutenant, however highly he disapproved the giving the toast on public occasions, did not think it became him to take any further step, having taken care that the king's authority should not, in his presence, be insulted by it. Another subject, or rather another part of the subject, called his attention.

The statue of King William, you all know, has been, for some years back, bedaubed with ridiculous painting and tawdry orange colours—a ludicrous specimen of bad taste, with which, however, his excellency did not feel himself called on to intermeddle. But beyond this, a set of low persons, whose names were not avowed, had been for some years back in the habit of mounting the statue in the night of the 3rd of November, and of the 11th of July, and putting on it a fantastic drapery of orange scarfs, in themselves ridiculous, if they had not been meant as a mark of triumph over a certain portion of their fellow-subjects. This being done by a party of sworn Orangemen, and for the avowed purpose of insult, had been resented by the Roman Catholics whom it was intended to insult; and on the 12th of July last a serious riot had occurred, the insulted party conceiving that they had as good a right to undress, as the other had to dress, the statue of King William. In the course of this affray lives had been endangered, the peaceable inhabitants of College-green seriously alarmed, the tranquillity of the metropolis disturbed, and evil passions of the most furious kind engendered in the minds of the parties. It is obvious that one of these three courses was to be pursued. Either the dressers of the statue were to be protected by public force and the constituted authorities; or they were to be forbidden and prevented; or the parties were to be left to fight it out, till outrage, riot, and bloodshed arrived at such a height that the civil power must act against both. I have never heard it distinctly stated, or that it was distinctly stated by any person, that either the first or the last of these courses ought to have been proved; either that the public authorities should have been called to assist the nightly party in making the toilet of King William, and to apprehend any person who should presume to interrupt them; or that the streets of the capital should be disgraced by the continuance of these senseless brawls. The first question on which his excellency had to satisfy his mind was, whether the continuance of the practice of dressing the statue might, under such circumstances, be legally prevented.

He was advised that it clearly might; that these mummers had no right to lay their hands on this public ornament, whether for the purpose of decoration or dedecoration. 'Gentlemen, I remember that on one occasion a set of ruffians mounted this statue, and daubed it over with lampblack. Neither they nor any other persons had a right to meddle with the public ornaments, either to adorn or disgrace them. But independently of this, his excellency was advised that this being proposed to be done, not in discharge of any acknowledged duty, or in the prosecution of any known business, or in the exercise of any right of property or franchise, either by grant or usage, and being found by experience to have a tendency to produce and to have actually produced a breach of the peace, and it being proved on oath that it had done so, and that its continuance excited well-grounded apprehensions for the safety of their persons in the minds of the king's subjects residing in the neighbourhood, several of whom, persons of known respectability, and Protestants too, had made affidavit to that effect, his excellency was advised, that he would be well warranted in using the civil force to prevent the dressing of the statue.

I am ashamed to think that it should be necessary to say, in a court of justice, that they were Protestants. I say this, because there are persons weak enough to imagine that the oath of a Catholic is not to be attended to on this subject, and because it has been untruly stated that these were affidavits of Catholics of the lower order. I owe an apology to the good sense and feeling of the court and the jury for stating what their religion was; it is a disgrace to our country that such topics should be adverted to. Gentlemen, I have been public prosecutor in this country at a period when the passions of men were most alive; and never in the course of my official experience have I given any other advice to the solicitor for the crown than to select honest and fair men, without reference to their religious opinions, and I have never felt myself disappointed in the result; and therefore you will not suppose that the circumstance of these persons being Protestants was necessary to prop their credit in my estimation.

I am glad to have this opportunity of stating, that being called on in the discharge of my sworn duty for my opinion, I gave it as I have stated, and I challenge any man who respects his character as a constitutional lawyer to correct its soundness. It is no light matter to charge the executive government with acting contrary to law against any portion of the people; it begets in their minds the notion, that in resisting the civil authorities they are resisting not law, but power—such a course is calculated to bring the government of the country into contempt; and when the acts so spoken of have been done in pursuance of the king's instructions, it is a violation of the personal respect which is due to him, independently of its tendency to weaken the authority of his government in this country.

His excellency was, independently of any respect which his kindness might dispose him to attach to the opinion of his law adviser, perfectly satisfied of the illegality of the practice in question; and I am authorised to take this public opportunity of stating, that having communicated on the subject with the king's government in England, he was sanctioned by their unanimous opinion in using the civil power for the prevention of these illegal practices. I am further authorised to state, that since his excellency adopted the measures which are so publicly known for the carrying that opinion into effect, his conduct has received the unanimous approbation of the entire British cabinet, and has, above all, been crowned by the highest reward which a subject can receive for the faithful discharge of his duty—the personal approbation of his sovereign, whose commands he executed, and whose government he sustained.

Before his excellency resorted to any public means for the suppression of this practice, he tried every expedient, by persuasion and remonstrance, to obviate the necessity of public interference. It is but justice to say that many, very many of the principal persons who were supposed to have an influence over the Orange associations did exert their authority for the purpose; but whatever were their exertions, they were unavailing; they found they could not govern the party with whom they had associated themselves. So must it ever be, when rank and station and education condescend to combine in a secret bond with the vulgar and the ignorant. They must not expect to govern them; so long as they run in the same course of party and opinion, they may be suffered to lead; but in vain will they endeavour to alter the direction or moderate the violence. When the evil spirit is unchained and let loose, the spell that raised it will be unavailing to allay it: for the purposes of a greater excitement they may be powerful and dangerous; for those of repression and restraint altogether impotent. The lower classes of these persons declared they would disobey the lord mayor's proclamation and resist the magistrates. Furious and absurd speeches were made at public meetings, filled with vulgar invectives against the constituted authorities; and preparations were made for resistance to the law. The dressing of the statue on the night of the third and day of the fourth of November was prevented; but on subsequent nights, particularly on the night of the 6th of November, several of the party assembled for the purpose, and were not dispersed without considerable disturbance and difficulty. On this occasion the traverser Henry Handwich was particularly active; he headed a party who arrayed themselves against the magistracy for the purpose of dressing the statue. He was, it seems, the regular mantua maker to King William. He collected subscriptions on the night between the fifth and sixth of November; he mounted on the statue, and nailed upon it the tawdry ornaments with which he was furnished. With some difficulty he and his party were suppressed; they were dispersed before morning. Two or three similar attempts were afterwards made, but the firmness of the magistrates was sufficient to put them down.

In this situation of affairs, the lord lieutenant availed himself of the first opportunity which the various claims of public care allowed him, to announce his intention of honouring the Theatre Royal with his presence; a play was accordingly announced, and notice given.

I shall now state the facts of this case, which will be so clearly proved, and placed so far beyond all doubt, that no gentleman whom I have the honour of seeing in that jury box, can leave it with a doubt upon his mind as to the real nature of the transaction. Certain persons met together, and conceived that this would be a good opportunity of marking their public indignation against the Marquess Wellesley, for presuming to enforce the king's command in forbidding the dressing of the statue. One of those persons, gentlemen, (melancholy, if this be so, is the situation of the lord lieutenant) holds high situations under the king's government, a place in the post office, and another in the customs, producing nearly £800 a year. I allude to a man named William Heron. This person, and another of the name of M'Cullogh, who holds a situation in the Meath hospital; a man named Atkinson holding a situation in the custom house, and others, on the night of Wednesday or the morning of the Thursday before the play, consulted as to the best means of dealing with the subject. The result they came to was, that this would be a proper opportunity for acting in the theatre in such a manner, as to evince the unpopularity of the lord lieutenant and his government, and make it necessary for him to leave the house, and eventually to leave the country. It was determined that a subscription should be raised to purchase tickets. Well knowing that the true expression of the public sentiment would be strong in favour of his excellency, they resolved, in order to thwart it, to collect a party and pack the theatre. They thought the persons who were associated would of themselves be sufficient for the pit and the middle gallery; but that for the inferior orders, seats must be purchased. Accordingly a subscription of £2 was collected by Heron, and sent by him to Atkinson. This was to be communicated to an Orange lodge, assembled at the house of one Daly in Werburgh-street, in what is called the Purple Order of the lodge. That, gentlemen, is not conferred upon any person until he has been for a certain time a member of the General Institution. This subscription was given to the parties present at the lodge, and an additional subscription was raised by them. Two of those lodges were concerned. The traverser, James Forbes, is a member of the lodge 1660. He is deputy master of that lodge. William Graham is secretary of the same. Henry Handwich and Matthew Handwich are members of the lodge 780, of which Henry is deputy master; and William Brownlow is a member of 1612. Although it is necessarily my duty to show who and what these persons are, I do not meddle with the general character of Orange lodges in Ireland, the merits of which are for another place. I am well satisfied that the great body of Orangemen feel as much abhorrence at this crime as any individual can do. With this subscription a number of pit tickets were purchased on Saturday morning from the box keeper at the play house. This was for the purpose of filling the upper gallery. It was thought that the members who were able to purchase tickets for themselves would be sufficient for the pit and middle gallery. One pit ticket was to be given to every three. Forbes was present when this subscription was raised. On the Saturday morning, Forbes, M'Culloch, and Atkinson went together to the theatre, and purchased the tickets. They regularly proceeded to fashion the conspiracy in all its parts. It was determined that an inferior Orange Lodge, to which Handwich belonged, and which met at Mrs. Daly's in Ship-street, should be ready to go to the Theatre to execute the plan. Application was made in the morning to Matthew Handwich at his work, and he was desired to communicate with his brother Henry. Accordingly, about four o'clock in the evening of Saturday the parties met—Forbes, Atkinson, the Handwiches, and others. They were first supplied with drink. They came armed with sticks. Handwich had been asked, if he could furnish sixty men. He said he could. He had not quite so many at first, but the number was completed in the passage to the Theatre. They were dispatched from the place of meeting in parties of three, each with a pit ticket. The number was at first sixty, but afterwards increased to near an hundred. They were armed with bludgeons. The residue of the whiskey they had been drinking they put into a bottle and carried to the theatre. The last words of Handwich, on leaving the place of meeting, were "boys be wicked." It was settled that the duty of Lodge 1612 should be, to go to the pit door, and beset it before it was open, and to rush in in a body, and occupy that part of the pit next to his excellency's box. Their directions were, that as soon as "God save the King" was played, the "Boyne Water" should be called for, and if it were refused, that the play should be stopped, and that a system of hissing, groaning, and violence should commence. One of the party had a large rattle in his hand, for the purpose of riot. I should tell you, that at the meeting held of the Purple Order, on Friday evening, and at which Forbes was present, the plan was fully announced of compelling the lord lieutenant to leave the theatre, and if possible, the country. One of the party even offered to lay a wager that before March he would be out of the country. Finding that these conspirators entertained such serious views, that their object was to make such a demonstration of hostility as to compel his excellency to quit the country, and that this was to be effected by resistance, by riot, and even by personal violence, one of the parties engaged took the alarm. He was shocked at the extent to which their fury might go. At one time he had formed the resolution of going to the lord lieutenant, and apprising him of the truth, and the danger to which he was exposed. He went to the park; a sentinel at the gate of the viceregal lodge asked him his business; his mind was in that situation, in which a trivial circumstance makes an alteration—he hesitated, and returned, and the disclosure was not made.

Gentlemen, the party (1612) which had been arranged for the purpose, rushed into the pit, and occupied that part of it which was nearest the viceregal box; the upper gallery party, to the number of 60, went there with the pit tickets. They had fixed upon a watchword, "look out;" they seated themselves on the left hand side of the gallery, where the violence was carried on during the night. Forbes placed them at their posts in the upper gallery, armed with bludgeons; the police occupied the opposite side of the house, and like faithful watchmen fell asleep on their posts; no interruption was given to the merriment or to the mischief of the party. To show the deliberation of their plans I should mention, that previously to the play, handbills were struck off, containing expressions insulting to the lord lieutenant; such as "Down with the Popish government," &c., and other expressions insignificant and contemptible, except as evincing deliberation and concert. These handbills were brought to the theatre, and disposed of by the members of the conspiracy; several were thrown by M'Culloch, from the lattices over the lord lieutenant's box, and others from various parts of the house. It will be proved, that from the opening of the theatre, the grossest system of insulting and offensive expressions was commenced; groans were raised for "the Popish Lord Lieutenant," and cries of "no Popish Government." There were also groans for the house of Wellesley. They did not confine themselves to the noble lord at the head of the government—they extended to the Duke of Wellington, and the other branches of his illustrious family. Not satisfied with that, those advocates of religion gave " a clap for the Calf's Head," an allusion to a monstrous outrage committed in or near Ardee, by some ruffians who profaned a Roman Catholic place of worship by placing such a thing upon the altar. They applauded also Sheriff Thorpe, with the Calf's Head. There was " a groan for the bloody Popish Lord Lieutenant." I cannot remember all the terms of outrage which were used. Some persons, not connected with the gang, cried out "Shame, shame"—of these some were severely beaten, and one man had a narrow escape by getting down from the upper into the middle gallery; several were alarmed and left the house. When the lord lieutenant came in, there was a general expression of approbation from the audience, which for some time bore down the hisses of the conspirators. But when an opportunity arose, a violent hissing and groaning were set up. These things went on till " God save the King" was played; at that period, a bottle was thrown from the upper gallery, which hit the stage curtain. The fact will be proved by a variety of witnesses, who will leave no doubt upon it in your minds. It was flung from the gallery by Henry Handwich. He will appear to have been a leader of the party. You will have the testimony of several distinct and independent witnesses, who can have no other object than to tell the truth. Several persons saw the bottle in its progress. Amongst the idle reports which have been circulated as to this transaction, it has been said, that this came from the carpenters' gallery—and from the pit—but gentlemen, we shall put the fact beyond all controversy. As to the precise point where it hit the curtain, there is a diversity of opinion; but that it hit somewhere nearer to the lord lieutenant than to the centre, all the accounts concur. Some of the witnesses say it struck within four feet of the side next the lord lieutenant, and within four feet of the stage. Another says, that it was the breadth of a festoon. But all concur in this, that it was thrown, and that their impression was that it was directed against the lord lieutenant. It was thrown from the same side on which his excellency sat. You will ask why did they get to that side. The right hand side had been early occupied by other persons; and the conspirators feeling it necessary to be in a body, were obliged to go to the left. The precise situation in which Handwich was placed when he threw the bottle, will be proved to you. He threw it under him, or by a side motion, and not over him. Any person who will attend to the position in which he was, as well as to that of the lord lieutenant, will easily account for the aberration of the instrument. All the witnesses agree in stating it to be their impression that the bottle was directed against his excellency. Besides the general proof to show that the bottle came from the upper gallery, there are three witnesses who distinctly saw Henry Handwich throw it. One whose arrival we hourly expect, had his attention excited by some expression of Handwich, and immediately marked him. He swears positively to his having thrown the bottle. George Graham was one of the principal rioters. He had a large rattle which he used at first for the purpose of making a noise; and when it had performed its services in that department, he converted it into an instrument of personal attack. He broke it into two pieces, and it will be distinctly proved, that he came forward and took deliberate aim at the lord lieutenant's head; so good an aim, that it struck the cushion of the next box, and with such force, that it cut the cushion and rebounded on the stage. If it had taken effect, in all probability it would have put an end to his life. When I state that a bottle was thrown at the king's representative, and that implements of violence were flung at his person, such is the state of the public mind, that it is listened to as if it were a mere bagatelle, a *jeu d'esprit*, a trifle of which the lord lieutenant need not take any notice, and which is below the attention of the government and the law officers.

Why, gentlemen of the jury, are we awake? Can we be insensible to the effect of such occurrences upon the honour and safety of the country? Can we reflect without indignation that such an outrage should be committed in a civilized country against the person of his majesty's representative, because he had the presumption, in opposition to a desperate gang, to execute the parting injunctions of the king, in a manner not calculated to give offence or excite animosity? The sentiments of the audience were roused; some rushed up to the gallery. Graham first flung the heavy part of the rattle, and then the light. It will be produced to you. Forbes, as I have already stated, was a party to the entire system of the party, and was present at the sending the men from Daly's to the gallery with bludgeons. He stationed them in the upper gallery at their post. After the bottle and rattle had been thrown, he was observed in the lattices or pigeon-holes, immediately adjoining the left side of the upper gallery, in which he had previously stationed the party; he was separated from them only by the spikes, dividing those two parts of the house. He was seen actively encouraging the rioters; he held in his hand a whistle with which he sounded the alarm, and gave a signal which was answered through the whole house. He was asked by a magistrate, why he used the whistle, to which he replied, "for fun." He was then arrested, but liberated on promise to give bail. It will be proved that he went from the theatre to a tavern in Essex-street, kept by a person of the name of Flanagan. He and William Graham, one of the distributers of the bills, and who was active in the riot, William Brownlow, the Atkinsons, and others, went in a party to this public house. They communicated together as persons well acquainted with each other, and talked about what had passed at the theatre. Some one said to Brownlow, "Why did not you go to your place in the gallery?" He said he was as well where he was in the pit; and afterwards boasted of the share he had had in the business, saying, that others had not done so much. A conversation ensued as to the occurrences at the theatre. Forbes referred to the part he had taken. This conversation was overheard by two gentlemen, Mr. Farley, an attorney, and a Mr. Troy, who will be produced to you. Forbes spoke as a person conscious that he had committed a crime. He said he had only one life to lose, but that he was ready to sacrifice that for the accomplishment of his one object. He was ready, he said, to go to Botany Bay, but that if he did, he would establish an Orange Lodge there. Nay, he said he would be willing to go to hell, but that one great drawback to his happiness there would be, that he was sure to meet a Papist in it.

This is a specimen only of his sentiments; but, what is more material for our present purpose, he expressed his regret that the bottle had missed its aim, but he trusted and hoped that the next time their plan would be better laid, and the attempt be more effectual. Here, gentlemen, is a person engaged in planning the whole attack; who collected bludgeons and ruffians to execute it, who directs violence against the lord lieutenant, and who, after his excellency's life was endangered, expressed his regret, not that they went beyond their instructions, but that they had not executed them in their full extent. Am I now to justify myself in your opinion, and in that of the public, for the exercise of my discretion in this *ex officio* information by which I have been enabled for the first time to bring these facts before the public? I ask any man who has a principle of candour or honesty in his composition, whether he is not bound to acquit me, and whether I should not have basely betrayed the king whom I serve, and the office with which he has honoured me, if I suffered public justice to be stifled and obstructed? When these transactions were brought under the consideration of the government, the law officers were consulted by the magistrates. We bestowed the most patient attention and laborious investigation on the case; for five or six days we were occupied at this business; every day some new light was thrown upon it, until it at length assumed an aspect so formidable, as to lead us to the apprehension that his excellency's life had been directly aimed at. When we learned that Forbes had avowed his approbation of the act; when after the conspiracy had shown itself in its most desperate effects, he expressed his regret at its failure, and his determination to make another attempt more effectual—we felt, when called upon for our advice upon his application to be discharged, that we could not justify it to our conscience and our sworn duty, or to the respect due to the high personage and illustrious character who had been offered at, if we had suffered him to go at large till we knew the whole of the transaction. There was at that time evidence, not only sufficient to warrant a grand jury for finding a bill for conspiracy to murder, but even for a petty jury to found a verdict for conviction. It was one thing to consider the proper species of committal, and another in what way we should ultimately proceed. When that point came to be finally decided on, and we had reason to believe that the whole of the evidence was before us, our determination was not to proceed on the capital charge. It was infinitely better we should be censured for the tameness of our proceeding, than that we should be arraigned for its rigour. We felt that before we sent up an indictment containing a capital charge, we should be clearly satisfied that the primary object of the conspiracy was to take away the life of the lord lieutenant, and that if any doubt rested on the case, it would be better to be blamed for the timidity and forbearance of the prosecution than exposed to the heavy charge of exerting a rigour beyond the law; we were glad to show in the instance of the most illustrious personage of the realm a strict observance of the law. What satisfied my mind against sending up a bill of indictment on a capital charge was this, that the object of driving the lord lieutenant by violence from the theatre, and from the country, though it involved the imminent hazard of the life of the lord lieutenant, was distinct from the notion of a conspiracy to murder him. When it clearly appeared that the object was to put down the lord lieutenant's government, and force him from the country, although this plot involved in it an outrage on his person, I did not think that in a capital case a jury could be called upon to say that murder was the aim of the conspiracy. Under these circumstances, therefore, we thought it right to send up the indictments for the misdemeanors, which the grand jury have thrown out.

The nature of these informations has already been laid before you.

There are two distinct informations; one is for a riot and the other for a conspiracy to riot. The counts vary; but in each there is alleged, first, a conspiracy to riot, and then a conspiracy to hoot, groan, hiss, and assault the lord lieutenant. In point of law, either or any part of these charges, if proved, will justify a verdict. I have no doubt of being able to prove the whole. I have stated this case without exaggeration against the traversers at the bar. I have no feelings in the discharge of my duty, except the desire faithfully to acquit myself of what I owe to my country and to my sovereign. I may have expressed myself with warmth, I hope not with intemperance. But after I have disabused your minds of the ten thousand falsehoods which have been circulated on this subject, I feel it would be trifling with public justice to say, that this was the act of a few misguided ruffians, growing out of any sudden impulse. It is a proceeding originating with a gang within the limits of this city, associated for the purpose of putting down the king's government, of driving the lord lieutenant from this country, and of showing that he has not the power, against their wishes and their authority, to discharge the duties belonging to his exalted station.

The trial, with its long muster of witnesses and its eloquent array of counsel— an oration for each traverser—went on, and ended in a disagreement of the jury. The traversers were let out upon bail, Plunket threatening to prosecute again; but the proceedings were never revived.

EX OFFICIO INFORMATIONS.
April 15, 1823.

THE umbrage excited among the Orange party by the high-handed manner in which Plunket had proceeded against the bottle-rioters soon vented itself in pamphlet and speech, and Saurin, whose party spirit was seasoned by private spite, zealously fomented the attacks upon him. I will quote Sheil's sketch of this feeling, of which he was a keen spectator.

"Saurin," he says, "protested (and he is in the habit of enforcing his asseverations by appeals to the highest authority, and by the most solemn adjurations) that in his opinion the conduct of Mr. Plunket, in proceeding by *ex officio* informations, was the most flagrant violation of constitutional principle which had ever been attempted. He seemed to think that the genius of Jefferies had by a kind of political metempsychosis been restored in the person of William Conyngham Plunket. He became so clamorous in his invocations to liberty, that he almost verified the parable in the Scriptures. The demon of Whiggism, after a long expulsion, seemed to have effected a re-entry into his spirit, and to have brought a seven-fold power along with it. He was much more rancorously liberal than he had ever been, even at the period of his hottest opposition to the Union. Little did he think, in this sudden but not unaccountable paroxysm of constitutional emotion, that his own authority would be speedily produced as a precedent, and that his great rival would find a shelter under the shadow of so eminent a name. It was not, however, to convivial declamations that his invectives were confined. The press was resorted to, and a pamphlet entitled 'A year of Lord Wellesley's Administration' appeared. It was written with skill, but without power. It was destitute of real eloquence, but exhibited that species of dexterity which a veteran practitioner in Chancery might be expected to display. It was believed that if not actually written by Saurin, he supplied the materials. The poison was compounded by other hands. This book was a good deal read, but owed its circulation rather to the opinions which it inculcated, than to the language in which they were conveyed.

Having succeeded in exciting the public mind to an adequate tone of irritation, Mr. Saurin resolved to push his attack into his enemy's territory, and to invade him in the House of Commons. The selection which he made of one of his instruments for this purpose was a little singular. His oratory illustrates a phrase of the satirist, 'tenero supplantat verba palato.' The spirit of Saurin, however, breathed some of its masculine nature into his soul, and he exhibited a sort of Amazon intrepidity in his encounter with Mr. Plunket. His coadjutor was more appropriately chosen, and a certain noble lictor was felicitously selected for the scourging of the attorney-general.* That the latter was guilty of some indiscretion in revenging the affront which was offered to the viceregal dignity, his firmest advocates do not now dispute. He was probably actuated by an honest desire to pierce into and disclose the penetralia of Orangeism, but this object he might perhaps have attained without committing the rioters for high treason against the representative majesty of the noble marquis. He lent himself not a little to the personal exasperation of that distinguished nobleman. Lord Wellesley regarded the bottle affair not only as a violation of his honour, but as an attempt upon his life."

The attack, as Sheil states, was led by Mr. Brownlow, who, on the 15th of April, moved :—

"That it appears to this house that the conduct of his Majesty's attorney-general for Ireland, with respect to the persons charged with a riot in the Dublin theatre, on the 14th of December last, particularly in bringing them to trial upon informations filed *ex officio* after bills of indictment against them for the same offence had been thrown out by a grand jury, was unwise; that it was contrary to the practice, and nor congenial to the spirit of the British constitution; and that it ought not to be drawn into a precedent hereafter."

MR. PLUNKET said, that in rising on such an occasion as the present, the house would naturally suppose that he felt some degree of embarrassment. He had listened with great attention to the speech of the honourable gentleman. Many of the observations which had fallen from him were entitled to his entire approbation, and, allowing

---

* Mr. Charles Brownlow (the late Lord Lurgan) was the leader of the parliamentary attack upon Mr. Plunket. The "noble lictor" was Colonel Barry, an officer of militia, and representative of the county of Cavan. He succeeded to the barony of Farnham upon the death of his cousin, the fourth baron, in July, 1823.

for some undue warmth which had characterised a portion of his
speech, he was rather disposed to thank than to blame the honourable member for the temper in which he had brought forward this
subject. But, at the same time that the honourable member had
entitled himself to this acknowledgment, he could not but observe
that he had indulged himself, in a very considerable degree of latitude, in the charge which he had felt it his duty to bring against the
individual who now addressed the house. He could not help complaining, that when the honourable member brought forward a specific charge against him for having filed an *ex officio* information,
after a bill of indictment had been ignored by the grand jury, he
should have endeavoured, by all the powers of his eloquence, to involve him (Mr. P.) in all the odium which attached to the system
of *ex officio* informations in general. The argument of the honourable member went the length of arraigning the power of the crown
to file *ex officio* informations in all cases, whether through its law
officer or the Court of the King's Bench. The honourable member had
contended, that a grand jury was the constitutional barrier between
the prosecutions of the crown and the safety of the subject; but, if
it were essential to the safety of the subject that a party should in
no case be put upon his trial without the intervention of a grand
jury, the whole system of informations must fall to the ground. If
the proceeding by information were odious, illegal, and unconstitutional, he (Mr. P.) was not liable to the charge of having imported
it from Ireland; for among all the institutions incorporated into the
law of this country, there were none of more unquestioned antiquity
and admitted legality than the proceeding by information. If such
a proceeding were opposed to the genius of our free constitution, it
was somewhat extraordinary that it should not have been abolished
in the lapse of a thousand years. He would admit, that no length of
antiquity could sanction a practice which could be shown to be
wrong but he must think it somewhat hard; that he should be
selected as the object of censure, and that his conduct should be
compared with that of Sir George Jefferies, of infamous memory—
with that of Empson and Dudley, and all persons who had inflicted
misery on their country, and whose acts had brought down vengeance
on their own heads. It was rather too hard that the accumulated
odium of a thousand years should be reserved for this day, and
thundered on his devoted head. The honourable member had contended, that the functions and privileges of a grand jury were impeached by this proceeding. It was impossible that anything could
be more eloquent, or more calculated to excite an auditory, than the

observations of the honourable gentleman. He had touched a string which could not fail to vibrate. But, to what extent did the honourable gentleman mean to lay down the principle. Did he mean to say, that no criminal proceeding could be instituted without the intervention of a grand jury? He admitted that the functions of a grand jury ought not to be called in question, nor could any public functionary be guilty of a more gross breach of decorum than by vilifying a grand jury for the exercise of that discretion with which the constitution had invested him. But, was there anything in his (Mr. P.'s) conduct which would justify a comparison with that of the odious Jefferies? When the grand jury returned their verdict, he was free to say, that he, in common with the court and auditors, was filled with astonishment, and that he did say on that occasion— "They have a duty to discharge within their province on their oaths, and they have exercised their discretion; I also have a duty to discharge, and, with the blessing of God, I will discharge it fearlessly and honestly!" After hearing all the arguments which had been urged against him, he did not feel that he had been guilty of anything that was inconsistent with the law and constitution of the country. He would put it to the candour of the honourable member whether it was fair to couple any observations upon his conduct, with a reference to the filthy and disgusting Billingsgate which flowed from the lips of Sir G. Jefferies, when he reprimanded the grand jury, and sent them back a second and a third time? But, said the honourable gentleman, though Jefferies sent the grand jury back a second and a third time, he did not venture to file an *ex officio* information. The reason why Jefferies did not proceed to this extremity had not occurred to the honourable gentleman, but it was a very simple one; Jefferies was not then attorney-general, but chief justice of the Court of King's Bench, and had no more right to file an *ex officio* information than the honourable gentleman had.

Another ground of complaint against the honourable gentleman was, that it was utterly impossible to collect the extent of the charge which he had brought against him. The honourable gentleman had introduced a charge unconnected with the present question; namely, that of his (Mr. P's) having advised the committal of the parties for a capital offence, who were afterwards prosecuted only for a misdemeanor. This question had been already disposed of by the house, nor was there, in point of fact, any evidence to show that the parties were committed at his (Mr. P.'s) desire. The honourable member had brought forward a motion for censure, without any evidence to support it, but he would not act so unworthy a part as to shelter himself behind the total want of evidence. The magistrates who committed those individuals were responsible for their own act, and there was no evidence that they had resorted to his (Mr. P.'s) advice. He would frankly avow, however, that the magistrates did resort to his advice. The honourable member said, he had been assured by high legal authority, that no man ought to be committed on a capital charge, unless there was irresistible evidence of his guilt. He begged to say that no such irresistible evidence was necessary to warrant a committal upon a capital charge. In the present case, he had held himself bound to advise the committal upon a capital charge, although he did not think it advisable to follow it up by a capital prosecution. The information upon which he had advised the committal had not been laid before the house. It had been very properly withheld ; not for the purpose of screening himself, but for the purpose of protecting the magistrates. He, however, was perfectly ready to meet the honourable member, and to state the grounds upon which he had given that advice. He was perfectly ready to state again the grounds upon which he had acted; and he felt it due to his own character and honour to show that he had not subjected any man to the deprivation of his liberty, on hasty, light, or insufficient grounds. When the parties had first been taken up, they had been committed upon the charge of misdemeanor. He (Mr. P.) had at that time only heard the circumstances attending the riot; and, although he had thought them daringly outrageous, he had not thought that they amounted to what would constitute a capital charge. Some persons in the theatre had done that which endangered the life of the lord lieutenant; but he had not seen anything to warrant his believing that there had been a conspiracy to take away the life of the lord lieutenant. In the course, however, of the seven days' examination which followed, facts had come out which tended to show that the riot had been the result of premeditation, and that the person who had been the principal agent in the conspiracy, and who had assisted in packing the house for the purpose of making the riot, had connected himself with the attack upon the person of the lord lieutenant. It had been attempted to throw ridicule upon that attack, through the implements with which it had been made. It was easy to make jokes upon a rattle or a bottle ; but neither a rattle nor a bottle would be a very pleasant joke, if flung at the head of any honourable gentleman. If that bottle had struck the lord lieutenant on the head, instead of striking the cushion of the box in which he sat, it would in all probability have taken away his life. And what followed the throwing of these weapons? Why, Mr. Forbes at once expressed his regret that they had missed. One of the offenders declared that they were determined to hazard their lives for the attainment of their object, and hoped, on another opportunity, that they should be more successful. It was said that this man was infuriated with drink, and that he should not be made responsible for words so inconsiderately spoken. But, the same intemperance, the same uncontrolled fury of passion, which allowed him to use these expressions against the lord lieutenant, might prompt him to deeds which would put the life of his excellency in peril; and he (Mr. P.) would not have discharged his duty, if he had not advised that the parties should be held in custody until full deliberation upon the proper mode of prosecution could be had. Accordingly, three persons were arrested; the man who flung the bottle, the man who flung the rattle, and the man who had made use of the expressions before mentioned.

There was one thing to which he would entreat the attention of the house, and particularly that of the country gentlemen; and that was the state of the law and the practice with regard to grand juries. He trusted he should be able to satisfy the house, that it was no novel, violent, or unconstitutional thing to question their decisions. He hoped to be able to show that there was nothing in it so very hostile to freedom, or so adverse to the spirit of the constitution as had been alleged. In doing this, he would, in the first place, point out that trials upon information were really the law. This was the more necessary, not only on account of what had been said by the honourable gentleman, but on account of what had been detailed in newspapers, and taken up and repeated till the ears of the country had rung again. On this account he felt it necessary to go at some length into the proof of the legality. In the first place, there was no point of the law more clear than this, that the ignoring of a bill by a grand jury was no bar to subsequent proceedings by indictment. Nay, the bill might be again and again sent to the grand jury, and again and again ignored, *toties quoties*. It might be questioned by the same grand jury or another, and from this it was evident that the verdict of a grand jury was not a sacred thing. In the next place, he hoped he would be able to show, that the method of proceeding by indictment upon information was as old as the constitution, and, as such, formed part of the constitution itself; that it formed a part of the general administration of justice as much as anything else which belonged to that administration; and not only that, but the reason was distinctly assigned; namely, to guard the crown and the public against the defects of the administration of justice. Before the revolution, this power of filing informations was assigned to two officers—the king's attorney-general and the master of the crown office. The attorney-general exerted it for offences which were peculiarly against the king's person or government. The master of the crown office exerted it for the prosecution of offences of a lower degree, which were not so easily rendered amenable to the ordinary process of law. Each of these officers was at liberty to exert the right of filing informations; their power was co-existent; one of them could do it to the same extent as the other; nor had one of them greater authority than the other. This was the case down to the time of the revolution. The honourable member had referred to this power, as if it were a remnant of the jurisdiction of the star-chamber, so justly odious. Whereas, at the abolition of the star-chamber tribunal, a period remarkable for the constitutional jealousy of parliament, it had been expressly stipulated, that nothing in those proceedings should impeach the right of the crown to proceed in particular offences by filing informations. This of itself proved, that the power, even in the period of the greatest jealousy as to the liberties of the country, was held to be quite compatible with the constitution. The right of the crown had been exercised in the manner he had before described, down to the period of the revolution. The act of the 4th and 5th William and Anne introduced some new regulations. In the debates upon that act, the mode of proceeding by information was brought into question. Some members were of opinion, that it would be a good thing to get rid of it altogether. Repeated conferences were held upon the subject; and especially upon that part of it which related to informations consequent upon parliamentary proceedings. The act at length passed, by which the power before enjoyed by the master of the crown office was brought under very considerable restraints, and that officer was disabled from proceeding by information, except under the permission of the Court of King's Bench, to which he must address his application under affidavit. But the power of the attorney-general was reserved unmolested, and was to exist in just the same extent as before the passing of the act; and therefore the attorney-general must be considered as having the same power and discretion in proceeding by information, as the master of the crown office had before the statute of William. The act gave the attorney-general no power which was not enjoyed by the master of the crown office. It did not enlarge the jurisdiction of the King's Bench in any degree. He prayed the house then to attend to the direct and reasonable inference. If the attorney-general had a power co-extensive with that of the master of the crown office before the passing of the statute, so he must be held, as far as the right of filing informations went, to hold a power coextensive with that of the Court of King's Bench. At any rate, this could not be disputed with him in regard to that class of informations which went to prosecute offences against the state. If this were not admitted, they would be driven to the monstrous conclusion, that before the statute of William, the master of the crown office had greater power and authority than the attorney-general, a proposition much too wide for discussion; and therefore he would not involve the house in it. He thought he might safely assume that the attorney-general enjoyed this power in a concurrent degree with the Court of King's Bench, and that he was at liberty to proceed by information or indictment, according to his discretion. He appealed to the professional members, if there was a single case in the books which affected to establish a difference, as to the rule of law, between proceedings by indictment and by information. It was the clear and established principle of law, that no subject could be called on to plead to, or be tried for, the same offence twice. But there was no protection from further proceedings until after the trial. Now, the presentment before a grand jury was no trial; it was only a proceeding towards putting the defendant on his trial; and therefore he must show, not the decision of a grand jury, but the acquittal by a petty jury. He defied any lawyer to show that the application of the principle had ever admitted any distinction between proceedings by indictment and by information. Ignoring the bill was no bar to a new prosecution either way; nor anything short of an acquittal by a tribunal competent to try the information.

To establish these points, he had had recourse to that place where alone it was possible to come at the precedents which guided him; and he would now proceed to state what were the results of that investigation. The case had all along been treated as if it were something quite new to have recourse to an information after the ignoring of an indictment, and as if he had acted in a manner highly indecorous in making any remark on, or attempting any opposition to, the finding of the grand jury. The house would see how this assumption accorded with the fact. The crown office had been searched, and he was now to inform the house what was the result. The first case was, the "King against Hope" (Trinity Term, 8 and 9 George 2nd). The motion was for an information on a charge of trespass and assault. It was insisted in the defence, among other things, that the prosecutor had already proceeded by indictment, which was ignored by the grand jury. This was the very case on which they were now at issue. Yet there was no condemnation on those who questioned the exercise of these functions by the grand jury—there was no complaint of throwing a slur or attempting to discredit them. It had been asked, was it not most unjust to impeach the conduct of those who, being sworn to secrecy, could not be allowed to explain. This, if true, was equally applicable to the Court of King's Bench. But the fact was, that neither the court nor the grand jury were called on for a defence. The question was not between the court and the jury, but between the criminal and the public—whether offenders should be allowed to escape through a failure in the exercise of the functions of grand juries or not. The defendant in the case before-named pleaded that an indictment which had been presented was ignored. The answer given by the court was, that the ignoring of the bill was the very reason why the information should be granted; and that it was one of the great privileges of the subject to be secured, by this mode of proceeding, from the loss of his just remedy on cases where, from little party heats and local irritations, that was likely to happen; and this was assented to *per totam curiam*. It appeared from the report that the grand jury attempted to send the witnesses away; that they were unwilling to ask them any questions, and appeared to wish to turn the whole matter into ridicule. Here was not only the case of passing by the decision of the grand jury, but the particular grounds of conduct in the grand jury were also alleged. Here were reasons given which went beyond the statement just now made by the honourable member. And who said this? He could assure the house he was not using the words of Judge Jefferies, nor of Empson or Dudley; nor of any other of the odious authorities with whom he had been compared. This was the decision of Lord Hardwicke, in which it was declared that the attainment of justice was not to be frustrated through little party heats and local irritations. The next case to which he would allude was that of the King against Thorpe. This was a prosecution for a nuisance. In this case it was alleged that an *ignoramus* had been returned by the grand jury. This was not a case in which there were political ferments, and in which the jury had got into little party heats; yet Mr. Bearcroft said there was reason for filing the information, and Lord Mansfield made the rule absolute, upon the ground that some of the grand jury had been influenced in favour of Thorpe. The next case was that of the present king against the inhabitants of Berks, in the matter of the repairing of a bridge. From the affidavits, it appeared that this case had been sent to the grand jury, and had been ignored.

A second presentment was made, when Lord Folkestone was in the chair. This was again ignored; and it was presented a third time, when Mr. Dundas was in the chair; and it was a third time ignored, upon which an information was filed. He hoped he had now adduced cases enough to prevent the notion from becoming universal, that the inoculation of this obnoxious right had not been communicated by him; that the taint to the constitution could not be of his giving, but that it was as old at least as the time of Lord Hardwicke. Now, if in this country it was necessary to have a check over the local heats and the misconduct of grand juries, he would appeal to the house whether it would be safe that a similar check should be withdrawn in Ireland? He had looked over files of the records of the courts in that country, and he had found no fewer than thirteen cases since the year 1795, and these had had the sanction of Lord Clanwilliam, Lord Kilwarden, and Chief Baron Downes. The first to which he would allude was in February, 1795, and it was for perjury. Some of the other cases were trivial, but if in the strong ones there was misconduct, that was sufficient to establish the necessity of the right. In another case, the grand jury of Westmeath had thrown out the bill; and the affidavit stated that this had been done by the address of one of the grand jury. He would pass over the other cases, except two, which were valuable; inasmuch as the affidavits upon which the informations were filed contained no charge of misconduct. These cases were, the King against Paterson, and the King against Crawford, and they were both for sending letters with a view to provoke challenges, and in neither of them was any accusation made against the grand jury, further than that they had ignored the bills by some influence unknown to the deponent. He should trouble the house with one more case, the more important as it referred to the very grand jury who had ignored the bills preferred by him. What would the house think when he informed them that at that very hour a conditional order of the Court of King's Bench of Ireland existed, to set aside the finding of that very grand jury, on the ground of misconduct at the very same sessions? He had the copies of the affidavits on which that conditional rule was granted; but as the case was still pending, he felt some difficulty as to the manner of expressing himself from a reluctance to mention names. The affidavits allege the misconduct of the grand jury as the ground for setting aside their finding. The bill in which they found *ignoramus* charged A. and B. with a conspiracy to defraud a third party. A. got B. to make oath that he had received a sum of money for the purpose of defeating the claim of C. Two witnesses were examined. The grounds of misconduct, as alleged in the affidavits, were, first, the refusal to receive a letter of one of the accused, because they would have nothing to do with a written document; and next, that they would not admit conspiracy, because the witnesses would not swear that the parties committed perjury. The interrogatories were curious. "Did poor M'Mahon," said the jury (that was not the real name), "to your knowledge commit perjury." Witness—" No, the charge is for conspiracy." The witness was then shown the door, and the bill was ignored.

He had now concluded his reference to cases, and should next apply himself to the argument that was drawn from the want of precedent. He had been asked, if he was justified in the course he had taken; where were his precedents? Where, he would ask, in all the cases he had alluded to, could they have looked for a record? The truth was, that where, after a bill being ignored, an attorney-general subsequently filed an *ex officio* information, it was impossible that, either on the information, the evidence, or the defence, the finding could be found; as it was wholly immaterial to all. When, therefore, he was asked for precedents, his answer was, that from the nature of the question, it was impossible to produce them. And yet the honourable mover had been pleased to taunt him with having pursued a course for which he could produce no precedent in the history of the country. Every man acquainted with the subject was aware, that it was rarely that an attorney-general felt it necessary to seek the intervention of a grand jury. He had, however, in the present instance, deviated from the custom, and made a reference to that "constitutional barrier;" but, after the lesson that had been read to him, he was free to confess that he did not feel much disposed to repeat the application. No man would deny that the treatment the king's representative received at the theatre at Dublin, was of that marked character, as to have justified his majesty's attorney-general in having recourse to the habitual practice of both countries, and filing an *ex officio* information. What, then, was his crime? Not that he had filed such an information, but that he had gone to a grand jury. It was for this crime that he had been assailed with all the lightning of the honourable mover's eloquence; it was for this that all the terrors of the violated constitution had been arrayed against him. But it was said, "it was a mockery to go to a grand jury, unless you were determined to abide by their finding." Such an observation was inconsistent with the first principles of justice. He could, were it necessary, refer to cases where it was laid down by judges on the bench, that, with the view of saving expense to parties in the country, the reference to a grand jury in the first instance was desirable. But he could easily suppose a case where an attorney-general would feel a desire to have his own judgment backed by the opinion of a jury of sound and honest men. Was it therefore to be concluded, that if that functionary had reasons to know that, in place of that sound and honest opinion, the case submitted to that jury had been decided under sinister and improper feelings, he was therefore to allow the principles of justice to be defeated—that he was bound by a step in the pursuit of justice, to allow the ends of justice to be subverted? He would suppose the case of a grand jury, who, when a number of witnesses were introduced for examination, placed their hands on their ears, and threw their legs across, in evident demonstration of the determination to pay no attention—would any man, under such circumstances, assert that the principles of justice were satisfied? If, in addition to this, it could be shown, that the finding of such a grand jury was wholly disproportionate to the evidence produced before it, would any sound mind venture to pronounce that such a jury had arrived at a legitimate decision? Admit the opposite inference, and what must be the consequence? It would be this—that the very constitutional barrier, emphatically dwelt upon by the honourable mover, and with the violation of which he (Mr. P.) was accused, would become inoperative. If while it was open to the subject, redress was refused to the crown, no future attorney-general would venture to go before a grand jury; and thus by the very argument of the advocate of that great constitutional security, all its valuable results would be lost to the subject. It was, perhaps, unnecessary to state, that after the finding of a grand jury, the crown could obtain no redress from the Court of King's Bench. The language of the court was, that " We will not do it, because you, the king's attorney, can do it yourself." If, therefore, it was illegal, after a grand jury had ignored a bill, for an attorney-general to file his information, to the king would be denied a right of redress, to which the meanest subject was entitled. The right honourable gentleman then proceeded to read from Burrow's Reports, cases in which the Court of King's Bench had refused to interfere with the finding of a grand jury where the crown was a party, on the very ground that its interference was unnecessary, as the king's attorney possessed the power. With respect to the case of Moore, he should first say, that it was by accident, and from the peculiarity of the circumstances which arose out of it, that it was possible to cite it as a precedent. The grand jury had, in that instance, found the bill where they intended to find *ignoramus*. They subsequently made affidavits, stating it to be a clerical error, and with the hope of being allowed to rectify it. The court refused the application. The attorney-general, unwilling to put the party on his trial after such an admission from the jury, quashed the indictment, by issuing a *noli prosequi*. He then filed his information *ex officio*. The circumstances excited considerable public attention; the notice of parliament had been attracted to it. After an examination of the question, parliament petitioned for the removal of the judge (the house would mark that fact), while no complaint whatever was even suggested against the attorney-general, for filing his information. Here, then, he might rest his defence, did he not know that far more important considerations demanded of him to show, that in the case of the Dublin grand jury, had he acquiesced in their finding, the ends of public justice would have been defeated. He would first apply himself to the finding. It appeared from the papers, only that night presented to the house, that thirteen witnesses had been examined before that grand jury, exclusively of other witnesses produced on the trial of the traversers. He had no hesitation in saying, that any impartial person, looking at the evidence, would at once declare that there was no part of that bill of indictment, whether it referred to the conspiracy, to the riot, or to the assault, that was not completely and demonstratively proved. There was no sound mind that would not admit that the men who could have brought themselves to such a conclusion as the Dublin grand jury had, could not have arrived at it by legitimate means. It had been distinctly proved, that a plan had been formed to commit a riot; that in furtherance of that plan, a number of persons assembled at the theatre; that a missile had been thrown by Graham; that Forbes had gone the day before to the theatre to buy tickets for the purpose of packing an audience—that Forbes was taken with the whistle in his hand with which he incited the rioters; that at a subsequent meeting at a tavern, he had expressed his concern at the failure of their purpose, and his hopes of success on a future occasion. Yet, with such evidence, the grand jury ignored the bill. He would candidly put the house in possession of what he felt to be the impressions under which that jury acted. It was his conviction—a conviction which he felt with all the force of a moral certainty—that they, the grand jury, conceived the plan of these rioters to be a very right and proper plan. They conceived that, when the lord lieutenant, in compliance with the expressed desires of his sovereign, had exerted himself to conciliate the various classes of the Irish people, and to put an end to the heart-burnings which had so long embittered that community, it was extremely proper and lawful, that certain persons, whom, for something or for nothing, he (Mr. P.) had designated as a "gang," should seize the first opportunity that presented itself, for marking their powerful disapprobation of such an acquiescence in the express commands of his majesty. To that extent they felt it highly proper the opposition should proceed; though they were not prepared to go the length of thinking that it was right to fling bottles and rattles at his majesty's representative. That, in his conscience, he believed to be the decided conviction of the grand jury—a conviction, he also believed, which the greater portion of the Dublin corporation did not consider erroneous. Such, indeed, was the statement of one of the counsel, who, on the subsequent trial, defended the traversers. It was, however, not the opinion of the chief justice who tried them; from whose charge he would read a short extract :

"Before I proceed to sum up the evidence, it will be necessary for me to examine a doctrine asserted by the traverser's counsel, in opposition to what I have announced as the opinion of the court up n the law of the case. It has been insisted that in a public theatre, any man has a right to disturb and terrify the audience by expressing his censure or approbation of public and political characters; that such right has been constantly exercised and enjoyed in the theatres of both countries; and that such a disturbance of the peace, under such circumstances, loses its illegal character, and becomes excusable. There is no such right. It is a position not founded in point of law. If allowed to go abroad uncontradicted, it would be productive of the most dangerous consequences. The rights of an audience at a theatre are perfectly well defined. They may cry down a play or other performance which they dislike, or they may hiss or hoot the actors who depend on their approbation, or their caprice. Even that privilege, however, is confined within its limits. They must not break the peace, or act in such a manner as has a tendency to excite terror or disturbance. Their censure or approbation, although it may be noisy, must not be riotous. That censure or approbation must be the expression of the feelings of the moment. For, if it be premediated by a number of persons confederated beforehand to crydown even a performance or an actor, it becomes criminal. Such are the limits of the privileges of an audience, even as to actors and authors. But if their censorial power were to be extended to public or political characters, it would turn the theatre into a den of factious rioters, instead of a place of cultivated amusement, or, as some conceive, of moral improvement. What public man in any department would himself go, or would take his family to a theatre, if he were to incur the risk of being hissed or insulted by a rabble, instigated by ruffians, exasperated perhaps against him by the discharge of some public duty? We are, therefore, anxious to disabuse you as to this topic, which has perhaps not unjustifiably been used by the counsel for the traversers, but which we are bound to discountenance; and to tell you, that no length of time during which licentiousness may have remained unpunished can be sufficient to sanction so mischievous a pretension, or protect it from the reprehension of a court of justice."

Such was the view of the law as taken by the chief justice of the King's Bench. Such was not the view of the law taken by the Dublin grand jury. They, in their wisdom, thought the public conduct of the king's representative a fit and proper subject of animadversion and outrage at a public theatre. When they had ignored the bills, they had determined to throw their protection around those who had seized the first occasion of showing that the experiment of governing the people of Ireland under the protection of equal laws, was a dangerous experiment to him who had the virtue and the courage to try it; they had determined to give a decisive proof that in Ireland there was a power hostile to its population, and superior to the throne itself. It was in opposition to such feelings and such a determination that he appealed to the law, as the functionary of the crown. Were he even on the ground of form to be made the object of the censure of that house, the principles on which he had acted would nevertheless be to him the source of unceasing consolation. It had been said, that he had no right to justify himself for the course he had pursued by any reference to what the evidence on the subsequent trial disclosed. To that he must reply, that if any man found the conclusion to which he had arrived borne out by results, he was entitled to refer to those results, in order to prove the propriety of the course he had adopted. What, then, was made manifest on that trial? It was proved, that a plan had been concerted at a meeting of an Orange lodge. It was with reluctance he introduced Orangeism into the discussion. He had lived many years in the city of Dublin, and in habits of intercourse with very respectable persons, supposed to be attached to such associations, and never in his life had he had any altercation with them. I have, however, (said Mr. Plunket) ever deprecated their existence. I hold them to be illegal, and subject to the penalties of the statute law. I consider an association, bound by a secret oath, to be extremely dangerous on the principles of the common law; inasmuch as they subtract the subject from the state, and interpose between him and his allegiance

T

to the king. As an exclusively religious association, their unequivocal tendency is, to defeat the power to govern by equal laws, and to keep the various classes of the population in a state of positive war. The natural consequence of their existence has been, and must be, to produce exclusive Catholic associations, equally hostile to good government, each arrayed against the other, and both against the law. As a public officer of the constitution, I have felt it to be my duty to enforce the law against Catholic secret associations. From that duty, when circumstances called for its exercise, I have never shrunk. But how should I reflect upon my own actions, if I were capable of visiting with the terrors of the law the one class of the community, while I shrunk from its application to the other? It is the system of Orange associations that places the Protestants of Ireland in imminent danger. The support of the Protestant is in the law.

It was only when he stepped beyond the precincts of law, and challenged the population of Ireland to hostility, that he endangered his safety and risked the security of the establishment. It is because I wish well to that establishment that I deprecate the existence of Orange societies. But, to suppose that I could descend from my rank and character in society to prostitute both, through rancour against any party, is an imputation of which I feel myself to be undeserving. If my life and character is not a shield against such a suspicion, no defence that I can offer would be entitled to the attention of this house.

To return to the evidence: it was proved that five persons, one of them enjoying a lucrative office in the post-office, had arranged the outrage against the lord lieutenant. They had determined to give a proof of the unpopularity of his administration, on the first opportunity. The visit of his excellency to the theatre furnished that opportunity. When apprised of that intention, it was determined by the rioters to drive him from the theatre, and by such a manifestation of opinion to compel him to desist from the course of rule that he had followed. It was to be remarked, that whatever private opinions the lord lieutenant might entertain on certain questions, he had abstained from mixing them up with his public acts. It did so happen, that from the control of events, without any reference to inclination or otherwise, he had not conferred a single office on a Roman Catholic from the commencement of his government. His offence was, that he had endeavoured to give effect to the mandate of the king. And yet, these were loyal, very loyal men, who assaulted the king's representative! On the trial it was proved by witnesses, and enforced by counsel, that there was not a more loyal subject to the king than Mr. Forbes, who packed the audience. Loyal no doubt he was, most loyal—so long as the king governed his subjects in the way that Mr. Forbes approved. In that acceptation of the word, there were not more attached members of the community than the Orange lodges of Ireland. And truly loyal, and most estimable in every consideration, they would prove themselves, would they but throw aside the follies of their secret associations. But it was the inevitable consequence of associations which confounded the respectable part of society with the low and the turbulent, that the first, by the unnatural connexion, lost their superiority and influence, while the other were emboldened in their violence. To resume his narrative: the theatre was packed; persons were sent to occupy different parts of it, whose admission was purchased, and who were inflamed with ardent spirits, according to the arrangement of Forbes, who went himself into the lattices, or upper-boxes, to keep up a communication with the rioters, who were to act under his direction. When such were the facts which had been established by evidence, was he not right in his opinion that the grand jury had acted upon a false principle in coming to the conclusion which they had done? The honourable member had called on him, on the supposition of a variety of facts which had nothing to do with the motion. He had not, however, made out his case. While he (Mr. P.) had not only grounds for impeaching the decision of the grand jury, but also the manner in which it had been impannelled. He had reason to know that the sheriff was related to two of the traversers, in the close affinity of first cousin. This, had he known it at the time, would have been ground of challenge to the array. He had also in evidence upon oath, that the sheriff declared that the traversers need not be afraid of the result of the trial, as he had a list of Orangemen for the jury in his pocket. Another circumstance would show the spirit in which the grand jury was empannelled. There was a person named Poole, who was desirous of serving on the grand jury. The sheriff promised him previously to the riot, that he should be on the jury; but, after the riot, he found that his name was not on the list, and when the sheriff was applied to on the subject, he said, "Do you suppose I would allow a man to be on the grand jury, who said he would abide by the king's letter?" He (Mr. P.) did not mean by such statement to inculpate the members of which the grand jury was composed. It was, indeed, a gross impropriety in the sheriff, if he selected jurors under manifest prejudice; but as to the jurors themselves, they were not perhaps aware of the prejudice, or if they were they would forego it. There was another objection to the mode of empannelling the jury. When he found that a whole day had passed without finding the bills, he procured the panels of the five preceding years. He found on inspection that there were from about 70 to 100 on each panel, and that on calling the panel it was with difficulty the requisite number of the jury was made up after calling the whole list. In the present instance the number was only about 50, of which there were about 26 names that he did not find on any other panel, and the whole number attended, with the exception of two or three; they answered in regular order, and before the 26th name was called the jury was completed. He would put it to the candour of the house if he would have been justified in going back with the case to such a grand jury. He would ask the honourable member himself this question, as a man of honour, and he was sure he would answer it fairly. He would put it to the candour and honour of the house, whether he had acted in a manner which the circumstances of the case did not justify. He had the affidavit of a person who assisted in the office of sheriff, to the effect, that when the jury was about to be struck, according to the usual course of the office, the sheriff ordered the panel to be brought to him, and said he would prepare it himself—he who was a relation of two of the traversers; and the deponent swore that he believed this course was taken to enable the sheriff to deal with the panel as he pleased, though he was sworn to do impartial justice between the parties! The right honourable gentleman then adverted to the evidence of a person named Farley before the grand jury. He was a person who had overheard, at the tavern in Essex-street, a conversation respecting the riot in which Forbes was principally concerned. That person deposed that he saw a man in the tavern who stated certain things—that man was Forbes; though the deponent did not know his name at the time. He was asked by the jury if he knew the man's name; he said, "No, but that he saw the man in the traverser's box that morning, and he now knew his name to be Forbes." He was told by the jurors that it was no matter what he knew now; he should confine himself to what he knew at the time. This person went back two or three times to give his evidence, and it was always received as evidence against a person unknown. This evidence had been confirmed by that of a man named Troy; and it would be seen by his examination, that the jury were determined the question should be considered as exclusively Irish. The jury wished to throw some imputation on Farley, who was a Protestant, as being a Roman Catholic, and this they attempted to do through the evidence of Troy. They wished to learn from the oath of Troy, who was a Catholic, whether Farley was a Catholic also, that he might be disregarded on his oath; when Troy was so interrogated, he said he believed not. A juror said, tell us what you know, not what you believe. Troy answered, "I believe you to be a Protestant, and in the same way I believed Farley to be one;" but on that ground the jury would not believe that Farley was not a Catholic. He next alluded to the evidence of a person named Ryan, who was asked whether he was counselled or instructed to appear there? He declared he was not; he was asked what motives he had in coming forward to give his evidence? He was also asked, whether he could be mistaken as to the person of the man who threw the rattle? He said it was impossible. He was asked what description of person he was? He said he was a sallow-looking young man, whom he should know again, though he never saw him before. He was asked were there not many men alike. He was asked, did he not say that he might be mistaken in the person? He said no. The juror replied, you did, for I have it down in my notes. He believed he had succeeded in showing the legality of the power which he had exercised; if, however, it was allowed that the power was legal, but the exercise of it unconstitutional, he professed he could not understand the distinction. If it was unconstitutional to exercise a prerogative, it ought to be taken away; but it might be said, the power was both legal and constitutional, yet it had not been exercised with a sound discretion, and for such exercise the party was answerable. The cases were very different. If the power was illegal, the fact of having exercised it would have been a *prima facie* case against him, and the very statement would have put him on his defence. But, if the power was legal, and to be exercised on a sound discretion, then it lay upon his accuser to show that he had acted culpably in its application. And what evidence was there of this? There was no evidence but what came from his own lips. His own explanation furnished the evidence; and on that evidence he was sure, that, in the opinion of the house, he should stand acquitted. The mode pursued was not a fair way of dealing with a public functionary. He should not be condemned for the exercise of a discretionary power, unless it was shown that he made use of it as an instrument of oppression and injustice. But, where was there any evidence to show that he had turned the prerogative of the crown to party quarrels, or private resentment? He would allow that others might have acted more wisely in the same situation than himself; but he denied that any could have acted more honestly. If he had acted on a mistaken motive, let it be shown; but no man could prove that he had acted unconstitutionally. He disdained the imputation of an improper motive. He had spent a long life connected with politics, and every man who knew him was aware that he never had been actuated by the feelings and sentiments of party. Much of the obloquy which he had lately endured, and endured, too, from those who were never before united on any one point, was occasioned, he believed, because he would not lend himself to party views. He, however, had never sought to benefit himself by treading in such crooked and devious paths. He was opposed to zealots of every party. He was inimical to the little sects and the little policy which did so much mischief in his native country, and he should feel happy if they were done away. The present question was one of great importance. It involved the proposition, whether in future the laws were to be administered in Ireland on the principle of impartial justice—whether the king was to be permitted to exercise, for the benefit of the people of that country, the gracious disposition which he had shown towards them; or whether they would tolerate a party which was alike calculated to put down the king and the law? He had now put the house in possession of his case; and he would leave it to their honour and justice. As it nearly concerned him personally, his situation was one of great delicacy; he should withdraw during the discussion, and leave the house to the free and unconstrained exercise of its judgment. The right honourable gentleman then withdrew, amidst loud cheering.

After Plunket had withdrawn, Mr. W. Courtenay with a brief and manly defence of his conduct, moved that the other orders of the day be read. In the course of the debate, the English attorney-general declared his opinion curtly, that the proceeding had been perfectly legal and proper. Finally, the original motion was withdrawn, on the undertaking of Sir Francis Burdett to move an inquiry into the conduct of the sheriff of Dublin.

THE ROMAN CATHOLIC QUESTION.

April 17, 1823.

THE "annual farce," so designated in this debate by Sir. F. Burdett, of presenting the Catholic petition happened this year under angry auspices. Plunket at this time was in the complete confidence of the Irish Catholics. But the Radicals sympathised with the Tories in reprehension of his conduct as attorney-general, and the ministry was divided by diametrically opposite views of the Catholic question. A few days before the motion came on, Canning (then secretary for foreign affairs) had used language which created the impression that it was hopeless to think of inducing any English government to carry Catholic emancipation. It certainly looked like an absurdity to see a member of the government, in which Lord Liverpool was premier, Lord Eldon chancellor, and Peel home secretary, appearing as the Catholic parliamentary champion; and Plunket had upon this ground left himself peculiarly open to attack, by denouncing, in his speech of 1813, the dishonesty of any ministerial compromise on a topic so momentous.

At the very beginning of the debate, Sir Francis Burdett declared that he would give no countenance to the present motion. "They had heard not longer than two nights ago from the former eloquent advocate of the Catholic claims, (Canning) that there was not the least chance the question would be carried in favour of the Catholics; if this was the case, why consent to practise a deception upon the house and the country. He had stated that it was impossible a government or rather an administration should ever be formed in which this question should be carried; and that if it was possible to form such an administration, he, to accomplish it, would willingly leave office, but in fact his acceptance of office had really been the cause of all this compromise of the public safety." As for Plunket, "In bringing forward their claims that night he thought the right honourable gentleman was not doing a service to the Catholics either of England or of Ireland." Finally, in declaring that he would withdraw from the house when the motion was introduced, he justified the course he meant to take by reading the passage from Plunket's speech of 1813, which was directed in fact against the very same cabinet, into which after ten years he had entered by virtue of its last coalition, in which he describes "one half of the king's ministers encouraging the Catholics to seek without enabling them to obtain; the other half not decided; some holding out an ambiguous hope, others announcing a never-ending despair;" and in which he denounced the consequences of such a course as "disastrous, not merely in the tumult and discord which they are calculated to excite, but in their effect upon the character of the government and the times." There was loud and long continued cheering at this apposite quotation.

The petition was ordered to lie on the table. The Speaker then called upon Mr. Plunket, upon which Sir F. Burdett, Mr. Hobhouse, Lord Sefton, Mr. Bennet, Sir R. Wilson, and several other members on the opposition benches left the house. After a short interval,

MR. PLUNKET rose. He commenced by observing, that it was his intention to have that day presented a petition from the Roman Catholics of Ireland, which had been agreed to by a considerable number of gentlemen—considerable, not merely with reference to their numbers, but also with reference to the rank and station which they held in society. Owing, however, to some mistake in furnishing the names of the petitioners, it was impossible for him, that night, to lay the document before the house. This circumstance did not, however, conclude him from introducing the Catholic question, because he was authorized by the Catholics of Ireland to appear in that house as their advocate. Never in his life did he address the house under circumstances of such extreme difficulty as those under which he was placed at the present moment. He found he had to sustain the cause of the Catholics, not only against those who had been always opposed to them, but also against a considerable portion of those who had been ever looked upon as their friends. The cause had sustained a severe loss by the secession of a large portion of honourable members who were in the habit of giving it their support, and who had very ostentatiously withdrawn themselves, for the purpose of marking their sense of the impropriety of the manner in which it was brought forward. But, if the cause had sustained a loss from the secession of those honourable members who had retired, it had suffered a still heavier loss from the speech of the right honourable gentleman (Mr. Tierney) who remained within the house, with the intention of giving his vote in its favour. The right honourable gentleman had always been the friend of the Roman Catholic claims; he had always acted so; and he did not mean to impeach his sincerity. But he would say, that the greatest enemy which that cause ever had never gave it so deep a wound as had that night been inflicted upon it by its ancient friend. It was in vain that the right honourable gentleman and others endeavoured to throw on him the responsibility of the failure of the question. The responsibility of that failure lay upon those who had foretold in such ominous tones its defeat, and who treated the subject as a mockery, a farce, a delusion, while they animadverted on the personal demerits of the individual who was to bring it forward. Under these circumstances, he felt that he should not be considered, in the just and honest minds of the Roman Catholics either of England or of Ireland, as acting an insincere part when he introduced this question; and he was not at all afraid of encountering, and throwing aside, those imputations which honourable gentlemen had been pleased to level at him. He was really at a loss to furnish himself with any plausible reason why the right honourable gentleman should think that this question was not now entitled to support from every member of that house, because it was in the hands of a divided administration. The right honourable gentleman had, in his recollection, from the year 1807, supported the Catholic cause, though the administration was divided. The cause, during that period, had made regular and daily advances, though only a portion of the cabinet was in favour of it. He did not find, when the question was brought forward by any individual on the right honourable gentleman's side of the house, that he had ever damped the cause or thrown out such disheartening presages of failure as he had indulged in on the present occasion. He would ask the right honourable gentleman how he could reconcile it to his feelings as a patriot—as a man who viewed this question, not as it referred to party, but as it respected the people—to embarrass the proceedings of those who were friendly to it, merely because the individual who brought forward the motion sat on the ministerial, instead of the opposition side of the house? He had always considered the Catholic cause as being too high for party. He ever considered it as separate from all petty interests; and he was proud to say that his coming over from one side of the house to the other, had not injured him in the opinion of the Catholics of Ireland as the advocate of their cause; and he could state that it had not in the least effaced the impressions of unalterable zeal with which he had ever come forward to support their claims. The right honourable gentleman appeared to think that there was something extraordinary in the circumstance of his having moved from one side of the house to the other. He was not aware that there was anything in this alteration which ought to surprise the right honourable gentleman; for, if his recollection did not fail him, the right honourable gentleman himself had performed the figure of moving from one side of the house to the other and back again, as gracefully and adroitly as it could be executed by any honourable member. He did not, however, know but his votes might afterwards have been very correct. Doubtless, he could give a very satisfactory reason for them. But, if he were asked, why he was not now sitting on the same side of the house with the right honourable gentleman, he thought he could make out a case that would be equally satisfactory. Words which he had used ten years ago, had been quoted in the course of the debate, and had been introduced with much sarcastic observation. He had on that occasion expressed strongly the feelings which he strongly felt, and he did not think his present conduct was inconsistent with those expressions. He did then certainly point out in strong terms the dangerous consequences of a divided cabinet on this question; for he believed a large portion of the cabinet of that time were utterly and entirely insincere. He thought so from the manner in which that administration had come into office, and other circumstances; and he did not hesitate to express what he felt. He might, however, remind the right honourable gentleman, that he had the honour of holding office under an administration of which the right honourable gentleman was a distinguished member. That was a divided cabinet. They were content to bring forward a very contracted measure on this subject, and even that they would have abandoned at the time, if the feelings of his majesty could have been propitiated, and the necessity for their going out of office avoided. He did not censure them for that conduct; indeed, he thought they had acted wisely on that occasion. In making the change which the right honourable gentleman had alluded to, he had not been influenced by any mean or mercenary motives. He came to that side of the house on which he now sat, feeling that he was perfectly justified towards the Catholics in doing so; knowing that those members of the cabinet who advocated the Catholic claims were decidedly and conscientiously sincere in their opinions; and seeing that the Catholic cause was making rapid strides under that portion of the administration, so divided, who were favourable to it. The right honourable gentleman did him too much honour, if he supposed that his (Mr. P.'s) conduct was of such extreme importance to the views and objects of the Catholics of Ireland; but he would say that, humble as he was, if he thought his coming over to the ministerial side of the house was likely to injure the Catholic cause in the slightest degree, the right honourable gentleman would never have seen him where he then was. He had made sacrifices in that cause. He had not rested on theatrical words or rhetorical flourishes; but he had willingly consented to sacrifices, which gentlemen ought to have remembered. Yes! he had made sacrifices which rendered him invulnerable to the attacks that had been that night directed against him.

He feared he had too long trespassed on the house, in referring to a matter which was personal to himself. He would here drop it, and proceed with the important motion itself. He owed it to the house, perhaps, to offer some explanation, why he had not brought forward this question during the last session, and also why he refrained from postponing it now. With respect to the motives of his own conduct, he was always ready to sacrifice his own views and his personal feelings to the paramount interest of the great question itself; and he could not help feeling that on the present occasion, the cause which he had so much at heart was perhaps placed at some risk by the secession as well as by the forebodings of some of the honourable gentlemen opposite. Notwithstanding this untoward circumstance, he owed it to the country to redeem the pledge he had given, and he felt he should do essential injury to the cause itself were he, because some ten or twelve gentlemen chose to pronounce a funeral elegy upon it, and then withdraw, to abandon that ground, the maintenance of which honour and duty had imposed upon him. His reasons for postponing the question last year were simply these. The friends of the question, whose views he was bound to consult, were, from the then state of Ireland, divided in opinion as to the propriety of agitating the subject at that moment, and the Catholics of Ireland were disposed to leave the decision in the hands of their friends. Thus placed, he yielded to the wishes of some, and postponed the renewal of the discussion. And here he must beg leave to deprecate the idea, that he was bound to make this an annual question. He had never looked upon it in that light, nor had his great predecessor, Mr. Grattan. He had never considered it as strictly an annual topic of discussion; but rather thought that great advantages were derived from giving the people of England time for periodical reflection upon the subject, an opportunity of which, to their honour, they had amply availed themselves. His own opinions had been early formed upon it—long before he had a prospect of taking a part in public life; and the opinions which he had at first instinctively formed had been confirmed by his education and professional studies, and fixed and strengthened by a thirty-five years' residence in Ireland. Indeed, he thought the question rested upon principles so demonstratively clear, so congenial with the principles of the constitution, and so cogent upon grounds of public necessity, that he was astonished to find it still in any quarter pertinaciously opposed. He by no means meant to say that the refusal of emancipation would be followed by any thing like insurrection or rebellion in Ireland. The Roman Catholics were too sensible of the value of the privileges they had already received, to put them in risk by any such intemperate and ill-advised proceeding. They were grateful for what had been bestowed upon them; they were aware of the progress of public opinion in their favour; they were satisfied that, sooner or later, the question must be carried. No man could say that the question could remain where it was. To retrograde was impossible; the march must be progressive. Let no man say that the subject only affected one class of the community. It was impossible such an exclusion could fail to be felt as a degradation, by the humblest as well as the highest individual of the class affected by it. The history of Ireland showed that the consequence of perpetuating these disabilities must always be felt in the perpetual watching and feverish vigilance attendant upon a state of discontent, which kept that country out of its natural place in society, affected the resources of the British empire both in peace and in war, and diminished her consequence in the scale of Europe.

The right honourable and learned gentleman then took a rapid review of the parliamentary history of the Catholic question, and adverted to the sanction by the House of Commons of the principle of concession in the year 1821, and in the bill of last year. The numbers and property of the Catholics had, he said, been exaggerated in their reference to the result of the measure; and he was convinced that, were the bill passed, the youngest man now alive would not in his time see **twenty** Catholics returned to parliament. However, although the danger from their admission to the House of Commons was, in his opinion, visionary, yet he was ready to declare that were the bill in a committee he would not abandon it, if any gentleman thought proper to limit the number of Catholics to be admissible into parliament. Twice, then, by specific bills, had the House of Commons sanctioned the principle of concession; but those bills had been stopped elsewhere. It was irregular for him to allude to the cause of that obstruction; but the alleged reasons had gone abroad, and he might be permitted to notice them. It was said, that these bills introduced a new principle, hostile to the Protestant establishment of the country, and subversive of the settlement laid down at the Revolution, and to which the house of Brunswick owed their security upon the throne. But, was it true that the House of Commons had twice sanctioned a principle of so alarming and unconstitutional a nature: or were they to be told that the throne rested on a separate parliamentary basis, of which the House of Commons formed no part? He positively denied that the throne was exposed to such a risk; and contended with great earnestness that the principle which he advocated was not only congenial with, but inseparably involved in the great principles which were declared and established at the Revolution.

Before he proceeded to speak of the bill, for leave to bring in which he should wish to move, he was desirous of making two or three further preliminary observations. And first with respect to securities. Securities had hitherto been the subject of much difference and discussion. By some they had been considered useless; by others those which had been offered had been deemed insufficient. For himself, he had always been decidedly of opinion that some securities were absolutely and indispensably necessary; so much so, indeed, that he should object to passing any bill without them. Another objection to former bills was, that they did not contain any provision in favour of Protestant Dissenters; but that they relieved the Roman Catholics from disabilities to which they left the Protestant Dissenters. He was glad of an opportunity to disabuse the public mind on that point. Nothing could be less true. The tendency of the bills was, to put the Roman Catholics on the footing of the Protestant Dissenters, and nothing more. It was singular how uninformed the public were in many respects. It was generally imagined that the Protestant Dissenters had no right to sit in the House of Commons. On the contrary, he had as much right to sit in that house and in the House of Lords, as the member of the Pro-

testant establishment. It was also contended that if the measure
which he proposed were carried, the test and corporation acts must
also be repealed. That he denied. There was no necessary connexion between Catholic emancipation and the repeal of the test and
corporation acts. Besides, the test act had been repealed in Ireland
for forty years ; and that repeal had not only failed in increasing,
but had actually very much cut down the dissenting interest in that
country. If at some future period, the repeal of the test and corporation acts were proposed, he would most cordially support the
proposition ; but he must decline mixing it up with the Catholic
question.

He would now call the attention of the house to the argument
founded on the principles connected with the Reformation. He admitted that from the Reformation must be justly dated the rights and
liberties of the people. But he claimed it as an admitted position,
that the exclusion of the Roman Catholics or the Dissenters from
office, or from constituting any part of the government, rested on
statutable prohibition, and was in direct contradiction to any presumption founded on constitutional principles. They must look at the
statute law alone, then, as the ground of the exclusion. The act of
uniformity of Elizabeth must be regarded as an isolated statute, to
be construed by the light of history. At the period of the Reformation three principles were operative: the first was the unalienable establishment of the Protestant religion in these realms as far as human
regulation could affix permanence ; the second was to put down and
prevent the exercise of all religious professions, as contumacious, which
were at variance with the religion so established : the third was, to
give the state a power of distinguishing the well-affected from the
disaffected, and to disable and disqualify the latter from being admitted into its high offices. Of those principles the first was the most
important, and was inalienable ; the second, after having been contended against for three hundred years, was at length abandoned by the
repeal of the law against recusancy ; the third was intended as a test
to separate the well-affected from the disaffected, and for that purpose the oath of supremacy was framed. What the friends of emancipation sought was, a qualified oath of supremacy, such as might be
taken by a conscientious Roman Catholic, who must always acknowledge a certain degree of spiritual authority in the head of his church.
The right honourable and learned gentleman then referred to three
documents, at the period of the Reformation, to show the sense in
which the spiritual jurisdiction of the crown was understood at that
time. The first was the act of supremacy, by which the crown was

invested with the jurisdiction over its subjects which was claimed by a foreign power. Now, he contended, that interference in the spiritual concerns of a sect was not claimed or given by that act; and, even if the Roman Catholics gave it at the present day, it could not be exercised by the crown. The only authority which that act gave to the sovereign, was the power over the Established Church, which was claimed by the Pope, and which was denied to him. The next document was the declaration of the queen, by which, in explanation of the act, she claimed only such a jurisdiction as would exclude the admission of any foreign authority over her subjects. The third document was the act dispensing with the taking of the oath in certain instances by Roman Catholics: the queen being, as was stated, otherwise assured of their loyalty. This, then, was all the act required; it was not looked upon as a test of religion, but as a guarantee of loyalty. The oath of supremacy required the person who took it to declare, that no foreign prince, prelate, state, or potentate, hath or ought to have any jurisdiction, ecclesiastical or spiritual, or any authority whatsoever within these realms. Now, the oath in the bill of 1821 (and which he proposed to continue) was to the same effect, but it added—"hath or ought to have any jurisdiction, &c., contrary to the allegiance due to the sovereign of this country." The Roman Catholic was now ready to take this oath: and he would ask what farther would be required of him as a test of his loyalty?

The right honourable gentleman then went on to cite several authorities, for the purpose of showing that this was the sense in which that test was understood at its first enactment; that it applied, not to religion, but to loyalty; and that several noblemen and gentlemen took the oath in Elizabeth's time, not conceiving it to compromise their religion. This was further proved by the act of the 27th of Elizabeth, in which severe penalties were enacted against Jesuits and priests exercising their clerical functions; but these penalties were dispensed with in the cases of such as took the oath. Now, it was clear that these priests were Roman Catholics, and the legislature of that time could not have been so absurd, could not have added insult to injury, by requiring them to purchase their exemption from penalties, by taking an oath which no Catholic could take, if it had the meaning which was now sought to be put upon it. It was not until there was added to the oath a declaration, that the Catholic worship was superstitious and idolatrous, that it was understood to be against the religion, and that Catholics, generally, refused to take it. The Pope, at the time of passing the act of supremacy, claimed an authority over the whole English church—the power of appointing to bishoprics—

of receiving the profits of the sees while vacant—of deposing the king —of excommunicating him and the people. The act denied to him any such authority: and the Roman Catholics were all ready to swear, that he neither had nor ought to have such authority, and they were willing to take any stronger oath to the same effect if it could be devised.

The right honourable gentleman then went on to answer many of the usual objections urged against the measure; amongst others, that the dispensing with the oath to Catholics, while it continued it to Protestants, would be inconsistent. But, the Protestants would not be in a worse situation than they were at present. They all took it; but none took it in the sense that the Pope had no authority in these countries, for it was clear he had some spiritual power; but it was ready to be sworn by all Roman Catholics, that he neither had nor ought to have any which was inconsistent with the power and sovereign authority and supreme jurisdiction of the king of England, or in any manner opposed to it. All the researches which had been made in connexion with this subject, had produced but one solitary case in which the head of the Roman Catholic church could act in opposition to the law of the state. Persons of that degree of consanguinity, which admitted of their marrying without offending the laws of the Protestant church, could not marry by the laws of the Roman Catholic church. From this circumstance, in a particular case where the restoration of conjugal rights might be decreed by our laws, the laws of the Roman Catholic church might oppose it. But those laws could not deny the validity of the marriage, nor the legitimacy of the children of such marriage, nor could they do anything that might affect the rights, liberty, or property of the subject. They could merely exclude the parties from participation in the rights of their church. The power of the Pope was no longer what it used to be. His devouring lion, as it had been called when the oath of supremacy was framed, had become tame and harmless in our time—had in fact been rendered innocent as a suckling lamb. Whatever danger might be supposed to attach to the influence which the Pope, as head of the Catholic church, might exercise in his realm, the danger existed now in as great a degree as it could rationally be expected to exist after the claims of the Catholics should have been granted. If the Catholic were disposed to trifle with his conscience, what could prevent him from misconstruing the oath which he was now called upon to take. If he were honest, the new oath to be proposed to him would bind him, if dishonest, the oath at present proffered would not.

The right honourable gentleman again referred to the reign of

Elizabeth, and quoted the letter of Lord Burleigh to her majesty, in 1583, in which he stated, that considering the urgency of the oath of supremacy must in some degree beget despair, for many Catholics must in taking it either do that which they thought unlawful or be deemed traitors, he submitted to her majesty's consideration, whether it would not be better for her security, and for the satisfaction of the Catholics themselves, to let the declaration be, that whoever refused to swear that he was ready to bear arms in her majesty's defence against all foreign powers or states opposed to her, should be deemed traitors; this would be a better proof of their loyalty. But (Lord Burleigh added) if it should be said, that in an oath of this kind they might dissimulate, or expect that the Pope would absolve them from its observance, he would reply, so they might in the oath of supremacy; and they who would keep one, might be trusted with the observance of the other. These were the sentiments of that great and wise statesman, above two hundred years ago; but it seemed we grew wiser as the world grew older, and refused to have any reliance upon the faith of oaths. We, who admitted that the whole security of the state—the safety of society—depended upon the sanctity of oaths, now refused to place any reliance upon them. To be consistent, if we distrusted the oaths of the Catholics, we should undo what had been already done in their behalf—we should go back to the full severity of the penal laws, and proceed against them even to extermination; we should wield the iron rod of conquest, and when we had got the strong man down, we should not content ourselves with cutting off his hair, which would grow again, but should cut off his head which could not be replaced.

He now proceeded, with reluctance, to notice the arguments drawn from the revolution against Catholic emancipation. There was no greater mistake than that which was fallen into by those persons who supposed that the revolution and settlement had anything to do with the system established by the 25th and 30th of Charles 2nd. So far from this being the case, the revolution was at right angles with that system. The fact was, Charles 2nd had ceased to be the protector of the state; the crown had formed the project of overturning the established religion. The acts of the 25th and 30th of that reign were not intended to make the throne fundamentally Protestant, but were framed as a substitute for such protection. It was obvious that such a system could not be lasting. The parliament, in effect, said to the king, "we cannot trust you; we will keep you on the throne, yield you dutiful obedience; but we will not suffer you to change the religion of the state." The first measure of the Revolution was in direct opposition to the system of Charles 2nd. It altered the law by making the throne fundamentally and essentially Protestant. King William's parliament altered the oath of supremacy, and proposed to repeal the test and corporation acts. Now, his (Mr. P.'s) measure proposed no such innovations on the act of William, as William had made on those of Charles 2nd or as Charles 2nd had made upon those of the reformation. These alterations were made according to the altered circumstances of the times; and it was upon the alteration in the circumstances of the country at the present period, that he founded the expediency of the proposed measure. It was said, that the settlement at the revolution ought not to be shaken—that the principles then established were principles of toleration, of civil and religious liberty, and of equal protection to all. The revolution was not marked by any such principles of pure and religious toleration. It quite shut out the Roman Catholics of England and Ireland: it enacted severe penalties against priests being engaged as schoolmasters; so that the Roman Catholics were not made objects of toleration, but victims of persecution. The age of pure and religious toleration did not in fact begin until the 18th of the late king; and then were the true foundations of civil and religious liberty first laid. Those who opposed these claims on what they called the principles of the revolution, by a perverse sort of chemistry, extracted from it, for the sake of their argument, all that was bad and intolerant, and left behind all that was great, glorious, and free in it, as a useless residuum. It had been often argued, that Mr. Locke was good authority against the admission of Catholics to the full enjoyment of the constitution; it was urged that Mr. Locke had laid it down as a principle, that so long as the Roman Catholics delivered themselves up to the supremacy of a foreign prince, whose commands they held themselves bound to obey, even to the prejudice of the state, they were not entitled to the privileges of toleration. Mr. Locke was right in stating, that any portion of the community who were leagued with a foreign power against the interests of their own country were not entitled to a participation in its constitution. But, who would venture to say, that the Roman Catholics of the present day were not entitled upon such ground? And if so, what became of the argument of Mr. Locke? Mr. Locke went on to say, that while the Roman Catholics acknowledged a foreign power, superior to the laws of the country, they were not deserving of toleration, and could not complain of not being considered good subjects. Now, he would ask, who would venture to say, that the Roman Catholics of these realms were not good subjects? Were they to consider the concessions which already appeared on the statute book as mere flattery, and not at all deserved by the parties to whom those concessions were made? But, if the Roman Catholics were considered to be good subjects, then he would ask, what became of the authority of Mr. Locke? It was natural for the great men, who watched as it were the cradle of the constitution, to feel considerable alarm at the conduct of the Roman Catholics, and to consider them as bad subjects, in consequence of their readiness to join a foreign power. This was the doctrine of Lord Somers among others. But if the Roman Catholics of the present day were loyal and firm supporters of the constitution, why should they go back to former periods for a justification of a line of conduct which, though perfectly right and reasonable then, was perfectly wrong and unreasonable at present? It was true that the great men of that period, such as Lord Clarendon, Lord Somers, Mr. Locke, and others, were decidedly hostile to the Catholics; but then gentlemen who referred to the writings of those men should take into consideration the circumstances of the times in which they wrote. He would next call the attention of the house to the doctrines held by Blackstone with respect to the Catholics. That great writer, speaking upon the subject, said, "the sin of schism, as such, is by no means the object of temporal coercion and punishment. If through weakness of intellect, through misdirected piety, through perverseness and acerbity of temper, or (which is often the case) through a prospect of secular advantage, in herding with a party, men quarrel with the ecclesiastical establishment, the civil magistrate has nothing to do with it; unless their tenets and practice are such as threaten ruin or disturbance to the state. He is bound indeed to protect the Established church; and if this can be better effected by admitting none but its genuine members to offices of trust and emolument, he is certainly at liberty so to do; the disposal of offices being matter of favour and discretion. But, this point being once secured, all persecution for diversity of opinions, however ridiculous or absurd they may be, is contrary to every principle of sound policy and civil freedom." This was exactly the doctrine upon which he now called upon the house to act. The same author went on as follows:—" As to Papists, what has been said of the Protestant Dissenters, would hold equally strong for a general toleration of them; provided their separation was founded only upon difference of opinion in religion, and their principles did not also extend to a subversion of the civil government. If once they could be brought to renounce the supremacy of the Pope, they might quietly enjoy their seven sacraments; their purgatory, and auricular confession; their worship of relics and images: nay, even their transubstantiation. But while they acknowledge a foreign power superior to the sovereignty of the kingdom, they cannot complain if the laws of that kingdom will not treat them upon the footing of good subjects." So that if it appeared that the Roman Catholics were at present good subjects, as he contended they were, then there was at once an end to all the arguments both of Mr. Locke and Blackstone. Was it not a formidable argument to set up, that out of a population of seven millions in Ireland, five millions were bad subjects, disaffected to the government, and undeserving of a participation in the constitution? If it could be shown that there were in Ireland five millions of men disaffected to the government, then he would say, that the right honourable the secretary for foreign affairs would be furnished with a stronger argument in favour of neutrality, than any which even his own powerful and argumentative mind had been able to urge. If they were obliged to employ the forces of the country in watching over a disaffected population of five millions in Ireland, then adieu to the power and glory which had hitherto distinguished this country. They might live on in a state of feverish discontent and uncertainty; but it was impossible that great or permanent good could be effected in such a state of things. The right honourable and learned member went on to quote Lord Hardwicke, for the purpose of showing that the real security to the Established church of this country was to be found, not in the oath of supremacy, not in the declaration, but in that wise and salutary law which made the crown of these realms essentially Protestant.

Before he sat down he owed it to Scotland to say a few words upon the law upon this subject as it now stood in that country. The measure which he proposed only went to remove the oath of supremacy, and the declaration. But, there was a Scottish law which went to disable Catholics from being electors or elected, in choosing or being elected to serve in certain public offices. This law he believed was still unrepealed; and he should feel happy if any honourable representative of that country would propose a clause in the bill, for the repeal of this law of disqualification. By the eleventh article of the Scottish union, it was provided, that the British parliament was competent to abolish any Scottish law, for the purpose of assimilating the constitution of both countries, and every alteration of private law was admitted which tended to the advantage of that country. Having gone through the various topics, he could not sit down without saying a word or two upon the declaration. It was satisfactory to know, that neither clergyman nor layman had opened his lips in favour of it. He hoped that this blot would not much longer be allowed to remain upon the statute book; for he did not believe that a single human being existed, who would assert that it was warranted by any principle of religion. The enemies of the Catholic claims feared those who worshipped the same God, and acknowledged the same Redeemer—for his part he dreaded only those who worshipped no God, and acknowledged no Redeemer. They feared that the Roman Catholics were disloyal—he only dreaded lest severity and injustice should make them so. The right honourable gentleman concluded with moving, " that this house do resolve itself into a committee of the whole house, to consider the state of the laws by which oaths or declarations are required to be taken or made, as qualifications for the enjoyment of offices, or for the exercise of civil functions, so far as the same may affect his majesty's Roman Catholic subjects; and whether it would be expedient, in any and what manner, to alter or modify the same, and subject to what provisions or regulations."

The reports proceed to say, that "after the motion had been read from the chair, a loud and general cry of 'question, question,' was raised." Several speakers attempted to prolong the debate amid an impenetrable uproar—each side of the house appearing equally anxious to hustle the question aside. As Mr. Lambton closed a short emphatic speech with a declaration that he looked upon the "manner in which the question was brought forward by the Irish attorney-general, as a gross deception upon the Roman Catholics," the cries changed to "adjourn," "divide," "clear the gallery," and strangers were ordered to withdraw. The house remained with closed doors for an hour and a half, and, after dividing on a motion of adjournment to the following day, in which the noes had 292 votes to 134 ayes, it was moved that the debate be adjourned for six months. Whereon a motion was made and the question put, "that the house do now adjourn," which was carried. Thus the present motion dropped ineffectual.

This debate demonstrated to the Catholics of Ireland the necessity of pressure from without in assisting parliament to come to a conclusion. The Catholic Association was formed in the following month, and gratefully passed in its first proceedings a strong vote of thanks to Plunket. On the day after the debate, he was asked in his place whether he meant to renew the question this session. He said he was in the hands of its friends, but that for his own part he was averse to a renewal of the notice this session.

CONDUCT OF THE SHERIFF OF DUBLIN.
April 22, 1823.

The following week, Sir F. Burdett's motion for inquiry into the conduct of the Sheriff of Dublin was brought forward. In introducing it, he passed a liberal eulogy upon Plunket's conduct—" The first law officer of the crown endeavours

ing to reduce a party to the government of the law that had long domineered over the people, and anxious to secure the multitude against the vexation of long imposed and organised oppression." Plunket followed him.

Mr. PLUNKET said, he meant to trouble the house with a few observations on what had fallen from the honourable baronet. He begged leave, in the first instance, to assure him, that he did not mean to offer any opposition to the motion. He was, indeed the last person in the house from whom such an opposition could be expected. He thought, however, that his case did not stand on the ground on which the honourable baronet had thought fit to place it. He had, it was true, in the discharge of his duty, exercised a power which appeared to give offence to some persons; and the question ultimately resolved itself into this—whether he had exercised a sound discretion in the application of that power? The opinion of the house was called for on this point—whether he had used his discretion unduly, oppressively, or improperly? It was not, whether under the same circumstances, he should again exercise the same power—or whether, in the peculiar situation of Ireland, it was necessary to resort to his legal prerogative? These were not the disputed points. The question was—whether he had exercised the power intrusted to him with a fair and honest intention? It was not because others would, perhaps, under similar circumstances, have acted differently, that he was to be censured. Different individuals would take different views of the expediency or inexpediency of exercising a discretionary power; but still their intentions might be equally pure and upright. The situation of a public functionary would be most lamentable, if, because he differed from others in the use of a discretionary power, he was, therefore, to become the object of censure, no matter how just and proper his motives were. In order to make a public functionary the fair object of censure, the house must arrive at this conclusion—that he had acted on some sinister principle. If what he had done, and which he considered neither unconstitutional nor illegal, come to be inquired into, no censure could be directed against him, unless the house was of opinion that he had acted from a love of oppression, from a malicious intention, or from some other base and unworthy motive. If they could not arrive at this opinion, he was discharged from all matter of accusation. He thanked the honourable baronet for the fair and candid mode in which he had brought forward this proposition; and he would do him the justice to say, that on no occasion did he ever forsake that gentlemanly urbanity of manners which he had displayed that night. Under the circumstances of the case, he (Mr. P.) had, on a former evening, stated the reasons which induced him to act as he had done. He, however, knew, that the statement which he had then made for the purpose of absolving himself, must of necessity draw after it this inquiry. But he would ask whether this brought the question to the point—whether, in exercising his legal power, he was, or was not censurable? In his opinion it clearly did not. If he brought forward charges against individuals, he might on that account, lay himself open to the censure of the house; but that censure could have nothing to do with his conduct in the exercise of his legal prerogative. Having stated the general grounds on which he conceived his conduct to have been justifiable, he next stated the particular grounds on which, as it appeared to him, it became peculiarly necessary that he should adopt the discretion which had given rise to so much animadversion. In the course of that statement, he certainly had advanced matter which involved a very high censure on an individual holding a situation of great importance. What he asked of the house to give him credit for on that occasion was, not that the charge was exactly as he had stated it—not that he knew it of his own knowledge to be a perfect truth—but that it was conveyed to his mind in such a manner as fully impressed him with an idea of its truth. Now, he would ask, if he were completely satisfied in his own mind that those facts were true, was he not justified in acting on that impression? It was a case of very great importance to the country—it was a case in which he felt that justice ought to be done as speedily as possible; and therefore he proceeded by the readiest mode. Was he, under all the circumstances, to forego any proceedings against the rioters until he could procure affidavits which would enable him to institute a prosecution against the sheriff? If he had done so, he thought it would have been a gross violation of his duty. The only question, therefore, was—whether he had that reasonable conviction in his mind of the truth of those facts which would form a fair ground for adopting the proceedings to which he had resorted? He certainly felt that conviction; and therefore he contended that the proposed inquiry was one in which he had no more interest than the honourable baronet, or any other person in that house; except that he should be sorry if, by any chance, it could be supposed that he brought a charge against a public officer lightly or unadvisedly. He meant not to allege anything which could give rise to acrimonious feeling; but this he would say, that his suspicions with respect to the conduct of the sheriff were not removed, but were considerably strengthened, by what had since taken place. He had no hesitation in declaring, that he thought the conduct of the sheriff was a very proper object for prosecution. He deemed it right now to state, without meaning to interfere with any course which the house might think proper to pursue, that if the business were not taken out of his hands by the house, it was his intention to institute such a prosecution, for the purpose of arriving at the real justice of the case. He agreed with the honourable baronet that it would be an essential denial of justice, if the sheriff were not afforded an opportunity of entering on his defence. If the house proceeded with this inquiry, the case would, of course, be taken out of his hands. If, however, the house declined interfering, he would institute such a prosecution as the case called for. Having said thus much, it would, perhaps, be expected that he should give some explanation to the house as to his not having proceeded sooner. It might be asked, " Why did you not proceed against the sheriff before, if you considered him liable to prosecution?" He would, in answer to that question, state what must appear to every candid mind a full and sufficient reason. He had received the information with respect to the conduct of the sheriff from different quarters. As that information reached him, he communicated it to the lord lieutenant; and it was from time to time communicated to his majesty's government. To show that the idea of a prosecution was no after-thought, he had to observe, that he had stated to the government that it would be a matter of grave and serious consideration whether a prosecution should not be instituted against the sheriff, for his conduct in empanelling the grand jury. From the first moment the information was given to him relative to the manner in which the sheriff had conducted himself, the impression was strong on his mind that the matter must be probed to the bottom. The trial of the rioters commenced on the 24th or 25th of January, and certainly that was not the fit time for instituting a prosecution. Mr. Sheriff Thorpe was the person by whom the panel for the grand jury was returned. At his (Mr. P.'s) desire, he wished the two sheriffs to join in that panel, the thing being perfectly legal: he conceived that would have been the better way, as two of the traversers were related to Mr. Sheriff Thorpe. The fact, however, was, that the panel was signed only by Mr. Sheriff Thorpe; for, though he showed it to his brother sheriff, no alteration was made in it. He, however, had hoped that the petty jury for the trial of the traversers would have been differently returned; and that thus a fair trial would take place. Therefore it was that he did not think it necessary to stop the proceedings for the purpose of prosecuting one of the sheriffs. Soon after his arrival in town, the honourable member for Armagh gave notice of a charge which he meant to bring against him in that house. He asked whether he would have been justified if, when accusations were pending against himself, he had instituted a prosecution against the sheriff. When the honourable member for Armagh gave notice of his motion, he (Mr. P.) entreated that it might be brought forward immediately. He complained of having that charge suspended over his head for two months. Until five minutes before he stood up to defend himself, he did not know what the specific accusation against him would be. If, under these circumstances, he had instituted a proceeding against the sheriff, would it not have been said that it was intended as a set-off against the accusation levelled at himself? As regarded himself, he thought the question had been completely disposed of the other evening; as the proposition that he was not influenced by any undue motive in the exercise of his discretion was acquiesced in. As regarded the sheriff, he repeated, that if the nouse did not take the matter out of his hands, he would institute a prosecution. He must do it also by the unfavourite mode of an ex-officio information; for as to applying to a grand jury of the county of Dublin to find a bill against the high sheriff, that would be utterly useless. He should file an ex-officio information, and he should next apply to the Court of King's Bench, that the case might be tried at the bar of that court, but that the venue might be directed to come from another county. The sheriff would then have an opportunity, by the testimony of witnesses, and by other legal means, to make his defence. If, on the other hand, the house resolved to enter on an immediate inquiry, to that course he could not possibly entertain the slightest objection. But, as in the event of the institution of a prosecution he should be called upon to prosecute, it was not his intention to give his vote either for or against the motion. He, however, perfectly agreed with the honourable baronet, that it would be rank injustice if the sheriff, who wished to vindicate his character, were shut out from a fair opportunity of entering on that vindication.

EX OFFICIO INFORMATIONS.
May 2, 1823.

Mr. Spring Rice moved that Mr. D. Macnamara and Mr. T. O'Reilly, attorneys in Dublin, be summoned to attend as witnesses at the bar of the house on the 9th of May.

Mr. Plunket readily embraced the opportunity which this motion

afforded him of stating a fact which had some connexion with it. It had been charged that in filing an *ex officio* information after bills of indictment had been ignored by the grand jury, he had acted in his office of attorney-general for Ireland without precedent, and had introduced into the administration of the law a practice of which no instance had occurred since the Norman conquest. He had upon that occasion suggested, that from the authority of the Court of King's Bench, in cases which he cited, a fair analogy was to be traced, and sufficient to justify his proceeding. He had remarked that it was unfair, because he could not produce the precedents for the reasons he then stated, to suppose they did not exist. He had since received a letter from a Mr. Foley, an attorney of Ireland, a gentleman whom he had not the honour of knowing, in which that gentleman stated, that seeing the reports of those debates in parliament in which this subject had been mentioned, and the manner in which the argument had been used, he was induced, from a sense of justice to inform him that he believed a case took place in Ireland twelve years ago, in which an *ex officio* information had been filed by an attorney-general after bills of indictment for the same offence had been ignored by the grand jury. He (Mr. Plunket) replied to this letter by thanking Mr. Foley, and requesting him to inquire into the subject; he had done so, and the following were the particulars which he had transmitted:—
In October, 1811, bills of indictment were preferred against a person of the name of Leach, for writing a letter to Sir Edward Littlehales, soliciting the appointment of the place of barrack-master. The bills contained three counts; the first was for sending a letter, proposing to give a bribe; the second for offering money by way of bribe; and the third for offering securities by way of bribe. These bills were ignored by the grand jury; the court was surprised, and ordered fresh indictments to be sent again to the same jury, who again ignored them. In November following, the then attorney-general, his predecessor, Mr. Saurin, filed an *ex officio* information containing the same counts, acting under the power which he (Mr. Plunket) had exercised; and the case was tried in the same court. He held the papers in his hand, which he did not mean to lay on the table, because he would not seem to inculpate the character of the right honourable gentleman who had preceded him; but he owed it to his own character to state, that twelve years ago the same thing had been done for which he had been censured, and in which he was charged with having acted unprecedentedly. The conduct of the attorney-general at that period had never been impeached, nor had any doubt been entertained of its legality or justice. He felt that this bore most strongly upon his own

ease, because that honourable gentleman had supposed he was only acting in the course of his duty.

Mr. DENMAN asked if any judgment had been passed in the case mentioned by the right honourable gentleman.

MR. PLUNKET replied, that judgment had been signed for want of a plea; and it appeared, in consequence of the contrition expressed by the defendant, and of his having lost a valuable appointment, that no further punishment had been visited upon him, and the affair was dropped.

Mr. ABERCROMBY had heard this statement with the greatest astonishment. There were two persons to whom, *ex necessitate rei*, all the particulars of this case must have been known—the then attorney-general and the crown solicitor. He would ask the house to consider how the attorney-general for Ireland was served in the discharge of his duty, when no communication of this fact had been made to him? If Mr. Saurin did not think fit to inform the right honourable gentleman, this was a matter of courtesy of which he (Mr. Abercromby) had no right to complain; but that the crown solicitor should not have informed him of it, seemed something more than accident. It was for the purpose of impressing upon the house the situation in which the right honourable gentleman was placed, the inconveniences of which, he believed, were also shared by the lord lieutenant himself, that he called their attention to this singular conduct of the crown solicitor.

Mr. PLUNKET was bound in justice to the crown solicitor to state that two gentlemen of the same name had held that office—they were father and son; the father was dead, and the son must have been a very young man at the time to which he had alluded.

This short scene closed Plunket's vindication in the Bottle Riot case. His statement is described as having electrified the house. It was notorious that Saurin was the real promoter of the proceedings against him throughout, and the fact now discovered, that Saurin had himself, in precisely similar circumstances, resorted to the use of the *ex officio* information, at once marked the utter unfairness of the whole proceeding. On the same day the committee, obtained by Sir F. Burdett, commenced their inquiry. It sat for nine days, on the last of which Plunket was examined. The chairman was directed to report the evidence to the house; and on the 8th of June, Mr. J. Williams, for Sir F. Burdett, who was absent through indisposition, gave notice of a motion founded on the evidence. On the day fixed for the debate, Sir Francis was still indisposed, and the session ended, nothing done, on the 19th of July.

IRISH INSURRECTION ACT.
May 12, 1823.

IN a despatch dated January 23, Lord Wellesley, referring to the tithe jacquerie which at this time affected Clare, Limerick, Cork, and Tipperary, with selvages of several of the adjoining counties, asked for a renewal of the Insurrection Act. Lord A. Hamilton attacked Plunket for inconsistency, in sustaining measures which he had formerly stigmatised as an extinction of the constitution—also for his conduct on the Catholic question—and for the spirit in which he opposed any attempt to abate the payment of tithes.

Mr. PLUNKET said, that as he had been much misrepresented, but no doubt unintentionally, by the noble lord who had just sat down, he must take the liberty of addressing a few words to the house upon this question. He could not be fairly charged with inconsistency for the support which he was now giving to this bill, inasmuch as he had advocated it last year, and also in 1806, when he was connected with the Duke of Bedford's administration in Ireland. He allowed that it contained a most unconstitutional principle, seeing that it annihilated the trial by jury; and he lamented, as much as any man could do, the melancholy necessity which compelled the government to inflict it at present upon Ireland. Still, the measure was to be only of a temporary nature, and was much better than the introduction of martial law, which appeared so desirable to the honourable member for Cork. The introduction of martial law, he, for one, did not like; because it was sure to produce irritation, and it could not be attended, either directly or remotely, by any conciliatory or beneficial consequences. The great evil under which Ireland at present laboured, was the reluctance felt by individuals to come forward to give their evidences. Would the introduction of martial law cure that evil? And if it would not, would martial law justify those who resorted to it in punishing individuals without any evidence at all? If evidence could be procured, the present law would be sufficient to meet the grievance; but, unfortunately, there existed at present in Ireland a terror superior to the terror of the law, and which paralysed every effort to carry it into execution. The learned gentleman then proceeded to defend himself from the charge of inconsistency which had been brought against him for his conduct in respect of the Roman Catholic claims. He contended, that to that question he had clung with adhesive grasp both in its good and in its bad fortune.

The noble lord had said that, considering his conduct regarding that important subject, it was quite impossible to repose any confidence either in his sincerity or in that of any of his colleagues. Unfortunately for the noble lord's assertion, he had received from the Roman Catholics of Ireland, since the late unfortunate decision on their claims, the most satisfactory assurances that they approved of every thing he had done to forward them. It was true that, in 1813, he had expressed his opinion of the disadvantage of bringing their claims forward with a divided cabinet. He would again repeat what he had then said, that, in his opinion, Catholic emancipation ought to be a *sine qua non* with every administration, and that it was a measure upon which the safety and tranquillity of Ireland principally depended. He thought that there was nothing in his expressions at that time which precluded him from obeying the orders of his sovereign in taking office under the present ministry. In 1813 he had entertained doubts of the sincerity of the ministers who then advocated Catholic emancipation. Those doubts had since been removed, in consequence of the great exertions which had been made to forward that cause by a noble lord now no more, and also by a right honourable friend (Mr. Canning) who was now seated near him. In 1813 he had also thought it feasible to obtain a cabinet whose members should be unanimous in their opinions upon that subject. At present he was convinced of the impossibility of ever seeing any such prospect realized. When, therefore, he saw that his majesty wished conciliatory measures to be adopted towards Ireland, and also that the government in that unhappy country was determined to discountenance the system by which its grievances and discontents had been so long fomented, he felt that he should not be weakening the cause of Catholic emancipation, by going over to the side of the house on which he now sat; and he therefore had gone over to it, retaining all his old, and not adopting any new opinions for the guidance of his political conduct. He had made these remarks in consequence of what had fallen from the noble lord, whose observations appeared to him to press more upon the individual who then addressed them, than they did upon the question immediately before the house. He would now say, that were he inclined to vote for the inquiry proposed by the noble lord, he would not vote for it as an amendment to the present motion. Without saying whether he would or would not vote for that inquiry, were it brought forward as a substantive motion, he would say this—that it deserved a separate discussion, and that at any rate it ought not to be obtruded on the house as a secondary consideration, when it was necessary to obtain an unanimous vote from it, in favour of the insurrection act, in order to dispel any illusion which might exist in the mind of any misguided wretches, respecting the light in which they were regarded by either house of parliament. The learned gentleman then proceeded to argue that he was not inconsistent in giving his support to the present tithe bill, after the opinions which he had formerly expressed regarding the inviolability of church property. The noble lord had complained of the asperity with which he had condemned the propositions submitted to the house by the honourable member for Aberdeen.

He begged leave to assert that he had never intended to use any such tone as the noble lord had attributed to him. All that he had then said was, that the property of the church was not public property, to be cut up and carved at pleasure; and what he now maintained was this, that though the property of the church was as sacred as any private property, it was still liable to those regulations of the legislature to which other private property was liable. In conclusion, he again lamented that this act should be necessary, and if any honourable member could propose a better, he would willingly adopt it. One proof that the powers which it gave had not been improperly employed had been furnished them that evening by the honourable member for Cork, who had complained that they had been administered with too much lenity. He thought that, under such circumstances, the house might fairly bestow those powers once more upon the Irish government; seeing that the only complaint which had been made against it arose out of the discretion and moderation with which it had exercised the extraordinary powers committed to its charge.

Leave was given to renew the bill, by 162 ayes—noes 82, and the power of suspending the constitution was shortly afterwards placed in the hands of Lord Wellesley and his heterogeneous administration. It cannot be complained that they abused their powers—nor was Plunket ever a merciless prosecutor. There was very little hemp used, considering the times, in his campaign against the Threshers. He never countenanced the packing of juries; and the Bottle Riot case and Emmet's are, perhaps, the only cases that can be shown where he exhibited an avenging animus in vindicating the law. In his report, indeed, upon which Lord Wellesley founded the application for renewing the Insurrection Act, he asks instead for the extension of an English Act which would enable him only to transport for seven years. "With such an instrument to work with," says he, "I should entertain a confident hope of entirely subduing this offensive and disgusting association." But the halter was the only weapon that the law then recognised for dealing with Irish grievances.

BURIALS IN IRELAND.
March 22, 1824.

This measure, it may be seen, had the useful and charitable design of diminishing the asperities of sect in Ireland, by modifying the power possessed by the Protestant clergy over the service of burials.

MR. PLUNKET rose to move the order of the day for the second reading of the Burials in Ireland bill. The right honourable and learned gentleman observed, that he would not have brought it forward at that moment, if he had not had some reason to flattter himself, from the general opinion which he had collected from all sides of the house on the measure, that there was no likelihood of any material objection being offered to it, nor of any discussion arising that would be at all calculated to produce a protracted debate. The house was already aware of the general scope and object of the bill. It related to the burials, in Ireland, of persons dissenting from the doctrines and discipline of the Established Church, with those forms and ceremonies which were peculiar to the religion professed by them. Every one must feel, that this was a subject of extreme importance, as it related to the moral feelings, passions, and prejudices of the great bulk of the population of Ireland; and they must also perceive, that it was a question of the greatest delicacy, because, as it referred to circumstances which must occur in the precincts of Protestant churchyards, it would naturally excite the attention of those who felt an interest in the security of the Protestant establishment. He therefore approached the subject with a considerable degree of caution, he would not say of alarm; because the measure had been so maturely considered, and so nicely prepared, with reference to both sides of the question, that while it would make the law easy, as to the burial of Dissenters, it would not create any just alarm in the minds of those who were connected with the Established Church. But, when he stated that it was a subject of great difficulty and delicacy, he begged to observe, that it was not on that account that he had taken it out of the hands in which it had been previously placed. Whether he considered the question with a view to its importance, its difficulty, or its delicacy, he knew of no hands better suited to bring it forward effectually than those of his right honourable friend (Sir J. Newport). The course which his right honourable friend had taken in the debate relative to education in Ireland, which occurred a few evenings since—the tone of temper and moderation with which he had introduced that delicate subject, proved clearly that no man was more fit to conciliate the opinions and soothe the passions of all parties. Still, however, he thought it would be felt, that it was better that this question should be taken up by one who spoke the sentiments of the government of the country, rather than by any individual unconnected with the government. Many reasons could be adduced in support of this position. It was right, in the first place, that the public should know the anxious solicitude which the government entertained, with respect to the welfare of the people of Ireland; and next, it was important that the question should be now brought forward in such a manner as to reconcile all classes to it. This end could be much better attained by the government, than if the measure were introduced by any individual, however respectable. Having said thus much to excuse the government of the country for entertaining this measure, it would perhaps be expected that he should state some reason for its not having been taken up sooner. Many circumstances existed in Ireland which would have made it unwise in government to have interfered with a question of this kind at an earlier period. Whatever inconveniences existed in the actual state of the law—and he admitted those inconveniences to be many and considerable—yet still it was found that very few of them were of a practical nature. Government, therefore, had not thought it necessary to legislate on theoretical principles, so long as the existing law appeared to work well. But a new state of things had sprung up, and it was now found expedient to make some change in the law. The first thing it was proposed to do was, to repeal the act of the 9th William 3rd, cap. 7. He believed, with respect to this point, there was an universal consent on the part of every person concerned. He would now state what the object of the act of William was. It was probably known to most gentlemen in that house, that there were in Ireland a number of abbeys and convents, the sites of places formerly used for religious worship, and vested in ecclesiastical persons. These venerable places were looked on with considerable respect, if not reverence, by all classes of people in Ireland. They had been founded from motives of piety, and though sometimes tenanted by superstition and bigotry, yet it could not be denied, that they were often the abodes of genuine religion and pure charity. From them, in former times, the blessings of hospitality had been disseminated amongst the poor and the needy. Those places had long since been taken out of the possession of the ecclesiastical proprietors, and vested in the several members of the state. But they were still viewed by the people with feelings of respect and veneration. Though no longer used as places of religious worship, they were much resorted to as places of burial, not merely for the Roman Catholics of the country, but very frequently for the Protestants; and he felt, that the remains of those ancient edifices were not the least interesting objects of contemplation to those persons who visited Ireland. Looking to the disturbances, religious and political, by which that country had been torn, it was a point on which the mind reposed with some degree of pleasure, when it reflected, that in those cemeteries the Protestant and the Catholic, persons of all ranks and persuasions, were buried in common. However they might have differed in life, in death they were suffered to repose together; and the place of their interment was not made a scene for the display of acrimonious feeling and unseemly asperity. This state of things had prevailed, he believed, more or less, ever since the Reformation. It must seem extraordinary that, under these circumstances, the act of the 9th of William was passed, by which burials in those places were forbidden, as well to Protestants as to Catholics. It seemed extraordinary, when the practice was carried on without offence to any party, that it should have been interfered with by this law. He believed it was not with a view to any direct interference with the rights of sepulture of any religious sect that the law was enacted, but that it was framed in a spirit of jealousy, which could not bear that any religious feeling should be kept alive with respect to those old places of worship. Certainly, whatever might have been the object of the act, its provisions were opposed to those affections and decencies, with reference to the deceased, which ought always to be respected. The act was framed, but it fell still-born, as all measures must do when opposed to the feelings and sentiments of a country. In no one instance, for a series of years, had the custom which had so long prevailed been interfered with—in no one instance had this obnoxious law been carried into effect. If, then, there was an act on their statute-book, to enforce which would be considered a crime, and to infringe it would be looked on as a duty, it ought not to be suffered to remain; and one object of the measure now before the house was, to repeal this act. The house would, however, observe, that there was a clause regulating and narrowing that repeal. The reason of this was, that many of those places were diverted from their original purpose, and were possessed by individuals; and care should be taken, that no interference with private property was admitted under this measure; which would be the case if persons, who were not in the habit of using particular places of this description for burying grounds, were suffered to do so now. He would now, as shortly as he could, apply himself to the more important provisions of this bill, so far as it professed to give the right of burial in Protestant churchyards, according to the religious ceremonies of the parties whose friends were brought there for interment. The noble lord who presided over the government of Ireland, and who had applied himself to this, as well as to every other subject connected with the interests of that country, felt the deepest anxiety for the success of this measure; and he (Mr. P.) knew of no other reason why he now addressed the house, except that, from his constant intercourse with the noble lord, he had the best means of learning his views on the subject. This measure originated with the noble lord, and had received the unanimous sanction of his majesty's government. The two great objects of the bill were these, to secure to Dissenters of every denomination the right of interment according to their own forms and ceremonies, and to take care, at the same time, that nothing was done offensive to the dignity, or subversive of the security, of the Protestant religion. Before he proceeded further, it was necessary that he should describe what was the state of the law on this subject as it now existed. In the first place, he would endeavour to put the house in possession of what was the situation of the Protestant parson as to the right of burial. Gentlemen, doubtless, knew, that the freehold of the churchyard was vested in the rector. The churchyard was his freehold, and no person could enter it, unless by his leave, without committing a trespass. But, besides the right which belonged to him as the possessor of the soil, he was, as the parson, empowered by law to superintend the mode of granting Christian burial in the churchyard. He was to grant the right of interment; and, by the act of Uniformity, he was to read the burial service of the church of Ireland, as by law established, and no other. He could not, himself, read any other service; neither could he depute any person to read a different service in the churchyard. He could employ another gentleman in orders to read the service of the church of Ireland; but he could not allow any layman, or a member of any other community, to read it. If this law were acted on, and the Protestant clergy were in every instance to insist on reading this service, and going through the rites and ceremonies prescribed by the church of Ireland, it would virtually deprive the great body of the people of the right of interment. Considering what their religious opinions were, such a practice would amount to actual exclusion. He did not mean to argue, whether their feeling on this subject was a right one or not: it was his duty merely to state the fact. The opinions, feelings, and prejudices of the people of Ireland were such, that if the principle were insisted on, it would actually amount to an exclusion from the right of interment of all the Catholics, at least, if not of all the Dissenters. This was the situation of the law on one side; now let the house mark what it was on the other. According to the laws of the land, every person had a right to interment in the Protestant churchyard of the parish where he died. His relatives had a right to claim it; but they were entitled to claim it, subject to that right of the Protestant parson which he had just mentioned. But, suppose he performed the rites of the Protestant church, or that he waived their performance, there was no law which, in either case, prohibited the performance of dissenting rites in a Protestant churchyard. There was no law, where the

Protestant parson had discharged his functions, or waived them, to prevent Roman Catholic ceremonies from being performed in the churchyard, however ostentatiously celebrated, or however calculated to produce feelings of pain in the mind of the Protestant clergyman. There were a number of laws passed in Ireland, after the Reformation on the subject of the Catholic priests. By those laws, besides inflicting penalties on priests coming from abroad, there were others which also imposed penalties on all priests who were not registered in a regular manner. By the 21st and 22nd of the late king, the greater part of these penalties were removed, under certain restrictions and conditions. One of them was, that the benefit of those acts should not extend to any Catholic priest who officiated in a Protestant churchyard. It was supposed, that under this clause it was a criminal or penal act for a priest to perform the burial service in a Protestant church-yard: but the supposition was entirely erroneous: it had no other effect than saying, that the Catholic priest who performed the service in a Protestant churchyard, should not have the benefit of that particular law. He was liable to be indicted, not for having performed the service, but for not having duly registered himself under the former act; which he was not required to do, provided he obeyed the restrictions enumerated in the 21st and 22nd of George III. But, whatever might have been the state of the law on this subject, growing out of the 21st and 22nd of George III., all difficulty was removed, in Ireland, by the law of 1793. By that law it was not an illegal act for the Catholic priest to officiate. He could not be indicted for it; he could not be prevented from doing it. If the contrary were admitted: if the Protestant clergyman had a right to insist on performing the service of the church of Ireland, it would totally exclude the whole body of Roman Catholics from interment. If the Protestant clergyman chose to come in and perform his service, or if he waived his right to officiate, there was no law to prevent the Catholic priest from exercising his functions. This was the state of the law; and, considering the situation of the parties, it was fraught with all the seeds and elements of discord and dissension. But though such was the fact—though the state of the law was calculated to produce conflictions and collisions between those opposing parties—it was pleasing to state, that with very few and rare exceptions, those elements of discord and dissension had not created any of those effects which might have been expected from them. One would, indeed, almost praise this state of the law; since it gave an opportunity to people of all sects, and of all religious opinions, to display feelings the most liberal and charitable. He must say, and he said it with great respect for the parochial clergy, that, until of late years, they had not, in the smallest degree, interfered with the right of interment in Protestant churchyards. They had forborne to exercise a duty which was imposed on them by the common law of the country, and by the act of Uniformity, because they felt that it would create uneasiness and dissatisfaction. The Catholic clergymen also had conducted themselves in a most exemplary manner. He believed the Catholic body in general were buried without any ceremony; but it was customary, on the interment of Catholics of the better orders, to have, more or less, a sort of service performed by the priest. Sometimes he appeared in the stole, a sort of black robe, and sometimes he officiated in his plain clothes; but he never presumed to offer anything offensive to the Protestant Church. This was the way in which the matter remained, until lately, without any degree of offence being taken by the Protestant clergy. This would be particularly stated; because it proved that there was not that unmanageable texture in the sentiments of those who held different religious opinions in Ireland, that ought to shut out all hope of accommodation, that ought to lead the house to believe that it was impossible to smooth down those religious feelings, the asperity of which had been the bane and curse of Ireland. When matters remained thus—when, on the one hand, there was no interference, and on the other, no offence—he thought it would have been unwise if government had legislated for prospective evils, that perhaps might never have arisen. But, about four or five years back, the performance of religious ceremonies by a Catholic priest in a Protestant churchyard was resisted. At the time this took place, such occurrences were extremely unfrequent; and government thought it better to get rid of them by giving them conciliatory advice, rather than by exerting the strong hand of authority, or by calling on parliament to take the business up. In the course of the last year, however, the complaints on the subject had greatly increased. Whether the right was more frequently claimed by the Catholic clergy, or contended for in a different degree or manner from what had been customary, he could not say; but a good deal of alarm had certainly been excited. Whether that alarm was just or not he could not discover; and he believed it would be very difficult to ascertain the fact. If one person were asked, whether the ceremony were the same as was heretofore performed, the answer was in the affirmative; but the next individual of whom inquiry was made would state exactly the reverse. In fact, individuals seemed to be guided rather by their prejudices, than by any desire to elicit the truth. He therefore thought it would be much better to leave the circumstances out of which this alarm had arisen, in the ambiguity in which they were placed at present, than to attempt to explore them. Whatever had been done by the Protestant clergy, was, he felt convinced, performed in the discharge of a conscientious duty. He paid a most ready and willing homage to the forbearance manifested by the great body of the parochial clergy of Ireland; and he was certain, wherever they had recourse to resistance, they were impelled to it by a sense of duty alone. The government, as he had already observed, were anxious to soothe all differences, by friendly and conciliatory advice; but it at length became necessary to examine what the real state of the law was on this subject. If the law were clear and plain—if its operation appeared calculated to produce peace and union—then it was right that the people should know it; but the case was greatly altered when the law carried within itself the elements of hostility: when the concord which had so long prevailed arose, not from a knowledge of the state of the law, but from an ignorance of it. It would have been productive of the most unpleasant consequences, if it had been boldly stated, " You, the priest, have a right to bury this man—you may enter the churchyard with bell, book, and candle, and perform the service in the most offensive manner possible." If the priest had the power to exclaim to the Protestant clergyman, " I am doing this by the authority of the government, who have told me what the law is on the subject," it would be the cause of constant feuds. This pernicious knowledge of their rights must end in continual conflicts between the parties; and therefore it was necessary, that the law should not remain in its present situation. Heretofore, the law had not been insisted on—the proceedings of the Catholic clergy had been little interfered with. Had it been otherwise, the Catholics of Ireland would be driven from the tombs of their ancestors. It was not a claim of ambition which they put forward—it was not a political privilege which they demanded. What they contended for was the offspring of those feelings of devotion and piety, which were inherent in the nature of man, which were wholly independent of adventitious circumstances. There was no crime so barbarous, no ignorance so profound, no philosophy so arrogant, as to deny the justice of that feeling which was implanted in the nature of man, and which induced him to look with affectionate regret to the spot where the remains of his ancestry were deposited. It was not the creature of philosophy: it was the voice of that Being, who, when he had doomed us to the grave, inspired our hearts with the confident hope, that our affections and feelings would exist beyond that goal. If, however, the Roman Catholic priest were openly told, that he might perform his ceremonies in the most ostentatious manner, such a proceeding would give alarm, and not unjustifiably, to the Protestant. It was therefore necessary that some alteration should be made in the law; and the question was, which was the best mode of dealing with the subject? There were three modes in which the existing law might be altered. First, it would be possible to give separate burial-grounds to the Roman Catholics and the Protestants; and this idea had, in fact, occurred to some Catholics of influence; but he thought, for his own part, and he was convinced the house would go along with him in the feeling, that, of all remedies for the present evil, no other so objectionable could be found. The allotment of separate burial places would not only, like the giving separate places of education, tend to strengthen the line of demarcation already subsisting between the two religions, and to preclude for ever all hope of that union in heart and political opinion which every sincere lover of Ireland must hope for, whatever he might think as to its immediate probability, but it would go to outrage the very commonest and yet most sacred feelings of humanity. It would have the effect, the house would see, in many cases, of separating families as to their place of burial. A husband could not be buried with his wife, a brother near his brother, a father by the side of his son. It would hardly be necessary to say more upon the impracticability of introducing such an arrangement. The next proposition then, he would suppose to be this—to make the right of interment to the Dissenter in Ireland an absolute right—to have it a stern and unbending mandate upon the Protestant parson, to admit him to burial, and then to restrict the exercise of this absolute right, so as to prevent its being used in a manner offensive to the feelings of the Protestant. This plan certainly did not carry, upon the face of it, so much positive unfitness as the former; but still the house would hardly find it to be a wise one, even if it was practicable, which he doubted: for the great difficulty in the way of such a regulation would be, not the unwillingness of the Protestant parson to give up the absolute right, but his disability to do so. By the act of Uniformity, and the canon law of the country, he was bound to perform the right himself, and could not make over absolute power to another to do it. This, however, was as the law now stood; the new act authorised the parson to give the desired permission; but if it was said, that the spirit and the terms of the act ought to be—not he *may* give permission, but he shall give permission, he (Mr. P.) denied the fitness of that course, because the house should be aware, that, even for the admission of a Protestant to burial, there was nothing upon the parson mandatory. The Protestant himself could not be buried without permission from the parson. True, the parson might not withhold his permission, unless upon some satisfactory reason; but, even if he did withhold it wrongfully, he could not be indicted, or made liable to a civil action for so doing; he could only be censured in the Spiritual Court. Cases might be put, however, in a moment, in which the parson was entitled to refuse. He was not bound to bury a person who died excommunicated; or who had never been baptised; or one who had committed suicide. In fact, he was generally to judge of the time, the convenience, and the fitness of the thing being done; and if the assent was not compulsory in the case of a Protestant, there were additional reasons in abundance why it should not be so in the case of a Roman Catholic. When a dissenting clergyman applied to a Protestant clergyman for permission to bury, the Protestant clergyman was bound to judge, first, whether it were one of the applicant's flock. He must ascertain whether the deceased was really a Roman Catholic or not; because there had been cases, and not very uncommonly, in which that point had been disputed. There were other circumstances to be considered. Who was the applicant, for instance? Was he, as he professed himself, a Protestant clergyman? He might be some mad fanatic Jumper, who had no right to make any such application. All these were matters of which the Protestant clergyman had to judge; and, if an absolute mandate was to be given, they would all be special matters to be provided for. Further specialities would have to be considered—the mode and manner of performing the ceremony, the tapers, and other circumstances of ostentation in the Catholic, which went beyond the modesty of the Protestant church. But the present bill made arrangements which could hardly fail to satisfy all parties; for, as its avowed intention was, to give the Dissenter the benefit of interment according to the rites of his own church, in a Protestant churchyard, the Protestant clergyman could no longer allege the difference of religion as a reason for withholding the permission to bury. He repeated that the present act was one for which the Catholics of Ireland ought to feel most grateful; for it was in fact a charter of toleration, a direct declaration, that every person in Ireland, of whatever religious belief, was entitled to interment according to the rites of his own persuasion. The law, as regarded its effects, was put into the strongest practical shape. The Protestant clergyman was to be applied to. If he thought fit to refuse permission- he was bound to state in writing to the applicant, and immediately, the cause of his refusal; and moreover, forthwith to certify the same cause to his ordinary, or the bishop of his diocese, who was to forward it again without delay, to the lord lieutenant, or chief government of the country. Thus there could be no reason to apprehend refusal on the existing ready ground—that of the difference in the religion in the party making application; and still less would there be any danger of a light or frivolous objection, because it would be known that that objection was at once to go before authority. And further, with regard to the extent of the act, it was virtually mandatory, though not mandatory in terms, for he stated it as a principle of law, and if he was wrong he might be contradicted, that where a public functionary was legally enabled to do certain acts which were for the good of the community, the law which made it lawful for him to do those acts, in fact made it his duty to do them. So that, on the one hand, the act was mandatory, for the clergyman stood bound, in such a case, to do that which it was lawful for him to do; and on the other hand it would be observed, that in the provision for the service to be performed, there was no permission for the burial service generally, but specially for the service of the grave—an important point —because, in the Roman Catholic liturgy, the service of the grave was not the burial servi e, the burial service involving the most pompous display of the rites of the Catholic religion; and the service of the grave being merely a short prayer and psalm, attended with no parade of ceremony whatever. Still the law, no doubt, as it would stand, might by possibility be abused. He did not deny that it might. It was possible, on the one hand, that a Protestant clergyman might, in defiance of consequences, capriciously withhold his permission; and on the other hand, there might cases arise, in which the privilege granted might be taken gross advantage of. But it was not, in his view, the spirit of legislation, to make laws to meet extreme and barely possible cases. He rather preferred, in all arrangements, to leave such cases to be dealt with as they arose; and he had no fear, upon the present question, but that the law would work perfectly well. With regard to the Protestant establishment, he was not surprised that they should feel some alarm as to the new law at first. It was certainly, up to a certain point, the introduction of a new right and power; it was giving the Catholic church a right in the churchyard of the Protestant church: but a great deal of this objection vanished when gentlemen considered, that the law in fact only took away a right which the Protestant clergyman had never exercised. If it was said that the Protestant parson had only abstained from using his right, because the ceremony performed had been performed in the private house of the Catholic, and not openly, as it would be now, in the Protestant churchyard—this might be said, and the case still would be exactly where it was before; for the very avowal conceded a principle just as strong as that he now contended for. The ceremony was performed in the private house? True; but the Protestant clergyman knew that it was performed there. He not only knew it, but he must, of necessity, be taken by his own act, to be cognizant of it; because he could never be supposed to be permitting bodies to be interred without any ceremony of Christian burial. We could not bear that the Protestant parson had been permitting human bodies to be thrown into the ground like so many dogs; he could only stand justified in his forbearing to perform the rites of Christian burial according to his own religion, by the knowledge that those rites, according to another form, had been performed already; so that, in fact, he acknowledged that the performance of certain rites, according to the manner of the Catholic faith, gave a body that title to come into his Protestant churchyard, which, without those rites, it could not have had. The act before the house went, in principle, no further than this. There was nothing new in the effect of what it did, the novelty was only in the form. No rational Protestant parson would complain of being permitted by law to waive that right, which he had been all along accustomed to waive, with the law against him in so doing. In the confidence that his measure would satisfy all parties, he should sit down by moving that the bill be read a second time.

UNLAWFUL SOCIETIES IN IRELAND BILL.

February 11, 1825.

Early in the year 1823, O'Connell proposed to Shiel and a party of friends who were dining with Mr. T. O'Mara at Glancullen, the plan of an association for the management of the Catholic cause. At the aggregate meeting of the Catholics, which took place in April, a resolution of the same design was carried; and on Monday, the 12th of May, the first meeting of the Catholic Association was held at "Dempsey's rooms in Sackville-street." Thenceforward the Association in frequent sitting met at Coyne's, the Catholic bookseller's; and before a month had passed, was in active working order.

From small beginnings it became, in the course of a year, the most formidable popular organization that the world ever witnessed. Its influence ramified into every parish in Ireland. Its capacious sphere found place and work for every member of the Catholic body, the peer, the lawyer, the merchant, the country gentleman, the peasant, and the priest—petitions to be accumulated, rent to be levied, deputations to the throne and to parliament, vigilant administration of justice between Catholic and Protestant, stormy electioneering—and every week the passionate eloquent outbursting in speech and address of that fierce sense of wrong and longing for freedom, which, for a century, had been smouldering in the hearts of the people. Over all, the voice of O'Connell, like some mighty minster bell, is heard through Ireland, and the empire, and the world—through all time too.

Its historian says well, "It guided the people and thus raised itself in raising the people. In the short space of two years, what had long defied the anxious exertions of all preceding bodies was tranquilly accomplished. The 'three hands,' the three classes were found in one, the penal statute was the *force* which clasped them. The entire country formed but one Association."

Emancipation had ceased to be the "open question" of English statesmen. It had become the purpose of a people—a people, which from a mere mob, trodden to the helot level of the law, had become as carefully arrayed, and as animate with the sense of organization as an army. English statesmen felt that their "open question" would soon be wrested as a right, no longer conceded as a grace; and prepared to cover their retreat. It was determined to accompany emancipation with the suppression of the Catholic Association, and the disfranchisement of the Catholic peasantry—the stout-hearted forty-shilling freeholders.

The bill for the first purpose was introduced by Goulburn, under the above heading, and was defended by Plunket in the following speech.

Mr. PLUNKET said, he stood in a situation which required the utmost indulgence of the house. The subject before the house had been so fully discussed in all its parts, that he felt it impossible for him to add to the arguments that had already been adduced in its favour; and he should not have obtruded himself on the house in the course of this debate, if it were not to declare his view of the state of that country to which this question immediately related. That was his object, rather than the hope of throwing any additional light on the subject then before the house. He confessed that he never had risen in that assembly with emotions of greater pain, nor did he ever approach any question with feelings of deeper apprehension than he approached this. It was said, that the measure now proposed was contrary to the popular principles of the constitution; and that it was intended, through a breach of those principles, to wound the cause of the Roman Catholics. The measure had been denounced, by gentlemen whom he highly respected, as one that was likely to be attended with circumstances of the most ruinous nature. These, certainly, were very heavy imputations on the proposition made by his right honourable friend; but he must say, that down to the present moment, they rested on mere assertion, and were unsupported either by argument or proof. Coming, however, from persons of so much sincerity and ability as those to whom he had alluded, he was led almost to doubt the evidence of his senses, and to distrust the proofs which the converse of the proposition laid down by those gentlemen was capable of receiving. He trusted that, upon consideration, it would appear to the house, that the proposed measure did not interfere with any of the popular privileges of this country; he trusted also it would be found that it did not affect the Catholic question; and he confidently trusted that none of those disastrous consequences would flow from it, which some gentlemen seemed to anticipate. The question rested not on ordinary grounds; it rested on the ground of imperious and essential necessity. The safety of the state made the adoption of this measure absolutely necessary. Before he proceeded further—before he touched on incidental points, he would call the attention of the house to the real nature of the question which was proposed for consideration. It had been argued very generally on the opposite side of the house, that this measure attacked, most materially, the privileges of the Catholic body; but he begged leave to say, that it went to attack all illegal and unconstitutional institutions, whether arrayed on behalf of the Roman Catholics or against them. This was not a single measure—it was not a measure hastily taken up: it was adopted in consequence of a communication from the throne, which communication also recommended, that the entire state of Ireland should be taken into consideration in the course of the session. The situation of that country was to be considered, not with reference to any particular point, but with reference to all points; and from those of course it was impossible the Catholic question could be excluded. It was necessary to pursue this course, for the purpose of curing the evil, of which the Catholic Association was only a symptom. He could not, therefore, conceive, let the individual be ever so sincere a friend to Catholic emancipation, how he could object to the proposed measure, accompanied as it was by the declaration contained in the speech from the throne. It was said, and truly said, that, at the moment when the peace of the session was likely to be disturbed by the bringing forward of this measure, Ireland was in a state of peace and tranquillity. And his honourable friend who spoke last, wondered why such a measure, under these circumstances, had been resorted to. He would admit that Ireland was in a state of peace and prosperity. She had participated in the general prosperity of the empire. She had been enabled, by the noble lord at the head of the government, and by the measures which he had matured (measures of the most wise and temperate description), to enjoy the blessings which were the offspring of internal tranquillity. Those measures had been properly administered; and public confidence had, in consequence, been restored. The noble marquis, when sent to Ireland, had found that country in a state nearly bordering on rebellion. He softened down the feelings of exasperation that existed, and the people soon placed confidence in the justice and benignity of his administration. It was a great blessing —it was a most gratifying object—to behold that country now floating on the tide of public confidence and public prosperity. She was lying on the breakers, almost a wreck, when the noble marquis arrived; and if he had not taken the measures which had been so successfully adopted, she never could have floated on that tide of public prosperity.

He could not agree with the honourable and learned member for Winchelsea when he asserted, that the return of peace and tranquillity to Ireland was attributable to the exertions of the Catholic Association. But, even if that position were true, still it formed a reason for adopting the present measure; because, as the honourable member for Galway (Mr. Martin) had very properly said, all argument as to the necessity of this measure was at an end, if once the existence of so formidable a power was admitted. If the Catholic Association could put down those who were illegally inclined, could they not raise them up again, if they thought proper? *" Tollere seu ponere vult freta."* And here he would beg leave to say, that amongst the persons who were most active in effecting this restoration of order and tranquillity, and in convincing the people of the advantages which were derived from an equal administration of the laws, were the Catholic priests of Ireland, not the Catholic Association, who arrogated to themselves all the merit, who wished to run away with all the praise that was due to the nobility, clergy, and gentry of the country. The Roman Catholic clergy had, without any dictation from that body, preached to the people the principles of religion and of peace. He said this in justice to that most useful and most calumniated set of men. Having borne this testimony to the tranquillity and prosperity of Ireland, the question naturally was— " Why, when the state of things is so flattering, do you bring this measure forward?" He would answer, that, although he never remembered a period when greater prosperity prevailed in Ireland, yet he never recollected a time when so great, when so violent a degree of excitation existed in that country; and he knew that much alarm was felt on account of the danger that might arise, if the present system were allowed to go on with a progressive increase of strength. That very considerable alarm existed in the minds of many Protestants, it was impossible to deny. He did not mean to contend that this alarm had not been exaggerated; that it had been very much raised by wicked and interested persons, he readily admitted; but the desperate conduct of this society had tended to verify the justice of the fears and apprehensions that had been conjured up. An honourable member had, in the course of his speech, admitted that in the parts of Ireland in which he had been, he had observed that this excitation was powerfully alive. He further said, that amongst the Roman Catholic population he had observed more excitation and expectation than he ever remembered to have witnessed before; and he asked, whether this was not a reason for immediately granting the Catholic question? He (Mr. Plunket) sincerely wished to grant the claims of the Catholics; but if they could not grant them, were the legislature, therefore, not to make provision for any circumstances of danger which they might have reason to apprehend?

[Hear, hear, from Sir F. Burdett.]

The honourable member for Westminster appeared to notice this proposition. He wished him to do so. If this measure of Catholic emancipation were not granted by the house, was the refusal, he would ask, to be submitted to, or to be resisted? Because the answer to that question involved the justice or the reprobation of the measure now before the house. The fact was, that if the Catholic question was felt to be of that paramount importance which called for instant adoption (and to that point he went), there was no necessity for this institution; but if the measure of Catholic emancipation was not adopted, and if the refusal was to be resisted by the physical force of Ireland, then, he contended, that this was an association which ought to be opposed as well by the friends of the Catholics as by those who were adverse to their claims. Before he proceeded further, he would very shortly remind the house of the nature of this Roman Catholic Association. He did not mean, after the luminous statement of his right honourable friend, and the remarks which he had made in the course of the debate, to give more than an outline of the association; confining himself strictly to those points which he deemed essentially necessary. It appeared that this society was formed on a plan different from those numerous defiances of the law which had existed in Ireland. A number of gentlemen had, it seemed, formed themselves into a club, not merely for the purpose of forwarding the Roman Catholic question, but "for the redress of all grievances, local or general, affecting the people of Ireland." He quoted the words of their own address; and he must say, that those parties undertook, on the moment, as many important subjects as ever engaged the attention of ary body of legislators. They undertook the great question of parliamentary reform—they undertook the repeal of the Union—they undertook the regulation of church-property—they undertook the administration of justice. They intended not merely to consider the administration of justice, in the common acceptance of the term, but they determined on the visitation of every court, from that of the highest authority down to the court of conscience. They did not stop here. They were not content with an interference with the courts; they were resolutely bent on interfering with the adjudication of every cause which affected the Catholics, whom they styled " the people of Ireland." Here was a pretty tolerable range for their exertions. He did not deny, that if a set of gentlemen thought fit to unite for those purposes, it was in their power to do so; but then comes the question as to the means which they employ; and those means I deny to be constitutional. They have associated with them the Catholic clergy—the Catholic nobility—many of the Catholic gentry, and all the surviving delegates of 1791. They have established committees in every district, who keep up an extensive correspondence through the country. This association, consisting originally of a few members, has now increased to 3000. They hold permanent sittings, where they enter upon the discussion of every question connected with the peace and tranquillity of Ireland. This I think is a pretty strong case in favour of the opinion, that their existence is not compatible with the security of the state. With this, however, they were not satisfied. They proceeded to establish a Roman Catholic rent; and in every single parish of the two thousand five hundred parishes into which Ireland is divided, they established twelve Roman Catholic collectors, which, taken together, makes an army at once of 30,000 collectors; unarmed I admit; unarmed in every thing but prayers, entreaties, and influence. Having raised their army of collectors, they brought to their assistance two thousand five hundred priests, the whole ecclesiastical body of that religion; and thus provided, they go about levying contributions on the peasantry. Now, I say that this is a direct violation of the principles of the British constitution. I do not say that it is illegal in the strict sense; for if it was, the Irish government would be able to prosecute, and need not have come here for a remedy; but it is going far enough to say, that parliament is the recognised legislature, and that the association has gone so far as to assume its functions, to justify the position, that they had violated the principles of the constitution.

In proceeding to state my view of the constitutional question, I am aware of the high authorities in whose presence I speak, and of what I owe to them and to myself. But, nevertheless, I will say, that an association assuming to represent the people, and in that capacity to bring about a reform in church and state, is directly contrary to the spirit of the British constitution. Let me not be misunderstood. Do I deny the right of the people, under this free constitution, to meet for the purpose of promoting the redress of grievances in church and state, by discussion and petition? Most certainly not. Do I mean that they have a right to increase their numbers, and to form themselves into clubs and bodies? Certainly not. But I do deny that any portion of the subjects of this realm have a right to give up their suffrages to others—have a right to select persons to speak their sentiments, to debate upon their grievances, and to devise measures for their removal, those persons not being recognised by law. This was the privilege alone of the commons of the United Kingdom; and those who trenched upon that privilege acted against the spirit of the British constitution. I will not assert that there may not be cases where no danger would be likely to arise from such an assumption of authority. But I must treat the case now before the house as it really stands; and I contend, that if there be a body of people in Ireland—I care not whether they amount to 6000 or more—who stand forward as the representatives of six millions of their fellow-subjects, such an assembly is illegal. That is the point which the house has to consider. So far as that assembly is opposed to the authority of the House of Commons, it is, I maintain, guilty of a daring infraction of their rights. It was not (Mr. Plunket said) the amount of " the rent" that he complained of: it was the principle that he complained of. For some purposes, such a contribution might go on fairly : but, in this instance, might not the Association, through the medium of the priests, declare, " We are the persons who represent the Roman Catholics, and we have a right to wield the power of the state." Was this a state of things to be endured? If they did not put it down, would it not, on the part of the legislature, be an abandonment of that duty which they took upon themselves to discharge for the benefit of the country? Could the government answer such a dereliction of duty to the country at large? If the power of the country was seized and wielded by those individuals, who could answer for the consequences? Even if they were the wisest and worthiest men that ever wielded the resources of any state, he would not allow them to have a government of this description. He would allow this species of power to no man, unless he was subjected to that wholesome control, to that salutary check, which was formed for a purpose the most beneficial

—that of preventing those abuses which might exist under any system of government. But, to whom were these individuals accountable? Where was their responsibility? Who was to check them? Who was to stop their progress? By whom were they to be tried —by whom were they to be rebuked—if found acting mischievously? If the executive in the state wielded great powers, the constitution pointed out the mode in which it was to be done. But, in this instance, the society assumed the power both of the legislative and executive bodies, and rejected all the checks by which the latter was hemmed in and surrounded. Let the house look to the nice balance which was preserved in this (for so he must denominate it) our popular constitution. If the House of Commons could assemble whenever it pleased—if it could continue to sit as long as it pleased—why, in a short time the entire authority of the state might be swallowed up in the representative body. In that case, however, there was an efficient check; but these gentlemen were subject to no control. They met when they pleased; and in point of fact they were in the habit of sitting from January to December, and of exercising their powers with as much strictness and severity as any absolute monarch could do. Gentlemen in that house who did not know what was passing in Ireland were not aware of the formidable instrument—more formidable than the sword or the purse—which was exercised by this association in Ireland. Individuals connected with them went into every house and every family; they mixed in all the relations of private life, and afterwards detailed what they had seen or heard with such a degree of freedom, with such a degree of publicity, with so great a want of restraint, that it really required more courage than belonged to ordinary men to express a fair and candid opinion. The numbers of the association were increased, in consequence, from time to time, by a body, he believed, of right unwilling conscripts. That body which, in its outset, was viewed without jealousy, had increased to three thousand, who had actually met.

There was but one other topic, and on that his right honourable friend the secretary for Ireland had already touched, to which he felt it necessary to refer—he meant the interference of the Catholic Association with the administration of public justice. He could not conceive a more deadly instrument of tyranny, or a proceeding more irreconcileable with justice, than this was. The association claimed to represent—whom? To represent six millions of the people of Ireland; and then they claimed the right of denouncing, as an enemy to the people of Ireland, and of bringing to the bar of justice, any individual whom they chose to accuse (no matter on what grounds) of having violated the rights of that people. Was not this a mockery? Could the party so accused come safely to trial, when the grand inquest of the people of Ireland were his accusers? and when those accusers had in their power the application of money levied on the people of Ireland? The consequence must inevitably be, that magistrates and persons in authority must yield to such a power, or else they must array themselves against it. Looking to the consequences, he knew not which was the worst alternative. In either case the country must be a prey to wretchedness. The courts of justice would be converted into so many arenas, where the passions of those who appeared in them would be displayed with the utmost malignity. There party would be opposed to party, and thus would those courts become scenes of factious contention. And, when such was the state of things, the Marquis Wellesley must be content to lie under the heavy reproach, the painful imputation, of not having allowed this institution to die of its own follies! The noble marquis, in accordance with the rest of the government of Ireland, wished to put that association down; and, in his (Mr. P.'s) opinion, the determination was a wise one. Was it, he asked, to be desired, that an institution of this kind should be kept up, merely because it was supposed by some individuals, that it was impossible to carry the measure of emancipation by any other mode? Of what materials did gentlemen think the Protestants of Ireland were composed, if they imagined that the Protestant body would not establish a counter-association? Would they not seek the means of defending themselves? He did not believe that amongst the Catholics there was any present intention of having recourse to force. He believed they were peaceable in their intention, but he would say they were not their own masters. They must obey the command and behests of those under whom they had placed themselves. Was it the intent of those leaders to adopt violent measures? He did not say it was; but he would say that even those leaders were not their own masters. If they got the dregs of the population under their command, and if that population became irritated, they might rest assured, however good their intentions might be, that desperate men would take the lead of them, and produce a catastrophe which they did not now contemplate. They would be forced down that precipice where they now meant to stop, as surely as a man, placed on the brink of a steep rock, and pressed from behind by a million of persons, must give way to the power which pushed him onwards. It was, therefore, no answer to his argument to say that the intentions of the association were now honest and peaceable.

He would now turn to another part of the subject. The convention act, notwithstanding all the reprobation that had been bestowed upon it, was a very useful act. It was framed by one of the ablest lawyers of the day—the late Lord Kilwarden, at that time Mr. Wolfe. He was an honest man, a sound lawyer, and an ardent lover of the constitution. At the very period of his death, he proved his attachment to the constitution. He expressed a wish that no man should be brought to trial, or punished for his murder, except in accordance with the established and known law of the land. The convention act provided for the case of election and actual delegation. It did not, however, touch the Catholic Association, where no election or delegation actually took place. But did it not come to the same thing, if an individual assumed to act on behalf of a great body, and called meetings in every county throughout the country? Was not the principle precisely the same? Here were persons who proposed to act in the name and on the behalf of the people. Surely those against whom the convention act was directed did no more. It was not too much to say—as he had said in the outset—that they were called on to legislate in the spirit of the constitution. The *salus populi*, which was truly the *suprema lex*, demanded that they should put an end to this institution.

But gentlemen said, "although the mischief is great, you ought not to proceed, because there is another remedy—that is the granting of Catholic emancipation." He would state his opinion once for all on this subject. He considered Catholic emancipation, and he had always done so, as that measure, without which all other measures to render Ireland contented and tranquil must be ineffectual. He looked upon the emancipation of the Roman Catholics as a claim of right and justice. It would baffle human ingenuity to furnish any good argument against it. On public grounds of justice emancipation ought to be granted; and he thought it was utterly impossible much longer to delay it. Early in life he had set out with that impression, and he was daily more and more convinced of the accuracy of his opinion. He felt the policy as well as the urgency of granting it. These were his sentiments. They were such as he had always expressed, and which he never would abandon. But, when this alternative was proposed to the house instead of the measure now before them, the question was, "Can we have it?" He thought not. But those who opposed the proposition now under discussion, turned round and said, "Because we cannot have that measure, do not put down the mischief, the existence of which we admit." This appeared to him to be bad reasoning. The question, then arose. "By whose fault was it that we could not have it?" Let that question be examined, and let those by whose fault it arose give the answer; but, whether or not they could name those with whom the fault lay, if fault did exist, still there were circumstances which obliged them to resort to the present measure, as the only one which could immediately give an effectual check to a great growing evil. He would repeat, if there were persons who had the power to do away with the necessity for the present proceeding, and neglected the means, they were answerable for the consequences.

He would now, with the leave of the house, endeavour to examine that question and to meet it fairly, and would be ready to take his own share of responsibility on the occasion. Before he proceeded, he entreated of honourable gentlemen on the opposite side, that if in anything which he might feel it necessary to say for his own justification, he should appear even for a moment to bear hard upon them, they would not consider it as an intentional attack. He assured them he had no such intention. Nothing was further removed from his wish than any inclination to attack any members for the line of conduct they might have thought proper to adopt; but it was necessary that he should state all that bore fully upon the point. He only wished that, while he thus placed his own conduct under examination, and put himself upon his trial, he might be allowed to file a cross-bill, and put those who accused him on their trial along with him. The right honourable and learned gentleman then alluded to his former conduct with respect to the Catholic question and to ministers, in nearly the following words:—Sir, in the year 1813, I was, as I trust I ever have been, a zealous friend of the Catholic question. In that year the question was introduced by my lamented friend Mr. Grattan, to whom the Catholics had already owed so much. My friend, on that occasion, was pleased to put a value on my services to which they were not entitled; but undoubtedly he could not overrate the zeal which dictated them. Sir, at that time, I argued the question on its plain and firm grounds—those on which it had formerly been so ably urged by others. The speech which I then delivered was afterwards published. Honourable members may be familiar with parts of it, for they have, from time to time, been quoted here by several gentlemen. A part of it was last night read by the honourable and learned member for Lincoln (Mr. J. Williams), and a part on a former occasion by the honourable member for Westminster (Sir F. Burdett). I do not mention this as having any objection to it; I would not even object to the whole being entered among the standing orders of the house, to be read by gentlemen as often as it answered any purpose. In that speech, I said, that it was to be lamented that the cabinet were so divided upon the question of Catholic emancipation. I added, that if after having given the subject their most mature consideration, they could not, as a body, make up their minds upon it in one way or another, they were answerable to the public for the consequences of leaving such a measure as a constant source of irritation. If the honourable baronet (Sir F. Burdett) does not think that this is the meaning of what I said—if I added anything more, that might seem to militate stronger against my subsequent conduct and my present opinion, let him point it out, and I assure him I will read it to the house immediately. I admit, with him, that the fair import of my observations on that part of the subject was, that as a friend to Catholic emancipation, I did not think I could, with honour, join any administration so divided upon it as the then cabinet was. This, sir, is, I think, a full and fair admission of what were my sentiments in the year 1813. Now, sir, I as frankly and distinctly declare, that I have since changed that opinion. I once did think that I could not with honour join an administration, divided as were the cabinet of that day on the question of emancipation. I have now altered that opinion. This declaration cannot be considered an evasion of the charge brought against me. It does not extenuate it, when I say that once I firmly held a strong opinion, which I have since changed and have acted on that change. But here I admit the question arises—Am I justified in having made that change? Have any circumstances occurred since then, which called for that change on my part? I think I shall satisfy the house that there have; and, in defending myself on the ground of those circumstances, I cannot avoid throwing some blame on the conduct of honourable members opposite. In my observations, in 1813, I stated, that I did not think the support given to the question by some members of the cabinet was much to be depended upon.

Mr. Plunket here turned round towards Mr. Canning who sat near him, and said:—

I can assure my right honourable friend, that my opinions in this respect had never any reference to him, whose sincere support of the measure could never be doubted for an instant. My doubts had reference to the conduct of a noble friend, now no more (Lord Londonderry); and I confess I did at that time believe that in the support which he gave to the Catholic question, he was not so sincere as I afterwards found him. My noble friend, on that occasion, stated that I myself was inconsistent in expressing my unwillingness to act with a cabinet divided on the question of emancipation, as I had before acted with a ministry who were not all united on that question—I allude to that which existed when the Duke of Bedford was lord lieutenant of Ireland. In the Grenville administration, it was urged by the noble lord, that there were some who were decidedly opposed to the Catholic question. Lord Sidmouth was one, and Lord Ellenborough another. I own I did not think, at the time this argument was urged, that it was sufficiently conclusive to alter the opinion which I had formed. I did believe that the administration of 1813 were unfriendly to the claims of the Catholics; and I doubted, at that time, the sincerity of some members of it, who appeared to be favourable to those claims; but I did think that an administration altogether disposed to the concession of those claims might be formed out of that side of the house with which I had then the honour to act. Sir, in making this declaration of my former sentiments, and of the change which has since taken place in them, I beg to be understood as doing so, solely in justice to my own character and motives. I do not consider that I am bound to give an explanation of my conduct to any man or particular set of men in this house. There was not one of the gentlemen with whom I had formerly the honour to act, by the wisdom of whose counsels I would in all matters be guided, except Lord Grenville. With respect to all the other members of that administration, I might have departed from them at any moment, without incurring the risk of being upbraided as having given up a party to whom I stood pledged.

But to return to the progress of the Catholic claims. The measure founded upon those claims continued to make its way. Through the zeal and activity of Lord Castlereagh, it obtained an extent of legislative support which, while it left me no doubt of its ultimate success, also removed every suspicion that I had entertained of the sincerity of that noble lord in its support. It was at that time argued with reference to the objections supposed to exist on the part of the people of England, but not with reference to what were, or what were not, the opinions of any boards or committees which had been constituted to support it. As the discussion of the measure proceeded, the number of its advocates increased, and before the death of Mr. Grattan it had already gained very considerably on the public attention. After the lamented decease of my valued friend, I had the honour of introducing the measure. It was warmly supported by some of his majesty's ministers, and though opposed, conscientiously, no doubt, by others, it passed this house, and was carried to the Lords, and there, after a warm discussion, it was rejected, only by a very inconsiderable majority. Now, sir, when I saw those things take place, had I not a right to believe that the question could be carried by a divided administration? I had seen it pass this house, and I saw it accidentally negatived by a small majority in the other? Was not this one fair ground for the alteration of the opinion I had formed in 1813?

But, I had other reasons for the change of that opinion. The gentlemen who sit on the opposite side of the house will do me the justice to believe, that, whether as a body, or individually, I entertained and do entertain the highest respect for them. I respect the manly manner in which they put forward their objections to what they conscientiously believe to be wrong on this side. I do not for a moment assert that because I may differ from them, they must be wrong and I right; but, whichever was right, it must be remembered, that without ceasing to sit on their side of the house, and joining them where I could, I had frequent occasions to dissent from their opinions. They no doubt adopted the course which they honestly believed to be best. I claim the same construction of my conduct in that which I pursued. In that which I looked upon as the best, I had daily occasions to differ from them. On the question of the continuance of the war—a question the most important in its nature—I differed from them. On the question which arose out of the disturbances in 1819, I felt obliged to take my stand; and, on public grounds, I differed wholly from the view which they took of the situation of the country. On the question of parliamentary reform, I also differed from them. In short, upon almost all the cardinal points connected with the general administration of public affairs, I found that our opinions were wholly different. But, it was not I alone who differed from them in their views on many important questions; I found the public also differed from them on many most material points; and that, not possessing the confidence of the public on so many questions, they did not contain within their body the materials out of which a cabinet could be formed with any prospect of carrying the question of Catholic emancipation. When I thus found, that on the one side there were a set of men, who, though not altogether agreed on the subject, could carry that question—when I found on the other a party, who, though agreed upon that point, did not possess sufficient influence to carry it—and when I knew that on many very leading questions of great importance I was conscientiously opposed to that party, to which I had never stood pledged, where, I ask, was my inconsistency in taking office, in obedience to the gracious commands of my sovereign? I have thus stated the reasons which induced me to take office, and to change the opinion I had expressed in 1813. I am not ashamed of those reasons, or unwilling that my conduct should be judged by them, either in this house or before the public. And though I think those reasons a sufficient justification of the course I have pursued, yet, if there should still exist any one who, directly or by implication, should impute to me that I have accepted office merely for the sake of place or of profit, and without any regard to political consistency, I will appeal to the history of my life, and to the sacrifices I have made for that consistency, for a proof of the fallacy of the imputation. Let me but be judged by the facts connected with my whole public conduct, and such imputations will fall as unfounded calumnies.

It was stated, sir, in the first discussion of this session, by the honourable and learned member for Winchelsea, that the influence of the Catholic Association originated from a feeling, on the part of the Catholics, that they were deserted by their old friends. If this was intended as an allusion to any supposed conduct of mine, or to any supposed irritation on the part of the Catholics at that conduct, I must say that the honourable and learned gentleman's statement is not borne out by the fact. I have on four occasions, since I accepted office, received the public thanks of the Catholics, assembled in aggregate and other public meetings, for my services in their cause, and those thanks accompanied with expressions of confidence in my continuance of those services. I here hold in my hand these published resolutions to that effect, but I will not read them. I should rather that were done by any other than myself. At a time when the Catholic petition was sent to me to be presented, I refused to undertake it, unless it were left to myself to use my own discretion as to the time when I should present it, and whether I should bring the question forward in that session or not. Those terms were conceded, and the confidence of the Roman Catholics in my exertions on their behalf remained unabated. That confidence was not withdrawn, even when I refused to present the petition as from the association. In November last, when it was resolved that the Catholic petition should be confided to the care of the honourable baronet opposite (Sir Francis Burdett), Mr. Wolfe, a gentleman of whom it is but justice to say, that a man of greater merit or more promising talent did not exist in that association—I say, that in November last, on the motion of Mr. Wolfe, it was resolved, that the Catholics though they had confided the petition to another, still relied confidently upon the continuance of my usual support of the measure. I do not think they could have placed their cause in more efficient hands than those of the honourable baronet; and I beg to assure him, that when he brings the question forward, he shall have my unaltered support. When he introduces the measure to the house, he may feel assured that I shall not get up and walk out, leaving him in the unpleasant situation in which I was placed on a former occasion. When I say this, I am far from intending to cast any imputation upon the motives of the honourable baronet on that occasion. He did that which he thought best. I do not blame him; for I do not believe that either in or out of parliament there exists a more just, consistent, and honourable character, whether viewed in the various relations of public or private life. I am aware that the honourable baronet needs not any praise of mine, but justice compels me to say thus much.

I beg pardon for having occupied so much of the attention of the house in speaking of matters personal to myself; but what I have stated was, I submit, called for by the fact of my being mentioned, day after day, as one cause of the existence of this association, as if that could have proceeded from my alteration of an opinion which I expressed twelve or thirteen years ago. The right honourable and learned gentleman then adverted to an extract from his speech in 1813, which had been read yesterday by the honourable and learned member for Lincoln, as a sort of evidence of another act of inconsistency on his part. He would now repeat the passage which the honourable and learned gentleman had quoted, and show the very unfair advantage which had been taken, by separating two passages which followed close one upon the other in the speech. The passage was—" Sir, it appears to me most unfair to visit on the Roman Catholics the opinions and the conduct of such public assemblies as profess to act for them; if they labour under a real and a continuing grievance, and one which justifies on their part a continued claim, they must act through the medium of popular assemblies, and must of course be exposed to all the inconveniences which attend discussion in such assemblies. In all such places, we know that unbounded applause attends the man who occupies the extreme positions of opinion, and that the extravagance of his expression of such opinion will not be calculated to diminish it. That there may be many individuals anxious to promote their own consequence, at the expense of the party whose interests they profess to advocate, is an evil inseparable from such a state of things; and amongst those who sincerely wish to promote the interests of the cause, much may fairly be attributed to the heat naturally generated by long-continued opposition; much to the effects of disappointed hope; much to the resentment excited and justified by insolent and virulent opposition."

The arguments which he (Mr. P.) then used were by no means inconsistent with those he now held. He then condemned such associations; so he did at present; but he thought now as then, that the conduct of a few individuals ought not to be visited upon the whole body. If this was the whole of what he had then said on the subject, it would not prove inconsistency, but would show that he was consistent on both occasions; but, as he had made another remark at that time which would more fully explain his present meaning, he thought it a want of candour in the honourable and learned gentleman not to have made any reference to that part of the speech. When he attacked a man for the inconsistency of his present opinions with those which he had delivered thirteen years ago, he ought, in common justice, to have stated what those opinions were. If he had only read the paragraph of his speech immediately preceding that which he quoted, it would have put his present and former sentiments on this point in their proper light, and shown that in both he was perfectly consistent. The passage omitted by the honourable and learned gentleman was this : " Sir, the conduct of the Roman Catholics of Ireland has been resorted to as an argument for abandoning the pledge of the last session. Sir, I am not an advocate for their intemperance ; I am free to say that there have been some proceedings on the part of the public bodies who affect to act for them, altogether unjustifiable. Their attempts to dictate to the entire body how they are to act on each particular political occurrence—their presuming to hold an inquisition on the conduct of individuals in the exercise of their elective franchise, and putting them under the ban of their displeasure, because they vote for their private friends, and abide by their plighted engagements—all this is a degree of inquisitorial authority, unexampled and insufferable ; and this by persons professing themselves the advocates of unbounded freedom and unlimited toleration, at the moment when they are extending their unparleying tyranny into the domestic arrangements of every Catholic family in the country." One would have thought, in reading this passage, that by a happy anticipation he was foreseeing at that period that which was happening at the present. The passage proceeded thus : " Sir, I am equally disgusted with the tone of unqualified demand, and haughty rejection of all condition or accommodation so confidently announced by them; nor can I palliate the intemperance of many of their public speeches, nor the exaggeration and violence of some of their printed publications. To this tone I never wish to see the legislature yield ; but as this indecent clamour is not to compel them to yield what is unreasonable, I trust it will not influence them to withhold what is just." Now, he thought that if he had been endeavouring, without the appearance of egotism, to procure some gentleman to introduce his former conduct as compared with his present, he could not have selected any person who could have been more effectual in showing his consistency than the honourable and learned gentleman on this occasion.

One word more as to the effect of the association. It was, he thought, calculated to check the disposition of the people of this country, which he perceived was daily inclining them in favour of the Catholic claims. He differed from his right honourable friend (Mr. Peel) on this point, and thought that the public feeling on this point was not so confined as his right honourable friend had supposed. The people of England were beginning to see the question in its proper light. They perceived that the game of governing by division would no longer succeed, but that to have any hope of success in the mode of treating that country, a system of conciliation must be adopted. They began to be aware, that if a great deal was not done to blight the gifts which Providence had bestowed upon that country, Ireland would not hang as a burthen on, but become one of the most fertile sources of, British prosperity. The idea of the separation of the two countries was idle and absurd. It was possible, that in the lapse of ages England might share the fate of other great empires. Whenever she did fall, Ireland would most certainly fall with her; but separate they never could be. To hold out the idea of their separation as a threat to this country was puerile nonsense. In the event of a war England might rely upon Ireland. It was but an act of justice to his countrymen to say, that they would be ever found foremost amongst the defenders of the empire. But foreign nations not having the same means of knowing the real state of that country, but judging from slight appearances, might be led to form opinions with respect to its disposition towards England, as might involve us in a foreign war. So that to the people of England the state of the sister kingdom was of great importance, inasmuch as it might be the means of inducing other nations to disturb our peace.

He would not trespass longer on the attention of the house. It was almost unnecessary to add, that amongst the mischiefs which the association was calculated to produce, that was not the least which removed the discussion of the Catholic question from the ground of sound argument and good policy, on which they were invulnerable, and substituted an idle display of physical force, as if physical force were intended to be arrayed against them. As a sincere and zealous friend of the Catholics, he would advise them to leave off the high tone which they had so long used. Their cause had great merits, and needed not such adventitious aids. With respect to the effect of the proposed measure, he was decidedly of opinion that it would be most favourably received by the best-informed and most respectable of the Irish nation. He did believe that people in that country were beginning to see the advantage which would result to them, from taking their cause out of such hands. But it was said that the association spoke the sentiments of the Irish people. So they did—so did he (Mr. P.), and so would every man who advocated the cause of emancipation. But, beyond that, the association did not represent the feelings of the country; and he most positively denied that the people of Ireland would think of resenting the abolition of that association. The clergy and the country gentlemen were beginning to get tired of seeing their just influence with the people taken from them by this body; and must naturally be favourable to any measure by which it would be restored. Even the members of the association itself would acquiesce quietly in the law which would put an end to their power. Very many of them were sensible and clever men, and must be aware of the inutility of opposition to the will of the legislature. The gentleman who was the most prominent member of that body—Mr. O'Connell—would himself be of this opinion. Mr. O'Connell was a man of great talent and acquirements. He filled the highest rank at the bar which the laws permitted a gentleman of his religion to occupy; and was deservedly considered as a man of eminence in his profession. He only knew him professionally; but he had reason to believe him to be most amiable in all the relations of private life. In his political sentiments, he looked upon him as wild and extravagant; but, nevertheless, he was persuaded that if this bill passed, neither he, nor Lord Fingall, nor Lord Gormanstown, nor any other gentleman connected with the association, would ever descend to any pettyfogging tricks to evade its operation. He believed that the great body of the people of the country would gladly seize the passing of the proposed bill as a favourable opportunity for getting rid of the influence of that body.

<small>The debate was one of the ablest that occurred upon the Catholic question, and was particularly distinguished by a masterly narrative statement of Canning as to his own policy, and that of various cabinets in which he had acted, towards the Catholics. Brougham, who followed him, contrasted the language of Plunket's Union speeches with the alleged violent debates of the association—a home thrust which Plunket did not attempt to parry. Leave was given to introduce the bill by a majority of 155, and it passed in the course of the month, unaccompanied, however, by any measures of relief, at which great indignation was felt in Ireland, until O'Connell "drove a coach and four" through the act, and</small>

formed the new Catholic Association " for purposes of public and private charity, and such other purposes as are not prohibited by the statute." When the attorney-general returned to Ireland, he found the association there before him, quite impregnable to indictment and if possible more powerful than before.

THE CATHOLIC CLAIMS.
February 28, 1825.

ON the day after the third reading of the Unlawful Societies Bill, Sir F. Burdett, by authority of the Association, presented the Catholic petition. The government divided in the debate—Canning for, Peel against the motion—the English solicitor-general also against, after whom the Irish attorney-general. The imperfect report of this great speech is much to be regretted.

MR. PLUNKET said, that after the repeated discussions, year after year, which this question had undergone—after the recent protracted debates upon Irish affairs—and more particularly after it had fallen so often to himself individually to claim the indulgence of the house upon this very subject, he should have been strongly disposed, on the present occasion, to have repeated his opinion by a silent vote. There were, however, peculiar circumstances which compelled him, though reluctantly, not to allow this debate to pass without giving the reasons which still governed his vote. In doing so, he still felt that it would be bad taste to increase his trespass on their kindness by taking a wide range of observation on this occasion, or to do more than to take a few leading points, and confine himself strictly to their necessary consideration. He thought himself peculiarly called upon to deliver his sentiments, as the management of the question had been transferred from himself to the honourable baronet opposite. He trusted that no man would suppose he harboured a motive so mean or unworthy, as to suffer his sentiments to be warped by the change of hands into which the petition of the Catholics had passed. He was ready to bear testimony to the judicious and discreet manner in which the honourable baronet had introduced the motion—to the temper, the perspicuity, the reason, and the justice, with which he had recommended it to their consideration; and he should endeavour to imitate the conciliatory tone, of which the honourable baronet had set so eminent an example, and in arguing this question to keep clear of all topics of irritation on either side. As to the particular time when they were called upon to discuss the Catholic claims, he did not mean to express what would have been his opinion had he been consulted on that point; he should have found it, what he had no doubt the honourable baronet had done, a point of much embarrassment, not as relating to his own opinions, but to those of others, entitled to some degree of deference. For himself, he had long since made up his mind on this question. With deep and intense feelings for the maintenance of the best rights of the empire, his decided and unalterable conviction was, that this measure could not be too speedily carried. No time was too early for its adoption; none could arrive when it should not have his most zealous support. With respect to what had fallen from his honourable and learned friend, the solicitor-general, why did he recur to the time of discussing the question—why did he call upon those who differed from him to consider that part of the consideration? He must ask his honourable and learned friend, before he assented to go into that argument with him, at what time he would be prepared to give his consent to such a motion as this? He feared that his honourable and learned friend had made up his mind to a perpetual opinion upon this question, which would render, so far as he was concerned, any argument as to the expediency of time a useless waste of words. Were the time one of perfect calmness and tranquillity, doubtless his honourable and learned friend would say, " Why agitate the topic now—*non quieta movere*—nobody calls for such a discussion." Were the time one of trouble and difficulty, then the expression would be the other way—" This is no time for embarking in such matters; every thing is too unsettled." So that in calm or in storm, there would be found no time that was not quite inopportune, in his honourable and learned friend's view of the matter. He entirely agreed in the observation of the honourable and eloquent member for Yorkshire, that there was a peculiar grace and fitness in the present time, for the concession of these claims to the Catholics. Some of the friends of that body had been induced, by what they felt to be a most painful necessity, to enact a measure of restriction against certain parts of that body. It was, therefore, just the time to show the Catholics generally, that, notwithstanding what he alluded to, parliament was ready to consider the justice of their claims. He had not the same means of judging as other gentlemen had, what were the sentiments of the people of England upon the subject; but he had of late spoken with men of various habits of thinking respecting it, and not one had he found who was prepared to say that this question was never to be carried. He had others to contend against, and they were the most formidable opponents of the measure, because they met it boldly upon its own merits, and disdained the paltry trick of appealing to the passions or prejudices of any classes of the people; who declared, that if they thought the accomplishment of such a motion as this would effect the tranquillity of Ireland, they would at once yield. These candid and able opponents were among the best friends of the Established church, and when he heard that declaration from their lips, must he not believe that, in the measure which he advocated, there was nothing—there could be nothing—calculated to endanger the stability of the church of Ireland? He solemnly assured the house, that, though this measure was as dear to him as it could be to any man, if he thought it could risk in any degree the security of the church of Ireland, instead of being its advocate, he should be found among the foremost ranks of its warmest opponents. He supported the question, because of its perfect reconcileableness with the stability of the Protestant church; and he supported it further, because he thought the passing of this bill would be found a measure eminently calculated to support that church.

Some allusion had been made to former bills, and, among the rest, to one of his own, upon this subject. To show how clearly on all these occasions the security of the Established church was provided for, he would beg leave to read a paragraph from his own bill of 1821, which was copied from the preceding bill of Mr. Grattan. It was as follows: " And whereas the Protestant Episcopal Church of England and Ireland, and the doctrine, discipline, and government thereof, and likewise the Protestant Presbyterian Church of Scotland, and the doctrine, discipline, and government thereof, are, as between Great Britain and Scotland, severally and respectively, permanently and inviolably in these realms." These were the recitements of the two bills. How, then, could it be said, that no adequate provision had been made for the security of the Established church? His honourable and learned friend had promised to argue this question upon its constitutional bearings; but he had listened in vain for the promised argument. He had heard, indeed, from him a good deal about the Catholic Association; a good deal about the avowed intentions of the Catholic clergy; but nothing, or nearly nothing, of the constitutional grounds on which he meant to resist the question. The claim of the Roman Catholics was a claim to be admitted members of a free representative government—to be admitted to institutions, the advantages of which belonged equally to every subject of that government. He did not say that the right would admit of no exception or control. There was nothing in the social fabric concerning which he would venture to make that assertion. Even the enjoyment of natural rights must be qualified, in a state of society, with conditions. Still more must this be connected with the artificial rights given by the mere existence of society: but these conditions ought only to be imposed in the degree which would be the most likely to protect and preserve the rights and privileges of all. Whether the rights enjoyed by individuals were of the character of natural or of chartered rights, they were liable to be withheld on the ground of general expediency. But, then, the expediency must be clearly and unquestionably made out; and this was a maxim of the constitution, which went no less, though upon more circumspection and discrimination, to affect the most obvious rights of individuals. He directed the attention of the house to the circumstances under which our ancestors had thought it necessary to limit those rights, in a very peculiar manner, with respect to Roman Catholics. At the Reformation, it was found necessary to deal with those rights which were fully permitted before that period. The main object, then, was to protect the rights of the throne against the claims of a foreign power, and against the disaffection of those subjects who might reserve their allegiance for that foreign power, to the detriment of the throne, and of the state in general. This being the object, how did they proceed? They guarded, in the first place, against the evils existing. There were the claims of the Pope to interfere with the interest, not simply of the Roman Catholic religion, which then was the established religion of the state, but he claimed also the right of disposing of benefices, of naming the clergy, of deposing the monarch, and of absolving the people from their allegiance. The legislature accordingly provided—first, for the absolute and unconditional integrity and inviolability of the church; further, for the spiritual prerogative of the crown, forbidding at the same time the exercise of any other than the established religion. What were the mischiefs dreaded, and what the provisions of the legislature? To prevent the claims of the Pope, or any other foreign power, to interfere with the church. Did they hear of any claim to that interference, or to the right of deposing kings, or absolving their subjects from their allegiance? Was that believed or asserted by any man in either kingdom? Dangers there were still; but of a different kind. Those enactments were, therefore, gradually done away. The law forbidding the exercise of any other religion was done away by the repeal of the act against recusancy. The only remaining one which could be at all supposed to contain that spirit, was the act of uniformity; which could not be at all affected by the proposed measure. Thus far did parliament go, down to the time of the Reformation. The wisdom of our ancestors watched the progress of time, and took their measures accordingly. In the reign of Charles the Second they observed a new danger—a monarch careless about religion, or secretly affected to an unconstitutional one, who was to be followed by a Popish successor. Here their providence was as remarkable as before. They provided a remedy, not adapted entirely to meet the evil, but the only one they could obtain; which was to require certain oaths to be taken by those who were ready to take seats in parliament. That was found insufficient on the accession of James II., who openly maintained the Roman Catholic religion against the constitution and the rights of his people. The legislature finding this resource fail, then prudently shifted their ground, and had recourse to a measure at once wise, bold, and salutary. They drove the monarch from the throne, for violating the constitution, and they resolved that the sovereign power should be held inviolable and unalterable in Protestant hands. Did he deny that the throne must be Protestant? Was he doing anything to weaken its Protestant supremacy? No such thing. Was there any mode or device to make that supremacy surer, which the genius of any man could suggest? He was ready to incorporate it with the proposed bill, or to have it introduced as a separate, yet concomitant measure. What were the dangers which afterwards threatened the establishment? The claims of an exiled family driven from the throne, and the plots and agitations of a disaffected party retained in its interests. He admitted, freely, that the Roman Catholics of that period were suspected justly. What was the course taken by parliament? All the former measures against the Papists were continued. They were held to be not good subjects, and were to be trusted neither with honour nor power in the state. They were coerced in their persons and property—they were deprived of their civil rights—they became sunk and degraded into that wretched state, from which they were relieved by the benignity of the last reign. This was a natural course of reasoning, though he did not conceive it to be a very wise one; but it showed that our ancestors adapted their remedies to the evils then existing, and pressing upon their apprehensions.

In 1791, a new danger and an entirely new difficulty presented themselves. The Roman Catholics had proved themselves truly submissive—they had been uniform in their peaceable conduct. Though rebellion had twice raged in Scotland, no movement was made in Ireland in favour of the exiled family. It had been found that the Catholics, so sunk and degraded, were ineffectual to the protection of the government—that by the depression and privations imposed upon them, the heart's blood of the state was impoverished. The landlord found that the lands could not be sufficiently cultivated. The valuable energies of labour were everywhere paralysed. If the annals of that period were to be properly read and considered, the late king would be for ever illustrious in history, entitled as he was to the especial gratitude of every Roman Catholic in Ireland. That system of beneficence which he introduced had been now in practice for the space of forty years. It had raised the Roman Catholics of Ireland to a state of affluence, comfort, and respectability. It had given them a perfect equality of civil rights. It had caused them to participate in the advantages of the institutions. What was the danger which they had now to dread? Not the Pope—not the claims of foreign potentates—not the assumption of a power to dissolve the allegiance of the people—not the interests of an exiled family. The Roman Catholics had perfected the proofs of their obedience, and had been admitted to their civil rights, as good subjects who were entitled to everything which they could reasonably claim. The danger now to be apprehended was perfectly new, though not inferior, he admitted, to that of a dispute concerning the supremacy or the succession to the crown. Better measures had prevailed—the state had acquired sounder health—a current of wholesome blood was felt—feelings of conciliation had been manifested—the Roman Catholic subjects, though not directly raised to power in the state, had acquired possession of the means of danger, and were on a par with themselves. The honourable member for Louth had spoken alarmingly of the six, or five, or four millions of persons in the communion of the Roman Catholic church. Now, what we feared was, to see four millions—taking them at the lowest—of subjects, having wealth, power, and respectability on their side, and awakened to a full sense of their condition, coming up, year after year, to claim the rights and privileges enjoyed by their fellow-subjects, and retiring dejected and disappointed. That was the danger which the house had to cope with. Yet the honourable member for Louth would persist in telling them that they were not to look at the dangers of their own times, but to go back to the Reformation, to the reign of James II., and to the Revolution. He would say that the present danger was the greatest, perhaps the only one for them to consider.

The other argument proves a want of acquaintance with human nature; it bespeaks our ignorant use and application of the manual of history. Time, as has been said by one of the clearest observers of his effects, is the greatest innovator of all. While man may sleep or stop in his career, the course of time is rapidly changing the aspect of all human affairs. All that a wise government can do is to keep as close as possible, to the wings of Time, to watch his progress, and accommodate their motion to his flight. Arrest his course you cannot; but you may vary the forms and aspects of your institutions, so as to reflect his varying aspects and forms. If this be not the spirit which animates you, philosophy must be impertinent, and history no better than an old almanack. The riches of knowledge would serve no better than the false money of a swindler, put upon us at a value which once circulated, but had long since ceased. Prudence and experience would be no better for protection than dotage and error. Did he admit that the danger here was serious? He did not therefore inculcate dread. If the Catholics were to come down to the bar to claim their rights with clamour and shouts, he would laugh at them. Should they use threats and defiances, he would despise them. Parliament could subdue any force raised on their side. But if they merely claimed the rights of free constitution, he had no armour to oppose to them. He had no mode of dealing with them, but to open the arms of friendship—to admit them, as allies, as equals, to share the benefits and join with him in the defence of the constitution; be it against foreign or domestic enemies; be it in peace, or be it in war.

They were told that there was a bar—that the principles of the constitution were opposed to the admission of the Roman Catholics. He had read with eagerness—he had carried on his researches with deep anxiety—he had endeavoured hard to find out where that principle could be discovered, and he solemnly declared that he could not discover it. Referring to the distinction which had been taken between civil and political rights, was the fact so, that the constitution did not admit any to political power, however completely in the possession of their civil rights, unless they subscribed the doctrines of the Established church? Did not every day's experience disprove that assumption? Was not the honourable member for Norwich (Mr. W. Smith), whom they listened to day after day with satisfaction, an example of the contrary? Where was the alarm for the disjunction of the interests of church and state? Had there not been a lord chancellor of England who was a Dissenter? A man who refused to subscribe the doctrines of the church of England had, in his official capacity, issued writs of summons to the peers of Great Britain, and appended the great seal to them. He alluded to the late Lord Rosslyn. Were honourable members who contend for this ignorant of what had been doing in Ireland? The test laws had been there repealed for fifty years, and the dissenting influence had been on the decline ever since. When that repeal was talked of there was great alarm. Dean Swift, with all his wit and talents, felt and spoke of it with horror and desperation, and prognosticated from it the immediate downfall of the state. For forty years past it had not been heard of, and was almost forgotten by the house; the Dissenters had ever since declined. Had the Roman Catholic influence declined in the same period? The former had been ever since withering under the hand of liberty; the latter had been fostered and cherished by severity.

But, it was said, the Roman Catholics might have their civil rights, they must not, however, expect political power; that the constitution prohibited. Was there nothing of political power in what they possessed? They had the right of electing members to serve in parliament. Was that no exercise of political power? They acted as magistrates. Was that no exercise of political power? They served as jurors. Was not that exercising political power? This country had liberally imparted education to them. Did not that put the means of political power within their reach? Where was this line of distinction between civil and political power marked in the constitution? The warmth of discussion apart, he denounced the doctrine as inconsistent with the principles of our free constitution, and only fitted for the meridian of a despotic government. He had once endeavoured to define civil liberty to the house; he had used the description which he found in the books—"Civil liberty consists in doing all that which the law allows a man to do." But he went beyond that. There is a civil liberty, the enjoyment of which is given by the laws themselves. Once admit men to enjoy property, personal rights, and their usual consequences, and on what pretence could they be excluded from the institutions by which the whole of those possessions must be guarded?

It was asked, what have the Roman Catholics to complain of? they are only excluded from the parliament, the bench, and the high offices of state; which meant that they were only excluded from the making and administering of the laws, from all posts of honour and dignity in the state. These were bagatelles, for which, according to the argument, it was not worth while for the Catholics to contend—and, therefore, it was scarcely worth the while of the parliament to refuse. How would the honourable and learned gentlemen who used this argument like to be excluded from their chance of obtaining these trifles? He begged to ask if these were not the very nothings for which Englishmen would cheerfully lay down their lives?

Did they still talk of the danger of admitting the Catholics? He put it to the house to consider, whether they would willingly see such a body represented anywhere but within the walls of parliament. To shut them out from parliament, after giving them everything which rendered them consequential short of it, was to teach them to array themselves elsewhere. Somewhere else they must go, if the house could not make room for them. God forbid the recurrence of bad times! but it might happen that a bad prince might mount the throne, and then perhaps, being refused admission where they had a right to it, they would range themselves behind the throne, and assist in the sacrifice of the public liberties. His honourable and learned friend the solicitor-general was satisfied as to the laity, whom he considered as sufficiently good subjects. The danger which his honourable and learned friend apprehended was from the Roman Catholic priests. He dreaded, in a country where the majority of the people differed from the religion of the state, the uncontrollable and all-controlling influence of the priests, who were themselves detached from the state. France, it had been said, had of late shown herself particularly tenacious on the subject of religion; and, looking at what might be her views with regard to Ireland, it was said that there might be great danger. He supposed that the bill was intended to diminish so much of the influence of the Roman Catholic clergy over their flocks as arose out of their present grievances. Here was a danger admitted on both sides to be actually existing, and here was a measure proposed by the honourable baronet to meet that danger. Let the measure for bringing those priests within the pale of the constitution be proved to be calculated to increase their influence, and he would say something to it.

Before I go further, I would ask those honourable members who admit the dangers which exist, whether they are prepared with a remedy? Some may, perhaps, tell me that I am to trust to time and to proselytism. I admit that much may be expected from proselytism, and that it is likely to be increased by the pious and exemplary lives, the kind and charitable behaviour, and the religious example of the Protestant clergy; and I am of opinion that the time will come when the religious differences between Protestants and Catholics will be much lessened, and, though we may not see it, that our children's children may be witnesses of it. But, sir, this prospect is distant and uncertain; the dangers which surround us are pressing and imminent. So long as you continue a line of demarcation between Protestants and Catholics, so long do you hold up the latter as aliens to the state. And, while you do this, let it be considered that your proselytism will be at a stand. For any man who should become a Protestant under such restrictions would be considered an apostate, a wretch who changed his religion only for purposes of gain. Before I conclude,

I must take the liberty of stating shortly to the house a few of the measures which I consider calculated to remedy the existing evils. First, I would take away all grounds of grievance, by placing the Roman Catholic on an equal footing with the Protestant. I would do this in order to prevent their union in one body against one common oppression. Next, I would, as has been recommended by an honourable friend of mine, make a suitable provision for the Roman Catholic priesthood. I have been told that the Roman Catholic priest would not consent to such an arrangement. Let me assure my honourable friend that he is deceived in his statement. The Roman Catholic clergy would not, it is true, purchase a permanent provision by the disgrace of having abandoned their flocks. But if Catholic emancipation were granted—if the laity were once relieved from the disabilities under which they laboured—the Catholic priesthood would anxiously and gratefully receive a permanent provision. Honourable members are much mistaken, and know but little of Ireland, if they imagine that the Irish people or the Irish priesthood wish to usurp the property of the Established church. The church of Ireland may be in danger of being pulled down from other causes; but if it were pulled down to-morrow, and the livings offered to the Roman Catholic priests, the laity would not allow them to accept them. I speak this in the hearing of many who are acquainted with Ireland, and who must know that it is not the wish of the laity to have their priests raised to influence and authority by such means. The gentry of Ireland respect their priesthood, but I can assure the house they are not priest-ridden.

Before I sit down, sir, I must say one word more as to the danger which I conceive to exist at the present period. If the priesthood were to express a desire to get possession of the church property, the laity would at once cry out against them. But, I would ask, are the Protestant clergy right in saying, that they are determined to resist the claims of the Roman Catholics so long as they themselves existed? What was this but giving a form and substance to that which was before but a wild chimera? What was it but compelling the Catholics to say, we must now oppose the Protestant clergy in self-defence, for, until they shall be deprived of their property, we have no chance of obtaining our political rights? All who know me, know that I am, and ever have been, a zealous supporter of the Established church; but never, even when I have been most zealous in its support, do I conceive myself to have rendered it better service than in giving it this warning, and placing its ministers on their guard. Sir, I feel convinced, that if a foreign enemy were landing on our coast to-morrow, this house would not grant to the Roman Catholics anything which it could not concede with honour and with safety to the Established church. I trust to God no such period may arrive. I feel that if it ever does, it must be far, very far distant. But I know that, were it to come, such would be your firm and irrevocable determination. And, sir, it is because I know there exists no such danger —it is because I feel that we are in a time of perfect safety and security, that I call upon you to do that now, which a sense of justice ought to compel you to do even in a time of the greatest danger. Let me not be told, sir, that the people or the priesthood of Ireland will refuse to accept any concession which we may make to them. I say, in the language of my honourable friend the member for the county of York, that it is for us to legislate; that it is for us to do what is right; and if the Catholics of Ireland should refuse to accept what we offer them, they will be deprived of all power to do injury, because they will be deprived of all power to make just complaint. One word more, and I have done. The alarm which exists with respect to the Roman Catholics of Ireland, is, I can assure the house, unfounded. The Roman Catholics of Ireland are not only tranquil but loyal. Nay, more, they are determined to continue loyal, no matter what may be the result of their application to parliament, because they feel satisfied that the growing feeling of liberality towards them, and the enlightened policy of England, will not allow them to labour long under their present disqualifications. For myself, I feel perfectly convinced of the loyalty of the Roman Catholics; and if the government of France were speculating upon their disloyalty, be assured of it, they will find themselves much mistaken; for, should the day ever come when that loyalty would be put to the test, they would be found to a man rallying round the standard of the British constitution. And why is it that such conduct is to be expected from them? It is because they have under that constitution enjoyed thirty-five years of conciliation and progressive improvement. It is because they trust to the kindness and the wisdom of the British legislature. But, sir, we want something more from the Irish people than mere loyalty; we want their affection; we want their confidence; we want their cordiality; we want to induce them to deal with us as friends and brothers, in order to put an end to those anxieties which disturb us, and free us from that feverish state, in which we have so long been placed. I beg pardon, sir, for having trespassed at such length upon the attention of the house, and conclude by giving my most cordial support to the motion of the honourable baronet.

 Canning had come down to the house from a sick bed, and on a crutch, to give his support to the motion. The opposition could afford to look on and allow the government to fight the question out, for Peel took upon himself the audacious task of replying to both his illustrious colleagues. Brougham closed the debate, and the motion was carried by a majority of 13. Resolutions upon which to base a bill were instantly assented to, and a committee formed to prepare the same. It passed the Commons, and was lost on the second reading in the Lords; with all its accompaniments, except the bill against the Association.

ELECTIVE FRANCHISE IN IRELAND BILL.
April 26, 1825.

THIS is the debate upon the forty-shilling freeholders. Brougham had passionately referred to the Duke of York's famous declaration in the House of Lords on the preceding day, that in every position wherein he might be placed by Providence, he would resist the measure of Catholic emancipation—the apprehension of which had caused the insanity of his father. Plunket rose to order. Brougham denied that he had been disorderly. "In the parliament to which the right honourable gentleman formerly belonged, such a course might have been pursued; but not in an English parliament. * * * An honourable and learned gentleman (himself the most disorderly in the world), shall get up and complain that you are out of order, not because anything irregular has been said, but *quid timet*, merely because he apprehends something possibly may be." Sir John Newport spoke just before Plunket, but had to leave the house from indisposition.

I SHALL not detain the house long; and I confess, sir, that I never rose to address the house with more painful feelings than at the present moment. I am particularly glad that my right honourable friend, whom indisposition has just compelled to leave the house, has preceded me on the present occasion; because I feel greatly cheered by the reflection, that the sentiments of one of the best and most tried friends of his country differ, in almost every particular, from those of my honourable and learned friend. I am desirous of explaining to the house the ground on which I took the liberty of calling my honourable and learned friend to order. I do not regret the course that I took; on the contrary, I feel its propriety still more strongly after what has fallen from the honourable and learned member since I adopted it. I do not, either from my habits in the Irish parliament, to which my honourable and learned friend thought proper to allude, or from the little experience I have acquired in this house, think he was entitled to say that I called him to order before he had really committed a breach of it. He seems to have interpreted rather too largely the declaration from the chair, because, sir, you delicately avoided telling him in direct terms that he was grossly out of order. I am fully aware that though it is not strictly regular to allude to what passes in the other house of parliament, it would be absurd to watch over-anxiously particular instances of deviations from strict regularity, provided they remain within reasonable and proper limits. But I will call to the recollection of any body who heard my honourable and learned friend, whether this was not an occasion on which mischief was about to be done, and on which I was warranted on an interference, which, on another occasion, might have appeared punctilious and pedantic.

In one sentiment which fell from my honourable and learned friend I agree entirely. I agree in the necessity of passing this important measure; and of passing it without the delay of an hour. I must take the liberty, however, of saying, that many of the sentiments which fell from my honourable and learned friend were, in my judgment, eminently calculated to defeat this measure of emancipation. I agree with my honourable and learned friend, that it is most essential to the success of the Catholic cause, that the question of emancipation should be carried by a large and overwhelming majority. But I confidently appeal to every member of this house, whether the speech of my honourable and learned friend was not calculated to defeat that object, and to interfere with the success of the cause. I was somewhat surprised, sir, when my honourable friend, the member for Louth, came forward with arguments, which he thought proper to urge in direct contradiction to his own evidence, under the solemn obligation of an oath. I would not, of course, be supposed to throw the slightest imputation on the honourable member, nor even to insinuate that that additional sanction would be more binding on him than his own sense of honour; but, it certainly did sound strange in my ears, to hear my honourable friend put forward arguments, completely in the teeth of everything he had recommended to the committee of the House of Commons. I shall not enter into the evidence from which such copious extracts have been read by my honourable friend, who brought forward this subject with so much ability; but, I wish to place before the house the argument of the honourable member for Louth, and the conclusions he has drawn, so much at variance with his own evidence.

The honourable gentleman's complaint against the measure is, that it does not go far enough, but that it should be extended to the disqualification of all holders in fee; but, does my honourable friend mean, that we should carry our principle to the length of disfranchising a body of men like the yeomanry of England? Now, what is the ground upon which the honourable member supports his opinion? Why, forsooth, because certain vagrants have settled in certain commons in Ireland; who, by acts of rapine and disseisin, have obtained a title to certain lands. Why, then, if this be so distressing an event to the honourable member, let him bring in a bill to disfranchise them. He admits there is a great existing evil, which this measure, as far as it goes, is well adapted to remedy; but, because a parcel of travelling tinkers have migrated to the bogs of Drumskele, in the county of Louth, he turns round upon us and says, that, unless we so change our measure, as to render it impossible for any rational man to adopt it, he will resist it with all his might. Now, if the speech of the honourable member, surprised me, the house may judge of my consternation, when I heard my honourable and learned friend, the member for Winchelsea, adopt his argument; nay, more, misrepresent it, and carry it to a length which the honourable author himself never contemplated. Of course I do not mean for one moment to assert, that my honourable and learned friend would be capable of wilfully misrepresenting anything, either here or elsewhere, but so it is. Such is the wonderful power of his talent and eloquence, that, whatever argument is favoured with his adoption, receives a force and extent of which its originator was wholly unconscious; and when my honourable and learned friend felt himself in that cruel and grievous situation which he has so feelingly depicted —impelled by a sense of duty to do that which might be detrimental to a measure to which I know he is attached; I really do lament most heartily, that instead of applying all those powers of ridicule in which he is unrivalled, and that faculty of exposure which belongs to him, in a degree that I never witnessed in any other man in any house, to demolish the argument of the honourable member for Louth, he should have exercised his transcendent abilities to embellish and support it. But to come to the argument—I think I have some ground to complain of my honourable and learned friend. That he is an ardent friend to Catholic concession, does not rest upon his assertion or on mine; he has given proofs of it too strong for any man to doubt his sincerity. The extent of his services cannot be over-rated; but, I have perceived on this occasion, and with great regret, what he has never shown on any other. His extreme rapidity of conception and wonderful facility of utterance, has, by unremitting exercise, become a weakness, which leads him into statements, which, in the sober reflection of his cooler moments, his own excellent judgment would disavow. I appeal to the recollection of this house, whether my honourable and learned friend has not pressed into his service, in opposition to this measure, which, for aught he knows (as he himself declares), may be sound and salutary; for my honourable and learned friend set out by stating his entire ignorance of the merits of the measure, of which, I must do him the justice to say, he gave the most convincing demonstration as he went along—I would appeal, I say, to all who hear me, whether the effect at least of his address was not to awaken prejudices which might defeat the measure, the success of which we all have at heart?

My honourable and learned friend says that the object of the measure is to put down perjury, and he asks what right we have to interfere in such a question, when every man in the house perjures himself? And then, in one of his flights, he takes a range amongst the army and clergy; but what has all this to do with the question? And, to come to the real argument, even admitting that the qualification for sitting in this house does lead to perjury, and supposing the army and church not exempt from the stain, are we in no instance to cure the evil when we have it in our power? If any other member had pursued such a line of conduct, would not my honourable and learned friend have called it a jump? Why should he resort to such a line of argument? I cannot suppose he could have been desirous to press into his service popular topics for the purpose of exciting prejudice. Have I not a right to complain that my honourable and learned friend has all through his speech assumed as facts what he was bound to prove were facts? He has condescended to nickname this measure, and then calls upon you to reject it. But, what right has he to call this a measure of disfranchisement? Catholic emancipation, he says, would be a great good, and although not immediately felt, would be materially beneficial, and would conciliate Ireland; whereas, this measure would be immediately felt by the people, and felt as an injury. The whole scope of his argument is, that instead of producing content in Ireland, this measure will excite a ferment amongst the Catholics themselves; but, sir, let me inform my honourable and learned friend that this measure does not go to disfranchise a single human being now alive. If this be so, I would ask, what is there in the bill to justify the ferment which my honourable and learned friend anticipates amongst the Catholics; or how can he reconcile his desire for conciliation with this glowing appeal to their prejudices? He seems to apprehend that the Catholics of Ireland will be more alive to constitutional jealousies than to their own interests; in the heat of argument he has prevailed upon himself to believe that their constitutional feelings will be aroused by abstract considerations. In his estimation, they must be most powerful and acute reasoners, for they will overlook the general benefit to be conferred, whilst their feelings will be directed to the immediate operation of a measure which can affect no man living. My honourable and learned friend seems to suppose, that the Irish parliament differed from all others on points of order; and I should infer that he thinks the Irish people differed from the inhabitants of all other countries, and entertained opinions repugnant to all the principles which regulate human actions. But, says my honourable and learned friend, "I do not know whether this bill is good or bad—I have kindly feelings towards it—I am not opposed to it." But, to my mind, he presented as ugly an appearance as I ever witnessed; he exhibited very little of that affection and endearment which distinguish a zealous friend from an adversary. One thing he could not at all endure: he could not bear the idea of joining this measure with any other; he was opposed to it, because it had the appearance of a bribe. But, the time presses—a large majority even will not carry the measure—nothing short of unanimity will accomplish the object—still he could not consent, such was his sense of duty, to the proposed measure. This really appears to me standing a little too much on the knight-errantry of logic. He will not consent to unite a measure which may be good, for aught he knows, to another measure, which, he contends, if accomplished, must be beneficial to the empire. This appears to me the very romance of delicacy, and if my honourable and learned friend, in addition to his other numerous avocations, should devote his talents to the writing a novel, he might, no doubt, found a very interesting tale on his delicate embarrassment, and introduce some 'sentiments, which, although extremely suitable there, were ill adapted to the sober discussions of an assembly like the House of Commons.

Now, I will frankly state my opinion of this measure; and, in doing so, I am not afraid of leaving my character for frankness in the hands of the house. My decided opinion is, that this measure is in the abstract good; but even if I thought it, to a certain extent injurious, not unjust, but faulty in some respects; or if I thought it calculated to accomplish a greater good, I would adopt and support it, for the purpose of obtaining the higher benefit. That is my creed: —I openly avow it, and there is not an honest man in the house who will condemn it. My honourable and learned friend complains, that we have joined this measure to the emancipation of the Catholics, which has no natural connexion with it; and he states it as a grievance, that it should be placed close by the side of the larger measure, and that the motions of the one must wait upon the progress of the other. But have they, in fact, no connexion? Now, we propose to admit the Catholics to the participation of the constitution; and how are we met? "What, (say our opponents) will you emancipate this immense Catholic population, and allow the mob to rush in and take possession of those seats?" And am I to be told that a measure which takes away this power from the hands of the mob has no natural connexion with the great question of Catholic emancipation? But, take the other view of the question. Suppose the question should not be carried, I know of no other way in which the Catholics can advance their cause, than through the agency of the 40s. freeholders; so that, in fact, in every way in which the measure can be contemplated, it is strictly and inseparably connected with the question for removing the Catholic disabilities. My honourable and learned friend complained bitterly of the cruel situation in which he was placed; but I never saw a man in such circumstances who appeared more happy, or who drew upon his own rich resources in higher perfection. I never knew him disdain more completely the consideration before him, and throw himself upon the energies of his own mind, and the extraordinary powers of his fancy and eloquence, than upon this rack of torture on which he placed himself, complaining of us for having taken him by surprise, by the unexpected introduction of a measure which, for the last three months, every body well knew was intended to be submitted to the house. But now let us come to the measure itself; and I would beg of gentlemen, whatever their opinions may be, to examine it in its own abstract shape. But, before I enter upon this part of the subject, I wish to make one observation. Should my right honourable friend near me (Mr. Peel) think this measure not bad in itself, but likely to produce good, yet holding his particular opinions on Catholic emancipation, I should not blame him if he resisted this measure, on the ground that his opposition would defeat the more extensive question, which to his mind appears fraught with evil; at the same time, I must say, and I speak it not in the niggardly spirit which is sometimes displayed of admitting sincerity on the ground of courtesy; I shall not use that uncourteous courtesy towards my right honourable friend; but in the honest sincerity of my heart I say, that no man would be less disposed than my right honourable friend to defeat a measure which is good in itself, on account of its connexion with any other measure to which he might be opposed. We complain of the act of 1793, which has been so truly described by the honourable member for Louth, as having begun at the wrong end, by letting in the rabble and shutting out the higher classes; the consequence of which has been, that the country gentlemen of Ireland let out their land, and subdivided it into small freeholds. This was the system which led to all the unfortunate consequences. If one of those poor wretches was prosecuted for perjury, his landlord went bail for him, and he was never heard of afterwards.

Was not this in itself an evil of a serious nature? The next proceeding is this; and let the house observe, all these facts are emphatically detailed in evidence, although my honourable and learned friend complains of want of information. The landlord gives this wretched being a freehold, which may not be worth forty pence, comprising, perhaps, an acre of land and a miserable hovel, the rent of which he could never pay without the addition of his own labour; but if he can earn 40s. a year on his land, he then swears he is a 40s. freeholder; but should he refuse, the landlord tells him, " you must give up your land; I'll not keep an idle, lazy, lubberly fellow, who will not swear he is worth 40s. a year." Is the house, then, to be told that they are not to provide a remedy for this flagitious evil, because the clergy or the army, or even members of parliament, do not always adhere to the truth?—topics which form good subjects for amusement when my honourable and learned friend wishes to indulge his fancy, but which are very feeble arguments against remedying this crying evil. I could not help thinking that my honourable and learned friend displayed somewhat of the alacrity of an advocate, in selecting from the wide range of his own imagination all those popular topics that could be plied against the cause. The present system leads to the most painful consequences. At an election, the landlord says to his agent, " Send those 500 men to the market." Generally speaking, they neither know nor care for whom they vote; but, should his religious feelings be aroused, should the priest be called into action, then arises a contest between the priest and the landlord, neither of them seeking to elevate the poor peasant, but to get possession of him. The consequence of which is, to insult the landlord and degrade the priest. But after the heat of the contest has subsided, the poor wretch retires from the religious excitement, and has to settle with his landlord, he has to make up his rent, he is unable to do it, and is dismissed; and the result is, that the poor man is ruined by yielding to his religious feelings, and resisting the tyranny of his landlord. Thus the peasant is habituated to a perpetual contest with his landlord, in which the landlord always succeeds.

Are these things disputed in the evidence? Do we want witnesses to prove that perjury has been committed? Why, it was distinctly proved before the committee of this house—a committee composed of persons of all opinions, who were inclined to probe the subject to the bottom. I have no recollection of any measure in support of which such satisfactory evidence was adduced before a committee. Do we, by the measure we propose, affect the independence of elections? No such thing. On the contrary, we secure the purity of election.

I hold in my hand an account of the number of persons registered for eight years in thirty-two counties, from which returns were made, and what was the proportion? In the year before the election, the proportion was of the 40s. freeholders, 18 to 1 of the 20l. and 50l. freeholders. The consequence of all this was, that the independent freeholders were overlaid, and the principle of election was wholly destroyed. 'The honourable member for Corfe Castle (Mr. Bankes) was so fired with constitutional zeal, which the courtesy of the house compels me to admit is great, but one particle beyond which I am not prepared to go, has declared, that he would rather expire on the floor of this house, than sacrifice one portion of his fine Runnymede feelings. I do admire most exceedingly the fine spirit of the ancient barons, when it bursts out through the honourable member for Corfe Castle. But I hope it will be some consolation to him to learn, that this measure is not intended to affect England. There may be modes of managing votes in some of the towns in England; but with English towns I profess myself wholly unacquainted. At present, I address myself to the honourable member for Corfe Castle, and I trust his feelings will be appeased by the circumstances to which I have adverted. We propose no violent change; the measure is to be slow and gradual in its operation; the result of it will be the raising up a class of sturdy, independent yeomanry in Ireland, who, in the fulness of time, will be fitted for the same rights which are enjoyed, and wisely exercised, by the people of this country. This is the principle of the measure; it disfranchises no man; it will produce no violent effect on the country; and it is entitled to support, because it appears calculated, from the evidence which has been received, to give general satisfaction.

Sir, with respect to one part of the evidence, my honourable and learned friend has been much mistaken, I mean the evidence of Mr. O'Connell. I have read that evidence lately; and the meaning of it appears obviously to me to advise the committee not to meddle with the subject; but this I understood to apply to the operation of the measure by itself without any other—which no man would advise. I do not wish to attach to the character of Mr. O'Connell more value than I think properly belongs to it. I must do him the justice to say that he enjoys a large portion of the confidence of the people of Ireland. I had very little intercourse with that gentleman until after the recent discussions in this house; but, from what I have seen of him, I cannot hesitate to declare, in the face of parliament, that I do not believe there is any man less disposed than Mr. O'Connell to abuse the extensive confidence he enjoys amongst his countrymen, or more desirous to employ it for the benefit of his country. I myself have been lately in Ireland, and have had much intercourse with people of various opinions as to the policy of the measure. They appeared to me to approve of it. It has also the support of my right honourable friend (Sir J. Newport). There are many other Irish members sitting round my honourable and learned friend, who can inform him as to the operation of the measure; for although I cannot sympathise with him, or suppose him in any unpleasant predicament, arising from a want of acquaintance with the great general principles of this or any other important question, yet, on the details of the measure, I must give him credit for the most absolute ignorance. However, he is surrounded by those who can best inform him; and they, I believe, with one or two exceptions, are persuaded the measure will give general satisfaction. Let him consult them, and still more his own excellent judgment, flinging aside, for the present, the aid of his rhetoric, and he cannot fail to arrive at a sound conclusion.

Sir, I need not attempt to describe the solicitude I avow myself to feel for the success of this bill. I hail its accomplishment, not alone as it advances the hopes of the Roman Catholic, but I sincerely hail it with reference to the satisfaction it is calculated to impart to the Protestants of Ireland. I mean, that it is calculated not only to conciliate that portion of the Protestants of Ireland who are friendly to the repeal of Catholic disabilities, but even those who still continue adverse to its accomplishment. And here it is impossible that I should not express the heartfelt gratification that I, in common with all those who look forward to the completion of the great measure of Catholic relief, have felt at the great advance that question has received, by the accession of such support as has been afforded to us by the vote of my honourable friend the member for the county of Armagh. If any one thing could excuse a feeling of envy or jealousy in my mind it would be, I confess, towards him; enjoying, as he does, the proud consciousness arising from his generous, manly, and honest declaration. Returning to this measure, my honourable and learned friend has asked, even though it should be coupled with the accomplishment of Catholic relief, who is the bold man that would venture to say that this measure will afford relief to Ireland? I meet the interrogatory of my honourable and learned friend; and, though I do not profess myself as the votary of that extreme political courage, which I have often found to be more an indication of rashness than firmness, yet, with my conviction of the propriety of the measure—with my knowledge of the general impressions that exist in Ireland as to its necessity—I am that bold man. I do in my conscience believe, that, coupled with the substantial measure of relief, it will not only conciliate the Catholics, but give increased security to the Protestants of Ireland. And here I have to complain of my honourable and learned friend, that in the whole of his excursive speech, he has altogether thrown out of his view what that security demanded. But, though he disregarded it, it is a consideration that I confess has never been out of my calculation. To obtain the great measure of relief to the Roman Catholics of Ireland has been the object of my utmost anxiety. I have been always solicitous for that great accomplishment—now, more than ever. I feel that a day should not be lost before the house carries this vote into effect. But, strongly as I feel its necessity, I am still persuaded, that if it were carried into effect, leaving an existing distrust in the minds of the Protestants of Ireland, it would be a curse instead of a blessing. Let it be recollected, that in the progress of this great cause, every foot of it has been reclaimed ground. It has made its way gradually—the triumph of enlightened views and irresistible argument. And therefore it is that, since first it was introduced to the consideration of the legislature, there never was a moment when the result of such continued exertions was more likely to be frustrated—when the cup was more likely to be dashed from the lip on the brink of enjoyment—than at the moment I address you, by any indiscretion on the part of any honourable member. I beg my honourable and learned friend to believe, that I think him incapable of any such intention. I never can forget his super-eminent services to the great cause. No man who feels for the prosperity of Ireland and the security of the empire, can forget the important benefits which, in the exercise of his powerful talents, my honourable and learned friend has given to those great objects. But, without presuming to pronounce on the reasons, it was impossible not to see with regret, that even he is labouring this night under an effort which was eminently calculated, though not intended, to defeat the great object for which he had heretofore so powerfully struggled, and by so doing to dash from Ireland the blessing, the very moment that it anticipated its fulfilment. There are many other topics connected with this great question which press themselves on my consideration, but I feel that neither my own strength, nor my feelings of respect to the attention with which I have been honoured, will permit me to intrude further on your patience. I leave, therefore, the question to the enlightened judgment of the house.

The Bill was read a second time by a majority of 48, and proceeded *pari passu* with the other wings. On the 2nd of May, the house resolved on the motion of

Lord Francis Levison Gower, that it was expedient to pension the Irish Catholic clergy. All English statesmen have had a conviction, since the Catholics first began to grow into a political power, that the pension would be the real "golden link" between the countries. We find even Peel in this debate almost advocating its adoption—urging only the necessity of obtaining some church patronage to the crown. "It was too hard if the King were to have no voice in the appointment of a bishop with a salary of £1000 a year." The scale of pension proposed was, £1500 to an archbishop; £1000 to a bishop; £300 to a dean or vicar; from £200 to £120 to a parish priest; and £60 to a curate. Plunket warmly supported it with a few pithy sentences—ending the debate by declaring, that such a measure would be "a buttress to the Established church." On the 11th the Relief Bill was read a third time and went to the Lords—where, as we have already stated, it was rejected on the second reading.

CATHOLIC RELIEF.

June 10, 1828.

In May, 1828, Sir F. Burdett, after three days' debate, carried a motion for Emancipation in the House of Commons by a majority of 12. Immediately afterwards a conference with the House of Lords was agreed to, and on the motion of the Duke of Wellington, lords were appointed to confer. On the 9th of June, the Marquis of Lansdowne introduced a motion for legislation on the basis of the Commons' resolutions, and Plunket, who had been called to the upper house in the preceding year, made his first appearance in the House of Lords in support of the motion. He was preceded in the debate by Lord Manners, whom he had so often bewildered in the mazes of his marvellous logic in the Irish Court of Chancery, and whose unflagging hatred to the Catholic claims was just beginning to relax under the weight of that tremendous popular pressure, which caused Wellington and Peel to give way. Lord Lansdowne's motion was rejected, but in the next month, O'Connell was returned to parliament for Clare, and the positions ceased to be tenable.

I AM anxious to take the first opportunity that fairly occurs, of repeating my unalterable conviction upon this question. The noble and learned lord behind me (Manners), last night stated the result of his observations, after a residence of twenty years in Ireland, and I am satisfied that he uttered, with perfect truth and candour, the conclusion at which his mind had arrived. I hope that your lordships will permit me, after forty years spent in that country in active life, public and private, official and unofficial, in parliament and out of parliament, with the fullest opportunities of observing the deportment of all classes, to state my unalterable conviction, that unless this agitating question be disposed of by some conciliatory adjustment, there is no hope of prosperity, tranquillity, or even safety for Ireland. If any person has arrived at this decision, that under no circumstances, at no time, and accompanied by no conditions, he can and ought to do anything for the Roman Catholics—that person is entitled to vote against the proposition to-night. Unless he has arrived at that decision, I do not see how it is possible to refuse his support to the motion of the noble marquis.

I have listened with the most profound attention to the able, temperate, and dignified statement of my noble and learned friend who has just taken his seat. Part of it I heard with the most gratified feelings; because I did think, and I still hope I am not mistaken in so thinking, I saw in the resistance he felt it necessary to make to the proposition, some distant gleam of comfort, some secret hope, some latent opinion in his mind, that there were circumstances and securities, if time were given to look after them, and if the search were made at the proper season, which might render the adoption of some measure in favour of the Catholics admissible. On the other hand, I felt extreme regret and disappointment at other parts of his speech, because, if I could agree with him in believing that we can take no step for the admission of Roman Catholics into parliament, and into office, without the destruction of the Protestant establishment in Ireland, I, who have supported these claims almost from the first moment I could think, would abandon my ancient and confirmed opinions, would change my side and become as determined an opponent to concession, as I have been its most anxious advocate.

I look on the Protestant establishment of Ireland as a fundamental principle of our imperial constitution. I take it to have been unalterably settled at the Union, and that to talk of changing the Protestant religion of Ireland without shaking the Protestant establishment of the empire is idle. I speak no new language, now that for the first time I have had an opportunity of delivering my sentiments 'n the presence of the right reverend bench; I utter but the opinions I have entertained and expressed in the other House of Parliament. I think a religious establishment essential to our well-being, and that without a dignified establishment in times like these, religion itself would be degraded. I am, therefore, persuaded, not only that the establishment is necessary, but that the rank, affluence, and dignity of the hierarchy are important to our best interests. I think further, that its power and influence are and ought to be so great, that unless that hierarchy be connected with the state, it may be too powerful for the state; and hence the necessity of maintaining that connection for the benefit of the state. On these grounds, and not for any fanciful and theoretical reasons, assigned by some writers upon this subject, I never for a moment would consent to anything which should endanger the Protestant establishment.

I further feel that the Protestant establishment of Ireland is the very cement of the Union; I find it interwoven with all the essential relations and institutions of the two kingdoms; and I have no hesitation in admitting that if it were destroyed, the very foundations of public security would be shaken, the connection between England and Ireland dissolved, and the annihilation of private property must follow the ruin of the property of the church.

I should be happy to suppose that I had misunderstood my noble and learned friend, in the interpretation I put upon the latter part of his argument; and I repeat that if I thought with him, that the consequences of admitting the claim of the Roman Catholics would be such as he anticipated, I would now and for ever resist them. I am most anxious to relieve my own mind, and to state the grounds on which I can do so satisfactorily, from this terrible alternative; and I trust your lordships will excuse me, if I go a little back, and briefly call your attention to that period of our history so much adverted to by my noble and learned friend—I mean the period of the Revolution.

The general circumstances under which that glorious event occurred are so well known, that it is unnecessary for me to do more than shortly advert to them. At that date, this Protestant country took up arms in support of its civil and religious liberties, against the bigotted and despotic monarch who had endangered both. She took up arms, as she had a right to do, for that purpose, and she succeeded; but let me remind your lordships, that that success would probably have been more than problematical, if the energies and patriotism of the people of this country had not been sanctioned and stimulated by the strongest motives of religious duty. The union of patriotism and religion produced that success. What was then the situation of Ireland, of Popish Ireland—of the unfortunate natives of that country? I do not advert to this point for the sake of reviving ungrateful recollections, but because it is necessary to my argument. When we come to sit in judgment upon the conduct of the natives of Ireland, we should do it not with feelings of resentment against them, but of shame, remorse, and self-accusation against ourselves. These are the assessors whom we ought to call in, to aid us in arriving at a decision, and in passing a just sentence of atonement.

Ireland was once in possession of an undefiled religion; free from

Popery and Papal usurpation. You forced upon her pure christianity your own corruptions and superstitions, and you taught her to consider herself yours, not merely by right of conquest, but by Papal right. Without reference to her habits or opinions, you compelled her to receive your corrupted religion. As knowledge advanced, we became prepared for a change; and here the Reformation was effected with the full consent and approbation of the people. They understood and appreciated the blessing of the reformed religion; but the other unfortunate portion of the empire had been left in a state of ignorance and barbarism, and in this condition they naturally turned and adhered to the corruptions and superstitions which, in the first instance, you had forced upon her. Then you forced the Reformation upon her, without any regard to the habits and opinions of the people. When, therefore, she some time afterwards found a Popish monarch on the throne of England, she refused to take up arms against him, because he professed the same religion. Had the Irish possessed an enlightened philosophy, they might, perhaps, have known that it was better to sacrifice their religion to their patriotism, than their patriotism to their religion; but, in such times, that was too much to expect from human nature, and accordingly, not only did they not take up arms against a Popish king, but they took up arms in his behalf. They were subdued; and what were the duties, at that period, devolving upon the English government? The great men of that day had a most difficult task to accomplish. It was impossible that they should treat the Roman Catholics of Ireland as good subjects; they had been, not as against the king, but as against the English government, in a state of armed resistance, and they could not safely be admitted into parliament or into office. It therefore became requisite by an act, strictly speaking, of injustice, but injustice compelled by rigid necessity, to exclude them from parliament and from office. But let me remind your lordships, and particularly the learned earl (Eldon), who is taking notes of what I say, of what was the state of the law, as it existed at that time. At the Revolution the Irish Catholics were in undoubted possession of the privileges of sitting in both houses of parliament. I shall presently have occasion to observe upon the application of these two laws to the English; but I am now speaking only of the Irish. The 5th of Elizabeth, by which, for the first time, the oath of supremacy was made necessary for admission into the House of Commons, never existed in Ireland. From the Reformation down to the 2nd William and Mary, a period of 130 years, the Irish enjoyed the undisputed privilege, not merely in point of law, but practically, of sitting in parliament; they were also, though not, perhaps, to the same degree, admitted into office. The first of Elizabeth was adopted by the 2nd Elizabeth in Ireland, and it required the oath of supremacy to be taken on accepting office; yet among the Roman Catholics it was not for a long time considered a barrier to their admission. It has been truly stated by my noble and learned friend, that many Roman Catholics took the oath of supremacy, and I may add, they did so, both in this country and in Ireland; for the first twelve years of the reign of Elizabeth, they took it without difficulty in this country, and it was not until after the attempts of the Popish priests, sent over from the Continent to deprive Elizabeth of her throne and life, that any difficulty of the kind arose. The act of the 2nd of William and Mary was the result of stern necessity superseding the ordinary dictates of justice, and even the faith of treaties. But what was the course it became necessary then to pursue?

Those enlightened persons, those lovers of freedom, then at the head of affairs, saw their difficulty and became satisfied of the truth of this proposition, that it was utterly inconsistent to shut any class of individuals out of parliament and office—to deprive them of franchise and of the privileges of the constitution, and yet to leave them in possession of wealth and power. The two principles were utterly inconsistent; if you separate wealth and knowledge from the state, wealth and knowledge must overturn the state. Therefore those profound statesmen saw in all its bearings the proposition I am now submitting to the house; and what was the course they pursued? I am not stating it for the purpose of casting any imputation upon them; they were in a situation of great embarrassment, and I have not met with any suggestion in any writer as to the mode in which they ought to have proceeded. Treat them as good subjects they could not; admit them to parliament and offices in the state they could not; and then began that system which was pursued for seventy years—the system of keeping the Irish Roman Catholics in the lowest extremity of poverty and ignorance. It was pursued to that limit, where the art of grinding down a people must end; and then what took place? The good sense and good feeling of this country recoiled with pain and disgust from the termination of their own system of government. They were shocked to see one of the fairest portions of the empire reduced to so destitute a condition.

Let the house recollect, that the whole period from the Revolution was one continued scene of severe but necessary infliction; and let the house recollect also the conduct of the Irish under it. While Scotland, and even England, had been subjected to more than one insurrection in favour of the exiled family, Ireland remained resigned and patient, and never raised an arm or a voice in its behalf. The people of England were softened and subdued by the resignation and forbearance of the people of Ireland, and became satisfied that something ought to be done for them. A new system then began; and for the last fifty years, you have been retracing the steps taken for the 70 or 80 years preceding, and endeavouring to replace the Irish in the situation which they originally occupied. Support, encouragement, privileges—constitutional privileges—to a great extent were given to them, and accordingly we now no longer find them in the abject and ignorant wretchedness to which we formerly reduced them. Your own acts of justice and policy have raised them to the situation of a great, powerful, and reflecting people. The English government and the Irish parliament made some mistakes in endeavouring to alter their course. Many of the provisions of the act of 1793 were most wise and salutary; but others were introduced of a decidedly objectionable tendency. By that act, all disabilities, all incapacities, either with respect to landed property, admission to office, or to other privileges of the state, were absolutely repealed, with certain exceptions, extending to a considerable number of offices, and above all, to seats in parliament—that highest privilege in civil life. You gave to Roman Catholics the right of returning members to sit in parliament, but you withheld from the Catholic aristocracy the right of filling those seats themselves; that is to say, you created a Roman Catholic constituency for Protestant representatives. It was impossible that this discordant state of things could arrive at any consistent termination, and by that error of the act of 1793 you laid the foundation of further evils. Under this new system of government, it was almost miraculous how Ireland continued to revive and to recover from her state of moral and physical degradation; so much so, that at length England became apprehensive of the growing power of Ireland, and in 1800 the Union was proposed, and took place. It was effected avowedly on this principle, that by uniting the two countries under one religion, security might be given to the two establishments; and that by uniting them under one constitution, happiness and freedom might be ensured to both.

Beware, my lords, how you paralyse that Union; consider how impossible it is effectually to preserve that Union by consolidating the two establishments, and yet at the same time not to render it perfect by giving equal rights to the people of both countries. That these were the opinions of the illustrious statesmen under whose auspices the Union was commenced and concluded, will not now be disputed. I do not mean to assert, that the distinguished individual then at the head of the government held out expectations to the Roman Catholics, that they would be admitted to political power; but at that period hopes were encouraged that the Union would be the means of facilitating the acquisition of privileges which they could otherwise never have a chance of enjoying. When the act of Union was carried I had a seat in the Irish parliament; I was then a young man, and I felt it my duty to oppose it; I am now an old man, but under the same circumstances, were they again to occur, I should adopt the same course. As, however, the Union was carried, we ought to do our utmost to render it perfect and permanent. I thought in the year 1800, that it was a measure of party; that it would not be acted upon fairly, and that the inferior country would be obliged to suffer without redress. I have been most happily disappointed. I know of no instance in which the interests of Ireland have been brought under the consideration of the Imperial Parliament, in which those interests have not been attended to with justice, with favour, and almost with partiali·y.

Then, I may naturally be asked, if both countries have been so prosperous under the Union—if many privileges have been given to Ireland by it—if the markets of this country have been thus opened to her produce, why is she not satisfied, and why, by making these claims, does she attempt to disturb the harmony of the empire? I answer that the Irish Catholics, by making these claims are evincing their gratitude for benefits conferred upon them, and that they are the necessary consequence of the situation in which they are placed. If they aspire after the honours of the state, in order that they may serve their common country with advantage, it is not only consistent with the policy but with the dictates of human nature. If, as you say, you have given the protection of the law to the Catholic—if you have admitted him into the possession of wealth and power, and yet have excluded him from office on account of his religion, which you say necessarily makes him a subject not worthy of confidence, not worthy of a seat in parliament—is he to feel himself satisfied, or rather, does he not show his gratitude by asking for more? I should think him most base and unworthy to be free, if he were not to ask for more if he were sincere; but I should not believe in his sincerity, and should think him a base and deceitful hypocrite, I should think him a disgrace to the country, if he were not to ask for all the privileges of the rest of his countrymen.

I have been told, and it has been more than once mentioned in the course of this debate, that there is a difference between civil rights and political power. There is, in my opinion, no position more at variance with the fundamental principles of the constitution. Political power is the guardian of civil rights. The civil rights of subjects are not founded on any written law, but arose out of the essence of the constitution. Where is the law on which the rights of Protestants to seats in parliament are founded? There may be, and there are, laws for regulating the right; but the right itself rests on the common principles of the constitution. That right, like others, may be modified according to circumstances; but still, enjoyment is the general rule, exclusion is only the exception; and those who defend the exclusion are bound to prove its justice by making out its expediency. Our constitution is anything but an establishment of castes. The whole of it rests and is supported on the free admission of all the people to its benefits. The Throne, the Commons, and the House of Lords, all rest on this fundamental principle of our constitution, and by this it has been preserved from the fate of other countries. We have heard of public councils in other countries, which have been changed into oligarchies by trenching too much on the executive, or into courts of justice by permitting the executive to intrude too far upon their privilege; but the grand principle of our constitution is, that the several orders fall back upon the people, and are, I may say renewed by them. What is the construction of your lordships' house? Is it not gradually renewed and strengthened by an infusion from the body of the people—of those who are conspicuous for their merits, for having served the country, or the power of serving it by their wealth? The basis they rest upon is that of public opinion; and their improvement is founded on popular stamina. The lowest man in the state may, by his own merits and the exercise of his prerogative on the part of the sovereign, become a member of this house. What a proportion of your lordships have been elevated to the rank of the peerage in the late reign! And does it become those who have been thus taken from the people to talk of castes? With what face could I think of using the privilege which has been conferred upon me by putting my back to the d or to shoulder out the Duke of Norfolk? Shame on the ingenuity which could so construe the four corners of the great charter, as to turn it to the exclusion of the descendants of those freemen by whose wisdom and valour it was obtained! The position against which I contend, is that most erroneous one—that one set of men in a free state should have political power, whilst others should be excluded. This is a state of things so intolerable, that it is not in human nature to bear it. The subjects of the most absolute despot may, under a beneficent ruler, be happy; but it is impossible that men living under a free government can feel themselves otherwise than in a state of degradation, when they find they are debarred the exercise of their privileges as freemen, because they are said to believe in a religion which is superstitious and idolatrous. In such a state every comfort and enjoyment they may have will be smothered with indignation at the privations to which they are exposed, and the grounds on which their exclusion is defended. Can your lordships then be surprised, that you are called upon, year after year, by the Roman Catholics, for the removal of the disabilities under which they labour? I have at all times endeavoured to moderate the zeal of my Roman Catholic countrymen, by recommending them to make their approaches with temperance to the hostile opinions, and even the unjust prejudices, of those who are opposed to them in this country; but I should greatly abuse any influence which I may possess amongst them, if I were to advise them to cease their application altogether. The best advice I can give is, that they should never cease to pursue the assertion of their claims, until they obtain a full recognition of their rights. If there is any effect of their exclusion which I should view with the greatest alarm, it would be, that their voices shall be no longer heard in support of their just claims. That, indeed, would be a danger worse, not only than any which result from their exclusion, but than any which could well be imagined from their admission. What, I would ask, is the state of Irish feeling now on this subject? It is well known that in the pursuit of this one object of emancipation, an intensity of feeling pervades the whole of the Catholic population of Ireland, no matter what their rank, condition, or state in society. They all join in this pursuit with a degree of unanimity which has no parallel. Laity and clergy are alike associated in following the same object. Over a body thus united, a few individuals have acquired an influence, by which they have the power to excite them to almost any object they may think proper. I would ask your lordships whether that is a state of society which ought to continue in Ireland? Are we to hold our laws, our liberties, our safety, at the discretion of those individuals? Is it a state in which so important a part of the empire should be allowed to remain? Your lordships may complain, that a few persons should possess this power over so large a portion of the people. Why, it is not unreasonable to ask, should a few lawyers, who have only their zeal and their talents, possess this extraordinary influence? Your lordships will find, in answering this inquiry, that you yourselves are the cause. The people are united, because they are aggrieved. They associate and send forth their complaints, because they consider themselves injured; and your lordships may as well endeavour to avert the current of the blood in the human body, as to prevent those complaints, as long as you suffer the grievances out of which they spring to exist. As long as there are wrongs to be redressed, there will be public assemblies of the people to seek that redress; and, in those public assemblies there will be leaders, vying with each other in the race for vulgar popularity. If one sees that he is outstripped by another, he will endeavour to do something to render himself more agreeable to the passions, which, for that purpose, he will be disposed to excite. Do your lordships object to this state of things? Their demagogues are the spawn of your own wrong. You yourselves have created it, and, instead of looking on persons thus engaged as objects of justice, you should rather consider them as victims to injuries of long standing.

The question then, to be considered is, what are we to do in this case? Are we to stand still, or go backwards, or go forwards? To stand still is impossible. We must then either go forward, or go backward. "Go backward," said the noble lord, "Go backward! re-enact the penal laws, and outlaw a large portion of the people." Excellent tyranny, if it were possible. Make war on your own resources, and tarnish the honour of the country, by weakening it in such a cause. War, my lords, and for what? War, which, when you had carried to a certain extent, you would have to begin again. War, which would leave you a guilty spectacle to scoffing and exulting Europe. Do your lordships suppose that what is passing in Ireland, is an object of indifference to the continent of Europe? Do you suppose that our excellent constitution, and the unexampled prosperity of our career, has made us the love and not the envy of the world? There may be some foreign statesman who, taking up his glass, and viewing the dark spot in the western horizon pregnant with the materials of the coming storm, thinks not that it will break on him but for him; but I would answer for it with my life, if there should be an invasion of Ireland, that the Irish people will be found true to the king and the constitution. But, why so? Is it by virtue of the oath of supremacy, or the oath against transubstantiation? They may invoke all the saints in the calendar without giving you much benefit by it; but you will be entitled to their support, by reminding them of the events of the last fifty years, during which, in measures of their improvement, you have endeavoured to counteract the blighting effects of the penalties and persecutions of the preceding eighty. You will be entitled to it, by the hope of freedom which they see yet held out, and the prospect that their difficulties will, at no distant day, be wholly removed by your liberality.

I am most anxious not to introduce any topic which has not a tendency to conciliation, but I cannot help remarking on the inconsistency of the arguments of divided allegiance, and that which is admitted on all hands, namely, that the Roman Catholics are good subjects. This admission is made without your lordships' house; but then it is notorious that out of this house a strong feeling is excited against the assumed disposition of the same individuals, by the recital of the persecutions and fires of Smithfield. I do not mean to state that any of your lordships would be disposed to avail yourselves of the prejudices arising on this ground; but it cannot be overlooked, that while many of you oppose the Catholics on one ground, the only tie they have on the public voice in their support arises from another. I cannot pass over in this place, the use which has been made of the name of Mr. Pitt, and the manner in which the authority of his alleged opinions have been dealt with. This statesman, whose acts are well known—whose speeches and opinions are recorded and matter of history—is now held up by some of his admirers in support of a cause which he never advocated. The principles of that right honourable gentleman on this question were, I should have imagined, well known, they caused his retirement from the councils of a sovereign who loved him, at a time, too, when the country was engaged in war, in the issue of which his fame was committed. Yet, with all this, his name has been made the watchword of those by whom the very contrary opinions are held. I do not mean to impute to those noble and honourable persons who have been made, perhaps, in many cases, the unwilling sharers in those orgies; but I must say, that they are deeply responsible by whom this unfounded cry has been set up.

Lord Eldon—I claim my share of that imputation.

Lord Plunket assured the noble and learned lord, that all he felt it his duty to state on this subject, he said in good feeling towards him, and without meaning it in any way offensively to him, for no man had a higher respect for the character of the noble and learned lord, than he entertained. His argument was, that it was extremely unfair to hold out Mr. Pitt as the enemy of Catholic emancipation, and to associate the general principles of that statesman with opposition to the measure.

Lord Eldon denied that he had so held out the opinion of Mr. Pitt.

Lord Plunket—That is exactly what I wanted to hear. But whoever sent forth such an erroneous opinion to the country is deeply answerable for it. Another insinuation is, that Protestant ascendancy is opposed to radicalism, and the inference sought to be obtained is that those who support the one are opposed to the other. This also is extremely unfair; because it is well known, that many who are sincerely opposed to radicalism are as sincere in support of emancipation. I will now call the attention of your lordships to a book which has been laid before the public, containing a number of letters which passed between the late king and one of the members of his council, relating to the conscientious scruples entertained by the sovereign, as to whether he would be justified in refusing his assent to certain measures which might be proposed by the houses of parliament, and whether such assent would not be a violation of his coronation oath. Now it appears to me, that in the lifetime either of the late king, or of the member of the council to whom the letters were addressed, their publication would not have been justifiable; and I also think, that the representatives of the noble lord in question were not justified in placing them before the public.

LORD KENYON—May I be permitted to say a few words? (cries of " order, order.")

LORD PLUNKET—I meant distinctly to convey to the noble lord my opinion, that the publication of these letters was not proper; but in doing so I never intended to convey anything that was personally offensive. I must repeat, that the publication of letters tending to influence a measure before parliament, by putting in opposition to it the opinion of the late king, was not a fair mode of dealing with the subject. When I say this, I mean no insinuation against the sincerity of his late majesty. They are the conscientious opinions of an honest man, and the mode in which they are put is calculated to endear his memory to the people, and prove him a worthy member of the house of Brunswick. But it is miserable to think of the use that has been made of that opinion, and how the ear of royalty may be abused in some cases; for his majesty was made to believe, that he had no right to assent to the measure to which the letters referred, and that such assent would be a violation of his coronation oath. The opinions of Lord Kenyon were those of a sound lawyer and an honest man. What he said was, that it was not incumbent on his majesty to refuse his assent to the repeal of those acts, when the house of parliament in proposing that repeal considered it for the benefit of the country. In the same view he mentioned that the repeal of the Test Act might take place without any breach of the coronation oath or the act of Union. His lordship added—it seems to me, that the judgment of the person who takes the coronation oath must determine whether any particular statute proposed does destroy the government of the Established church. It seems that the oath, couched in the general terms in which it is found, does not preclude the parties sworn from exercising a judgment whether that he is bound to maintain will be essentially, or in any great degree, affected by the proposed measure. The noble lord thus left it as a case which might be decided by the exercise of his majesty's judgment, acting by the advice of his responsible ministers.

I now come to an act upon which much stress has been laid—I mean the 30th of Charles II. That act has been made to bear an overwhelming influence on this question; for it is contended, that it forms one of the fundamental principles of our constitution. If that be so, what a frightful step has been already taken; for the House of Commons has more than once passed a bill for the repeal of part of that act, and therefore has agreed to a measure contrary to the principles of the constitution. It will be necessary to relieve your lordships from such a dangerous consequence as must follow, if the principle to which I advert be true. Now I deny that the 30th of Charles II. is such a measure as it has been described. It was not an act passed with reference to Ireland ; for the exclusion of Roman Catholics from seats in parliament in that country did not take place till some years after. But I will prove, from legislative records, and from the history of those times, that the 30th of Charles II. was not then, nor afterwards, considered a fundamental principle of the constitution. It was passed at a period after the Restoration, when the sovereign was suspected, and not unjustly, of being imbued with Roman Catholic principles. Your lordships know, that the first attempt made at that time, in consequence of the supposed opinions of the monarch, and those that were known of his probable successor, was the bill of exclusion, and that having failed, the 30th of Charles II. was substituted. Now, what does that act say? It states that many of the mischiefs that had accrued to the country had arisen from Popish recusants having access to the throne; and declares that as a reason why the oath of supremacy should be taken as a qualification for seats in both houses of parliament. I do not deny that such an oath may have been necessary at the time; but I will ask, whether that measure has ever been declared permanent and unalterable? The first legislative measure which referred to it afterwards was the 5th of Anne, when provision was made for the demise of the crown; in the absence of the successor, a regency was provided, and the regent was declared to be disabled from giving assent to the repeal of certain acts. The first of these was the act of Uniformity. Mention was made of the 30th of Charles II., but that was rejected. Is not this a proof that the act was not considered permanent and unalterable? The act that was considered permanent, the regent was prevented from repealing; but with respect to the other, it was left, like an ordinary act, to the discretion of the government of the day. The next act to which I shall refer is that of the Union of England and Scotland. It was by that act declared, that the church of England and the church of Scotland were to be considered permanent and unalterable in those countries. But no mention was made of the 30th of Charles II.; and when the commissioners proposed that the oath should be taken in Scotland, it was refused, and the words were added—until parliament shall otherwise provide. I have thus, I conceive, redeemed my pledge of proving that that act was never considered a fundamental principle of our constitution. It was, as I have observed, passed to prevent the danger of Popish recusants having access to his majesty. Now, the 31st of the late king took away recusancy, and gave to Popish lords the privilege of access to the sovereign; and if that act had gone a little further, it would have repealed the whole of the 30th of Charles II., and left your lordships little trouble on the subject. This act of the 31st of the late king, was two years afterwards extended to Scotland. Here there was a repeal of the very ground on which the 30th of Charles II. was passed. The object of all these acts, and their only object, was, to exclude the temporal power of the Pope: and in all the acts which have been passed relating to Ireland, there has been an express provision that they shall continue until parliament shall otherwise provide.

I think I have now disposed of all that relates to the 30th of Charles II., and redeemed the pledge which I set out by giving. The noble and learned lord who preceded me, seems to put upon the oath of supremacy an interpretation different from that which I put upon it. I think it impossible to take it. My idea of the oath of supremacy is, I confess, that, in the strict and literal sense of the words, it is impossible to be taken by any person; for it not merely denies that any foreign power "ought to have any authority, ecclesiastical or spiritual, within this realm;" but it denies even that any foreign power "hath" any such authority. Now if we admit that there are Roman Catholics in this country, the Pope must have spiritual authority here. In the nature of things he must exercise it. We may deny his right, but we cannot deny his power while there are Roman Catholics in the country. The intent of the oath, no doubt, was, that it should be an absolute denial that any foreign power exercised any temporal or spiritual authority, as to the established religion of this country. It is perfectly correct, with reference to that church, to say, that no foreign potentate hath or ought to have any power or authority, temporal or spiritual, over it; but, as to the spiritual concerns of a sect, which was not at that time recognised by the law, we did not prevent them from submitting to foreign authority, nor could we do it. And, my lords, I will ask, does the king of England exercise any authority in the spiritual concerns of this sect, or could he do so without the sanction of parliament? Certainly not, according to the words and nature of that oath; and, as long as it continues, the Pope must have that power. I only state that, according to the words of the oath, and to the nature of things, this must be; but do I mean to advance that this oath is uncontrollable? No; on the contrary, I think it most important that this power should be placed under the control of the state. I think it is a danger for which a remedy ought to be provided. I think it a formidable thing that there should be an intercourse between the Roman Catholics of Ireland and a foreign power—an intercourse which, at present, may be innocent, but for the mischievous effects of which hereafter nobody can pretend to answer. I say, that, when any specific measure comes before your lordships for discussion, I shall join most heartily in requiring that the appointment of the Catholic clergy should substantially, if not by direct form, rest with the present system of domestic nomination, under the control of the state. I agree with noble lords in believing that danger may result from the authority now exercised by the Pope in these appointments; but the noble lords feel that this furnishes them with a good argument against removing the Roman Catholic disabilities, and they had rather have the danger and the argument, than adopt a course of proceeding which would have the effect of doing away both. For myself, my lords, I cannot conceive how anybody, anxious to guard the Protestant establishment, can refuse entertaining this proposition, or joining hand in hand with me in carrying it into effect. On the subject of additional securities, I am strongly impressed with the conviction that some arrangement ought to be made with the see of Rome, by which, in the appointment of the Roman Catholic clergy, a substantial control should be given to the government; they should be rendered respectable in the eyes of their flocks, and, for that purpose, a competent provision should be made for them by the state, not absolutely and independently, but, like the Regium Donum, granted to the Protestant Dissenters. To this last point some objection may be made on the score of our finances, but I can assure noble lords, that they will incur much greater expenses by keeping up an army, which, in quieter times, would be wholly unnecessary, than would be necessary to support the whole of the Catholic clergy. If caution and jealousy be thought to be unfounded on the part of the Protestant governors of the country, still that is no reason that they should not at once be conceded.

I listened with deep attention the other evening to the observations made by a right reverend prelate (the Bishop of Durham) on the subject of divided allegiance; but I have not been able to collect what has been the exact danger that he apprehends, or what he thinks likely to happen inimical to the constitution of this country, through the interference of the Pope. The only instance I have heard of, in which the authority of the see of Rome is at variance with the law of this country, relates to marriages. It is held by that power, that certain marriages which, according to the law of this country, are perfectly valid, are wholly illegal according to the canonical as it is there professed. But this is merely an opinion which does not interfere in any degree with the civil rights of parties; it does not affect the legitimacy of children, nor their right to inherit their parents' property, but only expresses the censures of the church against parties who are living in what is thought to be a state of sin. This is the single instance which has been adduced; but if there had been more, they would have added little weight of argument, if they had been of a similar character. They are altogether too insignificant, as well as too few, to weigh in the minds of statesmen who have an object so important to gain as the restoring peace and tranquillity to Ireland.

My noble and learned friend on the woolsack has said that the Roman Catholics decline to give any securities whatever, and that this circumstance decides him in voting against them. He says, that it entitles him to take away from the ranks of the advocates of Catholic emancipation, the great names of Pitt, Fox, and others. All that I can say to this is, that they did support the measure, and although the event has not happened, to which the noble lord alluded, in their lives, it does not follow that they would have refused to continue their support, because it had happened subsequently. As to one of them, my view of the matter is borne out. It was in 1813, that the securities proposed were refused by the Catholics; but Mr. Canning continued to support their cause, and this encourages me to hope, that, if they had lived, they would also have continued their support, even if the Catholics had refused what was demanded of them. But I do not think they did refuse. It is said to be the opinion of the great body of the Catholics, that they ought not to give these securities; but the opinion of the Catholics as a body should not be taken from what is said in public meetings, or from what falls from the demagogues and leaders at those meetings, into whose hands we have thrown them. Neither ought it to be inferred from their silence when those opinions are expressed; in which, they do not perhaps, concur, although they dare not contradict them. I confess I think they ought to do so. But it is really a matter of no importance, whether they do or not agree to the securities. It is for your lordships to do what you feel to be right and just. If you think that the measure may be safely adopted if accompanied by securities, it is your duty to pass it, without any regard to what the Catholics may think of those securities. This, I contend, is one sound principle of legislation. Every great body ought first to ascertain what is right and expedient to do, and this being ascertained, to carry it into effect. I am as certain as I am of my existence, that the great Catholic body would not hesitate for a moment to adopt the securities that may be proposed to them.

But we are asked, how is it to tranquillize Ireland? I answer, that if any noble lord thinks the sole object of this measure is to tranquillize Ireland, he is totally mistaken. The object of it is to do an act of justice. The tranquillity that may ensue is accessory, and not the principal object. Ireland no doubt will then be tranquil, but nobody can suppose that this proposition is by itself to be considered as a *panacea* which is to produce immediate and everlasting peace. Ireland will still be liable to be disturbed by the angry passions; but there will not be that hectic fever which makes Ireland a dead weight upon this country, instead of being, as it might be, an accession of strength and wealth. There are some other topics on which I wish to touch; but I have occupied so much of your lordships' time, that I will now conclude. I meant to have made some observations on the Catholic Association. I brought a bill into the other house of parliament for putting down that association; but it must be remembered, that I did so in the belief that that measure would be accompanied by others of a salutary nature. It has not been accompanied by any such measures; and I am free to say, that if the bill for putting down the Catholic Association were now to be brought down to the house, I should not feel myself bound under existing circumstances to vote for it. I am convinced that any measure, other than that which is intended to be founded upon the resolution before the house, will fail of accomplishing the tranquillization of Ireland. If the discontents and disturbances are stopped up in one place, they will break out in another. Nothing can repress them but expedients so rigorous that they will be inconsistent with a free country. The only effectual method of calming and defeating discontents is by taking away from the discontented that pretext which their wrongs give them.

ROMAN CATHOLIC OATHS.

March 13, 1829.

At last the hour of victory arrived. The king's speech of 1829 recommended parliament to review the laws imposing civil disabilities on the Catholics, with a view to their removal. A second bill for suppressing the Catholic Association having passed both houses unanimously, on the 5th of March Peel made that great act of humility, his speech introducing the measure of Catholic emancipation. His motion for a committee was carried by a majority of 340 to 160 votes, and in a few days the bill was introduced. Meantime the intolerants in the upper house uneasily watched the proceedings of the Commons, and Lord Eldon tried to pass the time by a motion for an account of the Roman Catholics in England who have taken the oaths under the act of 1791, and in Ireland under the act of 1793. The Chancellor spoke on the other side, and was followed by Plunket.

Lord Plunket said, that after what had fallen from the noble lord who had just sat down, and after the observations which had been made by the noble and learned lord who had preceded him, he could not avoid trespassing upon their lordships' attention for a few moments. He should feel it his duty, in the first instance, to apply himself to some part of that very extensive range, into which the noble and learned lord who had introduced this motion, and the noble lord who had just sat down, had thought fit to go; and, with regard to many of the observations which had fallen from those noble lords, he must say, notwithstanding all his respect for those noble lords, that they wandered much from the subject immediately before the house. Many of the observations of those noble lords applied to a measure which had passed that house, and which was now beyond their lordships' reach, and to another measure, which was not as yet before them, and respecting which any discussion for the present was, to say the least of it, out of place and irregular, and one into which he did not imagine the noble and learned lord would have strayed. He had supposed, that the word "constitution" would have been struck out of the observations of the noble and learned lord for that night; and yet all the observations made by that noble and learned lord were founded on the assumption, that the measure which had been recommended from the throne to the consideration of parliament would be subversive of the constitution of Great Britain. If this were not the proper time (as the noble lord himself acknowledged) to discuss that measure—if the period for its regular consideration had not as yet arrived—was it, he would ask, right or fitting, that observations like that should go forth amongst the lower orders in this country, and that the poor, the ignorant, and the uneducated, should be taught to believe that a measure which had been deliberately recommended from the throne would violate the coronation oath, and subvert the Protestant constitution of this country? He would confess that he was somewhat alarmed when he heard the noble and learned lord say, that "upon his own knowledge he could say that his majesty's consent would never be given." His apprehensions were greatly excited when the noble and learned lord had proceeded thus far in the period; but the sentence ended in a way perfectly satisfactory to him, and he was sure to all noble lords in that house; namely, "that his majesty's consent would never be given—to any measure calculated to subvert the Protestant constitution of this country." The noble and learned lord might, if he pleased, exercise for the future his talent at prophecy, but he was not much inclined to attend to the noble and learned lord's lucubrations in that way; for he could not forget that last year the noble and learned lord had thought proper to give utterance to a prophecy, when the bill for the relief of the Dissenters was before their lordships, and the result only proved—how much the noble and learned lord had been mistaken. The other noble lord had contended, that the government of Ireland ought to have put down the Catholic Association, and that they possessed the power to effect that object. He was sure it would be some consolation to the noble marquis who had lately held the reins of government in Ireland, and to his noble friend who sat behind him (the Marquis Wellesley), that they shared the censure pronounced by the noble lord, with all the governments that had existed in that country since the reign of Henry II., and that the censure had been spread out by the noble lord on so large a space, that but a small division of its weight could be allotted as their respective portions. He should endeavour to rescue the government of that country—the two noble personages that had been alluded to, and the distinguished persons that had preceded them in the government of Ireland, from the unfair aspersion which had been cast upon them. He never remembered a period, as long as he was connected or acquainted with the government of Ireland, when the laws were not fairly administered; and he would maintain that the vices which prevented the full, and complete, and satisfactory administration of the laws of that country, were to be found in the laws themselves; and that it was absolutely impossible for any government to administer such a system of laws, so as to give satisfaction to the country. And here he could not avoid remarking, that no observation had ever done more mischief amongst the people of Ireland, or had diffused so great a disrespect for the laws of that country, as an observation which had fallen from the noble lord who spoke last;—namely, that "in Ireland there was one law for the rich, and another law for the poor; and that both were equally ill-administered." That observation had passed into a proverb, and it was regularly brought forward in every case of attack upon the constituted authorities of the country. Now, he would say, that no such principle had been acted upon in Ireland. He had had a better opportunity of observing the system of government pursued there, than the noble lord's two years' residence in that country afforded him, and he would say, that no charge could be more unfounded, and that the law in Ireland had been administered equally and impartially. The noble lord had arraigned the Irish government for not putting down the Catholic Association. It was impossible for the government of that country to put down the association by force of the existing law, or by any law, through the ordinary medium of the legal tribunals of the country. He was therefore of opinion, that the mode of proceeding recently adopted for putting down the association was a wise one, inasmuch as it armed the government with a summary power to put down that body, and to repress any manifestation of feeling which its extinction might be calculated to excite. If hereafter there should be evinced a disposition in Ireland to rebel against that law, or to evade it, let not such disposition be imputed to the framers of the law, but to those who told the people that they could drive not merely a donkey-cart but a coach and six through it. The noble and learned lord, instead of giving his assistance to render that law effectual, told the people of Ireland that it was a flimsy act, which they could easily evade. Was it the duty of the noble and learned lord—of a person of great experience and legal research—instead of devoting his attention to this law, with a view to render it calculated for the objects it was intended to accomplish, to come down, as he had done, to that house, after it had been passed, and to state that it was so imperfect that it would be easily evaded? The noble lord who spoke last had insinuated, that, under the principles of the existing common law of the land, the association could have been put down. Now, it would be satisfactory to him, and no doubt to their lordships generally, to learn from that noble lord any proceeding at common law, by which that body could have been put down. He would not say, that a great portion of the proceedings of the association was not contrary to the common law, but he would maintain that an indictment against the association would be utterly untenable as a principle of common law. It was the law that the people could only be represented in parliament. If, therefore, any body assumed a representative capacity, and performed the functions of parliament it would, in so doing, violate the spirit of the common law. But the assertion that where particular laws were framed to exclude a people from being represented in parliament, any body that represented them for the purpose of petitioning for redress of their grievances, came within the principles of the common law, he would utterly deny. If the noble lord would point out to him a page in the common law—in that body of tradition and written law in which it had been handed down—in which it was laid down as a principle, that any portion of the people of this country should be permanently excluded from parliament, he would engage to show the noble lord, in the next page, a principle recognizing the perpetual existence of a committee for sending forward complaints and presenting petitions. In looking at the petitions from the people of England, he was satisfied that they were entitled to the utmost respect, and they were more entitled to respect, as they manifested the strong attachment of the petitioners to the Protestant constitution of this country. So far the petitioners were entitled to respect and attention; but when they proceeded to express their fears, that a measure for Catholic relief would endanger the Protestant constitution of this country, he did not think that this house was at all called upon to defer to their judgment on that subject. The privilege sought by the Roman Catholics was admission to the constitution. They sought not to do away with any means of security, or to take away any of the privileges possessed by the people of this country. But if it were a portion of the privileges of the people of this country, that any portion of the people should be shut out from the benefits of the constitution, and if, to take away from the Catholics the privilege of sitting in parliament, or of filling offices in the state, was to confer a privilege on the Protestants, he would say, that it was downright robbery and injustice. If you should take a thing from A and give it to B, that was an act of unqualified injustice; and so the principle which recognized the exclusion of the Catholics as a privilege belonging to the Protestants was one of robbery and injustice.

Did the noble lord mean to say that the people who had assembled at these meetings to prepare anti-Catholic petitions, who were gathered at parish vestries and parish meetings, were persons competent to instruct parliament as to the true law on these points? Let the noble lord, when he came to argue this question at the proper time, go himself into all the points connected with the laws and the constitution; and let him then show, if he could, that the measure for the removal of Catholic disabilities was calculated to shake the foundations of the constitution of these realms; but to say that the lower orders of the people could give information to the house on these mysterious, he would call them, and higher classes of public policy, was ludicrously absurd. Let noble lords but for a moment reflect upon the nature of the union between Great Britain and Ireland, and they must at once perceive, that it was a dangerous mistake, to say that the opinion of the people of England should be committed against the rights and privileges of the people of Ireland. He would not say, that at the period of the Union, there had been an express understanding and agreement with the people of Ireland that it would be followed up by the measure of emancipation, but there was certainly a very general expectation that, as soon as the Union was passed, a measure of that description would follow. Lord Cornwallis, Lord Castlereagh, and Mr. Pitt, who had been principally instrumental in having the Union carried in Ireland, when they found that it was not to be followed by emancipation, retired from the councils of his majesty. Now, let their lordships suppose, that the Union had never been carried, and that the parliament of Ireland still existed; and suppose a measure, restoring their rights and privileges to the great body of the Irish people, had obtained the assent of the crown and of the parliament of that country, would it be endured by the Irish people, that they should not regulate their own concerns, because the opinion of the lower classes of the people of England was against the measure? The persons who ascribed dangers to the constitution from this measure would never think of doing so, if the Union had not existed; those persons adopted a line of proceeding calculated to shake the foundations of that Union, and to raise up a principle of national hatred, which, combined with the principle of religious hatred, would operate doubly against the liberty, happiness, and peace of the country. He would now take the liberty of making a few observations, in reference to the motion which had been introduced by the noble and learned lord. • He must say, that that noble and learned lord had not dealt with the question with his usual frankness. The noble and learned lord said, that his measure did not deal with Ireland at all, while the greater portion of the noble and learned lord's observations were applied to the system which had been adopted in Ireland, to give the Catholics the opportunity of obtaining admission to certain offices and privileges, on complying with certain conditions imposed by the legislature. With regard to the argument which the noble and learned lord had raised on the point respecting the succession, it was sufficient to state the simple facts, to afford a full answer to the noble and learned lord. In the year 1774 an act was passed which required from the Roman Catholics a declaration to support the succession of the royal family. After that act was so framed in Ireland, the act of 1778 was framed, and he would call their lordships' attention to the form of oath which was employed in that act—the 18th George III., c. 6. By that act the exact phraseology of the Irish act of the 13th and 14th of the king was adopted; and he would beg their lordships' attention to the mode in which that act of the 18th of the king was passed in this country. It was introduced into parliament, not by the advocates of the Roman Catholics—it was brought forward by two distinguished men at that time, who were remarkable for their devoted attachment to the Protestant establishments of this country; he alluded to Sir George Saville and Mr. Dunning. That act was taken up by Lord Thurlow, who was then attorney-general; who said, he would give his best attention to it, and would follow it up through all its details. Under such circumstances, that act was passed in Great Britain, and, unfortunately, it was afterwards followed up by the Irish parliament, and its very phraseology adopted. What object could there be for that conspiracy, the existence of which the noble and learned lord would seem to suppose? They pledged themselves to support the succession to the throne in the House of Hanover, but as the words " being Protestants" were omitted, it was at once to be assumed, that these Catholic conspirators had provided for an occasion when some member of that house might become a Papist, and when, the other members remaining Protestants, it would be open to the Catholics to join the professor of their own creed, and support his claims to the crown. It was for such an improbable, such a wild and ludicrous purpose, that they must believe the existence of such a conspiracy. After the act of 1778 had been adopted in England, then came the act which passed in the Irish parliament in 1782; and he would beg to call their lordships' attention to that act. The act of 1782, finding that the previous act of the 13th and 14th of the king had already provided a declaration for the Catholics, and that the language of that act had been adopted in the English act, proceeded upon the authority of the act of the 13th and 14th of the king, strengthened by the act of 1778 in England, to enact in these words:—" that, whereas, all such of his majesty's subjects in this kingdom, and all persons whatsoever, who shall hereafter take and subscribe the oath and declaration prescribed by the 13th and 14th George III., ought to be considered good and loyal subjects of his majesty." There was the conspiracy! These were the conspirators who, by taking this declaration, were entitled to be considered good and loyal subjects of his majesty!

The act then proceeded to enable those who subscribed and took that oath to fill those situations and obtain those privileges, which were then opened to them on such conditions. He next came to the Irish act of 1793. In the meantime, the English act of 1791 had been passed, in which the words "being Protestants" were introduced after the words "the Princess Sophia, and the heirs of her body." The noble lord who spoke last had said, that he had known Catholics object to take that oath. He knew not upon what authority the noble lord stated that circumstance; but it was remarkable, that it was the first time that he had ever heard of the objection having been made. As for the act of parliament itself, it was strong enough. The noble lord contrasted it with the Irish act of 1793. Previous to the passing of that act, the Roman Catholics of Ireland had published a declaration, disavowing, in the most unequivocal terms, the odious and revolting doctrines which had been imputed to them. The act of 1793 was not introduced by an advocate of the Roman Catholics. It was an act brought forward on the authority of government, and introduced into parliament by Mr. Secretary Hobart. A right honourable gentleman, now no more, at the time said, that it would be a good thing to embody in it the declaration made by the Catholics disavowing the odious tenets imputed to them. The suggestion was adopted, and that was the only oath to be found in the act of 1793. The oath framed for Roman Catholics by that act, and required to be taken by them, must be considered by them as a degradation in itself; for it contained the disavowal of the most abominable and odious doctrines. But the act of 1793 did not first introduce the other oath which was at present taken. The act of 1793 said, that the persons who abjured those obnoxious tenets, and who took the oath prescribed by the former act—the 13th and 14th of the king—should be entitled to all the privileges which the laws then conferred on Roman Catholics. From what he was now going to state, their lordships would see what credit was due to the assertions of the noble lord. In the year 1813, a bill for Catholic emancipation was introduced by his lamented and eloquent friend, the late Mr. Grattan. The bill was criticised by the agitators in Ireland. They quarrelled with a great part of its enactments; and they cavilled most against the details of the bill; yet, though the oath proposed by Mr. Grattan was similar to that contained in the act of 1791, they never mentioned it among their objections to the bill. What had taken place between 1792 and 1812 to cause such a change in the sentiments of the Catholics? It remained, indeed, for the noble lord, and those who had informed him that the Catholics objected to the oath in the act of 1791, to state what had occurred between 1793 and 1813, that had effected such an extraordinary change in the opinions of the Roman Catholic body. In the Catholic bill which he (Lord Plunket) proposed in 1821, the oath of the act of 1791 was not introduced in terms; for the frame of that bill was different from that of the bill of 1813. In that bill of 1821 that oath was not introduced, as he proposed a common oath to be taken both by Catholics and Protestants. The oath which he proposed in that bill was intended, with slight alterations, to be taken respectively by Protestants and Catholics; and such an oath rendered that of 1791 unnecessary. In the bill which he introduced in 1825, and which passed the House of Commons, the oath of the 13th and 14th of the king was again resorted to. In the year 1825 there was no such conspiracy of Catholics as that represented by the noble lords to have existed in 1793. Indeed there was not the shadow of a conspiracy ever suspected by any one, until those noble lords went so far back as 1778, endeavoured to rake up the ashes of fifty years past, and thought it fit and proper to cast imputations on the loyalty of the Roman Catholics, who, he would take the liberty to say, were as little open to such an imputation, and had evinced as strong and unimpeached loyalty, as those noble lords themselves. They had evinced their loyalty by deeds, by oaths, and by the continued probity of their entire character. Surely the noble lord would not descend to the level of the vulgar and ignorant crowd, and join them in asserting that the Catholics were not to be trusted on their oaths? If the noble lord would join in such a vulgar and unfounded prejudice against the Catholics, and would then require them to swear to abide by a Protestant sovereign, the noble lord would, in that case, be obliged to say, that they had sworn falsely; and where then was the utility of the noble lord's precautions? He had no objection to the production of the returns moved for by the noble and learned lord; but if the noble and learned lord, from the scantiness of those returns, should attempt to draw an argument against the Roman Catholics, he would tell him that he was much mistaken. The argument would be the same against Protestants as against Roman Catholics. The oath prescribed would not, in any instance, be taken by a Roman Catholic, except for the purpose of obtaining some office, or getting rid of some penalty under the act. With regard to the Roman Catholic priesthood, it would be found that, in every instance, they had taken the oath prescribed by the act of 1793. Their object in doing so was to remove the penalty of premunire, to which they otherwise would be liable. So when an office, situation, or livelihood, was to be obtained by a Roman Catholic layman, for which the taking of this oath was one of the qualifications, it would be found that, in every such instance, it had been taken With respect to the Roman Catholic clergy in the College of Maynooth—upon which college heavy and unfounded slanders had been thrown out, which he would take another occasion to refute and expose—not one of them had been three months in that college without being obliged by the superior to take this oath. In order to show that oaths of this nature had been only taken where a necessity for taking them as a qualification arose, he would move, as an amendment on the motion of the noble lord, for a return of the number of Protestants of the Established church of Great Britain and Protestant Dissenters who had taken the oaths of allegiance, abjuration, and supremacy. It would then appear, that Protestants as well as Catholics only took those oaths prescribed by law when they found them necessary as a qualification for some office or employment. Under the 1st of George I., c. 13, the Protestants of Great Britain were obliged to take the oaths of supremacy and abjuration; and this act was extended to Ireland by the 6th of George III., c. 55 (confirmed by the 21st of the same reign), which rendered it obligatory on the Protestants and Protestant Dissenters of that country to take oaths of abjuration. Now, in order to show that those men, of undoubted loyalty to the House of Brunswick, the Protestants and Protestant Dissenters, only took those oaths when, like the Catholics, with regard to the oaths of the acts of 1791 and 1793, they had a particular purpose for so doing, he would move, that, in addition to the returns called for by the noble and learned lord, returns should also be made of the number of Protestants and Protestant Dissenters who had neglected to take oaths enjoined by the 1st of George I., and by the 6th and 21st of George III., in Great Britain and Ireland, since 1813, the period of the noble and learned lord's motion.

CATHOLIC RELIEF BILL.
April 4, 1829.

The Catholic Relief Bill came to the upper house on the 1st of April, and was debated for a second reading next day. The Duke of Wellington led the discussion with a distinct intimation that the king's government in Ireland had become impossible without Catholic emancipation. The two Protestant primates, Canterbury and Armagh, followed in opposition. The Bishop of Oxford and the Bishop of Salisbury succeeded—the first offering his resolute support, the other his "cordial negative" to the bill. After a debate of not very remarkable length or ability, the house adjourned to the following day. The great authorities of the Lords then, and on the third day, delivered their opinions. The Archbishop of York and the Bishop of Durham commenced the discussion in sermons saturated with a thorough *odium theologicam*. The Duke of Sussex supported the government with a very learned and a very amiable essay on legal persecution. The lofty and statesmanlike argument of Earl Grey immediately preceded Lord Eldon raging with baffled bigotry, and uttering weird predictions of the endless evils which toleration of Popery would be sure to introduce. Plunket appears to have been on the watch for the old Chancellor, and for a signal opportunity of closing the great argument to which for so many years he had devoted his mind. This speech ends the debate, which decided the liberties of the Catholic people of the empire. After a few explanations, and a brief formal reply from the Duke of Wellington, the house divided, and the bill was read a second time by a majority of 105.

My lords—I assure your lordships that I have not reserved myself for this late period of the debate, under the impression that I have any claim to review the arguments which have been adduced in the course of it by noble lords who resist the proposed measure. But, my lords, the noble and learned lord who has just sat down, having repeatedly declared in this house, at an early period of your discussions, and having through the medium of this house loudly and decidedly proclaimed to the people of this country, that the measure announced by his majesty's government was opposed to the Protestant religion and the safety of its establishment, and subversive of those fundamental principles of the constitution which had been established at the periods of the Reformation and Revolution, and having undertaken to demonstrate the truth of these assertions whenever the proper time should arrive for so doing, I did think myself justified, if not bound, to wait for the fulfilment of that pledge.

My lords, after the commanding arguments of my noble and learned friend on the woolsack, and of my noble friend behind me (Earl Grey), I own I did listen with intense curiosity to the observations of the noble and learned lord; but I must say that that curiosity has been completely and agreeably disappointed. The noble and learned lord must excuse me for saying—and I say it with every feeling of personal respect for him—that the alarming denunciations of danger and destruction to our religion and our constitution, with which the noble and learned lord at the outset assailed this measure, rest at this moment where they originally did, upon the high authority of the noble and learned lord, but unsupported either by fact or argument, or by parliamentary or historical documents. Before, however, I apply myself particularly to this legal part of the subject, your lordships will, I trust, excuse me, if I venture to make some general observations on the subject; I shall not do so at any great length; but, my lords, after having anxiously watched the progress of this momentous question for more than thirty years, and seeing it now approaching, as I trust it is, rapidly and certainly to its final consummation, I think I owe it to the house, to the subject, and to myself to state some of the grounds on which I rest my support of it.

My lords, I wish to proceed at once to the consideration of the actual state in which the country is now placed, and to justify the proposed measure on the ground of its adoption being necessary for the safety, if not for the actual existence, of Ireland in connexion with Great Britain. But a right reverend prelate has stated, that expediency is not a principle on which a statesman is justified in acting; but I think the right reverend prelate was under the necessity of finally admitting the exactness of the proposition stated by one of his right reverend brethren, the Regius Professor of Oxford, that where no principle of justice is violated, expediency is a sound principle of political action. If this be so, I ask what principle of justice is violated by the present measure? Is it a violation of justice to admit millions of the inhabitants of these countries to the privileges of citizens. I have always understood the principle of our constitution, and of every sound and free constitution, to be that laid down by my noble friend (Earl Grey) and, as I now collect, not dissented from by the noble and learned lord; namely, that admission to parliament, to office, and to franchise, is the principle, and that exclusion from any of them is the exception, and that such exception can be justified only upon grounds of necessity or of political expediency of the highest degree. The people in this case claim a right to share in the making and administering those laws by which they are to be governed, and this right can be resisted on no other ground than that of a clearly demonstrated expediency. They are excluded it is admitted by acts of the legislature, excused or justified only on the supposition that they were expedient at the time of their enactment. But if it can be shown that the expediency on which the exclusion was founded has passed away, or that there are motives of expediency for the repeal of those laws, infinitely transcending those which led to their enactment, what pretence can be found for precluding us from acting on the principles of right, of justice, of expediency, and of necessity, in the adoption of such measures as are applicable to the actual circumstances of the country?

What then, my lords, is the state of Ireland? My lords, it is a great mistake to suppose, that for the last fifty years Ireland has, with respect to her civil concerns, been badly governed. On the contrary, it is but justice to the British government to say, that during that period a wise and liberal system of policy has, in that respect, been adopted. You have opened to her, without distinction of Protestant from Catholic, all those channels of wealth which flow from unrestricted freedom of trade—you have given to all classes of her people an equality of civil rights—you have enabled her to accumulate all the great materials of national strength—you have raised her from the state of wretchedness and poverty, and ignorance and abjectness, in which the penal code had sunk her—you have associated her with yourselves in the concerns of this great empire, and have kindled in the minds of her people all those proud and independent feelings which belong to a powerful nation, associated with yourselves in those high duties which so materially affect the destinies of the civilised world.

See then, my lords, what has been the consequence. It is this —that having advanced in this full tide of civil prosperity, with a rapidity surpassing your most sanguine calculations, she is at this moment in a state of political danger and disorganization without a parallel in the history of any other country in Europe. What is the cause of this strange result? My lords, the statement of the evil unfolds the cause and demonstrates the remedy. The state of things is "unexampled civil prosperity, and unexampled political danger." Where is the cause of this disproportion between the advance of national prosperity and the attainment of happiness and safety? I answer, "in the laws;" in this, my lords, that the uniform course of the laws which regulate the civil rights of the subject, has been, for more than half a century, not only in advance beyond those which regulate their political rights, but in irreconcilable contradiction to their principles. Why, then, if you see the mischief and the cause, there can be but one course as to the remedy, "put down the mischief, and correct the laws which produce it." The noble duke at the head of the government has, therefore, most wisely proposed, and you have most wisely passed, a law for putting down the Roman Catholic Association; but I say "wisely," only because you follow your process of coercion with the great measure of relief, which alone can render it effectual. That, or any other expedient which human policy could devise, must be impotent for any purpose of lasting good, so long as you leave the great body of the people compressed into union, by grievances galling and insulting, and which it is not in the nature of freeborn men to endure without complaint.

My lords, the truth and extent of these mischiefs and miseries cannot be duly appreciated by noble lords who have never personally witnessed them. It is not that parties are opposed to parties, or sects to sects, or one part of the kingdom to another; it is not like anything that I can trace in history; it mixes itself in every transaction in public or in private life, obstructs every duty, embarrasses every dealing, poisons every enjoyment, haunting every movement of business, of obligation, or of social intercourse.

My lords, the violent reclamation against the projected measure which has been made on the part of many of the Protestants in Ireland, does not grow from a religious panic, or any apprehension for the safety of the Protestant establishment, as in this country; nor again, from a sordid desire of monopoly, which I do not believe exists to any considerable extent in either country. No, my lords, the feeling which, I frankly own, bursts spontaneously from the hearts of the great body of the lower classes of Protestants and Protestant Dissenters, especially in the north of Ireland, is that of resentment at being deprived of the enjoyment of a sense of superiority, which has been bred by the law, and in which they have indulged for more than a century; the right of putting out their hand and pushing back their equals in their progress to an honourable station in society—a privilege from which they derive no substantial benefit, no advantage other than the luxury of insulting and degrading their fellow-citizens. My lords, it is this perpetual consciousness of legal superiority which elevates the brow of the Protestant, and corrodes the heart, and breaks down till it rouses to fury the elastic spirit of his Roman Catholic neighbour.

My lords, in the higher classes of society, this feeling is corrected by courtesy and by those habits which belong to rank and to education. In this house (although I think I have heard the topic of idolatry pushed rather beyond its due limit,) the exclusion is justified on principles of state policy. It is said, "You are very worthy and honourable people, we respect you very much, but we are sorry that there are political reasons which require the continuance of your exclusion from the state." But in Ireland, my lords, and amongst the classes which compose the great body of the persons who exult in their legal superiority, the language is more offensive than even the exclusion. "You are an idolater—you are not to be believed on your oath—your religion is odious, and corrupt, and unchristian. What claim can *you* have to be associated with us in the exercise of the privileges of freemen?" "What!" says the Protestant shopkeeper, "shall I think myself safe, or fairly dealt with, if a Roman Catholic judge has any share in the administration of the laws by which I am to be governed?" What must the Roman Catholic gentleman feel, on the other hand? "Am I fairly dealt with, and am I to feel thankful when the law by which I am to be governed is administered *exclusively* by Protestants?" It is not that they are not well and fairly administered, but the claim and the principle are founded in folly and insolence, and it is not in human nature that this daily and hourly claim of unmeaning superiority can be patiently endured, and the very circumstance that the refusal of the participator is so worthless to the Protestant, and that he forfeits no advantage by the participation, aggravates the resentment of the Roman Catholic, by marking more distinctly that the exclusion rests upon a principle of useless and gratuitous insult. Why, then, my lords, every individual whose resentment is kindled by these privations is sensible that the brand which stigmatises him as an individual, is a religious brand which dishonours his entire sect ; why then there needs no plan of organization to combine all these individual discontents. The combination, and hostile combination, of the entire Roman Catholic population is formed by the laws; the insult is given by the laws. And then when you see all these individual resentments embodied in one great national confederation, you wonder at this monster of your own creation, and cry out against those who do not put down the existence of this force, which is beyond the reach of the ordinary power of the state. My lords, persons who, I doubt not, meant well, but who were utterly mistaken as to the real state of Ireland, told you, " never mind, the people don't care about the thing." A noble earl now no more, of whom I must ever speak with the highest respect, was misled by those assertions, and the answer to the question on the secret committee in Ireland was relied on, " Do the Roman Catholics attach the value of this drop of ink, or of this pen to the obtaining of Roman Catholic emancipation ?"

The noble and learned lord who spoke last, has even now stated, that Catholic emancipation was a pretence used by Jacobins and Radicals to cover their real designs against the constitution.

[Here Lord Eldon said that he had alluded only to the period of 1798.]

My lords, if the period of 1798 has no bearing on the present times, or on the present question, why did the noble and learned lord call it to his aid ? In whatever degree he applied it, I think I am justified in meeting it, and I cannot but observe that it seems whimsical to suppose that, if Roman Catholic emancipation was a subject devoid of interest, it should be resorted to as a colour for the purpose of exciting interest.

[Lord Eldon made some further observations in the nature of a disclaimer of the topic.]

My lords, I do not press the subject further on the noble and learned lord; nothing can, in my opinion, be more unjust than to seek to fasten, either on individuals or on classes of individuals, opinions which they disclaim. But, my lords, the fact is now beyond controversy, that these absurd and useless exclusions have united the whole body of the Roman Catholic people, from the highest to the lowest;

and you have formed into a confederation against you, a powerful people, agitated by the two most active stimulants that can affect the mind of man—resentment for insult to their persons, and for insult to their religion. How then do they, and must they act? By continual claim against continual grievance—continual meetings must be had to give expression and effect to those claims—leaders distinguished by their enthusiasm and talents must acquire an ascendancy; to maintain that ascendancy they must invite or yield to everything that is extravagant and seditious; and thus you have the Roman Catholic Association, with all its dangers and all its licentiousness, necessarily formed and perpetuated by your own laws.

My lords, you can no longer affect not to see this terrifying state of things. There exists at this moment, or did exist when this measure of grace and justice was announced—for it fled, like a troubled spirit, at the very dawn of conciliation—but there exists, sleeping or waking, a power beyond the state; not a transient tumultuary movement, nor a casual rising against the peace, but a permanent confederation, resting on the sympathies of the great body of the people, indissolubly combined for the attainment of just objects which they never can abandon; growing out of the essence of your legalizing—involving in their constitution every principle of misrule, sucking into their vortex everything which is involved in the common grievance, or which chooses to attach to it its own interests and passion, bidding for all the rank and property and talents and enthusiasm and virtue, and for all the folly and sedition and madness which are scattered through the great mass of society; which shall predominate, depending on the accidental character of their leaders; holding all the component parts of society in a state of solution, uncertain what may be raised to the top or what may sink to the bottom; exciting the occupiers of the soil, putting aside the proprietor, arming itself with all the powerful energies of religion, or defying all its wholesome influences as best may suit the purpose of the hour. These, my lords, are the terrible ingredients of that unnatural power which the vices of your exclusive system have engendered. That these desperate elements of mischief have not burst upon us, we owe to the vigilance of our government, to the wholesome effects of the liberal policy by which you have ameliorated the condition of the people, to the confidence they have felt in the growing liberality of parliament, to the unwillingness of the leaders to involve themselves in any act of violation of the public peace, by which they themselves and the country might be desperately committed; but above all, under God's providence, to the continuance of peace, and the absence of any foreign enemy.

But, my lords, this is a precarious tenure by which to hold the peace and safety of these countries. This state of things cannot endure. The scenes which have passed in Ireland within the last two years must not be reacted.

Noble lords say, "Trust to time, and to wise institutions for improving the condition of the people." My lords, there are evils for which time or wise institutions can bring no cure; on the contrary, they must be more deeply aggravated every day and every hour My lords, in a wholesome and natural state of society every accession of wealth is a new pledge of public safety; but, in the unfortunate perversion of principles which constitutes the character of the existing laws, the dangers and the mischiefs grow in exact proportion to the increase of all the ordinary ingredients of public prosperity. If I am asked, who are the most discontented and dangerous members of society in Ireland? I must answer, and no person acquainted with that country will contradict me—"Those who have most recently and rapidly been raised to comfort and opulence." Increase the prosperity of Ireland threefold, and she will be three times as dangerous. The vice of your laws changes wholesome nutriment into poison. You must abandon the chimerical attempt to separate political power from those civil rights which are the foundation and substance of all power. You have undertaken the impossible problem of governing rational beings, surrounded by free institutions, upon the principle of their not being worthy to share in them; to govern a free people on the principle of their being bad subjects, or to shut out the people who are admitted to be good subjects from all share in the political constitution of our representative government; to rest the frame of government neither upon substantial power nor upon public opinion; these are solecisms gross, and exploded by the universal consent of mankind; false in theory, and condemned by the acknowledged policy of every free government in the world except our own.

My lords, I cannot say that I have ever met with any person who directly asserts that the present state of things can continue. The noble and learned lord, indeed, has intimated that these evils may be cured by the force of the common law. My lords, I have again and again applied my mind to what has been asserted, or hinted by the noble and learned lord; I have endeavoured to ascertain his meaning, and to find some practical application of it; and with every degree of respect for him, I am obliged to declare, solemnly and unaffectedly, that I am not able to arrive at the most distant guess at what he proposes, even as a means of punishment; but with respect to the quieting or governing my unfortunate country, it is a perfect mockery. My lords, I defy the ingenuity of any man to find a principle to arrest the vital current of a people's justified feelings, or to prevent the demonstration of them. It has all the effect of cruel trifling (though I am sure not so intended) with the feelings of those whose lot is cast in the midst of the terrible crisis, to talk of applying the latent principles of the common law to the throbbing temples and to the dry and burning frame which is consuming under this unremitting hectic. Let us not disguise the bitter alternative; this terrible state cannot continue, and it must be put down, either by force of arms or by the repeal of the laws which inflict the grievances.

My lords, of this alternative his majesty's ministers have chosen the latter part; and in obedience to his majesty's gracious communication, in which he has called on us to find a remedy for those evils, consistently with the safety of our establishments in church and state, the noble duke has proposed a measure which, in my judgment, is appropriate and adequate; finding the evil in the unsuitableness of the law to the existing state of the country, he proposes to correct the law, and to do that which is the basis of the whole science of legislation—to accommodate the law to the circumstances of those on whom it is to operate; and instead of leaving us exposed to the risk of some fearful hour of public difficulty, in which those thunderclouds that hang over us might rush into collision, he has availed himself of this auspicious moment, while we are in profound peace abroad, and while yet the hostile parties into which Ireland is divided are unstained with the guilt and horrors of civil war, to submit to the consideration of your lordships the measure which is now before you. Whether it is fitted to produce those glorious results, it is for you, my lords, to judge; but in this respect at least, it appears to me strictly to preserve the condition pointed out in the royal speech, that it cautiously abstains from touching any part of our religious establishments, or from making any the slightest innovation upon any part of our Protestant institutions.

It has, indeed, been very confidently asserted, that the Protestant church is endangered, and the Protestant religion attacked, by the present measure. I shall beg leave very briefly to address myself to the right reverend bench on this subject; and I do assure them with no unfriendly voice. I am sure they will do me the justice to acknowledge that my uniform conduct in respect to them entitles me to say so; and I should be willing, my lords, to lay this bill alongside the coronation oath, and I would ask to have any one iota pointed out in which the one interferes with the other. Does it propose to take away from the bishops or clergy of this realm, or from the churches committed to their charge, any property or privilege which by law appertain to them? Does it propose to meddle with any article of their faith? Does it introduce into their religious establishment, or to any of its offices or emoluments, any person who does not acknowledge their creed or subscribe to their articles? Does the admission of freeborn men and loyal subjects to constitutional rights violate the laws of God or the true profession of the gospel? But, my lords, the argument grounded on the coronation oath has been, I think, in the course of the present discussions nearly if not altogether abandoned, and I shall not at this hour consume your lordships' time by any further observations upon it.

But it is urged, that though the present measure does not directly attack the church, yet, by the admission of Roman Catholics into parliament, it may lead to such consequences. My lords, the right reverend personages who state their apprehensions need not be reminded of the caution which is necessary in the application of an argument; which refuses a present good, or submits to a present evil, solely from the apprehension of a remote and future danger; what is present we know; what is future we can only conjecture; and every right reverend person will, I am sure, candidly admit to me that he should be well satisfied of the grounds of probability on which his anticipations rest, and of the reality of the dangers or mischiefs which he forbodes, before he refuses to act on the demands of present duty and expediency. What, then, are the grounds on which these apprehensions rest? First, on the supposition that the Roman Catholics, if admitted to power, would aim at the subversion of our establishment; and second, that they might be able to effect that object. I will briefly advert to each branch of the supposition. On what principle is it assumed that the Roman Catholics are enemies to our establishment? A most reverend prelate (the Archbishop of York) has candidly borne testimony to the virtues of those Roman Catholics with whom he has happened to be acquainted; indeed, the right reverend bench in general have, in a manner which reflects credit upon them as gentlemen and as Christians, acknowledged the honour and probity of the great body of the Roman Catholics Why, then, my lords, they are willing to swear, and by this bill they are required to swear, that they will not use their privileges to disturb or weaken the Protestant establishment. Now, I really cannot understand what is meant by saying that a man is amiable, exemplary in the discharge of all the duties of life, and that he is a most worthy moral character, and yet that you will not believe him on his oath. Why then, if you will not believe his oath or his assertions, look to his acts. Have the body of the Roman Catholics done any act of hostility to the church establishment? It is true, as has been stated by the noble and learned lord, that in the eager prosecution of their political claims, very foolish and angry speeches have been made at public meetings, both by priests and laymen, with reference to the Protestant church; and with great deference to the noble and learned lord, I have seldom known a public political meeting in which very idle and foolish speeches have not been made; and it is not perhaps much to be wondered at, if upon such occasions the Roman Catholics have retorted with violence and indiscretion, the acrimony with which they had been assailed. But it is too much to say, that because two or three angry priests or demagogues have expressed themselves intemperately or indecently at public meetings, the feelings so expressed by them are in accordance with those of the whole Roman Catholic body. My lords, no body of people of any persuasion could stand such a test. The Roman Catholics, rely on it, whatever may have been said by any individuals of their body, have never attempted to offer any injury to the Established church, and they are ready to swear that they will not. "No," the opponents say, "this will not do;" for they know the sentiments of the Roman Catholics better than the Roman Catholics themselves, and that they are bound in conscience and duty to subvert our establishment. My lords, this assertion is purely gratuitous; it is not only unproved, but it cannot be proved. To show this it would be necessary, first, to show that the establishment of any religion is a matter of conscience or of duty. It is no such thing; it is admitted by every one to be a matter of policy and of state regulation; some will say of unwise policy, others, and I entirely agree with them, of most wise policy. But, wise or unwise, it cannot be a matter of conscience or duty, in the members of any one religion to make it an established one; still less can it be a matter of conscience or duty in the members of any one religion to overthrow the existing establishment of any other religion.

But, my lords, the question is not truly put. I will not take upon me to say, whether, if the question were put abstractedly to a Roman Catholic, does he prefer a Protestant or a Roman Catholic establishment, he would not answer that he would prefer the latter. The Roman Catholic can have no particular fondness for the Protestant establishment as such, or so as to give it a preference to all others; but the question which an honest and rational Roman Catholic has to ask himself is totally different; he says, here I see the Protestant establishment subsisting in these countries for three hundred years.

I see it embedded in the state, and all its institutions, that it could not be overturned without the subversion of the state itself, and along with it, of all the privileges, and rights, and liberties which I enjoy, and expect to transmit to my posterity under it; and therefore I have no hesitation in preferring a Protestant establishment accompanied by all these enjoyments and blessings, to the wild projects of seeking for a Roman Catholic establishment, at the risk of forfeiting them all —at the risk, do I say? no, but with the certainty.

My lords, every Roman Catholic well knows that the Protestant establishment of Ireland is indissolubly wound up with the establishment of England, and that neither the church of England nor the government of England will ever permit the Protestant church of Ireland to be subverted. My lords, I take upon myself to say, that such extravagant notions, which could not be accomplished without heaving the British empire from its centre, do not enter into the contemplation either of priests or laymen of that persuasion.

So much, my lords, for the supposed principle of hostility. Let me now offer a few words as to the means of effectually acting upon it. The apprehension rests upon the supposition that such members of the Roman Catholics as will be admitted, that they will be enabled to sway the majority of both houses of parliament, for the purpose of overturning or essentially injuring the Protestant establishment; that a constituency, of which the great majority is Protestant, will elect a number of Roman Catholic representatives, sufficient to effect this purpose, in the House of Commons; that a Protestant king will raise to the peerage a number of Roman Catholics, sufficient to effect the same purpose in this house; that a Protestant king, bound by his solemn duty and interest to protect his own religion, and that of the state and its establishment, will join in this conspiracy. If this apprehension refers to the representation from England, do they really fear that the Protestants of England will become parties to this league against their religion? If to Ireland, is it to be supposed that any Roman Catholics returned after the passing of this bill, would be more devoted to the interests of the Roman Catholics than the Protestant members now returned by a Roman Catholic constituency. I cannot bring myself to believe that such apprehensions are seriously entertained. Do they forget the bill of rights, the corner-stone of our constitution, which has made one branch of the legislature essentially, and unalterably, and exclusively Protestant; giving thereby a perfect and absolute security against even the possibility of any legislative measure subversive of the Protestant religion and establishments? Do they forget that the fountain of all executive power in these countries is essentially, unalterably, and exclusively Protestant, affording thereby a perfect security, that no person shall be appointed to any office under the crown, of whose loyalty and determination to support the Protestant institutions that exclusively Protestant king shall not be entirely and conscientiously satisfied? But above all, my lords, let it be recollected, that all these exclusive powers of protection are exercised in the face of open day under the control of enlightened public opinion, and subject to the jealous criticism of the Protestant people of this country, possessing the fullest information of everything which passes within these walls, and of all the acts of all our public functionaries.

I would then, my lords, request them to look at the petitions which have been laid on your table; petitions, I admit, of little value, when you consider them as arguments, but of incalculable value as conveying the clear expression of the devoted attachment of the people of England to the Protestant religion and to the Protestant church. My lords, in that sentiment I find the true and unconquerable security of the Protestant religion. If, my lords, the wild and extravagant dream of such a nefarious confederation of King, Lords, and Commons were to be realized, and were even the right reverend bench to become parties to such an act of suicide, must they not be controlled and overwhelmed by the indignation of the Protestant people of this country? These, my lords, are fancies on which no rational man would place the difference of a day's purchase in dealing for his estate; they are suppositions transcending the limits of moral possibility, and on which no sober mind can rest, as a motive for action in this great concern. My lords, I own it does affect me with astonishment unspeakable, that acute and reasoning minds can be so sensitive to these possibilities of theoretical and distant, and consequential dangers, and that they can rest at ease under, and pray for a continuance of, the immediate and direct, and practical dangers in which they are at this moment placed. In what does the real danger consist? In this, my lords, that the Protestant hierarchy in Ireland rests on a very narrow basis, on a very small proportion indeed of the population of the country. Where is our safety to be found? In the interest which the great body of the population feel in the state, and in its laws. Millions of people desire admission to the privileges of citizens, from which the argument I have now to deal with admits they ought not to be excluded on mere political grounds. They do not seek to meddle with any of the rights or possessions of the church, and they offer to bind themselves by solemn oaths, not to use their privileges for the purpose of doing so directly or indirectly. No; the heads of the church say, these privileges which you seek, are incompatible with the existence of the church. You have not done anything hostile to us; you do not purpose to do anything hostile to us; you offer to swear that you will not do anything hostile to us; we know you to be very worthy and honest people, but on certain maxims which we have laid down, we will not believe either your oaths or your actions; and we frankly tell you, that as long as our establishment continues, you never shall obtain your political privileges. Are these, my lords, safeguards for the church? Where millions of our fellow-subjects are indissolubly united in pursuit of rights, as sacred as any institutions in the state, when the throne and the great body of the wealth and intelligence of the Protestants of Ireland are not opposed to them, is it for the clergy of the Established church to say, we put ourselves in the breach, the only obstruction to your march, and you never shall obtain your object until you put down our establishment. My lords, this is a fearful alternative to hold out to the Roman Catholics; but it is very wise on the part of the church, to tell the Protestant proprietors there can be no tranquillity for your country, you shall not be relieved from the apprehension of civil war; British capital shall not flow into your country, to raise the value of your estates, and to give employment to your people, so long as the Protestant establishment exists.

My lords, I do address myself most earnestly to the right reverend bench, most particularly, my lords, to the right reverend prelate who is at the head of the Church of Ireland, whose opinions I know and lament are so different from mine on this great question, but whom I cannot address without the expressions of respect and esteem to which his unpretending good sense, and mild and dignified and conciliatory discharge of the duties of his high station so justly entitle him. My lords, it has been said, that the Roman Catholic religion remains unchanged, and that they hold opinions of exclusive salvation, which disable them from living in charity with others. My lords, harsh and exclusive doctrines may be found in almost all creeds, and amongst angry theologians, but such, my lords, are not the doctrines of our Roman Catholic fellow-subjects; nor can anything be more unlike to another, than the Roman Catholics of the present day to the Papist of the days of Queen Mary. My lords, no person of any church can be so wicked or senseless as to hold or to act upon the opinion, that his fellow-creature is doomed to eternal punishment by a merciful God, because he differs from himself in speculative opinions! The materials of truth and nature extinguish such monstrous folly and impiety.

My lords, I will not at this hour dwell on the most extraordinary arguments that have been founded on the most extravagant suppositions—that the whole parliament may be Papists—that all the king's ministers may be Papists—and then what is to become of the Protestant religion and constitution. I cannot well imagine how these things can happen, unless all the people should become Papists, and then, indeed, it must be owned, the Protestant establishment would be in some danger, and from which it would not find effectual protection in any act of parliament. So it is said, what if we have an hypocritical king, an hypocritical minister, or cabinet of ministers? My lords, it is impossible to deal with such fancies. I know of no law which can control hypocrisy—our present laws do not profess to do so, nor can the measure now proposed expose us to any additional danger in that respect.

My lords, I have to congratulate your lordships on the altered tone which is now assumed with respect to the fundamental principles of the Reformation and the Revolution, which it was so confidently asserted the present measure would subvert. I think I may safely appeal to your lordships, whether the professions so repeatedly made by the noble and learned lord, that he would, at the proper time, demonstrate for the satisfaction of the people of England, that the sacred principles established by the Reformation and the glorious Revolution of 1688, would be overturned by the admission of Roman Catholics to parliament and to office. These assertions have been in every part disproved by the powerful and unanswerable arguments of my noble and learned friend on the woolsack, and of my noble friend behind me (Earl Grey). These assertions rest now, as they did at the time when they were first made, solely upon the authority of the noble and learned lord, and he must excuse me if I say they have not been supported by any proof. The noble and learned lord has, indeed, vehemently asserted his entire belief in those opinions, and his determination to live and die in them. I most sincerely hope that it may be very long before he affords this last proof of his sincerity; but in the meantime, I think the public who had been so loudly appealed to, were entitled to, and did expect some arguments drawn from our history and our laws, to show that they had not been alarmed without grave and sufficient cause. My lords, the convincing and irresistible reasoning of the two noble lords to whom I have just alluded, makes it unnecessary for me to go into any minute or lengthened consideration of those great constitutional points to which they have applied themselves; a few observations, however, I trust, your lordships will permit me to offer. It has been asserted, that the Roman Catholics were excluded from the House of Commons at the period of the Reformation, and that the oath of supremacy was intended to produce that effect. No assertion can be more unfounded. They were not intended to be so excluded; they were not, in fact, so excluded; and the oath of supremacy had no such object. The oath of supremacy was intended as a test of loyalty, not of religion; the statute of 5 Eliz., which imposes the oath as a preliminary to sitting in the House of Commons, demonstrates that it was merely a test of loyalty; it does not impose it as a condition for sitting in this house, because it says, the queen was otherwise assured of the loyalty of the peers. They accordingly sat without interruption until the 30th Charles II. But it was not any part of the policy of Queen Elizabeth to exclude Roman Catholics either from the House of Commons or from office. She was a sound Protestant, as sound as the noble and learned lord, or as any right reverend person in this house; she had proved her sincerity by adhering to her religion at the peril of her life and of her throne. Her policy was not to exclude, but to woo and win her Roman Catholic subjects. She framed the oath of supremacy, with a view of its being taken by them. She altered the liturgy from the form of Edward VI., by excluding those passages relative to the real presence. which would have made it impossible for the Roman Catholics to join in communion with the church of England. She restrained the intemperate zeal of her ecclesiastics, and forbid the use of offensive expressions such as "Papist" or "schismatic," and accordingly this wise policy was completely successful; for the first thirteen years of her reign, the Roman Catholics *did* take the oath of supremacy, and *did* join in communion with the church of England, and did serve in her fleets and in her armies, and were confidentially employed in the highest offices in the state. The noble and learned lord will not, cannot contradict me; he knows those facts to be true; they rest not in assertion, but on the evidence of the statute book, of the public records, of the letters of the queen's ministers, and on the uncontradicted testimony of lawyers and historians. I will not mar, by recurring to it, the eloquent and magnificent statement of the noble earl, of the loyal gallantry of Lord Howard of Effingham, leading the fleets of his excommunicated Protestant sovereign, against the consecrated banner of the Pope. James the First, as Mr. Hume informs us, appointed indifferently Roman Catholics and Protestants to office. It is undoubtedly true, my lords, that the policy of Queen Elizabeth was interrupted and disappointed by political intrigues, set on foot by foreign emissaries, and fomented by seminary priests and Jesuits; but it is equally true, that this disappointment arose, not from religious, but from political motives. My lords, it is well known, that in the latter part of the reign of Charles I., and after the restoration, the Roman Catholics became suspected, when the throne became suspected; certainly not suspected of disloyalty, but deservedly suspected of adhering to the crown in its designs, first, against the liberties, and latterly, against the religion of the people—still they were legally admissible to the House of Commons, although the spirit of the times was such, that in point of fact, very few were admitted. Still those who got admission on taking the oath of supremacy, could not be directly excluded, and the Protestant leaders were under the necessity of recurring to this device; the laws against recusancy were in force, and one of the penalties attaching on conviction, was a disability to come within ten miles of London or Westminster. A person under such a disability could not perform his duties as a member of the House of Commons, and they accordingly proceeded against him for recusancy, and then, on producing the record of the conviction, a new writ was moved for—all this appears on the journals of the Commons.

Such, my lords, clearly, was the state of the law as to parliament, from the Reformation to the 30th Charles II., and so much for the assertion, that Roman Catholics were excluded by the principles of the Reformation. Now as to the statute of 30 Charles II., it recites the dangers which had arisen from Popish recusants having free access to the king, and it contains two enactments; first, that no person shall sit in either house of parliament without taking the oath of supremacy and subscribing the declaration; and second, that persons refusing to do so shall not have access to the king: and it subjects the parties offending to the same penalties (amongst others) which attach upon persons convicted as Popish recusants. Such was the law. What has become of it? First, all the laws against recusancy have been repealed, there is one member of this immortal law lopped off; and second, the clause which forbid the access of such persons to the king, is also repealed; so there is a second member of this immortal law also hacked off, and sent to follow its companion. And it is this mutilated part of Titus Oates which we are now called on to venerate as the statute of the great King William, and which forms the foundation of all our rights, as settled at the glorious period of the Revolution.

My lords, I do not mean to say that this act of Charles II., however disgraceful the circumstances which accompanied it, was not necessary, or that the Roman Catholics were not at that time a body dangerous to the state, or that there was any intention of repealing it at the period of the Revolution; on the contrary, many additional and severely penal laws were enacted against the Roman Catholics immediately before and after the period of the bill of rights; but I call for the proof of any intention expressed in the bill of rights, or to be inferred from it, that any of those penal laws were to have perpetual continuance, or were to be considered as incorporated into, or forming part of, that glorious transaction. Does the bill of rights concern itself with the doctrine of transubstantiation, or the sacrifice of the mass, or the invocation of saints? No, my lords, the wise men who were actors in that great event, had no lumber room in their heads for such trumpery. They state the various points in which the rights of the subject had been invaded—they do not profess to be systemmongers, or grinders of theories—they give no abstract dogmas on the constitution—even in the statement of the invasion of the right of petitioning they do not state generally the right of petitioning, but merely that of petitioning the throne, because that was the right which had been invaded in the case of the seven bishops; and then, having distinctly stated the rights which had been actually attacked, and insisted on them as their birthright, they proceed to remedy the great grievance which had been derived from the religion of the king being different from that of the state, and for this they provide a remedy which they declare to be intended to endure for ever, and they declare the crown unalterably Protestant. But how, my lords, do they effect this great object? not by laying down any pedantic maxim or abstract dogma, but recurring to those lights by which common sense and true philosophy apply the experience of the past to the circumstances of the present; they say "whereas it has been found by experience, that it is inconsistent with the safety of this Protestant kingdom to be governed by a Popish prince, or by any king or queen marrying a Papist, therefore they enact, &c." They call it, it is true, " this Protestant kingdom;" and I hear it repeatedly asked, "is not this a Protestant kingdom, and a Protestant parliament, and a Protestant government?"—I say yes, and that ours is a Protestant parliament and government, exactly in the same sense in which it is a Protestant kingdom, that is not exclusively Protestant, but with the great majority of the population, and of the wealth, and of the knowledge of the empire Protestant, possessing that character of ascendant but not exclusive Protestantism which must always belong to it. The position then that there is anything in the bill of rights, or in the settlement at the Revolution, directly, or by implication, establishing the principle of exclusion, cannot be maintained. Does the assertion then mean, that the restrictive laws which were in force at the time, or which were enacted shortly after it, are to be considered as partaking of the same fundamental character? Never was a more untenable proposition uttered.

I do not mean to take up your lordships' time by again going over the ground which has been so fully occupied by my noble friends, but I would beg to call your attention to one or two particular statutes. An act was passed in the 1st year of William III., forbidding Papists to carry arms; and that being the state of the law when the bill of rights was enacted, the grievance stated in the bill of rights is, that Protestants have been deprived of arms whilst Papists have been allowed to carry them. Now it is worthy of observation, that this only point in which it might, with any degree of plausibility, be contended that the bill of rights contained any principle of exclusion against Roman Catholics has been absolutely repealed. My lords, the act of 1817, sanctioned by the noble and learned lord, by which the necessity of taking the oath and declaration previous to the obtaining commissions in the army has been done away, has been fully stated by the noble duke, and by my noble and learned friend on the woolsack. I shall therefore only make an observation upon it. By the law of 25th Charles II. it was not necessary that the oath or declaration should be taken or made previous to the obtaining the commission; this was not thought a sufficient security, and therefore expressly for the purpose of curing this mischief, the act of 1st William, cap. 8, was passed, making it necessary to do those acts previously to obtaining the commission. The act, therefore, of the noble and learned lord is a precise repeal of the statute of William, and a restoration of the act of 25th Charles II., which the act of William was expressly introduced to repeal; and observe, no statement in the act of 1817, that any law of King William was in existence or intended to be touched.

My lords, it would be unpardonable in me to go into any discussion on the acts of union with Scotland and with Ireland; they have been so fully observed upon, and the demonstration of my noble friends having been so complete, that the acts of Charles II. were not intended to be perpetuated by them; to one document only on that subject, I shall beg to call the attention of your lordships. In the journals of this house of the 3rd July, 1706, on the bill for securing the church of England, which was afterwards inserted as one of the fundamental articles of the Union, there is this entry—
"Question put, that it be an instruction to the committee of the whole house, to whom the bill for securing the church of England is referred, that there be inserted in the said bill, as a fundamental

condition of the intended Union, particular express words, declaring perpetual and unalterable an act of parliament made in the 25th of Charles II., entitled an Act for preventing Dangers which may happen from Popish Recusants." It was resolved in the negative. I have other entries of a similar character, but I shall not now detain your lordships by referring to them. I will merely state, with reference to observations that have been made on the act for regulating the election of the sixteen peers and forty-five members for Scotland, and which is declared as valid as if it had been part of the act of Union, that that act is not, like the two acts for securing the churches of England and Scotland, made a fundamental part of the Union, but, on the contrary, the article of the Union which directs that all future elections shall be according to the provisions of that act, is qualified by the words, "until the parliament of Great Britain shall otherwise direct."

My lords, there is only one other topic to which I think it necessary to advert. Many noble lords have said they would be disposed to waive their objection to the proposed measure, if they could believe it would afford a reasonable hope of giving tranquillity to Ireland. A noble earl, who always speaks with distinguished ability (Lord Mansfield) has applied himself particularly to this consideration. He will excuse me if I say, that he does not appear to me to have taken that high view of the subject to which his eminent abilities might have led him. He has, I think, overlooked the question—"Ought it to satisfy the Irish people?" My lords, I do in my conscience believe that it will satisfy the Irish Roman Catholics, because I am sure it ought to satisfy them, and this, my lords, is the true question for a statesman. If he is satisfied that he is rendering justice, he may confidently expect tranquillity. Hitherto the Roman Catholics have been engaged in the honourable pursuit of legitimate objects; they have been unanimous in that pursuit—the great body of the intelligent Protestants in Ireland have gone along with them. But if unfortunately they should not be satisfied with obtaining what is just and reasonable, or if factious and designing agitators should endeavour to rouse them to acts of disturbance of the public tranquillity, our position will be totally altered—the rational portion of their own body will not join with them; the Protestants to a man will be united against them; you will no longer have an entire people to contend against—turbulent individuals you can punish by the law, and if unfortunately the ordinary power of the law should be found insufficient, my noble friend may confidently come to parliament and call for its co-operation, in arming the executive with extraordinary powers—by being honest he is enabled to be strong.

But, my lords, I will hope for better things; the Roman Catholics appear already to be tranquillized even by the announcement of this measure. I trust also that now that the association and all its irritations are at an end, the Brunswick Clubs will disappear.

My lords, much allowance is to be made for them. They have been goaded and irritated; they have been alarmed for their own safety. On the part of many of them their association has been merely in self-defence—like their adversaries associating for a lawful purpose, they have been led into excesses which cannot be justified; but I am full of hope they will speedily subside into tranquillity. There does not exist in any part of the world a finer race of people than the Protestants of the north of Ireland—I speak from personal knowledge of many of them—and of large bodies of them—religious, sober, industrious, intelligent men. When they come to understand the real nature and operation of this measure, I am persuaded, that instead of considering themselves as sufferers, they will feel relieved from the infliction of the nominal and useless superiority over their fellow-subjects, which the impolicy of our laws had imposed on them; and I well know, that those amongst your lordships, and in the other house of parliament, who have most strenuously opposed this bill, will be among the foremost to exert themselves to ensure its beneficial operation.

PARLIAMENTARY REFORM.

March 28, 1831.

The great seven days debate in the commons commenced on the 1st of March, and on the 7th, the English Reform Bill was read for the first time, without a division. The second reading was taken on the 21st and carried on the 22nd by a majority of 1. The commons then proceeded to discuss the Irish and Scotch bills. The lords intensely agitated, on the motion of Lord Wharncliffe, began to debate the question without waiting for the decision of the lower house. A disorderly controversy between Lords Sidmouth, Eldon, and Wharncliffe, occupied the early part of the sitting, after which Lord Durham delivered the ministerial declarations. He was followed by the Duke of Richmond and the Marquis of Londonderry, after whom—

LORD PLUNKET said, that the question had been argued by so many noble lords upon the side of the house upon which he had the honour to sit, and they had spoken so strongly and so effectually upon the subject, that it might appear that he rose to add to the triumph they had obtained, if he addressed the house at any length at such an inconvenient period of the discussion. Under such circumstances he should not detain their lordships long, nor should he have taken the liberty of offering himself to the notice of the house, if he had not felt apprehensive that he might not have the opportunity of expressing his sentiments when the question came regularly before their lordships, and he might therefore labour under the imputation of shrinking from the duty of declaring his opinions, and of supporting the measure. He certainly could not say that he had approached the consideration of this momentous question without a very considerable degree of alarm, but he must avow that he now felt a very great relief from that alarm, for he found that what was originally stated to be an inroad upon the constitution, and a principle pregnant with every danger—what was declared to be a measure which ought to be met resolutely in the very first outset, as calculated to introduce a new system subversive of all constitutional practices—was now no longer so formidably denounced, and all such grounds of opposition were entirely abandoned. It was at first stated that the measure was calculated to introduce a new system; but, after a short time, that enunciation was given up. At first it was stated that there was no necessity for any reform, and it was now four months since that opinion was announced. It had been persevered in to nearly the end of a seven days' discussion, and had never been formally relinquished. At the close of that period, with a tardy candour, or he might call it a reasonable prudence, it was admitted that all reform was not revolutionary. The principle, then, of reform was no longer knocking at the outer door and refused admittance; it had been admitted within doors, and its demands, it was allowed, were not altogether unreasonable. Those who did not agree in those demands did not deny them altogether—they only wished to avoid prompt payment, and asked to pay by instalments. He was at a loss to understand how noble lords and honourable and right honourable gentlemen meant to meet the question under these circumstances. He had not heard of one person who did not agree that reform was just and proper, only they quarrelled with the degree and extent of the reform proposed. They abstained, nevertheless, from stating how far they were willing to go. The noble lord who had introduced the question to their lordships' notice with great ability, and, he would add, with great fairness, had employed a tone in discussing the subject, and made admissions which were not calculated to obtain for him the support of those noble lords who sat around him, and he had not found a secender. That noble lord had stated that the claims of the people were irresistible, and that some degree of reform was absolutely necessary. The noble lord had referred to the opinion of Mr. Canning, but he did not think the supposition of what the opinions of dead men might be, were they now alive, ought to guide the opinions of living men. How could he or any man say, that if Mr. Canning were now alive, his opinion would not be changed like the opinion of the noble lord? and how could he say that Mr. Canning would not now think some reform necessary? The noble lord, who was warmly attached to Mr. Canning, was as much opposed to reform at one time as Mr. Canning. They ought, therefore, to consider the nature of the question before them, and not endeavour to guess at the opinions of those who were not alive to speak for themselves. What then did he find? Why, that the persons who were lately at the head of the government of this country, of whom he wished to speak with great respect, particularly of the noble duke who was then at the head of that government—he found that these gentlemen—and he did not say it as exciting feelings of degradation—he found these gentlemen obliged to resign the government, and obliged to resign it because they could not resist the pressure of reform. To that pressure the present government had acceded; and now their opponents pressed on them because they had taken up the principle of reform. Under these circumstances, what was to become of the country? Did the persons who, under such circumstances, resisted the plan of reform, look at the consequences? What medium party was to succeed? Did those who resisted reform—the reform proposed by his majesty's ministers, and who acknowledged the necessity of some reform—come forward with any plan or principle of their own? Why did they not introduce a bill into the other house, or even into that house, if it could be done consistently with the principles of the constitution and the laws and usages of parliament? Those who were of opinion that the present plan went too far, should bring in a bill of their own, and should let the two lie side by side, and thus the public would be able to form some judgment of the comparative merit of the two measures. Was this fair and honourable course adopted? Was it expected that his noble friends, and the distinguished persons who originated this plan of reform, could stoop and degrade themselves so low as to belie their principles, and abandon the measure? His noble friends had been accused of endeavouring to excite in the people of the country discontent with the government, and at all our institutions. But he would ask all those who had made use of such language, were the grievances of the country any secret, or were the sources of those grievances so concealed that a veil could be drawn over them to hide them from the public odium? He would maintain that his noble friends had not excited the people of England; but, on the contrary, by bringing forward this great and satisfactory measure, they had done much to quiet the people, by meeting the general sentiments, and by removing the permanent and just sources of discontent. If his noble friends should abandon their plan, they would cover themselves with irretrievable disgrace, and they would bequeath a most bitter legacy to those who came after them, by teaching the people that no confidence whatever was to be placed in any set of public men. There would then be no means left of governing the country, and it would be plunged in all the horrors of anarchy. He therefore felt himself much relieved from the embarrassment of making a choice. He was compelled to embrace the plan of reform. His noble friends had come into power on account of the evils which oppressed the country, and the danger arising from the conviction of those evils upon the public mind. They had found the people excited. The storm was growing, the surges were lashing, the vessel was heavy laden and labouring in the troubled waters, and the helm had been abandoned by those who had been placed at it, and whose duty it was to have steered with skill and science. His friend it was, who had seized upon the helm, and who with mature experience had said, " I will undertake what they won't undertake; I will meet the danger, and with a firm hand I will point out to you the haven to which your course ought to be steered." Every honest man in the country was bound to assist in this great effort, upon the success of which depended the safety of the state. His noble friend was calling upon them not to proceed through unexplored latitudes, and upon devious courses, but to steer cautiously, but boldly, to the only port that was capable of affording protection and safety. He (Lord Plunket) was not inclined to trouble their lordships at any great length at that hour of the night, and under the circumstances of the question, but he must address a few more observations to their lordships before he sat down. The reform bill had been termed a revolutionary measure. The term revolutionary was the most ridiculous, the most dishonourable, and the most offensive that it had ever been his unfortunate lot to hear in any public assembly. It was true that this charge had been abandoned in all the mortification of defeated artifice, and in all the shame of detected folly; but still it was said, that if the measure was not actually revolutionary, it was what was almost as dangerous—it was a great and an extensive change. Did any noble lord who heard him, and who was in the least acquainted with the history of his country, believe that great political changes were either unusual, unconstitutional, or bad? Did they not owe, and was not every stage of society indebted for, all they possessed to some great change from what had been precedent? He had not been an inattentive observer of the progress of society, and the nature of his studies had pretty well acquainted him with the history of this country; and the page of history showed nothing more clearly than that from the beginning of its political existence there had been a continued course of changes, when the circumstances of the country required changes to be adopted. He found the people of England at all times clinging to one great principle; the polar star which guided them at all times—at least through a period of 1000 years, during which the constitution had been preserved—was the principle, that it was the people's birthright that the freedom of their persons and the enjoyment of their property was not to be injured or affected but by their own consent. They had at all times given effect to that great principle. That was the basis of their free government, and that principle all the rules and regulations, which were the offspring of times and circumstances, were intended to carry into effect. They never had the folly to say that this great principle should bend to rules and regulations, but they always adapted their rules and regulations to this principle. Nothing could be more revolutionary in relation to this great principle than to adopt some stickfast resolution, which would prevent this principle from being at all times acted on. Looking at facts, did not our history abound with great changes? Was not the Reformation, which altered all the property of the church, a great change—a salutary change indeed, but a great change? Was not the act of Henry VI, by which the great body of the freeholders was excluded from the privilege of voting, and the franchise conferred on those who held a freehold of 40s., a great change? What did their lordships say to the Union with Scotland, which altered the whole parliamentary constitution of the country? or what did they say to the Union with Ireland? Were not these great and extensive changes? He could enumerate many more changes, but he would content himself with adverting to that last and great change which admitted the Catholics into the bosom of the state. These were all great and rapid changes. What would their lordships say to the king's power and prerogative to issue writs for new places? That was a permanent machinery for perpetual change. That power had been, perhaps, unduly exercised, and there had resulted a great abuse; and were they not to exercise the prerogative of parliament, and get rid of that abuse? Persons who did not see these things must explore history, not with the eyes of

2 D

statesmen or of philosophers, but merely with the curiosity of antiquaries. They did not look at the great lesson which history afforded, but they stereotyped it, or, like antiquaries with coins, they did not care for the legend inscribed on them—they valued them for the rust.

Great and most important changes had taken place in England since the Revolution of 1688. The rapid and astonishing influx of wealth had absolutely changed the whole state of the middle classes of society. Those middle classes now consisted of persons well acquainted with every useful branch of art and science; they were fully capable of forming enlightened views and sound principles upon all political and moral questions, and upon all points connected with the state. This class of persons had been raised in England into astonishing power, and they now came forward and demanded a reform with an irresistible pressure. Parliament had to choose between two alternatives. Would they oppose their present institutions, enfeebled as they were by abuses and tottering with corruption, so often and so ably pointed out and exposed, to stand the shock of these great rushes of public opinion, or would they receive these people, the middle classes, into the pale of the constitution, and by giving them their due share in the representation, claim them as friends and allies, instead of opposing them as aliens and enemies? The spread of intelligence among the lower orders, and even amongst the middling classes, was considered by many to be dangerous to the state. Widely different were his opinions upon the subject: but he would only say, that whether it were or were not dangerous, certain it was that there were no means of stopping it. He did not consider the diffusion of knowledge to be dangerous to society, but the most fatal proofs existed of the inconvenience and dangers arising from a population in a state of ignorance. The spread of imperfect light might be attended with danger; but it was a danger to be removed only by a diffusion of more perfect information. Purify the institutions of the country, and no safety-lamps would be required. It had been said, in terms of exultation, that the constitution of England was an admirable constitution—that it worked well—that it produced the most perfect moral and intellectual state of a population, and it was the glory and happiness of the country, and the envy of all foreign nations. He would avow, with the greatest satisfaction, that he did not believe, with all its defects, that there could be found, in the page of either ancient or modern history, a single constitution that had worked so well even for the good of the people. He would acknowledge with pride and satisfaction, that the constitution of England was the envy of all less favoured nations. All this was perfectly true. He believed that every civilized nation admired in the English constitution the bill of rights, the institution of the jury, the *Habeas Corpus* act, the independence of the judges, and the impartial administration of the laws by judges who were independent of the influence of the crown, and lastly, the theory of our representative legislature. Having acknowledged all this, he would now only beg leave to ask, who among these foreign admirers of the British constitution ever fell in love with the corporation of Old Sarum, or was enamoured of the free representation of Gatton? Who would say that the British constitution had ever been admired, out of England at least, because there existed the practice of trafficking in boroughs, and the privilege of buying and selling the rights of the people? These were not the subjects of admiration with anybody—they were plague-spots to be purified, or vices to be held in execration. If the constitution worked well, it was not from the variety of its abuses, or the number of its deformities, but in spite of them. Remove these, and they would restore it to its proper form and vigour. How did the constitution work well? Although the system of borough corruption was acknowledged to be a gross abuse, a hideous deformity and vice, still was it repeated that many distinguished persons who possessed boroughs were people of virtue, and who disdained to use their privileges, or to prostitute their possessions to bad purposes. Many persons in whom these borough properties were vested did not act upon the same views, and therefore some sat upon one side of the house, and some upon the other. These things happened very frequently, but was the British constitution to be for ever dependent upon such accidents? Let them, as soon as they could, take away accidents and introduce a system of securities. The physical system of the human body presented a beautiful economy of nature, and worked well; and if any accident occurred, such as an injury to a blood-vessel, nature accommodated herself to the change, and some substitute of organ or of function was produced. But when nature resumed her power, she dispelled all substitutes. The well-working of the political constitution of England was the growth of happy accidents and lucky chances; but these would be dispelled when sound and enlarged principles were resumed. His only object in getting up in his seat that night was, to explain himself upon this great measure of reform, and he apologized for having detained their lordships so long.

PARLIAMENTARY REFORM.
October 6, 1831.

ACCORDING to Mr. Roebuck, the Reform Bill was carried by a *coup d'etat*— struck by Lord Brougham and Earl Grey. History will, however, probably ascribe the violent, almost unconstitutional momentum, given to that measure in its passage through parliament, rather to the democratic energy and dashing courage of the chancellor, than to the serene and stately patriotism of the premier. On the 18th of April—in a parliament six months old—ministers were defeated by a majority of eight in committee on the bill for England. After four days deliberation, they determined to dissolve; and on the instant Brougham ordered the crown and robes, the great officers of state, and the guards to accompany the king to the house. Then, and not until then, the premier and chancellor waited upon his majesty, and called upon him to carry out the resolution of his ministers—Brougham managing the whole proceeding. The king at first declined—asked how could he dissolve a parliament which had just given himself so good a civil list, and settled so handsome an annuity on his wife. The chancellor admitted it was very hard to annoy so good-natured a House of Commons, but the king's government could not be carried on with them, and without ceremony they must go to the country that very day. The king tried to temporize. How could parliament be dissolved without the regular paraphernalia, robes, heralds, and army. When he was told that all had been ordered without consulting him, he flamed and charged the chancellor with having committed high treason. Brougham answered with exquisite intrepidity, that he was perfectly well aware he had, and was ready to take the consequences; but first of all, the safety of the State demanded that parliament should be dissolved. To the *sang froid* of this declaration, the bluff sailor-king could find no angry answer. He agreed to dissolve, and a general election took place under the auspices of the *Times* Newspaper. "Plaster the enemies of the people with mud and duck them in horseponds," said that absolute organ of the *Vox Populi Brittanicci*. A Radical parliament, elected amid revolutionary riots, carried the whole Bill to the upper house by majorities wonderful in an era of close boroughs. In the debate on the second reading, Plunket spoke the following ill-reported speech, of which Brougham has recorded his intense admiration. The debate was one of wonderful brilliancy, and Plunket rose in reply to an exceedingly able attack by Lord Carnarvon upon the whole conduct of the measure by ministers.

LORD PLUNKET said, that he was induced to obtrude himself on the attention of the house, with the view of attempting a reply to the very able and powerful speech of the noble earl who had just addressed the house. He should in some respects differ from the course taken by the noble earl, for he would attempt to argue the principle of the bill. With every respect to the noble earl, and paying the full tribute of admiration to the talents which he had displayed, he must assert, and before he sat down the house would be able to judge whether he was justified in making the assertion, that he had left the principle of the bill untouched. The noble earl said, that he had reluctantly entered into a discussion in which he was opposed to those for whom he professed strong esteem and regard. The noble earl had also stated, that he had listened to the arguments in favour of the bill, with a strong desire to be convinced by them. Had it not been for these direct assertions of the noble earl, which he was bound to believe, and did believe, he should have supposed, from the tone of severity and the strain of sarcasm which pervaded his speech from the beginning to the end, that the noble earl's reluctance was not so very strong as he had led the house to imagine that it was, and that something more than a logical difference on the subject had dictated the noble earl's observations. He really could not recollect one objection which the noble earl had made to the principle of the bill. The noble earl had said, that ministers were building a new constitution. He had also said, that the bill, if carried, was one which would render it impossible for his majesty's government to be carried on. These were positions which the noble earl had adopted and not laid down himself for the first time. They had been reiterated from the commencement of the discussion up to that moment; and now that the noble earl had ceased to speak, they remained as they did before he began to speak, resting only on mere assertion. It had been stated of this measure, which had been brought forward by ministers, and sent up to their lordships backed by the authority of the other house of parliament, that it was founded on fanciful theories, that the grievances which were complained of were ideal, and that the bill would destroy a system which was working well for all purposes of public utility, and endanger the constitution of the country. To every one of those assertions he would take upon himself to give a positive denial. He would not rest on his mere denial, but would state further, that the theory which was opposed to the bill was improper, and at direct variance with the ancient established and acknowledged principles of the constitution. The persons who complained of injustice being done to them, were themselves the usurpers of the power of the realm. He believed that the rejection of this remedial constitutional measure, which had been sent up to their lordships from the Commons of England, would be attended with dangers not imaginary, remote or trivial, but immediate, vital, and overwhelming. All considerations personal to himself were lost in the deep and anxious alarm which he felt upon this subject. There had been a degree of personal rancour accompanying the attacks which had been made upon the bill and its authors, which proved that something more than apprehension for the constitution influenced the opposition to the measure. Assertions and attacks, such as he alluded to, must not rest upon the authority of those who made them, or on the pertinacity and perseverance with which they were reiterated. They must be tried by the test of reason and argument. There was one circumstance to which he could advert with some degree of pleasure—namely, that the tone originally assumed by the opponents of the bill had been abandoned. He could not avoid observing, that the opposition to this measure had descended from that high tone which it had assumed at the commencement; and he found that this measure of parliamentary reform, which had been at first encountered as an audacious measure of corporation robbery, and as directly tending to overturn the state, was now met by an admission from every person who had spoken from the other side of the house, with one single exception, that reform, and in some considerable degree, too, was necessary ["*no, no*"]. He certainly thought, that the only person who had denied that reform was necessary was a noble earl opposite (the Earl of Mansfield) ["*no, no*"]. The noble earl was the only person, of all who had spoken on the subject, that entertained such an opinion ["*no, no*"]. It was, of course, impossible for him to conjecture what was passing in the minds of noble lords opposite, but among the persons who had taken part in the present debate, or spoken on the presentation of petitions, the noble earl was the only person who had avowed himself the uncompromising foe to any kind of reform whatever. The noble earl to whom he alluded, and of whom he wished to speak with the greatest respect for his talents, had certainly taken a very whimsical course in establishing his position against all reform, and against this specific measure in particular; for, after joining in the general cry of its tendency to overturn the monarchy, and all the institutions of the state, he proceeded further, and said, that the present measure would have the effect of establishing the ministers in their places, and that by reform of parliament they would be enabled to carry on all their injurious measures against the interests of the country. The first use, said the noble earl, which ministers would make of their new power, would be to go to war with Portugal; and the next step to be taken by ministers was to commit the equal outrage—as he believed it would appear in the estimation of some noble lords—of not going to war with France. Then the ministers would proceed to put an end to all the rights of primogeniture, of hereditary property, and, in short, to adopt every one of those measures which were perpetrated in the wildest days of disturbance and folly that ever afflicted the French nation. This really appeared to him to be a sweeping course of objection, and one which he was not quite prepared to follow. He was only prepared to argue this measure of reform on its own grounds and principles. With the exception of the noble earl, all the noble lords who had spoken on the other side of the house, had declared themselves friendly in some degree to parliamentary reform ["no, no," from Lord Falmouth]. He really thought that the noble lord had, in part of the speech which he had delivered that night, expressed himself in favour of some kind of reform; but he found that he was mistaken, and he certainly had no wish to fix on the noble lord so odious an imputation.

An explanatory interruption here took place on the part of Lord Falmouth, and almost immediately a discussion followed, as to the reasons for the resignation of the late ministry, in the course of which the Duke of Wellington twice rose to explain; Plunket continuing to comment upon a descrepancy which he had detected between the statement of the Duke on the subject and that of Sir Robert Peel.

It appeared to him that a studied mode of expression was adopted by the right honourable baronet (Sir R. Peel); for he said, that the late cabinet were not then prepared with a measure of parliamentary reform, the ministers, under those circumstances, having been defeated on the question of the civil list, and apprehending what might be the result of meeting the House of Commons on the question of reform, did not choose to encounter the event. Their lordships would observe, that the right honourable baronet said, "that the cabinet were not prepared with a measure of reform;" while the noble duke said, "they were not only not prepared with a measure, but that as long as he formed part of his majesty's cabinet, he should feel it his duty to oppose any proposition for reform." The result of this was, that the late administration was broken up under the impression that in the circumstances in which they were placed, they were not able to meet the question of parliamentary reform in the House of Commons. This was the inference which he drew from the declarations made by the late ministers, and he thought it a very important one. Upon the dissolution of the late government, the present administration came into office, avowedly on the principle that some measure of parliamentary reform was absolutely necessary; and that the government of the country could not go on without it. This was all he wanted to establish. The noble duke and his colleagues unanimously resigned office, because they could not meet parliament, in the then state of feeling on the subject of parliamentary reform. The head of the government was determined to oppose all reform as long as he continued in the cabinet, but his right honourable colleague only said, that he was not prepared with a measure of reform. They both, however, resigned, and it did not appear that any measure of reform, of however modified a nature, had been suggested to their sovereign, in the possession of whose confidence they at that time stood. Therefore, he had a right to say, that their retirement from office, and the coming in of their successors, were connected with the ques tion of parliamentary reform. Was it any ground of attack on his noble friend at the head of the government, that when called upon by his sovereign—whom his former servants, he would not say had abandoned, but had declared their inability to serve any longer, to form a government—he did not refuse to obey that call, and did undertake to carry on in that difficult crisis the public business of the state, on the known and avowed principles on which he had been in the habit of acting? His noble friend had, in the first instance, explained the principles on which he accepted office, and amongst them were, the principles of economy, of non-interference, and, primarily and particularly, of parliamentary reform. In consequence of the declarations made by the noble earl, a measure of reform was introduced to the consideration of the late parliament. The noble lord who had just sat down had said, with respect to parliamentary reform, " that the breeze had been fanned into a hurricane by the noble earl," from whom he was so unwilling to differ. Did the noble lord conceive that the noble duke opposite was likely to be moved by such a breeze? He rather inferred from the change of government, that the breeze had previously assumed the character of a hurricane, and if his noble friend, now at the head of affairs, in endeavouring to allay the hurricane, rode on the whirlwind, he could not be said to be directed by the storm. A measure of reform, the same in substance and for efficiency of purpose as the one now before their lordships, was introduced into the late House of Commons. It was there canvassed in all its parts by friends and enemies; it underwent a most severe scrutiny, and the principle was adopted by what he could not call a very large majority, for it was carried by a majority of one only. His majesty's ministers afterwards, finding that they were about to be baffled, took his majesty's pleasure upon the subject, whether, for the purpose of ascertaining the sense of the people, not with respect to that particular measure (but still it so happened that that measure was in the singular position which he had stated), the parliament should not be dissolved. The people, thus appealed to, expressed their opinions with a degree of assent amounting almost to unanimity, and though the entire subject of parliamentary reform had been opened, their opinions applied to that particular measure which had been so rigidly canvassed in parliament, and they exercised their suffrages so directly in reference to that measure, that their representatives had been termed delegates. He appealed to those noble lords who recollected what had passed in the country, whether they ever recollected elections to have been conducted with a greater degree of order and regularity? With respect to Ireland, he was sorry to say, it was difficult to mention at random any period of the history of that country, during which a state of perfect tranquillity might be found; but still there had been no disturbance there since the dissolution, connected with the elections The same thing might be said with respect to England. He mentioned this circumstance, because attacks had been made in connection with this measure of reform, not merely on the government, but also on the people of the country, who had been accused of unfitness to form the basis of free representation. The elections having been conducted with such tranquillity and propriety, the discussions in the House of Commons having been conducted, on the part of those who introduced this bill, with as much deliberation as any debate in the history of parliament, and the bill having passed, after some amendments, by an overwhelming majority, it certainly did surprise him to hear a noble baron (Lord Wharncliffe) take upon himself to say, that after this specific measure had been submitted to parliament, and the opinion of the people taken on it, when petitions were presented declaring their approbation of this measure, those petitions only meant to convey approval of reform generally. On what authority the noble baron made such a statement he did not know; but he was sure that if the petitions referred to any measure, it could be no other than the one before the house. This measure having been brought forward under the sanction of government, and under the sanction of his majesty, as implied in his authorising the government to propose it, and having passed through the House of Commons, certainly was entitled to be treated with a great degree of courtesy by their lordships. He did admit that their lordships were fully entitled to canvass the measure in all its parts, freely and fearlessly, in the exercise of their duty. But although their lordships were in the exercise of their undoubted privilege in the present circumstances, they were to recollect that they were sitting in judgment on the people of England, and on a subject peculiarly—and so far as any subject that could come before their lordships could, be, exclusively—relating to the privileges of the other house of parliament. He, therefore, could not too anxiously implore their lordships to consider well, before they adopted the desperate experiment of rejecting this measure, what were the consequences which might result from that rejection. He was satified their lordships would think, that whatever might be the ultimate fate of the measure, it was entitled to receive the most respectful attention of the house. A good deal of sarcasm had been thrown out in that place against the people of England. He again said, that there had been some smart

sarcasms and polished epigrams thrown out against the people of
England; the noble lord opposite had got up a great deal of
pointed irony and polished epigram, though he had omitted to touch
any real part of the subject, at the expense of the people of England.
But he (Lord Plunket) would say, that that people, whose petitions
had been sent up in such numbers to their lordships, and whose rights
were involved in this question, were no light, giddy, and fantastic
multitude—no rabble labouring under a temporary delusion, but a
great nation, intelligent, moral, instructed, wealthy—a nation as much
entitled to respect, and with as many claims to favourable consideration, as any nation in ancient or modern times. Therefore when
noble lords attacked this measure, and said that if it was carried, it
would give the people of England the means of overthrowing the
throne and the church, and abolishing all our venerable institutions,
he would ask those noble lords, if such were the effects to be apprehended from the measure if it were carried, what would be the effects
if it were not carried? But he affirmed that the charge was totally
untrue. The people of England had no such objects. They were
too sensible to indulge any such rash schemes. But if our institutions were such that they could not be sustained without repressing
the just complaints of the people, why, he would say, they were not
worth the tax we paid for them. But he again said, that the charge
was a libel upon the people of England; it was an attack upon the
character of the country, which was as dangerous as it was untrue.
Then the matter for their lordships' consideration was, whether they had
reason to think that this was a mere popular burst, which would soon
die away, and that all would become calm again in (as a noble lord
said the other night) about two years; that they were consulting the
interest, and the tranquillity, and the safety of the country by rejecting this measure; that the Commons house of parliament, which had
passed this bill by a large majority, was ready to recede from the
measure, and that the people of England were disposed to abandon
it. If their lordships rejected the measure, and they got locked in
the wheels of the other house of parliament, so that they could not
go on, what would be the consequence? The noble lord had said
that the only consideration for their lordships was, whether this was
or was not a right measure, and that they were not to look at consequences. This was a doctrine almost too monstrous, he should have
thought, for a sane man. If the wheels of the government were to
be stopped in the way he had mentioned, how could the government
go on? The noble baron did not argue the principle of the measure,
but he went into the details, and contended that the inconveniences

of the measure being certain, their lordships were bound to shut their
eyes against the consequences of rejecting it, and to stand secure
amidst the wreck of elements—

> " Should nature's frame in ruins fall,
> And Chaos o'er the sinking ball
>   Resume primeval sway,
> His courage chance and fate defies,
> Nor feels the wreck of earth and skies
>   Obstruct his destined way."

Those lines of the poet exactly described the feelings and conduct of
the noble lord. But he (Lord Plunket) would affirm, that they
were bound to consider consequences; and he would call the attention
of their lordships to what the consequences would be if they rejected
this bill, under circumstances which would prevent the introduction
of a measure of equal efficacy. Where, he would ask their lordships,
were they to look for strength, on the dissolution of the present government? The noble duke opposite was one of the first persons to
whom the eyes of the public would be directed in such a case. It
was with reference to this that he had been so particular in endeavouring to ascertain the exact words used by the noble duke on a
certain occasion. But if the noble duke was then unable to go on
with the government of the country, because at that period he had
lost the confidence of the House of Commons, and was apprehensive
of what might be the result of that loss of confidence, did the noble
duke conceive that he was now restored to the confidence of the
House of Commons, and that he had a better chance now than before
of parrying the question of reform? He (Lord Plunket) did not
think so; and great as might be the misfortune to the country, that
the noble duke should be prevented from carrying on the business of
the country, he did not conceive how the noble duke could join other
members of his own party who had declared for partial reform. As
to the noble earl (the Earl of Carnarvon), the noble duke could not
calculate on him, because he had not got into the kitchen. He
would ask their lordships whether they seriously thought there was
any chance of safety to the country if this measure were rejected?
When noble lords made violent appeals, and called upon the reverend bench to attest their solemn appeal to Providence, he hoped
they would ask their own conscience, at that retired hour, when the
still small voice of nature was heard, and then consider whether they
were satisfied with their own conduct, and were convinced they were pursuing a course which was likely to be productive of safety and benefit
to their country. Let him (Lord Plunket) not be accused of offering

a threat; it would be presumptuous in him to hold such language. No threats were likely to influence their lordships; no threats of popular violence or insurrection should have, or ought to have any effect upon the noble lords in that house. He trusted that any one there would be ready to join heart and hand in giving assistance to the government of the country, in resisting everything tending to insurrection. But the danger was, that things might come to such a pass that the government could not go on—that we should be reduced to a state of utter anarchy. These were questions which noble lords, who made those appeals to the reverend bench, should put to their own minds; for though they might withstand a sudden explosion of popular fury, there was a deeply-seated sense of wrong ready to burst forth in the hour of danger, which impressed minds of most fortitude with a sense of terror. Many of their lordships, he thought, might be reconciled to the measure, if he could find arguments to show that it was necessary to the security of the institutions of the country. He should, therefore, in pursuance of the promise he had made, now proceed to call the attention of their lordships to the nature of the case before them. What was their lordships' place in the constitution? They were invested with noble and high privileges as a branch of the legislature; they were the hereditary counsellors of the crown; they were the highest judicial court of appeal in civil and criminal cases, and, from their character, growing out of their station, rank, and place in the country, they were entitled to the respect and reverence of the country. Their lordships must not believe that he flattered them, when he assured them, that they stood as high in the opinion of the country as any branch of the legislature. Then, were any of these high privileges assailed? No; but what they claimed was a share in the representation of the country. There might be cases in which, for the sake of avoiding mischief, and in discharge of their duty to themselves and to the crown, they ought to resist the demands of the people. But was this one of those cases? If a struggle took place, could their lordships resist the right of the people to a full and fair representation in parliament? "Do as you would be done by," was a simple and sublime maxim which vindicated its divine origin; "Do as you would be done by," and he would ask their lordships if the people claimed any of the privileges of the crown or of the House of Lords, if they interfered with their lordships' hereditary titles, would their lordships be disposed to submit quietly to the invasion? Suppose, they had got possession of those privileges, and an act of parliament was introduced for restoring them to their rightful owners, would their lordships think themselves fairly treated if the House of Commons, standing on no other plea than their power to do so, threw out the bill? Their lordships in such a case must submit; but would it be a sincere, a cheerful submission? They would submit, but it would be only because they could not help submitting. Then the two cases ran exactly parallel; the people of England were as much entitled by law to a full and fair representation in the House of Commons as their lordships to their seats in that house. The principle contended for by noble lords was an unintelligible principle; it was a claim on the part of an oligarchy—to what? to a right to return a part of the democracy. The principle was wholly unintelligible; and he defied any phrenologist to point out an organ which could comprehend such an anamoly. He did not think that the accidental circumstance of some members of that house having got possession of a few places in the other house of parliament, was any reason why their lordships should consider it unjust to restore them. He had thus got rid of the objection as to any operation of this measure against the privileges of that house. He then came to the rights of the throne. All knew what the rights of the throne were. This measure did not interfere with any of the rights of the throne. He was not aware that any language had been used to deny the rights of the throne, the prerogative of dissolving parliament, or calling up to that house those in whose favour it might think fit to exercise that prerogative. There was no doubt that the king had the right and prerogative of making himself known to his people and erecting a throne in their hearts. He thought that what had been said upon this subject was unconstitutional trash. The king's name was not to be used to impute personal blame and responsibility. The king could do no wrong; but, to say that the King of England, the representative of the house of Brunswick, which had been invited to this country to protect its rights and liberties, had not a right to make himself known to his subjects as their father and protector, was trash. The King of England was not like an eastern monarch; we were not to look at a king as an abstract idea; he was entitled to make himself known, and to show that a King of England could be the father of his people. He had said more than was necessary on this point, because so much had been said respecting the dangers which threatened the rights of the crown, and history had been resorted to for no other purpose than to pervert facts. Our kings in former times had issued their writs, calling on certain inhabitants of counties to return members to parliament, in order to advise the king as to what taxes should be laid on. A right had been given to places to return members, and other places had ceased to have representatives. An instance of the latter had not occurred since Richard II., but the former practice continued till a much later period. All this, however, had no concern with the subject, and it was throwing away time to discuss it. But, although the prerogative of the king was not affected by the abolition of nomination boroughs, yet it was said, if the government could not be carried on without them, what was to be done? He should like to know, how the power of buying and selling seats, and the sellers putting the money in their pockets, could have any bearing on the king's government. Was it quite certain, that though one set of buyers of boroughs might be well disposed to the crown, and might combine together for the king's service and the public good, there might not be other combinations not quite so pure? If the king's government could only be carried on in that manner, he thought it would be quite as well that the king should carry on his own government. But it was not necessary for the king's government. But it was said that these boroughs were not only a necessary protection against the king, but against the people; for, that if the people were fairly and properly represented, the government could not go on, and the House of Commons would swallow up all power. This was a most extraordinary doctrine. It came to no more nor less than this—that this was not a representative government, and he would ask, if that was a thing to be received by the people of England with acquiescence and satisfaction? Ours was essentially a representative government. In such a government the people had no right to intervene in the duties of the executive government; if they did, that would be a democracy; but they had a right to be fully and fairly represented. If the people were altogether excluded, the government would be an aristocracy; if they regulated the whole government, and interfered with the executive, that would be a democracy. A full and fair representation of the people, united with an aristocracy and an executive with which the people did not interfere, was the true nature of our government; and one element of that government, without trenching on the others, this bill restored. It gave a full and fair representation to the people adapted to the present circumstances of the country. It had been said by noble lords opposite, that this was a new constitution—that ministers were unmaking the constitution—and they were indeed doing so, if the doctrine he had referred to was not correct. It was said, that if the people were fairly represented, the king would not be safe on his throne; but the doctrine was too monstrous to be maintained. It was not at that period of enlarged knowledge and reflection, that such a doctrine could be promulgated, without the danger of arousing in the country, from one end to the other, the deepest excitement. So far from innovation, they were reverting to the old and established, and acknowledged theory of the constitution, and those who opposed the change were hostile to that established theory. When the noble earl (Falmouth) called on the reverend bench to defend the present system, he called upon Christian prelates to defend a system of hypocrisy; but he (Lord Plunket) called on that bench, by the same strong and sacred obligations, to join him in supporting that which was the real constitution. If their theory was the true one, where was it proved to be so? For it was not one of those truths which lie upon the surface. None of our own writers; some foreigner had discovered it. How the noble lord had come by it, it was not possible to imagine. Here were gentlemen buying and selling places in parliament for 5000$l.$ or 12,000$l.$, which enabled them to come in there, and move on the axis of their own particular interests. They revolved in cycles and epicycles, with more satellites about them than any planet discovered by Olbers or Herschell or any one else; and when it was intended to deprive the favoured inhabitants of A and B of the light of those luminaries, it was supposed that the laws of nature were about to be repealed. These were the men who, in defiance of the king and the country, would uphold this system for the exclusive benefit of themselves, and oppose a measure which had received the sanction of the House of Commons and of the country. And now one word with respect to the allegations—for to call them arguments would be bitter irony—of noble lords, founded on the great changes which the bill, according to them, would introduce into the established institutions of the country. " These institutions," say they, " have been framed by our wise and venerated ancestors to last for ever—the country has flourished under their influence, and oh! beware, you puny moderns, and do not touch with your rash hands what has received the sanction of time, and been formed in the spirit of the wisdom of antiquity." Now, let him ask these sapient expounders of the wisdom of our ancestors, whether the world had grown older or younger since our ancestors followed their ancestors to the tomb? To believe these noble lords, the world was every day growing younger, and the old age of the world was its infancy. With them, groping in the dark, was light and wisdom; and experience but another name for youthful ignorance. Indeed, he was sure that if he divided the house on the question, whether the world was not actually younger and less experienced in the year 1 than in 1831, he was sure that many noble lords opposite must vote in the affirmative.

What, if our ancestors were as blind worshippers of their ancestors as noble lords, wise in their generation, would fain just now persuade us to be of theirs, was no advantage to be taken of increased knowledge —of increased experience—of the relations of society being better understood because contemplated under a greater variety of aspects? Were circumstances, the growth of time, and change, the growth of both, in the habits of thought and action in the people—and the increased and increasing diffusion of knowledge—and, above all, was time, the great innovator, of no influence? And what was the change? Why, that change should be effected in the machinery of a branch of the constitution. Pray what was the history of the constitution? Were noble lords who objected to all change, at all read in that history? It should seem not, for otherwise they must know that the history of the constitution was nothing but the history of its changes, and the English constitution might be shortly denominated a succession of legislative changes. Such it would be found by any man who went about writing its history. But of all these changes, the most numerous and most extensive—that is, the chapter of the history of change, which would be found to be most various and diversified—would be that of the change of the constitution of parliament. Why, the very peerage, as at present constituted, was a change from its original character under our infallible ancestors. Were noble lords aware that their original right to sit in that house was derived from a species of tenure, of which the whole peerage now contains but one instance—a tenure derived from the possession of certain lands or tenements? If so, must they not admit that their right to sit there, being different from the original one, their actual constitution was a great departure from the wisdom of our ancestors? Was not, he repeated, the whole history of parliament a history of change? Was not the sweeping away some thirty mitred abbots from that house by Henry VIII., a great change? Then, was not the addition of sixteen representative Scotch peers by the union with Scotland, and of twenty-eight representative Irish peers by the union with Ireland, great changes?—the rather as the nature of their tenures of seats in that house were wholly different, not only from that by which the English peers exercised their functions, but also from each other. The English peers were hereditary, that is, they sat there by descent and possession : the Scotch peers sat there by neither descent nor possession, nor for life, but for a single parliament; while the Irish peers were elected to sit for life, but, as with their Scotch brethren, not from descent or possession. Look then again at the rotation system of the Irish bishops, so different from that which regulated the

English bishops, with respect to the right to take a part in the proceedings in that house—in itself a great change from the original constitution of our ancestors. Again, let them consider the numberless changes which had been made in the oaths taken by members of parliament since its first constitution, all showing, that the history of the English constitution was the history of a succession of legislative changes. But, say noble lords, " This is all very true; but these changes in the constitution were gradual and imperceptible, while that now proposed by the noble earl was of unparalleled rapidity." The answer was simple: rapid was a term of degree that was relative to circumstances, and change was a term different in its meaning from restoration. The bill proposed no change not rendered imperative by circumstances, and only effected the removal of abuses which had been the growth of two centuries. The circumstances which at present justify the change explain the rapidity. But then, again, say noble lords, " admitting the necessity of some change, and that it should even be a rapid one, why should it be so extensive? Was not such extent fraught with danger to all existing institutions?" His answer was, that the safety was to be found only in the extent of the measure. For mark the reasoning of these noble objectors to an extensive measure of reform : " We all," say they, " admit the necessity of some measure of reform ; not, be it understood, because we conceive that justice or sound policy recommend it, but because the public demand is so pressing, that, judging by the signs of the times, we cannot help making some concession." Now was it possible for the veriest enemy of the institutions of the country to teach a more dangerous lesson than was contained in this admission? Does it not teach the people, that though nothing would be granted on the score of justice, much would be yielded to importunity? And was this the language befitting a British statesman ? The duty of a statesman worthy of the name was of a far other character. He was not to be merely watching and veering about with every breeze of the popular will, to borrow a metaphorical illustration from the noble earl, and to merely shape his measures as the popular vane indicated. No, a statesman should take his stand upon an eminence, from which great general principles and lofty views revealed themselves at every step, from which he could, uninfluenced by mere temporary exigencies, clearly see the people's rights and his own duties, and, while seeing them, perform the one by granting the other. From this position he should only descend to counsel and to decide, to see that the people should enjoy their right, and if he found himself capable of effecting this good, he was bound not to await the bidding of the public voice, but to raise the standard of political improvement in the advance of the people. His duty it was, to devise for the wants of the people, to advise them, to moderate them, to be their leader and conductor to freedom and happiness. This was the duty of a statesman, and he who was incapable of it, or who neglected it, however he might win favour with noble lords so —if we took their own word for it—infallible, disinterested in their judgment, would be held in just contempt by an enlightened posterity. The statesman who had discharged his duties in the manner which he had just glanced at, alone could turn round to the people— in the case supposed by the noble earl (Harrowby) opposite—and say to them, should they unfortunately be induced by mischievous advisers to exceed the limits of discretion, "I have been no ill-natured spy upon your actions; I have honestly endeavoured to execute the trust confided to me for your benefit. I stand here as your friendly adviser, and tell you for your own sakes, to arrest yourselves in your progress, and thereby enjoy the blessings which Providence has bestowed upon you." Such an appeal would be irresistible. He felt confident in the good sense of the people of England, and was convinced that such seditious papers as those circulated at a Westminster meeting some years ago would, so far from influencing the people to mischievous ends, recoil upon their promulgators. And now he begged to touch upon one other topic before he sat down. It was an old argument with the opponents of reform, that the constitution worked well, and could not be bettered. This was partially true, so far as it applied to many of the institutions of the country—it was false as it applied to the subject matter of the present bill. It was true, that the constitution worked well, if by the term was understood the several institutions of the country; it was equally true that it worked ill so far as the representation of the people was concerned. He entirely subscribed to the several panegyrics which had been made upon the practical working of most of our institutions. The laws were sound, and ably administered; the judges were learned and honest; juries impartial; magistrates upright; the clergy pious and well informed; the finances judiciously managed; and the several offices of state ably filled; but, with all that, the people were not satisfied; the great good was wanting of contented subjects, and they could probably only be made so by receiving that share in the constitution which was by law assigned them. All these eulogiums, then, had nothing to do with the question before them, which was, whether the people were or were not duly represented? No man pretended to deny that our representative system required some amendment, so that it could not be said that the "work-well" eulogy could be predicated of it. It was true, that a noble earl (Carnarvon) opposite maintained that it could, that the representative branch of the legislature did work well in practice ; and he quoted passages from speeches of Mr. Fox and his noble friend (Earl Grey), delivered many years ago, in order to show that they also had been of the same opinion. But the noble earl strangely overlooked the very important fact, that the speeches to which he referred as containing eulogies on the British constitution were actually made for reform in parliament, and that these eulogies were a part of the argument for that reform. It was plain, then, that some of the institutions of the country might be, or they actually were, very good in principle and efficient in practice, while others, the representative one, might be neither one nor the other. It had been asked, but what, after all, would be gained by this bill? He answered that the people would be satisfied, and that hardly a greater benefit could be conferred upon a nation than to remove all sources of dissatisfaction. Need he add, that no dissatisfaction could be more dangerous than that of an enlightened and wealthy people with those who would deny them the means of a pure system of representation. The truth was, that no argument could be more fallacious than the work-well one, for it would be found that beneficial results had grown up under circumstances of a most baleful nature, to which it would be absurd to attribute them. For example, the Irish parliament, for thirty or forty years before its gross and scandalous profligacy led to the act of Union, was a mockery of the very name of representation, containing as it did 200 members, over whose election the people of Ireland had as much control as the people of Siberia, and who had no principle but venality, and no occupation but sordid self-aggrandizement; and yet that parliament, perhaps he should say in spite of it, owing chiefly to the exertions of a band of patriots and orators, of whom Lord Charlemont and Mr. Grattan were the leaders, was instrumental in raising Ireland from barbarism to comparative civilisation —from poverty to comparative wealth, and in enabling Ireland to make the most rapid strides towards commercial importance. That profligate parliament passed wholesome measures with respect to trade—repealed bigotted laws—removed several of the penal disabilities against the Catholics—and yet, surely, not even the noble marquis (Londonderry), who was so eccentric in his political idiosyncrasies, would venture to say, that the Irish parliament was a faithful representation of the people. The Union put an end to that monstrous system of profligacy, and, as completed by the admirable measure of Catholic emancipation, for which the friends of Ireland never could be too grateful to the noble duke opposite, had effected much towards improving the representation of the Irish people. But much remained to be done which only a measure like the present could accomplish. The noble and learned lord proceeded to observe, that though he had, when early in his political career, raised his voice with vehemence against the measure of the Union, and though he was far from regretting his conduct on that occasion, he, now that the measure had been completed, would resist its repeal to the last moment of his existence. Notwithstanding its monstrous abuses, the Irish parliament effected some good as, notwithstanding the monstrous absurdity of the present representation of Scotland the people of that country had advanced in wealth, intelligence, and national prosperity. But would any man deny that the people of Scotland were dissatisfied with their representative mockery of a system? Could he deny that they would be thrown into a state of frenzy and fury by having their hopes of reform disappointed? It required no very minute acquaintance with that country to be able to answer the question with confidence; all that was wanting was, a knowledge of the ordinary workings of human nature. That knowledge showed, that the natural result of increased wealth and intelligence was an increased anxiety for the possession of that right without which these advantages lose half their value, namely, political freedom. There were other topics which he was anxious to touch upon, but felt unwilling to trespass longer on their lordships' attention.

The debate for the day closed with this speech. It was resumed on the following day, Lord Eldon once again reappearing in the house, and warning his peers that if this bill were carried, the British constitution would indeed be annihilated. There is something intensely pitiable in the frantic agony with which the old Wezeer of George the Third resists Reform—something half-ludicrous, half-terrible, in the contrast between the old chancellor and the new. Eldon tells them he comes from the verge of the grave, to warn and entreat them to reject the Bill. On the same day, Brougham delivers from the woolsack the grand oration in which he ends by imploring the Lords, on bended knees, as they value their honours, privileges, and estates, not to reject the Bill. Nevertheless, not having the fear of God and the people as yet sufficiently before their minds, they did reject it, by a majority of 41 proxies.

In the month of May next year they succumbed to terror, the influence of the Duke of Wellington, the entreaties of the king, and the determination of ministers to create peers until the hostile majority was swamped.

This desperate determination was mainly due to Brougham, who literally compelled the king to give himself and Lord Grey absolute written control of his prerogative for the purpose. "I wonder," said the premier as they left the presence, "how you could have the heart to press him for a written permission when you saw the state he was in." But through these transactions, Brougham seemed to be possessed by the soul of Oliver Cromwell.

TITHES.

February 27, 1832.

It occurrs to me that this speech, of no remarkable oratorical merit, may be interesting to the reader for an evidence of Plunket's opinion of the great Catholic and the great Orange agitator of his day. He speaks in answer to Lord Roden.

LORD PLUNKET said, that, as he was connected with the Irish government, and as an attack had been made on that government, he thought the house would excuse him for wishing to say a few words on this subject, and in defence of the conduct of the government of which he formed a part. He wished that the noble earl who had just sat down had presented the petition to which he had alluded, for the points it contained were involved in this irregular discussion, the only object of which was, to hold out to the people of this country, that the government was opposed to the maintenance of the Established church in Ireland, and was the enemy of the Protestant interest in that country. He was certain, however, that whatever was done with respect to tithes, there was no such effectual encouragement given to agitators, the value of whose promises the people well appreciated, as such opinions as those he had just alluded to, put forth by persons of character and property. Those opinions came with great gravity and weight, and were calculated on that account, to be most mischievous. With respect to what had been said of Mr. O'Connell, he would remind their lordships that that gentleman could not be considered as having been legally convicted of any offence; he had not been found guilty by the verdict of a jury. The state of his position with regard to the law was this: he had been indicted under a certain act of parliament—he had suffered judgment by default, and the act on which he had been indicted expired shortly afterwards. Now, if the noble and learned lord opposite would produce any authorities to show that, under such circumstances, a conviction could legally be carried into execution, he should be ready to meet the noble and learned earl on that question. He was himself ready to maintain the negative, both on principle and on authority. If he was right in that opinion—that the judgment suffered by default, under such circumstances, left Mr. O'Connell at liberty to move in arrest of that judgment, surely they would not say that punishment, which could not be visited on him in point of law, should be visited on him in his professional character. He was responsible for having affixed the great seal to the patent of precedence to Mr. O'Connell. He did not stand up there as his advocate, nor for the agitators of either side, from both of whom he had received nothing but obloquy, which he valued for this reason, that, next to the approbation of good men, he most esteemed the obloquy of bad men. He, therefore, rested his defence on the same grounds as those who sat beside him. But he might also observe, that that proceeding was totally unconnected with any question of politics, and the patent of precedence was given to Mr. O'Connell only on account of his professional eminence. The ordinary way of granting a patent of precedence in Ireland was, to enable the man to whom it was granted to rank next after the king's attorney and solicitor general. That, however, had not been done for Mr. O'Connell. He had only been named to take rank above those gentlemen much his juniors, whom he had seen promoted over his head. Whatever he might think of Mr. O'Connell in a political point of view, it was impossible to deny that, in his profession, no individual exhibited higher attainments, nor was any man more worthy of the distinction he had received. That being the case, the government was bound to accord him the distinction. It was the object of a rational government not to be vindictive, but just, and the gift of the patent of precedence was required by justice. He should have been happy if, by that mark of kindness, not incompatible with their duty, Mr. O'Connell had been induced to betake himself to his profession, in which he was entitled to expect the highest honours, but he could not regret what had been done. The noble earl opposite had expressed his disgust at the conduct of agitators. They were to be condemned, undoubtedly; but if he was asked, who was the greatest agitator, he should say, that it was the person who collected together large mobs of ignorant persons—who addressed them in a manner calculated to raise their jealousies, and revive their prejudices—who addressed English people, and called on them to form Protestant Associations—telling them that he loved the Catholics as men, but that they were a set of people who wished to put down the Protestants and their religion. Such a person was the true agitator. Such a person, who thus collected these ignorant assemblages together, and scattered among them ambiguous—no, not ambiguous, but unfounded assertions; such a person risked the making of Irish agitation not only formidable but desperate! To accomplish that fearful object in Ireland, all that was wanted was—not a war against the state—not a war against the tithes—but a war between the Protestants and Catholics.

The noble and learned earl opposite had again indulged in prophecies. The noble and learned earl had followed this course for forty years, according to his own showing. He sincerely hoped that the noble and learned lord might live for forty years more to prophesy; and he sincerely hoped, too, that the noble and learned earl's prophecies might be, at the end of that time, as visionary as they had been up to this moment. But, passing from that, he begged to make a few observations on the statement which the noble and learned lord had made, that the law was not vindicated in Ireland, the noble and learned lord had said, that the law was the same in both countries. He believed that it was in the abstract—that, as far as the letter of the law went, the guilt of entering into a conspiracy to refuse payment of tithes was in both countries the same; but it was a very different thing for the chancellor to furnish the attorney-general with the abstract principle of the law, and to tell him that such was the law, and for the attorney-general to carry on a prosecution under it. In these prosecutions there were such things as witnesses, and jurors, and the public, all of whom were to be considered; but he would venture to say, that, in every instance in which an outrage had been committed, a prosecution had been instituted, had been successful, and the authority of the law had been vindicated by the punishment of the offender. Although he was not the public prosecutor, he was not insensible to the duties of the office. He had communicated with the law officers of the crown in Ireland, and with the distinguished and very learned person who filled the office of attorney-general; and he would venture to assert, that, in no instance in which a prosecution could be successfully instituted had that prosecution been neglected. If the noble and learned earl opposite would ask for the papers connected with this subject, he would undertake to show, from those papers, that what he had stated was really the case. He assured the noble and learned lord, that if he would communicate with him upon any case in which he thought a prosecution advisable, he would undertake either that a prosecution should be instituted, or that he should satisfy the noble lord's mind that it could not be effectually done, and that he would point out to the noble lord the difficulty which would prevent such a prosecution. This he would readily do if the noble lord would do him the honour of making to him such a communication.

THE LORD CHANCELLOR OF IRELAND.

March 2, 1831.

PLUNKET contrived to provide for six sons and several nephews at the expense of Church and State. It was Cobbett's delight, after he had begun to hate him heartily, to parade the long pedigree of places and pensions, and to taunt the old anti-Union orator with the passage in which he declares that if that infamous measure should be carried, he would pledge his children, like young Hannibal, upon the altar of their country, to eternal hostility against the enemies of its freedom. Through the latter years of his life, when having once taken place, he took to it in earnest, and with all the eagerness and energy of his character, after the long self-denying ordinance which he had imposed upon himself, from the fall of Lord Grenville to the viceroyalty of Lord Wellesley, the "young Hannibals" furnished an easy hit for newspaper scribes and platform Pharisees. Plunket felt, or affected a vast disdain for such folk, and if annoyed, never condescended to reply or retaliate. However, in the *furore* of the Reform excitement, Lord Londonderry was tempted to utter the same imputations in his place in the house, and further to declare that he agreed with one of O'Connell's opinions, uttered apparently at random in a passion, "that there was not a more pernicious legislator for Ireland, or a more venal politician than Lord Plunket." After speaking for some time, the marquis took his seat, offering no resolution or petition, and Plunket rose to propose a vote of censure upon him.

My lords, I rise, with your lordships' permission, to address myself to the question before the house, and for the purpose of replying to one of the most unjust and most unwarrantable attacks that has ever been made on any individual within these walls. The noble marquis began his observations with a declaration—which I give credit to, as I am bound to believe any statement made by a noble lord—that he had no personal hostility to me; but I leave it to you, my lords, to say, whether his conduct is consistent with that disclaimer of personal hostility. The noble marquis, under the pretence of asking me a question, has not thought it unbecoming in him to go into a recital of all the falsehoods which newspapers have collected with regard to me or to my family. He has made himself the organ of all the calumnies which have been uttered against me, and, without the slightest pretence whatever, has made an attack as bitter, as severe, and as unwarranted, as the slender abilities of the noble lord will allow him to do. Fortunately for me, the ability of the noble lord to strike lags behind his inclination, as, in natural history, we see that the most venomous are among the least powerful of the animal creation. The noble lord complains that I cried "hear" to some observation of his. I certainly did so: but still am unconscious of having committed very great offence, the rather as I am not apt to complain myself when the noble lord deigns, in his own peculiar tone, to cry "hear" to any remark of mine. My "hear" I beg leave to remark, was at least not a scream—not a sound pushed beyond the usual limits of human exclamation—in fact, was not much calculated to alarm the ears or the feelings of my auditors. In this, I confess, there is a marked difference between us; but surely my vocal inability to cope with the noble lord ought not to be charged upon me as an offence. A noble baron opposite (Ellenborough) has defended the noble marquis's proceedings as not inconsistent with the usages of the house. "My noble friend," said he, "having thought better of it, was by no means irregular in withdrawing the petition he rose to present." In this, the noble marquis, then, is only appearing in a new character, exhibiting his dramatic versatility. Allow me to congratulate him in eclipsing even himself as an orator and a logician. It is conceived to be a notable result of most specimens of human eloquence to convince others against their preconceptions, and persuade them to act according to the wishes of the speaker. For the first time, however, in the history of logic and oratory, we now have a "learned Daniel" who, in the course of his oration, actually persuades, not others, but himself, to act contrary to his own predetermination. The noble lord has frequently before persuaded others, who might otherwise have voted on his side, that to do so would be acting in the teeth of common sense; for it is one of the shining attributes of the noble lord's genius, that his support is injurious only to those who have the misfortune to count him as an ally; but this I believe is the first time that his *per contra* persuasive powers have been successfully directed against himself. Long, I trust, will they be so harmlessly directed, and long may they be as successful in persuading others to the reverse of his intentions as they have in the present instance, with himself. Before the noble lord had ventured to attack me as he did, and complain of the remuneration which I have derived from the public for my services, he ought to have made himself somewhat better acquainted with simple facts. Had he been present the other evening when I moved for returns of the appointment of secretary to the Master of the Rolls in Ireland, he would have heard me state the object of my motion, and thereby have avoided wasting his time and eloquence this evening. I now tell the noble lord—not for his personal satisfaction, for with him I will hold no terms, and will offer no explanation whatever with a view to removing his dissatisfaction, but for the satisfaction of the house—the object I had in view in moving for these returns. Aspersions, the most unwarranted and injurious, were thrown out in another place against me with reference to the appointment of my secretary, and a notice of motion was given in the House of Commons for documents connected with that appointment. I, accordingly, for the purpose of meeting any calumniator who would dare to repeat these aspersions to my face in this house, came down and moved for similar returns to be laid before your lordships, so as to afford any noble lord who might be disposed to repeat the calumny an opportunity of doing so, and myself an opportunity, which, with God's blessing, I will never shrink from, of meeting, and exposing, and chastising my calumniator. In moving for the returns, I also moved for returns of the similar appointments made by my two predecessors in office, in order that your lordships and the public might clearly see, that the aspersions and calumny applied as much to Lords Chancellor Manners and Hart, as to Lord Chancellor Plunket.

The noble lord has thought proper, on the authority of a newspaper statement, which, I assure your lordships, I have never read, and to which I am wholly indifferent, to state, that my family derive £36,000 a year from the public, and concerning which he calls upon me for an explanation. I will not stoop to refute so extravagant a falsehood. I envy not the structure of understanding which could bestow upon it a moment's credence. What! are noble lords to be called upon to defend themselves in parliament against every stupid calumny which mortified but most impotent vanity, or the virulence of faction, may insert in a newspaper. I am surprised that even the noble lord could entertain such a monstrous proposition. He asks me, have I made any inquiry as to the source or authenticity of the statement; I answer him, no. I would not lower myself in my own estimation by treating it otherwise than with silent contempt. I ask the noble lord, have any statements ever appeared in newspapers touching his own personal affairs? And, if so, has he been called upon, as he calls upon me, in his place in parliament, to explain them away? Was it ever, for example, stated—no doubt without any foundation—that the noble marquis applied to a certain prime minister for some remuneration or pension, which the said prime minister was cruelly unjust enough to refuse? Was the noble lord, in a word, ever called upon explain to the public the amount and distribution of the large sums of public money which found their way to the pockets of the Stuart family? Certainly not; it was reserved for himself to set the precedent of making a most senseless newspaper calumny the occasion of as senseless an attack on the individual calumniated. I state, then, that the newspaper allegation, on which the noble lord has grounded his attack, is totally and absolutely a falsehood. Whether it is quite fair and consistent with the usage of parliament and good society to make the allegations of a newspaper the pretext of calling upon any noble lord to enter into a statement of his family affairs, I leave it, after this emphatic denial, to the good taste and gentlemanly feeling of your lordships. I take leave of the calumny, with this assurance to the noble lord, that I am one who have never been a hunter after favours from any minister or government whatever. I am not one who has given his support or his opposition in parliament according to the mere dictates of vanity or personal interest, and I am one who never made a demand for public money which the individual from whom it was demanded was forced to stigmatize as "too bad." The noble lord professes to entertain no feelings of personal hostility against me. I profess to entertain no such feeling against him; but this I tell him, by way of wholesome warning, that if he, on any future occasion, venture to indulge in rash attacks on my character, though I will not degrade myself by following the example of personal invective, he may perhaps have little reason, so far as the vanguards are concerned, to congratulate himself with a large balance on the credit side of the account between us. The noble lord has thought fit to catechise me as to the advice which I may have felt it to be my duty to give my sovereign in matters connected with the office I hold under him. What right has the noble lord, or any noble lord, to ask me such a question? Or, on what ground should he venture to charge me with having deprived him of the confidence of his majesty, and to have given his majesty counsel displeasing to a party who arrogate to themselves exclusive loyalty, while they are thwarting, by every means in their power, the king's government? Such questions and such charges are the mere ravings of distempered vanity, and are not to be reasoned with by those who are capable of sound ratiocination. I can assure the noble lord that, so far from occupying the time of my sovereign with discussions of the noble lord's transcendent merits as a statesman, an orator, or a logician, I never have wasted a moment of even my own time on either, and that the noble lord's affairs are to me a matter of as utter indifference, as I am sure they must be to the rational portion of the public. This declaration may not be flattering incense to the noble lord's estimate of his own public merits, but it is a simple fact, which I trust will spare him much future fretfulness. I do not recollect whether there is any other point on which the noble lord is anxious to "obtain some explanation." If there be, and that he will have the goodness to remind me of it, I shall be very happy to afford him all in my power. Perhaps the little I have afforded will suffice him for the present; if not, let him hoist the flag, and I am ready for the combat. With respect to the members of my family, I have nothing to conceal in regard to any of them. If they hold public situations, they fulfil the duties attached to them, and are not therefore, an improper burthen on the public. I have six sons, and I have certainly endeavoured to provide for them, as it is my duty to do. Two of my sons are in the church, two at the bar. I defy even calumny to impeach their conduct at either. My eldest son derives no emolument from the public, and all my family occupy but that station in society to which I am persuaded they are fully entitled.

After Plunket sat down, Lord Londonderry rose again to explain. A short angry scene followed. Plunket's temper had been fiercely stirred, and the marquis was at the best of times rather disorderly. The debate that followed was a series of interruptions of the most laconic character. "The noble lord," complains Lord Londonderry, "calculates what I have received during ten years diplomatic service, compares it with his own, and draws a large balance against me."

LORD PLUNKET—I did no such thing.

THE MARQUIS OF LONDONDERRY—I ask you, my lords, is that a fair way of meeting the charges?

LORD PLUNKET—I repeat I did no such thing.

Again the marquis returns to the list of places.—"As the noble lord has provoked me to it, I will read what is stated of him by which it will be seen whether the economical and retrenching administration with which he is connected take care to feather their own nests. The first item is, the Lord Chancellor of Ireland £10,000." "That," said Plunket, "is the first falsehood." After a little, Lord Grey and Lord Ellenborough interfered; Lord Londonderry apologized for the breach of order he had been guilty of, and the motion was withdrawn.

FAREWELL TO THE BAR.

June 21, 1841.

UPON the last day of Plunket's appearance in court every portion of its space was densely thronged. He decided some few cases, and in one of them referred "to the person who was to succeed him in the office he then filled." At the conclusion of the business of the day, Sergeant Greene, as the senior of the Bar present, addressed him thus:—

"I presume, my lord, it is not your lordship's intention to sit again in this court; I therefore rise, as the senior in rank of the members of the Bar now present, and with the full concurrence of the brethren of my profession (here all the members of the Bar rose simultaneously), to address your lordship a few words before your retirement from that bench over which your lordship has for many years presided."

Lord Plunket rose from his seat, and advanced to the front of the bench.

"My lord, we are anxious to express to your lordship the sense we entertain, not only of the ability, the learning, the patience, and the assiduity which have marked your lordship's administration of the high and important functions committed to your lordship's charge, but also, my lord, of the courtesy, kindness, and attention which we have all personally experienced at your lordship's hands, in the discharge of our professional duties in this court. We gratefully acknowledge, my lord, the disposition you have ever shown to accommodate us all—a disposition by which we all admit your lordship was ever actuated, without regard to personal circumstances or to our political feelings or predilections. We trust, my lord, it will be said that this feeling on our part will be as general and as uneversal, as the kindness on your part has been uniform and uninterrupted. My lord, it is needless for us to dwell here, for the purpose of commenting upon the talents and endowments which have raised your lordship to the high position from which you are about to retire. They are, my lord, recorded in our history, and they will long live among the proudest recollections of our countrymen. From a sense of these, we offer to you our present tribute of the profoundest admiration and respect; and, my lord, it is gratifying for us to add, that at no period of your lordship's career have they ever shown in greater lustre than at this moment. My lord, with warmest wishes for your lordship's happiness in that retirement, which none is more fitted than your lordship to adorn, we respectfully bid your lordship farewell."

When the Bar had concluded their address, the Attorneys presented theirs, at the close of which Plunket said—

It would be great affectation on my part if I were to say that I do not feel to a considerable degree at the prospect of retiring from a profession, at which I have for a period of more than fifty years of my life been actively engaged—a period during which I have been surrounded by friends, many of them warm ones ;

His lordship then paused evidently much affected.

without exception: many of them are now no more; some of them, nay many of them I see at this moment around me. This retirement from the active scenes in which I have been so long engaged, and which have become as it were incorporated with my life, I cannot help feeling, and feeling deeply. It has, however, in some degree been alleviated by the prospect of the repose which is probably better suited to this period of my life, and which perhaps would have earlier induced me to retire but for events of a particular description which have latterly occurred; but independent of this I must say, that any pain I would have felt has been more than alleviated by the kind and affectionate address which has been offered to me by my friend Sergeant Greene, and which has been so cordially assented to by the members of both professions.

I am not unconscious that in the discharge of those duties, my ability for which has been so over-rated by my friend Sergeant Greene, I have been led into expressions of impatience which had been much better avoided. For any pain that I have given in doing so, or any feelings that I have hurt, I sincerely apologize, and I am grateful to the profession for not having attributed to inclination any such observations; and I must say, that whatever any such expressions may have been, they never have influenced me. It is a sentiment that I trust never will influence me ; and I am now able to say, that in retiring from my profession, I do not carry with me any other sentiment than that of affectionate consideration for all and every member of the profession.

Now with respect to the particular circumstances which have occurred, and the particular succession which is about to take place in this court, it will become me to say very little. For the individual who is to occupy the situation I now fill, I entertain the highest political and personal respect—no one can feel it more so—but I owe it as a duty to myself and the members of the bar to state, that for the changes which are to take place I am not in the slightest degree answerable ; I have no share in them, and have not directly or indirectly given them my sanction. In yielding my assent to the proposition which has been made for my retiring, I have been governed solely by its having been requested as a personal favour by a person to whom I owe so much, that a feeling of gratitude would have rendered it morally impossible that I could have done otherwise than to resign.

When I look at the Bar before me, and especially the number of those who might have sat efficiently in this judicial place, I am bound to say, that for all those great ingredients which are calculated to enable them to shine as practitioners, and as members of the Bar, or as gentlemen, for candour, for courtesy, knowledge, and ability—I challenge competition—I challenge the very distinguished Bars of either England or Scotland, and I do not fear that those I have the honour of addressing would suffer in the comparison. To them, for their repeated kindnesses I am deeply indebted. I do assure them that when I retire into quiet life, I will cherish in my heart the affectionate kindness and attention which I experienced at their hands.

Plunket was deeply affected during the delivery of this parting address. At its conclusion he bowed to the Bar, and left the court, leaning upon the arm of his friend Sir Michael O'Loghlen, Master of the Rolls.

The profession which he had so long adorned, added to its parting honours a levee. Nearly all the practising members of the profession waited upon him at his mansion in Stephen's green. "So numerous a bar levee had never before been witnessed in Ireland;" writes the author of *Ireland and its Rulers.* "It was thronged by Tories, Conservatives, High Whigs, Low Whigs, Radicals, Corn Exchangers, and Repealers. Several of the judges were present ; the Master of the Rolls, who hated all kind of pomp, put on his state-robes for the occasion, and since the days when Charlemont House was in its glory, so many influential persons had never gathered under the roof of a private individual in Ireland." The old man, it is said, was full of animation and energy, and in perfect possession of all his fine faculties, on this day, the occasion of his last appearance in public life.

APPENDIX. 443

THE KING AGAINST WALLER O'GRADY.

I have printed the following celebrated speech as the most perfect specimen upon record of Plunket's consummate power of pleading. I have not willingly consigned so much space to a dry legal argument, but I could not help feeling that it was due to his high professional fame.

Old Chief Baron O'Grady, in the year 1817, appointed his son Waller to the situation of Clerk of the Pleas in the Court of Exchequer. Saurin, instigated it was believed by a personal animosity, which was sometimes supposed to stimulate his official conduct, astonished the Four Courts, by instituting proceedings on the part of the crown, against the new officer—on the ground that the king, not the court, had the right of appointment. The Chief Baron resisted with the first abilities and energy to be had at the Irish Bar, and the case became a regular legal tournament—in which Saurin and Bushe, on the part of the crown, and Plunket and Burton on that of the court, debated every point of law, vestige of tradition, and atom of precedent, that could by possibility be brought to bear upon the case. The following is Plunket's speech to the jury.

It is now my duty to lay before you the case of the clerk of the Pleas of the Court of Exchequer: and my lords and gentlemen, I am apprehensive, that in so doing I shall be obliged to claim a larger share of the time, of the attention, and of the indulgence of the court and jury, than I should be disposed to do. But this case is one of very great importance to the parties, and to the public; and I should not satisfactorily discharge my duty to my client, to the learned judge who has appointed him, or to the Court of Exchequer who have justified that appointment, and who are now brought before the bar of this court upon a criminal information to answer the charge of having usurped upon the rights of the crown, which they are by their oaths bound to maintain, were I not to enter with some minuteness into every part of this extraordinary case.

You already know, my lords, from the statement of the counsel for the crown, that this is a claim of right by Mr. Waller O'Grady as the clerk of the Pleas of the Court of Exchequer; a claim put upon an appointment by the chief baron of that court, which has been ratified and acted on, and admitted as an authority, by the whole Court of Exchequer. It is a claim on his part, I allow, against a long usage by the crown, and I do not scruple to admit it to be right and proper that that claim should be carefully examined. It is certainly the right and the duty of the king's law officers to take care that his rights shall not be usurped, or his just prerogative diminished; but it must be equally admitted, that if the claim of the chief baron be a well-founded one, it is fair upon his part to urge it: nay more, that it would be a most gross dereliction of his duty to suffer any of the rights intrusted to him by the law to be diminished or impaired.

I agree with the proposition laid down by the attorney-general, that according to the constitution of these countries, the king is the fountain of all office; and I agree further, that it is the duty of the king's attorney-general to provide that this right of the crown, so far as it remains, shall be guarded from encroachment. But if by this position it is meant to be insisted, that all offices in this country are derived immediately from the crown, I beg leave totally to deprecate such a doctrine. All offices are certainly derived from the crown mediately or immediately; but it is equally, true, that there are many offices vested by the constitution and by the common law in other persons, as incident to offices derived by them from the crown, and over which the king can have no control. With respect to those offices which are exercised in courts of justice, whether the persons who are to fill them be appointed by the courts or not, in all cases where they are to be admitted by the court, the care of them is intrusted to that court and to that alone. If the crown conceives itself injured by such an admission, the attorney-general has no right to proceed by a prerogative information, but the only legal mode of trying the right, is by the crown's appointing an officer and having his title tried in the first instance in the court to which he is appointed, and if their decision be unsatisfactory, then by appealing to another. This proposition I pledge myself to demonstrate to the court and the jury.

Having premised so much, I shall call the attention of the court to the admitted facts of this case : namely, that the office of clerk of the Pleas is an ancient office in the Court of Pleas of the Exchequer, the duty of which is to enrol pleas and judgments of that court, and which is of high concern to the administration of public justice, that the present defendant has been appointed by the chief judge of that court, and that he has been regularly admitted by the entire court. Having stated so much, I must beg leave to say, that this proceeding is unprecedented, vexatious, unwarrantable, and illegal in every particular. I state once for all, to my learned friend the attorney-general, that I am sure he will not suppose, that in so speaking, I mean any personal disrespect to him. I am sure that in instituting this proceeding, he has been actuated solely by considerations of duty and a laudable desire to maintain what he conceives to be the just rights of the crown. Nor is there any man for whose legal knowledge and information upon general subjects I entertain a higher respect.. But I must say, that in the present instance, by some fatality, he has acted in direct violation of the best established principles of the constitution ; and that a proceeding of this nature can have no other tendency than to bring humiliation and disgrace on courts. of justice, and odium upon the prerogative of the crown. And I say this now, because I conceive this is the place and the time—when the judges of the land are brought to the bar of this court to answer for their conduct, upon a criminal information—when the judges of a superior original court are called as culprits and usurpers before the tribunal of another and a co-ordinate jurisdiction.

Wherever a court of justice is created, of necessity the judging of the admissions of the persons who are to be their clerks is vested in such court. They are the persons intrusted by the law to judge of the sufficiency of the persons to be admitted, and also the legality of their title. Unless they are satisfied of both, they ought not to admit. Upon this, I shall refer your lordships to the treatise on the authority of the Master of the Rolls, a book, your lordships are aware, of very high authority, and which, it is well known, was written by Sir Joseph Jekyll. In the second section, 64, 65, it is laid down, " The admission of officers of courts of justice, by whomsoever nominated, belongs to those courts, who are to judge of their qualifications. And accordingly, though the nominated officer is usually admitted, yet in some instances, he has been rejected, as in Dyer, 150, in the case of the clerk of crown, who is nominated by the king under the great seal. For the nomination, admission, and swearing of officers, is an act of the court." And for these positions he cites the year book 9. Edw. IV., p. 5, which I have examined, and which is direct on the point. The case referred to in Dyer is Hunt *v.* Allen (Dy., 149 a. 152 b.), which was an assize by Hunt against Allen, the question turning on the validity of the nomination of Hunt. And the case of Fogge, chief clerk or custos brevium, in 18 Edw. IV. was cited, "where the justices would not allow the patent of the king to encumber the place, because there cannot be two chiefs in one office." And the court accordingly refused to admit him. There is a further case in Dy. 150 b. upon the same subject. The crown appointed Croxton and Vynter clerks of the crown; Croxton died, and Vynter came into court and showed the king's patent, and prayed to be admitted, &c., but the court refused to admit him, and appointed another person. I am now showing the authority of courts to refuse admission if they think proper. The admission of the officer is "an act of the court," judging of the fitness of the person, and the legality of the appointment. The latter of the above cases in Dyer is an instance of rejection on account of unfitness in the person, and the former for the illegality of the appointment. And in further confirmation of this right I beg leave to cite to the court, Cavendish's case, 1 Anderson, 152. There the crown appointed a person to execute writs of supersedeas in the Court of Common Pleas. The judge of that court refused to admit him, because in point of law the grant was void, inasmuch as the duty of making such writs belonged to the chief prothonotary. It appears that this case was attended with much difficulty on the part of the court, and much exertion on the part of the crown. But yet no idea was entertained that such a proceeding as a *quo warranto* would lie, notwithstanding that great efforts were made on the part of Cavendish. The justices, however, refused to yield to either menaces or importunities, and the crown was at length obliged to acquiesce. This was in the reign of Elizabeth. Now, according to these doctrines and these precedents, I take upon me to say, that the uniform course and practice has been, in every case where it is conceived that the right of the crown or of any other party has been affected by the admission of any officer by a court, to try the right by the nomination of an officer on the part of the party complaining, and to have the title of that officer in the first instance tried by the court which has given such admission. The present proceeding is without even the colour of precedent in the whole history of the law; in England or in Ireland; before the Revolution or since the Revolution; there never before was an example in which the act of a superior court of justice admitting its own officer has been questioned at the bar of another court; much less by such a proceeding as a criminal information; and I must again repeat, that the direct tendency of it is to throw disgrace upon the administration of justice, and odium upon the prerogative of the crown. I thought it my duty to apprise the attorney-general, that we consi-

2 F

dered this proceeding so mischievous and unconstitutional, that we should be called upon to arraign it. I do not find that the attorney-general has stated any other reason in its vindication, than an usage on the part of the crown to appoint to this office for 400 years. It is not only the privilege, but the duty of the king's officer to assert his right; I do not mean to say there is anything criminal in it; but why the staleness of this demand should now for the first time justify a proceeding in the teeth of all decency and all precedent, I do not see the semblance of a reason. If it be said, no action has been brought, because if it had, it must have been tried in the first instance in the Court of Exchequer; the answer is, that the law has said so. And it has said so, for the best reason, in order to avoid a clashing of jurisdictions, which must be the consequence of allowing one court to be called before another, as is done here, to answer for the exercise of its discretion in the appointment of its own officer. Nor is it in the power of the crown to defeat this courtesy of the law by resorting to such a proceeding as a criminal information. The privilege of correcting an erroneous decision (if this was so), is as great a privilege as that of affirming it. If the Court of Exchequer had done anything amiss, if on the trial of an action they should decide against the just rights of the crown, they are liable to be corrected by way of appeal, and in no other way. No other court has any original jurisdiction. Suppose an application had been made to this court, not as is now done, by a prerogative information, but for liberty to file such an information, the court must have refused it. They must have refused it, in analogy to every principle of law; for there is no instance to be found of one court of justice questioning the act of another, of co-ordinate jurisdiction, especially in the appointment of its own officers. This court never had, in any shape, an appellate jurisdiction over the Court of Exchequer. This doctrine is fully laid down in 4 Inst. 71, 105, 106, where it is said, that the crown could not grant such a jurisdiction. So that this is an attempt to give originally to this court the right to reverse the decisions of the Court of Exchequer, a right which even the crown could not give by way of appeal.

Suppose judgment of ouster given by this court against the officer of the Exchequer, where is the jurisdiction in this court to arm its officers with the power of enforcing it? Suppose, after such a judgment, the Court of Exchequer were to say that the officer should still act, where is the power, either in this court or in the crown to restrain him? Is a party to be brought into court by criminal information as an usurper, because he acts under the authority of a superior court, a court which has exclusive jurisdiction over his office, and which can commit him to prison if he refuses to perform it? What authority has this court to punish the officer of the Court of Exchequer, any more than the Court of Exchequer has to punish the officer of this court?

I have complained that this proceeding is vexatious: I say again, it is vexatious in every part of it, and that it cannot be attended with any advantage to either the king or the public. It not merely puts the defendant to prove his title, as has been said by Mr. Attorney-General, but it hampers him in point of pleading: so that even if his title were good, he would be liable to be defeated by a trivial irregularity. He is precluded from pleading double matter: so that if he had ten defences, he must yet resort to only one, and if the issue be found against him on that one, it is fatal to his case. If he be successful, he can have no costs, but is compelled to defend himself at his own expense: and if he fails, he has costs to pay. I say, it is a prerogative of so severe a nature, that it ought not to be resorted to, unless where there has been a direct and manifest usurpation of the rights of the crown. Had the attorney-general inquired, he would have been informed of the nature of this appointment. He would have learned, that it was not a claim set up by a stranger, but made by the chief baron, and ratified by the court. Immediately upon the making of this appointment, my lord chief baron waited upon the lord lieutenant, and informed him that he felt himself bound by his oath to maintain the rights of the crown, and proposed that the case should be referred to the principal law officers: offering at the same time to waive any advantage gained by the appointment. That proposal, for what reason I know not, has been declined. I do not mean to say that any blame upon this subject is imputable to the lord lieutenant, of whom I wish to be considered as speaking with every sentiment of personal respect. The first intimation given to the chief baron after this communication of the intention of the crown, was by the filing of this information.

Allow me now to ask, whether, if the Court of Exchequer refused to admit another officer, a mandamus could issue from this court to compel them? To show that it could not, I beg to cite Lee's case, Carth. 169, 170. 3 Mod. 332, 335. S. C. In that case, a mandamus to admit a proctor into the Ecclesiastical Court was refused, and on this ground "that (3. Mod. 335.) officers are incident to all courts, and must partake of the nature of those several and respective courts, in which they attend; and the judges, or those who have the supreme authority in those courts, are the proper persons to censure the behaviour of their own officers, and if they should be mistaken, the King's Bench cannot relieve: for in all cases where such judges keep within their bounds, no other courts can correct their errors in proceedings." And the sole question raised in that case was, whether the court had acted within its jurisdiction. Sir Bartholomew Shower, who was counsel for the mandamus, in his argument endeavours to distinguish the case, as being that of an inferior jurisdiction: admitting that it would be otherwise in the case of the Court of Common Pleas. This case will be material in a subsequent part of my argument, as showing that the course of the court is the law: but at present I use it only to show that one court is not subject to the control of another of co-ordinate jurisdiction.

Again, this proceeding is most vexatious; for even if judgment of ouster should be pronounced against the defendant, there could not be judgment for the king to put him into possession of this franchise, because he cannot exercise it himself. Rex *v.* Stanton, Cro. Jac. 259, 260. From the entry in 1 Lill. 6. Woodhouse *v.* Twyford, it appears, that when a plea of privilege is put in by an officer of the court, he is not obliged to go into the right of appointment, but need merely state his appointment and admission. Thus this proceeding is additionally vexatious. If the crown gets a judgment of ouster, the consequence will be, that it will appoint a person to execute this office, who must go back to the Court of Exchequer, and according to the course of law, submit to them the validity of that appointment. Nor is this merely a wanton conjecture; for in the late act of parliament passed in the last session, making provision for the fees of this office, it is recited, " And whereas his royal highness the Prince Regent, in the name, &c. proposes to make a grant of the said office," which is a direct intimation that the crown is to grant. " And whereas a suit has been instituted, and other suits may hereafter be instituted respecting the right of a grantee of his majesty, &c." So that this proceeding is to end in a grant by the crown to try the right. Should these suits which are spoken of, be instituted, where are they to be tried? Can they be tried any where but in the Court of Exchequer? Unless, indeed, in the spirit of these proceedings, an act of parliament is to be passed for transferring the jurisdiction. If these suits are to be conformable to precedents from the earliest times, they can follow no other course than that which I have suggested. And can it be thought a wholesome or a sound exercise of that discretion which is placed in the crown, instead of trying the right in the first instance, to institute a proceeding which is to deprive the party of the benefit of pleading, to subject him to costs, and to call down condemnation upon the Court of Exchequer? And this for the purpose of again submitting the same question to that same court, thus degraded and vilified? It can only bring the law into disgrace: and if my learned friend the attorney-general were now addressing your lordships, he would disclaim such an imputation. I am sure he is incapable of sanctioning so revolutionary and jacobinical a doctrine: and if these shameful consequences had struck his mind, he would never have prosecuted such a suit. So firmly was I impressed with the weight of these consequences, that I advised the chief baron to call on this court to enter a remanet upon this record, till the opinion of the twelve judges could be had upon it, and until (if necessary) the twelve judges of England should be consulted. He has, however, declined to do so, and desires his case to go before a jury but I should not have conceived I had done my duty, had I not advised him as I did.

There are three material issues before the court and the jury. The first is upon an uniform usage alleged by the attorney-general to have existed in the crown from time immemorial, to appoint to this office. The second is upon a right of the chief baron as chief judge of the court (which he is by this pleading admitted to be,) and by the usage and course of the court, namely, that he should appoint to all such offices as the court were at any time entitled to appoint to: and the third is simply upon that usage. These issues are all nearly connected with each other. In order to have a determination upon the second, we must previously dispose of the first: and accordingly this course has been taken by the crown. The argument of the attorney-general is this: that if the court has such a right, it must be, either by the original constitution of the court, or by prescription, or by act of parliament: and he says that there is no evidence of this being the original constitution of the court. Again he says, that even if the right ever were in the court, yet, first, it could not be legally transferred, and secondly that in point of fact it was, not transferred. This, if I mistake not, comprehends the sum of his argument. The words used by him in stating the right of the court, are somewhat ambiguous: he says that if there be such a right, it must be either "by the constitution of the court, or by prescription, or by act of parliament." What is meant by the original constitution of the court, I do not exactly know. If it means the common law, then I heartily subscribe to the position: but if it means some positive institution of the court, as implying some attributes which the common law does not allow to it, then I must deny it. And here let me remark, that by a singular and unaccountable felicity, the attorney-general has not once in the whole course of his argument mentioned the name of the common law. That this should be the case, I am not surprised: because the attorney-general has found himself under the necessity of falling foul of Lord Coke and Lord Holt.

There is a difference between the two modes of expression, common law and usage. According to the one, it would be necessary to show the right had always existed: but not so in the other. The common law is the protection of the inheritances and the liberties of the subject. It is a body of immemorial usage; not arising from prescription—nor from act of parliament—nor from charter: but growing out of the immemorial usages which have prevailed in these countries. As they existed in England they were imported here, as a grand code of law, by King John, in the 12th year of his reign. The attorney-general has alleged, that although by the common law of England these rights were established in the chief justices there, yet it would not be so here. I deny that; for I say the subjects of this country are purchasers of the common law of England, and of all its properties and all its benefits. It was not arbitrarily imposed upon them by conquest: they were purchasers of the entire benefit of it; and therefore if by the common law of England this right is vested in courts of law, it is necessarily so here also.

In order to learn what is the common law, I know of no other mode, than by inquiring into the reasonableness of the thing, the ancient usage of the country in that and in analogous cases, the declaration of the legislature, the expositions of wise and learned men, and finally the decisions of courts of justice. I shall refer to all these criterions for the purpose of seeing whether there is any common law upon this subject, and if so, what it is. The first circumstance for your lordships' attention is thdeclaration in the Stat. of Westm. 2 c. 30, 13 Edward I., anno 1285; the words of which are, " All justices of the benches from henceforth shall have in their circuits clerks to enroll all pleas pleaded before them, *like as they used to have in times past.*" By the common law, wherever a court of common law exists, the judges of that court, or one of them, must have a power of appointing the clerks who are to enroll the pleadings and judgments. My Lord Coke, in his comment on the above passage,* says, "Hereby it appeareth that the justices of courts did ever appoint their clerks, some of which after, by prescription, grew to be officers in their courts : as *here it is put for example*, that the justices of the benches in their circuits had clerks that enrolled all pleas pleaded before them, as anciently they used to have, that is, as by the common law." So that by this comment, Lord Coke declares that the statute is in this respect but confirmatory of the common law; and further, that the case to which the legislature had applied this declaration, is only put by way of example. He then proceeds, " Now the cause of making this branch was, that the king was informed that he might erect offices for entering and enrolment of records in his courts of justice, and especially justices of assize, which this branch declareth to belong to the justices, and that they had enjoyed this of ancient time, that is, by common law." Here then Lord Coke declares the common law, and expressly states the encroachments of the crown: and that for the remedy of this particular encroachment, the statute declared the common law. "And the reason (says he) is twofold. These reasons of Lord Coke the attorney-general has treated as ludicrous. I think I am sufficiently alive to the ridiculous, and have a due sense of the facetious powers of my learned friend the attorney-general; but in this instance I am so dull and stupid as not to feel the ludicrous effect of these reasons. The first of them is, "for that the law doth ever appoint those that have the greatest knowledge and skill, to perform that which is to be done." Now, for the life of me, I cannot see the joke. On the contrary, if I were looking for a grave and satisfactory reason, fit to come from the lips of one of the sages of the law, and to be incorporated in that great comment, which is, more than anything that I know, the evidence of the common law, I could not have found one more so in every respect than this. These were the feelings of ancient times—the presumption then was in favour of the wisdom and integrity of judges, and that they would exercise their offices with honesty and judgment. But it is in these days to be supposed, that judges will not exercise their rights with impartiality and integrity! Such were not the feelings of Lord Coke, or of that day, or under which our common law has grown.

The second reason given by Lord Coke is, that "the officers and clerks are but to enter, enrol, or effect that which the justices do adjudge, award or order, the insufficient doing of which maketh the proceeding of the justices erroneous, (this is a precise statement of the

* 2 Inst. 425.

duty of the clerk of the pleas in the several courts), than which nothing can be more dishonourable and grievous to the justices, and prejudicial to the party: therefore the law, as here it appeareth, did appropriate to the justices the making of their own clerks and officers, and so to proceed judicially by their own instruments; and that this was the common law, the king cannot grant the office of the shire or county clerk (who is to enter all judgments and proceedings in the county court) for that the making of the shire clerk belongeth to the sheriff by the common law, as in Mitton's case it appeareth, *et sic de cæteris.*" If a century had been employed in condensing the reasons of this common law principle, it could not have been done in words more emphatical than those of Lord Coke. The attorney-general says, the court has no interest in the proceedings but only the party. This is not the law. The judges are interested, first in the propriety of their own judgments, and next in the faithful entering of them. They are interested in having their judgments duly taken down and enrolled by their own instruments. They are likewise interested in the safety and rights of the subjects, suitors in their courts. They are the persons to guard that safety and those rights. From the moment that courts of justice are framed, from that moment the rights and the duties of protecting the subject devolve upon them, and it is their interest as well as their duty to protect his rights. And yet we are now told, that courts are not proper judges of their duty, but are to be called to the tribunal of some other court, to answer for their discharge of those duties of which the law has constituted them the only judges. It is a doctrine in the highest degree illegal and unconstitutional, fraught with the most mischievous consequences, and one which ought to be instantly met and put down.

For the doctrine thus laid down by Lord Coke, he refers to Mitton's case, 4 Rep. 32. In that case, the crown appointed a sheriff, and then appointed a shire clerk. The question was between the sheriff (who claimed a power of appointing the shire clerk) and the appointee of the crown. This was in 26 Elizabeth, 1584. The argument for the crown admitted, that if the sheriff were the judge of the county court, the right by common law belonged to him. The whole question turned upon this, whether it was the sheriff's court or not. The attorney-general says the question was whether it was the property of the sheriff or not; and with some degree of triumph asked, "if the Exchequer was the chief baron's court?" No one ever said that it was; but in the same sense as the sheriff's court is his, the Exchequer is the court of the barons. They are both the king's courts, though these judges preside in them. The true and only inquiry was this, was the sheriff the president of the court? And it is then laid down, "that law and reason require that the sheriff, who is a public officer, and minister of justice, and who has an office of such eminency, confidence, peril, and charge, ought to have all rights appertaining to his office, and ought to be favoured in law before any private person for his singular benefit and avail." To this case Lord Coke adds a decision by Anderson and Popham with regard to gaolers, to the same effect. All are parts of the same principle and analogy, namely, that a derivative office is inseparably incident to its principal. In Mitton's case many precedents of appointments by the king were stated; but what was the answer? "*judicandum est legibus, non exemplis,*" that is to say, that if the law be clear, instances the other way are to be considered not as precedents, but as usurpations. Now apply these principles to this case: although the king may have the power of appointing the judges who constitute the court, yet having once constituted them to be a court, the appointment of their clerks must be incident to their office, and the crown cannot take it from them. In Mitton's case, though the crown had the appointment and removal of the principal, yet it was held not to have the appointment of the subordinate officer.

In the case of Harcourt *v.* Fox, cited on the other side (1 Show 526) this doctrine is still more strongly exemplified. There the king might by virtue of his prerogative appoint any of the justices custos rotulorum; but the moment he did appoint one, then, *ex necessitate* and by the common law, such custos must have the appointment of clerk of the peace.

Such is the law as laid down by C. J. Holt, who was one of the most distinguished men in the history of our law. He suffered under the tyranny of James II., for his integrity and principles, and for his efforts in establishing our civil and religious liberties. After the Revolution he was made by King William chief justice of the King's Bench: and by his learning and talents he dignified and adorned that high situation to which he had been raised by his integrity and independence. It is therefore (allow me to say) a flippant mode of getting rid of the authority of such a man to say that he had a cause involving a similar point on his own part, and was therefore influenced in giving his judgment. His words are (530) "the clerk being the person that must be trusted with the rolls to make entries upon, to draw judgments, to record pleas, to join issues, and enter judgments, then of common right, by the common law of the land, it belongs to him that hath the keeping of the records, to nominate this clerk, and not to any one else." Here the keeping of the records is relied on as if the right of appointment grew out of it. The case of the custos rotulorum was peculiarly circumstanced. All the justices were of equal degree, and they could not agree amongst each other, which of them should have the right that must belong to one, namely, of nominating the custos rotulorum. If they could have agreed, it would have become the usage of the court that the one so agreed upon should appoint, and there would then have been no pretence for the interference of the crown. But this not having been done, the crown of necessity appointed the custos, and he, when so appointed, had of course the nomination of the clerk of the peace.

The powers of superior courts do not grow out of the keeping of the records, but the keeping of the records belongs to them as judges of the courts. The custody of the records is incident to the pronouncing of the judgments. Thus it is said "that all the justices being judges of record, the records of the court must belong to them, and certiorari's to remove them must be directed to the justices in general, &c."* I take this case to be a most governing one upon this subject. Your lordships see that the right of having the custody of the records is not derived from the act of the crown appointing a custos, but the law annexes the custody of the records to the merely being judges in the court. And in like manner Lord Coke states this right of appointment to be in the court from its constitution, and without reference to any custody of the records; he deduces it not from any such custody, but solely from their being judges.

All the points in this case of Harcourt v. Fox are important; because justices of the peace, custos rotulorum, and clerk of the peace, are all offices created within time of memory; they did not exist at common law; their origin was recent. But yet the consequence of the common law principle that wherever a court is created they are to appoint their own clerks, did, when this new jurisdiction was created, attach to it; and this is the reason why the attorney-general was so unwilling to allow this right to be in the court by common law, but would have your lordships suppose it must have been in them, if at all, by what he calls the original constitution of the court. At all times, and under all circumstances, the court, who are to pronounce the judgment, must nominate the clerk; so that even if other persons had originally been the judges, and then new persons should be appointed, the common law principle would attach, and those new persons would have the nomination. For instance, your lordships see, that upon the creation of this new jurisdiction of justices of the peace in the time of Edward III., there did not result to the king a right of nominating their clerks, but the common law principle took it out of the king, and put it into the court; and so by the common law, the justices of the peace had the appointment of the custos; but they not being able to agree upon the particular person who should exercise that right, the king nominated one; but even then, the king could not nominate a man who was not in the commission. And yet if he be the fountain of all office, except so far as a court has the appointment from its original constitution, or by prescription, (as has been asserted) he might have done so. Why is it then that he could not? because when the legislature had once created a new court of record, the appointment of its clerks necessarily belonged to that court. Your lordships will find that Lord Holt has expressly stated these courts to have been created within time of memory. He says, "the commission of the peace did commence in time of memory, and the justices were appointed by the crown, not before the 1st of Edward III., and then they were made in lieu of the conservators of the peace, who were as ancient officers as the law knew." The conservators were at common law, and to them of right belonged the nomination of their own clerks. Then the constitution of the court was changed; instead of conservators, there were appointed justices of the peace; but still the common law attributes of judges were transferred to those new officers,

* 1 Show. 528.

and in virtue of them, they also had the nomination of their clerks. So in 4 Mod. 173. S. C. "It is plain that it was not an office time immemorial, because the commission of the peace is not so." It then mentions the original of the office of custos, and goes on, "Afterwards it became incident to the office of the lord keeper to nominate the cust. rot. and then because of the necessity of one to make entries and join issues, the custos appointed a clerk for that purpose, who is now called clerk of the peace; and this seems very agreeable to the statute of Westm. 2, by which it appears, that such officers and clerks who are to enter and enrol pleas, were always appointed by the judge or chief minister of the same court."

The next authority to which I shall call your lordships' attention, is Skroggs *v.* Coleshil, 1 Dy. 175. a. b. The office of exigenter of London and other counties became vacant, and afterwards the chief justice of the common bench died, and during the vacancy of both offices, the queen granted to Coleshil the office of exigenter, and then appointed Brown chief justice, who refused to admit Coleshil, and admitted Skroggs his nephew. The queen commanded Sir Nicholas Bacon, keeper of the great seal, to examine and report the title of Coleshil. And he having convened the judges of the Queen's Bench, the chief baron, the attorney-general, and the attorney-general of the duchy, "took a clear resolution after a long debate and hesitation of all the premises, that the title of Coleshil was null, and that the gift of the said office by no means, and at no time belongs or can belong to our lady the queen, but is only in the disposal of the chief justice for the time being, as an inseparable incident belonging to the person of the said chief, and this by reason of prescription and usage. And it follows from this, that our lady the queen herself cannot be chief justice in the said bench." It appears however, that the queen was not satisfied with this exclusion to which she was subjected, for "notwithstanding the said resolution of the judges aforesaid, the queen upon importunate suit, directed her commission to the Earl of Bedford and nine others, giving them authority to hear and determine the interest and title of the said office, &c." And afterwards, "Coleshil exhibited a bill to those commissioners stating his title, and Skroggs demurred to the jurisdiction, for which he was committed to the fleet, and there remained for two weeks: and then request was made by three serjeants in the bench to grant a *corpus cum causa*, directed to the warden of the fleet. And upon consideration of the court, the request was held reasonable, and to be granted, because he was a person in the court, and a necessary member of it. And note the words of the statute West. 2. c. 30, for the origin of clerks of assize, &c. All justices shall have in their circuits clerks to enrol all pleas pleaded before them, like as they used to have in times past. And so it seems in reason, that the justices were before the clerks, and made clerks at their pleasure."

I do not mean to quit this argument without explaining the words "prescription and usage," above used; because it has been argued from them by the attorney-general, that this right of appointment was vested in the chief justice by a personal prescription. The term "prescription" in this instance means this, that by the common law the right of appointment was necessarily vested in all the judges of the court, but that the personal right of appointment as exercised by the chief justice alone, was founded upon "prescription and usage," which transferred that power which was originally in the whole court, to him individually; exactly what we say has been done in the present case. Upon this part of the case, the authority already cited from Anderson* is material, as also the case of Brownlow v. Cop and Michell, Mo. 842. Brownlow was the prothonotary of the Court of Common Pleas; the crown appointed another person, and Brownlow brought his assize against the appointee of the crown. He waived his privilege, and brought his assize in the King's Bench. The king directed his writ to the justices, reciting that he had by his patent granted the making of supersedeas's to the defendant, and requiring the justices not to proceed *rege inconsulto*. It was insisted that the writ should be quashed, and there was a long argument upon it. The mode of arguing does not exactly appear, but the crown admitted they had not the right, by entering into an undertaking with the court, not to appoint in future, thus clinging to their usurpation at the very moment they were obliged to admit that it was a usurpation. And an indenture was actually executed to that effect.

After all these authorities and all these principles, it might well be supposed that in England this question would be set at rest. But it was not so; and the crown once more attempted to raise it in the case in Show P. C. cited by the attorney-general.† This was the case of Bridgeman v. Holt, reported also in Skinn. 354. And this case itself contains the principles upon which the common law right of the chief justice has been established. I wish to apprise you, gentlemen of the jury, that the uniform usage in England is, that the crown has no right to appoint, and in fact never does appoint, the officer called clerk of the Pleas, either in the King's Bench, or the Common Pleas, or in the Exchequer.

From the statement of this case of Bridgeman v. Holt by the attorney-general, your lordships might imagine that C. J. Holt had pleaded a prescriptive personal right, and not a right at common law. Now, the first thing material to be observed in that case is, that it was an action of assize, and the general issue was pleaded; so that it did not appear from the pleading, whether the defendant's claim rested on prescription or on common law. The whole case came out upon evidence, of which it will be necessary to trouble the court with the detail. The first piece of evidence given by the plaintiff was the patent from the crown. The defendant insisted that the office of clerk of the Pleas was not grantable by the crown, but that the right of appointment belonged to the chief justice of the King's Bench. And to prove this, it was shown that the business of the officer is to enrol pleas between

---

* Cavendish's Case, 1 And. 152. † 11L

party and party only, that is to say, common pleas, and had nothing to do with pleas of the crown: that all the rolls and records in this office were in the custody of the chief justice: that all the writs to certify or remove records in this clerk's office are directed to the chief justice: and from the nature of the employment, it was insisted, that in truth he was but the chief justice's clerk: and that consequently the office must be granted by the chief justice. Thus, they first state the nature of the office, and then the particular reasons which gave the right of appointing to it, to the chief justice. "And for further proof it was shown by the records of the court, that for the space of 235 years past, this office, when void, had been granted by the chief justice." It has been asked, why, if the chief justice had really this right by common law, should he be so absurd as to go into evidence of the usage? I would be glad to know whether there is any common law right claimed by the crown in this case? Or has such a right been abandoned by the counsel for the crown? For the whole of this day, and part of yesterday, has been employed by them in giving evidence of the usage. If the crown have no common law right, then let them give up any claim to it; and if they have, they cannot lay any stress upon Lord Holt's going into evidence of usage. The fact is, that Lord Holt did no more than the attorney-general has done in this very case, or than any prudent man would. He first showed his common law right, and having the usage in his favour, he offered that usage in evidence in farther confirmation of his common law right. But I undertake to show that his right was determined on the ground of common law, and not of any personal prescription.

In the first place, his counsel "insisted upon the mere right of granting the said office, viz., that it was not grantable by the crown, but was an office belonging to the chief justice of the King's Bench, and grantable by him." In the next place, "it was observed on behalf of the defendant, that in all these records produced and read in court, after the mention of the surrender to the chief justice, there are these words, 'to whom of right it doth belong to grant that office whensoever it shall be void.'" Again, "it was further insisted and proved that there are, in the nature of clerks, three considerable officers of the Court of King's Bench; the first and chiefest is the clerk of the crown." And here let me answer the objection that our argument would go to prove too much, as according to it the clerk of the crown ought also to to be appointed by the court. We mean only to say, that in the case of Common Pleas the court has such a right. The clerk of the crown (Shower 113) is the attorney-general and prosecutor of the crown, and is to draw all indictments, informations, &c., in pleas of the crown, and this without the interference of the court. The crown might therefore justly enough say, that an office of this nature should be in its own disposal; but yet even in that case, so strong was the leaning in favour of the general common law principle, that this clerk also was originally appointed by the court. Com. Dig. "Courts." B. 4. A statute was afterwards framed (15th Edward III.) to this effect: "It is consented that if any of the offices aforesaid (which are mentioned in the act) or the controller or chief clerk in the Common Bench or King's Bench, by death or other case, be ousted of their office, the king, with the consent of the great men, &c., shall put another fit person in such office." After the making of this statute, the king appointed the clerk of the crown, which he had never done before; and though the act has since been repealed, yet it having been considered as in this respect declaratory of the common law, the crown has continued still to appoint the clerk of the crown in the King's Bench; but on the circuits the senior judge appoints the clerk of the crown.

"The second officer (say the counsel in the case in Shower) is the prothonotary or chief clerk for enrolling pleas between party and party in civil matters; he and his under clerks do enrol all declarations, pleadings, &c., in civil causes, especially where the proceedings are by bill. This clerk files in his office all the bills, declarations, &c., and all the writs of this court in civil matters are made by him and his under clerks, and tested by the chief justice; and he hath the custody of all returns of elegits, executions, scire facias's, and the filing of all bills, every of which are, in the eye and judgment of the law, in the hands of the chief justice, whose clerk this officer is.

"The third is the custos brevium, who keeps all the rolls and records of judgments in this court, which are also said to be in the custody of the chief justice; and this office, when void, is in his gift and disposal."

The defendant then insisted on the statute of Edward VI. against the sale of offices,* which contains a salvo to the two chief justices and judges of assize to dispose of the offices in their disposition, as they used to do, and so far recognizes the common law right of the judges.

And then to prove the defendant's title, the grant of the chief justice was produced and read and proved, and that the defendant was admitted and sworn.

To answer all this evidence, there was produced the copy of an act of parliament made in 15 Edw. III., allowing the king, as already mentioned, to fill certain places when vacant, and it was urged, that by virtue of this act, the king had the right of appointing to the office.

Upon this evidence, the court declared they would nonsuit the plaintiff. Now if this were a case in which the right of the chief justice had rested (as alleged) upon a personal prescription, it was a case to go to the jury, but if on the other hand, it were a right at common law, then it was a question for the court itself to decide. Having put the act of parliament out of the way, the court would nonsuit, because there was a clear common law right in the chief justice, which if not taken out of him by the act, would bar the plaintiff. The counsel for the crown did not deny, that if the act were out of the way, the court were right, but they insisted that it was impossible to get rid of the act, and prayed the court that it should go to the jury. The court did what they ought not to have done, and did suffer it to go to the jury; and the jury found that this office did not pass to the crown under the act.

* 5 and 6 Edward VI. c. 16.

The plaintiff's counsel then tendered a bill of exceptions, on the ground that the court and not the jury ought to have judged of the act of parliament, which bill the court very properly refused to sign, inasmuch as this was done at their own instance and desire, whereupon they went to the House of Lords. In the report of this case in Skinn. 355, it is said the counsel pressed it should go to the jury, and the judges accordingly left it to them.

What then was the case of Chief Justice Holt, on the whole of this trial? Your lordships will recollect he was not hampered by any particular pleading, but was allowed to give everything in evidence under the general issue. The opinion of the court clearly was, that (the act being once out of the way) there was a principle that enabled them to decide in favour of the defendant. This could only be a common law principle, which was a question for the court and not for the jury. The defendant did in evidence, what we have been obliged to do in pleading, that is, he showed a common law right in the court at large, and then a transfer of the exercise of that right by usage and prescription to the person of the chief justice. Had Chief Justice Holt spread his title out upon the record, he would not have called it a prescription. It was nothing more than an usage. He would have stated his title exactly as we do here, namely a right at first inherent in the court, but by usage to be exercised by the chief justice.

There is a great distinction between prescription and usage. A prescription implies a grant: an usage implies no such thing. On the contrary, the idea of a grant would be inconsistent with it. An usage is a customary mode of modifying or qualifying an existing right. But in no case does it imply a grant. It is merely what becomes a practice. Hence it is not necessary, for the validity of an usage, or in order to constitute the practice of a court, to go beyond time of legal memory. Forty or fifty years, or any time which is long enough to show the court, that such a thing is the practice, will suffice. A course of the court when ascertained, is the law of the court, and is binding not only upon that court itself, but upon all other courts.

We have been driven to strictness in pleading, and been obliged (perhaps fortunately) to state our title with a degree of accuracy, to which Lord Holt was not bound. He showed in evidence first the law, and then the usage grounding his own right. And just so have we done in pleading. In fact, the usage of a court must be decided by the court, and in Lord Holt's case there could be no question for the jury upon that point. Had the question been upon a personal prescription, it must have gone to the jury, but the court negatived that supposition, by expressing their determination to nonsuit the plaintiff.

I think therefore that the case establishes two points for me: first, that the defendant there set up and established a common law right in the court: and next, that besides that, he showed an usage to give that right to the chief justice, that is to say, an usage of which the court, and the court only were to judge.

Tuesday, November 19.

My lords and gentlemen of the jury,—The head of argument of which I treated yesterday, was the common law right of the court to appoint to this office, and in investigating that head, and the authorities referred to in support of it, I have endeavoured to show that the ground on which the right is vested in the chief justice of the King's Bench and Common Pleas in England, must be a principle of the common law, which annexed the right to the court, and then an usage enabling the chief justice to appoint, and that the right cannot be founded upon any personal prescription in the chief justice. I do not think it necessary now to recapitulate these arguments. The last argument I submitted from the case in Shower, was, that the court could not have proceeded upon the notion of a prescription, inasmuch as they declared their intention of nonsuiting, and would have done so, had it not been for the importunity of the plaintiff's counsel.'

In addition to that argument, I have a few more remarks to offer upon this case, which appear to me to be most material. If the title there relied upon had been a prescription against the crown, your lordships know it must have been founded upon the supposition of something which the crown might lawfully grant, for every prescription implies a grant. The argument on the other side is, that it was not the usage of the court that was relied on, but a prescriptive right in the person of the chief justice. This right, if not derived from the court, must have been derived from the crown. It will be necessary therefore to probe this position, that the right is vested by prescription.

Let me ask in the first place, had the king a right to make a grant of his power of nomination? And secondly, if he had, might he have granted it to an absolute stranger, or was he bound to grant to one of the court? If he had the right at all, it must be either generally and without restriction, or in the modified way I have just stated, namely, a right to grant to one of the court, and to no other. If the former is asserted, and if the proposition be, that the king has a right to grant to any person at his pleasure, I must beg leave totally to deny it; because I think your lordships will find, that where there are any certain rights and prerogatives remaining in the crown, and undeparted with (I am now, for argument's sake, supposing the right of nominating this officer not to be out of the crown,) these are original and inherent prerogatives of the crown, and cannot be divested by the constitution of the King's Bench. If this particular right was vested in the crown, it was so vested for the public benefit, and could not be departed with. If this be so, though the king, it is true, might grant the office, yet it is equally true, he could not grant to another the power of granting the office. For I lay it down as a principle of law, that though the king may depart with his lands, which are his private property, and though as to them there might therefore have been a prescription against him even prior to the *nullum tempus* act, yet from the nature of the thing, such prescription must be confined to such things as the king may lawfully grant.

It is so laid down by Lord Mansfield in the case of the Mayor of Hull *v*. Horner, Cowper, 102. He refers to the case of the King *v*. Brown, and says, that even before the *nullum tempus* act, he had always held, that there might be a prescriptive right against the crown. But he confines it to cases where the crown might lawfully grant.—This indeed is so clear upon principles of reason, of analogy, and of policy, that it is scarcely necessary to cite authorities in support of it. To instance a familiar case; if I appoint a trustee to act for me, he may do anything necessary for the execution of his trust, but he cannot transfer the trust itself. That is a personal confidence, and cannot be conveyed to another. So it is with regard to the crown, which is a public trustee. Though it may grant an office to any person it thinks proper, yet it cannot transfer the right of nominating to such office. If (as we are now supposing) the right of appointing to the office of clerk of the Pleas was not attached to the Court of King's Bench, and if the exercise of it in the crown was not confined to any member of that court, then it must be an original right in the crown, for the benefit of the public, and therefore the crown must be disabled from granting it. Your lordships will find, that the moment anything is vested in the crown, which in the contemplation of law is for the public good, that moment is the crown disabled from transferring it. In the case of the temporalities of a bishop, they are vested in the crown during the vacancy of the see. It does not very clearly appear that the public benefit requires that such a right should not be granted away. It might at first be well supposed, that it was a sort of private property in the crown, and accordingly it was not originally clear, but that the crown might have transferred it. But yet it is declared by Magna Charta, that these temporalities shall not be sold. From the moment it was ascertained by this declaration, that such a prerogative was a public one, from that moment was the crown incapacitated from deputing it. And Lord Coke, in his commentary on Magna Charta (2 Inst. 15.) lays it down, that there can be no prescription for these temporalities against the crown. The same thing is laid down, Com. Dig. Grant G. 2. And indeed this is strictly consonant to the spirit of our civil polity. And in confirmation of this doctrine, I beg to refer your lordships to the case of Colt and Glover *v.* Bishop of Coventry. Hob. 140, 154. The court there say, "But a lapse (as I have said) is an act and office of trust reposed by law in the ordinary, metropolitan, and lastly in the king (who is *certum et stabilimentum justitiæ*) the end of which is to provide the church of a rector, in default of the patron; and yet as for him, and to his behoof. And therefore, as he cannot transfer his trust to another, so cannot he direct the thing wherewith he is trusted, to any other purpose; and therefore, though the king or bishop may suffer the church to stand void (which yet is *culpa*) yet they cannot bind themselves, that they will not fill the church, for that were *injuria et malum in se;* and therefore shall be judged in law, in deceit of the king; for *eadem mens præsumitur Regis, quæ est juris, et quæ esse debet, præsertim in dubiis.*"

Allow me now to apply this general analogy of the law to the present question, namely, whether the case in Show. could have been decided on the ground of a personal prescription. To suppose it was, necessarily infers that the right of nominating to the office was a prerogative not departed with by the crown; and then the claim of the chief justice must have been this, that the king being intrusted with this right, had delegated that prerogative to another person; just in the same manner (though less in degree) as if he had delegated the right of appointing his judges or other ministers of justice. Now this, I say, he could not do; because such a prerogative is for the public advantage, and cannot be deputed.

I have put this supposed **right** of delegation alternatively, either as a general one, or as modified in a particular way. Let us now consider the second supposition, viz., that the right is to be granted only to one of the court. What is it that has so restricted it? If there be nothing in the nature of the court or the common law to restrict it, I do not know what else can. And if it be by the common law, the right of granting the office necessarily belongs to the court. It is impossible for ingenuity to confuse this argument or to get out of it. If this supposed prescription be not void as asserting a general right of delegation in the crown, it must inevitably admit a right in the court.

The cases in England have decided this very point; that is, that there is a right by common law in the court, but that it is exercised by one only, namely the head, of the court. Whether this be said to be by prescription or by usage, (if it be granted there is a common law right in the court,) is a matter perfectly indifferent, as to either the rights of the parties, or the determination of the question. If it were clear that there was a right in the court, though it might be erroneously stated in the pleading, that the chief justice's right is founded on usage instead of prescription, yet still the crown having no right, this *quo warranto* information could be wholly unwarrantable.

It appears from the pleadings here, that the chief baron is the chief judge of the Pleas side of the Court of Exchequer; that the chief baron has named this defendant as the officer, and that he has been admitted as such by the entire court. So that if I am right in saying there is a common law right in the court, and that that right is some way or other (no matter how) vested in the chief judge, there is here a complete title admitted upon the record. Nay, if it be even alleged that that right never could be taken out of the court, yet still I say there is a clear title on this pleading, because the court made this appointment.

A prerogative process to question such an appointment is an abuse of the prerogative. What concern is it of the crown's, in what manner the court have exercised their right? They have exercised it, and the crown has nothing to do with it. See whether the grantee of the chief baron has not done what he was bound to do in pleading. The attorney-general admitted that if this right was by common law in the court (and this will be most material in another part of this case) it could not be taken from them by grant, or prescription, or anything short of an act of parliament. It is true, that being once vested in the

2 G

court, it could not be divested out of them, either by grant, or by prescription, which implies a part. Therefore when we plead our title according to the nature of this proceeding (not give it in evidence as we were entitled to do, and as was done in the case in Shower) as a title arising from a usage or practice of the court it must avail; for although no usage can divest the court of its right, yet it may modify such right, and determine by whom in particular it may be exercised. This is not a grant, nor a prescription, but the usage (which is the law) of the court; a law to be recognized not only by the court itself, but by all other courts.

The argument of the attorney-general against this claim is, first that no such usage in point of fact exists; and secondly, that it is not a lawful usage. I have already mentioned, that a usage differs from a prescription, in that prescription supposes a grant, whereas usage does not, but on the contrary, cannot be supported by a grant. And in proof of this distinction, I beg leave to refer to Gateward's case, 6 Rep. 61, where it is said, "that every prescription ought to have a lawful beginning, but otherwise of a custom; for though that ought to be reasonable, it need not be intended to have a lawful beginning, as custom of Gavelkind Borough, English, &c. The common law is the general usage of the entire land; but a particular usage (such as Gavelkind,) is only a reasonable act which need not to have had such beginning as a prescription." And therefore when we talk of the usage of a court it is totally different from a prescription, and cannot have originated in a grant; it grows merely by admitting such a certain practice. Nor is it necessary, that such a usage of a court should exist from time immemorial; for this would be tying up the hands of a court, and preventing it from altering its practice, however inconvenient it might be found to be. Indeed it is monstrous to assert that the usage of a court requires to be from time beyond memory; and the contrary was expressly decided in Deverell's case, 2 Anstr. 624. The question in that case was whether Deverell should be confirmed in the place of clerk in the remembrancer's office. It was relied on that he should not be passed over, and it was argued, as here, that the usage insisted on against him, was not a usage from time immemorial. But Chief Baron Macdonald's answer to that is as follows: "It has been argued that no usage can have effect to bind this question, unless such as could be legally set up as a prescription. I cannot agree to this argument. In offices in every court, new customs and new usages grow up, and get firm root by continuance much short of legal prescription." It was not necessary for me to have cited this authority, because it stands to common sense, that a court of justice must cease to be such, where it is not at liberty to alter its own practice, and to appoint such officers as it thinks fit.

Upon this part of the case, your lordships will find that the argument of C. J. Treby in Owen v. Saunders, 1 Lord Raym. 163, is very material. He is speaking of the office of custos rotulorum, and supposes that he may have been originally named by the justices themselves, and that the clerk of the peace may have been nominated by him, with the consent of the court. His words are: " The original of this office of cust. rot. is not very clear ; but in all probability, the trust of the conservation of the Rolls was committed to one of the justices of the peace, and then he was called custos rotulorum : and probably by the consent of his brethren he nominated the clerk of the peace. He is called so, 13 Hen. IV., 10 pl. 33. And in Dyer 175 b. it is said that it seems in reason that the justices were before clerks. 12 Ric. 2, c. 10, calls him clerk of the justices, and appoints him wages. 2 Hen. VII. 1, first makes mention of the custos rotulorum, &c." Now, in this, two things are important to be observed. First, that all this is alleged to be within time of memory ; the establishment of justices of the peace is so, and consequently so must this usage. And secondly, that the power of nominating the clerk of the peace may have been given by the justices at large, and by their consent, to one of their brethren ; and this, by a usage of the court. And it is also to be remarked, that no doubt is here entertained of the legality of such usage. The only doubt is as to the fact.

I take it, therefore, that the usage of a court with respect to matters within its jurisdiction, makes the law; it binds the court itself and every other court: and every court is bound *ex officio* to take notice of it, just as much as if it were the law of that particular court. It is a thing not questionable—not traversable—nor for a jury to decide upon —but is a question for the consideration of the court. This is clearly exemplified in Lane's case, 2 Rep. 16, a very strong case. By the general law of the land, the lands of the king cannot pass unless by grant under the great seal. But nevertheless, by the usage of the Court of Exchequer, the king's lands may pass under the seal of that court. And this is so, not by any general law of the country, but by the usage of that particular court, which, in that instance, makes the law. Lane's case arose in the Common Pleas, and three points were there resolved by the court. First, "that although by the common law no grant of any land by the king is available or pleadable but under the great seal of England, and although in this case it was not alleged that in the Exchequer the common course of the court was to make such leases under the seal of the court ; yet it was adjudged that the said lease under the Exchequer seal was good, and that by the common usage of the Court of Exchequer : for the customs and courses of the king's courts are as a law, and the common law for the universality thereof doth take notice of them : and it is not necessary to allege in pleading any usage or prescription to warrant the same. And so it is holden in L. 5, E. 4, 1, a. and 11 E. 4, 2 b. that the course of a court is a law: and in 2 R. 3, 9, b. it is holden that every court of Westminster ought to take notice of the customs of the other courts: otherwise it is of courts in *patriá*." Now, after reading this case, I cannot help feeling and complaining of it as a monstrous hardship in the present case, upon the defendant, upon the Court of Exchequer, and upon this court, that by this proceeding we should be called upon to establish in evidence the usage of the Court of Exchequer. Suppose the present defendant were an officer of this court, and your lordships had admitted him, the crown claiming the right of appointment: by the very same right of prerogative by which this information is filed, it might have been filed in the case I have just put. The one is as much a supreme court as the other; both have the same right of admitting their own officers: and both are equally uncontrollable in the exercise of that right, unless by way of appeal. Suppose, then the attorney-general had thought fit to do so in the case of an officer of this court, and this without any claim on the part of the crown (for we are now supposing the right to be absolutely vested in the court), and suppose he had called on your lordships to send up an issue to the jury, to try what was the course of the court, what would your lordships, what would the jury, what would the public say to so gross an abuse of the royal prerogative? I put it to the good sense and feeling of the counsel for the crown themselves, whether they will involve this court, the Court of Exchequer, and the public, in the monstrous consequences of such a proceeding—whether they will put upon this court the odious task of deciding upon the customs of another superior court—or whether they will expose the Court of Exchequer to the humiliation of submitting to such a censure? I appeal to them, whether they will persevere in such a course of proceeding, when they see it thus dilated into its monstrous disproportions, until it at length assumes the gigantic form of unconstitutionality? If your lordships think it right, send your tipstaff into the Court of Exchequer, to drag the judges of that court from the bench, in order to give this court an account of their conduct. If this proceeding is to be persevered in, we shall be compelled to produce one of the learned judges of that court to prove the usage; if the court can submit to the indecency of such a spectacle, if we must be forced to do so, we shall produce Mr. Baron George, and your lordships shall see what has been the usage of the Court of Exchequer, and in what various instances rights and duties, which were originally vested in the court, have been exercised by a particular individual of it.

Every court is bound to notice the usage of another. If it were stated in a book of entries, that by the requisition of the court, the chief baron had the right to a certain appointment, would not that be considered as a sufficient authority? That is what is done on the record here: for it is stated that the officer was admitted. If we are obliged to resort to the proof of that usage, we shall show, that the taking and signing of all recognizances—the signing of all writs after judgment—of every writ of *Habeas Corpus*—the examining and signing of every taxed bill of costs—the signing of every writ of privilege, of all commissions of rebellion, all *venditioni exponas's*, all writs of supersedeas, and all injunctions in cases of estrepement, are, by the usage of the court, confined to the chief baron alone. Every writ of error directed to the Court of Exchequer is, by the same usage, allowed by the chief baron alone. On his allocatur alone the clerk of the Pleas is authorised to transmit the record, and without his allocatur he cannot do so.

In all those cases in which any patronage is vested in the court, (for example, in the appointment of crier and tipstaff,) by the usage of the court, such patronage is exercised by the chief baron alone. And not only in the Court of Exchequer, but in every court in England and Ireland where any patronage is exercisable in the appointment of its officers, it is, in point of fact, exercised by the chief judge alone. And yet we are now told, it is impossible that this can be done.

I hope the court will not consider me as endeavouring to create any unnecessary embarrassment in this case. I have stated what appears to me to be a most serious one, growing out of this proceeding. I trust the opposite party will tell the court how they are to get out of it. There is an issue joined here upon the usage of the Exchequer: do the counsel for the crown desire that a jury shall try that fact? Are they desirous of diverting a jury from its proper functions, for the purpose of ascertaining a right, which is admitted to exist in the court itself? We are ready to do in this respect as your lordships shall think fit.

I have now considered this case as resting upon the common law, and answered the cases which have been put by the attorney-general on the ground of prescription, as also the argument, that the right, supposing it to exist in the court, could not be exercised by a particular member of it: and I hope I have given to them a satisfactory answer. It now remains, in the first place, to advert to the argument, that there is something peculiar in the constitution of the Court of Exchequer, which makes the law there different from what it is in any other court, and then to observe upon the alleged usage contended to exist in favour of the crown.

In the first place, it is said, that by the peculiar constitution of the Court of Exchequer, the chief baron is not the keeper of the records of that court, nor even all the barons: but that the custody of them is in the treasurer and barons; and that in consequence of this peculiar constitution of the court, the records of the Exchequer must be considered as a parcel of the king's treasure, and as the muniments of his rights. Before I go into the examination of this argument, I should be glad to know in what manner, and with what view, it is to be applied? Is this a case between the crown and the Court of Exchequer? Or is it, under the pretence of a prerogative investigation, an experiment to try whether there can be a right in any third person, such, for instance, as the treasurer? I cannot conceive that the latter is the meaning of this information, because that would be an abuse of the prerogative, which I think the persons concerned for the crown would be incapable of advising. I must take it, therefore, that this is a proceeding, not for the purpose of knowing whether there be a title in the treasurer, but whether, by the constitution of the court, they can hold this title against the crown.

Now, as to the argument that the Court of Exchequer is established for the recovery of the king's debts, and that suitors can only sue in it on the fiction of being the king's debtors, and that, therefore, the common pleas of the Court of Exchequer are not the pleas of the subject, but the king's pleas. I hold all this to be the very quintessence of prerogative pedantry. If this doctrine were to be pushed to its extent, it would go to show that in the King's Bench also, the appointment of the clerk of the Common Pleas ought to be in the crown. For in that court also, a party is obliged to sue under a fiction, namely, that the defendant has been guilty of a breach of the peace. In like manner, in any case, the party, if he fails, is liable to be amerced "*pro falso clamore*," and he would thus be subject as a debtor to the king. If fictions of law are to be resorted to, and every remote degree in which the rights of the crown may be supposed to be affected is to be brought in aid of the claims of the prerogative, there is not a muniment of public justice which may not be considered as part of the king's treasure.

It was objected by the attorney-general, that the argument drawn from the keeping of the records would prove too much, because it would go to show that the custos brevium should also be appointed by the court. The custos brevium of the King's Bench in England is in the appointment of the crown, but not the custos brevium of the Common Pleas. And what is the reason of the difference? Because in the latter, the writs are original writs; whereas in the King's Bench they are judicial, or at least the greater part of them, and of consequence, in illustration of the common law doctrine, and according to what is laid down by Lord Coke, the court which pronounces the judgment has an interest in having these writs properly entered. They therefore appoint the clerk of the writs, where the writs are judicial, but not otherwise.

Now as to the constitution of the Exchequer. If the chief baron of that court has not, from the usage of the court, the right of appointing to this office—if, I say, he is precluded from it by the particular constitution of the court, it is to be inquired upon what other officer it could devolve. If the common law be as I have stated, it could not devolve upon the crown: it must devolve upon some other officer. It would suffice to answer to this part of the case, that there is no claim set up by any other officer of the court, but that the claim is made by the crown alone. It is to be observed, that no such argument can arise upon the issue on the usage of the crown, but only on the second issue. And on this issue, the only way in which it can affect the right, is by showing that by the constitution of the court it cannot be in the chief baron. If it cannot be in him, I cannot imagine any other person in whom it can be, except either the chancellor of the Exchequer, or the treasurer of the Exchequer. As to the first of these officers—he is no judge of the common law side of the Exchequer, and never was. He never exercised any judicial function on that side of the court. The pleas at the common law side are before the barons only : but on the equity side they are before the chancellor, treasurer, and barons. And as to the custody of the records, the chancellor of the Exchequer never had it, either actually or constructively. The only function which he ever exercises on the law side of the court is, that he is holder of the seal, there being but one seal for both sides, law and equity. As therefore he holds the seal, he must necessarily use it for the law proceeding. But yet, so careful was the law that this circumstance of his holding the seal should not entitle him to interfere in the law side, that by his oath he is precluded from using the seal in any law proceeding without the consent of the treasurer or chief baron, or some other baron: and in no act connected with the judicial power of the court can he use the seal without their concurrence. The form of his oath is, "the king's seal you shall carefully keep, and shall seal no process except such as shall be ordered by the treasurer or chief baron, or some other baron, except only original process." So that the chancellor of the Exchequer could not of himself have used the seal in appointing to this very office, unless by applying to the chief baron.

Now by what law is it, that the chief baron is in this instance substituted for the entire court? Is it by act of parliament? or by prescription? No: but by the usage of the court. But I only use this at present for the purpose of showing, that the accidental circumstance of their being but one seal induced the necessity of disabling the chancellor from using it without the warrant of the chief baron.

Another argument relied on is, that the chancellor of the Exchequer is the person who appoints to this office of clerk of the Pleas in England. I suppose it is so: but it is equally true that the king does not appoint to it. The office of chancellor of the Exchequer in England is in its nature different from ours. For a long series of years, the person exercising that office in England has also filled the office of under-treasurer of the Exchequer in England. The act of parliament giving him precedence, describes him as such. In all grants and acts of parliament where he is named, he is so described. And in the writ which issued for inquiring into the state of the public records in the country, and in which the two chancellors are named, the one (the English officer) is described as chancellor of the Exchequer and under treasurer, and the other simply as chancellor of the Exchequer.

The treasurer was originally the head of the law side of the Exchequer, and so long as he continued so, he had in virtue of that situation the appointment to such offices as were in the disposal of the law court. He has, however, from a remote period ceased to be the head of the law side; but in England, from the commencement, when he had that right of appointment, a prescription has prevailed in his favour of continuing to appoint; and from that period to the present, there has been an uniform exercise of the right by him in England; whereas throughout all that period, no such right has been exercised by the treasurer in Ireland. Nor is this an argument to be lightly dealt with. The chancellor of the Exchequer of Ireland has not been treasurer in Ireland, except by accident; the two offices have never gone together as they have done in England. The chancellor of the Exchequer in Ireland cannot have any law right; for a period of 400 years the offices of treasurer of the Exchequer and chancellor of the Exchequer have been separated. And hence, the chancellor of the Exchequer in

Ireland never has exercised the right of appointing to any of the law offices of the Exchequer. So that the chancellor of the Exchequer in Ireland has no common law right, and so far from having a prescription in his favour, he has never even set up a claim. The chancellor of the Exchequer in England on the other hand has always held the office which entitled him to grant the offices of the law side of the court.

It seems that originally, by the constitution of the Exchequer, this right of appointment would belong to the treasurer as head of the law side, and as long as he acted as such, the common law would have continued to him that right; but when he ceased to act, then of course it ought to devolve upon the next acting officer. At what period exactly the treasurer ceased to act, is involved in obscurity. It was not probably all at once, but by degrees; and thereupon the chief baron became the acting chief law officer. Had the treasurer continued ever since to this day, it is not for me to say whether or not he would still have had an actual right; that is a question with which I have nothing to do. I do not mean to pronounce any opinion as to whether the chief baron in England could controvert the right of the English treasurer; but he certainly could controvert the right of the crown. In England the chief baron would have a very different case from that which we make. He would have to say, that an officer who originally had this right of appointment, in virtue of his office, and who though he had ceased to exercise his office, had yet continued to exercise such right of appointment, was not entitled to appoint; perhaps he could not say so. But in this country an officer, such as the chancellor of the Exchequer, who never had the right, could not now in the first instance set up a claim. So that as to any argument drawn from the chancellor of the Exchequer in England, it is wholly (to use a phrase of my learned friend the attorney-general) a chimera. No claim is here made by the chancellor of the Exchequer, or on his behalf; the only ground of the case is an alleged right in the crown. And this right is stated, not as one derived from and incident to the right of appointing the chancellor of the Exchequer, but as inherent in the crown, and as part of its prerogative.

It remains to consider how far the treasurer can affect the right of the chief baron. Originally the treasurer perhaps had this right; but when he ceased to act, the chief baron, as the acting chief judge, then became entitled to appoint. In confirmation of this, allow me to mention the case of the creation of a new court. For example, the creation of a new Court of Error in this country by the act of 1800.* A new officer thereupon became necessary, namely, the clerk of the Pleas of that court. And so strongly felt was the force of the common law principle that the right of appointment would belong to the head of the court, that the act of parliament makes a special provision giving the right of appointment to the crown. Here is a direct legislative recognition of the common law right. This provision was considered as a

* 40 Geo. III. c. 39.

great hardship, and the chief justice of that day, (the late lamented Lord Kilwarden) complained of it, as an injury done to him, that he and the court were deprived of the right. And here I may observe, that in the former Court of Error, the chancellor who was the head of it, nominated his secretary to be the clerk.

Having premised so much, I shall proceed to consider how far, originally, the treasurer was a judge of the common law side of the Exchequer. The statute *de scaccario*, made in the 51 Hen. III., st. 5, sect. 7, enacts, " And the warden of the king's wardrobe shall make accompt yearly in the Exchequer in the feast of St. Margaret; and the treasurer and barons shall be charged by oath, that they shall not attend to hear the pleas or matters of other men, while they have to do with the king's business, if it be not a matter that concerneth the king's own debt." And the 8th section adds, " And the king commandeth the treasurer and barons of the Exchequer, upon their allegiance, and by the oath that they have made to him, that they shall not assign any in their rooms, but such as this act meaneth of, and that the Exchequer be not charged with more persons than is necessary." Here the treasurer and barons are alluded to as the persons who have the nomination of such people in the Exchequer; the chancellor of the Exchequer is not mentioned.

An act made 12 Rich. II., c. 2, to regulate offices, enacts as follows: " Item, it is accorded, that the chancellor, treasurer, keeper of the privy seal, stewards of the king's house, the king's chamberlain, clerk of the rolls, the justices of the one bench, and of the other, the barons of the Exchequer, and all other that shall be called to ordain" (this word " ordain" comes upon one rather by surprise, for the attorney-general has been insisting that ordination is not an appointment), " name, or make justices of peace, sheriffs, escheators, &c., shall be firmly sworn that they shall not ordain, name, or make justices of peace, &c., for any gift or brocage, favour or affection, &c." Not a word here of the chancellor of the Exchequer.

The 2nd Hen. VI., c. 10, makes all officers who appoint clerks, answerable for such clerks.

The next recognition of these officers is in stat. 6, Edw. 1, c. 14, whereby the king grants to the citizens of London that disseisees shall have damages by recognizance of assize, by which they recover. "And it shall be commanded unto the barons and to the treasurer of the Exchequer, that they shall cause it every year to be levied by two of them at their rising after Candlemas."

Then comes the 10th Edw. I. addressed, " The king to his treasurer and barons of the Exchequer, greeting." And in sect. 10, " Moreover we provide, that all debts whereunto the sheriffs make return that the debtors have nothing in their bailiwicks, &c., shall be estreated in Rolls, to be delivered to faithful and circumspect men, which shall make enquiry thereof, after such form as shall be provided by the treasurer and barons." This, your lordships observe, is a regulation as to common pleas returns.

In 13 Edw. I., c. 8, it is directed that the writs mentioned in it shall be enrolled, and at the year's end the transcripts sent into the Exchequer, that the treasurer and barons may see the sheriff's answer.

Maddox, in his History of the Exchequer, thinks it was the part of the treasurer to act with the barons in matters relating to the revenue.

I shall now show that these powers have long since ceased on the part of the treasurer. Your lordships will find in the statute 20 Edw. III., c. 2, " In the same manner we have ordained, in the right of the barons of the Exchequer, and we have expressly charged them in our presence that they shall do right and reason to all our subjects, great and small; and that they shall deliver the people reasonably, and without delay of the business they have to do before them, without undue tarrying as hath been done in times past." The barons of the Exchequer, your lordships will observe, are here enjoined, as the only persons concerned. In remarking upon this statute, Lord Coke, 4 Inst. 115, says, " Hereby it appeareth, that to them belongeth doing of right and reason in legal proceedings."

So the statute 31 Edw. c. 12, constituting the Court of Exchequer Chamber, recognises the barons as then the only judges of the law side.

Again the 5 Rich. II., c. 10, after reciting that certain complaints had been made of the officers of the Exchequer, gives to the barons full power to hear such complaints.

Lord Coke, 4 Inst. 118, in treating of the equity side of the Exchequer, says, " The judges of this court are the lord treasurer, the chancellor, and barons of the Exchequer: generally, their jurisdiction is as large for matter of equity as the barons in the Court of Exchequer have for the benefit of the king by the common law."

And in 4. Inst. 109, he lays it down, " All judicial proceedings, according to law in the Exchequer, are *coram baronibus*, and not *coram thesaurario et baronibus*.

In the Bankers' case (82) Lord Somers, (who we know was not interested to enlarge the jurisdiction of the barons), speaking of the court of Exchequer, says, " but if it be considered in its several parts, as to what is intrusted distinctly to the treasurer and chamberlains, and what is put under the direction and government of the barons, it comprehends distinct courts, and such as have no proper communication one with another; though, perhaps, as to some things, the treasurer, chamberlain, and barons are intrusted jointly: as my Lord Chief Justice Coke 4 Inst. 105, says they are with the custody of the judicial records." The passage of Lord Coke here alluded to is, " Albeit the barons, as hath been said, are the judges, yet the treasurer of the Exchequer is joined with them in keeping of the records, whereof the barons are judges, for they are parcel of the king's treasure." This passage of Lord Coke relates entirely to an information of intrusion into the king's lands, which, of course, are the king's treasure; and these records are kept not in the office of the clerk of the Pleas, but of the treasurer's remembrancer.

All writs of error, it is true, are, in the King's Bench and Common

Pleas, directed to the chief judges of those courts, whereas in the Exchequer they are directed to the treasurer and barons. But that we are not to be concluded by the form of the writ appears from 2 Inst. 381, where Lord Coke, speaking of the writ *ex parte talis*, says, " The writ in the register and *F. N. B. ubi supra*, is, *coram thesaurario et baronibus, nostris de scaccario*, but it ought to be *coram baronibus de scaccario*, according to the act, and that the rather, because the barons are (as hath been said) the soveraigne auditors of England, and herewith agreeth Fleta." So, though on the treasurer's ceasing to be the head of the court, the form of the writ should have been altered, yet it continued to be the same. But notwithstanding the direction of writs of error to the treasurer and barons, the records are in the custody of the barons only, and so in all records, removed by writ of error, it appears on the face of the pleadings. The writ itself mentions the judgment to be given by them only: and though directed to the treasurer and barons, yet it is allowed by the chief baron only, he being, in fact and of right, the head of the common law side of the court, and upon his allocatur alone is it that the clerk transmits the record. There are a variety of records in the Exchequer, which are the king's treasure, in which the king has an interest, and which are in the custody of the treasurer's remembrancer; there are others in which the crown is also interested, and which contain proceedings before the barons; and, thirdly, there is a class called common pleas, or pleas between subject and subject, and they are in the custody of the barons, and of the clerk of Common Pleas, as their clerk. But to argue from the records being in the treasurer's custody, as part of the king's treasure, is absurd, because the treasurer originally kept the records of the King's Bench and Common Pleas also, so far as the king's rights were concerned; so that if this argument be well founded, it would give to the crown or to the treasurer the right of appointing also the clerks of the pleas in those courts. But the treasurer never claimed that right, nor has he, since he ceased to be a common law judge, ever claimed to appoint the clerk of the pleas in the Court of Exchequer. The offices of chancellor of the Exchequer and of treasurer have been united immemorially in England, and the oath of the chancellor of the Exchequer in England is different from that of ours. It contains no restriction, as ours does, as to the use of the seal. Here there is no claim by the treasurer, and, in fact, no such officer has for some time existed, although the form of the writs continues to include him. The English treasurer is called in records by various names, sometimes the king's treasurer, sometimes the treasurer of England (2 Madd. 41). The treasurer of Ireland is sometimes called lord treasurer, treasurer, and the 33rd of the king calls him high treasurer; and he has been sometimes called treasurer of the Exchequer, and sometimes our treasurer of the Exchequer. The judicial duties cannot be put in commission. What is become of them? I cannot see. The last grant is to one of the Boyle family; and the office of vice-treasurer was formally abolished in the person of Mr. Clements, in 1795. The king now appoints a receiver-general. By the act of last session consolidating the offices of chancellor of the Exchequer in both countries, the same person is to execute the duties of both, which shows the impossibility of his being a judicial officer on the common law side of the Irish Exchequer.

Now as to the length of time which has been urged on the part of the crown, it will be conceded, that if this right was at first vested in the court, it could not be taken out of them but by act of parliament, or by prescription: no length of time short of a prescription can deprive them of it. A court of justice is not like an individual; no encroachment on its rights can bar them. Littleton (S. 413) says, "no dying seized (where the tenement come to another by succession) shall take away an entry. As of prelates, abbots, priors, deans, or of the parson of a church, or of other bodies politic, &c., albeit there were twenty dyings seized, and twenty successors, this shall not put any man from his entry." And Co. Litt. 250. a. says, this is applied to bodies politic, whose successors come in in the post, and not to natural persons, whose heirs come in in the per. And the same is also laid down, 2 Inst. 154. 155. "Wherefore should not the successors of a bishop, dean, abbot, prior, &c., be as well in the per, as the heir by descent? and the reason thereof is, for that the heir cometh in by his ancestor, and therefore a descent shall take away an entry, and the warranty of the ancestor shall barre the heir; but in case of succession, a dying seized taketh not away an entry, nor the warranty of the predecessor doth bind the successor." Here, too, I have to mention a case which occurred in this court, the King v. Carmichael. The crown had appointed the clerk of the peace for the county of Carlow in the time of Henry VIII., and from that time downwards. Mr. Bruen, as cus. rot. granted to Carmichael; the attorney-general filed an information against him; Carmichael pleaded the facts, and had judgment against the crown. The sole argument was, whether the clerk of the peace derived under the custos; for if he did, it was not disputed that the custos would have the appointment; and the right being shown to be in the custos, the length of time was held to make no title for the crown. That decision has been acted upon ever since.

I shall now apply myself to the question of usage, and will at present suppose there is a common law right in the court. I must suppose that, or the question of usage would be immaterial; for otherwise there must be judgment against the chief baron's grantee. This alleged usage is urged as amounting to a legal prescription. It is not contended on the part of the crown that there is any act of parliament to give them this right. If they mean to rely upon usage as evidence, whence to presume an act of parliament, I say that is illegal. The case of Hewett v. Parish of St. Andrew, in this court, is said to favour such a presumption. That case was afterwards on in Chancery, and it was stated to my Lord Redesdale (who then presided in that court) that such a doctrine had been acted on. It struck him with surprise, and he objected to it what cannot be answered, that if such a doctrine were allowed, there would be an end of all the ancient and received notions of prescription. According to them, no prescription can be admitted, except a legal commencement could be presumed; but if an act of parliament is to be presumed to make a new law, there is an end of all restriction upon prescription. Why is it that a prescription de non decimando, is not valid? because it could not have a legal origin. But we have only to suppose an act of parliament, and it could. In fact, such a presumption as this would amount to a power of legislating, and saying that length of time shall have the effect of making that law, which otherwise could not be so. Lord Redesdale denied there was any precedent for such a doctrine, and refused to act upon it.

But even if this were a case in which the court would submit such a presumption to a jury, it is hopeless to look for any evidence to warrant it. It is an usage against the common law, which I conceive could never have arisen in this country. The common law was introduced here, in the 12th year of King John's reign, and it abrogated every usage contrary to it; and as time of memory is previous to that period, it follows that in this country there can be no prescription against the common law. In the case of Tanistry (Davies 37, 38, 39, 40) it was held that the introduction of the common law into Ireland abolished these customs. And the same would have been the consequence of its introduction into Wales: but for the purpose of preventing it, the stat. of Wales (27. H. VIII. c. 26. s. 27.) appoints commissioners to inquire into the customs of Wales, and expressly saves them. And accordingly, in this country the custom of gavelkind prevailed before the introduction of the common law, as appears from Sir James Ware's antiquities, but it was then abolished. Gavelkind is good at this day in England, because it is a part of the local common law. Any custom that might have a legal commencement, may prevail in Ireland as well as in England: but the common law of England, when introduced here, abolished all customs at variance with it, notwithstanding those customs might be legal in England. If previously to that period, a subject had a grant of lands, that would not have been disturbed; in like manner of anything not contrary to the common law. It is to be remembered, that we are now taking for granted the right is in the court: it is contended that there is a prescription to take it out of them, and put it in the crown. Now I say that cannot be: that is a prescription which could not have a legal origin, and if not, it cannot have any validity.

Further, the pleading of this as a prescription in the crown, presupposes it has no common law right. For where a prescription is set up for anything, it is an admission that the law does not give it. Noy. 20, Pells v. Towers. Com. Dig. Prescription, F. 4. Wilson v. Bishop of Carlisle, Hob. 107.

Now, gentlemen of the jury, a word to you upon this question of usage. The evidence of it has been derived from a book of extracts agreed on both sides to be read. In the first place, there is no evidence of any exercise of this alleged right on the part of the crown until the year 1403, 254 years within time of memory. The first document showing by whom any appointment was made, is in 1375, and that was an appointment by the court. The first appointment by the crown was in 1403. Where the actual entries do not appear, to show by whom the earlier appointments were in fact made, the first presumption is that they were made according to law. If then the defendant be right in saying the court has a common law right, this court is bound to presume, in the absence of the records, that the earlier appointments were made by the court, who thus had the right. I admit it is a presumption liable, like all others, to be rebutted by contrary evidence, but it is good till so encountered. And in analogy to this, in the case in Shower, where Chief Justice Holt, in aid of his common law right, referred to the usage, he only produced the entries for 250 years, although the entries went farther back; and for this reason, that it was to be presumed the earlier entries were in conformity with the right.

Gentlemen of the jury, I have now to call your attention to the first of these entries, that is an order for payment to Bromley in 1332. Gentlemen, it has been argued that all these entries, showing that payment was made to this officer out of the king's treasury, are so many proofs that the appointments were made by the crown. But you will find that in the case where the appointments were made by the court, the entries are also for payment out of the king's treasury. So that this circumstance affords no evidence who it was that appointed. The crier of the Court of Exchequer, who is confessedly appointed by the chief baron, is also paid out of the treasury. I take it therefore that the case may be cleared of all these entries.

The next entry is in 1334, 8th and 9th Edward III., and is for payment to John de Carleton as clerk of the Pleas. This John de Carleton was also appointed chamberlain. The patent appointing him to this latter office appears, but no patent is to be found appointing him clerk of the Pleas. Here is an entry stating him to hold both offices, and yet the patent for one appears, and not for the other. It cannot be said that the patents are lost; for here is one. If we suppose him appointed by the court, it is natural enough that there should be no entry of the mode of his appointment, because nothing more would be necessary than his admission by the court. But, on the other hand, if the crown had appointed, a patent would have appeared, and that not being the case, the inference is irresistible, that he was not appointed by the crown.

The next document is an order for payment to Simon de Legaston, dated 14 Dec. 1342, and in the same year is one to Robert Baynard. It is here material to remark, that during this period there appears to have been a scramble for this office, and the appointments are involved in confusion. This circumstance of two orders for payment to two different persons in the same year sufficiently shows it.

In 1344, John de Hacksey appears to be sworn in before the treasurer and barons, and the same John de Hacksey is again sworn in in 1357; there is no reason to show why. There was evidently some contest for the office during that interval. And here let me observe, that the evidence of the swearing in has been preserved; then why not the evidence of an appointment by the crown, if any?

Then, in 1352, is an order for payment to John de Carleton, the same who was formerly appointed. You will recollect, gentlemen, that to support the allegation of the crown, of a prescription, there must be an uniform uninterrupted usage. After all this comes an order, in 1355, for payment to Robert Baynard; and again, 1363, for the same person, who held till 1375. It will not be contended that, up to this period, there is any evidence of an appointment by the crown, or indeed by any person. There is some evidence against the crown.

Now comes the entry in 1375, the first which is clear as to the mode of appointment. It is not surprising that, after the state of confusion in which the title to the office had been involved, it should be thought expedient to put an end to all doubt, by the ministers of the court joining in an appointment. Accordingly, in this entry it is stated, that John de Penkeston "stood ordained" by the chancellor and treasurer of Ireland, and the barons, and others "our ministers of our Exchequer aforesaid." Much has been observed upon this appointment. First, it is said, it was made by the lord chancellor of Ireland, and not the chancellor of the Exchequer. Let it be so; it is indifferent to me. But then a record is produced, to show that Robert de Emeldon was chancellor of the Exchequer, in order, by a subsequent entry, to show this appointment must have been by him. It clearly appears, however, that this first instance of an appointment is not by the crown, and that it was thought necessary that the treasurer, barons, and other ministers of the court should concur. Many expedients have been resorted to, to get rid of this record. It is said, the wind was unfavourable, the packet could not sail—the king's letter did not arrive, and the office was of so much importance, and the necessity for filling it so urgent, that all the principal officers met, and appointed. It is curious, that this appointment was made in 1375, and the entry was not made till two years after. Had the steam packet been delayed all this time? Another remarkable fact is, that no entry is to be found of the appointment itself, though it was certainly made by the court. And the king, when he orders payment to this officer, not only recites his appointment by the court, but expressly states that to be his title. It is conceded, that though an interruption in the possession will not destroy a prescription, yet an interruption of the right will. Here then is an entry on the part of the crown, acknowledging that Penkeston was lawfully ordained by the court. It cannot be said the law officers had not time to communicate with the crown before this entry was made. Now if the appointment was an extraordinary one, would not the king have asserted his prerogative? He does not do so. So that, in short, this is a prescription set up by the crown, to be maintained by uninterrupted usage, and the very first entry brought to prove it is destructive of the right. I really cannot help commiserating my learned friend who is to reply to me, for the hopeless task he has to encounter, of persuading you, gentlemen of the jury, that this is a clear, uniform, uninterrupted usage.

This appointment was in 1375. It is a curious fact in natural history, and one that deserves to be particularly recorded, that the wind blew in the same direction for eight and twenty years; for so long this Penkeston held the situation.

In 1403, it appears that William Sutton was appointed by the crown, and in 1423, (1 Hen. VI.) he was confirmed. This is the first instance in which the crown exercised the right. The grant of the office, 1 Hen. VI. recites an inspeximus of letters patent to Sutton, recognising the appointment of Penkeston, and concludes by confirming them, "any grant of the said office by our chancellor of the Exchequer or any other person or persons notwithstanding." So that this first instance of any appointment by the crown, begins by recognising the appointment by the court, and concludes by being validated by a *non obstante* clause. I protest, it is really difficult to continue an argument upon such a thing. If we suppose a right at any time in the chancellor of the Exchequer, that instant we destroy the king's claim: for the argument is not that the right is in the crown, as incident to the power of appointing the chancellor of the Exchequer: but that it has a distinct inherent, independent right by prescription. Is a grant by the crown with a *non obstante* clause, is that, I ask, to be evidence for the crown? It is not, it cannot be, evidence of anything but an unconstitutional usurpation. The *non obstante* doctrines, as we know from our history, were so rooted as to be admitted even in the courts of law, whether right or wrong, anything could have been done by a *non obstante* clause. It is wonderful our liberties could have survived such a doctrine. If there had not been a buoyancy in the British constitution which made it incapable of sinking, if there had not been a spring in the minds of the English nation too strong to be subdued, if they had not been predoomed to be a free people, their liberties could never have survived so deadly an instrument of tyranny and usurpation. It was urged and acted upon till the revolution, and to use the language of the luminous and classical commentator on the laws of England, "it did not abdicate Westminister-hall, till James the Second abdicated the throne." And shall such a thing as this, be sent up in our days to a jury, as evidence to the right of the crown?

Up to the period of Penkeston's appointment, all, as I have observed, was confusion. After this appointment there was none—no small evidence that where the court acted, their appointment was acquiesced in as rightful. But from the appointment of Sutton, the confusion begins again. James Blakeney is next appointed, it does not appear by whom, or when.

The next entry is in 1430, 27th July—a very important one. It states, that the crown had granted to Robert Dyke the office of chancellor of the Exchequer, "And moreover by reason that the said office of clerk of the pleas in our Court of Exchequer is member and parcel of the said office of chancellor of the green wax and annexed to the same; and the same office of clerk of the pleas has been held by Robert de Emeldon as chancellor of the said Exchequer, as may appear of record, and also by other persons as we are informed," it then grants to

Dyke the office of clerk of the pleas. Now, suppose it were true that the office of clerk of the pleas is member and parcel of the office of chancellor of the Exchequer, it destroys the right of the crown, because on that supposition the right belongs to the chancellor of the Exchequer: and if it be false, then it amounts to an acknowledgment that the crown did not claim by virtue of its prerogative. " And that the same office of clerk of the pleas has been held and occupied by Robert de Emeldon, as may be of record in our treasury, and by other persons, as we are informed." This is the crown's statement of its own title. Now, I say, that whether that statement be true or false, it equally destroys the right of the crown. The crown is clearly looking for arguments to support its usurpation. Robert Dyke appointed Stannaher and another his deputies. The recital of that appointment is, that Robert Dyke was nominated in 1 Hen. VI. At the very time of the grant to this Dyke, the office of clerk of the pleas was full, by William Sutton, to whom it was previously granted. So that the crown having appointed Sutton to the prejudice of the right of the chancellor of the Exchequer, then grants to Dyke the office of clerk of the pleas, as parcel of the very same office of chancellor of the Exchequer ; and the reason is " because it was so held by Robert de Emeldon," who had been in 1348, (a hundred years before), locum tenens of the treasurer. He is so recited 22 & 23 Edw. III. in a patent granting to William de Burton. When the crown had the right, the entry is made so early as 1348. In this grant of 1431, therefore, the crown rests its title on the office of clerk of the pleas being part of that of chancellor of the Exchequer, and refers to Robert de Emeldon, as the only instance in support of its being so : and upon referring to that, it appears he was also locum tenens of the treasurer, an office which might of itself have given him a right: and all this when the office was full by Sutton, the crown's own grantee. Even after this assumption of right, that is to say, in the year 1432, and in 1436, there are orders for payment to Sutton : so that this claim of title was clearly an usurpation by the crown, and not only that, but an usurpation by the crown on its own grantee. The whole proceeding is a complicated tissue of folly and usurpation, and affords no evidence whatever of any right.

After this, (1438) John Hardwicke is appointed chancellor of the Exchequer and clerk of the Pleas, and in the same year, notwithstanding this appointment, the chancellorship of the Exchequer is given to John Baynard. Again, in the same year, on the 5th of June, this office is granted to Richard de Waterton. Here are three different persons appointed by the crown in one year.

In the same year (1438) is an order to admit Cunningham and White as deputies, and on the 14th of December, in that year, an order to pay Sutton, the very man who was appointed in 1403. And yet, after all this confusion, it is gravely said, that this is a case of irrefragable, uniform, and consistent usage. It is really astonishing, that with such documents before them, the counsel for the crown should venture to state them as evidence of an uninterrupted possession in the crown.

I hold in my hand the draft of an act of parliament, which was presented to the House of Commons, before my lord chief baron could lay his case before the house. It was carried hastily and precipitately through that house, and presented to the lords on the very same day. It was read a first time—it was ordered for a second reading, and it would have been carried there also on the third day, but for one noble lord. This act, as it was first framed, and had nearly passed, recited, " Whereas the office of clerk of the Pleas in his majesty's Court of Exchequer in Ireland is an ancient office; and whereas the said office has hitherto been held under the appointment of his majesty and his predecessors." This really looks as if there had been some misgiving on the part of those concerned for the crown, that they could not maintain an uninterrupted usage, and therefore would not venture to state it to be immemorial. But the House of Commons, when they passed this statute, must have imagined there was such an usage. If, instead of the words used, the expression had been, " Whereas the crown has now and then enjoyed," the act would never have passed. However it was passed, the house having conceived there was an immemorial usage. It was thrown out in the Lords, and the new act which has been passed, does not recite any enjoyment by the crown. That was retracted, because it could not be maintained; and yet they now bring forward to influence a Dublin jury, what they had not the audacity even to assert to the legislature!

Gentlemen, there are a number of other entries. 29th September, 1439, Waterton is appointed clerk of the Pleas. 1st October he is sworn in in Chancery, and a writ issues from the chancellor to the barons to admit him. Is this a lawful mode of appointing?

In 1445 is a patent from the crown, confirming the deputy of Hardwicke. Then there is a grant of the office of chancellor of the Exchequer and clerk of the Pleas to Hardwicke and Shelton by authority of parliament. They were also appointed collectors of customs. The " authority of parliament" means this, that these officers' fees being charged upon the customs, this could only be by authority of parliament.

In 1448, we find a grant of the offices of chancellor of the Exchequer and clerk of the Pleas to Birmingham and Fitz Robert. Then an order to pay Fox and Powel as deputies. In 1451, Birmingham and Fitz Robert apply to be allowed their fees. Next is an order to pay Browne as their deputy. Then in 1452, an order to pay Toole, the deputy of Birmingham, and another to John Dennis in 1458.

In 1460, we find a grant to Pickering of the office of clerk of the Pleas. This is said to be " by bill of the lieutenant himself and by authority of parliament." Now if a presumption is to be made of an act of parliament, this would probably be relied on as such by those concerned for the crown. We can show the meaning of this authority of parliament. The Duke of York, the father of Edward the Fourth, was then lieutenant in Ireland. It was thought a desirable thing on the part of Henry the Sixth, who was then king of England, to induce the

Duke of York to accept the lieutenantcy of Ireland, in order to get him out of the way. He accepted the situation, but determined to fortify himself in it; for we find from Cox's History of Ireland (160) that he only consented to take it, on the express conditions, first, that he should be lieutenant for ten years; secondly, that he should receive the whole revenue, without accounting; thirdly, that he should have treasure from England: fourthly, that he should let the king's lands to farm; and fifthly, that he should appoint to and dispose of, all offices at his pleasure. And now I make the gentlemen a present of the authority of parliament.

The next appointment is by the crown to Delahide and Dartas. And there is a special act of parliament made for the purpose of ratifying that appointment. This single fact demonstrates that the crown had no right. If the king was entitled, why should he pray the legislature to give him what he had before? Will it be said that at that time there was any act of parliament enabling the crown? What now becomes of this presumption? What becomes of the king's inherent right? Gentlemen of the jury, if it be possible to have a plain document showing that up to a certain period the crown had no right, this act of parliament is that document. The crown cannot get out of it: it is vain to try. It cannot be said the act is for the purpose of enabling the two offices to be held together; that was often done before. No, gentlemen, it was clearly and manifestly for the purpose of enabling the grantee of the crown to hold against the general rule of law.

From this period till the statute of Henry VII. there is but one appointment, namely, to Woffer. When, or by whom that was made does not appear. It may be presumed to have been by the court. The statute of Henry VII.* was then passed, making the judges dependent upon the crown. If while they held during pleasure, and while the *non obstante* doctrine continued, the judges had questioned the king's right, they could not have prevailed; for the crown had the power by a *non obstante* to compel the admission of its officer. Whilst the *non obstante* claim existed, it was just the same thing as if it was exercised. Arguments, therefore, drawn from the acquiescence of the judges during that period weigh nothing. Would it, I ask you, gentlemen, have been advisable for them to go to law with the crown, while they were removable at its pleasure? What do you think would have been their fate, if they had? Do you think that my Lord Chief Baron O'Grady, if he had held during pleasure, would have set up the present claim? We know from history that Lord Coke lost his office for asserting his common law right, and insisting upon the appointment of Filazer in his court. It is sometimes accounted for otherwise; but this was his real offence; and it is so stated by Blackstone, and in the life of Lord Coke, in the *Biographia Britannica*. We now, thank God, live in better times. The affairs of this country are no longer considered as of the same provincial insignificance in which they were formerly held; and the rights of the court

* 10 Hen. 7, C. 2.

and of the subject in this country are on the other side of the water held as sacred as the rights of Englishmen. I am far from insinuating that even here there would be any disposition to take advantage of the dependent situation of a judge, if he were dependent. I sincerely believe there is not an individual in the profession, or in the community, more incapable of stooping to a base or unworthy action than his majesty's attorney-general. But to talk of acquiescence on the part of judges in former times, as affording a presumption in favour of the crown, is ridiculous; because the whole history of England from the period of the union of the Houses of York and Lancaster to the Revolution, is nothing but a series of usurpations by the crown on the rights of the people. Ware's history shows the usurpations committed on the rights of the treasurer and chancellor of Ireland, and when they were spoliated, it is not surprising that those of the judges should. It was not till the 22nd year of his reign, that the judges in Ireland were made independent of the crown; and in addition to this, from the time of the Revolution to the present, all the grants of this office from the crown have been in reversion, so that no vacancy has occurred to act upon, before the present appointment.

Gentlemen, I have exhausted my own strength and your patience. I shall not attempt to recapitulate. Our case rests upon the common law: we claim the same rights as the judges in England. As to an uninterrupted usage in the crown, gentlemen of the jury, if you think there is evidence of it, if you are ready to find upon your solemn oaths, that which has not been so much as asserted to the legislature, let it be so, and in God's name find a verdict for the crown.

THE END

www.ingramcontent.com/pod-product-compliance
Lightning Source LLC
Chambersburg PA
CBHW051847300426
44117CB00006B/290